PACEMAKER®

World History

PEARSON
AGS Globe

Shoreview, MN

Reading Consultant

Timothy Shanahan, Ph.D., Professor of Urban Education, Director of the Center for Literacy, University of Illinois at Chicago, Author, *AMP™ Reading System*

Reviewers

The publisher wishes to thank the following educators for their helpful comments during the review process for Pacemaker® *World History.* Their assistance has been invaluable. **Debora Hartzell,** Special Education and Vocational Teacher, Lakeside High School, Atlanta, GA; **Lenore Hoyt,** Social Studies Teacher, Centennial High School, Circle Pines, MN; **Stephen C. Larsen** (formerly of The University of Texas at Austin); **J. B. Whitten,** ESE Teacher, Lennard High, Ruskin, IL

Acknowledgments appear on page 798, which constitutes an extension of this copyright page.

ISBN-13: 978-0-7854-6391-7
ISBN-10:   0-7854-6391-7

7 8 9 10   V011   11

1-800-992-0244
www.agsglobe.com

Table of Contents

Reading Strategies

Maps

Maps, cont.

Timelines

Words from the Past

Learn More About It

Great Names in History

Technology Connection

How to Use This Book: A Study Guide

Welcome to the study of world history. You may be asking yourself, "Why do I need to know about people, places, and events that happened a long time before I was even born?" When we study the past, we can have a better understanding of why some things happened the way they did. We can learn from the mistakes and the successes of the past.

This book is a story about the world. As you read the units, chapters, and lessons of this book, you will learn about the important people and events that shaped world history.

Before you start to read this book, it is important that you understand how to use it. It is also important that you know how to be successful in this course. Information in this first section can help you achieve these things.

How to Study

These tips can help you study more effectively:

- Plan a regular time to study.

- Choose a desk or table in a quiet place where you will not be distracted. Find a spot that has good lighting.

- Gather all the books, pencils, paper, and other equipment you will need to complete your assignments.

- Decide on a goal. For example: "I will finish reading and taking notes on Chapter 1, Lesson 1, by 8:00."

- Take a five- to ten-minute break every hour to keep alert.

- If you start to feel sleepy, take a break and get some fresh air.

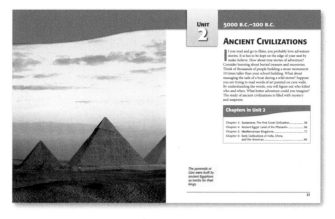

Before Beginning Each Unit

◆ Read the unit title and opening paragraph(s).

◆ Study the photograph. Do you recognize anything in the photo? Also read the caption and try to connect the ideas to the picture.

◆ Read the titles of the chapters in the unit.

◆ Read the Chapter Summaries to help you identify key ideas.

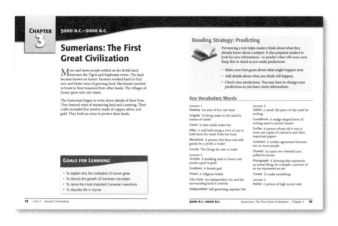

Before Beginning Each Chapter

◆ Read the chapter title and dates, as well as the opening paragraphs.

◆ Review the Goals for Learning. The Chapter Review and tests will ask questions related to these goals.

◆ Study the timeline(s). Timelines help you see the order in which key events in the chapter occurred.

◆ Read the information in the Reading Strategies box; it will help you become a better reader. Reading Strategy notes in each lesson will help you apply the strategy as you read.

◆ Read the words and definitions in the Key Vocabulary Words box. They are important vocabulary terms for the chapter.

◆ Read the Chapter Summary to help you identify key themes.

◆ Look at the Chapter Review. The questions cover the most important information in the chapter.

Note These Features

You can find complete listings of these features in this textbook's table of contents.

Reading Strategy:
Summarizing

Reading Strategy
Tips to help you understand and make sense of what you read

Map Study
Helps locate important features in a certain area of the world during a certain time period

Timeline Study
Aids in understanding the order of events in the chapter or lesson

Words from the Past
Presents written or spoken words related to the chapter that continue to affect the world today

Learn More About It
Provides additional information related to the chapter

Great Names in History
Highlights people who have made contributions to the world

Technology Connection
Highlights inventions at the time that made life better or easier

Before Beginning Each Lesson

Read the lesson title and restate it in the form of a question. For example, write: *What changes have happened throughout history?*

Look over the entire lesson, noting the following:

◆ bold words

◆ text organization

◆ photos and maps

◆ Lesson Review questions

As You Read the Lesson

◆ Read the major headings.

◆ Read the subheads and paragraphs that follow.

◆ Study the maps.

◆ Before moving on to the next lesson, see if you understand the concepts you read. If you do not, reread the lesson. If you are still unsure, ask for help.

◆ Practice what you have learned by completing the Lesson Reviews.

Artifact

A handmade object, such as a tool or weapon

Using the Bold Words

Knowing the meaning of all the boxed words in the left column will help you understand what you read.

These **vocabulary words** appear in **bold type** the first time they are mentioned in the text and are often defined in the paragraph.

They find handmade objects, called **artifacts,** that have long been underground.

All of the words in the left column are also defined in the **Glossary**.

Artifact (är´ tə fakt) A handmade object, such as a tool or weapon (p. 9)

Word Study Tips

◆ Start a vocabulary file with index cards to use for review.

◆ Write one term on the front of each card. Write the definition, chapter number, and lesson number on the back.

◆ You can use these cards as flash cards by yourself or with a study partner to test your knowledge.

History

Chapter 1, Lesson 1

The record of past events and the story of what happened to people in the past.

Taking Notes

It is helpful to take notes during class and as you read this book.

◆ Outline each lesson using the subheads as the main points.

◆ Always write the main ideas and supporting details.

◆ Keep your notes brief.

◆ Write down important information only.

◆ Use your own words.

◆ Do not be concerned about writing in complete sentences. Use phrases.

◆ Do not try to write everything the teacher says.

◆ Use the same method all the time. Then when you study for a test, you will know where to go to find the information you need to review.

◆ Review your notes to fill in possible gaps as soon as you can after class.

Using a Three-Column Chart

One good way to take notes is to use a three-column chart. Make your own three-column chart by dividing a sheet of notebook paper into three parts. In Column 1, write the topic you are reading about or studying. In Column 2, write what you learned about this topic as you read or listened to your teacher. In Column 3, write questions, observations, or opinions about the topic, or write a detail that will help you remember the topic. Here are some examples of different ways to take notes using the three-column chart.

The topic I am studying	What I learned from reading the text or class discussion	Questions, observations, or ideas I have about the topic
Sumer	• civilization grew between the Tigris and Euphrates rivers • Sumerians invented many things that we use today	• It makes sense that Sumer grew between two rivers because water is important to all life. • I wonder what people did before the wheel was invented.

Vocabulary word	Definition	Sentence with vocabulary word
Merchant	a person who buys and sells goods for a profit; a trader	Sumerian **merchants** traded crops for gold, silver, and pearls from other lands.

Topic	Facts	Page number
Sumerian city-states	each city-state was independent and had its own government	p. 43
	built walls around their city-states (for protection)	p. 43
	Ur was one of the greatest Sumerian city-states; it had a ziggurat (a gigantic temple)	p. 44

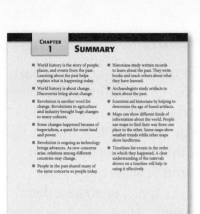

Using the Summaries

◆ Read each Chapter Summary to be sure you understand the chapter's main ideas.

◆ Review your notes and test yourself on vocabulary words and key ideas.

◆ Practice writing about some of the main events from the chapter.

Using the Reviews

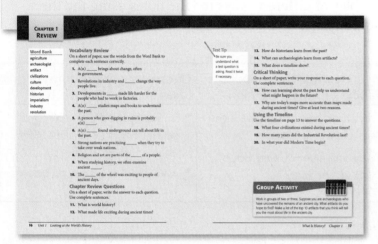

◆ Answer the questions in the Lesson Reviews.

◆ In the Chapter Reviews, answer each fill-in-the-blank, short-answer, critical-thinking, and timeline question.

◆ Review the Test-Taking Tips.

Preparing for Tests

◆ Complete the Lesson Reviews and Chapter Reviews. Make up similar questions to practice what you have learned. You may want to do this with a classmate and share your questions.

◆ Review your answers to Lesson Reviews and Chapter Reviews.

◆ Reread the Chapter Summaries.

◆ Test yourself on vocabulary words and key ideas.

Reading Checklist

Good readers do not just read with their eyes. They read with their brains turned on. In other words, they are active readers. Good readers use strategies as they read to keep them on their toes. The following strategies will help you to check your understanding of what you read. A strategy appears at the beginning of each chapter of this book.

- **Summarizing** To summarize a text, stop often as you read. Notice these things: the topic, the main thing being said about the topic, important details that support the main idea. Try to sum up the author's message using your own words.

- **Questioning** Ask yourself questions about the text and read to answer them. Here are some useful questions to ask: Why did the author include this information? Is this like anything I have experienced? Am I learning what I hoped I would learn?

- **Predicting** As you read, think about what might come next. Add in what you already know about the topic. Predict what the text will say. Then, as you read, notice whether your prediction is right. If not, change your prediction.

- **Text Structure** Pay attention to how a text is organized. Find parts that stand out. They are probably the most important ideas or facts. Think about why the author organized ideas this way. Is the author showing a sequence of events? Is the author explaining a solution or the effect of something?

- **Visualizing** Picture what is happening in a text or what is being described. Make a movie out of it in your mind. If you can picture it clearly, then you know you understand it. Visualizing what you read will also help you remember it later.

- **Inferencing** The meaning of a text may not be stated. Instead, the author may give clues and hints. It is up to you to put them together with what you already know about the topic. Then you make an inference—you conclude what the author means.

- **Metacognition** Think about your thinking patterns as you read. Before reading a text, preview it. Think about what you can do to get the most out of it. Think about what you already know about the topic. Write down any questions you have. After you read, ask yourself: Did that make sense? If not, read it again.

Using Globes and Maps

A globe is a model of Earth. Looking at the globe, you can see that Earth is round. You can see Earth's features and surfaces. A globe is the best way to show Earth. However, how do you show the round features of a globe on a flat page? You use a map.

You also can see that geographers divide Earth into halves or **hemispheres**. The **equator** divides Earth into the Northern Hemisphere and the Southern Hemisphere. The equator is an imaginary line that circles the middle of Earth.

The **prime meridian** and the **international date line** divide Earth into the Eastern Hemisphere and the Western Hemisphere. The prime meridian is an imaginary line that circles Earth from the North Pole to the South Pole. The international date line is on the side of Earth you cannot see here. It is directly opposite the prime meridian.

Geographers measure distances from the equator and the prime meridian. These distances are imaginary lines called **latitude** and **longitude**.

The Hemispheres

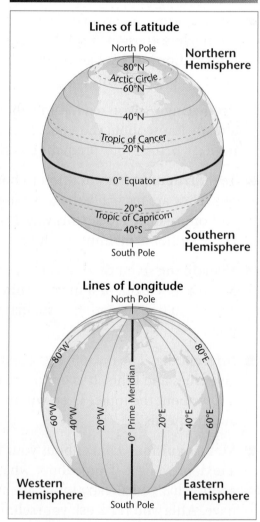

Lines of Latitude

North Pole
80°N
Arctic Circle
60°N
40°N
Tropic of Cancer
20°N
0° Equator
20°S
Tropic of Capricorn
40°S
South Pole

Northern Hemisphere

Southern Hemisphere

Lines of Longitude
North Pole

80°W
60°W
40°W
20°W
0° Prime Meridian
20°E
40°E
60°E
80°E

Western Hemisphere

Eastern Hemisphere

South Pole

Cartographers, or **mapmakers**, have created different map projections. Some of these map projections show the true size of a place, but distort, or change, the shape. Others show the true shape, but distort the size. All maps show some kind of distortion. Therefore, geographers must choose the best maps for their purposes.

A **Mercator projection** stretches the lines of latitude apart. It does not show the true size of landmasses. A Mercator projection does show true shape, however.

Landmasses in a **Robinson projection** are not as distorted as in a Mercator projection. However, there is some distortion in the size of the landmasses.

Mercator Projection

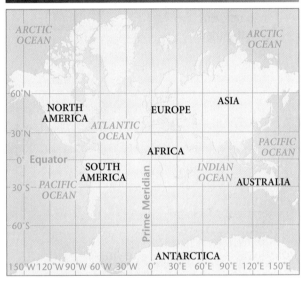

Robinson Projection

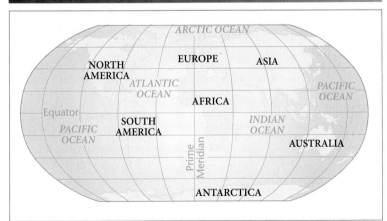

Critical Thinking

Why would a mapmaker choose to use a Robinson projection instead of a Mercator projection?

Reading a Map

To understand history, you need to know how to read maps. To read a map, you need to understand its parts. The main parts of a map are a title, a key, a compass rose, and a scale. Many of the maps you see are **general purpose maps**. These are political maps and physical maps. A **political map** shows features that people determine, such as country boundaries, cities, and capitals.

The **title** of a map tells the area the map covers. →

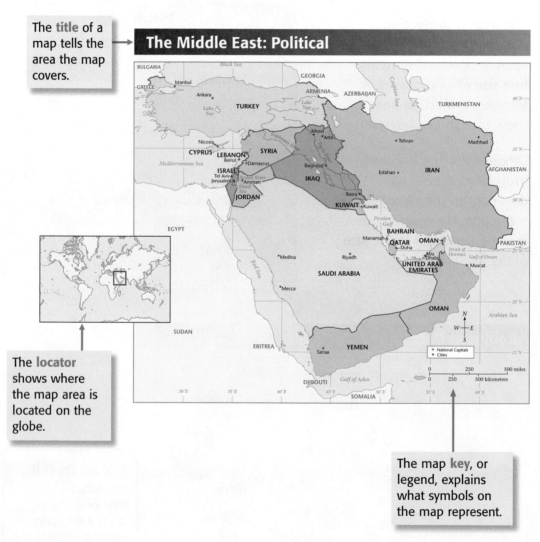

The Middle East: Political

The **locator** shows where the map area is located on the globe.

The map **key**, or legend, explains what symbols on the map represent.

A **physical map** shows how high a landmass is. It also shows natural features such as rivers and oceans. Some of the maps you see show specific kinds of information. These maps are called **special purpose maps**. There are many types of special purpose maps. For example, a map that shows where early civilizations lived is a special purpose map. Look at the Early Civilizations of North America map on page 323.

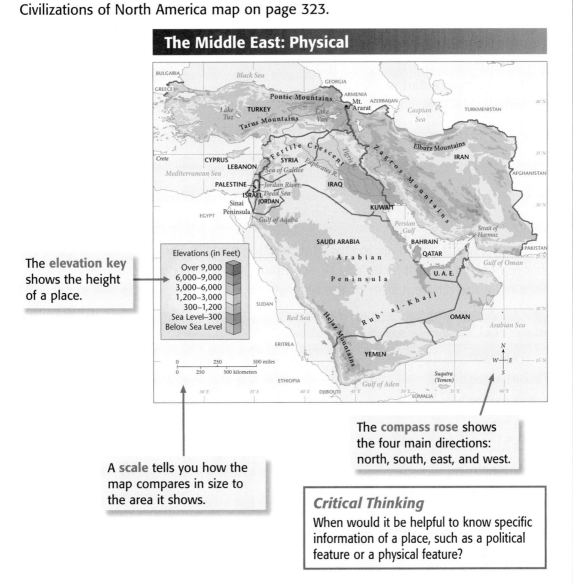

The Middle East: Physical

The **elevation key** shows the height of a place.

Elevations (in Feet)
Over 9,000
6,000–9,000
3,000–6,000
1,200–3,000
300–1,200
Sea Level–300
Below Sea Level

A **scale** tells you how the map compares in size to the area it shows.

The **compass rose** shows the four main directions: north, south, east, and west.

Critical Thinking
When would it be helpful to know specific information of a place, such as a political feature or a physical feature?

Reading Graphs and Charts

Graphs and charts organize and present information in a visual way. There are different types of graphs and charts.

A **circle graph** is sometimes called a pie graph. It is a good way to show the sizes of parts as compared to a single whole. This single whole is represented as a circle. Each piece of the circle represents a part of the whole.

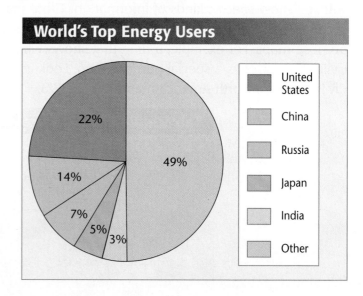

A **bar graph** is a good way to show information visually. Each bar represents a set of facts. You can compare sets of facts by looking at the different sizes of the bars.

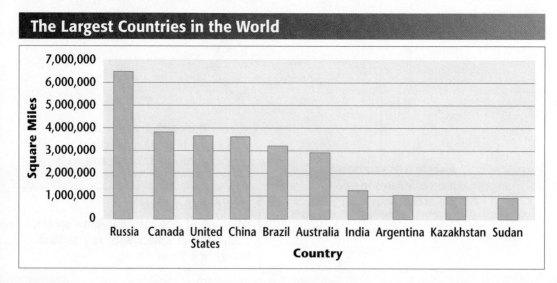

World Facts

Fact	Place	Location	Size
Highest Mountain	Mount Everest	Nepal and China	29,035 feet high
Longest River	Nile	North and East Africa	4,160 miles long
Largest Island	Greenland	North Atlantic	840,000 square miles
Largest Body of Water	Pacific Ocean	From west of North and South America to east of Asia and Australia	63,800,000 square miles

A **chart** can also be called a table. Charts are organized into rows and columns. Charts can help you to compare information.

A **line graph** shows the relationship between two sets of information. A point is placed at the intersection of every fact. When all the points are on the graph, a line is drawn to connect them. You can get a quick idea as to the trend, or direction, of information by looking at the ups and downs of the line.

World Population Growth: Historical

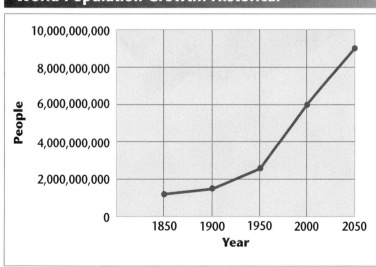

Critical Thinking
If you were to organize information about your classmates into categories such as age and gender, would you use a chart or a graph? Explain.

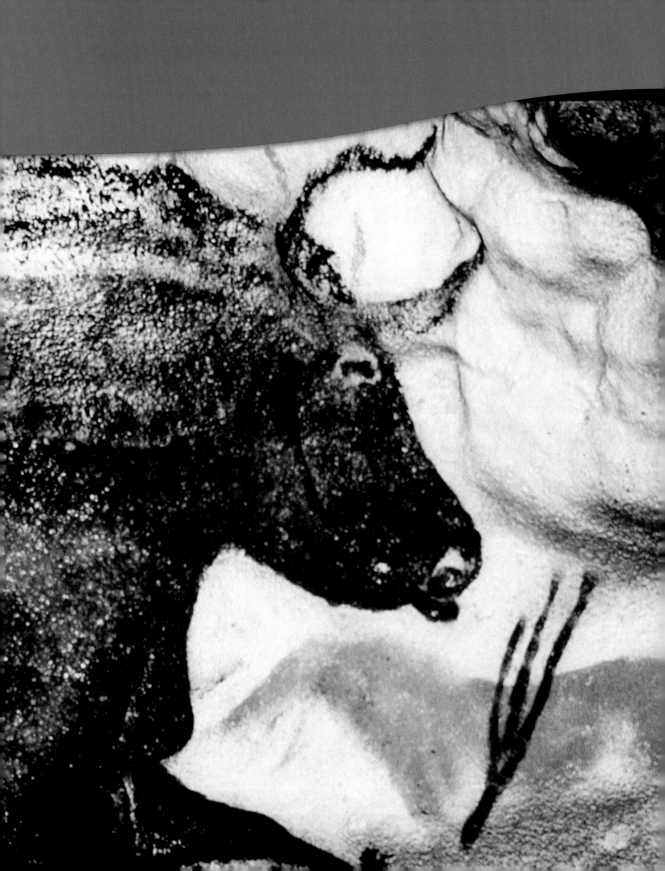

LOOKING AT THE WORLD'S HISTORY

When two people want to get to know one another, they may ask, "Where were you born? Where did you go to school? From what city did you move?" They want to know history. It could seem that studying world history is not important, but it is. Like many leaders from history, you may want power. That power could well be the power to understand. You can have the power to better relate to today's world news. You can travel to far-off places and have a clearer idea of how a another culture developed. You can plan your future with a broader vision of how you want to create your own history.

Chapters in Unit 1

This cave painting in Lascaux, France, is thousands of years old. People of Stone Age cultures often painted pictures of animals they hunted.

What Is History?

You are reading a book about the history of the world. For centuries, now, your ancestors have been recording their history for future generations. Their forefathers did the same for them. Before those people, however, earlier inhabitants of the planet were not writing history books. They were too busy trying to live.

The information in this first chapter comes from clues left in or on the earth. Thanks to the efforts of curious explorers such as archaeologists, you can learn quite a bit about the earliest people. Who knows? Your own curiosity may someday cause you to go exploring, too.

GOALS FOR LEARNING

- To explain why life in ancient times was just as exciting as life today
- To describe how historians and archaeologists learn about the past
- To explain why people make maps and how to use a timeline

Reading Strategy: Summarizing

When readers summarize, they ask questions about what they are reading. As you read the text in this chapter, ask yourself the following questions:

- Who or what is this chapter about?
- What is the main thing being said about this topic?
- What details are important to the main idea?

Key Vocabulary Words

Lesson 1

History The record of past events and the story of what happened to people in the past

Slavery The owning of human beings with the belief that they are property

Revolution A complete change, especially in a way of life or a government

Industry Business and manufacturing

Agriculture The use of land for growing crops and raising animals; farming

Development Growth of something

Imperialism The practice of conquering other lands, forming colonies in other lands, or controlling the government and wealth of weaker lands

Culture The way of life—religion, ideas, arts, tools—of a certain people in a certain time

Lesson 2

Historian Someone who writes about the past; an expert in history

Border The dividing line between two countries

Primary source A first-hand account of a historical event

Civilization A group of people who have cities and government

Archaeologist A scientist who studies cultures of the past by digging up and examining the remains of ancient towns and cities

Artifact A handmade object, such as a tool or weapon

Lesson 3

B.C. (Before Christ) Dating from before the time Jesus Christ was born

A.D. (Anno Domini) Dating from the time Jesus Christ was born

History Is All About Change

History

The record of past events and the story of what happened to people in the past

Slavery

The owning of human beings with the belief that they are property

Revolution

A complete change, especially in a way of life or a government

World **history** is the story of how the people of different times and places lived. It is the record of discoveries such as better ways of farming and new machines. It is also the story of the building of cities and nations, and of the creation of beautiful art and music.

What Changes Has the World Gone Through Since Ancient Times?

History is all about change—changing times and changing ideas. Long ago, for example, owning human beings as property, **slavery**, was an accepted part of everyday life. The ancient Egyptians made their slaves (the people that they owned) their prisoners. So did the Greeks, the Romans, the Aztecs, and many others. However, today, people in much of the world believe slavery is wrong.

About 500 years ago, there was a big change in the way people pictured their world. People realized that the Earth is round, not flat. Explorers set out from Europe on long ocean voyages. They discovered a huge body of land where they had thought there was only ocean. North and South America took their role in the story of the world.

Another word for change is **revolution.** Ideas of freedom, democracy, and independence swept across the world. This led people in many countries to rise up against their government. In both the Eastern and Western hemispheres, people rose up and demanded freedom.

Industry
Business and manufacturing

Agriculture
The use of land for growing crops and raising animals; farming

Development
Growth of something

Imperialism
The practice of conquering other lands, forming colonies in other lands, or controlling the government and wealth of weaker lands

Culture
The way of life—religion, ideas, arts, tools—of a certain people in a certain time

More than 6,000 life-sized clay soldiers were buried with an ancient Chinese emperor.

Revolutions in **industry** (business and manufacturing) and in **agriculture** (farming) changed the way people lived. Discoveries and inventions often helped people lead better lives. Sometimes changes made life harder. For example, the **development**, or growth, of industry in England made life better for many people. However, life became harder for the people who worked in the factories.

Out of the age of exploration grew an age of **imperialism**. Imperialism is the search for more land and power. Strong nations set out to rule weaker ones. Weaker lands were forced to accept foreign ideas and **cultures**, or their way of life. Europe tried to set up colonies all over the globe.

Many countries tried to fight this. People wanted to control their own lands and lives. The spirit of nationalism led people to unite under their own flags.

As histories must, this book talks about wars. Down through the ages, there have always been wars. Tribe fought against tribe, city fought against city, and nation fought against nation. World Wars I and II in the 20th century were the worst wars of all time. Sometimes history seems like nothing but a long list of wars. This book tells how wars happened and how they changed nations. Some nations became weaker; others found new power.

You Decide
The invention of television in the 20th century changed the way many people lived. If there were no TV, would your life be better or worse? Explain.

Remember
All human beings have the same basic needs for food, clothing, and shelter. In different times and places, people have met these needs in different ways.

We are still in the process of revolution. Each day, there are changes in science, in technology, and in relations between countries. There are still many difficult problems that need to be solved.

To us, ancient times may seem simple. That is not really so. About 5,000 years ago, the Sumerians in the city of Ur were very busy. They worried about feeding their people and making lands produce crops. They struggled to defend themselves against their enemies. They also faced the dangers of nature, like floods. They invented new ways to get from one place to another faster. They set up governments and made laws. They tried to explain their existence through religion. They also educated their children. They celebrated life through art and writing.

Are we really so different today? People go into space. They use the great power of the tiny atom. However, the events of ancient days were just as exciting to the people who lived then. What about the day a human being first put ideas down in writing? Was the first wheel any less exciting than the first rocket engine? People in ancient times must have found discovery and changes to be just as exciting as we do today.

The cultures of the past are our best clues to history. By looking at yesterday's people, we can better understand the world as it is today—and as it might be tomorrow.

Christopher Columbus claimed land in the West Indies for Spain in October 1492.

Match the definition in Column A with the term in Column B. Write the correct letter on a sheet of paper.

Column A

1. the way of life of a certain people in a certain time

2. a complete change, especially in a way of life or government

3. the practice of conquering, forming colonies, or controlling the government and wealth of weaker lands

4. the use of land for growing crops and raising animals; farming

Column B

A agriculture
B culture
C imperialism
D revolution

On a sheet of paper, write the letter of the answer that correctly completes each sentence.

5. In ancient times, Egyptians, Greeks, _____, and Aztecs made people their slaves.

   A Romans   B Sumerians   C English   D French

6. In ancient times, revolutions in _____ and agriculture changed the way people lived.

   A exploration B industry   C science   D slavery

7. World War I and _____ were the worst wars in human history.

   A Civil War   C World War II
   B Seven Years' War   D Gulf War

On a sheet of paper, write the answer to each question. Use complete sentences.

8. What change has taken place over the years in the way people feel about slavery?

9. What did Europeans discover after they knew the world was round?

10. How was life in ancient times like life today?

Historians and Archaeologists

Objectives

- To identify types of documents historians use to learn about the past
- To identify types of objects archaeologists use to learn about cultures of the past

Historian
Someone who writes about the past; an expert in history

Border
The dividing line between two countries

Primary source
A first-hand account of a historical event

We find out about the people of the past by looking at the things they left behind.

How Do We Learn About the Past?

The easiest way we can look into the past is by reading papers and books of days gone by. **Historians** look at old maps that tell how the dividing line between countries, or **borders,** and the names of countries have changed. They study letters, diaries, speeches, news articles, and other documents. These types of writings are called **primary sources.** Then they write books about their findings.

LEARN MORE ABOUT IT

The Trojan War

Thousands of years ago, the Greek poet Homer wrote the *Iliad.* It was about a mighty city called Troy. He wrote that Paris, son of the king of Troy, was visiting Sparta in Greece. There, Paris fell in love with Helen, the wife of King Menelaus. Paris took Helen home with him to Troy. The Greeks swore revenge. A huge army set sail for Troy. For 10 years the Greeks fought the Trojans, but the Greeks were not able to capture the city. Then they built a gigantic wooden horse. The Greek soldiers hid inside it. The Trojans were curious about the horse and dragged it inside the city walls. The Greeks climbed out and killed most of the Trojans, including Paris. Then the Greeks looted and burned the city. Helen returned to Menelaus in Sparta.

Did all of this really happen? Was there ever a city called Troy? A German archaeologist named Heinrich Schliemann believed there was such a place. In 1870 he traveled to Turkey with a team of assistants. There they began digging in a mound that seemed to fit the location described in Homer's *Iliad.* Sure enough, they uncovered the ruins of several cities piled on top of each other. At least one of the cities had massive stone walls. Schliemann had discovered Troy!

Civilization

A group of people who have cities and government

Archaeologist

A scientist who studies cultures of the past by digging up and examining the remains of ancient towns and cities

Artifact

A handmade object, such as a tool or weapon

Reading Strategy: Summarizing

What is the main idea of this lesson?

This hoe was used for farming by an ancient Plains people in North America. It was made from the shoulder blade of a buffalo.

What about the cities and governments of people, or **civilizations,** from long ago? There were times when no one wrote books or drew maps. How do we know so much about the ancient days? People called **archaeologists** dig in the ruins of ancient civilizations. They find handmade objects, called **artifacts,** that have long been underground. They study each artifact they find and piece bits of information together. In this way, they come up with a picture of the past.

Scientists have many ways of deciding how old things are. A piece of cloth, an iron tool, and a painting on a wall may all be pieces of the puzzle. As the pieces come together, bit by bit the story is told!

GREAT NAMES IN HISTORY

Louis Leakey and Mary Leakey

Louis and Mary Leakey made exciting discoveries about early humans. Louis Leakey believed that humankind had developed in Africa. The two British scientists worked in East Africa for about 40 years. They collected stone tools and pieces of bone, skulls, and teeth. These were clues to what early people were like.

Match the definition in Column A with the term in Column B.
Write the correct letter on a sheet of paper.

Column A

1. a handmade object
2. a group of people who have cities and government
3. someone who writes about the past
4. a scientist who studies past cultures by digging up and examining the remains of ancient towns and cities

Column B

A archaeologist
B artifact
C civilization
D historian

Word Bank

Homer
horse
maps
primary sources
Troy
weapons

On a sheet of paper, write the word from the Word Bank to complete each sentence correctly.

5. Writings from the time about things that happened are called _____.

6. Historians often use _____ to learn how borders and country names have changed.

7. Tools and _____ are examples of artifacts.

8. _____ was a Greek poet.

9. The *Iliad* is about a mighty city called _____.

10. In the *Iliad*, the Greeks hid inside a gigantic wooden _____. They built it to trick the Trojans.

Maps and Timelines

Objectives

- To explain why maps are important
- To describe the information that maps can show
- To explain how a timeline works
- To identify the different units and intervals that can be used on a timeline

You will notice many maps and timelines as you read. The maps will help you locate the part of the world you are learning about. Locators and other features on the maps will help guide you. They show you where the area you are looking at is in relation to the rest of the world. Timelines in each chapter help you understand the order of the events you read about.

What Do Maps Show?

The maps in this book show how countries have changed and how groups of people have moved. They show that cities were built along rivers and on seacoasts. They show how waterways made it possible for different people to come together.

The World

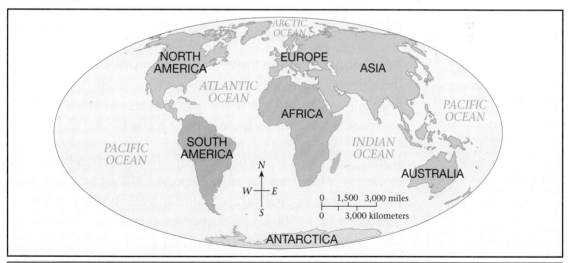

MAP STUDY

1. What are the names of the continents?
2. Which oceans border Africa?

B.C. (Before Christ)

Dating from before the time Jesus Christ was born

A.D. (Anno Domini)

Dating from the time Jesus Christ was born

Reading Strategy: Summarizing

What are some important details about things different types of maps may show?

People have been making maps for a long time. They drew maps to try to understand their world. They also used maps to find their way from one place to another. Since ancient times, the art of mapmaking has come a long way. Maps of today are more accurate, or correct. Now there are maps to show landforms, maps to show weather, and maps that picture continents, countries, and cities.

Mapmakers, however, have more work ahead. Think about the maps of the future. Will maps be needed to help people find their way among the stars?

What Do Timelines Show?

The history of the people of the world is a long and exciting story. The timelines in each chapter will help you keep events clear and in order. Look at the timeline on page 13. It gives some idea of just how long the story is. The timeline shows some of the time periods and people you will read about as the story unfolds. If you look closely at it, you should be able to find where you fit on the timeline of history.

When looking at the timeline, you will notice some differences in the way the dates are written. **B.C.** represents the time in history *before* Jesus Christ was born. **A.D.** represents the time in history *after* Jesus Christ was born.

It may seem as if some of the civilizations in this book came and went very quickly. However, the timeline shows that the Roman civilization lasted for 1,250 years (from 750 B.C. to A.D. 500). The Sumerian civilization lasted about 1,500 years (from about 3500 B.C. to 2000 B.C.). The timeline also shows that the "modern times" period is only about 500 years old so far. How does the period in history that we call ancient times compare in length with medieval times and with modern times?

You can use the same method to read most timelines.

1. Look at the whole timeline to figure out how much time it covers. Look for the earliest date. It is the first date on the left. Look for the latest date. It is the last date on the right. To read most timelines correctly, you will read the dates from left to right.

2. Remember that a timeline is like a ruler. It is divided into equal units. These equal units are called intervals. An interval may be one day, one month, one year, five years, or any other amount of time. To read any timeline correctly, you need to know how much time each unit or interval represents.

Reading Strategy:
Summarizing

What are some important details that help you read timelines?

TIMELINE STUDY: **ANCIENT TIMES TO MODERN TIMES**

Which civilization came first, the Greeks or the Sumerians?

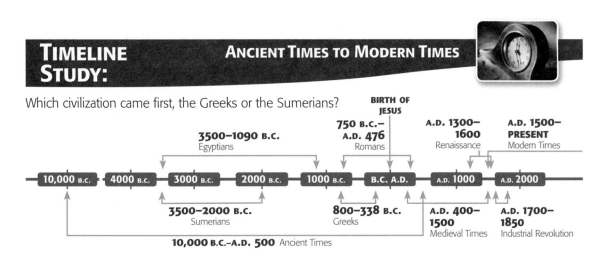

REVIEW

On a sheet of paper, write the answer to each question. Use complete sentences.

1. What are two reasons why people first started making maps?

2. What information can a map show? (List at least three things.)

3. Why is a timeline useful?

Word Bank

A.D.

B.C.

events

intervals

left

rivers

way

On a sheet of paper, write the word from the Word Bank to complete each sentence correctly.

4. People make maps to find their _____ from one place to another.

5. Maps can show many things, including: country borders, cities, and _____.

6. _____ represents a time in history before Christ was born.

7. _____ represents a time in history after Christ was born.

8. On a timeline, the earliest date is on the _____.

9. The equal units on a timeline are called _____.

10. Timelines list _____ in the order in which they happened.

- World history is the story of people, places, and events from the past. Learning about the past helps explain what is happening today.

- World history is about change. Discoveries bring about change.

- Revolution is another word for change. Revolutions in agriculture and industry brought huge changes to many cultures.

- Some changes happened because of imperialism, a quest for more land and power.

- Revolution is ongoing as technology brings advances. As new concerns arise, relations among different countries may change.

- People in the past shared many of the same concerns as people today.

- Historians study written records to learn about the past. They write books and teach others about what they have learned.

- Archaeologists study artifacts to learn about the past.

- Scientists aid historians by helping to determine the age of found artifacts.

- Maps can show different kinds of information about the world. People use maps to find their way from one place to the other. Some maps show weather trends while other maps show landforms.

- Timelines list events in the order in which they happened. A clear understanding of the intervals shown on a timeline will help in using it effectively.

CHAPTER 1 REVIEW

Word Bank

agriculture

archaeologist

artifact

civilizations

culture

development

historian

imperialism

industry

revolution

Vocabulary Review

On a sheet of paper, use the words from the Word Bank to complete each sentence correctly.

1. A(n) _____ brings about change, often in government.

2. Revolutions in industry and _____ change the way people live.

3. Developments in _____ made life harder for the people who had to work in factories.

4. A(n) _____ studies maps and books to understand the past.

5. A person who goes digging in ruins is probably a(n) _____.

6. A(n) _____ found underground can tell about life in the past.

7. Strong nations are practicing _____ when they try to take over weak nations.

8. Religion and art are parts of the _____ of a people.

9. When studying history, we often examine ancient _____.

10. The _____ of the wheel was exciting to people of ancient days.

Chapter Review Questions

On a sheet of paper, write the answer to each question. Use complete sentences.

11. What is world history?

12. What made life exciting during ancient times?

13. How do historians learn from the past?

14. What can archaeologists learn from artifacts?

15. What does a timeline show?

Critical Thinking

On a sheet of paper, write your response to each question. Use complete sentences.

16. How can learning about the past help us understand what might happen in the future?

17. Why are today's maps more accurate than maps made during ancient times? Give at least two reasons.

Using the Timeline

Use the timeline on page 13 to answer the questions.

18. What four civilizations existed during ancient times?

19. How many years did the Industrial Revolution last?

20. In what year did Modern Time begin?

GROUP ACTIVITY

Work in groups of two or three. Suppose you are archaeologists who have uncovered the remains of an ancient city. What artifacts do you hope to find? Make a list of the top 10 artifacts that you think will tell you the most about life in the ancient city.

Early Humans: The Story Begins

Millions of years ago most of the world was frozen. This was the Ice Age.

Over time the ice began to melt. Small groups of people hunted for food in the warmer, southern parts of the world. This time is known as the Stone Age.

People started to plant food. They learned how to tame animals. They started to build homes in small villages. Much of the earliest farming took place in an area known as the Fertile Crescent. This was the area of the Middle East between the Tigris and Euphrates rivers.

GOALS FOR LEARNING

- To understand how humans began to hunt and what happened after the Ice Age
- To explain how the development of agriculture changed the world
- To describe the area known as the Fertile Crescent

Reading Strategy: Questioning

Asking questions as you read will help you understand and remember more of the information. Questioning the text will also help you to be a more active reader. As you read, ask yourself:

- What is my reason for reading this text?
- What decisions can I make about the facts and details in this text?
- What connections can I make between this text and my own life?

Key Vocabulary Words

Lesson 1

Ice Age A period of time when much of Earth and Earth's water was frozen

Glacier A large, slow-moving mass of ice and snow

Stone Age The earliest known period of human culture where people used tools and weapons made from stone

Lesson 2

Settlement A small group of homes in a newly established place or region

Specialize To work in, and know a lot about, one job or field

Craft A trade or art that takes special skill with the hands

Lesson 3

Fertile Crescent The area of land in the Middle East shaped like a quarter moon

Fertile Able to produce large crops, as in rich soil

The Hunters

Objectives

■ To define the Ice Age and glacier

■ To describe the people of the Stone Age

Reading Strategy:
Questioning

What do you think you will learn about in this lesson?

Ice Age
A period of time when much of Earth and Earth's water was frozen

Glacier
A large, slow-moving mass of ice and snow

Our story of the world's history begins more than one million years ago. It was a time called the **Ice Age.** Most of the world was frozen then. It was covered with thick sheets of ice called **glaciers.** These glaciers had formed in the north.

In the northern parts of Europe, Asia, and North America, ice piled up about 10,000 feet thick. The weight of all that ice caused the glaciers to spread out. As they moved, the glaciers pushed soil and rocks out of their way. Many valleys and lakes were formed. Slowly, the glaciers moved farther and farther south.

People of the Stone Age lived in caves and used simple weapons to hunt.

Stone Age

The earliest known period of human culture where people used tools and weapons made from stone

How Did Humans Begin to Hunt?

Over time, in the southern parts of the three continents, the ice melted some during the short summers. Little groups of people lived there, scattered about. They were hunters. They had learned to make spears and other simple weapons and tools. They used wooden sticks, bones, and stones. They had not yet learned how to use metal. So historians call these people and their way of life the **Stone Age** culture.

Such was life on Earth for tens of thousands of years. The hunters left their caves in the summer to move around. They could not settle down for good. They had to follow the herds of wild animals. They also gathered some food from shrubs and trees, such as nuts, berries, and fruits. However, they mainly counted on animals for food and clothing. Hunting was the most important thing in their lives. Without a good hunt, they would die. Just staying alive was a constant struggle for people during this time.

LEARN MORE ABOUT IT

Cave Artwork

Stone Age art has been discovered in caves in France, Spain, Italy, and other places. Most of the time, the caves were discovered by mistake. In 1940, for example, three teenage boys stumbled down a hole and discovered Lascaux Cave in France.

In 1994, three men discovered Chauvet Cave in France. Some of the paintings were created more than 30,000 years ago! The artwork included animals not usually pictured on cave walls. Horses and bison were there, but so were leopards, hyenas, rhinos, and bears. In addition, there were many pictures of cave lions. These pictures showed that the artists knew the habits of the cave lions well.

It is possible that even older cave art has been discovered. In 2000, painted slabs of rock were found at Fumane Cave in Italy. The art, which includes a half-human, half-beast figure, may be 32,000–36,500 years old.

Words from the Past

Humans Learn to Say "Hello"

What did early humans sound like? What language did they speak? No one can be sure. Scientists think that humans developed language over millions of years. Very early humans probably used a "call system." They made sounds with a certain meaning, like those that some animals use. Calls showed feelings. "Look out! There's a lion!" "I'm scared." "This plant tastes good."

Then life changed for early humans. For one thing, they began to walk upright on two feet. This allowed their hands to be free to make tools. People also began to live in larger groups. They worked together to find wild plants. Groups of hunters tracked animals. Now people needed a better way to share ideas. Hunters had to plan for the next day's hunt. A skilled potter needed to teach younger workers their art. The bodies of humans also changed. Their brains and larynx, or voice box, developed. By about 100,000 years ago, some early humans were ready for a different kind of human speech.

On a sheet of paper, write the letter of the answer that correctly completes each sentence.

1. The Ice Age was more than one _____ years ago.

   A hundred   **B** thousand   **C** million   **D** billion

2. A glacier is a _____.

   A cave painting   **B** thick sheet of ice   **C** valley   **D** shrub

3. The _____ Age was a time when people hunted and made simple weapons and tools.

   A Ice   **B** Information   **C** Cave   **D** Stone

4. People of the Stone Age did not yet learn how to use _____.

   A metal   **B** sticks   **C** bones   **D** stones

5. People of the Stone Age hunted wild animals, and _____ food from shrubs and trees.

   A armed   **B** planted   **C** cooked   **D** gathered

On a sheet of paper, write the answer to each question. Use complete sentences.

6. Where did the glaciers form?

7. What caused the glaciers to spread out?

8. What helped form the valleys and lakes during the Ice Age?

9. Where did people live during the Stone Age?

10. Name three countries where Stone Age art has been found.

The Agricultural Revolution

Objectives

■ To explain two things people learned when the glaciers melted

■ To describe how taming animals helped people in their everyday life

■ To explain why the Agricultural Revolution helped develop trading

■ To name the three basic human needs that were met because of the Agricultural Revolution

Settlement

A small group of homes in a newly established place or region

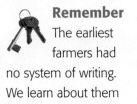

Remember

The earliest farmers had no system of writing. We learn about them from the artifacts that archaeologists find.

The Ice Age ended about 10,000 B.C. The glaciers began melting. The land was no longer frozen. People now learned how to grow food. They no longer had to chase wild animals across the lands. Once they learned to raise their own food, they could settle down. That change, from hunting to farming, made civilization possible.

How Did Humans Begin to Farm?

The people of long ago watched the winds blow seeds across the ground. They noticed that new plants grew where the seeds landed. This is how the people learned to farm. They tried planting seeds themselves. They broke up the ground to make it soft. They chose the best seeds, and they grew plants. Next, they made tools to use in farming. They used flint sickles to cut grain and wooden plows to help them dig up the ground.

Once the glaciers were gone, life became easier for people. Now they could count on a ready food supply. Often they grew more than they could eat in one winter. They could store food for the future. They would not have to move away from their homes to search for food. People began to form small groups of homes, called **settlements,** and live there.

They also learned to tame animals. Some say the dog was the first animal tamed. Next came cows, goats, sheep, and pigs. With their own herds, people had a steady supply of meat, milk, and wool. They now had animals that could live side by side with them. The animals could carry loads and help people work.

TECHNOLOGY CONNECTION

Ancient Farming

The earliest known farmers had some interesting methods. They used short-handled hoes, or sickles, to loosen soil and plant seeds. This was difficult work.

Farmers harvested grain using sickles made of flint. They gathered the grain onto areas of hard-packed earth. Then oxen, pulling sleds with flint points underneath, crushed the husks away from the grain. Grain was moved in bags carried by people, oxen, or donkeys.

Carts with solid wood wheels were used by about 3500 B.C. Wheels with spokes were invented by 2000 B.C. for two-wheeled carts. Farming wagons with either type of wheel were not likely used by the early farmers.

What Effect Did the Agricultural Revolution Have on People?

When people began to farm about 11,000 years ago, their lives changed. The change brought about by agriculture was great. For this reason, the change is often called the

Agricultural Revolution. Now people could settle in large groups, in one place. They chose areas with plenty of water and good soil. They built houses out of whatever materials were nearby. Often the houses were built of mud.

Now the people could plan on how much food to plant each year. They could decide on how many animals to raise in the herds. Now they had more control of their own lives.

For thousands of years, people have tamed animals to carry loads and help them with work.

Specialize
To work in, and know a lot about, one job or field

Craft
A trade or art that takes special skill with the hands

You Decide
There are still craftworkers today. Are craftworkers needed as much today as they were long ago? Why or why not?

Reading Strategy: Questioning

What sort of job might you have wanted to have those thousands of years ago? Why?

Having a large enough food supply and staying in one place gave people spare time. Not everyone in the group was needed to raise food or care for the animals. This allowed people to learn a lot about one job, and they began to **specialize.** Some people farmed. Others took care of the animals.

Now there were also chances to do things they had never done before. People had time to work on their **crafts.** Weavers wove grass into fine baskets. Others made pottery from mud and clay and baked it in ovens. With wool from the sheep, some people learned to spin thread and to weave cloth.

As different jobs developed, so did trading. Weavers might trade their cloth for food from farmers. A goat might be traded for an ax from the toolmaker. First, trading was carried on within the village. Later, people traded from one village to the next.

With the Agricultural Revolution, people's most important needs—food, shelter, and clothing—were easier to meet. However, now people owned things. Potters had their jars and bowls. Herders had their animals. Now there were things to protect! New laws were needed. Most likely a group of the oldest, wisest people in the village would meet. They would decide on rules for the rest of the people.

People started to worry when their villages grew rich. Someone might attack them and try to steal some of their riches. Therefore, people formed armies to protect their villages.

As time went on, villages grew into cities. Later, cities joined together to form small kingdoms. Agriculture is what made this development possible.

REVIEW

farming

kingdoms

laws

specialize

tame

On a sheet of paper, write the word from the Word Bank to complete each sentence correctly.

1. The change from hunting to _____ made civilization possible.

2. The Agricultural Revolution allowed people to _____.

3. People learned to grow food and to _____ animals when the Ice Age ended.

4. When people started to own things, new _____ were needed.

5. As time went on, villages grew into cities, which grew into _____.

On a sheet of paper, write the answer to each question. Use complete sentences.

6. Why were people able to live in settlements?

7. How did taming animals help people in their everyday life?

8. How did the Agricultural Revolution help develop trading? (Provide examples.)

9. What three basic human needs were met because of the Agricultural Revolution?

10. Why did people start to form armies?

LESSON
2-3

The Fertile Crescent

Objectives

■ To locate the Fertile Crescent on a map
■ To explain how the people of ancient Jericho tried to protect their town

Fertile Crescent

The area of land in the Middle East shaped like a quarter moon

Fertile

Able to produce large crops, as in rich soil

 History Fact
By about 8000 B.C., Jericho had between 1,000 and 2,000 people. Archaeologists have found wheat and barley in the remains of the town.

The success of farming depends on rich soil and the presence of water. For this reason, early human settlements arose near rivers.

What Is the Fertile Crescent?

The earliest known farming took place along the great rivers of the Middle East. These lands include what are now the countries of Jordan, Syria, Iraq, Iran, Kuwait, Lebanon, Israel, and Turkey. This area is called the **Fertile Crescent** because it is shaped like a quarter moon. The Tigris and Euphrates rivers provided plenty of water for the land. The soil was rich, or **fertile.** The land between the Tigris and Euphrates was called Mesopotamia. That name means "land between two rivers."

Within the Fertile Crescent was the town of Jericho. It is one of the earliest known towns. By about 8000 B.C., Jericho was probably a farming village. Its people built rounded houses of mud and bricks. Archaeologists have found remains showing that the people of Jericho buried their dead right under their houses.

The land around Jericho was very fertile. The people grew many crops and became rich. The town grew. Jericho now had to protect itself. The people built a stone wall around their town.

The wall was not enough protection. Around 7000 B.C., archaeologists say, Jericho was probably captured. The houses built after that time were no longer round but had square corners. This clue suggests that a new group of people must have taken over and settled there.

The wall built to protect Jericho was destroyed and the town was captured.

Geography Note

Archaeologists believe that people were farming the Nile Valley as early as 10,000 B.C. By 6000 B.C., farmers there were harvesting grains such as sorghum, millet, and barley. Beginning in about 4000 B.C., the area became increasingly dry. The Sahara grew. Many of the former Nile Valley farmers moved to southwest Africa.

Reading Strategy:
Questioning

Study the maps and the timeline. Ask yourself how they relate to what you just read.

More is known about the early farming villages of the Fertile Crescent than anywhere else. However, farming was developing in other parts of the world, too. By 6000 B.C., farming had spread to Europe. By 5000 B.C., a culture of rice farmers had grown up in China. Between 5000 B.C. and 2000 B.C., agriculture spread across northern Africa.

People began to settle wherever there was good soil and plenty of water. Now they had food and clothing. They had time to learn. Certain cities began to grow into great civilizations.

Compare the maps on the next page. Notice how the Middle East changed over time.

TIMELINE STUDY:
THE AGRICULTURAL REVOLUTION

How many years passed between the beginning of agriculture and the first use of the wheel?

10,000 B.C.
End of Ice Age

6000 B.C.
Farming spreads to Europe

5000 B.C.
Rice farming develops in China

| 10,000 B.C. | 9000 B.C. | 8000 B.C. | 7000 B.C. | 6000 B.C. | 5000 B.C. | 4000 B.C. | 3000 B.C. | 2000 B.C. | 1000 B.C. | B.C. A.D. |

9000 B.C.
Taming of animals and beginning of agriculture in Fertile Crescent

7000 B.C.
Pottery-making begins; Jericho probably captured

5000 B.C.
Agriculture spreads across northern Africa

3500 B.C.
First use of wheel

BIRTH OF JESUS

The Middle East: Then

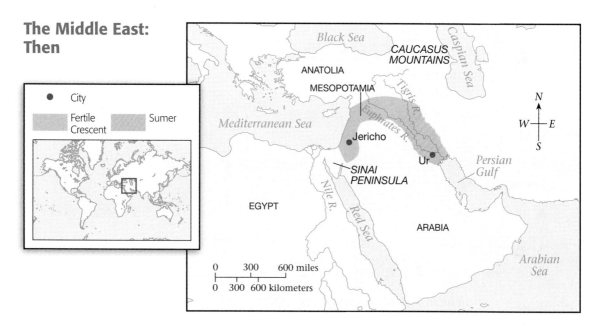

The Middle East: Now

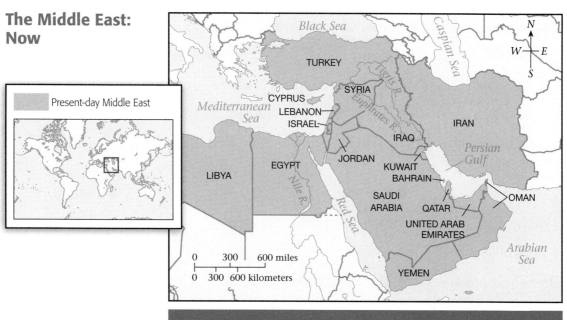

MAP STUDY

1. Which names of places are on both maps?
2. Look at both maps. In which present-day country was Sumer located?

On a sheet of paper, write the letter of the answer that correctly completes each sentence.

1. The land with rich soil and that produced large crops was known as the _____.

   A Middle East **B** Mesopotamia **C** Fertile Crescent **D** Jericho

2. The land between the Tigris and _____ was called Mesopotamia.

   A Jordan **B** Euphrates **C** Iraq **D** Lebanon

3. _____ means *land between two rivers*.

   A Mesopotamia **B** Tigris **C** Euphrates **D** Iraq

4. A town within the Fertile Crescent was _____.

   A Israel **B** Iraq **C** Jericho **D** Tigris

5. People in Jericho built rounded houses made of _____ and bricks.

   A sticks **B** straw **C** bones **D** mud

6. The people of Jericho tried to protect their town by building a stone _____.

   A wall **B** weapon **C** house **D** road

7. By _____ B.C., farming had spread to Europe.

   A 6000 **B** 5000 **C** 4000 **D** 2000

On a sheet of paper, write the answer to each question. Use complete sentences.

8. What Middle Eastern countries does the area known as the Fertile Crescent include?

9. What do archaeologists believe the people of Jericho did with their dead?

10. What evidence is there to suggest that Jericho was captured?

SUMMARY

- During the Ice Age, most of the world was frozen. In some places, the ice was 10,000 feet thick.

- In southern areas, groups of people hunted for food during the short summers.

- Hunters could not form long-term settlements. They had to follow the animals. They gathered some wild foods such as nuts and berries.

- People began to see that the wind scattered seeds and became new plants. They started to plant seeds on their own. They made tools for farming.

- People began to tame animals.

- Farming meant people could control their own food supply. They could build houses and settle in one place. Some people call this the Agricultural Revolution.

- In the new settlements, people had different jobs. New crafts developed.

- As people created more and different products, trading began and villages became richer.

- Villages formed armies to protect their valuables.

- Villages grew into cities, cities joined to form kingdoms.

- One of the earliest areas of farming was in the Middle East, along two great rivers. This area is called the Fertile Crescent.

CHAPTER 2
REVIEW

Word Bank

craft

fertile

Fertile Crescent

glacier

settlement

specialize

Vocabulary Review

On a sheet of paper, use the words from the Word Bank to correctly match each definition below.

1. The area of land in the Middle East where the earliest farming took place

2. Arts and skills such as weaving and making baskets

3. Rich soil that is suitable for farming

4. To work in a job that takes a certain kind of knowledge

5. A moving body of ice and snow

6. A small village in a newly established place or region

Chapter Review Questions

On a sheet of paper, write the answer to each question. Use complete sentences.

7. What was the Stone Age culture?

8. Why were people able to live in settlements?

9. What did people begin to do after the Ice Age ended?

10. How did farming make life easier for people after the Ice Age ended?

11. Why did the people of Jericho build a wall around their town?

12. How did archaeologists know Jericho was captured?

13. Where did the earliest known farming take place?

14. What is Mesopotamia?

If a question asks you to describe or explain something, try to answer the question as completely as possible. Use complete sentences.

Critical Thinking

On a sheet of paper, write your response to each question. Use complete sentences.

15. Why do you think people made pictures in caves thousands of years ago?

16. Why did trading develop after people began to specialize?

17. Why is the change from hunting to farming called the Agricultural Revolution?

Using the Timeline

Use the timeline on page 30 to answer the questions.

18. Which came first, pottery-making or the first use of the wheel?

19. Where and when did rice farming develop?

20. How many years after the end of the Ice Age was Jesus born?

GROUP ACTIVITY

Form a group of three or four students. Discuss the ways life in early villages was like life in towns and cities today. Make a list of the ways they were alike. Share the list with the rest of the class.

ANCIENT CIVILIZATIONS

If you read and go to films, you probably love adventure stories. It is fun to be kept on the edge of your seat by make-believe. How about true stories of adventure? Consider learning about buried treasure and mummies. Think of thousands of people building a stone monument 10 times taller than your school building. What about managing the sails of a boat during a wild storm? Suppose you are trying to read words of art painted on cave walls. By understanding the words, you will figure out who killed who and when. What better adventure could you imagine? The study of ancient civilizations is filled with mystery and suspense.

Chapters in Unit 2

The pyramids at Giza were built by ancient Egyptians as tombs for their kings.

Sumerians: The First Great Civilization

More and more people settled on the fertile land between the Tigris and Euphrates rivers. The land became known as Sumer. Farmers worked hard to find new and better ways of growing food. Merchants traveled in boats to find treasures from other lands. The villages of Sumer grew into city-states.

The Sumerians began to write down details of their lives. They learned ways of measuring land and counting. Their crafts included fine jewelry made of copper, silver, and gold. They built an army to protect their lands.

GOALS FOR LEARNING

- To explain why the civilization of Sumer grew
- To discuss the growth of Sumerian city-states
- To name the most important Sumerian inventions
- To describe life in Sumer

Reading Strategy: Predicting

Previewing a text helps readers think about what they already know about a subject. It also prepares readers to look for new information—to predict what will come next. Keep this in mind as you make predictions:

- Make your best guess about what might happen next.

- Add details about what you think will happen.

- Check your predictions. You may have to change your predictions as you learn more information.

Key Vocabulary Words

Lesson 1

Swamp An area of low, wet land

Irrigate To bring water to dry land by means of canals

Canal A man-made waterway

Dike A wall built along a river or sea to hold back the water from low land

Merchant A person who buys and sells goods for a profit; a trader

Goods The things for sale or trade

Lesson 2

Temple A building used to honor and praise a god or gods

Goddess A female god

Priest A religious leader

City-state An independent city and the surrounding land it controls

Independent Self-governing, separate, free

Lesson 3

Tablet A small, flat piece of clay used for writing

Cuneiform A wedge-shaped form of writing used in ancient Sumer

Scribe A person whose job it was to write out copies of contracts and other important papers

Contract A written agreement between two or more people

Chariot An open two-wheeled cart, pulled by horses

Pictograph A drawing that represents an actual thing; for example, a picture of an eye represents an eye

Create To make something

Lesson 4

Noble A person of high social rank

The Sumerian Civilization

Objectives

- To locate the land of Sumer on a map
- To describe the Sumerian method of farming and irrigating
- To name three items that Sumerians got through trading
- To identify how Sumerians carried goods to and from Sumer

The land that would one day be called Mesopotamia lay between two rivers. The rivers were the Tigris and the Euphrates. Sometimes the rivers flooded and washed rich bottom-soil up on the land. This made the land good for farming. People settled on this rich land. They grew their crops and raised animals. In the south, in a land called Sumer, a great civilization grew.

How Did the Sumerians Farm?

The people of Sumer were called Sumerians. Although the land they settled was fertile, it was not a perfect place to live. The weather was very hot in the summer. In spring there was always the danger of the rivers flooding.

The Sumerians

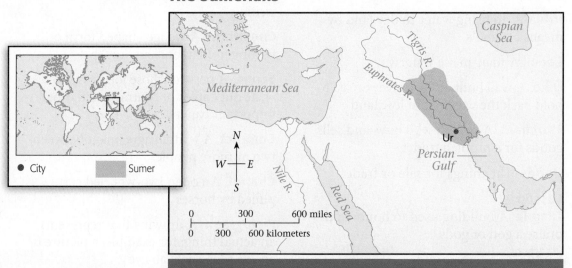

● City ▨ Sumer

MAP STUDY

1. What four large bodies of water are on the map?
2. What three rivers are on the map?

Swamp

An area of low, wet land

Irrigate

To bring water to dry land by means of canals

Canal

A man-made waterway

Dike

A wall built along a river or sea to hold back the water from low land

Merchant

A person who buys and sells goods for a profit; a trader

Goods

The things for sale or trade

 History Fact
Sumerians with the same jobs often lived and worked on the same street.

Reading Strategy: Predicting

Based on what you have just read, predict what you think you may learn from the next lesson.

Sometimes whole villages would be washed away. Many people would die.

Part of Sumer was **swamp** land, meaning it was quite wet. Other parts were very dry. Land that was flooded in the spring dried hard under the late summer sun. It was necessary to make the land ready for crops. The Sumerian farmers had to get water from the rivers to their fields.

The farmers found a way to **irrigate,** or bring water to, their fields. They made cuts in the river banks and dug waterways, called **canals.** The canals carried the river water out to the crops. The Sumerians also built a wall, called a **dike,** to hold back the flood waters.

A Sumerian farmer worked hard from early morning until late at night. Oxen were the farmer's treasure. They pulled the farmer's plow and carried the crops in from the field. Sumer was a wealthy, or rich, land. Its wealth lay in farming.

How Did the Sumerians Trade?

The people of Sumer had different jobs. While some were farmers, others were traders, or **merchants.** Sumer had little metal, stone, or timber of its own. Sumerians depended on trading to get these things. They sent their fine crops to other lands. In return, they brought back the **goods,** the things for sale or trade, they needed at home.

Boats carried the goods to and from Sumer. The Sumerian boats were among the first ever used. There were two kinds of boats. River boats were small. They moved along under the power of long oars or poles. Trading ships were much longer, and they were narrow. They had big sails. The trading boats brought home treasures of gold, silver, pearls, and copper from other lands.

Match the definition in Column A with the term in Column B.
Write the correct letter on a sheet of paper.

Column A

1. a man-made waterway

2. a person who buys and sells goods for profit; a trader

3. a wall built along a body of water to prevent flooding

4. to bring water to dry land by means of canals

5. an area of low, wet land

Column B

A canal

B dike

C irrigate

D merchant

E swamp

On a sheet of paper, write the letter of the answer that correctly completes each sentence.

6. The land of Sumer is located between the Tigris and _____ rivers.

   A Mediterranean   **B** Caspian   **C** Nile   **D** Euphrates

7. _____ were the farmer's treasure. They pulled the plow and carried crops in from the field.

   A Slaves   **B** Oxen   **C** Children   **D** Boats

8. The people of Sumer had to trade to get metal, _____, and timber.

   A stone   **B** weapons   **C** crops   **D** slaves

9. _____ were used to carry goods to and from Sumer.

   A oxen   **B** canals   **C** boats   **D** plows

10. Sumerians used two kinds of boats: river boats and _____.

    A trading ships   **B** canals   **C** plows   **D** merchants

Sumerian City-States

Objectives

■ To describe the earliest Sumerian houses

■ To name and describe one of Sumer's greatest city-states

Temple
A building used to honor and praise a god or gods

Goddess
A female god

Priest
A religious leader

City-state
An independent city and the surrounding land it controls

Independent
Self-governing, separate, free

In the beginning, the Sumerians lived in the hills northeast of Mesopotamia. Gradually, however, they moved into the river valleys.

How Did the Villages Grow Into City-States?

The earliest Sumerians lived in houses made from reeds. The reeds, or tall grasses, grew in the swamps. Later, the people learned to make bricks from mud. They dried the bricks in the sun and built houses from them. The brick houses stayed cool inside during the hot summers.

Each Sumerian village was built around a **temple.** The temple was where people would honor and praise a god or **goddess,** a woman god. The people believed a god or goddess lived in the temple and protected the village. The farmers took part of their crops to the temple to offer to the god or goddess. The **priests,** or religious leaders, of the temple became very wealthy and powerful.

Over the years, the villages grew. They became **city-states,** each one with its own government. The city-states were **independent,** meaning they were each separate and free. A temple still stood at the center of each city-state. There was farmland all around the edge of the city. The city-states often fought among themselves. For protection, the Sumerians built walls around their cities.

Reading Strategy:
Predicting

Think about what you
predicted earlier. Does
your prediction still work,
or do you need to revise
your prediction?

One of the greatest city-states of Sumer was called Ur. A gigantic temple, called a *ziggurat,* was built in Ur. This tall temple-tower was built to honor the god who watched over the city. The people of Ur came in great numbers to bring gifts to the temple. They believed that if their god was happy, the city would be wealthy.

The ziggurat was built to honor the Sumerian god who watched over the city of Ur.

REVIEW

Word Bank

bricks

city-state

gifts

god

government

reeds

temple

Ur

walls

ziggurat

On a sheet of paper, write the word from the Word Bank to complete each sentence correctly.

1. Early Sumerians lived in houses made of _____.

2. Sumerians learned to make houses from _____ that they made from drying mud in the sun.

3. Sumerian villages were built around a(n) _____.

4. A(n) _____ is an independent city and the surrounding land it controls.

5. Each city-state had its own _____.

6. Sumerians built _____ around their cities for protection.

7. _____ was one of the greatest city-states of Sumer.

8. A gigantic temple is known as a(n) _____.

9. Large temples were built to honor the _____ that watched over the city.

10. Sumerians brought _____ to gods to make sure they were happy.

Sumerian Inventions

The Sumerians' inventions were their gifts to the world. All the civilizations that followed used inventions of the Sumerians. There are still things in the world today that date back to Sumer.

What Was the Greatest Gift the Sumerians Gave to the World?

The greatest gift the Sumerians gave to the world was the invention of writing. The Sumerians were a wealthy people. They needed some way to keep track of what they owned. They began by drawing pictures. They used a reed as a pen. They drew on soft pieces of clay. The soft clay was then dried in the sun. The small, flat piece of clay, called a **tablet,** became a permanent (lasting) record. Later, the Sumerian drawings changed into wedge-shaped symbols. This kind of writing is called **cuneiform.** By putting symbols together, the Sumerians could write whole sentences.

Not all Sumerians knew how to write. Only wealthy parents could afford to send their children to school. Very few girls received an education, so students were often called school-sons. Their teachers were called school-fathers. Specially trained people called **scribes** learned how to write. The school-sons learned to write by copying texts over to tablets of clay.

A clay tablet

Contract

A written agreement between two or more people

Chariot

An open two-wheeled cart, pulled by horses

Remember

Before the Agricultural Revolution, most people did not have other jobs besides farming.

You Decide

What if the wheel had never been invented? What would the world be like today? How would people travel?

The scribes were paid well for their special skill. They were among the richest of the Sumerians. They drew up business agreements, called **contracts,** for the farmers and merchants. Some scribes learned to add, subtract, and multiply; they could become tax collectors.

We know a great deal about this earliest of civilizations. This is because Sumerian scribes wrote down their ideas and kept records.

What Other Gifts Did the Sumerians Give the World?

The Sumerian farmers had to pay a tax on their property. To figure the taxes, they invented a way of measuring land. Fields were divided into even squares. Then the squares were counted to decide how much tax a farmer owed. Since the Sumerians used silver as money, payments were made in silver. The value of the silver was measured by its weight.

The Sumerians also learned to measure time. The 60-second minute and the 60-minute hour probably come from the Sumerian way of counting time.

Historians believe that the wheel was first used in Sumer. Sumerian armies rode in wheeled **chariots.** A chariot is an open two-wheeled cart, usually pulled by horses. However, there were no horses in all of Sumer. Therefore, wild donkeys were taught to pull the chariots.

Irrigation canals came to us from the Sumerian farmer. Sailboats came from the traders.

There was little metal in Sumer itself, so the Sumerians traded for metal. They became skilled metalworkers. They learned to make fine jewelry of copper, silver, and gold.

Sumerian ideas and Sumerian inventions brought about changes that would affect life for ages to come.

Words from the Past

Pictograph
A drawing that represents an actual thing

Create
To make something

How Writing Changed

If you were trying to communicate with someone and you did not have a written language, how would you do it? You might use pictures to tell a story. That is how writing began in Sumer.

At first, **pictographs,** or drawings that represent actual things, were used. For example, a picture of a fish represented a fish. These early pictographs were drawn in vertical columns with a pen made from a sharpened reed.

In time, these pictographs began to look less like the real objects they represented. Instead, they became simple symbols that were easier to draw. These marks eventually became wedge-shaped strokes, or cuneiform. The Latin word for "wedge" is *cuneus.* People then began to write in horizontal rows. A new type of pen was used. It was pushed into the clay, forming the wedge-shaped symbols.

Writing eventually developed into something closer to an alphabet by other groups of people. However, it was the Sumerians who **created,** or made, the first efficient form of writing. There were symbols, or cuneiform writing, for thousands of words!

Word	Early Pictograph	Late Pictograph	Cuneiform
Bird			
Fish			
Ox			
Sun			

This chart shows how writing changed from simple pictures to symbols, called cuneiform.

REVIEW

Match the definition in Column A with the term in Column B.
Write the correct letter on a sheet of paper.

Column A

1. a legal written agreement between two or more people

2. an open two-wheeled cart, pulled by horses or donkeys

3. a person whose job was to write out copies of contracts and other important papers

4. a small, flat piece of clay used for writing

5. a wedge-shaped form of writing used in ancient Sumer

Column B

A chariot

B contract

C cuneiform

D scribe

E tablet

On a sheet of paper, write the answer to each question. Use complete sentences.

6. Why was cuneiform so important?

7. How could a Sumerian become a scribe?

8. Why did Sumerians have to invent a way to measure land?

9. What animal pulled the chariots in Sumer?

10. What are three gifts, besides writing, that the Sumerians gave to the world?

Life in Sumer

Although it may be hard to imagine, life in Sumer was
quite exciting.

What Was Life Like in Sumer?

A Sumerian boy might awaken to a hot, dry summer
day in the city of Ur. If his father were a farmer, the boy
would go with him to work in the fields. The two of them
would leave their small house with the earliest rays of the
sun. Perhaps that day the father and son would clean the
irrigation canals. Even if the day were very hot, the boy
would work hard. Those canals were important to the
farm. Without them, nothing would grow. The boy might
work alongside other farmers. They would have help from
the slaves from one of the larger farms.

Boys from wealthy families could go to school. If a
boy learned well, he might become a scribe. A scribe
could work in the king's palace or perhaps in the great
temple itself.

*Sumerian boys from wealthy families went to school, where
they learned to write.*

Noble

A person of high social rank

The king ran the city of Ur. He ruled in the name of the city's god. Priests, scribes, and **nobles** helped him rule. These people were very rich. They lived a fine life. They were members of the highest classes in Sumer.

The people of Ur believed that when they died, they went to another world. Archaeologists have discovered graves filled with fine gold jewelry. Some graves of the nobles hold many skeletons. It may be that other people killed themselves, or were killed, when the nobles died. This way they could follow the dead nobles to that other world.

What Brought an End to the Sumerian Civilization?

The Sumerian city-states fought with each other. That is why, after a while, Sumer grew weak. Around 2000 B.C., Sumerian cities came under attack. The Sumerian armies, even with their wheeled chariots, were not strong enough to save Sumer. Ur was destroyed. The city's wealth was stolen. Men and women were killed. Children were taken as slaves.

Reading Strategy: Predicting

Think about your prediction. What details can you now add to make your prediction more specific?

Soon other Sumerian cities fell, too. The invaders (attackers), called the Babylonians, built new cities. Later, some of those cities died away. Dust and dirt covered them over. Today archaeologists dig into great mounds that still stand in the Middle East. Under the mounds of dirt lay all that is left of these ancient civilizations.

TIMELINE STUDY: SUMER: 5000 B.C.–2000 B.C.

How many years passed from the rise of Sumerian city-states to their fall to the Babylonians?

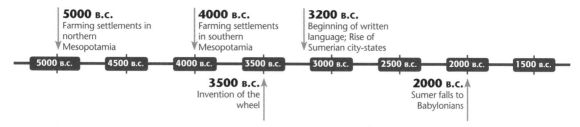

5000 B.C.
Farming settlements in northern Mesopotamia

4000 B.C.
Farming settlements in southern Mesopotamia

3200 B.C.
Beginning of written language; Rise of Sumerian city-states

5000 B.C. — 4500 B.C. — 4000 B.C. — 3500 B.C. — 3000 B.C. — 2500 B.C. — 2000 B.C. — 1500 B.C.

3500 B.C.
Invention of the wheel

2000 B.C.
Sumer falls to Babylonians

REVIEW

On a sheet of paper, write the letter of the answer that correctly completes each sentence.

1. On a typical day, boys from wealthy families might _____.

   A work on the farm   **C** go to school
   B praise their god in the temple   **D** go sailing

2. A _____ could work in the king's palace or even in a temple.

   A boy   **B** farmer   **C** king   **D** scribe

3. The _____ ran the city of Ur.

   A gods   **B** king   **C** nobles   **D** farmers

4. Priests, scribes, and _____ also helped rule Ur.

   A nobles   **B** slaves   **C** farmers   **D** young boys

5. Archaeologists have found graves filled with _____.

   A weapons   **B** gold jewelry   **C** chariots   **D** mummies

6. Sumerian cities came under attack around _____ B.C.

   A 5000   **B** 4000   **C** 3000   **D** 2000

7. The _____ invaded Sumerian cities and built new cities.

   A slaves   **B** scribes   **C** Babylonians   **D** archaeologists

On a sheet of paper, write the answer to each question. Use complete sentences.

8. What was a typical day like for a Sumerian farm boy?

9. What did the people of Ur believe happened to them when they died?

10. Why did Sumer grow weak?

- The first great civilization grew up between the Tigris and Euphrates rivers in the land of Sumer.

- The Sumerian civilization was based on farming. The Sumerians had to irrigate their land. They dug canals and built dikes to control the water supply.

- The Sumerian merchants traded with other lands for the goods they needed. They traveled in some of the world's first boats.

- Sumerians lived in brick houses built around temples. They honored gods and goddesses with their own crops as gifts.

- The Sumerians lived in city-states. Each city-state had its own government.

- One of the greatest Sumerian city-states was called Ur. The people there built a huge ziggurat, or temple, there.

- The Sumerians invented writing. They used wedge-shaped symbols in a kind of writing called cuneiform. Their trained writers, or scribes, became wealthy by writing down records and helping with business agreements.

- The Sumerians also invented the wheel, the sailboat, irrigation, canals, and a way of measuring.

- The Sumerian city-states were attacked and fell, but their ideas lived on.

- The invaders, the Babylonians, built new cities.

Word Bank

chariot

city-state

contracts

cuneiform

goods

irrigate

merchants

scribe

swamp

temple

Vocabulary Review

On a sheet of paper, use the words from the Word Bank to complete each sentence correctly.

1. Sumerians believed a god or goddess lived in the _____ and protected the village.

2. Sumerians depended on _____ to get metal, stone, and timber.

3. Each _____ had its own government.

4. Sumerians used boats to carry _____ to and from Sumer.

5. The Sumerian system of writing based on wedge-shaped symbols was called _____.

6. A(n) _____ was a person who was trained to write.

7. Scribes would draw up business _____ for farmers and merchants.

8. Sumer had fertile land; some parts were _____ land and other parts were very dry.

9. Sumerian farmers found a way to _____ their fields.

10. Sumerians used wild donkeys to pull their _____.

Chapter Review Questions

On a sheet of paper, write the answer to each question. Use complete sentences.

11. How did Sumerians farm the land?

12. Why did the Sumerians trade with other lands?

13. What did the Sumerians use for money?

14. How did the Sumerians invent writing?

15. What were five inventions of the Sumerians?

16. Why were scribes members of the richest and highest class of Sumerian culture?

Critical Thinking

On a sheet of paper, write your response to each question. Use complete sentences.

17. How do you think the Sumerians might have been able to prevent the fall of their cities?

18. How were Sumerian schools different from schools today?

Using the Timeline

Use the timeline on page 51 to answer the questions.

19. What two things were invented between 3500 B.C. and 3000 B.C.?

20. How many years passed between settlements in northern and southern Mesopotamia?

GROUP ACTIVITY

Choose five items found in your classroom and draw a symbol for each. Work in small groups to see if you can guess what one another's symbols represent. Once you have determined what each symbol means, create a sentence by putting certain symbols next to each other in a row. Present your group's sentence to the class to see if your classmates can guess what it says.

Ancient Egypt: Land of the Pharaohs

The story of the ancient Egyptians is quite interesting. The first farmers there lived in the Nile River Valley. Their villages joined to form larger settlements. By 3100 B.C., all of Egypt was ruled by King Menes. He became the first of the great Egyptian pharaohs.

Egyptian pharaohs led lives of great wealth and power. When they died, their bodies were preserved as mummies. They were buried in tombs surrounded by giant pyramids. The pharaoh's favorite things were buried with him or her. The Egyptians believed that after death people went on to another life.

GOALS FOR LEARNING

- To explain why people settled along the Nile River
- To explain why the pharaohs had their people build the pyramids
- To describe Egyptian culture

Reading Strategy: Text Structure

Understanding how text is organized helps readers decide which information is most important. Before you begin reading this chapter, look at how it is organized.

- Look at the title, headings, boldfaced words, and photographs.

- Ask yourself: Is the text a problem and solution, description, or sequence? Is it compare and contrast or cause and effect?

- Summarize the text by thinking about its structure.

Key Vocabulary Words

Lesson 1

Desert Dry, sandy land with little or no plant life

Upstream In the direction against the flow of the river; at the upper part of a river

Unite To bring together as one

Pharaoh A ruler of ancient Egypt

Tax Money paid to support a government

Lesson 2

Tomb A grave, usually one that is enclosed in stone or cement

Pyramid A huge stone structure with a square base and four triangular sides that meet in a point at the top; Egyptian rulers were buried in the pyramids

Transport To move from one place to another

Mummy A dead body kept from rotting by being treated with chemicals and wrapped in cloth

Lesson 3

Hieroglyphics A system of writing using pictures or symbols to represent objects, ideas, or sounds

Papyrus A writing paper the Egyptians made from water plants of the same name

Translate To change the words of one language to another

Egypt and the Nile

Objectives

■ To describe what happened to the Nile River Valley every July

■ To locate upper and lower Egypt on a map

■ To describe what a pharaoh did

Reading Strategy:
Text Structure

Preview this lesson, including the headings, features, and boldfaced words.

Desert

Dry, sandy land with little or no plant life

At one time the area now called the Sahara was a green plain. People lived there. There was water and wildlife. Over time the weather changed. The plain dried up and became a **desert**—a dry, sandy land with little or no plant life. The people living there went looking for water. Some of them went to a land called Egypt.

What Was the Importance of the Nile?

A great river called the Nile ran through Egypt. The Nile River Valley was a swampland. It was a dark jungle filled with dangerous animals. The people needed water badly, so they cleared the land anyway. They built their villages along the river where the jungle used to be.

Like the Sumerians, the people of Egypt built a civilization along a river. They were able to do this because the land along the Nile had what they needed. The Egyptians learned to farm, to tame animals, to make pottery, and to weave. They learned to make tools from metal.

The weather in Egypt was hot. Each year, in July, the Nile River spilled over its banks in a great flood. Land that stood dry all year was suddenly under water for several weeks. The floods left the land very fertile.

Farmers learned to use the floods to help them. They saved some of the flood waters to water their crops the rest of the year. Like the Sumerians, they learned to dig canals to irrigate their fields.

Each July the farmers moved to higher ground, taking their animals with them. They knew that the floods would be over in a few weeks. They waited until the Nile once again flowed peacefully within its banks. Then they planted their seeds in the rich, soft ground.

Upstream
In the direction against the flow of the river; at the upper part of a river

Reading Strategy:
Text Structure

Study the map in this lesson. How does it help you to understand what the lesson is about?

How Did Lower Egypt and Upper Egypt Become One?

The civilization along the Nile did well. Villages joined together to form larger settlements. There came a time, around 3200 B.C., when two kings ruled all of Egypt. One king ruled Lower Egypt, in the north. Another king ruled Upper Egypt, in the south. A look at the map below shows each of these areas. The Nile River flows northward. A person in Lower Egypt who followed the Nile south, or **upstream,** would come to Upper Egypt.

Upper and Lower Egypt

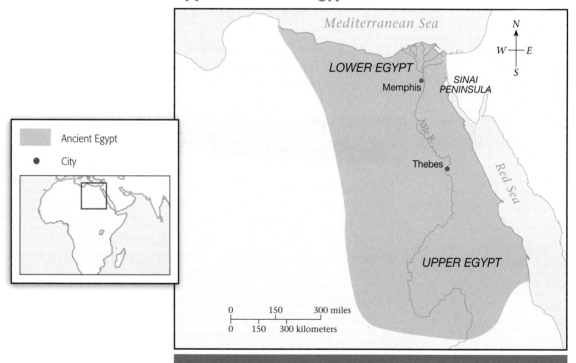

MAP STUDY

1. What are two ancient Egyptian cities on the map?

2. Which part of Egypt, Upper or Lower, bordered on the Mediterranean Sea?

Unite
To bring together as one

Pharaoh
A ruler of ancient Egypt

Tax
Money paid to support a government

 You Decide
People today still have to pay taxes. What do you think would happen if a government official used tax money to live a rich life?

The king of Lower Egypt wore a red crown. The king of Upper Egypt wore a white crown. The two kings ended up fighting to control all of Egypt. Around 3100 B.C., King Menes of Upper Egypt conquered Lower Egypt. Now Menes wore a "double" crown. He ruled and **united,** or brought together, all of Egypt.

King Menes became the first great ruler, or **pharaoh,** of Egypt. The Egyptians called their ruler *pharaoh*, meaning "The Great House."

The pharaohs were powerful rulers. Each year they collected **taxes**—huge taxes—from all the people to support the government. Farmers had to give the pharaoh a large part of their crops as a tax.

The pharaoh had many men to help carry out orders and collect taxes. The pharaohs lived rich, splendid lives.

LEARN MORE ABOUT IT

Farming Along the Nile
Egypt's success depended on thousands of peasants. But raising good crops depended on the Nile flooding every year. These floodwaters covered the land along its banks, making a strip of rich farmland. The rich soil came from farther up the river. The Nile also provided water for irrigation. The rest of Egypt was desert.

Men and women worked in the fields during the day. They grew grains such as wheat and barley. The flour from these grains was mixed with honey to make sweet bread. Farmers grew grapevines and picked dates too. Other peasants tended herds of sheep, goats, or cattle. They also hunted deer and water birds.

Besides food crops, Egyptian farmers grew cotton and flax, a plant that was used for its fibers. They spun the fibers to make cotton and linen cloth. Most farmwork was done by hand. Tomb paintings show farmers using metal tools to cut grain. Oxen were used for heavy work, such as turning water wheels.

REVIEW

On a sheet of paper, write the answer to each question. Use complete sentences.

1. Why did people settle along the Nile River?

2. How did farmers use the floods to help them?

3. What was the life of a pharaoh like?

On a sheet of paper, write the letter of the answer that correctly completes each sentence.

4. The Nile River Valley flooded every July, leaving the land very _____.

   A dry   **B** sandy   **C** barren   **D** fertile

5. Upper Egypt was in the south, and Lower Egypt was in the _____.

   A north   **B** east   **C** west   **D** bottom

6. King _____ was the first great pharaoh of Egypt.

   A Tut   **B** Menes   **C** Cleopatra   **D** Nile

Match the definition in Column A with the term in Column B. Write the correct letter on a sheet of paper.

Column A	Column B
7. in the direction against the flow of the river	**A** desert
8. money paid to support a government	**B** pharaoh
9. dry, sandy land with little or no plant life	**C** tax
10. a king of ancient Egypt	**D** upstream

The Pyramids

Objectives

- To explain how archaeologists think the Egyptians built the pyramids
- To tell what archaeologists found inside Egyptian tombs
- To detail how Egyptians prepared a dead body to be placed in a tomb

Tomb
A grave, usually one that is enclosed in stone or cement

Pyramid
A huge stone structure with a square base and four triangular sides that meet in a point at the top

Transport
To move from one place to another

The Egyptian pharaohs wanted people to remember just how rich and how powerful they were. Some had huge statues of themselves made. They also had their people build great **tombs,** or graves, for them. When the pharaohs died, their bodies were placed in the tombs. Jewelry, food, clothing—all the pharaoh's favorite things—went into the tomb, too. The Egyptians believed that a person would need those things in the next world.

These great, towering Egyptian tombs are called **pyramids.** The pharaohs of Egypt, from about 2650 B.C. until 1637 B.C., were buried within those huge pyramids. There are many pyramids still standing in Egypt today. They are considered one of the Seven Wonders of the Ancient World.

How Were the Pyramids Built?

The most famous pyramid is the Great Pyramid near Cairo. It covers an area larger than 10 football fields. It contains more than 2 million stone blocks, each weighing about 2.5 tons. Somehow, the stones had to be cut into shape and then moved, or **transported,** to the building site. Then the stones were raised into place. They were laid so that they fit together exactly. From a distance, the pyramid looks as if it were cut out of a single stone. The Egyptians of 4,500 years ago had no machinery or iron tools. So how did they do it? We do not know for certain. In fact, we do not know if we would be able to build pyramids today, even with our modern building methods.

The ancient Egyptians did use copper chisels. They also probably hauled the stones on some sort of wooden sled.

Most likely, they built a system of ramps and wooden planks to haul the stones into place. Mostly they had to rely on human muscle power. The ancient Greek historian Herodotus wrote about the pyramids. He said that 100,000 men worked each year for 20 years to build the Great Pyramid. Archaeologists doubt these numbers, but we will never know for sure.

Tombs within the pyramids have served as a wonderful record of the Egyptian civilization. However, robbers have broken into some tombs and stolen the artifacts. Fortunately, archaeologists have discovered some tombs still filled with goods from daily Egyptian life. The walls of the tombs are covered with picture-writing. The pictures tell the story of the ancient Egyptian world.

What Else Has Been Found in Tombs?

Archaeologists found more than bowls, pictures, jewelry, and pottery within the tombs. They found the pharaohs themselves! The Egyptians used certain chemicals to keep the dead body from rotting away. Of course, only the rich Egyptians could afford this special treatment.

This Egyptian tomb contains the mummy of Tutankhamen, an Egyptian pharaoh.

Burying people this way was not a simple matter in ancient Egypt. First, the brain and organs had to be removed from the body. Then the body was treated with a special chemical. It was then wrapped around and around in cloth bandages. A body wrapped like this is called a **mummy**. Many mummies were found deep within the Egyptian tombs. Scientists have removed Egyptian mummies and artifacts from these tombs. They are on display today in museums around the world.

REVIEW

On a sheet of paper, write the answer to each question.
Use complete sentences.

1. Why did the Egyptians build the pyramids?

2. Why did the pharaohs want all of their favorite things to be buried with them?

3. How do archaeologists think the Egyptians built the pyramids?

4. How did Egyptians prepare a dead body for burial?

5. What did archaeologists find inside Egyptian tombs?

Word Bank

Herodotus

iron tools

picture-writing

rich

wonders

On a sheet of paper, write the word from the Word Bank to complete each sentence correctly.

6. Greek historian _____ wrote about the pyramids.

7. Only _____ Egyptians could afford to bury a mummy.

8. Egyptians did not have machinery or _____ to build the pyramids.

9. Tomb walls are covered with _____ that tell the story of the ancient Egyptian world.

10. The pyramids are considered to be one of the _____ of the world.

Egyptian Culture

Geography Note

Many ancient Egyptian writings tell of voyages through the Red Sea to the Land of Punt. This land had beehive-shaped houses on stilts. Travelers returned with new and different plants and items. They brought back the skins of animals such as giraffes or cheetahs. Many believe the Land of Punt was in eastern Africa, probably in present-day Ethiopia.

The Egyptian pharaohs and their nobles lived rich lives. However, all the rest of the people led very simple lives.

What Was Egyptian Life and Religion Like?

The farmers worked hard in their fields. There was usually plenty of food. This meant that Egypt's craftworkers had more time to improve their skills.

The Egyptians were concerned about the way they looked. Drawings and statues show Egyptian women with long, dark hair worn in many braids and ringlets.

Both men and women wore makeup. They painted their lips red. They drew around their eyes with a dark green or gray paste called *kohl*. The Egyptians also liked perfume. Both men and women rubbed sweet-smelling oils into their skin.

Most ancient Egyptians believed in many gods. Just as in the land of Sumer, each city had its own special god. Osiris was the powerful god of death.

The river played an important part in Egyptians' lives and their belief about death. They believed that the dead were ferried, or transported, across a great river. There they would meet Osiris in the next world.

Egyptians cared about their looks. Both men and women lined their eyes with kohl.

Hieroglyphics

A system of writing using pictures or symbols to represent objects, ideas, or sounds

Papyrus

A writing paper the Egyptians made from water plants of the same name

---

 History Fact

The Egyptian calendar was based on the sun. There were three seasons of 120 days each. There was a five-day celebration at the end of the year.

Reading Strategy: Text Structure

How does the timeline help you understand this chapter?

What Did Egyptians Invent?

The Egyptians invented a system of picture-writing called **hieroglyphics.** They learned to make paper from river reed called **papyrus.** Our word *paper* comes from the word *papyrus.*

The Egyptians learned to chart the stars. They also decided that there were 365 days in a year.

The Egyptians made jewelry of gold and precious stones. They used metals for tools and weapons. The Egyptians made music, too. Archaeologists have found ancient Egyptian instruments and the words to songs. The Egyptians built ships. They traded with other people.

Most of all, the ancient Egyptians are remembered as the builders of the pyramids. The Egyptian builders have left us what may be the most amazing works of any civilization. Most likely, many of their secrets still lie buried within the pyramids.

TIMELINE STUDY: EVENTS IN ANCIENT EGYPT

How many years did it take for a unified Egypt to become the world's greatest power?

5000 B.C.
First farming settlements in Egypt

3100 B.C.
Upper and Lower Egypt united under King Menes

2700–1450 B.C.
Time of wealth and development in Egypt

1450 B.C.
Egypt is world's greatest power

5000 B.C.   4000 B.C.   3000 B.C.   2000 B.C.   1000 B.C.

1200 B.C.
Egypt's decline begins

2650–1637 B.C.
Pyramids built

66   *Unit 2   Ancient Civilizations*

Words from the Past

Translate
To change the words
of one language to
another

The Rosetta Stone

Hieroglyphics can still be seen in many places in Egypt.
Yet for many hundreds of years, nobody could read them.
The meaning of these ancient Egyptian symbols had been
lost sometime in the distant past. Then in 1799, a French
engineer in Egypt discovered a large stone. It was half
buried near the mouth of the Nile River.

The Rosetta Stone, as it came to be called, was completely
covered with writing. Carved into the stone were three
languages: hieroglyphics, a second Egyptian language, and
Greek. A French historian named Champollion **translated**
(changed the words from one language to another) the
Greek portion first. Then he carefully compared this to
the other languages. He realized that the same message
was written in the three languages. He was finally able
to learn the meaning of the hieroglyphics. In 1822 he
published the results of his work.

Champollion had developed a system of sounds
and meanings that could be applied to other
hieroglyphics. For the first time, scholars could go
into an Egyptian tomb or temple and read the name
of a king and something about him. With hard work,
a skilled translator could read a papyrus roll that had
not been read for thousands of years.

Today, the Rosetta Stone is in the British Museum in
London, England. Many visitors come to see the black
stone that provided the key to understanding ancient
Egyptian hieroglyphics.

*The Rosetta Stone has the
same message written in
three languages.*

REVIEW

On a sheet of paper, write the answer to each question. Use complete sentences.

1. What was the Egyptian belief about death?

2. What were some important Egyptian inventions?

3. How did translating the Rosetta Stone help scholars?

On a sheet of paper, write the word from the Word Bank to complete each sentence correctly.

Word Bank

hieroglyphics

kohl

looked

music

Osiris

papyrus

perfume

4. Egyptians were quite concerned about the way they _____.

5. The green or gray paste Egyptians used to draw around their eyes was called _____.

6. Egyptians used _____ to smell good.

7. _____ was the powerful god of death.

8. The Egyptian system of picture-writing is known as _____.

9. _____ was the writing paper made from river reed that Egyptians used.

10. Archaeologists have found instruments and words to songs, suggesting that Egyptians made _____.

SUMMARY

- When the Sahara became a desert, people went to live along the Nile River. They cleared jungle land there and built villages.

- The river flooded each year. This caused the land around it to become more fertile. Farmers used the rich land and dug canals to bring water to their crops.

- Lower Egypt and Upper Egypt were united under King Menes. Menes was the first great ruler, or pharaoh, of Egypt.

- Egyptians paid taxes to their powerful pharaohs who, in turn, became wealthy.

- The pharaohs' tombs were inside giant pyramids. The most famous is the Great Pyramid near Cairo.

- Ancient Egyptians believed in life after death. Many of the things they owned were buried with wealthy Egyptians.

- A special treatment was used to bury the bodies of some wealthy Egyptians. A wrapped body treated with chemicals is called a mummy.

- We know a lot about Egyptians from the mummies and artifacts found in their tombs. We know they made jewelry, tools, weapons, and musical instruments.

- Both men and women of Egypt wore makeup and perfumes.

- The Egyptians invented a system of picture-writing called hieroglyphics.

- The Egyptians made paper from a reed called papyrus.

Word Bank

desert

hieroglyphics

mummy

papyrus

pharaoh

pyramid

tax

tomb

united

upstream

Vocabulary Review

On a sheet of paper, use the words from the Word Bank to complete each sentence correctly.

1. The area called the Sahara changed from a green plain to a(n) _____.

2. When pharaohs died, their body was placed in a(n) _____.

3. An Egyptian ruler was buried in a(n) _____, which is a great towering structure.

4. The dead body of a rich Egyptian might be preserved as a(n) _____.

5. The Egyptians made writing paper from a plant called _____.

6. A system of writing used by the Egyptians is called _____.

7. Follow the Nile River _____, and you will reach Upper Egypt.

8. Long ago, an Egyptian ruler was called a(n) _____.

9. Farmers gave a large part of their crops to the pharaoh as a(n) _____.

10. Egypt was _____ under King Menes.

Chapter Review Questions

On a sheet of paper, write the answer to each question. Use complete sentences.

11. What was the Nile River Valley like?

12. What happened to the Nile River every year in July?

13. How did King Menes come to wear a "double" crown?

14. What clues show that Egyptians were concerned about their looks?

15. How did the Egyptian pharaohs pay for their rich way of life?

Critical Thinking

On a sheet of paper, write your response to each question. Use complete sentences.

16. Why do you think so many people are fascinated by the Egyptian pyramids today?

17. Why is it important to understand the written records of ancient civilizations?

Using the Timeline

Use the timeline on page 66 to answer the questions.

18. How many years passed between the first farming settlements in Egypt and the unification of Upper and Lower Egypt?

19. When the pyramids were built, was Egypt rich or poor?

20. What year was Egypt the world's greatest power?

GROUP ACTIVITY

With a small group, create a trivia game about the pyramids of Egypt. Use information from this chapter, encyclopedias and other books, and the Internet. New information about the pyramids is available from ongoing archaelogical digs.

2000 B.C.–500 B.C.

Mediterranean Kingdoms

Many groups of people settled near the shores of the Mediterranean Sea. The Phoenicians sailed seas from their colonies on the eastern shore, trading with people in many lands. The ancient Israelites also lived on the eastern shores; they believed in one god called *Yahweh*. The Hittites, from the area of present-day Turkey, were warriors who made weapons with iron.

The Babylonians built a huge civilization near the Euphrates River inland, to the east of the Mediterranean. The Assyrians built their kingdom nearby, on the banks of the Tigris River. Like the Hittites, they were fierce warriors.

GOALS FOR LEARNING

- To explain the importance of the sea in the Phoenician civilization
- To explain the importance of religion to the ancient Israelites
- To understand why Babylon was one of the greatest cities of the ancient world
- To understand why the Hittites were so powerful in the eastern Mediterranean
- To describe the military society of the Assyrians

Reading Strategy: Visualizing

Visualizing is another strategy that helps readers understand what they are reading. It is like creating a movie in your mind. Use the following ways to visualize a text:

- Look at the photographs, illustrations, and words.
- Consider how your experiences may add to the images.
- Notice the order in which things are happening and what you think might happen next.

Key Vocabulary Words

Lesson 1

Navigate To plan the course of a ship; to sail or steer

Colony A group of people who settle in a far-off land but are still under the rule of the land they came from

Lesson 2

Worship To honor and praise a god

Bible The ancient Israelite and Christian book that is thought to be holy

Nomad A person who moves from place to place

Commandment A law or order, most often a religious law

Judaism The religion developed by the ancient Israelites that Jews practice today

Christianity The religion based on the teachings of Jesus Christ and the Bible

Conquer To get control by using force, as in a war

Capital A city or town where the government of a nation or state is located

Religious Having to do with a belief in a higher being

Lesson 3

Empire A group of lands all ruled by the same government or ruler

Code A group of laws

Lesson 4

Treaty An agreement, usually having to do with peace or trade

Lesson 5

Military Having to do with soldiers or the armed forces

Siege The surrounding of a city by soldiers who are trying to capture it so that food, water, and other supplies cannot get in or out

Tribute A payment or gift demanded by rulers of ancient kingdoms

The Phoenicians

The Phoenician civilization grew up along the eastern shores of the Mediterranean. It was unlike most of the other Mediterranean civilizations. The Phoenicians were not farmers. They built their cities on rocky shores; they were people of the sea. They were sailors and traders.

Few farm crops grew in Phoenicia. However, there were plenty of trees. The people cut down the trees to use as wood to build sailing ships.

What Did the Phoenicians Do on Their Travels?

The Phoenicians were the best sailors in the ancient world. They learned to use the stars to **navigate** (to sail or steer). This made it possible for them to sail beyond the sight of land. The Phoenicians sailed where no other people dared to go. Their ships went to every corner of the Mediterranean. They reached the coast of Spain. They even sailed out into the Atlantic Ocean, beyond Gibraltar. They sailed along the west coast of Africa. Then they probably went all the way around the continent of Africa.

Wherever they traveled, the Phoenicians set up **colonies.** A colony is a group of people who settle in a far-off land but are still under the rule of the land they came from. Their people settled in places all around the Mediterranean Sea. The Phoenician colonies became trading centers. One of the largest Phoenician colonies was Carthage. It was on the north coast of Africa. The people of Carthage traded their gold, ivory, and ebony for Phoenician pottery, glass, and beads.

Reading Strategy:
Visualizing

What words in this lesson help you visualize Phoenician life?

The colonies paid taxes to the Phoenician homeland. Great Phoenician cities—like Tyre, Sidon, and Byblos—grew rich and strong.

The Phoenicians were traders and sailors, not warriors. They paid soldiers from other lands to protect their cities. They built high stone walls to protect themselves from attack.

What Are Some Phoenician Inventions?

The Phoenician ships were powered by oars and sails. They sailed all about the ancient world. As the Phoenicians traded goods, they also traded ideas.

Phoenician Trading Routes

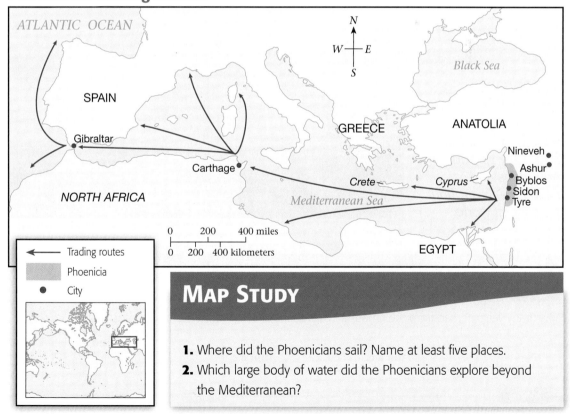

Trading routes
Phoenicia
City

MAP STUDY

1. Where did the Phoenicians sail? Name at least five places.
2. Which large body of water did the Phoenicians explore beyond the Mediterranean?

These are the Phoenician letters for A, B, C, D, and E.

One of the most important ideas the Phoenicians spread was the alphabet. They turned pictures into letters. In fact, our own alphabet comes from the letters the Phoenicians invented.

The Phoenicians became famous for another invention, too. It was a secret dye used to color cloth. The dye was made from snails that lived along the coast. The Phoenicians boiled thousands of snails to make just a tiny bit of dye. The dye was very costly. Named after the city of Tyre, it was called Tyrian purple.

The Phoenicians traded the purple cloth. Only rich people could buy it. Royalty decorated their palaces with it. They wore robes of Tyrian purple. The color purple came to stand for power and wealth. It became a royal color.

Phoenician explorers were the first people who could sail beyond the sight of land. They spread their ideas and inventions throughout the ancient world.

TIMELINE STUDY:

THE PHOENICIANS

How many years passed from the time the Phoenicians developed the alphabet until they rose to power?

| 2000 B.C. | 1500 B.C. Phoenicians develop the alphabet | 1500 B.C. | 1100 B.C. Phoenicians rise to power | 1000 B.C. | 600 B.C. Phoenicians may have sailed around Africa | 500 B.C. |

REVIEW

On a sheet of paper, write the letter of the answer that correctly completes each sentence.

1. Phoenician civilization developed along the _____ shores of the Mediterranean.

    A northern   **B** southern   **C** eastern   **D** western

2. Phoenicians were sailors and _____.

    A farmers   **B** traders   **C** warriors   **D** trappers

3. Phoenician sailors used the _____ to navigate.

    A compass   **B** map   **C** oars   **D** stars

4. Phoenicians would set up _____ wherever they traveled.

    A ships   **B** colonies   **C** temples   **D** crops

5. One of the largest Phoenician colonies was _____.

    A Carthage   **B** Tyre   **C** Sidon   **D** Byblos

6. Phoenicians paid _____ to protect their cities.

    A slaves   **B** farmers   **C** craftsmen   **D** soldiers

7. Phoenicians built _____ to protect themselves from attack.

    A weapons   **B** pottery   **C** stone walls   **D** ships

8. Phoenician ships were powered by oars and _____.

    A oil   **B** wood   **C** snails   **D** sails

9. One of the most important ideas Phoenicians spread was the _____.

    A alphabet   **B** ivory   **C** pottery   **D** ships

10. Another important Phoenician invention was a(n) _____ made from snails.

    A alphabet   **B** purple dye   **C** glass   **D** beads

The Israelites

Objectives

■ To explain how the Israelites' religion was different from that of other Mediterranean people

■ To describe the ancient Israelites' "Promised Land"

■ To name the two kingdoms that formed after King Solomon died

■ To explain why there is fighting over Jerusalem's land

Worship

To honor and praise a god

Bible

The ancient Israelite and Christian book that is thought to be holy

Nomad

A person who moves from place to place

Commandment

A law or order, most often a religious law

The ancient Israelites lived along the east coast of the Mediterranean Sea. Their civilization grew up just south of Phoenicia.

What Was Different About the Israelite Religion?

The ancient Israelites wanted their own land where they could honor and praise, or **worship,** their god. In the Mediterranean world, most people believed in many gods. There were gods of death, sun, and rain. The ancient Israelites believed in one god, Yahweh.

Their holy book, the **Bible,** says that a man named Abraham was the father of the Israelites. One day he left with his family to become a **nomad.** Abraham and his people moved from place to place, following their herds. They came to a land called *Canaan.*

Abraham's people were eventually treated as slaves in Egypt. The Egyptian pharaoh was cruel. A man named Moses became the ancient Israelites' leader. He led them out of Egypt, into the desert, away from the cruel pharaoh. On Mt. Sinai, Moses received the Ten **Commandments.**

Words from the Past

Judaism
The religion developed by the ancient Israelites that Jews practice today

Christianity
The religion based on the teachings of Jesus Christ and the Bible

The Ten Commandments

The ancient Israelites did not find their land of freedom right away. They wandered, searching, for many years. The Bible says that during that time, Moses was given the Ten Commandments. It says that the commandments came directly from God.

The commandments are laws to live by. They became laws for the people of ancient Israel. The first commandment says that people must believe that their god is more important than any other gods. "The Lord is One," the Bible reads.

The Ten Commandments also tell people how they must act toward each other. For example, children must honor their parents. The commandments forbid unfaithfulness, killing, stealing, or wanting what belongs to someone else.

Over time, the Ten Commandments became an important part of **Judaism** and **Christianity.** Today, some people want to display the commandments in public schools to remind students of the things they should not do. Other people feel that displaying them in school would make it look like the government is supporting a particular religion.

Moses holds the stone tablets which contain the Ten Commandments.

Conquer

To get control by
using force, as in
a war

Capital

A city or town where
the government of
a nation or state is
located

Religious

Having to do
with a belief in a
higher being

Reading Strategy:
Visualizing

What words in this
section help you to
visualize what happened
with the ancient
Israelites?

What Is the Promised Land?

The ancient Israelites finally reached Canaan again. They
called it the "Promised Land." They believed it was the
land that God had promised them. They settled there and
built towns. They followed their religion.

Holding onto the Promised Land was not always easy. The
Philistines lived nearby. The Philistines fought the ancient
Israelites for their land.

There were 12 tribes of ancient Israelites. At first, the
Philistines were able to gain control, or **conquer,** some
of the tribes. Divided, the ancient Israelites were weak.
In time, the tribes joined together under one king to fight
the Philistines.

There is a famous story of a shepherd boy named David.
He fought a Philistine giant called Goliath. David killed
Goliath with a rock from a slingshot. The ancient Israelites
then won the war against the more powerful Philistines.

David later became king of the ancient Israelites. The
town of Jerusalem became his **capital** city and was a
religious center.

When David died, his son, Solomon, became king.
Solomon built a beautiful temple in Jerusalem. He built
a group of fine sailing ships. King Solomon was known
to be good and wise. Under his rule, Jerusalem became a
mighty city.

What Happened When King Solomon Died?

When King Solomon died, his kingdom split. The tribes in the north made their own kingdom. They called it Israel. The tribes in the south formed the kingdom of Judah. Jerusalem was in Judah. The name of the Jewish religion came from the word *Judah*.

The two kingdoms were in danger! For the next 200 years they fought each other. They fought the powerful kingdoms that were all around them. These were the Egyptians, the Hittites, the Assyrians, the Babylonians, and the Persians. They all wanted control of the lands around Jerusalem.

At last the fierce neighbors were too strong. In 722 B.C., the Assyrians took over Israel. The Israelites were moved out or taken as slaves. In 587 B.C., Judah fell to a Babylonian people known as Chaldeans. The Babylonian king destroyed Solomon's fine temple in Jerusalem.

So it went. One power after another fought for the city that everyone wanted to control. Jerusalem was right in the middle of things. It came under many different rulers. Today it is more than 2,500 years since the Babylonians destroyed the temple. Very little has changed. Different groups of people continue to argue over who should control Jerusalem.

TIMELINE STUDY: THE ANCIENT ISRAELITES: STORY OF A PEOPLE

How many years passed before the ancient Israelites returned to Canaan?

| 2000 B.C. | | 1500 B.C. | | 1000 B.C. | | 500 B.C. |

1240 B.C. Ancient Israelites follow Moses out of Egypt

1200 B.C. Ancient Israelites return to Canaan

722 B.C. Assyrians conquer Israel

920 B.C. Israel and Judah become separate kingdoms

587 B.C. Babylonians take Jerusalem

Match the description in Column A with the term in Column B.
Write the correct letter on a sheet of paper.

Column A

1. the father of the Israelites, according to the Bible

2. the name of the one god the ancient Israelites believed in

3. the set of rules ancient Israelites lived by; came directly from God

4. the ancient Israelites' leader; led them out of Egypt, into the desert, to escape slavery

5. the son of David

6. the capital city and religious center; grew to be a mighty city

7. "The Promised Land"

Column B

A Abraham
B Canaan
C Jerusalem
D Moses
E Solomon
F The Ten Commandments
G Yahweh

On a sheet of paper, write the answer to each question. Use complete sentences.

8. How was the religion of ancient Israelites different from that of other Mediterranean people?

9. What two kingdoms formed after King Solomon died?

10. Why is there fighting over Jerusalem's land?

The Babylonians

The Babylonians built a great civilization in Mesopotamia, along the Euphrates River. Their empire eventually grew to include the land that had once belonged to the Sumerians.

What Do We Know About the Babylonians?

Babylon was the capital city of the Babylonians. It stood on the banks of the Euphrates River. Little remains of it today. There are a few ruins in the middle of some dirt mounds. Archaeologists have been digging through the ruins. They have learned that Babylon was one of the greatest cities of the ancient world. It contained some of the most beautiful temples and palaces to be found anywhere. They were decorated with blue glazed bricks and pictures of made-up beasts. People entered and left the city through huge bronze gates. Bronze is a hard metal made by blending copper and tin.

Near the center of the city stood the great Tower of Babel. This tower is mentioned in the Bible. Not far from the tower were the Hanging Gardens of Babylon. The gardens were one of the Seven Wonders of the Ancient World. They were built by a Babylonian king for his wife. She had been homesick for the beauty of her homeland in the mountains.

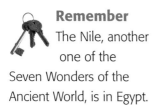

Remember
The Nile, another one of the Seven Wonders of the Ancient World, is in Egypt.

Beautiful gates such as this existed in ancient Babylon, which is now in Iraq.

Babylon became an important city about 2000 B.C. This was nearly the same time that the Babylonians were destroying the Sumerian civilization. The Babylonians went on to build a large **empire** in what had been the land of the Sumerians. An empire is a group of lands all ruled by the same ruler.

Reading Strategy:
Visualizing

Draw a picture to help you visualize some part of Babylon, such as the Hanging Gardens. How does this image help you remember what you are reading?

You Decide

How do laws today protect the rights of individual citizens?

GREAT NAMES IN HISTORY

Hammurabi

Hammurabi was one of the greatest kings of Babylonia. He ruled from about 1792 B.C. to 1750 B.C. Hammurabi created a system of laws called the **Code** of Hammurabi. These laws dealt with almost every aspect of life. There were nearly 300 laws. They applied to marriage and divorce, property and business, taxes, wages, loans, military service, and so forth. For anyone who broke a law, the Code listed harsh punishments in the form of an "eye for an eye" when seeking justice. The Code was created to protect the rights of the individual citizen.

In time, the Babylonians were conquered by other civilizations. However, some of their ideas about laws and justice have lasted through the ages. Some are included in our own laws today. The Code of Hammurabi can be seen in the Louvre in Paris, France.

TIMELINE STUDY:
THE BABYLONIAN EMPIRE

How long did the Babylonian empire last?

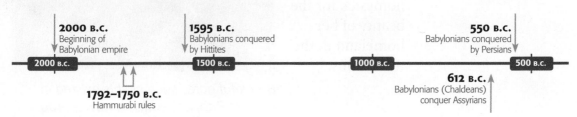

2000 B.C.
Beginning of Babylonian empire

1595 B.C.
Babylonians conquered by Hittites

550 B.C.
Babylonians conquered by Persians

| 2000 B.C. | 1500 B.C. | 1000 B.C. | 500 B.C. |

1792–1750 B.C.
Hammurabi rules

612 B.C.
Babylonians (Chaldeans) conquer Assyrians

REVIEW

Word Bank

Babylon
blue
bronze
citizen
Euphrates
greatest
Hammurabi
Hanging Gardens
Sumerian
Tower of Babel

On a sheet of paper, write the word from the Word Bank to complete each sentence correctly.

1. _____ was the capital city of the Babylonians.

2. Babylon was on the banks of the _____ River.

3. Babylon was one of the _____ cities of the ancient world.

4. Babylonian temples and palaces were decorated with _____ glazed bricks and pictures of made-up beasts.

5. People entered Babylon through huge _____ gates.

6. At the center of the city was the _____.

7. The _____ are one of the Seven Wonders of the Ancient World.

8. Babylon was an important city around 2000 B.C. This was at the same time the Babylonians were destroying the _____ civilization.

9. The Code of _____ was a system of laws. It addressed many aspects of life and was named for a great king of Babylon.

10. The Code was created to protect the rights of the individual _____.

The Hittites

Objectives

■ To describe the secret knowledge of the Hittites

■ To explain the peace treaty the Hittites and Egyptians signed

■ To explain what brought about the end of the Hittite empire

Reading Strategy:
Visualizing

How could this lesson be written differently to create a stronger picture in your mind?

Remember
When the Egyptians built the pyramids, they had no machines or iron tools.

The Hittites were warriors who came to the eastern Mediterranean around 2000 B.C. No one knows for sure where they came from, but they quickly swept through the lands called Anatolia. They found city-states already there. They conquered one after another. By 1650 B.C., the Hittites ruled all of these lands. Today this area is the country Turkey.

The Hittites were mighty fighters. They used their might to create an empire. After they conquered Anatolia, they began attacking neighboring lands.

What Was the Secret Knowledge of the Hittites?

The Hittites had a secret that gave them great power. For hundreds of years, they were the only people who knew how to make iron. Iron was a strong, heavy metal that was easy to shape. It made better weapons. No other people could beat the Hittite warriors and their iron spears.

The Egyptians looked upon the Hittites with great respect. They thought of the Hittites as the only other great power in the Mediterranean. In about 1269 B.C., after years of fighting with each other, the Hittites and the Egyptians made peace. To help keep the peace, a Hittite princess married an Egyptian pharaoh.

The Hittites and the Egyptians signed an agreement to keep the peace. It became the first recorded peace **treaty**, or agreement.

In time other people learned the secret of making iron. The Hittites were no longer the strongest. Around 1200 B.C., new people came and attacked the Hittites. They were called the *Sea Peoples*. They came from islands in the Mediterranean. They brought about the end of the Hittite empire.

The Hittites were mighty warriors. The ability to make iron was the secret to their power.

On a sheet of paper, write the letter of the answer that correctly completes each sentence.

1. The Hittites were _____.

   A farmers   **B** warriors   **C** traders   **D** trappers

2. The Hittites came to the _____ Mediterranean around 2000 B.C.

   A northern   **B** southern   **C** eastern   **D** western

3. The Hittites quickly _____ city-state after city-state in Anatolia.

   A conquered   **B** built   **C** traded with   **D** farmed

4. By _____ B.C., the Hittites ruled all of the lands in present-day Turkey.

   A 2000   **B** 1650   **C** 1258   **D** 1200

5. _____ was the secret that the Hittites had that gave them their great power.

   A The Code   **B** The Bible   **C** Sailing ships   **D** Iron

6. Even though they fought, the _____ looked upon the Hittites with great respect.

   A Sea Peoples   **B** Babylonians   **C** Egyptians   **D** Assyrians

7. To help keep the peace, a Hittite princess married an Egyptian _____.

   A king   **B** pharaoh   **C** god   **D** mummy

8. The peace agreement that the Egyptians and Hittites signed was the first recorded peace _____.

   A law   **B** tax   **C** treaty   **D** stone

9. In _____ B.C., new people came and attacked the Hittites.

   A 2000   **B** 1650   **C** 1258   **D** 1200

10. The _____ brought an end to the Hittite empire.

    A Sea Peoples   **B** Babylonians   **C** Egyptians   **D** Assyrians

The Assyrians

Objectives

- To describe how the Assyrian Empire grew
- To tell what the Assyrians did when they captured a city
- To name three Assyrian inventions

Military
Having to do with soldiers or the armed forces

Siege
The surrounding of a city by soldiers who are trying to capture it so that food, water, and other supplies cannot get in or out

The Assyrians were another warrior civilization. At first Assyria was a small kingdom. When the Hittite civilization ended, the Assyrians began to want an empire of their own.

The Assyrians built their capital city on the banks of the Tigris River. The city was named Ashur, after one of the Assyrians' many fierce gods.

Assyrian kings were hard rulers. They made their people pay heavy taxes. Assyrians lived under strict laws. Anyone who broke a law could be cruelly punished. Many law breakers were beaten. Some even had their ears cut off!

How Did the Assyrians Build Up Their Empire?

The Assyrians built up a great army. It was the best trained army of the ancient world. The Assyrians sent their army to attack the neighboring kingdoms. As more and more cities were captured, the Assyrian Empire grew.

The Assyrian civilization was a **military** one. Assyrian boys knew what their future held. Men had to go into the army. The Assyrians needed soldiers in order to keep their power. The Assyrians were builders as well as fighters. They built military equipment to help them conquer cities. They beat down city walls and gates with their huge machines called siege engines. They would surround a city with soldiers and try to capture it so that food, water, and other supplies could not get in or out. A city under **siege** from fierce Assyrians stood little chance.

Tribute
A payment or gift demanded by rulers of ancient kingdoms

Reading Strategy:
Visualizing

Study the photo of the sculpture from the Palace of Nineveh. How does this image help you visualize what you have read?

The Assyrians were not kind to the cities that they took. Sometimes they burned the city and killed the people who lived there. Often they took the people as slaves.

Sometimes, after they captured a city, the Assyrians acted as its new rulers. The people from the city had to pay **tribute** (give gifts or payments) to the Assyrian king. If they did not pay the high price, they were punished.

A relief, or sculpture, from the Palace of Nineveh shows an Assyrian king.

What Are Some Assyrian Developments?

The Assyrian civilization did leave some things behind besides a successful military record. They built fine buildings and statues. They invented machines that beat down walls and gates. They also built machines to help lift water from the river into canals.

The Assyrians were among the first people to have a library. The library stored clay tablets with writings from the ancient world.

Even the fierce Assyrians were defeated at last. By 670 B.C., the empire was so big that it was hard to control. It began to break up. In 612 B.C., the Assyrian city of Nineveh was under siege itself. The Assyrian Empire came to an end. The Assyrians had been conquered by a new Babylonian people—the Chaldeans.

Reading Strategy:
Visualizing

Study the timeline below. How does it help you visualize the change from Hittite to Assyrian power?

TIMELINE STUDY:

THE HITTITES AND THE ASSYRIANS

What happened in 1200 B.C.?

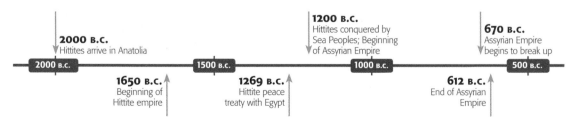

2000 B.C.
Hittites arrive in Anatolia

1650 B.C.
Beginning of Hittite empire

1269 B.C.
Hittite peace treaty with Egypt

1200 B.C.
Hittites conquered by Sea Peoples; Beginning of Assyrian Empire

612 B.C.
End of Assyrian Empire

670 B.C.
Assyrian Empire begins to break up

2000 B.C. — 1500 B.C. — 1000 B.C. — 500 B.C.

REVIEW

Word Bank

Ashur
builders
Chaldeans
laws
military
taxes
Tigris

On a sheet of paper, write the word from the Word Bank to complete each sentence correctly.

1. The Assyrians built their capital city on the banks of the _____ River.

2. The capital city of Assyria was named _____, after one of their many fierce gods.

3. Assyrian kings were hard rulers and made their people pay heavy _____.

4. Assyrians lived under strict _____.

5. The Assyrians had a(n) _____ civilization.

6. The Assyrians were _____ as well as fighters.

7. In 612 B.C., the _____ brought an end to the Assyrian Empire.

On a sheet of paper, write the answers to each question. Use complete sentences.

8. What did the Assyrians build to help them conquer a city?

9. What did the Assyrians do when they captured a city?

10. What are three things the Assyrians invented?

SUMMARY

- There were many kingdoms around the eastern Mediterranean Sea.

- The Phoenicians were expert sailors. They used the stars to help them navigate the seas.

- The Phoenicians were also active traders. They were not farmers or warriors.

- The Phoenicians set up many colonies. The colonies paid taxes to the Phoenician homeland. One of the largest colonies was Carthage.

- The Phoenicians developed an alphabet much like ours.

- The ancient Israelites gave us the Jewish religion. They were among the first to believe in one god.

- The ancient Israelites left slavery in Egypt to follow Moses to the Promised Land. They lived by rules called the Ten Commandments.

- David became king of the ancient Israelites. Jerusalem was his capital and religious center.

- David's son Solomon became a powerful king of the Israelites. When Solomon died, his kingdom split into Israel and Judah.

- A Babylonian King, Hammurabi, created one of the earliest systems of laws.

- The Hittites and the Assyrians were two groups who controlled the eastern Mediterranean Sea.

- The Hittites and the Assyrians both had warlike civilizations.

Word Bank

capital

colony

conquer

empire

navigate

nomad

siege

treaty

tribute

worship

Vocabulary Review

On a sheet of paper, use the words from the Word Bank to correctly match each definition below.

1. To defeat an enemy in war

2. In war, surrounding a city to prevent necessary items from getting in or out

3. An agreement, like the one the Hittites and Egyptians made to keep the peace

4. Something a ruler demands from the people

5. A large area of land controlled by a single ruler or government

6. A group of people who settle in a far-off land but are still under the rule of the land they came from

7. The city where the government of a nation or state is located

8. A person who moves from place to place

9. To plan the route of a ship

10. To honor and praise a god

Chapter Review Questions

On a sheet of paper, write the answer to each question. Use complete sentences.

11. How was the Phoenician civilization different from other civilizations on the shores of the Mediterranean?

12. How did purple become a royal color?

13. How were ancient Israelite beliefs different from those of most other people in the Mediterranean world?

14. What was the "Promised Land"?

15. How did the Egyptians and Hittites finally make peace with each other?

16. What other things, besides a successful military record, did the Assyrians leave behind?

Critical Thinking

On a sheet of paper, write your response to each question. Use complete sentences.

17. Why did the Hittites keep their ability to make iron a secret?

18. Do you think people liked living under the harsh rule of the Assyrians? Why or why not?

Using the Timelines

Use the timelines on pages 76, 81, 84, and 91 to answer the questions.

19. What period of time is covered on the four timelines?

20. How many years after the Phoenicians rose to power did Moses lead the ancient Israelites out of Egypt?

GROUP ACTIVITY

In a group of three or four, make a poster promoting one of the Mediterranean kingdoms. Be sure to talk about the religion, laws, or any special developments of that empire. Discuss what you think life would have been like in that kingdom. Share with the class the information from your poster about your chosen empire.

Early Civilizations of India, China, and the Americas

Another strong civilization grew up in the Indus River Valley of Asia. This culture thrived peacefully for more than 1,000 years. The Aryans gained power, bringing with them a system of separate social classes.

At about the same time, a civilization developed in the Huang He Valley of present-day China. These people wrote about history. Many dynasties, or ruling families, controlled China for hundreds of years.

Across the Pacific Ocean, the Olmecs were building a society in what is now Mexico. This civilization lasted for more than 1,000 years. The Maya people followed the Olmecs.

GOALS FOR LEARNING

- To describe civilization along the Indus River Valley
- To understand Buddhism and how it came about
- To describe the early Chinese civilization that lived in the Huang He Valley
- To understand life in the early Americas

Reading Strategy: Inferencing

Sometimes the meaning of a text is not directly stated. You have to make an inference to figure out what the text means.

What You Know + What You Read = Inference

To make inferences, you have to think "beyond the text." Predicting what will happen next and explaining cause and effect are helpful strategies for making inferences.

Key Vocabulary Words

Lesson 1

Conqueror A person who gains control by winning a war

Hinduism The main religion of India; Hindus worship many gods

Class A group of people according to social rank

Caste A social class in India

Soul A person's spirit

Reincarnation A belief that living souls are reborn in a new body

Lesson 2

Buddhism A religion based on the teachings of Buddha

Buddha A name meaning the "Enlightened One;" the name given to Siddhartha Gautama, the founder of Buddhism

Enlightened Knowing the truth

Emperor A person who rules a group of different countries, lands, or peoples

Foreign From another country; having to do with another country

Lesson 3

Ancestor A person from whom one is descended

Dynasty A family that rules a country for a long period of time

Barrier Something that blocks the way; a wall

Raid To attack suddenly; a surprise attack

Isolate To set apart from others; alone

Collapse To fall apart

Lesson 4

Shrine A place of worship believed to be sacred or holy

Ancient India

Objectives

- To describe life in the city of Mohenjo-Daro
- To describe the Aryan people
- To explain the Hindu religion
- To name the social classes of the Indian caste system

Reading Strategy:
Inferencing

What do you already know about present-day India or India of long ago?

One of the world's earliest civilizations grew up around the Indus River. These lands are now known as India and Pakistan. The people, like so many others, settled near the river. They learned to irrigate their fields and to grow crops. They made pottery, jewelry, and statues. They traded goods and ideas with the civilizations of the Fertile Crescent.

What Happened to the City of Mohenjo-Daro?

One of the main cities in the Indus River Valley was Mohenjo-Daro. Mohenjo-Daro was a neat, well-planned city. It had long, straight main streets. Covered drainage systems ran under the streets. The people built brick houses. They even built apartment houses.

Life was good in Mohenjo-Daro. There were public swimming pools and bath houses. People could cool off on hot Indus Valley days. Brick courtyards circled shaded wells so that people and animals could drink in comfort. Many houses in Mohenjo-Daro had their own indoor wells and tile-lined baths. Wheat and date palms grew on farms outside the city.

Mohenjo-Daro stood peacefully for close to 1,000 years. Then, around 1500 B.C., the city was attacked. People from the north, the Aryans, swooped down on Mohenjo-Daro. The Aryans showed no mercy. They ran through the streets of Mohenjo-Daro killing most of the people.

The Aryans believed that they were born to conquer and control. The word *Aryan* meant "nobleman" or "owner of land." The Aryans soon controlled all of the Indus River Valley.

Conqueror

A person who gains control by winning a war

Hinduism

The main religion of India; Hindus worship many gods

The Aryans were fierce **conquerors** who gained control of lands by winning a war. However, they also brought new ideas. They became known for making beautiful cloth decorated with gold and silver. They also became known for their skilled doctors and mathematicians.

What Religion Did the Aryans Bring to India?

The Aryans' religion was based on the idea that some people are born "better" than others. Their religion developed into the Hindu religion. Hindus, the people who practice **Hinduism,** worship many gods.

The Indus River Valley

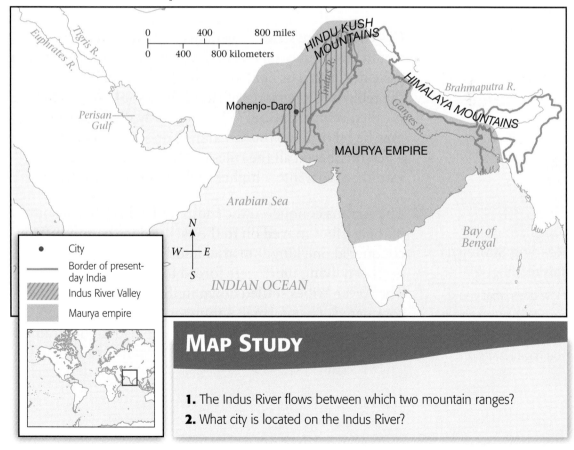

MAP STUDY

1. The Indus River flows between which two mountain ranges?
2. What city is located on the Indus River?

Class

A group of people according to social rank

Caste

A social class in India

Soul

A person's spirit

Reincarnation

A belief that living souls are reborn in a new body

Hindus believe that everything is God, or Brahman. They believe that Brahma, Vishnu, and Shiva are different faces of God. Brahma creates, or makes, life. Vishnu preserves life, and Shiva destroys it. Hindus believe these three faces show us the main powers of God.

The Aryans divided all people into four groups according to social rank, or social **classes.** They called these social classes **castes.** The highest caste consisted of priests and scholars. Rulers and warriors were the next in rank, followed by craftworkers, merchants, and farmers. Unskilled workers made up the lowest caste.

The Aryans called the people they conquered *outcastes* or *untouchables.* The outcastes had no place in society. Any Aryan who married one of the conquered people would also become an outcaste.

Caste laws were strict. A person born into a certain caste would always stay there. No one could ever rise to a higher caste during his or her life. Hindus, however, believed in the rebirth of a person's spirit, or their **soul.** This belief is called **reincarnation.** When the body dies, the soul may be reborn in either an animal or a human being. If a person obeyed all the rules of Hinduism, that person would be born into a higher caste in his or her next life.

The Aryans conquered the Indus Valley first. Then some of their tribes moved on to the east and to the south. They conquered one kingdom after another. The people who had been living there were forced to flee farther south. The Aryan tribes settled down in the lands that they conquered. They formed a number of city-states. Each one was ruled by a *raja,* or prince, who had highly trained armies to protect the lands.

Reading Strategy:
Inferencing

How does what you already know about India add to what you have just read?

Match the description in Column A with the term in Column B.
Write the correct letter on a sheet of paper.

Column A

1. a social class in India
2. prince
3. the God of the Hindu religion
4. a belief that living souls are reborn in a new body
5. a word that means "nobleman" or "owner of the land"

Column B

A Aryan
B Brahman
C caste
D raja
E reincarnation

On a sheet of paper, write the answer to each question. Use complete sentences.

6. What was life like in the city of Mohenjo-Daro?
7. What were the Aryan people like?
8. What are three different faces of God in the Hindu religion?
9. What are the four social classes of the Indian caste system?
10. How could a person change to a different social class?

Buddhism

Buddhism
A religion based on the teachings of Buddha

Buddha
A name meaning the "Enlightened One"

Enlightened
Knowing the truth

Buddhism is a religion based on the teachings of a man named **Buddha.** It began in India before Christianity or Islam, and quickly spread throughout Asia.

Who Was Buddha?

The man who would one day be called Buddha was born about 563 B.C., long before Jesus or Muhammad. He was the son of a wealthy Hindu in India. His father was a raja. Therefore, the boy, Siddhartha Gautama, was considered a prince. His life should have been one of riches and plenty. Instead, Gautama chose a different path.

He saw many of his people living in poverty and sorrow. He saw beggars in the streets. Gautama felt sorry for the unhappy people. Human life was full of suffering. The rich had so much; the poor had so little.

When he was a young man, Gautama gave up his own wealth. He left his father's palace and went to live in the forest. For about six years he lived simply, wandering around India. He spent his time thinking about how life could be better for people.

It is said that the truth came to Gautama one day as he sat under a fig tree. "The sorrows of the world are caused by selfishness," Gautama decided. If people could put aside their desire for riches, Gautama thought, the world would be a better place. So he developed a new religion, Buddhism, which is based on brotherly love. Gautama was called Buddha, which means the "**Enlightened** One." When someone is said to be enlightened, it means they know the truth.

Reading Strategy:
Inferencing

After reading this section, what inferences can you make about Buddhism? What words helped you make your inference?

What Did the Buddhist Religion Teach?

The Buddhist religion is known as a "gentle" religion. It teaches that the sacred (holy) life is found in unselfishness. People who get rid of all greed and selfishness will reach a state of mind known as *nirvana*. Like Hindus, Buddhists also believe in reincarnation. They believe that living beings, including animals, are reborn in another form after death. They see life as a continuing cycle of death and rebirth. A person can only break the cycle of death and suffering by reaching nirvana. Buddhists hope to reach nirvana someday. It is their idea of heaven.

Buddha, the "Enlightened One," had many followers.

Emperor

A person who rules a group of different countries, lands, or peoples

Foreign

From another country; having to do with another country

You Decide

Do you think that Asoka was a wise ruler? Why or why not?

Reading Strategy: Inferencing

What can you infer about the way the Indians reacted to the rise of Buddhism?

In 321 B.C., a new empire was created in northern India. It was called the Maurya empire. The third Maurya **emperor** was named Asoka. Asoka's rule began in about 268 B.C. He followed Buddha's teachings about brotherly love. Asoka made Buddhism the state religion. He taught that all people and animals were to be loved.

Buddha's teachings were very different for the Indians. They were used to Hindu ways. However, the Hindu caste system weakened during Asoka's rule. New laws treated all people more equally.

India's Maurya empire came to an end about 185 B.C. Then one **foreign** land after another invaded India. Most Indians went back to the Hindu religion. Buddhism, however, had spread. Followers of Buddha carried their ideas to China, Japan, and other parts of Asia. Beautiful Buddhist temples and pagodas are still standing today. They show that the gentle religion is still an important part of Asia's culture.

TIMELINE STUDY:

EVENTS IN ANCIENT INDIA

How many years did Asoka rule the Maurya empire?

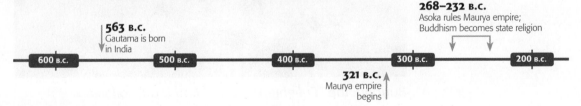

563 B.C.
Gautama is born in India

268–232 B.C.
Asoka rules Maurya empire; Buddhism becomes state religion

600 B.C. — 500 B.C. — 400 B.C. — 300 B.C. — 200 B.C.

321 B.C.
Maurya empire begins

On a sheet of paper, write the letter of the answer that correctly completes each sentence.

1. Siddhartha Gautama was born about _____ B.C., which was long before Jesus or Muhammad.

   A 563   **B** 321   **C** 268   **D** 185

2. Although Gautama was born a _____, he chose a different path.

   A slave   **B** farmer   **C** warrior   **D** prince

3. Gautama believed the sorrows of the world are caused by _____.

   A war   **B** selfishness   **C** unskilled workers   **D** kings

4. Gautama was called Buddha, which means _____.

   A "Enlightened One"   **C** "untouchable"
   B "nobleman"   **D** "gentle one"

5. The Buddhists believed that people should work to get rid of all greed and selfishness. In doing so, a person will reach a state of mind known as _____.

   A religion   **B** reincarnation   **C** nirvana   **D** Vishnu

6. The Mauryan emperor _____ made Buddhism the state religion.

   A Aryan   **B** Asoka   **C** Gautama   **D** Siddhartha

7. Buddhism has spread to China, _____, and other parts of Asia.

   A Egypt   **B** Babylon   **C** Japan   **D** Turkey

On a sheet of paper, write the answer to each question. Use complete sentences.

8. Why did Gautama give up his wealth and go to live in the forests?

9. What is Buddhism based on?

10. What does Buddhism teach?

Early China

Reading Strategy: Inferencing

What sorts of things can you infer the early Chinese wrote about?

Ancestor
A person from whom one is descended

They called themselves the *Black-haired People.* They lived in the valley of the Huang He, or Yellow River, in China. Their civilization grew up apart from the rest of the world. Steep mountains, wide deserts, and deep seas circled their lands. Northern China and the people of the Huang He Valley were cut off from other civilizations.

What Was Life Like in the Huang He Valley?

Most of the people in the Huang He Valley were farmers. They fought floods that were so terrible that the Huang He became known as "China's Sorrow."

They dug pitlike houses in the ground and wove roofs of grass. Their kings lived in palaces made of wood and mud.

In 1700 B.C., these early Chinese learned to write. They cut letters, or characters, into animal bones. They kept a record of their own history. It is one of the world's oldest written histories.

The people of the Huang He Valley made fine cloth. They raised silkworms. They carefully unwound the long, thin threads that the silkworms spun. They wove the threads into silk cloth.

The Chinese had a special feeling for their **ancestors,** the people from whom they were descended. They also showed honor toward their homes, their families, and their land. There were many rules of courtesy in the Chinese culture. Those rules made it possible for large families to live together happily.

Dynasty
A family that rules a country for a long period of time

The Chinese culture did not change for many thousands of years. This is because people honored the ways of their ancestors. Also, the land was cut off from the rest of the world.

What Dynasties Ruled China During Ancient Times?

A period of rule in China is called a **dynasty.** For about 500 years, Shang kings ruled the Huang He Valley. This period is called the Shang dynasty.

The Shang Dynasty, Huang He (Yellow River) Valley, China

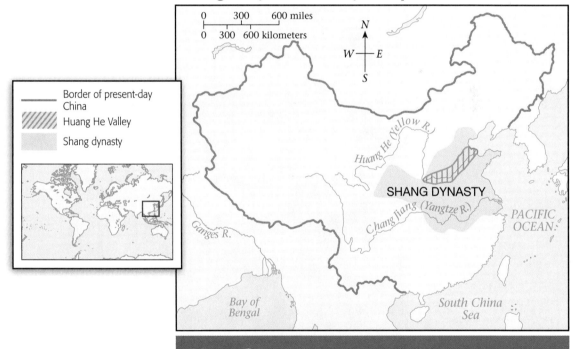

MAP STUDY

1. What two rivers flowed through the Shang dynasty of China?

2. Into which ocean do these rivers flow?

Around 1028 B.C., a warlike people, the Zhou, came to power. The Zhou leaders developed systems of irrigation and flood control. They also extended their rule southward. Chinese civilization now reached from the Huang He to the Chang Jiang, or Yangtze River. The powerful Zhou dynasty lasted for more than 750 years.

The name *China* may have come from Qin. The Qin family ruled China from 221 B.C. until 206 B.C. This period was called the Qin dynasty. Shi Huangdi was the first Qin emperor. His empire was the first Chinese empire with a strong central government.

The Great Wall of China is over 4,000 miles long. It was built to protect China from invading armies.

Barrier
Something that blocks the way; a wall

Raid
To attack suddenly; a surprise attack

Isolate
To set apart from others; alone

Collapse
To fall apart

Reading Strategy:
Inferencing

What did you already know about the Great Wall of China? Did this help you with your understanding?

History Fact
The Great Wall of China was built to prevent people from entering China. Another famous wall—the Berlin Wall—was built by East Germany in 1961 to prevent people from leaving the country. You will read about this in Chapter 29. The Berlin Wall was torn down in 1989.

Shi Huangdi planned the Great Wall of China. China had many natural **barriers** to keep people from other countries, or foreigners, out. Mountains and deserts lay all around. The only border that could be easily crossed was to the north. Enemies crossed this northern border to **raid**, or attack, Chinese farms. The Chinese of an earlier period had also tried to protect the border. Short walls had been built by the Zhou dynasty. Shi Huangdi decided to connect these walls. He wanted to build one great stone wall. Work on the wall continued on and off until around A.D. 1600.

The Great Wall of China is over 4,000 miles long. It is the longest structure ever built! The Great Wall is 30 feet high and about 20 feet wide at the top. The wall once had 2,500 watchtowers. It helped to protect the northern borders from invaders, especially those on horseback. It also further set China apart, or **isolated** them, from the rest of the world.

Shi Huangdi had planned a wall that would last for thousands of years. Unfortunately, the Qin dynasty only lasted a few years. It was expensive to build the wall. So Shi Huangdi forced people to pay high taxes. Many people began to hate the Qin dynasty. Soon after the emperor died in 210 B.C., a civil war broke out. The Qin dynasty quickly fell apart, or **collapsed.** By 206 B.C., the Han dynasty had gained control of China.

The Han dynasty is known as the first Golden Age of China. For more than 400 years, the Han dynasty (206 B.C.–A.D 220) changed China in important ways. The Han military expanded China's empire by conquering large areas of land. Today, the influence of the Han can be seen in the culture and people of China. More than 90 percent of people identify themselves as the "People of the Han."

Confucius

Confucius was born in 551 B.C. For more than 2,000 years, his ideas were the single strongest influence on Chinese life. Confucius gave people rules to live by. He was most interested in how people treated each other.

"Never do to others what you would not like them to do to you," Confucius taught. He taught that family life was most important. In China, large family groups lived together. Grandparents, parents, and children usually shared the same house. Therefore, if family members loved and honored each other, the family would enjoy good fortune. Old people were honored. Ancestors were respected. Respect for the ways of the ancestors kept Chinese culture from changing.

Confucius prized scholarship, or knowledge, and taught that a ruler should govern by good example. He thought that if a ruler used force to govern, the ruler had failed. In China, only well-educated people could be government officials. The greatest honor came to a family if a son became a scholar. Then he could study to take the government exams. The examination was based on the teachings of Confucius. A young man who passed the exams could become an official.

For centuries in China, people had to take tests to hold government jobs. China had the world's first civil service system.

The teachings of Confucius were so important that they were made the state religion of China.

On a sheet of paper, write the letter of the answer that correctly completes each sentence.

1. The Huang He Valley was surrounded by steep mountains, wide deserts, and deep seas. Because of this, the people _____ the rest of the world.

    A were connected to   **C** traded with
    B were isolated from   **D** fought with

2. People of the Huang He Valley fought terrible _____.

    A armies   **B** rodents   **C** floods   **D** storms

3. People in the Huang He Valley made fine _____ cloth.

    A silk   **B** reeds   **C** grass   **D** cotton

Word Bank

Han

Qin

Shang

Zhou

On a sheet of paper, write the word from the Word Bank to complete each sentence correctly.

4. The _____ dynasty ruled the Huang He Valley for about 500 years.

5. The _____ dynasty, a warlike people, spread their rule south toward the Chang Jiang.

6. Shi Huangdi, from the _____ dynasty, planned the Great Wall of China.

7. When the Qin dynasty collapsed, the _____ dynasty gained control of China.

On a sheet of paper, write the answer to each question. Use complete sentences.

8. Why did the Chinese culture remain the same for thousands of years?

9. Why was the Great Wall of China built?

10. What were three things that Confucius taught?

LESSON
6-4

Early America

Objectives

- To describe how scientists believe people came to the Americas
- To name two early civilizations in the Americas
- To name three new crops grown in the Americas

You Decide
Nobody knows for sure that American Indians migrated to North America over a land bridge. What do you think? Why?

There were faraway lands that the people of the Middle East and Asia knew nothing about. For the most part, these lands were wild, with thick woods and deep rain forests. They were lands that would one day be known as North and South America.

What Was the Land Bridge?

American Indians lived in the Americas. Many American Indians believe that their people have always lived there. Many scientists believe that the Indians first came from Asia. They say that the Indians traveled across a bridge of land and ice at the Bering Strait. Such a land bridge would have stretched 56 miles between Asia and Alaska. No trace of a land bridge exists now.

Why would these people have crossed the land bridge? Perhaps they were following animal herds. Then, over thousands of years, they kept on traveling south. Some stayed in North America. Others continued on to Central and South America.

For a long time, the people hunted and fished for their food. Then farming settlements began to spring up. This took place about 5,000 years after the people of the Middle East and Asia began farming. The new lands produced new crops. Farmers grew *maize,* or Indian corn. They grew squash, tomatoes, and beans.

South American farmers grew cotton as early as 3000 B.C. They raised herds of tall, woolly animals called llamas. They wove the llama wool into beautiful cloth.

Possible Route to the Americas

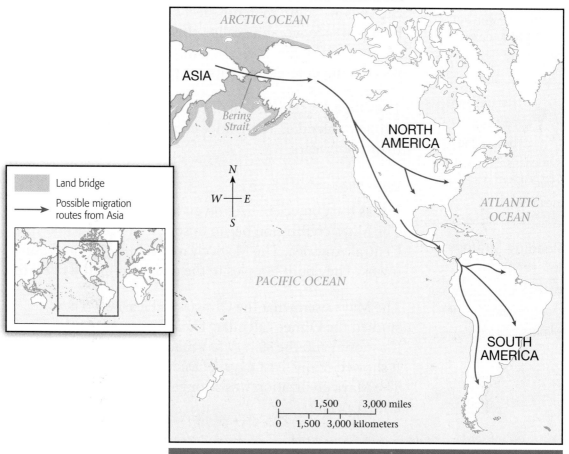

Land bridge

Possible migration routes from Asia

ARCTIC OCEAN

ASIA

Bering Strait

NORTH AMERICA

ATLANTIC OCEAN

PACIFIC OCEAN

SOUTH AMERICA

N
W—E
S

0   1,500   3,000 miles

0   1,500 3,000 kilometers

MAP STUDY

1. Which body of water did the land bridge cross?

2. Which America did the people from Asia reach first?

Who Were the Olmecs?

A people called the Olmecs built what might have been the first real city in the Americas. Their city was in Mexico, just west of the Gulf of Mexico. Archaeologists have discovered Olmec jade and pottery dating back to 1200 B.C.

Remember
Historians believe the Sumerians first used the wheel in 3000 B.C. on their chariots.

Reading Strategy: Inferencing

What inferences can you make in comparing the Olmecs and the Mayas?

The Olmecs carved giant heads out of stone. Some of their carvings are more than nine feet tall. The Olmecs also built places to worship, called **shrines,** atop high mounds of earth. The Olmecs did an amazing job. They worked without metal tools and without the wheel.

The Olmecs had a system of counting. They also invented a simple calendar. The Olmec civilization lasted for more than 1,000 years.

Who Were the Maya?

Just as the Olmec civilization ended, the Maya arose. The Maya civilization began in southern Mexico and Central America. The Maya cleared rain forests and built towns. They built temples to the gods of rain and of earth.

The Maya used what the Olmecs had learned. They studied the Olmec calendar. Then they watched the sun, the moon, and the stars. They made their own calendar. It showed many feast days set aside to honor their gods. The Maya civilization was strongest from about 250 B.C. until A.D. 800.

TECHNOLOGY CONNECTION

State-of-the-Art Communication

The Maya had one of the most detailed communication systems of their time. Their language had more than 800 different symbols. Their writings were carved on buildings, pillars, stairways, and wooden objects. They were written on paper as well as on walls and pottery.

The Maya wrote about cycles of time in detailed calendars. They wrote about traditions and customs. They described flowers and animals.

The Maya kept records of history, particularly their own rulers and ancestors. They told of victories over other cultures that usually included bloody human sacrifices to the gods.

Researchers have been studying Maya writings for over 100 years. About 85 percent of the writing found has been translated. Computers help compare findings in order to make more new discoveries.

The Maya temple is in Chichén Itzá, Mexico.

When the Olmecs built shrines in Mexico, what crop had been farmed there for 1,900 years?

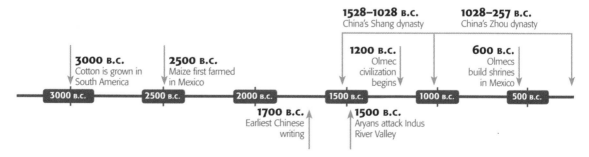

1528–1028 B.C.
China's Shang dynasty

1028–257 B.C.
China's Zhou dynasty

1200 B.C.
Olmec civilization begins

600 B.C.
Olmecs build shrines in Mexico

3000 B.C.
Cotton is grown in South America

2500 B.C.
Maize first farmed in Mexico

| 3000 B.C. | 2500 B.C. | 2000 B.C. | 1500 B.C. | 1000 B.C. | 500 B.C. |

1700 B.C.
Earliest Chinese writing

1500 B.C.
Aryans attack Indus River Valley

REVIEW

On a sheet of paper, write the letter of the answer that correctly completes each sentence.

1. Olmec jade and pottery have been discovered dating back to _____.

    A 1200 B.C.　**B** 600 B.C.　**C** 250 B.C.　**D** A.D. 800

2. The Olmecs built places of worship, known as _____, atop high mounds of earth.

    A rocks　　**B** anthills　　**C** temples　**D** shrines

3. The Olmec civilization lasted over _____ years.

    A 50　　　**B** 100　　　**C** 1,000　**D** 5,000

4. The Maya civilization began as the Olmec civilization _____.

    A began　　　　　　**C** was at its height
    B ended　　　　　　**D** started growing maize

5. The Maya built towns after clearing away _____.

    A rainforests **B** swampland **C** crops　**D** rocks

6. The Maya built _____ to the gods of rain and earth.

    A shrines　　**B** temples　　**C** churches **D** stone walls

On a sheet of paper, write the answer to each question. Use complete sentences.

7. How and why do scientists believe people came to the Americas?

8. What crops were grown in early America?

9. Why are the shrines the Olmecs built considered to be so amazing?

10. What did the Maya borrow from the Olmecs?

- An early civilization developed along the Indus River Valley in what is now India and Pakistan. One major city was Mohenjo-Daro. It grew peacefully for about 1,000 years.

- The Aryans from the north destroyed Mohenjo-Daro around 1500 B.C. They brought a caste system to India. The Aryans' religion developed from the Hindu religion. They believed in rebirth, or reincarnation.

- A prince named Siddhartha Gautama gave up his wealth to help the poor. He developed a new religion called Buddhism.

- The Maurya empire began in northern India in 321 B.C. Its emperor, Asoka, made Buddhism the official religion of the empire. The empire ended in 185 B.C. Followers of Buddha spread the religion to other parts of Asia.

- An early Chinese civilization grew up along the Huang He, or Yellow River. These people learned to write in about 1700 B.C. They left one of the world's oldest written histories.

- The Shang dynasty ruled China for about 500 years.

- The warlike Zhou dynasty came to power around 1028 B.C. The Chinese civilization grew under the Zhou leaders for about 750 years.

- The Qin dynasty ruled China from 221 B.C. to 206 B.C. Its first emperor, Shi Huangdi, began work on the Great Wall of China. Work on the wall continued on and off until around A.D. 1600.

- The Great Wall of China, at 4,000 miles long, is the longest structure ever built.

- American Indians may have descended from people who crossed a land bridge from Asia to the North American continent.

- The Olmecs of Mexico were one of the earliest civilizations in America. Their civilization lasted for more than 1,000 years.

- The Maya built cities in southern Mexico and Central America.

CHAPTER 6 REVIEW

Word Bank

ancestors

caste

class

dynasty

enlightened

foreign

isolated

reincarnation

shrine

Vocabulary Review

On a sheet of paper, use the words from the Word Bank to complete each sentence correctly.

1. Unskilled workers are the lowest _____, or caste, according to the Indians.

2. All people are descended from their _____.

3. A(n) _____ person knows the truth.

4. A social class in India is called a(n) _____.

5. A(n) _____ is a place of worship.

6. According to the belief of _____, a person who dies is reborn.

7. The Shang kings were a(n) _____.

8. The mountains and deserts surrounding China kept the Chinese _____.

9. India was invaded by many _____ lands.

Chapter Review Questions

On a sheet of paper, write the answer to each question. Use complete sentences.

10. What did the Aryans believe about the people they conquered?

11. Why is Buddhism known as a gentle religion?

12. Why was the Huang He, or Yellow River, known as "China's sorrow"?

13. What helped family members live together happily in China?

14. What is the longest structure ever built?

15. How might Asians have first traveled to North America?

16. What were four American Indian crops?

Critical Thinking

On a sheet of paper, write your response to each question. Use complete sentences.

17. Was it good or bad for China to be isolated for a long time?

18. How were the Olmecs and Maya like ancient civilizations in India and China?

Using the Timelines

Use the timelines on pages 104 and 115 to answer the questions.

19. Which was grown first in the Americas, cotton or maize?

20. How many years passed between the time the Olmecs built their shrines in the Americas and Gautama was born in India?

GROUP ACTIVITY

Form groups of three or four. Create a guidebook to the most interesting structures around the world. You might begin with the Great Wall of China or the Great Pyramid of Egypt. Ask classmates to name places they have been to or know about. Do some further research. Arrange your guidebook in some kind of order, such as alphabetical or geographical.

THE ORIGINS OF WESTERN CIVILIZATION: GREECE AND ROME

Many everyday elements of our world came from the ancient Greeks and Romans. As a theater audience member, you may smile at the plays from the ancient Greeks. You may stop at a post office building which is similar to the style of the Romans' buildings. Perhaps you are learning a foreign language that came from Latin of ancient Rome. By learning about the cultures of these ancient lands, you may better understand some things they gave us.

Chapters in Unit 3

The Colosseum, a brilliant example of ancient Roman architecture, still stands in Rome, Italy.

Greek City-States and the Golden Age

The people of ancient Greece were bold and determined. This was especially true in Greece's two most powerful city-states, Athens and Sparta. Athens was a city-state where its people asked questions. They thought about life and the power of gods, among many other things. They wanted to learn and create beautiful objects of art. The Athenians set up a democracy in which all of its citizens could vote.

Sparta was a very different city-state. Its leaders were members of the military. They focused on building a strong army to defend their lands. Citizens could not vote and many people kept slaves. Eventually the two city-states went to war against each other.

GOALS FOR LEARNING

- To explain the importance of the sea and trading in Greek life
- To compare life in Sparta and Athens
- To describe the series of wars the Greeks fought
- To identify the gifts that Greeks gave us that are part of life today

Reading Strategy: Metacognition

Metacognition means "thinking about your thinking." Use metacognition to become a better reader:

- Preview the text.

- Make predictions and ask yourself what you already know about the topic.

- Write the main idea, details, and any questions you have.

- Visualize what is happening in the text. If something does not make sense, go back and read it again.

Key Vocabulary Words

Lesson 1

Govern To rule

Tyrant A ruler who has complete power

Democracy A government that gives the people the ruling power

Citizen A person who has certain rights and duties because he or she lives in a particular city or town

Vote To choose leaders and pass laws

Expand To grow; to stretch

Hostility Feelings of hate or acts of war

Acropolis The hill on which the people in a Greek city built their main temple

Lesson 2

Myth A story, often about gods or goddesses, that is handed down through the years and sometimes used to explain natural events

Laborer A person who does hard work with his or her hands

Revolt To rise up against a government; to refuse to obey the people in charge

Constitution The basic laws and rules of a government

Jury A group of people who listen to the facts and decide if a person on trial is guilty or not guilty

Lesson 3

Democratic Having to do with a government in which all people have equal rights

Plague A deadly disease that spreads quickly

Lesson 4

Architecture The art of building

Athlete A person trained to take part in competitive sports

The Sea and Ancient Greece

Objectives

- To explain why each Greek city-state developed in its own way
- To contrast two ways that Greek city-states were governed
- To describe what the Acropolis is

Most early civilizations were mainly farming societies. The Greek civilization, however, was different. Greece is a very rocky land with many mountains. Much of Greece made poor farmland. The Greeks could not grow much wheat or other grains. Instead, they raised grapevines and olive trees. Greece is surrounded by the sea on almost every side. The Greeks took to the sea and became traders.

Ancient Greece

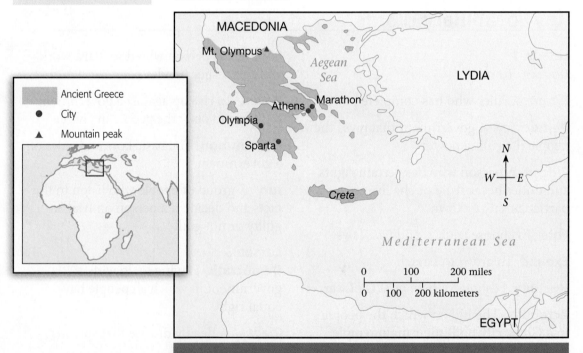

MAP STUDY

1. What are three Greek cities on the map?

2. Greece is surrounded by which two bodies of water?

Govern

To rule

Tyrant

A ruler who has complete power

Reading Strategy: Metacognition

Notice the structure of this lesson. Look at the title, headings, and boldfaced words.

What Did Greek Traders Do?

The Aegean and the Mediterranean seas made perfect travel lanes. The Greeks traded with most of the Mediterranean world. Greek traders set up colonies in the lands they visited. Greek culture spread across the seas.

Greek harbors were always busy. The air was filled with sounds. There was the clink of Greek coins and foreign coins. There was the chatter of many different languages as people of the world met. Merchants traded olive oil for wheat. Ships from Egypt unloaded papyrus. Ebony and ivory came in from Africa.

What Were Greek City-States Like?

The earliest people who settled in Greece began to build villages about 1500 B.C. As time passed, the small villages grew into city-states. Through trading, the city-states became wealthy. By about 750 B.C., the Greeks had begun to build colonies in other areas of the Mediterranean. Some Greeks settled on the Greek islands. Many others, however, traveled as far as southern Italy, France, Spain, and Portugal. They built cities there. Naples, Syracuse, and Marseilles began as Greek cities. Cities were also built in western Turkey and on the shores of the Black Sea.

On the Greek mainland, the city-states were becoming more powerful. The city-states were separated from each other by rugged mountain ranges. For this reason there was limited contact between the city-states. Each one developed in its own way.

Each city-state had its own government. Each had its own ideas about the way people should live. Some of the city-states were **governed,** or ruled, by a **tyrant,** a single powerful person. Some of the tyrants were cruel and unjust, while others ruled fairly.

Reading Strategy: Metacognition

Remember to look at the photographs and other graphics while you are reading. Also note the descriptive words. This will help you visualize what you are reading.

The first **democracy,** where the government gives people the ruling power, developed in the city-state. There, **citizens** could **vote** and have a say in government.

Because the city-states were so different from each other, they often fought among themselves. Tyrants with big ideas would decide that the time had come to grow, or **expand,** their rule. They would make plans to attack a nearby city-state. They might convince other city-states to join them. There was a constantly shifting pattern of friendship and **hostility** between the different city-states. This was a very unstable political situation. It would later lead to a major war between two of the largest city-states, Athens and Sparta.

What Is the Acropolis?

Each city-state was made up of a city circled by villages and farms. The farms provided food for the citizens. The city offered protection from invaders.

The Greeks usually built their city-states near a high hill. The hill was called the **Acropolis.** On that hill, they built special buildings, such as temples and theaters.

The people who lived in Athens built a beautiful temple atop their Acropolis. It was built to honor the goddess Athena. The temple was called the Parthenon.

The ancient Greeks built the Parthenon on a hill high above the city of Athens.

Match the description in Column A with the term in Column B.
Write the correct letter on sheet of paper.

Column A

1. a ruler who has complete power

2. a government that gives the people the ruling power

3. the temple built in Athens to honor the goddess Athena

4. the sea Greece was surrounded by (other than the Mediterranean Sea)

5. the high hill the Greeks built their city-states near; they often built special buildings, such as temples and theaters, atop this hill

Column B

A Acropolis

B Aegean

C democracy

D Parthenon

E tyrant

On a sheet of paper, write the answer to each question. Use complete sentences.

6. Why was farming difficult for the Greeks, and what did they do instead?

7. How did Greek traders help to spread Greek culture across the seas?

8. What were some items the Greeks traded?

9. Why did each Greek city-state develop in its own way?

10. Why did Greek city-states often fight with each other?

Athens and Sparta

Objectives

- To explain life in Sparta
- To describe the Athenian way of thinking
- To talk about democracy in Athens
- To name two Greek gods or goddesses

Myth

A story, often about gods or goddesses, that is handed down through the years and sometimes used to explain natural events

History Fact
Today we use the word *spartan* to mean "harsh" or "strict." The word comes from the Spartans of ancient Greece.

Athens and Sparta were the most powerful Greek city-states. Their citizens spoke the same language. They believed in the same gods. They told **myths** or stories about their gods and goddesses. However, life in Athens was quite different from life in Sparta.

What Was Sparta Like?

The Spartans lived in a military society. Sparta's government was led by a small group of men. They were most interested in keeping Sparta a great military power. Spartan children belonged to the state. A healthy boy was turned over to the government at the age of seven. He was raised to be a soldier. He was taught to fight and to stand up under pain. He had to obey orders without question. Soldiers defeated in battle were not allowed to return home.

If a baby boy were born with something wrong, he might be left on a hillside to die. The Spartans only wanted boys who could grow up to be soldiers. Spartans had little use for girls. Girls and women were seldom seen in public. They kept to their houses. The Spartans were great warriors. However, they left the world little in the way of ideas, art, or music.

The Spartans, like most of the Mediterranean peoples, kept slaves. Most of the work in the city was done by slave labor. The Spartan army was often kept busy fighting other city-states. At other times it had the job of keeping rebel slaves in line.

Although life was harsh in Sparta, things were very different in Athens. The Athenians gave less thought to warfare. They were more interested in enjoying life.

Laborer

A person who does hard work with his or her hands

The Greeks carved outdoor theaters into hillsides.

What Was Athens Like?

Athens was a wealthy city. The Athenians decided that their wealth gave them more time to enjoy the beauties of life. They wanted their city to be glorious. They built the Parthenon. Their marble statues show the human body in its ideal form. The Athenians put on plays in huge outdoor theaters. For the first time, plays were written about how people thought and acted. Some of these plays are still performed today.

The Athenians took time to ask questions about their world. Great teachers, like Socrates, led the Greeks to ask, "What makes people good? What makes people evil?" "Always ask questions," Socrates taught. So the Greeks questioned, and they learned.

You Decide

It is wrong for one person to own another. Why do you think slavery has existed, even though it is wrong?

Some Greeks even questioned slavery. That slavery might be wrong was a brand new idea. Most of the ancient world used slaves to do hard work as **laborers.** In Athens, too, work was done by slaves. A few Athenian thinkers, however, were possibly the first to ask, "Is it right for people to own other people? Is it right to force a person to labor for another?"

Revolt

To rise up against a government; to refuse to obey the people in charge

Constitution

The basic laws and rules of a government

Jury

A group of people who listen to the facts and decide if a person on trial is guilty or not guilty

Reading Strategy: Metacognition

Make a prediction as to what you think will happen next. Check your prediction as you continue reading and revise as needed.

In the early years of Athens, government was in the hands of landowners. If a man owned land, he was a citizen. He had a voice in running the city-state. As the city grew, many merchants and businesspeople, shippers and traders became wealthy. They did not own land, but they wanted a say in city government. They wanted to be citizens. Athenians rose up against their government. This **revolt** led to a new government. In 508 B.C., this government drew up an Athenian **constitution.** Under the new laws, all free men were citizens. Women and slaves, however, did not have the rights of citizenship.

A citizen had the right to vote. He was also expected to hold office if called upon, sit on a **jury,** and serve in the army. The Athenian democracy was a government "by the people." The problem was that so many of "the people" (women and slaves) were not allowed to be citizens.

LEARN MORE ABOUT IT

Greek Religion

The Greeks believed that people were important. They celebrated the human mind and the human body. Therefore, their gods were much like humans. The Greeks worshipped many gods and goddesses. They gave each one a name and a humanlike form and personality. The gods and goddesses, according to the Greek storytellers, lived on top of Mount Olympus. This is the highest mountain in Greece. There, they enjoyed life. They laughed and they argued just as humans do. They played tricks on each other and on the humans they ruled.

Zeus was the king of the Greek gods. His wife was Hera, queen of the gods. The Parthenon on the Athenian Acropolis was built to honor Athena. She was the goddess of wisdom and learning.

The Greeks told myths, which explained things in nature. They told of the doings of the gods and goddesses. Myths were told about jealous and angry gods and goddesses. Some fell in love with humans and others helped humans. Greek myths made exciting stories.

REVIEW

Word Bank

Athena

citizens

democracy

enjoying life

military

slaves

soldier

vote

women

Zeus

On a sheet of paper, write the word from the Word Bank to complete each sentence correctly.

1. Sparta was a(n) _____ society.

2. Athens was governed by a(n) _____.

3. Spartan children belonged to the state and boys were raised to be a(n) _____.

4. Athenians were less interested in warfare, and more interested in _____.

5. Spartans had little use for _____.

6. The Athenian constitution gave all free men citizenship and allowed them to _____.

7. In Athens, women and slaves were not allowed to be _____.

8. People in both Athens and Sparta had _____.

9. _____ was the king of the Greek gods, and Hera was the queen.

10. _____ was the goddess of wisdom and learning.

Fighting in Greece

Between 500 and 400 B.C., the Greek empire was tested in a series of wars. The first battles united the city-states as they fought the great Persian Empire. The next war set the Athenians against the Spartans. The war lasted 27 years and is known as the Peloponnesian War.

What Were the Persian Wars?

As Greek city-states grew strong and wealthy, another land began to look toward Greece. The Persian Empire under Cyrus the Great had become the strongest military power in the world. In 546 B.C., Persia attacked and conquered the Greek colonies in Lydia. This was along the coast of what is now called Turkey. About 50 years later, the Greeks in Lydia revolted. King Darius I of Persia crushed their uprising. Then he sent his huge army to invade Greece.

In 490 B.C., the Persian armies headed for Athens. On the plain of Marathon, the Athenians beat the mighty Persians! An excited Greek citizen ran 25 miles (about 40 kilometers) to Athens to spread the good news. An Olympic event of today is named after that run from Marathon to Athens.

But the Persians were not ready to give up. Darius's son, Xerxes, continued the war. About 10 years later, Xerxes led an even stronger force into Greece. The Greek city-states put aside their quarrels to fight the common enemy. Xerxes's navy attacked. The Greeks fought the Persian invaders long and hard. Yet the Persians were too strong. Xerxes's men attacked the city of Athens next. In 480 B.C., they destroyed the Parthenon and burned much of the beautiful city.

Democratic

Having to do with a government in which all people have equal rights

You Decide

If the Persians had conquered Greece, our lives today might be very different. Why do you think this is so?

History Fact

Athenians created their greatest art and architecture during the Golden Age.

Pericles helped Athenians fight for democracy.

Xerxes left Athens thinking that he had won the war. He was in for a surprise, however. His men met the Athenian navy off the harbor of Salamis. There was a great sea battle. The Persians were defeated. The Greeks sent the Persians back across the Aegean Sea. Greece was then left to enjoy a time of peace.

What Was the Time Known as the Golden Age?

The peace following the Persian Wars lasted for about 50 years. During that time, Athens grew in power and strength. It became the greatest city-state in Greece.

Athens collected money from the other city-states. The Athenians insisted that their navy must be kept strong in order to protect all of Greece.

A great Athenian leader named Pericles rose to power in 461 B.C. Pericles helped the Athenians continue their government in which all people have equal rights—their **democratic** government. He used some of the money collected from other city-states to rebuild the Parthenon.

Athens flowered with Pericles as its leader. It was a time known as the Age of Pericles, or the Golden Age of Athens. The Athenians, at peace now, had time to study science and geography. They wrote their greatest plays and created their finest statues.

Athens of the Golden Age was one of the most beautiful cities in the world. Many other Greek city-states followed the Athenians' way of life and their ideas of democracy.

Sparta, however, continued as a military state. The Spartans did not like the way Athens was building and growing. They were also angry that Athens had been collecting money from the rest of Greece.

Plague

A deadly disease that spreads quickly

What Was the Result of the Peloponnesian War?

Peace ended in 431 B.C., when Sparta led some of the other city-states against Athens. Sparta was a land power with a strong army. Athens was a sea power. Most of its strength was in its navy. Both cities fought for control of Greece. The war between Athens and Sparta was called the Peloponnesian War. It was named after the Peloponnesus, the part of Greece in which Sparta was located. This war went on for 27 years!

The Spartans tried to cut off supplies to Athens to starve the people. The Athenians held on even though the Spartans were among the world's best fighters.

Then a terrible disease, a **plague,** broke out in the city of Athens. One-fourth of the Athenian people died during the plague. Their leader, Pericles, was among those who died.

Athens could no longer hold out against Sparta. In 404 B.C., Athens surrendered to Sparta.

REVIEW

On a sheet of paper, write the letter of the answer that correctly completes each sentence.

1. The Persian Empire under Cyrus the Great was the strongest _____ power in the world.

   A military   **B** land   **C** sea   **D** weapons

2. After the Athenians beat the Persians, an excited Greek citizen ran 25 miles to Athens. The _____, an Olympic event, is named for that run.

   A triathlon   **C** marathon
   B discus throwing   **D** chariot racing

3. _____ led the Persian army in destroying the Greek Parthenon in 480 B.C.

   A Cyrus   **B** Darius   **C** Xerxes   **D** Pericles

4. The Persian Wars lasted about _____ years.

   A 10   **B** 27   **C** 31   **D** 50

5. The Peloponnesian War lasted _____ years.

   A 10   **B** 27   **C** 31   **D** 50

6. _____ was the great Athenian leader who helped Athens thrive under its democratic government.

   A Cyrus   **B** Darius   **C** Xerxes   **D** Pericles

7. Athens and Sparta fought the Peloponnesian War for _____.

   A control of Greece   **C** a democratic government
   B power over the sea   **D** the right to own slaves

On a sheet of paper, write the answer to each question. Use complete sentences.

8. How did the Greeks eventually defeat the Persians?

9. What is the reason for the name "Golden Age"?

10. Who won the Peloponnesian War and how did they do so?

Gifts from the Greeks

Architecture
The art of building

Reading Strategy:
Metacognition

Note the main ideas and important details in this lesson. Summarize what you have read to make sure you understand it.

The Doric, Ionic, and Corinthian columns are examples of classical Greek architecture.

The art and **architecture** of the Golden Age demonstrates the Greeks' love of beauty. In addition, it was a time when Greek thinkers questioned the world around them. The progress they made in art and their search for truth are their greatest gifts to civilization.

What Are Some Gifts the Greeks Gave Us That Are Part of Life Today?

Greek thought and Greek works are very much a part of life today. Greek ideas in building can be seen in modern buildings. Greek statues still influence today's artists. The style of art and architecture the Greeks developed is called the "classical" style.

Today's students still read the works of Greek thinkers like Socrates, Plato, and Aristotle. "Know yourself," the great teachers said. "Ask questions. Search for the truth."

The Greeks were the first people to ask, "What is the world made of? Why is it the way it is?" They developed ideas about the sun, the earth, and the stars.

"The earth is round," Eratosthenes said. "The earth moves around the sun," Aristarchus said. Euclid and Pythagoras helped invent geometry.

We can also thank the Greeks for a model of a democracy. "Our government is called a democracy because power is in the hands of the whole people," said the Athenian leader Pericles.

Greek words and ideas show up in our own language. *Astronomy, biology, geography,* and *geology* are all taken from the Greek language. So are the words *music, theater, drama, comedy,* and *tragedy.*

Athlete

A person trained to take part in competitive sports

The word **athlete** comes from the Greeks, too. It means "one who tries to win a prize in a contest." Our Olympic Games are athletic contests. They are modeled after those played by Greek athletes so long ago.

The first known Olympic games took place in 776 B.C. Early Olympic games were held to honor the gods and goddesses. They were held every four years at the temple of Zeus in Olympia. All wars in Greece had to stop when it was time for the games. The athletes came from Athens and Sparta and all the other city-states.

The earliest Olympic games were just foot races. Later the Greeks added events such as boxing, wrestling, jumping, discus throwing, and chariot racing.

Today, just as in early Greece, it is a great honor to win an Olympic event. Winners get medals of gold, silver, and bronze. In ancient Greece the winners were crowned with a circle of laurel leaves. The athletes brought glory to their city-state and themselves.

The Greek leader Pericles saw the greatness of Greece in the Golden Age. "Mighty indeed are the marks and monuments of our empire . . . ," Pericles said. "Future ages will wonder at us."

TIMELINE STUDY:

ANCIENT GREECE

What wars were going on when the Athenian Constitution was written?

776 B.C. First Greek Olympic Games

800 B.C. — **700 B.C.** — **600 B.C.** — **500 B.C.** — **400 B.C.**

546–449 B.C. Persian Wars

431–404 B.C. Peloponnesian War

508 B.C. Athenian Constitution

461–429 B.C. The Age of Pericles

On a sheet of paper, write the letter of the answer that correctly completes each sentence.

1. Greeks developed the _____ style of art and architecture.

   A "Athenian"   **B** "Spartan"   **C** "classical"   **D** "artistic"

2. The word *comedy* is an example of a word taken from the Greek _____.

   A Olympics   **B** theater   **C** government   **D** language

3. The Greeks provided us a model of democracy. In this model, the power of the government is in the hands of the _____.

   A nobles   **B** people   **C** king/queen   **D** military

4. Early Olympic games were held to _____.

   A honor the gods and goddesses   **C** win money for the athlete's city-state
   B keep the peace between city-states   **D** test the limits of the human body

5. In ancient Greece, all _____ had to stop when it was time for the Olympics.

   A thinking   **B** building   **C** governments **D** wars

6. Winners of an Olympic event in ancient Greece received _____.

   A medals of gold, silver, and bronze   **C** a bouquet of flowers
   B a crown of laurel leaves   **D** a trophy of Zeus (the Greek god)

Word Bank

Aristarchus

Eratosthenes

Plato

Pythagoras

On a sheet of paper, write the word from the Word Bank to complete each sentence correctly.

7. Great Greek thinkers, like Socrates, _____, and Aristotle, questioned their world.

8. _____ claimed the earth is round.

9. _____ said that the earth moves around the sun.

10. Euclid and _____ helped invent geometry.

SUMMARY

- Most of Greece's wealth came from trading rather than from farming. Traders set up colonies in places they visited.

- Greece was divided into city-states, each one with its own government. The city-states were very different from one another.

- Athens and Sparta were two powerful city-states. Athens was a democracy. Athens worked to make itself enlightened and beautiful.

- Sparta was a military government. Slaves were kept and most of life there focused on preparing for war.

- The Greeks worshipped many gods and goddesses with human qualities.

- The Persians attacked Greece many times beginning in 546 B.C. In 480 B.C., they destroyed much of Athens, but the Greek army drove the Persian army away.

- Pericles became leader of Athens in 461 B.C. This period became known as the Age of Pericles. People studied science and geography and created works of art. They made the city beautiful.

- Quarrels between Athens and Sparta turned into the Peloponnesian War. Sparta won.

- The Greeks were great thinkers. Because they questioned their world, they learned. The works of great thinkers such as Socrates, Plato, and Aristotle, are still read today.

- The first known Olympic games took place in Greece in 776 B.C.

Word Bank

architecture

athlete

citizen

constitution

democracy

jury

myths

plague

revolt

tyrant

Vocabulary Review

On a sheet of paper, use the words from the Word Bank to complete each sentence correctly.

1. Some Greek city-states were ruled by a powerful ruler called a(n) _____.

2. The Greeks told _____ about their gods and goddesses.

3. Athens developed a form of _____, or rule of the people.

4. In Athens, a woman was not a(n) _____.

5. A deadly disease that spreads quickly is known as a(n) _____.

6. A basic set of rules and laws is a(n) _____.

7. When citizens _____, they are refusing to obey the people that are in charge.

8. A(n) _____ is a group of people who decide whether a person has disobeyed the law.

9. In ancient Greece, the word _____ means "one who tries to win a prize in a contest."

10. The Greeks developed a style of _____ called the "classical" style.

Chapter Review Questions

On a sheet of paper, write the answer to each question. Use complete sentences.

11. What was the Acropolis in Greek city-states?

12. Why did Greek culture spread?

Test Tip

If you are asked to compare and contrast things, be sure to tell how they are alike and how they are different.

13. How did democracy develop in Athens?

14. What was the result of the Peloponnesian War and the plague in Athens?

15. Who participated in the Olympic Games in ancient Greece?

Critical Thinking

On a sheet of paper, write your response to each question. Use complete sentences.

16. Would you rather have lived in Sparta or in Athens? Give at least two reasons why.

17. Why is the period after the Persian Wars called the Golden Age of Athens?

Using the Timeline

Use the timeline on page 137 to answer the questions.

18. When were the first Olympic Games?

19. When did the Athenians get a constitution?

20. What came after the Age of Pericles?

GROUP ACTIVITY

Form a group of three or four. Make a poster about the most recent Olympics. Feature your group's favorite Olympic stars.

Alexander the Great

King Philip II of Macedonia built up the army of his poor, struggling kingdom. He conquered the Greek city-states, in hope of going on to win the Persian Empire. Upon his death, his son Alexander went on to carry out his father's wishes.

Alexander showed great power and even greater determination. The Macedonians under Alexander conquered many lands from Egypt to the Middle East. Alexander the Great defeated the Persian Empire before conquering the Aryans in the Indus River Valley.

GOALS FOR LEARNING

- To explain how Alexander became ruler of Greece
- To tell why Alexander was called the Great Conqueror
- To explain the reason for the end of Alexander's empire

Reading Strategy: Summarizing

As you read the text in this chapter, you will want to ask yourself questions to help you understand what you read.

- What is the chapter about?
- What new ideas am I being introduced to?
- Why is it important that I remember these ideas?

Key Vocabulary Words

Lesson 1

Assassinate To murder a leader or other important person

Campaign A series of battles all aimed at one military end

Ambition The drive to become powerful, successful, or famous

Lesson 2

Founded To have begun a country or city; to have built a city

General A high-ranking military officer

King Philip and Alexander

The Peloponnesian War was over. The Greek city-states were now under Sparta's rule. They still argued with each other, however.

Who Was King Philip of Macedonia?

To the north was a land called Macedonia. It was ruled by a king named Philip II. Macedonia had always been poor. Things changed, however, when Philip became king. Philip saw to it that Macedonians farmed their good soil. He sent out Macedonian traders. He built new roads. King Philip II had ideas.

Philip built up the Macedonian army. He built war machinery. He taught his men new ways of fighting. Philip soon had a strong army of foot soldiers and soldiers on horseback.

King Philip's plan was to conquer the great Persian Empire. To do that, Philip needed military strength.

He needed more strength than he had with only Macedonia behind him. Philip wanted the power of all the Greek armies.

King Philip told some of the nearby city-states about his plan. They agreed to join him. Philip, however, needed more power. He needed the largest city-states, Athens and Thebes, behind him. For that reason he used all his military know-how along with his well-trained men and their fine machinery. With this support, Philip conquered Athens and Thebes.

Soon all of Greece fell under Macedonian control—all except Sparta, that is. Philip never conquered Sparta.

You Decide

Philip never conquered Sparta. What do you think stopped him?

Assassinate

To kill a leader or other important person

Campaign

A series of battles all aimed at one military end

Ambition

The drive to become powerful, successful, or famous

Reading Strategy:
Summarizing

What are some important details about King Philip that help you understand this lesson?

Aristotle was a great thinker and teacher.

Now Philip was ready for war with the Persians. Yet King Philip II would never lead his men into Persia. By now he had made enemies. There was a plot to kill, or **assassinate,** him. Before he could begin his **campaign** against (or begin fighting with) Persia, he was killed.

Who Was Philip's Son?

Philip had a son, Alexander. Alexander was not an ordinary boy. From his father, Alexander inherited, or got, **ambition** and a love of power. Philip taught his son all about warfare and leadership. Alexander's mother, Olympias, was smart and hot-tempered. Alexander, too, was bright and easily angered.

As a boy, Alexander seemed almost fearless. Stories tell of the young Prince Alexander taming a certain horse. No other person in the kingdom could ride it. Alexander named that horse Bucephalus. Bucephalus would carry Alexander across an empire!

King Philip always thought highly of the Greek way of life and of Greek ideas. His son, Alexander, was to have the best of teachers—the Greek thinker, Aristotle. At age 13, Alexander began his lessons.

Aristotle taught Alexander to love Greek stories of heroes and adventure. He taught the boy about far-off lands and about other cultures. Aristotle saw to it that Alexander took part in sports, too.

By the time Alexander was 18, he was able to take a command in his father's army. Alexander was 20 when his father was killed. Now he was ready to take over as king of Macedonia and to become a conqueror.

REVIEW

On a sheet of paper, write the letter of the answer that correctly completes each sentence.

1. Philip II ruled a land called _____.

   A Athens   **B** Sparta   **C** Thebes   **D** Macedonia

2. Philip constructed _____ and taught his men new ways of fighting.

   A new roads   **B** war machinery   **C** an empire   **D** boats

3. To conquer the _____, Philip needed the military strength of all the Greek armies.

   A Persian Empire **B** Bucephalus   **C** Spartans   **D** Tyre

4. Philip II conquered all of Greece except for _____.

   A Athens   **B** Sparta   **C** Thebes   **D** Macedonia

5. Before Philip could lead his men into Persia, he was _____.

   A defeated   **B** made king   **C** assassinated   **D** campaigned

6. Philip's son, _____, inherited his father's ambition and love of power.

   A Aristotle   **B** Olympias   **C** Alexander   **D** Bucephalus

7. _____ was the great Greek thinker who taught young Alexander.

   A Aristotle   **B** Olympias   **C** Philip   **D** Bucephalus

8. Alexander was a fearless boy. _____ was the horse he tamed that no other person in the kingdom could ride.

   A Aristotle   **B** Olympias   **C** Philip   **D** Bucephalus

9. Alexander took command of his father's army at age _____.

   A 13   **B** 18   **C** 20   **D** 33

10. Alexander was only _____ years old when his father died.

    A 13   **B** 18   **C** 20   **D** 33

Alexander's Conquests

Philip II had planned to conquer an empire. Greece would be the center of that empire. Now that job fell to his son, Alexander.

What Is Considered One of Alexander's Greatest Military Victories?

Since birth, Alexander had been raised to be a ruler and a warrior. He was ready for the job. Alexander and the Macedonian army headed for Persia.

The next two years saw Alexander and his men crossing the Middle East. They conquered one land after another. Then in 334 B.C., Alexander began his campaign against Persia. In 333 B.C., Alexander did battle with the king of the Persian Empire, Darius III. Alexander won the battle, but King Darius escaped.

Alexander was the king of Macedonia at age 20. By the time he died at age 33, he expanded his empire and the whole world had heard of him.

On through the Persian Empire, to Syria, swept the conquering Macedonians. They attacked the great Phoenician city of Tyre. Alexander ordered his men to build a raised road over the sea to reach the city. The battle at Tyre was one of his greatest military victories.

What Was Egypt Like After Alexander Conquered It?

After taking over Phoenicia, Alexander moved south, toward Egypt. Alexander's army easily took Egypt.

The Egyptians had been under harsh Persian rule. They were glad to have Alexander as their new ruler. Some Egyptians even hailed Alexander as the son of an Egyptian god.

Alexander built a city on the Mediterranean coast of Egypt. He named it after himself, like many other cities he had built. Egypt's *Alexandria* became the most famous of the Alexandrias.

Founded
To have begun a country or city; to have built a city

Reading Strategy: Summarizing

What are some important details about Alexander's accomplishments?

LEARN MORE ABOUT IT

Alexandria

Alexander drew up plans for building the city of Alexandria in Egypt in 332 B.C. After his death, the ruling family carried out his plan. The city grew rapidly. It became one of the largest and most important cities of the ancient world. Within 200 years after it was **founded** (built), more than a million people were living in Alexandria.

It was a beautiful city. Many of its buildings were Greek in style. A giant lighthouse rose over 370 feet high. It was built of white marble and was known as one of the Seven Wonders of the Ancient World. The huge fire at the top of the lighthouse could be seen by sailors 30 miles away.

Alexandria was also famous for its fine schools and its library. The library contained more than 700,000 scrolls. A scroll is a roll of paper or parchment with writing on it. Scrolls were used instead of books. The library of Alexandria was the largest in the world. It became a famous center of learning and culture. The glory of Greece had come to Egypt.

General
A high-ranking
military officer

One of Alexander's **generals** (a high-ranking military officer) was named Ptolemy. Alexander chose him to rule Egypt. Ptolemy's family would rule Egypt for 300 years.

What Brought About the End of the Persian Empire?

Alexander was more interested in conquering than in ruling. Just as with Ptolemy in Egypt, he would set up many more rulers in other lands. When Alexander felt his work in Egypt was done, he moved on. He still wanted the whole world.

In 331 B.C., Alexander met King Darius III of Persia again. Alexander defeated Darius. Once again, however, Darius escaped. Yet Alexander had no more trouble with his old enemy. King Darius was to die that same year, killed by his own men. With Darius gone, Alexander was the ruler of all of the Persian Empire.

The city of Persepolis, in southwestern Persia, was the greatest city of the Persian Empire. Much of the wealth of the empire was stored in the palaces of Persepolis. Alexander and his army easily captured the city. They killed most of the people who lived there. They took the rest as slaves. The Macedonians took all the treasures and then burned the Persian palaces. In 480 B.C., the Persians had burned Athens. Now Alexander had gotten even.

Then Alexander looked east. What was left for him in the world? India would be next.

What Happened in the Valley of the Indus?

In 326 B.C., Alexander the Great arrived in India. The Aryan rajas (princes) along the Indus River battled the Macedonian soldiers. The Aryans rode great, lumbering war elephants. Yet Alexander's men, riding horseback, were faster. Alexander conquered the Indus River Valley. He wanted to go deeper into India, but his men were tired.

Heavy rains had come, and marching was hard. They wanted to go home.

"Back to Greece," the soldiers cried.

"On through India," Alexander demanded.

Alexander's armies insisted on turning back. They would go no farther. For that reason, Alexander had to give up his campaign.

Alexander's Empire

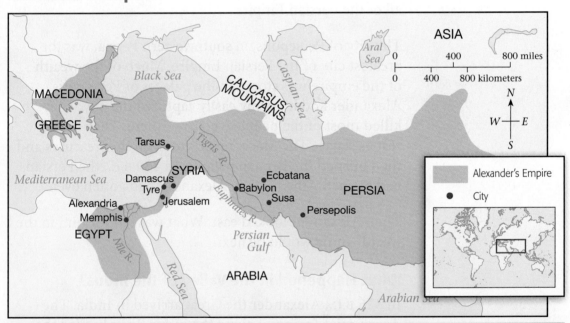

MAP STUDY

1. What are two cities in Egypt?

2. Which three rivers did Alexander have to cross to get to India (east of Persia)?

REVIEW

Word Bank

Darius III

Egypt

Egyptian god

India

Indus River Valley

Ptolemy

Tyre

On a sheet of paper, write the word from the Word Bank to complete each sentence correctly.

1. The battle at _____ is considered to be one of Alexander's greatest military victories.

2. Alexander conquered Persia and then went on to Egypt and _____.

3. The Egyptians were glad to have Alexander as their new ruler. Some even hailed Alexander as the son of a(n) _____.

4. Alexandria is the city Alexander built on the Mediterranean coast of _____.

5. Alexander chose his general _____ to rule Egypt.

6. King _____ of the Persian Empire escaped death when Alexander conquered Persia. Unfortunately, he was killed by his own men a few years later.

7. Alexander conquered the _____ easily. This is because his men, riding horses, were faster than the Aryans who rode elephants.

On a sheet of paper, write the answer to each question. Use complete sentences.

8. How did Alexander defeat the city of Tyre?

9. How did the Persian Empire come to an end?

10. Why did Alexander have to give up his campaign?

The End of an Empire

- To tell why Alexander made Babylon the capital of his empire
- To describe what happened to Alexander's empire after his death

Remember

At a much earlier date Hammurabi, a great ruler of Babylon, drew up a code of laws.

Alexander was 30 years old when he conquered the Aryan kingdoms in India. He had been fighting and building his empire for 12 years. In all that time he had never lost a single battle!

Alexander made his father's dreams real. He spread Greek culture and ideas over a large part of the world. Alexander's empire was the largest the ancient world had ever known.

Alexander imagined Europe and Asia as one big country, united under his rule. He wanted to blend the two into one. He chose Babylon as his capital city because it was in the center of his empire. He had plants brought in from one continent and planted on the other. Alexander married an Asian woman. He also rewarded his soldiers if they did the same.

Detail found on the tomb of Alexander the Great shows Persians and Greeks hunting together. It represents his desire for unity between people even after the fighting during his lifetime.

What Happened After Alexander's Death?

Alexander ruled a giant empire from his palace in Babylon. He had big plans for his empire. Then, in 323 B.C., he fell sick. He had a high fever. No medicines of the day could help him. Within a few days, 33-year-old Alexander the Great was dead. His soldiers placed his body in a gold coffin. It was taken to Alexandria in Egypt to be buried.

After his death, Alexander's lands were divided among some of his generals. The great empire was gone forever, split into separate smaller empires.

Yet the man who set out to conquer the world had left his mark. The lands Alexander touched would always show something of Greek style and Greek customs.

Reading Strategy:
Summarizing

What important event in history is this lesson about?

TIMELINE STUDY:

ALEXANDER THE GREAT

What does the timeline show about Alexander's short life?

356 B.C.
Alexander is born

338 B.C.
Philip of Macedonia wins control of Greece

336 B.C.
King Philip is assassinated

326 B.C.
Alexander invades India

360 B.C. 350 B.C. 340 B.C. 330 B.C. 320 B.C.

334 B.C.
Alexander begins Persian campaigns

332 B.C.
Alexander conquers Egypt

323 B.C.
Alexander dies

REVIEW

On a sheet of paper, write the letter of the answer that correctly completes each sentence.

1. Alexander was _____ years old when he conquered the Aryans in India.

    A 12   **B** 23   **C** 30   **D** 33

2. In his _____ years of fighting, Alexander had not lost a single battle.

    A 12   **B** 23   **C** 30   **D** 33

3. Alexander's _____ was the largest the ancient world had ever known.

    A army   **B** family   **C** empire   **D** slave population

4. Alexander wanted to rule Europe and _____ as one big country.

    A Asia   **B** Egypt   **C** Macedonia   **D** Persia

5. Alexander married a(n) _____ woman and rewarded his soldiers if they did the same.

    A Asian   **B** Egyptian   **C** Macedonian   **D** Persian

6. Alexander made _____ the capital city because it was the center of his empire.

    A Alexandria   **B** Babylon   **C** Persepolis   **D** Tyre

7. Alexander died at the age of _____.

    A 12   **B** 23   **C** 30   **D** 33

8. Alexander was buried in a gold coffin in the city of _____.

    A Alexandria   **B** Babylon   **C** Persepolis   **D** Tyre

9. After his death, the lands Alexander conquered were _____.

    A free to govern themselves   **C** divided among some of his generals
    B left to fight wars with each other   **D** given to his son

10. Alexander's empire _____ after his death.

    A turned to democracy   **C** grew
    B fought each other   **D** was over

- King Philip of Macedonia built up his army. He taught his men new ways of fighting. He planned to conquer the Persian Empire.

- Because Philip needed all of Greece behind him, he first conquered the Greek city-states of Thebes and Athens. He did not conquer Sparta.

- King Philip was assassinated, then his son Alexander led the Macedonian armies into Persia.

- Alexander set out to conquer the world.

- Alexander had a great victory at Tyre in Phoenicia.

- Alexander conquered Egypt. He built Alexandria on its Mediterranean coast.

- Alexander chose Ptolemy, one of his generals, to rule Egypt.

- Alexander became ruler of the Persian Empire after destroying the city of Persepolis.

- Alexander conquered the Indus River Valley area in India.

- Alexander brought Greek ideas and culture to the lands he conquered.

- Alexander died at the age of 33.

- After Alexander's death, his lands were split up among his generals.

Word Bank

ambition

assassinate

campaign

founded

general

Vocabulary Review

On a sheet of paper, use the words from the Word Bank to complete each sentence correctly.

1. Alexander the Great had the _____ to take over the world.

2. Alexandria was _____ in 332 B.C.

3. A(n) _____ has a top position in the military.

4. To win a war, a military leader must plan a(n) _____ of a number of battles.

5. The people who _____ a leader are murderers.

Chapter Review Questions

On a sheet of paper, write the answer to each question. Use complete sentences.

6. What did King Philip II of Macedonia need in order to conquer the Persian Empire?

7. How did Philip become ruler of Greece?

8. Why did Philip choose a Greek teacher for young Alexander?

9. Why was Alexander called the Great Conqueror?

10. What battle is considered to be one of Alexander's greatest military victories, and why?

11. Why did the Egyptians welcome Alexander the Great?

12. Why did Alexander choose Babylon as the capital of his empire?

13. What was Alexander's vision for his empire?

14. What happened to Alexander's empire after he died?

15. How did Alexander the Great leave his mark on the world he conquered?

Critical Thinking

On a sheet of paper, write your response to each question. Use complete sentences.

16. Why was Aristotle a good teacher for Alexander?

17. What was Alexander's greatest accomplishment? Explain why.

Using the Timeline

Use the timeline on page 153 to answer the questions.

18. What year was King Philip assassinated?

19. How old was Alexander when he began the Persian campaigns?

20. What is the order of the following: the conquest of Egypt, the invasion of India, the Persian campaigns?

GROUP ACTIVITY

In a group of three or four, write a mini-biography of Alexander the Great. Include basic information, such as his birth, accomplishments, and death. Include information from this chapter and from other books. In the last paragraph of your biography, express your opinion of Alexander. Tell why you think he was able to do so much during his short life.

The Rise of Rome

Over a period of 500 years, Rome grew to be a republic. It started as a group of villages and grew to be a mighty city. Its empire included lands on all sides of the Mediterranean.

The Romans had a strong civilization. They developed language, architecture, laws, and religion of wide range and strength. Their civilization was larger and more powerful than any that had come before it. The Roman Empire would have deep effects on many cultures that followed it.

GOALS FOR LEARNING

- To describe how Rome grew powerful
- To explain the role of Julius Caesar in early Rome
- To describe the beginnings of the Roman Empire
- To describe Roman society
- To explain the rise of Christianity in Rome
- To explain why the Roman Empire began to fall

Reading Strategy: Questioning

As you read, ask yourself questions. This will help you understand more of the information and become a more active reader. Ask yourself:

- What do I hope to learn from this text?
- What do the facts and details in this text tell me?
- Are there any people or situations in this text that connect to my life?

Key Vocabulary Words

Lesson 1

Peninsula A long piece of land almost completely surrounded by water

Republic A government in which the citizens have the right to choose their representatives to make laws

Elect To choose someone for an office by voting

Representative A person who is chosen to act or speak for others

Senate A governing or lawmaking body

Lesson 2

Province A part of a country, with its own local government

Governor A person chosen to run a province or territory

Civil war Fighting between people who live in the same country

Forum A public square in an ancient Roman city; lawmakers met there

Lesson 3

Pax Romana The Roman peace that began during the reign of Augustus Caesar

Lesson 4

Aqueduct A channel that carries flowing water over a long distance

Lesson 5

Gospel One of four books of the New Testament part of the Bible

Enslaved When a person is forced to become a slave

Persecute To treat in a cruel way

Convert Change from one religion to another

Bishop A high-ranking church official in charge of other priests and a number of churches

Pope The head of the Roman Catholic Church

How Rome Grew Powerful

Objectives

- To tell about the effect the Etruscans had on early Rome
- To describe how the Roman Republic was governed
- To explain what the Punic Wars were and what they did for Rome

Reading Strategy:
Questioning

What do you already know about Rome?

Peninsula
A long piece of land almost completely surrounded by water

Republic
A government in which the citizens have the right to choose their representatives to make laws

Seven hills rose up along the Tiber River in the center of Italy. Small villages dotted the seven hills. One of those villages was called Rome. It had been built by the Latins in 753 B.C. The Latins, or Romans, were one of several groups of people that had moved down from central Europe. They settled in the Italian **peninsula** around 1000 B.C. A peninsula is a long piece of land almost completely surrounded by water. Rome was not very important then. However, it would one day grow into a great city. That city would become the center of an empire.

Who Were the Etruscans?

From 750 B.C. to 600 B.C., the little Italian villages were ruled by a series of Roman kings. During those years, the Romans lived in peace. They were mainly farmers and herders. Things changed in about 600 B.C. North of the Tiber River lived a people called the Etruscans. They decided to conquer Rome and the other villages. The Romans did not stand a chance against them.

For about the next 100 years, Rome was ruled by Etruscan kings. The Etruscans had many skills. They built a wall around the city. They drained nearby swamps and laid the first sewer to carry away dirty water and human waste. The Romans even adopted the Etruscan alphabet. Slowly, Rome changed from a little farming village into a city-state.

Then, in 509 B.C., the people of Rome rose up against a severe Etruscan king. They took the government of Rome into their own hands and set up a **republic.**

How Was the Roman Republic Governed?

In a republic, the government is controlled by the people and there is no king. Roman citizens **elected,** or chose, men to make their laws and run their government. Three hundred elected **representatives** met in a **senate.** The senate was the part of the government that made laws. The Republic was democratic because citizens voted for the people who would represent them. The Roman Republic was a model for our own democratic system of representative government.

The members of the Roman Senate were usually wealthy landowners. Once elected, they held office for life. Some of the Senate members were quite old. The people thought them very wise. The word *senate* comes from the Latin word that means "old."

The early years of the Republic were not peaceful. At first Rome was attacked by armies from other lands. However, Rome grew more and more powerful. After a time, Rome wanted to gain more land.

What Did the Punic Wars Do for Rome?

The Romans became skilled soldiers. Almost every Roman male spent some time in the army. Rome's military power grew. The Romans began battling for more land. By about 270 B.C., Rome had taken over the whole Italian peninsula.

One of Rome's greatest enemies was Carthage. Carthage was on the north coast of Africa. It was a city settled by the Phoenicians. Carthage and Rome quarreled over Mediterranean trade routes.

Rome fought three wars with Carthage. These were called the Punic Wars. The first clash between the two states came in Sicily. They battled for the city of Messina. Rome finally won this war in 241 B.C., after 23 years of fighting!

Remember
Philip II and Alexander the Great were Macedonians.

During the second war between Carthage and Rome, Macedonia had sided with the Carthaginians. Macedonia was still the most powerful state in Greece. After taking Carthage, Rome sent armies into Greece. Roman armies conquered the Greek city-states. They brought Greek treasures back to Rome, introducing Roman citizens to Greek art and style.

The Romans made slaves of the conquered Greeks. Many of the slaves were used as laborers. Some of the Greek captives, however, were well educated. They became teachers and doctors in Rome. Many Greek slaves found themselves with kind Roman masters, masters who respected them. Some Greeks were able to earn their freedom. Therefore, in many ways, Roman culture was influenced by the Greeks.

Over the next 50 years, Carthage grew strong again. Once more, Rome felt threatened. So Rome declared war and sent its army back to Africa. This time, in the final Punic War, the city of Carthage was totally destroyed.

TECHNOLOGY CONNECTION

The Work of Archimedes

The Greeks lost a great thinker during the Punic Wars. Archimedes was a scientist, mathematician, philosopher, and inventor.

Archimedes worked for the state during the Punic Wars. During that time, he invented many weapons to defend his town of Syracuse, Italy. He developed a catapult that was used to throw stones at an enemy. Another tool he created could lift or tip an enemy's ship. Also, some claim that he invented a "burning mirror" to reflect the sun's ray toward an enemy.

However, Archimedes is most famous for another discovery. He learned that an item placed in water lost weight based on the amount of water it replaced. This idea was revolutionary for the time.

Archimedes eventually died at the hands of a Roman soldier.

By 140 B.C., Rome controlled all of the Mediterranean lands. Citizens of the Republic thought of the Mediterranean Sea as a Roman sea.

GREAT NAMES IN HISTORY

Hannibal

In 218 B.C., a fierce Carthaginian general named Hannibal arrived in Spain. He brought a huge army with him. He led his soldiers over the Pyrenees and the Alps. Many of Hannibal's soldiers rode elephants. The mountains were hard on the huge animals. Many elephants lost their footing on the narrow mountain paths and fell to their deaths. Most of them, however, made it to the Po Valley of Italy. Hannibal was a clever general. He caught the Romans by surprise and beat the Roman army. Thus began the second of the Punic Wars.

For the next 13 years, Hannibal led his army up and down Italy. He won more battles against Roman forces. Nevertheless, little by little the Romans grew stronger. Finally Hannibal was driven out of Italy. Then the Romans invaded Africa and defeated Hannibal's army in 202 B.C.

Hannibal crossed the Alps to invade Rome because he knew the Romans would be surprised.

Match the description in Column A with the term in Column B.
Write the correct letter on a sheet of paper.

Column A

1. the Carthaginian general who helped start the second Punic War

2. the people that ruled Rome for 100 years

3. the river Rome rose up along

4. the people who built Rome in 753 B.C.

5. the government the Romans set up after rebelling against a harsh king

Column B

A Etruscans

B Hannibal

C Latins

D republic

E Tiber

On a sheet of paper, write the answer to each question. Use complete sentences.

6. What effect did the Etruscans have on early Rome?

7. How was the Roman Republic governed?

8. What were the Punic Wars and why were they fought?

9. What did the Punic Wars do for Roman culture?

10. Why did the Romans think of the Mediterranean Sea as a Roman sea?

Julius Caesar

Objectives

- To explain the role of armies in Roman provinces
- To name some things Julius Caesar did for Rome
- To tell how Julius Caesar died

Province

A part of a country, with its own local government

Governor

A person chosen to run a province or territory

Senator

A person who is a member of the senate

Rome conquered many lands. Some of them were far from the city itself. To make the lands easier to govern, they were divided into sections called **provinces.** Each province had its own local government and was ruled by its own **governor.** Some people in the provinces accepted the Roman rule. Others were not happy with their new rulers. Furthermore, they did not like Roman customs.

To keep the people in order, Rome sent large armies to each province. A general was at the head of each of these armies. The soldiers in the provinces were a long way from Rome. They often felt more loyalty to their generals than they did to Rome. The generals became powerful men.

Sometimes the generals and their armies fought among themselves. The most powerful of the generals was a man named Julius Caesar.

Who Was Julius Caesar and Why Is He So Famous?

Julius Caesar was the Roman general in the province of Gaul. Gaul was a land to the northwest of Rome. It would one day be called France. People liked Julius Caesar. His soldiers were loyal to him. The people of Rome admired his success. He won many battles in Gaul and expanded Roman control. After a while, members of the senate in Rome, or **senators,** began to worry about Caesar's popularity. Was Julius Caesar becoming too powerful?

Fighting between people who live in the same country

The senate called Caesar back to Rome. "Leave your army in Gaul," the senators ordered. Caesar returned to Rome, but he brought his army with him. It was 49 B.C. The common people welcomed Caesar as a hero. Soon Caesar and his army took control of the Roman government.

Some of the other generals were not happy about this. They challenged Caesar's power. This led to **civil wars,** with one Roman army fighting another.

Julius Caesar was always the winner. He won battles in Greece, in Spain, and in North Africa. While fighting in Egypt, Caesar met the beautiful Egyptian princess, Cleopatra. He found time to fall in love with her. He helped her win the throne of Egypt.

By 45 B.C., Caesar controlled the Roman world. The people hailed him as their ruler. For the most part he used his power wisely. He made citizens of many of the people in the provinces. He even allowed some to sit in the Senate. He made sure the governors ruled the provinces fairly. Caesar made more jobs for the people of Rome. He set up colonies where poor Romans could start their own farms.

You Decide
Julius Caesar named a month after himself. What do you think it was?

Caesar even improved the Roman calendar. Borrowing from the Egyptians, he changed it to a system of 365 days in a year. He added an extra day every fourth year, creating "leap year." The new calendar was much better than the old one.

Julius Caesar was a powerful ruler in ancient Rome.

Forum

A public square in an
ancient Roman city;
lawmakers met there

The people of Rome cheered Caesar. They stamped his
picture on Roman coins and built a temple in his name.
At the Roman **Forum** (the public square where lawmakers
met), Mark Antony offered Caesar the crown of king.
Mark Antony was a senator and Caesar's friend. Caesar
refused the crown.

How Did Caesar Die?

Many of Rome's leading citizens were worried. It did not
help that Caesar had not accepted the crown. They were
still afraid he planned to make himself a king and put an
end to the Republic.

Reading Strategy:
Questioning

What details are
important to
understanding what
this lesson is about?

Some of the Roman senators, led by Brutus and Cassius,
plotted to kill Caesar. Many of these men had been
Caesar's friends. They did not want to lose the Republic,
however. Their first loyalty was to Rome. On March 15,
44 B.C., Julius Caesar was stabbed to death as he entered
the Roman Senate.

On a sheet of paper, write the letter of the answer that correctly completes each sentence.

1. Julius Caesar was the Roman general in the province of _____.

   A Carthage   **B** Gaul   **C** Greece   **D** Rome

2. Caesar was well-liked and popular, and soon he and his army took control of _____.

   A the province of Gaul   **C** the Mediterranean Sea
   B the Forum   **D** the Roman government

3. _____ were not happy about Caesar's control, which led to civil wars.

   A Other generals   **C** Roman senators
   B Citizens   **D** Farmers

4. Caesar controlled the Roman world by _____ B.C., and people hailed him as their ruler.

   A 202   **B** 140   **C** 45   **D** 44

Match the description in Column A with the person in Column B. Write the correct letter on a sheet of paper.

Column A	Column B
5. a senator who offered Caesar the crown of king	**A** Brutus
6. a Roman senator who, along with Cassius, plotted to kill Caesar	**B** Cleopatra
7. the Egyptian princess with whom Caesar fell in love	**C** Mark Antony

On a sheet of paper, write the answer to each question. Use complete sentences.

8. What was the role of armies in Roman provinces?

9. What are three things Julius Caesar did for Rome?

10. Why and how did Julius Caesar die?

The Roman Empire

Objectives

- To tell what happened after Julius Caesar died
- To tell what Emperor Augustus did

Reading Strategy: Questioning

As you read, notice details about the development of the Roman Empire. What questions do you ask yourself about these details?

Pax Romana

The Roman peace that began during the reign of Augustus Caesar

You Decide
Do you think it is a good idea to allow one person to have complete power? What would happen if that person were not a wise ruler?

Now that Julius Caesar was dead, the days of the Roman Republic were numbered. Most of the people had been happy under Caesar. They wanted a ruler who would continue with Caesar's policies and plans.

Who Was Augustus?

Once again there was a struggle for power, and civil wars shook Rome. First Brutus and Cassius fought against Mark Antony and Octavian. Mark Antony and Octavian had remained loyal to Caesar. When Octavian and Mark Antony won, they turned against each other.

Mark Antony fell in love with none other than Egypt's Cleopatra. They were determined to rule Rome together. Yet they were defeated by Octavian. The defeat led Antony and Cleopatra to kill themselves.

Now Octavian ruled all of the Roman world. It was the beginning of a new age for Rome. It was the start of the Roman Empire. Octavian became Rome's first emperor.

An emperor had even more power than a king. To his people, he was only one step below a god. In 27 B.C., the Roman Senate gave Octavian the title of "Augustus." The title meant that he was above all others. He was to be worshipped.

The Roman Senate continued to meet, but the Republic was as dead as Caesar. Augustus chose new senators to make his laws. Augustus, indeed, held complete power.

Under Emperor Augustus the Roman Empire thrived as never before. Augustus ended the civil wars. The time of peace that he brought about was called the ***Pax Romana*** (Roman Peace).

Augustus chose good, honest men as government leaders.
He built roads connecting all the provinces with Rome.
He improved harbors and made trade easier. Life became
better for most people.

The Roman Empire Under Augustus

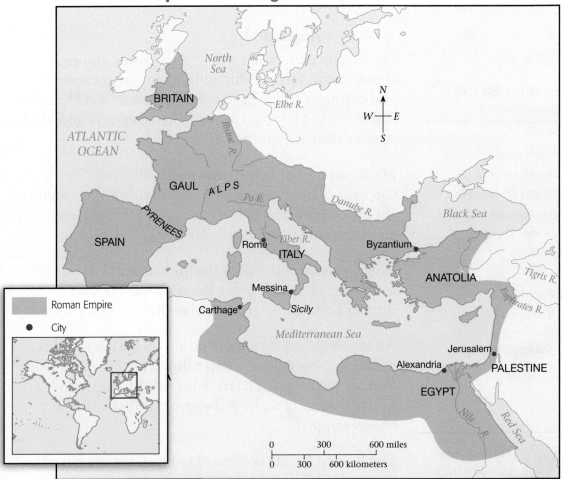

MAP STUDY

1. What five lands bordering the Mediterranean Sea were ruled by Rome?

2. Which two rivers formed the northern border of the Roman Empire?

REVIEW

Word Bank

Augustus

Cleopatra

emperor

king

Mark Antony

Octavian

power

On a sheet of paper, write the word from the Word Bank to complete each sentence correctly.

1. After Caesar's death, there was a struggle for _____.

2. Brutus and Cassius fought against Mark Antony and _____.

3. When Octavian and _____ won, they turned against each other.

4. Mark Antony fell in love with _____ and they were determined to rule Rome together.

5. Octavian became Rome's first _____.

6. In Rome, an emperor had more power than a(n) _____. He was one step below a god.

7. Octavian was given the title of "_____" by the Roman Senate. It meant he was above all others and should be worshipped.

On a sheet of paper, write the answer to each question. Use complete sentences.

8. Why did Mark Antony and Cleopatra kill themselves?

9. What changes did Augustus make to the Roman government?

10. Why did the Roman Empire thrive under Augustus?

Roman Society

As the largest city in the Roman Empire, Rome was a busy place. A million people lived in or near the city.

What Was Life Like in Rome?

Indeed, Rome had come a long way from that tiny village on a hill. It was a fine and beautiful place. The wide main streets were paved with stone. Fresh water came to the city through overhead **aqueducts.** The water was piped into houses and public fountains.

The Romans built beautiful temples to their many gods and goddesses. There were 300 temples in Rome alone. One of the most famous of these was the Pantheon.

The Roman Forum was a gathering place. It was there that the Senate met in the Senate House. Columned temples lined the edges of the Forum. Merchants built shops there.

The Romans also built huge public baths. They were more than a place to bathe in hot and cold pools. The baths were also a center of social life. The baths held libraries, gymnasiums, and even small theaters. The public baths were free of charge.

Wealthy Romans lived in big houses. These houses had swimming pools and large dining halls for parties. Many rich people also had country homes. They hired workers to live there and look after the land.

The average Roman family lived in a small house or apartment. The poorer people lived in tiny rooms in big apartment buildings. They often had to struggle for enough to eat.

Objectives

■ To describe Roman life
■ To tell some things the Romans built
■ To name the language of the Romans

Aqueduct
A channel that carries flowing water over a long distance

Reading Strategy:
Questioning

What experiences from your own life give you a better understanding of Roman society?

Geography Note

Appius Claudius Caecus became censor of Rome in 312 B.C. The censor was in charge of public works. He directed construction of the first major road from Rome. The Appian Way ran 132 miles (212 km) from Rome to ancient Capua. It was made of cemented lava stone and domed in the center for runoff of rainwater. In 244 B.C. the road was extended to Brindisi in the far southeast near the Adriatic coast. The road became a common route for Roman armies and merchants.

Reading Strategy: Questioning

What details about ancient Roman society tell you about its future?

Rich and poor people alike enjoyed the free entertainment provided by the emperors. The Romans celebrated many holidays—to honor their gods and goddesses or to honor military heroes. On these days they often held chariot races. These exciting races took place at a sports stadium called the Circus Maximus. The Romans loved to watch these events. They also enjoyed more violent forms of entertainment.

What Shaped Roman Art and Architecture?

The Romans admired the Greeks. They put up statues taken from Greek city-states. They copied Greek style in statues of their own. Many of the great buildings in Rome were also based on Greek style and form.

Roman builders liked to use arches, curved openings that supported something. Arches spanned streets, supported bridges, and held up great aqueducts. Visitors often passed under a great arch to enter a Roman city.

The Romans wanted their art and architecture to be useful. The 14 aqueducts that carried water into Rome were certainly beautiful. They were also useful—and they were built to last. Some aqueducts built more than 2,000 years ago still stand today.

Some roads of ancient Rome are in use today, too. "All roads lead to Rome," a famous saying goes. That means that Roman highways, paved layer upon layer, linked all the provinces to Rome. The Romans were fine builders. They built a sewer system to serve ancient Rome. Parts of it are still being used in the modern city.

This aqueduct was built more than 2,000 years ago to bring water to dry lands.

What Were the Languages and Laws of the Romans?

Italian, French, Spanish, Portuguese, and Romanian are all called Romance languages. They all come from Latin, the language of the Romans.

There are many words that we have taken from the Romans. We have *colosseums* today. Our government has a *senate*. The Russians changed the word Caesar to *Czar*, the Germans to *Kaiser*.

"Justice for all!" was an idea that came from the Roman Senate. Many of our ideas about laws and courts of law came from the Romans. Roman laws and lawmaking served as a model for many other nations.

Words from the Past

Borrowed Words

English-speakers use many words and phrases borrowed from Latin, the Romance languages, and other languages. In fact, about half of the words in present-day English come from languages other than English.

The Romance languages developed from Vulgar Latin. This was the spoken Latin of ordinary Romans. Soldiers and settlers brought Latin to areas throughout the Roman Empire. In each area, the language became a dialect of Latin. Over time, the dialect became a separate language. Italian, French, Spanish, Portuguese, and Romanian are national languages that developed from Latin.

England was a part of the Roman Empire, too. However, the English language developed from the language of Germanic tribes that invaded England in the fifth century A.D. Ever since that time, English has borrowed words from other languages.

Many words about the church came from Latin, such as *priest* and *bishop.* Many English words for technology also come from Latin. Even the word *computer* has Latin beginnings.

Many words about law and society come from French. A few words are *judge, jury, parliament, duke,* and *baron.* During one period of English history, the French-speaking Normans ruled England. English people cooked for the Normans. English names for animals, such as *cow, sheep,* and *swine,* are real English words. However, the names of meats from those animals—*beef, mutton, pork,* and *bacon*—are from French.

REVIEW

On a sheet of paper, write the letter of the answer that correctly completes each sentence.

1. The Romans built _____ to bring water to houses and public fountains.

   A arches   **B** public baths **C** aqueducts   **D** sewer systems

2. The Romans built beautiful _____ to honor their gods and goddesses.

   A houses   **B** temples   **C** arches   **D** aqueducts

3. The Romans built huge _____ that were the center of social life.

   A forums   **B** arches   **C** public baths   **D** temples

4. On the holidays Romans would celebrate, _____ would often be held.

   A Olympic Games **B** school   **C** big feasts   **D** chariot races

5. Roman builders admired the Greeks, and liked to use _____ when building.

   A arches   **B** aqueducts   **C** marble   **D** sewer systems

6. The Romans wanted their art and architecture to be beautiful as well as _____.

   A marble   **B** useful   **C** romantic   **D** big

7. The Romans built _____ in ancient Rome. Some parts are still being used today.

   A public baths   **B** houses   **C** apartment buildings **D** a sewer system

8. Italian, French, Spanish, Portuguese, and Romanian are _____ languages.

   A Romance   **B** European   **C** Roman   **D** Greek

9. The Romans spoke _____, which is what the Romance languages come from.

   A Romanian   **B** Latin   **C** Italian   **D** English

10. Many of our ideas about _____ come from the Romans.

   A romance   **B** language   **C** laws   **D** sewer systems

Christianity in Rome

Objectives

- To explain why Jesus's teachings appealed to the poor
- To tell how the Romans persecuted the Christians
- To describe how the Emperor Constantine helped the Christian religion grow in Rome

Gospel

One of four books of the New Testament part of the Bible

Enslaved

When a person is forced to become a slave

Reading Strategy: Questioning

What are the most important details that you will want to remember about the earliest days of Christianity?

Look at any of the timelines in this book. Each one shows how important a man named Jesus was to history and to the calendar we use today. All the dates before the birth of Jesus Christ are labeled B.C., or "Before Christ." All the dates after the birth of Christ are labeled A.D. The letters A.D. stand for the Latin words *Anno Domini,* or "in the year of our Lord."

Who Was Jesus Christ?

The Christian religion began with Jesus. Jesus was a Jew. He lived during the time of the Roman Emperor Augustus. He was born in Bethlehem, a little town south of Jerusalem. This was in a far-off province of the Roman Empire. Much of what we know about Jesus comes from the Bible. The first four books of the New Testament are about his life. These books are called the **Gospels.** The Gospels contain stories passed down over the years.

The Gospels say that Jesus taught people to love one another, to do good deeds, and to love God. If people were good, Jesus taught, they would be rewarded in an afterlife.

The teachings of Jesus were most popular with poor and **enslaved** people. His teachings offered some hope for happiness, if not in this life, then in the next. While other religions spoke of an afterlife, they said that princes would remain princes. Commoners would keep their lowly station—even after death. In contrast, Jesus spoke of a happy afterlife for all who were good on Earth.

Jesus's followers called him "Christ," or messiah. Jesus was 33 years old when he was sentenced to die on a cross. His crucifixion did not end his teachings. In the next years, the Christian religion spread to many lands.

Persecute
To treat in a cruel way; to hurt or injure

The Bible explains how Jesus taught others and performed good deeds as he traveled.

One man who carried word of the Christian religion was named Paul. Paul spent almost 30 years of his life traveling the Mediterranean world. He told people about Jesus's teachings. Paul could speak Greek. Therefore, he could take Christian beliefs to Athens and to other Greek cities. Paul started churches wherever he traveled. Even in Rome, Paul found people willing to listen. People were ready to accept a new religion that spoke of equal rights and hope.

How Were Christians Treated in the Roman Empire?

The Roman Empire had many religions. At first, one more religion did not seem too important. Therefore, the emperors allowed the Christians to worship as they pleased.

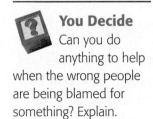

You Decide
Can you do anything to help when the wrong people are being blamed for something? Explain.

However, the Christians would not bow down to the Roman emperor. They would not call the emperor a god. Therefore, the Roman government decided that the Christians were a threat. The Roman emperors began to treat the followers of Christ cruelly, or to **persecute** them. They blamed the Christians for everything that went wrong.

A terrible fire burned in Rome in A.D. 64. This was the time when Nero was emperor. "The Christians started the fire!" Nero shouted. As a result, many Christians were killed. Paul, one of the men who had spread Jesus's teachings, was one of those killed.

The Romans persecuted the Christians for 300 years. Christian men and women were forced into Roman arenas to fight wild animals. Some of the emperors worried more about Christianity than others. Sometimes Christians were safe; other times they were in danger.

You Decide
Why do you think people risk their lives sometimes to follow their religion?

Christians often held secret church meetings. They met in tunnels, called catacombs, deep under the city of Rome. It was dangerous to follow the Christian religion. Yet even though it could mean death, people continued to join the Christian religion. At first only the poor Romans and slaves turned to Christianity. After a time, however, some of the Roman leaders became interested, too.

What Did the Emperor Constantine Do for the Christians?

Constantine became emperor of Rome in A.D. 306. In A.D. 312, a Roman general named Maxentius threatened to seize the throne. One night, Constantine dreamed that he saw a cross in the sky. He thought it was the Cross of Christ. He dreamed that if he carried that cross into battle, he would win a great victory. In response, Constantine rode into battle against Maxentius. He carried a flag that pictured the cross. He won that battle and Maxentius was defeated.

At the time Constantine became emperor, he had to share power with others. The Roman Empire had been divided into an eastern and a western part. In A.D. 286, the Emperor Diocletian decided the empire had grown too big to be ruled by just one man. Thus he set up a system of shared rule.

Roman Emperor Constantine was the first Christian emperor of Rome.

Legal

Lawful; based on the law of the government

Convert

Change from one religion to another

Constantine was not happy with shared rule. In A.D. 324, he clashed with Licinius, the ruler of the eastern part of the empire. That same year, Constantine became the sole ruler of the Roman Empire. In A.D. 330, he set up a new capital at Byzantium in the east. He renamed the city Constantinople. Today this city is known as Istanbul.

In A.D. 313, Constantine had made Christianity **legal.** Christians were no longer persecuted. More and more Romans now turned to the religion. Constantine himself **converted,** or changed, to Christianity. In A.D. 337, he was baptized and became the first Christian emperor of Rome. He built the first great Christian cathedral in Rome. He then built churches in Constantinople and in other cities.

The Eastern Roman Empire and the Western Roman Empire

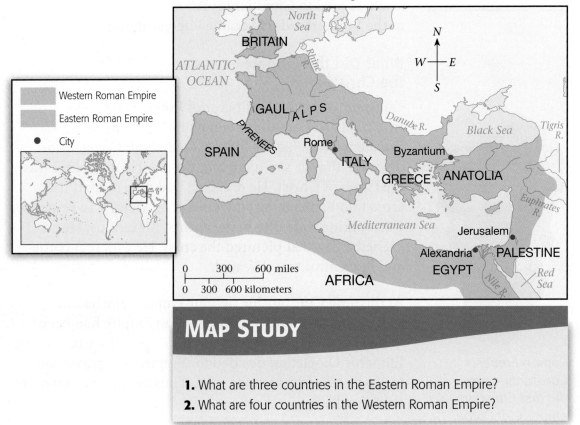

MAP STUDY

1. What are three countries in the Eastern Roman Empire?

2. What are four countries in the Western Roman Empire?

Bishop

A high-ranking church official in charge of other priests and a number of churches

Pope

The head of the Roman Catholic Church

The Roman government and the Christian church became very much a part of one another. Officials of the church were powerful men. The largest churches chose **bishops** as their leaders. The bishop of the Church of Rome became the head of the Roman Catholic Church, and was known as the **pope.** While the government of the Roman Empire was weakening, the Christian church was gaining power.

TIMELINE STUDY:

CHRISTIANITY AND ROME

When did Christianity become legal in Rome?

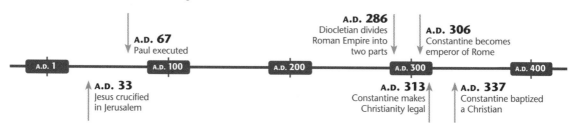

A.D. **67**
Paul executed

A.D. **286**
Diocletian divides
Roman Empire into
two parts

A.D. **306**
Constantine becomes
emperor of Rome

A.D. 1   A.D. 100   A.D. 200   A.D. 300   A.D. 400

A.D. **33**
Jesus crucified
in Jerusalem

A.D. **313**
Constantine makes
Christianity legal

A.D. **337**
Constantine baptized
a Christian

REVIEW

Word Bank

Constantine

Gospels

Jesus

Maxentius

Paul

On a sheet of paper, write the word from the Word Bank to complete each sentence correctly.

1. _____ was an important man in history. He is so important, that the dates on our calendar are named after him.

2. The books known as the _____ contain stories about Jesus's life.

3. A man named _____ carried the word of the Christian religion after Jesus's death.

4. A Roman general named _____ threatened to seize Constantine's throne, but was defeated in battle.

5. In A.D. 324, _____ became sole ruler of the Roman Empire.

On a sheet of paper, write the answer to each question. Use complete sentences.

6. Why did Jesus's teachings appeal to the poor?

7. Why did the Romans persecute the Christians?

8. How did the Romans persecute the Christians?

9. Why did the Emperor Diocletian divide the Roman Empire into an Eastern and Western Empire?

10. How did Emperor Constantine help the Christian religion grow in Rome?

The End of the Empire

■ To describe how invaders affected the Roman world

■ To explain how making the army larger caused a problem for the people

Reading Strategy: Questioning

In what ways does the timeline help you understand the order of events that led up to the end of the Roman Empire?

Not all of the emperors that followed Augustus were wise and good. Indeed, some were mad with power. Some were greedy. Royal families often fought among themselves over who would get the throne. Yet there were always skilled men to do the actual work of running the empire. The *Pax Romana* lasted for two centuries. During that time there were no serious threats to Rome's power.

How Did the Roman Empire Weaken?

Around A.D. 180, however, things began to go wrong. The Roman world faced invaders from northern and eastern Europe. Rome had to double the size of its army to protect the empire. A bigger army meant higher taxes—taxes that people could not pay! Prices of goods rose. Trading fell off. People were out of work. Life in the city was no longer good. More and more wealthy people left Rome to live in the country.

The Roman Empire did not fall in a day, or in a month, or even in a year. Yet the empire grew weaker with each passing year. Its fall was coming.

TIMELINE STUDY: RISE AND FALL OF THE ROMAN EMPIRE

How many years passed between the founding of Rome and its fall? (Remember to account for the change from B.C. to A.D.)

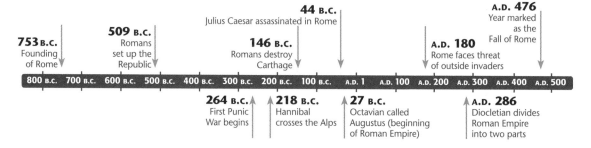

753 B.C.
Founding of Rome

509 B.C.
Romans set up the Republic

146 B.C.
Romans destroy Carthage

44 B.C.
Julius Caesar assassinated in Rome

A.D. 180
Rome faces threat of outside invaders

A.D. 476
Year marked as the Fall of Rome

800 B.C. 700 B.C. 600 B.C. 500 B.C. 400 B.C. 300 B.C. 200 B.C. 100 B.C. A.D. 1 A.D. 100 A.D. 200 A.D. 300 A.D. 400 A.D. 500

264 B.C.
First Punic War begins

218 B.C.
Hannibal crosses the Alps

27 B.C.
Octavian called Augustus (beginning of Roman Empire)

A.D. 286
Diocletian divides Roman Empire into two parts

On a sheet of paper, write the letter of the answer that correctly completes each sentence.

1. The emperors that followed Augustus were sometimes power hungry and _____.

   A wise **B** good **C** fair **D** greedy

2. Emperors struggled with each other over power. Still, _____ were always available to do the actual work of running the empire.

   A slaves **B** skilled men **C** nobles **D** kings

3. The *Pax Romana* lasted for _____.

   A two weeks **B** two months **C** 20 years **D** two centuries

4. There were no threats to Rome's _____ during the *Pax Romana*.

   A Republic **B** trading **C** power **D** architecture

5. Rome faced _____ around A.D. 180.

   A invaders **B** floods **C** civil wars **D** persecution

6. To protect its empire, Rome had to double the size of its _____.

   A empire **B** army **C** land **D** aqueducts

7. As a result, _____ were raised.

   A weapons **B** taxes **C** animals **D** churches

8. The price of goods increased while trading _____.

   A did not change **B** increased **C** decreased **D** doubled

9. Thus, more people left Rome to live in _____.

   A Gaul **B** Greece **C** the city **D** the country

10. The _____ of Rome was coming.

    A fall **B** rise **C** reign **D** peak

SUMMARY

- Rome grew out of settlements on seven hills along the Tiber River. For about 100 years it was ruled by Etruscans.

- In the Roman Republic, laws were made by elected representatives who met in a senate. There was no king. Members of the Roman Senate were usually wealthy landowners.

- Roman armies conquered many peoples. During the Punic Wars they took over the Carthaginians. They went on to conquer the Greeks.

- Conquered lands became Roman provinces. Each province was ruled by its own governor.

- Julius Caesar was a powerful general in the province of Gaul. He became the leader of the Roman Republic.

- Caesar won battles all around the Mediterranean. He met a princess named Cleopatra and he helped her gain the throne of Egypt.

- Roman armies battled one another, often over disagreements about Caesar's power. Some senators killed Caesar because they feared that he had too much power.

- Civil wars ended with Octavian as the head of the Roman Empire. The people called Octavian the Emperor Augustus.

- The reign of Augustus began a period of peace and growth known as the *Pax Romana*.

- The ancient Romans were great builders, lawmakers, and students of language.

- The Christian religion is based on the teachings of Jesus. Some Roman emperors persecuted the Christians.

- Constantine became the first Christian emperor of Rome.

Word Bank

aqueducts

bishop

convert

forum

peninsula

persecute

pope

province

republic

senate

Vocabulary Review

On a sheet of paper, use the words from the Word Bank to complete each sentence correctly.

1. The Romans settled on a piece of land called a(n) _____ around 1000 B.C.

2. The Romans built huge _____ to transport water.

3. The Romans conquered Greece, making it a Roman _____.

4. The Roman _____ made laws.

5. In ancient Rome, lawmakers met in a(n) _____.

6. Constantine chose to _____, or change his religion, to Christianity.

7. The _____ is the head of the Roman Catholic Church.

8. A(n) _____ is a high-ranking official of a church.

9. Roman emperors would _____ Christians.

10. In a(n) _____, citizens have the right to elect their own representatives.

Chapter Review Questions

On a sheet of paper, write the answer to each question. Use complete sentences.

11. Who controlled the government in the Roman Republic?

12. What were some of Julius Caesar's accomplishments as ruler of the Roman world?

13. What kind of leader was Augustus?

Prepare for a test by making a set of flash cards. Write a word or phrase on the front of each card. Write the definition on the back. Use the flash cards in a game to test your knowledge.

14. What happened to the language of Rome as the Roman Empire grew?

15. Who did Jesus's teachings appeal to and why?

16. What were two reasons for the fall of the Roman Empire?

Critical Thinking

On a sheet of paper, write your response to each question. Use complete sentences.

17. What was Nero trying to do after the fire in Rome?

18. Why was Constantine's conversion to Christianity important to the future of the Roman Empire?

Using the Timelines

Use the timelines on pages 181 and 183 to answer the questions.

19. What happened about 280 years after Jesus was crucified?

20. How many years passed between the founding of Rome and the setting up of the Republic?

GROUP ACTIVITY

Form a group of five or six. You are some of Rome's leading citizens in the Roman Republic. Caesar has been doing some good things in Rome, and he has just refused the crown. Still, you are worried that the end of the Republic is in sight. What will you say to your friends about your concerns? Write and perform a skit for the rest of the class.

fig. 5

fig. 6

fig. 7

fig. 1

fig. 4

A.D. 400–1400

THE MIDDLE AGES

The picture of a knight in armor atop a horse may get you interested. You may become more interested if a second knight is charging toward him with a lance. The Middle Ages was a period unlike any other before or after it. People were divided into classes to serve nobles and to protect the king. Traveling through many European countries you can still see the leftovers of many medieval estates. Throughout those same countries, you may still see shiny sets of armor or long threatening lances. However, the knights who once owned them are long gone with the Middle Ages.

Chapters in Unit 4

A country estate such as this included a feudal manor house. It was a place where a noble family could feel safe from enemies. Many estates included small villages and fields for growing crops.

The Barbarians and the Vikings

As the Roman Empire grew weaker, enemies beyond its borders were growing stronger. German tribes from the north, called *barbarians* by the Romans, threatened their borders. At last a tribe called the Huns invaded the Roman Empire. Meanwhile, other groups of warriors swept through Italy, Gaul, and Britain. The Western Roman Empire fell. The east became the Byzantine Empire. Strong new leaders such as Charlemagne came forward. Changes would begin with a new period called the Middle Ages.

GOALS FOR LEARNING

- To explain the role of barbarian tribes in the fall of the Western Roman Empire
- To tell why the Eastern Roman Empire did so well
- To explain how the Vikings influenced many parts of the world

Reading Strategy: Predicting

As you read a text, you can make predictions about what will happen next. It helps to preview the text and think about what you already know about the topic. As you make predictions, keep these things in mind:

- Make your best guess about what will happen next.
- Use what you know to predict what will take place next.
- Check your predictions. As you learn more information, you may find you need to change your predictions.

Key Vocabulary Words

Lesson 1

Middle Ages The period of European history extending from the Fall of Rome in A.D. 476 to about A.D. 1450

Frontier Land just beyond the border of a country

Uncivilized Without training in arts, science, or government

Primitive Of long ago; very simple

Barbarians Uncivilized, primitive people; people living outside Greece or Rome in the days of the Roman Empire

Lesson 3

Exiled Forced to live away from home in a foreign land

Saga A long story of brave deeds

Tradition A custom, idea, or belief handed down from one person to the next

The Fall of the Western Roman Empire

Reading Strategy: Predicting

Preview the lesson title. Predict what you will learn in this lesson.

Middle Ages

The period of European history extending from the Fall of Rome in A.D. 476 to about A.D. 1450

Frontier

Land just beyond the border of a country

Uncivilized

Without training in arts, science, or government

Primitive

Of long ago; very simple

The Roman Empire was growing weaker. The tribes that lived beyond the northern borders were growing stronger. The day was coming when these tribes would sweep across the borders. The empire would be destroyed. New people would come into power. These people had cultures very different from the Roman culture. A new period in history was being born—the **Middle Ages.** This period would last about 1,000 years.

Why Were the Germanic Tribes Considered "Uncivilized"?

Tribes of nomads lived just beyond the border of the Roman Empire—along the northern **frontiers.** These people were known as Germans. The Romans called the Germanic tribes **uncivilized** and **primitive.** The Germans wore clothing of rough cloth and animal skins. They carried spears, swords, and battle-axes.

The Germans' tribal laws were different from the well-ordered Roman system of law. An assembly of men ruled each German village. When villagers broke the law, the assembly would ask, "Guilty or not guilty?" If the villager said he or she was not guilty, a test was used to prove innocence or guilt. For example, the villager's hand might be thrust into boiling water. If the burn healed easily, innocence was proven. If not, he or she was guilty. The gods had spoken! This was not at all like the Roman courts of justice.

Barbarians
Uncivilized, primitive people; people living outside Greece or Rome in the days of the Roman Empire

You Decide
Under which system of laws would there be more justice—the German or the Roman? Why?

Germanic tribes often fought each other. The men took pride in their bravery in battle. They had fierce loyalty to the tribal chief. "I am a man now!" a German boy would shout when he received his first spear and shield. To lose his shield in battle would be his greatest disgrace.

The Romans called these German outsiders **barbarians.** Today this word is used to describe any uncivilized person. The Roman frontiers were protected from the barbarians by natural boundaries such as rivers and mountains. Where there were no natural boundaries, the Romans built forts and stone walls. The Roman Emperor Hadrian, who ruled between A.D. 117 and A.D. 138, built a huge wall. Hadrian's wall stretched across northern England.

The Germanic tribes lived just on the edge of the frontier. They were bound to cross over the borders. Therefore, the cultures mixed. The Germans learned to use Greek and Roman letters to write their own language. The Romans began to wear furs, as the Germans did. Many Roman women wore blond wigs made from German hair.

The Romans recognized the Germans' war skills. Some Germans joined the Roman armies. German soldiers sometimes married Roman women. It was all very neighborly at first. However, the Germans would not be friendly neighbors for long.

How Did Barbarians Contribute to the Fall of the Western Roman Empire?

The tribes from the north grew impatient. They wanted adventure. They wanted power of their own. They saw that they could take power, and riches, too, from the weakening Roman Empire. Barbarian armies began pouring across the frontier.

Besides being driven by greed, the Germans were fleeing an enemy of their own. A tribe of wild horsemen, called Huns, had swept out of Asia. Later, they were led by their fierce leader, Attila. They took more and more German lands. They forced the German tribes into the Roman Empire.

Barbarian invaders from the north attacked Rome in hopes of defeating the powerful empire.

A barbarian tribe called the Goths marched into Italy. Germans who had become Roman soldiers left their armies to join the Goths. In A.D. 410, the Goths, led by Alaric, entered Rome. The city was weak. The Goths took Rome with little trouble. They destroyed much of the city and stole what they could. Then they went on, leaving the ruins of Rome behind them.

Now other tribes of Germans swept through the Roman Empire. In A.D. 455, the city of Rome was attacked—this time by the Vandals. Like the Goths, they looted and destroyed everything in their path. Then they moved on into Spain and northern Africa.

Another army of Goths settled in Italy and Spain. Then the Angles, Saxons, and Jutes invaded the island of Britain. The Angles gave England its name. Their language would be called English. A tribe known as the Franks were on the move, too. The Franks settled in Flanders, just north of the province of Gaul.

The Roman Empire fell. Many Romans buried their treasures—including art and religious objects. They tried to save things from the barbarians. Long after that, people were still finding remains of the great empire. The treasures of Rome were buried in the fields and pastures of Europe.

The days of the Western Roman Empire were over. In A.D. 476, the German chief Odoacer overthrew the last of the Roman emperors. The fine cities were gone. There were no new schools. Few people studied art or literature or science. Barbarians set up new states. Their kings ruled, blending Roman law with tribal law. The Latin language changed. It became different in each of the different states. Only the Christian church kept its power and its organization.

History Fact
By A.D. 476, the Roman Empire was over. Barbarians had conquered all the Roman cities and states and set up their own states.

Reading Strategy: Predicting

Think about your prediction. What details can you now add to make your prediction more specific?

Review

Word Bank

assembly

Attila

buried

Christian church

mix

nomads

Odoacer

On a sheet of paper, write the word from the Word Bank to complete each sentence correctly.

1. The Germanic tribes were _____ who lived along the northern frontiers of the Roman Empire. They were considered by the Romans to be uncivilized.

2. According to German tribal laws, a(n) _____ tested villagers to prove their innocence or guilt.

3. Because the Romans and Germans lived so close, their cultures began to _____.

4. _____ was the fierce leader of the Huns.

5. Romans _____ their treasures to save them from barbarians when the Roman Empire was falling.

6. In A.D. 476, the German chief _____ overthrew the last of the Roman emperors. It brought about the end of the Western Roman Empire.

7. The barbarians took over the Western Roman Empire. After, the _____ was the only piece to keep its power and organization.

On a sheet of paper, write the answer to each question. Use complete sentences.

8. Why did the Emperor Hadrian build a wall across northern England?

9. What are the two reasons the German tribes moved into the Roman Empire?

10. What were two barbarian tribes that attacked Rome?

The Byzantine Empire

The Western Roman Empire fell to the barbarians. The Eastern Empire, with Constantinople as its capital, resisted attack. The Eastern Empire was known as the Byzantine Empire. It would last for almost 1,000 years after German tribes took the Western Roman Empire. Life in the Western Empire was grim. The Byzantine Empire, however, put up fine buildings trimmed in gold. A new university was built there. The people grew wealthy from trading.

The language of the Byzantine Empire was Greek. This became the official language of the Eastern church. In A.D. 1054, the Christian church split into two sections. The church in the west was called Roman Catholic. The church in the east was called Eastern Orthodox.

Who Was Charlemagne?

"A giant of a man! About seven feet tall! He had blond hair and a merry face." That is the way a writer of the time described Charles the Great, or Charlemagne. Charlemagne was king of the Franks, the German tribe that took Flanders. The Franks had continued their conquests. They ended up ruling all the lands that would one day be France.

Charlemagne's father was called Pepin the Short. He had died in A.D. 768. Charlemagne proved to be a fine ruler when he became king of the Franks. He conquered more land—much of Germany and part of Italy. He showed an interest in education and in the Christian religion, and won favor with the pope.

On Christmas Day, A.D. 800, the pope crowned Charlemagne "Emperor of the Holy Roman Empire." Although the empire was called "Roman," Charlemagne was still a barbarian. He dressed in the Frankish style and spoke the language of the Franks. His was a Germanic land rather than a Roman one.

Charlemagne's empire was a good one. Charlemagne built schools and encouraged artists. He learned to read Latin and worked closely with the church.

You Decide
Do you think Charlemagne was a fine ruler? Why or why not?

When Charlemagne died, his empire went to his son, Louis I. The empire began to crumble. It was finally divided among Charlemagne's three grandsons—Charles the Bald, Lothair, and Louis the German. The divided lands would one day become France, Germany, and part of Italy.

Charlemagne was crowned emperor of the Holy Roman Empire by the pope.

On a sheet of paper, write the letter of the answer that correctly completes each sentence.

1. The Eastern Empire resisted the barbarians' attack and would not fall for another _____ years.

   A 100   **B** 1,000   **C** 1,050   **D** 2,000

2. The Eastern Empire is known as the _____ Empire.

   A Greek   **B** German   **C** Frank   **D** Byzantine

3. _____ was the official language of the Eastern Empire.

   A Greek   **B** Roman   **C** Latin   **D** German

4. The Christian church split into two sections in A.D. _____.

   A 768   **B** 800   **C** 1054   **D** 2100

5. The church was called Roman Catholic in the west and _____ in the east.

   A Eastern Catholic   **C** Greek Orthodox
   B Roman Orthodox   **D** Eastern Orthodox

6. _____ was the king of the Franks.

   A Charlemagne   **B** Charles the Bald   **C** Lothair   **D** Louis the German

7. The Franks ruled all the lands that one day would be known as _____.

   A Italy   **B** France   **C** Sweden   **D** Denmark

8. The pope crowned Charlemagne "Emperor of the Holy Roman Empire." However, he was still a _____.

   A Roman   **B** Vandal   **C** barbarian   **D** Viking

9. After his death, Charlemagne's empire began to crumble under _____.

   A Louis I   **B** Charles the Bald   **C** Lothair   **D** Pepin the Short

10. Charlemagne's empire was divided, becoming France, _____, and part of Italy.

    A Norway   **B** Sweden   **C** Denmark   **D** Germany

The Vikings

People called the attackers Northmen because they sailed down from the north. They came from lands that are today Norway, Sweden, and Denmark. The Northmen were adventurers. They loved sailing and fighting. Their ships, powered by oars and sails, were swift. The sailors set their course by the stars and by the sun. They called themselves Vikings.

Who Were the "Raiders from the North"?

The Viking raids began in A.D. 793. The Vikings attacked an island off the east coast of England. This was followed by a wave of raids against England, Scotland, and Ireland. During the mid-800s the Vikings burned and looted towns on the coasts of France, Spain, and Italy.

For many years the Vikings kept on the move. They stole and took by force, or plundered, many towns, then sailed back home. Later, they settled in the lands that their ships reached.

Swedish Vikings settled in Russia. Other Vikings found homes in England and along the coast of France. The Vikings in France became known as the Normans. Their new land was called Normandy.

Some Vikings sailed the Atlantic Ocean and set up colonies in Iceland. In about A.D. 982, a red-haired Viking, Erik the Red, was **exiled.** In other words, he was forced to live away from his home in Iceland. In response, Erik decided to sail to Greenland to set up a colony.

Saga
A long story of brave deeds

Geography Note
Normandy is a region in northwestern France. It became a Roman province in about 50 B.C. The Franks took power in about A.D. 500. Vikings kept raiding the area until France gave it to them in A.D. 911. It was an independent kingdom for over 200 years. Due to several wars, control passed back and forth between England and France. It has remained part of France since A.D. 1450.

Erik had a son named Leif Eriksson. In A.D. 1000, Eriksson sailed as far as the east coast of North America. The Vikings stayed there for several years. Eriksson called the land Vinland (or Wineland), possibly for the grapes he found.

We do not know why the Vikings left Vinland. For centuries afterward, they made trips to North America, but they did not stay. They had to give up their colony in Greenland during the 1400s. By that time, the climate had become much colder.

Songs and stories of Leif Eriksson, Erik the Red, and other Viking heroes are called **sagas.** Much of what we know about the Vikings comes from these sagas. Some sagas tell of Norse gods like Odin and Thor. They tell of Valhalla, the hall of the gods, where dead Viking warriors live forever.

Many Vikings sailed from their homeland in the north in search of food and treasure.

Words from the Past

Tradition

A custom, idea, or belief handed down from one person to the next

Thor, Viking God of Thunder

Thor was the popular Viking god of thunder. The Vikings believed that thunder was the sound of Thor's chariot wheels as he flew across the heavens.

Thor was a son of Odin, king of the Norse gods. Thor was a great red-bearded fellow with a huge appetite. Thor wielded a magical axe-hammer called Mjollnir. Many Vikings and other Scandinavians carried small copies of this axe-hammer for their own protection. Thor could help sea voyagers and farmers because he controlled the sea, the wind, and the rain.

Thor had many adventures. Some of them were funny, and he did not always come out on top. Usually Thor used his hammer to smash his enemies' skulls. Sometimes he threw hot metal at them.

Stories about Thor and other Norse gods were part of the Vikings' oral **tradition.** A tradition is a custom, idea, or belief handed down from one person to the next. In the Middle Ages, these stories were written down in the Icelandic literature. Some famous stories featured Thor's battle with the serpent of the world. This serpent, or dragon, was said to wrap itself around the whole world under the sea.

When Christianity came to Scandinavia, the Vikings and other Norse people stopped worshipping Thor and carrying small axe-hammers. However, Thor's popularity continued in poems and stories. Today, our Thursday is Thor's Day. In literature and even in comic books, the adventures of Thor continue.

The hammer of Thor, Viking god of thunder.

Who Were the Normans?

The Normans were adventurous, like their Viking ancestors. In 1066 William, the Duke of Normandy, decided to make himself King of England. He waited for fair breezes to blow his ships across the English Channel. At last the moment came.

There was a savage fight known as the Battle of Hastings. William killed the English king, Harold. William became king of England and was named "William the Conqueror."

Why Did the Vikings Leave Their Mark on So Many Lands?

With new settlements and new languages, the Vikings turned to a new religion. They became Christians, leaving behind the Norse gods of the sagas. The Viking days of raiding ended.

The Vikings kept sea trade alive and booming. They used their fine ships and sailing skills to travel oceans and rivers. Their art is found throughout Europe. They decorated buildings, as well as ships, with carved animals and beasts. The adventurous Vikings settled in many lands; they left their mark on many cultures.

TIMELINE STUDY: THE NORTHERN INVADERS

How many years after Erik the Red settled in Greenland did Leif Eriksson reach North America?

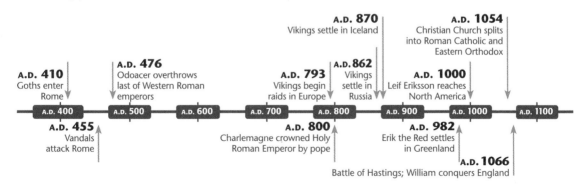

A.D. 410 Goths enter Rome

A.D. 455 Vandals attack Rome

A.D. 476 Odoacer overthrows last of Western Roman emperors

A.D. 793 Vikings begin raids in Europe

A.D. 800 Charlemagne crowned Holy Roman Emperor by pope

A.D. 862 Vikings settle in Russia

A.D. 870 Vikings settle in Iceland

A.D. 982 Erik the Red settles in Greenland

A.D. 1000 Leif Eriksson reaches North America

A.D. 1054 Christian Church splits into Roman Catholic and Eastern Orthodox

A.D. 1066 Battle of Hastings; William conquers England

A.D. 400 · A.D. 500 · A.D. 600 · A.D. 700 · A.D. 800 · A.D. 900 · A.D. 1000 · A.D. 1100

Word Bank

Christians

Denmark

Iceland

Normans

raiding

sagas

sailing

settled

Thor

William

On a sheet of paper, write the word from the Word Bank to complete each sentence correctly.

1. The Northmen, also known as Vikings, were attackers that came from Norway, Sweden, and _____.

2. The Vikings were adventurers who loved _____ and fighting.

3. The Vikings kept on the move, _____ towns and then sailing back home.

4. Vikings in France became known as the _____.

5. The Vikings explored and settled in many lands, including: Russia, France, England, _____, and Greenland.

6. The songs and stories about the brave deeds of Viking heroes are called _____.

7. _____ was the Viking god of thunder.

8. The Battle of Hastings made _____, the Duke of Normandy, the king of England.

9. The new settlements and new languages turned the Vikings into _____.

10. The Vikings left their mark on many cultures because they _____ in so many lands.

- Tribes of Germans lived along the northern border of the Roman Empire. The Romans called those people barbarians. German armies often fought one another. This made Romans fear invasion.

- Roman Emperor Hadrian built a huge wall that stretched across northern England. In other places, natural barriers provided some protection from the barbarians.

- A barbarian tribe called the Goths attacked and destroyed much of Rome. They were followed by the Vandals who destroyed much more. Angles, Saxons, Jutes, and Franks invaded and plundered Britain and other areas of the Western Roman Empire.

- The Western Roman Empire fell in A.D. 476.

- The Eastern Roman Empire was known as the Byzantine Empire. It lasted for another 1,000 years after the fall of the Western Roman Empire.

- Charlemagne, king of the Franks, ended up ruling the area that would become France.

- The pope crowned Charlemagne "Emperor of the Holy Roman Empire."

- Vikings sailed to other parts of Europe from Norway, Denmark, and Sweden. The Vikings settled in many of the places they raided. The Viking Leif Eriksson started a colony in North America.

- William the Conqueror, Duke of Normandy, conquered England.

- The Vikings influenced cultures in many parts of the world.

CHAPTER 10
REVIEW

Word Bank

barbarian

exiled

frontier

Middle Ages

sagas

tradition

uncivilized

Vocabulary Review

On a sheet of paper, use the words from the Word Bank to complete each sentence correctly.

1. A person living outside Greece or Rome was called a(n) _____.

2. The Vikings told _____ about their heroes, gods, and goddesses.

3. Erik the Red went to Greenland because he was _____, or forced from his homeland.

4. The Romans thought the Germans were _____ because they were more primitive.

5. The Vikings had an oral _____ of telling stories of Norse gods.

6. Explorers go beyond their country's borders to the next _____.

7. The period of history known as the _____ lasted about 1,000 years.

Chapter Review Questions

On a sheet of paper, write the answer to each question. Use complete sentences.

8. Who were the Angles, Saxons, and Jutes?

9. How did the Germanic tribes live before they invaded Rome?

10. What are two reasons that Germanic tribes attacked the Western Roman Empire?

11. Why was Charlemagne a fine ruler?

12. What was the Byzantine Empire like after the fall of Rome?

Test Tip

If you do not understand a set of directions, read them again and look at the questions that follow. If you still do not understand what you are expected to do, ask the person giving the test, if possible.

13. Where did the Vikings come from?

14. What are three places the Vikings explored or settled?

15. Why did the Vikings influence so many cultures?

Critical Thinking

On a sheet of paper, write your response to each question. Use complete sentences.

16. Could a barbarian become an excellent ruler in the Roman Empire? Explain your answer, using examples.

17. Are the sagas reliable sources of information about the Vikings? Explain why or why not.

Using the Timeline

Use the timeline on page 203 to answer the questions.

18. How many years after the Goths attacked Rome did the Vandals do the same?

19. When was Charlemagne crowned Holy Roman Emperor?

20. The Vikings began their raids in Europe before they reached North America. How many years passed between those two events?

GROUP ACTIVITY

In a group of two or three, research Viking life. Write a short account—a skit, story, or other piece of creative writing—about your topic. Then present your findings to the class. Sample subjects are:

- a news story of a Viking trade voyage or raid;
- a journal of a Viking discovering and settling in a new land;
- a Viking saga; and
- a skit about life in a Viking village.

The Lords and the Serfs

The strength and power of the Roman Empire had faded. So had the colorful way of life that the Romans spread throughout much of Europe, Asia, and northern Africa. Like the Athenians before them, the Romans had explored new ideas. They had created works of art and grand new buildings. They had set ambitious goals.

The next 1,000 years brought much change in the way people lived. Many lived a country life within the new feudal class system. In many cases, people were not "on the move" as much and life became more predictable. This would be a colorful time, but in a much different way.

GOALS FOR LEARNING

- To understand the feudal system people lived under during the Middle Ages
- To explain the role of religion in feudal life
- To describe the hard life of the Middle Ages

Reading Strategy: Text Structure

Before you begin reading this chapter, look at how it is organized. Look at the title, headings, boldfaced words, and photographs. Ask yourself:

- Is the text a description or sequence?
- Is it compare and contrast or cause and effect?

Key Vocabulary Words

Lesson 1

Organize To set up; to get a series or number of things in order

Feudalism A political and military system based on the holding of land

Vassal A noble who received land from a king in return for loyalty and service

Homage A pledge of loyalty; a promise to serve that was made to kings and lords during the Middle Ages

Lord A king or noble who gave land to someone else

Manor The lands belonging to a medieval lord, including farmland, a village, and the home of the owner

Estate A large piece of land with a large home on it

Freemen People who are free, not slaves, and who have the rights of citizens

Serf A poor farm worker who was bound to the land and whose life was controlled by the lord of the manor

Medieval Belonging to the Middle Ages

Fortress A building with strong walls for defense against an enemy

Lesson 2

Clergy The people who lead a religion

Monk A man who has taken religious vows and usually lives in a monastery

Nun A woman who has taken religious vows and enters a convent

Knight A high-ranking soldier of the Middle Ages who received his title from a noble

Lesson 3

Artisan A person who works with his or her hands to create something

Peasant A poor farmer or farm worker

Feudalism

Objectives

■ To describe the
life of the lord of
a manor

■ To describe the life
of a serf

■ To name the three
classes in feudal
society

Reading Strategy:
Text Structure

Preview the lesson.
Notice the headings,
features, and boldfaced
words.

Organize
To set up

Feudalism
A political and
military system based
on the holding of land

Vassal
A noble who received
land from a king in
return for loyalty and
service

Homage
A pledge of loyalty

When the Roman Empire fell, the period of European
history known as the Middle Ages began. Many people
in Europe moved from the cities to the country. The
splendor of the great cities faded. After a time, some towns
no longer existed. Trade all but disappeared. People no
longer used money. Education and learning became less
and less important. Only in the church was there an effort
to continue the reading and writing of Latin. The church
also saved many writings from ancient times.

What Was the Feudal System?

Life was now set up, or **organized,** under a new system
called **feudalism.** In a feudal society, a king ruled a whole
country. He divided the land among important men, or
of nobles. These nobles were called **vassals** of the king. In
exchange for land, the nobles paid **homage,** or pledged
loyalty, to the king. This meant that they promised to
serve the king. They swore to fight for and protect him.

A noble, or **lord**, lived in a **manor** house on a large piece
of land. This land was called an **estate**. The estate included
a small village and fields for growing crops. **Freemen** and
serfs lived on the feudal estate. They depended on the
ruling noble and his land for their living.

The manor fields were divided into strips of land. Freemen
were allowed to buy and farm their own strips. In return
they had to pay the lord of the manor a part of their crops.
Also, they had to promise to fight for the lord. A noble
always had to worry about attacks by neighboring estates.

The serfs did not own their own land. They worked for the
lord of the manor, farming his land. Serfs were tied to the
land on which they were born. They could not leave the
estate, even if they wanted to.

Lord

A king or noble who gave land to someone else

Manor

The lands belonging to a medieval lord

Estate

A large piece of land with a large home on it

Freemen

People who are free and who have the rights of citizens

Serf

A poor farm worker who was bound to the land and whose life was controlled by the lord of the manor

Medieval

Belonging to the Middle Ages

Fortress

A building with strong walls for defense against an enemy

 You Decide

Even rich people lived under harsh conditions during the Middle Ages. Would you have liked living in a castle? Why or why not?

The serfs provided every service for the lord of the manor and his family. The serfs grew crops and gathered wood. They took care of the lord's lands and his house. In the feudal system, each class owed loyalty and service to the class just above it.

What Was Life Like on a Feudal Estate?

Very little trade went on under the feudal system. Each feudal estate had its own village and met its own needs. Each village had a blacksmith who made tools and weapons, and a miller who ground grain into flour. The serfs had to use the services of the manor. They also had to pay whatever price was asked for these services.

Many nobles and their families lived in great houses made of stone. Some **medieval** manor houses were real castles. They were cold, however, and often gloomy. They had no glass in the windows or running water. They were dimly lit by burning torches made of twigs. The damp, shadowy castles were cold **fortresses** in which noble families could feel safe from enemies.

Many of the lords had several manors. They lived part of the year at one and part of the year at another. The lords chose managers to oversee the land when they were away.

While the noble family lived in the manor house, the villagers lived in small, smoky huts. They ate from wooden bowls and sat on backless, three-legged stools. They could not read or write. Their only contacts from outside the manor came when the village held a fair. Then merchants from around the countryside might bring their wares, or goods.

A manor lord could treat his serfs much as he pleased. "Between you and your serf there is no judge but God" was a medieval saying. Serfs had little protection from the lord's treatment.

On a sheet of paper, write the letter of the answer that correctly completes each sentence.

1. The Middle Ages began when _____.

   A the Vikings invaded England   **C** the church grew
   B the Roman Empire fell   **D** Charlemagne died

2. There were many changes during the Middle Ages. _____
   practically disappeared, money was no longer used, and
   education and learning became less important.

   A Trade   **B** The church   **C** The Vikings   **D** The sun

3. _____ was/were the main place where education and learning took
   place during the Middle Ages.

   A Huts   **B** Manor houses   **C** The church   **D** Fortresses

4. Life during the Middle Ages was organized under a system called _____.

   A homage   **B** feudalism   **C** manor houses   **D** country estates

5. In return for land, nobles had to _____ to the king.

   A give crops   **B** pay money   **C** give a serf   **D** pay homage

6. While freemen were allowed to buy and farm their own land, _____
   could not.

   A nobles   **B** lords   **C** serfs   **D** clergy

7. The noble family lived in manor houses, the villagers lived in small _____.

   A huts   **B** estates   **C** castles   **D** fortresses

On a sheet of paper, write the answer to each question. Use complete sentences.

8. What was the life of the lord of a manor like?

9. What jobs did the serfs have to do for the lord of the manor?

10. What were the castles like that some nobles and their families lived in?

Religion During the Middle Ages

Clergy
The people who lead a religion

Monk
A man who has taken religious vows and usually lives in a monastery

Nun
A woman who has taken religious vows and enters a convent

Knight
A high-ranking soldier of the Middle Ages who received his title from a noble

When the Roman Empire crumbled in A.D. 476, Europe broke into hundreds of small governments. Despite the unrest, the Church remained strong.

Who Were the Men and Women of the Church?

Medieval society was a Christian society. Higher officials in the church were nobles. Large pieces of land were often given to the leaders of the church, the **clergy.** The highest-ranking clergy were as wealthy and powerful as the most important lords.

Some men and women wished to devote their entire lives to serving God. These men became **monks** and lived in monasteries. These women became **nuns** and lived in convents. In monasteries and convents, they spent their days studying, praying, working, and taking part in religious services.

What Was the Purpose of a Knight?

Except for the church leaders, every important man in feudal society was a fighter. Even the kings were warriors. The estates fought each other. There were bands of robbers to be controlled. Tribes of people from other parts of the country often came looking for new lands.

Warriors of the noble class were known as **knights.** Knights fought to defend their own manors. They fought for their king as they had promised. They also fought to protect Christianity from being threatened.

Knights were noble warriors. They tested their skills in tournaments called jousts.

Reading Strategy:
Text Structure

As you read about becoming a knight, use a graphic organizer such as a word web to help organize the details.

LEARN MORE ABOUT IT

Knights in Armor

Being a knight was a costly business. Armor (the metal covering that protected a knight's body in battle) and weapons were elaborate and expensive. Serfs had to work hard to pay for their lord's fancy armor, many horses, and fine weapons. If a boy wanted to grow up to be a knight, he began training at age 7. He started out as a page. He learned to fight and to have the proper knightly manners.

The next step in becoming a knight was acting as a squire. A squire served a knight. He helped the knight with his armor and weapons. The squire also rode with his knight into battle. When he was 21, a worthy squire was "knighted"—or made a knight—by a noble.

The young squire became a knight when a sword was tapped on his shoulder.

Knighthood was both a military and a religious honor. A young man spent the night before he was knighted in a church. There he kept watch over his armor, as he knelt and prayed. He thought about the honor he was about to receive.

Knights kept their fighting skills ready by entering jousts, or tournaments. Two knights on horseback would fight each other with long lances. The goal of each knight was to knock the other one off his horse. The winner's honor was not only for himself. It was also for his favorite "lady," whose ribbon he wore into battle.

Word Bank

Christian

church leaders

clergy

king

monks

nuns

religious

7

squire

21

On a sheet of paper, write the word from the Word Bank to complete each sentence correctly.

1. Medieval society was a _____ society.

2. People trained or ordained for religious work are called _____.

3. Men who devoted their entire lives to serving God became _____ and lived in monasteries.

4. Women who devoted their entire lives to serving God became _____ and lived in convents.

5. Every important man in feudal society was a fighter except for _____.

6. The knights fought to defend their manors, their _____, and Christianity.

7. A boy wanting to be a knight started training at age _____ as a page.

8. The step after a page is a _____.

9. At age _____, the worthy knight-in-training would become a knight. It happened when a sword was tapped on his shoulder.

10. Knighthood was both a military and _____ honor.

Life in the Middle Ages

The feudal way of life was most widespread during the 1100s and 1200s. Life on a feudal manor was hard. There were floods and years of bad crops. There were always battles to fight. There were plagues, too.

What Was the Black Death?

In A.D. 1348, a ship from the east docked at an Italian port. Some sick sailors came ashore. They brought with them a terrible plague. This disease became known as the Black Death. It got its name because it caused spots of blood to turn black under the skin.

Little was known about medicine during the Middle Ages. There were few doctors, and those doctors that were around did not understand the causes of diseases or how diseases were spread. The villages were not very clean. A large population of rats lived off the garbage. Doctors today think that bites from infected rat fleas caused the plague. Doctors in the 1300s, however, did not know much about the prevention or treatment of disease. They had little help to offer.

The Black Death quickly spread across Europe killing thousands of nobles and serfs alike.

Artisan

A person who works with his or her hands to create something

Peasant

A poor farmer or farm worker

As a result of the plague, nobles and serfs alike fell sick and died. The Black Death also resulted in a shortage of labor. Because there were fewer workers, wages increased for **artisans** and **peasants.**

What Changes Were Happening in the Feudal System?

Feudal society lasted for almost 700 years. By A.D. 1400, however, the great manors had almost disappeared. Trade had picked up. Money had come back into use. Nobles no longer received land for services. People moved back to the towns.

New methods of warfare were being developed. Gunpowder and new weapons, such as cannons, were now available. In addition, foot soldiers were being used more effectively. Because of these changes, knights were no longer needed.

For hundreds of years, the picture of life in Europe had been the feudal manor. It was a world where most people fit into one of three classes: nobles, clergy, or serfs. "Some fight," a medieval bishop wrote. "Others pray. And others work."

Reading Strategy:
Text Structure

Study the timeline in this lesson. How does it help you to understand the sequence of events?

TIMELINE STUDY:

THE MIDDLE AGES

How long did the Middle Ages last?

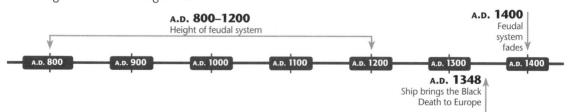

A.D. **800–1200**
Height of feudal system

A.D. **1400**
Feudal system fades

A.D. 800   A.D. 900   A.D. 1000   A.D. 1100   A.D. 1200   A.D. 1300   A.D. 1400

A.D. **1348**
Ship brings the Black Death to Europe

On a sheet of paper, write the letter of the answer that correctly completes each sentence.

1. Nobles, _____, and serfs were the three classes in feudal society.

    A knights   **B** kings   **C** lords   **D** clergy

2. Life on a feudal manor was hard with floods, bad crops, battles, and _____.

    A fires   **B** cannons   **C** plagues   **D** persecution

3. In A.D. 1348, a ship from the east brought _____.

    A the Black Death   **B** medicine   **C** cannons   **D** gunpowder

4. _____ were dirty and there were large populations of rats that lived off of garbage.

    A Manor houses   **B** Castles   **C** Estates   **D** Villages

5. There was little known about _____ during the Middle Ages.

    A farming   **B** medicine   **C** Christianity   **D** warfare

6. Doctors today think the plague was caused by _____.

    A bites from infected rat fleas   **C** the serfs
    B garbage   **D** bad crops

7. Feudal society lasted almost _____ years.

    A 700   **B** 1,100   **C** 1,300   **D** 1,400

8. Trade picked up, money was used again, and people moved back into towns by A.D. _____.

    A 700   **B** 1100   **C** 1300   **D** 1400

9. New methods of warfare were developed, such as _____ and cannons.

    A spears   **B** knives   **C** gunpowder   **D** bombs

10. Knights were not needed when _____ were being used more effectively.

    A serfs   **B** foot soldiers   **C** monks   **D** nobles

CHAPTER 11

SUMMARY

- During the Middle Ages many people lived under the feudal system. Each class owed loyalty to the class above it.

- Most medieval society was divided into three classes: the nobles, the clergy, and the serfs.

- In return for land, nobles were called vassals of the king. They paid homage to their king by agreeing to protect him.

- Medieval estates, or manors, included a manor house, a village, and fields. The noble was lord of the manor and the absolute ruler of the feudal estate.

- The manor house was like a fortress, designed to protect the noble from enemies.

- Serfs worked the land for the lord of the manor. They owned no land of their own.

- Members of the clergy were often given large pieces of land.

- Knights were warriors of the noble class. They were trained to protect the king and the king's interests.

- A plague called the Black Death killed many Europeans in the Middle Ages.

- By about A.D. 1400 the feudal system was weakening. Trade had increased and more people were living in towns. Better weapons meant that knights were no longer needed because armies were becoming more effective.

Word Bank

clergy

estate

feudalism

fortress

homage

knight

manor

medieval

serf

vassal

Vocabulary Review

On a sheet of paper, use the words from the Word Bank to correctly match each definition below.

1. A peasant who was almost a slave during the Middle Ages

2. A noble who received land from the king in return for loyalty and service

3. A pledge of loyalty that a noble gave to the king

4. A warrior trained to defend the manor, the king, and Christianity

5. A large piece of land that nobles, freemen, and serfs lived on

6. A way of life during the Middle Ages

7. Something that belongs to the Middle Ages

8. People who do religious work as their job

9. The house where a noble, or lord, lived

10. A building constructed so noble families would feel safe from enemies

Chapter Review Questions

On a sheet of paper, write the answer to each question. Use complete sentences.

11. What happened in Western Europe after the Roman Empire fell?

12. What were the main social classes in the feudal system?

13. Why was the feudal life hard for the serfs?

14. Where was the main place that education and learning were carried on during the Middle Ages?

15. What did men and women do if they wanted to give their lives to serving God?

16. Why did the Black Death strike all classes of feudal society?

Critical Thinking

On a sheet of paper, write your response to each question. Use complete sentences.

17. Why were knights so important in feudal society?

18. Do you think the serfs were more slave than free? Tell why or why not.

Using the Timeline

Use the timeline on page 217 to answer the questions.

19. When was the feudal system at its height?

20. When the feudal system faded, how long had it been since the Black Death arrived in Europe?

GROUP ACTIVITY

During the Middle Ages, each noble family had a coat of arms. The coat of arms used shapes, colors, and symbols to represent the family. Form a group with two or three other students. Brainstorm ideas and then design your own coat of arms. Use a favorite background color, or field. Draw a band of another color across the field. Draw a symbol for each family member.

Islam and the Crusades

The Middle Ages is sometimes thought of as a time of darkness, of little forward progress. In some ways, in some places, this was the case. However, there were major strides taken in many areas of Europe. The Crusades, or Holy Wars, caused a lot of people to move from one land to another. With the Crusades came new ideas and interests, as well as some new struggles. People began to question and challenge the people in power, such as kings. They also began to question the class structure they lived in. Christianity, Judaism, and the rise of Islam had large effects, too, particularly in the Mediterranean areas.

GOALS FOR LEARNING

- To discuss the importance of Muhammad
- To explain the struggle for power of the Holy Land
- To realize the costs of the Crusades
- To explain the changes in agriculture
- To describe the changes in city life
- To tell why the Magna Carta was important

Reading Strategy: Visualizing

Visualizing is like creating a movie in your mind. It will help you understand what you are reading. Use the following ways to visualize a text:

- Think about the order in which things are happening. That may be a clue to what will happen next.

- Look at the photographs, illustrations, and descriptions.

- Think about experiences in your own life that may add to the images.

Key Vocabulary Words

Lesson 1

Idol An image of a god that is used as an object of worship

Muslim A follower of the religion that Muhammad founded in Arabia in the seventh century

Prophet A religious leader who claims to speak for God; one who tells what will happen in the future

Holy Land Palestine

Koran The holy book of the Muslims that contains the teachings of Islam

Faith To believe in God; a religion

Lesson 2

Pilgrimage A visit to a holy place

Crusade Any of the military journeys taken by Christians to win the Holy Land from the Muslims

Truce A time when enemies agree to stop fighting

Lesson 3

Exploration The act of looking around some unknown place

Lesson 4

Surplus More than what is needed

Lesson 5

Migrate To move away from one country or region to settle in another

Guild An organization formed to protect the interests of workers in one craft or trade

Apprentice A person who learns a trade under a master

Lesson 6

Human rights The right to life, liberty, and pursuit of happiness

Charter A constitution

Muhammad and Islam

In A.D. 570, Arabia was a vast desert southeast of the Mediterranean Sea. The people who lived there, the Arabs, believed in many gods. They worshipped **idols**—images of a god—made of gold and silver. Tribes of nomads lived on the edges of the desert in tent camps. They drove caravans of camels across the sands. Wealthy people lived in fine homes in the cities. They dressed in rich silks and wore bright jewels.

It was not a peaceful land. Bands of thieves rode into the cities, waving swords. They looted and killed, taking riches off into the desert. The nomadic tribes also fought among themselves. More and more trouble spread throughout Arabia. Trade became harder and the people became poorer. Fewer people lived in fine palaces; more people struggled for even enough to eat.

Arabian people still ride camels great distances across empty deserts.

Muslim

A follower of the religion that Muhammad founded in Arabia in the seventh century

Vision

Something seen in the mind or in a dream

Prophet

A religious leader who claims to speak for God; one who tells what will happen in the future

Reading Strategy: Visualizing

Create a graphic organizer of the stages in Muhammad's life and the growth of Islam.

The **Muslim** religion was born in the desert land of Arabia. Today this land is called Saudi Arabia.

What Was Muhammad's Role in the Birth of Islam?

Around the year A.D. 570, in the Arabian city of Mecca, a man named Muhammad was born. Not much is known about Muhammad's early life. Yet Muhammad was to become a religious figure who would change the shape of the world.

When Muhammad was 40 years old, it is said, he had a **vision**. Muhammad believed he saw an angel on a hillside outside of Mecca. The angel spoke to him, saying that Muhammad was a **prophet** of God. "Teach your people," the angel said, "that there is one God, and that God is Allah."

Like Jesus, Muhammad became a teacher. He tried to teach people that Allah was the one true god. Most Arabs would not listen. They still worshipped their many gods.

Muhammad did have some followers. They heard his words about Allah. Muhammad promised that Allah would reward people for good deeds with a wonderful life after death. Poor people listened. Slaves listened. People whose lives were hard or sad listened to Muhammad.

The powerful leaders of Mecca began to worry. They had laughed at him at first, this man called Muhammad. Now he was growing popular. What if he stirred the commoners into a rebellion (revolution)? The leaders began to persecute Muhammad and his followers. The Muslims were forced to flee the city of Mecca.

In A.D. 622, Muhammad took his people to the Arabian city of Medina. Still, the number of Muslims grew. New converts became soldiers for Islam. With an army of followers, Muhammad returned to Mecca. They took the city in A.D. 630.

In A.D. 632, Muhammad died. By the time of his death, the prophet Muhammad had done his job. Most of Arabia was united under one religion. The religion of the Muslims was called Islam. The Islamic religion promised that any followers who died battling for Allah would go to paradise, or heaven. This idea alone created huge armies of enthusiastic soldiers. The Muslim soldiers were ready to carry the word of Allah throughout the world.

The Muslim Empire, About A.D. 750

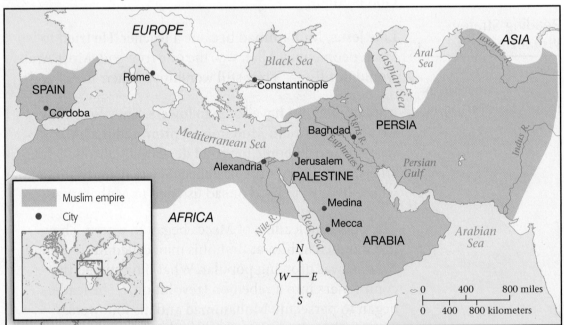

MAP STUDY

1. The Muslim empire extended across parts of which three continents?

2. Medina and Mecca were near which body of water?

Holy Land

Palestine; the area where Jesus of Nazareth lived

Koran

The holy book of the Muslims that contains the teachings of Islam

How Did Islam Spread?

Then came one of the greatest series of conquests, or take-overs, the world had ever seen. Between A.D. 640 and A.D. 660, Arab armies swept through Syria, Persia, and Egypt. They conquered Palestine, or the **Holy Land.** It included the holy city of Jerusalem. The Arab conquests continued for hundreds of years. Arab lands would stretch from North Africa and Spain to the Indus River and Central Asia.

Some of the conquered people welcomed the new religion with its hope of paradise. The Arabs, however, gave them little choice—the people must become Muslims or die. Only Jews and Christians were allowed to keep their own religion. The Muslims respected those who also worshipped one God and followed the words of a holy book.

Indeed, Muhammad was influenced early in his life by the Jews and Christians he knew. His God, Allah, was the one God of the Jews and Christians. According to Muhammad, God revealed himself to humanity through his chosen prophets. The major prophets were Adam, Noah, Abraham, Moses, Jesus, and, finally, Muhammad. God gave the Ten Commandments to Moses, the Gospels to Jesus, and the **Koran** to Muhammad. (Koran is also spelled *Qur'an*.) Even so, the Christians and Jews were forced to pay tribute to the new Arab rulers.

These are early Arabic numerals representing the numbers 1 through 5.

The conquering Arabs brought their culture as well as their religion. They built fine cities, new schools, and beautiful places of worship called mosques. Their language and writing became part of world culture. The Arabs made their mark on the world in many ways. The numerals that are used in the United States and Canada, for example, are Arabic numerals.

Faith
A religion

What Happened to Islam After Muhammad Died?

Muhammad died in A.D. 632. His death raised the question of who should succeed him. Different answers to that question led to the formation of two branches of Islam, the Sunnis and the Shi'ites. The Sunnis believe that Muhammad did not appoint (choose) a successor. Therefore, a new religious leader could be chosen by vote. The new leader did not have to be a relative of Muhammad. Shi'ites believe that Muhammad appointed Ali as his successor. Ali was married to Muhammad's daughter. Shi'ites believe that a new religious leader should be related to Muhammad. Eventually, these two branches developed different laws and religious practices.

Today Islam is one of the world's great religions. Most Muslims live in the Middle East, Pakistan, India, North Africa, and parts of Asia. They live in lands that the Arabs conquered during the seventh and eighth centuries. It is estimated that 1 percent of the U.S. population (5.75 million people) follows the Islamic **faith**. In Canada, that number is about 1.9 percent. It is believed that about 90 percent of Muslims are Sunnis.

TIMELINE STUDY: MUHAMMAD AND THE GROWTH OF ISLAM

After Muhammad died, what did the Muslims do?

A.D. 570 Muhammad is born in Mecca

A.D. 610 Muhammad has vision of the angel

A.D. 632 Muhammad dies

A.D. 660–720 Muslims conquer North Africa

A.D. 550   A.D. 600   A.D. 650   A.D. 700   A.D. 750

A.D. 630 Mecca taken by the Muslims

A.D. 640–660 Muslims conquer Syria, Jerusalem, Egypt, Persia

Words from the Past

The Koran

The Koran (also spelled *Qur'an*) is the sacred, or holy, book of Islam. The book is a collection of verses. The verses are said to be revealed (made known) to Muhammad by the angel Gabriel. His followers memorized his words or wrote them down. Later they were collected to form the Koran. Muslims believe the Koran is the word of God and cannot be changed in any way, although translations are permitted.

The Koran is made up of verses revealed to Muhammad.

The Koran says that Allah is the one and only God. Muslims must obey Allah and his word. Allah will judge each person by his or her deeds and obedience to him.

There are several things a good Muslim must do, according to the Koran. A Muslim must pray five times a day, facing toward Mecca. A Muslim must give to the poor. A Muslim must not eat or drink during daylight hours of one special month called *Ramadan*. A Muslim should, if at all possible, make at least one visit to Mecca. Today Muslim pilgrims from many lands still journey to the holy city of Mecca.

"There is no God but Allah," a Muslim declares, "and Muhammad is His prophet!"

Word Bank

conquests

culture

Koran

Mecca

poor

On a sheet of paper, write the word from the Word Bank to complete each sentence correctly.

1. Muhammad was born in the Arabian city of _____.

2. Muhammad's teachings appealed to the _____ and enslaved.

3. Islam spread by a series of _____ that lasted for over 100 years.

4. Conquering Arabs brought their _____ as well as their religion.

5. The _____ is the sacred book of Islam.

On a sheet of paper, write the answer to each question. Use complete sentences.

6. What did the Arabs worship in A.D. 570?

7. What did Muhammad see in his vision?

8. How does Allah reward good deeds?

9. Arab armies allowed Jews and Christians to keep their religion after they were conquered. Why?

10. What are the differences between the Islamic beliefs of the Sunnis and the Shi'ites?

The Crusades

Objectives

- To give four reasons people went on Crusades
- To describe the terms of the truce between Saladin and Richard
- To tell how the Holy Land came to be under Muslim rule

Pilgrimage
A visit to a holy place

Reading Strategy:
Visualizing

What clues help you to get a feeling about the way the Crusades progressed?

During the Middle Ages, the Christian religion was the strongest force in Europe. People made visits to a holy place, or **pilgrimages,** to show their faith. From Germany, France, England, and Italy they traveled to holy shrines. Thousands of pilgrims went on foot and on horseback.

Pilgrims traveled east to the holy city of Jerusalem. Jerusalem had been a holy city for the Jews since the days of Solomon's splendid temple. The Muslims had also called Jerusalem a holy city. Now it was a holy city for the Christians as well. Christian pilgrims flocked to Jerusalem. They went to see the place where Jesus had lived and taught.

Why Were the Holy Wars Fought?

When the Christian pilgrims of the Middle Ages journeyed to Jerusalem, that city was under Muslim control. The Arab Muslims respected the Christian religion. They allowed Christian pilgrims to visit Jerusalem.

In 1071, the Seljuk Turks, who dominated Syria, took power in Jerusalem. The Turks were Muslims, too. The Turks were not as friendly to the Christians. The Turks would not allow Christians to visit their city. They would not let them worship at the holy shrines.

An angry pope named Urban II stirred Europeans to action in 1095. He spoke before a gathering of important people. He reminded them that the Turks held Jerusalem. He told them that Christians there were in danger. It was their Christian duty, he said, to free the Holy Land.

Crusade
Any of the military journeys taken by Christians to win the Holy Land from the Muslims

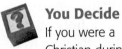 **You Decide**
If you were a Christian during those days, would you have wanted to go on the Crusades? Why or why not?

People listened. Feudal lords, knights, and commoners were all moved to action. Word spread across Europe. Soon armies of Christians were ready to travel to the Holy Land. They wore crosses on their clothing as a symbol of their mission. Then the Christian armies set forth on the **Crusades.** The Crusades were the military journeys the Christians took to win the Holy Land from the Muslims. The Holy Wars they started were to last for 200 years.

Many crusaders marched because of strong religious feelings. Some went on the Crusades for other reasons. Some were looking for adventure. Others were looking for wealth in new lands. Soldiers wanted military glory. Merchants wanted new markets for their goods. Criminals wanted a safe place to hide.

Crusaders came from every social class—kings and nobles, knights and lords. The serfs saw a chance to escape feudal manors. They joined the march, too. They all set out to take Jerusalem from the Muslims.

The earliest Crusade, in 1096, was led by a man called Peter the Hermit. This Crusade was made up of French and German peasants. They started out for the Holy Land before the huge armies of knights did. The peasants were not well organized. They had to steal food along the way to keep from starving. The Turks had little trouble defeating them. Most of the peasants were killed before they reached Jerusalem.

In the autumn of 1096, several armies of knights set out from Europe. Nobles from France led the march. It was a hard trip. Over the next two years, many died from hunger and disease. The knights had to fight many battles along the way. Those who made it to Jerusalem were ready for another fight. They started a bloody battle. It lasted six weeks. When it was over, the crusaders had taken Jerusalem and much of the Holy Land from the Muslims.

The Crusades

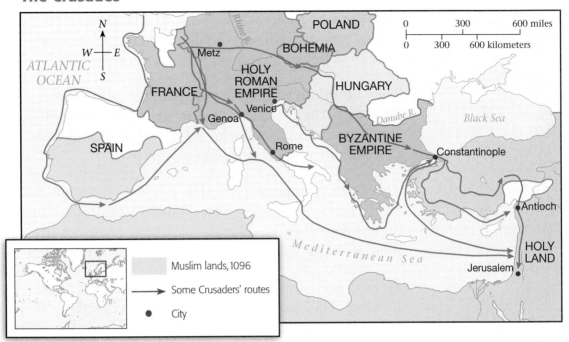

MAP STUDY

1. Which bodies of water did the crusaders cross on their way to the Holy Land?

2. According to the map, who did the Holy Land belong to in 1096?

The crusaders had killed many of the people who lived there—Jews and Muslims. The year was 1099.

The nobles from Europe set up several small states in the Holy Land. Christians back home were pleased. The Holy Land was under Christian control. Most of the crusaders returned to Europe.

Then European leaders in the Holy Land began to quarrel among themselves. The Turks launched new attacks. In response, more crusaders went off to help protect the Holy Land.

Truce

A time when enemies agree to stop fighting

History Fact

The German emperor Frederick I was called Barbarossa, King Philip II of France was called Philip Augustus, and King Richard of England was called Richard the Lion-Hearted.

What Was the Truce Between Saladin and Richard?

The Muslims' leader was Saladin, who was said to be strong and wise. Saladin's soldiers, or troops, won back the city of Jerusalem in 1187.

Then European rulers joined together to fight for the Holy City. The German emperor Frederick I, King Philip II of France, and King Richard I of England set off on a Crusade. Together they fought to take back Jerusalem.

The German emperor Frederick accidentally drowned on the trip to the Middle East. France's King Philip came home before the Crusade was over; he was too sick to fight. Richard the Lion-Hearted was left to face Saladin.

Richard and Saladin were both great leaders and brave warriors. They had much respect for each other's skills. When they met in battle, Saladin's forces gained the upper hand. Then word came that Richard was needed back in England. Saladin agreed to a five-year **truce** to stop fighting. Under the terms of the truce, Christians would be allowed to visit Jerusalem. They could also keep control of a few cities on the coast.

Saladin, a Muslim leader, seized Jerusalem from the Christian crusaders in 1187.

GREAT NAMES IN HISTORY

Saladin

Saladin was a Muslim leader. He became the ruler of Egypt and Syria. Saladin built schools and mosques (places of worship) there. He was so brave and honest that even crusaders admired him.

For years, the crusaders held Palestine. Saladin wanted those Muslim lands back. He united Muslims against the crusaders. His forces captured Jerusalem in 1187. Then they took back most of Palestine.

As a result, the Third Crusade began. It ended Saladin's two-year siege of the crusaders at Acre. But they never won back Jerusalem. Finally, Saladin and crusade leader Richard the Lion-Hearted met. Their truce let Christian pilgrims visit Jerusalem.

Independence
Being free; being able to govern one's self

How Did the Ottomans Gain Control of the Holy Land?

When Saladin died, the truce weakened. By 1291 the Muslims again held all of the Holy Land. In 1453, the Ottoman Turks took power in Constantinople and much of Anatolia. Like the Seljuk Turks, the Ottomans were Muslims. The Holy Land fell under their rule. The Ottomans also put an end to the Byzantine Empire. They changed the name of their capital city, Constantinople, to Istanbul. By 1500 the Ottomans would rule over a huge empire. The Middle East, North Africa, and much of eastern Europe fell to the Ottomans. The Ottoman Empire would last for hundreds of years.

LEARN MORE ABOUT IT

The Ottoman Empire

The Ottoman Turks first appeared in Asia Minor in the late 1200s. They were named Osmanli or Ottoman after their leader, Osman. It was under Osman that the Ottomans began to conquer the Byzantine Empire. The ruler of the Ottoman Empire was called a *sultan.* The sultan was a powerful man who ruled through a group of high officers.

The Ottoman Empire continued to grow after Osman's death. By the early 1400s, Constantinople was a Christian city surrounded by Muslim lands. Then the Ottomans, under the rule of their sultan, Mehmed II, captured Constantinople. Mehmed's troops also captured Bulgaria and parts of Hungary, and Mehmed II became known as "the Conqueror." In the 1400s and 1500s, the Ottoman Empire

extended into Asia and Africa. The Ottoman sultans took the title of *caliph,* or spiritual leader of Islam. Under the caliph known as "Suleiman the Magnificent," the Ottoman Empire grew. It now included Palestine, Egypt, and parts of Arabia, North Africa, Europe, and Persia.

The Ottomans continued to rule their vast empire for hundreds of years. During the 1800s, however, they began to lose territory. The government grew harsher. Minority groups in all parts of the empire suffered persecution. Many people wanted freedom, or **independence**, from Ottoman rule.

The Ottoman Turks joined Germany and Austria in World War I (1914–1918). With defeat came the loss of all non-Turkish lands. A free republic of Turkey was declared in 1923.

On a sheet of paper, write the letter of the answer that correctly completes each sentence.

1. Pope _____ stirred Europeans to action. He did so by telling them that Christians in the Holy Land were in danger.

    A Peter the Hermit   **B** Philip II   **C** Urban II   **D** Richard I

2. Christian crusaders fought to win Jerusalem from the _____.

    A Turks   **B** Ottomans   **C** Germans   **D** Muslims

3. Armies of Christians wore _____ on their clothing as a symbol of their mission.

    A Jesus   **B** crosses   **C** crowns   **D** hearts

4. In _____, the crusaders took Jerusalem and much of the Holy Land from the Muslims.

    A 1071   **B** 1096   **C** 1099   **D** 1187

5. Muslim leader _____ won back the city of Jerusalem in 1187.

    A Saladin   **B** Philip II   **C** Frederick I **D** Allah

6. The truce weakened when Saladin died. By _____, the Muslims held all of the Holy Land.

    A 1187   **B** 1291   **C** 1453   **D** 1500

7. In 1453, the Holy Land fell under _____ rule (who were also Muslim).

    A Ottoman   **B** Byzantine   **C** Turk   **D** German

On a sheet of paper, write the answer to each question. Use complete sentences.

8. Why did Christians go on pilgrimages?

9. What are four reasons people went on the Crusades?

10. What were the terms of the truce between Saladin and Richard?

The Costs of the Crusades

Objectives

- To name two ways the Crusades negatively affected people and their lives
- To explain how the Crusades affected European trade

Reading Strategy: Visualizing

Create a graphic organizer to list your own description of changes (new foods, for instance) that occurred with the Crusades.

Europeans found the Crusades costly in many ways. It took a lot of money to equip the warriors and send them such great distances. The Crusades were also costly in terms of lives. Many people—Christians, Muslims, and Jews—died bloody deaths fighting for the Holy Land. In the name of God, people looted, burned, and killed.

In the beginning, people thought the Crusades would lead them to glory. The Holy Wars, however, caused much suffering and misery. And this was all in the name of religions based on brotherhood and love.

LEARN MORE ABOUT IT

The Children's Crusade

One of the saddest of the Crusades became known as the Children's Crusade. In 1212, an army of 30,000 French boys and girls set out to fight. Most of them were 12 years old or younger. They were gathered together and led by a shepherd boy named Stephen.

At first it must have seemed like an adventure for the children. Sadly, however, few of them ever returned home. Nearly all of the 30,000 children died. Most fell sick along the way, or they starved to death.

Another army of German youths headed for Jerusalem. Led by a boy named Nicholas, these 20,000 children never saw the Holy Land either. When seven ships offered to take them to Jerusalem, they accepted. How lucky, they thought, to get a ride!

Unfortunately, the free ride was bad luck indeed. Two of the ships were wrecked in storms. All of the children aboard drowned. The rest of the ships were not headed for Jerusalem at all. The children had been tricked. The ships took them to Egypt, where they were sold as slaves.

Reading Strategy:
Visualizing

What words in this section help you visualize what you are reading?

What Changes Did the Crusades Bring to Europe?

By 1291 the Christians had lost all of the lands they once held in the Middle East. The crusaders brought back Middle Eastern ideas. Crusading merchants also brought home new products. The Crusades created a new Europe.

The merchants introduced Europeans to foods like lemons, rice, apricots, and melons. New spices, such as ginger and pepper, cloves and cinnamon, now seasoned European food. The merchants brought fine cloth. Europeans began wearing brightly dyed silks. With the new trading, Europe's whole economy became stronger.

When the crusaders left Europe, their journeys gave them fresh ideas. There was a new interest in travel and exploring new places, or **exploration.** People learned to make better maps. All the fighting that went on encouraged even more interest in warfare. Crusaders returned with new weapons and better battle skills.

The feudal society had kept medieval people tied down to the manors. The Crusades sent them out into the world. The Crusades were sad and costly. However, they also increased trade and brought a sharing of cultures.

Christians joined the Crusades to recapture the Holy Land from the Muslims.

REVIEW

Word Bank

children

economy

fine cloth

ideas

lives

maps

misery

spices

weapons

world

On a sheet of paper, write the word from the Word Bank to complete each sentence correctly.

1. The Crusades cost the Europeans a lot of money and _____.

2. The Crusades were meant to bring glory. Instead, the Holy Wars caused much suffering and _____.

3. _____ from France and Germany also went to fight.

4. The Crusaders brought back Middle Eastern _____ and new products.

5. The merchants introduced new food and _____ to the Europeans.

6. The merchants brought _____ and the Europeans began to wear brightly dyed silks.

7. With new trading, Europe's whole _____ became stronger.

8. The Crusades sparked people's interest in travel and exploration. As a result, people learned to make better _____.

9. The fighting also increased interest in warfare. The Crusaders brought back _____ and better battle skills.

10. In feudal society people were tied to their manors. The Crusades sent them out into the _____.

Changes in Agriculture

The world's first agricultural revolution had taken place long ago. It occurred along the Mediterranean Sea when people began planting seeds and raising animals. During the Middle Ages another farming revolution was going on. Now people were learning about new and better methods of growing food. These changes in agriculture also changed society as a whole.

How Did Farming Change During the Middle Ages?

During the Middle Ages, Emperor Charlemagne opened new iron mines. With more iron available, farm tools improved. Now there were new metal axes and hoes.

The new tool that most changed farming in the Middle Ages was the plowshare. A plowshare is the broad blade of the plow that cuts through the soil. Early plows had been little more than large sticks. These sticks were dragged across the ground by one or two oxen. They only scratched the earth. It took hours and hours of work to break up even a small field.

The new plowshare was made of sharp, curved iron. The plow itself was fastened to a heavy, wheeled frame. Eight oxen were needed to pull the plowshare. With the new, heavier equipment, farmers could till even the heaviest soil. Working in long, narrow strips, they could plow the land more quickly.

The plowshare meant that more land could be farmed and more food could be grown. People did not have to eat all that they grew. They had more food than they needed, or a **surplus** of food. They could use this surplus to trade for other goods.

Medieval farmers discovered that horses were better workers than oxen. Horses could work longer without rest. They moved faster. With more iron around, it was easy to make enough horseshoes.

The farmers invented a new kind of harness to fasten their horses to a plow. It fit over the horse's shoulders instead of across its chest. Now the horse could breathe easier and could pull heavier weights. It took fewer horses than oxen to pull the new plowshare.

Farmers learned to get more out of their fields. They maintained three fields now. They planted one field in the autumn and one in the spring. A third field was not used and lay fallow, or bare, each season. Each field was given a season to be fallow. This let the soil rest and grow rich again.

The three-field method of crop rotation worked well. If one crop failed, there was always a second crop to rely on. More food was produced.

**Reading Strategy:
Visualizing**

Study the art in this lesson. What does it say about agriculture in the Middle Ages?

During the Middle Ages, new tools changed the way people farmed.

REVIEW

On a sheet of paper, write the answer to each question. Use complete sentences.

1. What was the new tool that changed farming the most during the Middle Ages?

2. What was the new method farmers learned for growing crops?

3. Why did they let one field rest each season?

On a sheet of paper, write the letter of the answer that correctly completes each sentence.

4. The _____ revolution of the Middle Ages taught people new, better methods for growing food. It also changed society.

   A industrial   **B** farming   **C** feudalism   **D** warfare

5. Because _____ opened new iron mines, there was more iron available and farm tools improved.

   A Charlemagne   **B** Richard I   **C** Philip II   **D** Frederick I

6. The new plowshare, made of _____, allowed farmers to till heavy soil.

   A sticks   **B** stone   **C** leather   **D** iron

7. The plowshare created _____ food, which farmers could use to trade.

   A different types of   **B** a loss of   **C** a surplus of   **D** more demand for

8. Farmers discovered that horses were better workers than _____.

   A dogs   **B** oxen   **C** children   **D** slaves

9. Horses could work longer without rest _____.

   A and they moved faster   **C** but they were unproductive
   B and they complained less   **D** but they were ineffective

10. The farmers invented a new _____. It allowed the horse to breathe easier and pull heavier weights.

    A plowshare   **B** iron   **C** harness   **D** horseshoe

Changes in City Life

Objectives

■ To describe what life was like in a medieval town

■ To explain how the feudal system weakened

■ To tell how a person could become a member of a guild

■ To describe how cities like Constantinople and Antwerp grew during the Middle Ages

Population

People living in a place, or the total number of those people

Migrate

To move away from one country or region to settle in another

Reading Strategy: Visualizing

Draw a picture of a medieval town to help you visualize the ideas in this lesson.

During the 1000s, the number of people living in Europe, or Europe's **population**, began to grow. More people meant a need for even more farmland. Farmers cleared forests and drained swamplands in England and France. People began to **migrate,** or move, eastward. Germans colonized new lands in eastern Europe. Changes in agriculture caused people to live in new places.

What Was the Result of the Growth in Population?

As farm production increased, workers had more food to trade for goods. Beginning in the 1000s, craftworkers and traders began to settle in medieval villages to sell their goods. In addition to the blacksmith and the miller, there were now new shops in the villages. The villages grew into towns.

Medieval towns were usually surrounded by stone walls. Their narrow streets were often just mud. Sometimes the streets were paved with cobblestones. The towns were often dirty and dark.

With walls closing them in, the towns were small and crowded. People threw their garbage into the streets. There were no fire departments, no police departments, and no health services. Most of the houses were just huts made of wood. With these conditions, there was always a danger of fire and disease. The town of Rouen in France burned to the ground six times between 1200 and 1225! It is easy to see how the plague spread so quickly in such crowded, dirty towns.

History Fact
In the Middle Ages, a town that had a cathedral was known as a cathedral city. Many cathedrals grew to be large and beautiful.

In spite of their problems, the medieval towns grew. As they did, the workers, merchants, and craftworkers became more specialized.

People used money more often now. On the manors, services had been exchanged for goods. Now people paid money for new leather shoes, a pottery bowl, or a cake.

Serfs saw the town as a place to win freedom from manor lords. Sometimes serfs ran away and hid within the walls of a town. "Live free for a year and a day," the rule went, "and go free." A serf who could manage to escape his lord for that long became a free person.

Why Did the Feudal System Begin to Weaken?

During the late Middle Ages, business and trade increased. As the towns became stronger, and the merchants became richer, the feudal system weakened. The towns wanted to govern themselves—to be free of the manor.

Some feudal lords sold deeds of freedom to the towns. No longer were so many people "tied" to the land. Most towns were dirty and crowded. People, however, were freer than they had been on the feudal estates. It was not so surprising that they wanted to live in the towns.

What Was the Purpose of a Guild?

The towns offered opportunity. Peasants could work their way up in the world. They could learn a trade or a craft.

Each trade and craft had its own group, or **guild**. The guild helped set prices. It also set standards for workmanship. The guilds decided how long shops should stay open each day.

The guilds also offered a chance to learn. Boys and girls could become an **apprentice** and go to work for a guild member. The apprentice lived in the master's house and worked in the master's shop.

An apprentice served for seven years and received no pay. After that time, the apprentice could become a journeyman and earn wages. When the apprentice became skilled enough, the journeyman made one special piece of work for the master. It was called a "masterpiece." If the masterpiece was good enough, the journeyman might become a master and join the guild.

Streets in medieval towns often were named after different guilds. *Tailors Row* and *Boot Street*, for example, were typical street names.

What Were Some Big Cities During the Middle Ages?

Most Europeans lived in small, walled towns during the late Middle Ages. However, there were a few fine, wealthy cities. Trade flourished, or did well, in those cities. There were theaters and hospitals, schools and libraries.

There were cities like Constantinople, capital of the Byzantine Empire. One million people lived there. As many as one thousand ships might dock at Constantinople's harbor at the same time.

TECHNOLOGY CONNECTION

Silver and Medieval Business

In the 1160s more silver mines opened across Europe. Many of these were in Germany. As the number of mines increased, so did people's knowledge. Mining became more efficient and effective. More silver was brought into trade.

French and English merchants traded for German silver. Italians and other merchants from the Mediterranean traded goods brought from the East. More business was being conducted using silver money. Bankers from the south moved to growing northern trade centers.

Mines were expanded, or made larger. Small operations learned new technologies to mine greater amounts of silver. Jobs in industry became available to people. Those who did not want to be farmers now had other choices.

There were cities like Baghdad, center of the Islamic world. There, scientists studied mathematics and astronomy. Doctors made new discoveries in medicine. Geographers mapped the world.

There were cities like Córdoba, Spain. It was called the *Lighthouse of Learning.* Spanish Muslims and Spanish Jews studied there.

There were cities like Venice and Antwerp. Trade and manufacturing made these places wealthy.

All these cities grew during the Middle Ages. Trade kept them powerful and rich. They were centers for art, science, and education.

Constantinople was the capital of the Byzantine Empire. During the Holy Wars, it was raided by Crusaders.

On a sheet of paper, write the letter of the answer that correctly completes each sentence.

1. As towns grew, workers, merchants, and craftworkers became more _____.

   A wealthy   **B** in demand   **C** gifted   **D** specialized

2. As the medieval town population grew, people used money to exchange goods, rather than _____.

   A gold   **B** weapons   **C** services   **D** slaves

3. Towns offered _____, as peasants could work their way up in the world.

   A risk   **B** opportunity   **C** trade   **D** food

4. Streets in medieval towns were often named after different _____.

   A lords   **B** knights   **C** guilds   **D** clergy

5. Constantinople, Baghdad, and Antwerp are some examples of wealthy _____ in the late Middle Ages.

   A cities   **B** towns   **C** estates   **D** farms

6. _____ flourished in cities and helped to keep them powerful and rich.

   A Farming   **B** Trade   **C** The population   **D** Services

7. The cities were centers for art, science, and _____.

   A education   **B** weapons   **C** religion   **D** farm tool factories

On a sheet of paper, write the answer to each question. Use complete sentences.

8. What was life like in a medieval town?

9. How did the feudal system weaken?

10. What steps would a boy or girl need to take to become a guild member?

The Magna Carta

Objective

■ To discuss how the Magna Carta gave people justice

Reading Strategy: Visualizing

Create a graphic organizer of the events that led up to the signing of the Magna Carta.

Human rights
The right to life, liberty, and pursuit of happiness

Document
An important paper

Charter
A constitution; a set of statements that explains a group's purpose

There was little concern with **human rights** during the early Middle Ages. Indeed, the right to life, liberty, and the pursuit of (the attempt to get) happiness was not granted to everyone. A lord had much power over the lives of serfs.

What Progress Was Made During the Middle Ages in Human Rights?

When King John ruled England, he showed no interest at all in anyone's rights. He did not even treat the nobles very well! Suppose that King John did not like a certain noble. Perhaps he thought that noble was becoming too powerful. He might very well have the noble put to death.

Nobles were angry. In 1213 some powerful men met in England. They drew up a list of rights that they wanted the king to grant them. The final **document** would make sure that justice, or fairness, would not be denied to freemen.

King John did not want to give up any power. He refused to sign the list. In 1215 the nobles sent an army after him. King John saw that he could not defeat the army, so he finally gave in. At Runnymede, near the Thames River, King John signed the list of rights, or the **charter**. It became known as the *Great Charter*, or the *Magna Carta*.

TIMELINE STUDY: **THE CRUSADES**

How many years passed from the time of Pope Urban's sermon to the end of the Crusades?

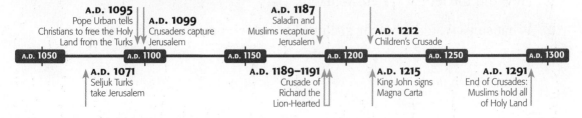

A.D. 1095
Pope Urban tells Christians to free the Holy Land from the Turks

A.D. 1099
Crusaders capture Jerusalem

A.D. 1187
Saladin and Muslims recapture Jerusalem

A.D. 1212
Children's Crusade

A.D. 1050   A.D. 1100   A.D. 1150   A.D. 1200   A.D. 1250   A.D. 1300

A.D. 1071
Seljuk Turks take Jerusalem

A.D. 1189–1191
Crusade of Richard the Lion-Hearted

A.D. 1215
King John signs Magna Carta

A.D. 1291
End of Crusades: Muslims hold all of Holy Land

Words from the Past

The Magna Carta

When King John signed the Magna Carta in 1215, he gave some rights and liberties to the nobles, or barons. He also reformed the legal system and gave a few rights to freemen. Most people in England, however, were not free—they were serfs. None of the liberties in the charter applied to them.

How could a charter giving most rights to barons become such an important document? One reason was that when King John signed the charter, he was admitting that even the king had to obey the law. For another reason, over time many people came to believe that the rights in the charter belonged to all English people. In England, future laws granting liberties to all English people were based on the Magna Carta.

King John signed the Magna Carta.

The Magna Carta said that:

- A freeman must be tried by a jury of his equals before being sent to prison.

- Taxes would be collected by legal means, not by force.

- Punishment should fit the crime.

The Magna Carta was important to the development of a new nation, the United States of America. The Magna Carta inspired colonists to fight for their rights against King George and Great Britain. The Declaration of Independence, the U.S. Constitution, and many U.S. state constitutions were based partly on the ideas of the Magna Carta.

REVIEW

Word Bank

equals

freeman

Great Charter

king

punishment

serfs

taxes

1213

1215

United States of America

On a sheet of paper, write the word from the Word Bank to complete each sentence correctly.

1. In _____, a group of powerful men met and drew up a list of rights. They wanted to ensure that justice would not be denied to freemen.

2. The Magna Carta is also known as the _____.

3. King John signed the Magna Carta in _____.

4. The Magna Carta changed the legal system and gave a few rights to _____.

5. None of the liberties in the charter applied to _____.

6. By signing the charter, King John admitted that the _____ had to obey the law.

7. The Magna Carta said that a freeman must be tried by a jury of his _____.

8. It also said that _____ should be collected by legal means.

9. According to the charter, the _____ should fit the crime.

10. The Magna Carta was important to the development of the _____.

CHAPTER 12

SUMMARY

- During the Middle Ages, many Christians made pilgrimages to holy places such as the city of Jerusalem. Jesus Christ had lived and taught in Jerusalem.

- Muslims were followers of Muhammad. He was born in Mecca in A.D. 570. Muhammad taught the word of Allah. By the time Muhammad died in A.D. 632, he had many followers. Their religion was called Islam.

- Muslims conquered many lands, spreading Islam and the Arabic culture. They conquered Palestine (the Holy Land), which included the city of Jerusalem. Jews and Christians were also living in Jerusalem at that time.

- Christian crusaders fought to win Jerusalem from the Muslims. They fought a war that lasted for six weeks. They took control of the Holy Land.

- In A.D. 1167, the Muslims regained control of the Holy Land. They made a truce with the Christians, who would be allowed to visit Jerusalem.

- The Ottoman Turks took control of the Byzantine Empire, the Middle East, northern Africa, and much of eastern Europe by 1500. This included the Holy Land.

- The Crusaders brought back new ideas, new products, and new plans for trade throughout Europe.

- A medieval revolution in agriculture meant new tools and better methods of farming. Many people migrated to the east.

- Medieval towns saw an increase in craftworkers and merchants. The craftworkers formed guilds.

- In A.D. 1215, King John signed the Magna Carta, giving new rights to the English.

Word Bank

apprentice

faith

guild

independence

migrated

pilgrimage

population

prophet

surplus

truce

Vocabulary Review

On a sheet of paper, use the words from the Word Bank to complete each sentence correctly.

1. Muhammad was a(n) _____.

2. A religious person might make a(n) _____ to visit the Holy Land.

3. Millions of people of the Islamic _____ live in the United States and Canada.

4. The new plowshare resulted in a(n) _____ of food.

5. A boy or girl could work for a master as a(n) _____.

6. Master craftworkers could belong to a(n) _____.

7. Germans _____ to new lands in eastern Europe.

8. Europe's _____ began to grow during the 1000s.

9. Saladin signed a five-year _____ that allowed Christians to visit Jerusalem.

10. Minority groups suffering persecution wanted _____ from Ottoman rule.

Chapter Review Questions

On a sheet of paper, write the answer to each question. Use complete sentences.

11. Who went on the Crusades to the Holy Land?

12. After the Crusades, who controlled the Holy Land?

13. Why did the feudal system weaken?

14. How did farming change during the Middle Ages?

Test Tip

Read test questions carefully. Identify questions that require more than one answer.

15. Why did towns begin to grow in the 1000s?

16. What did the Magna Carta say about the relationship of the king to the laws of the land?

Critical Thinking

On a sheet of paper, write your response to each question. Use complete sentences.

17. How did Muhammad affect the world beyond his own followers?

18. What do you think was the most important right in the Magna Carta? Explain why.

Using the Timelines

Use the timelines on pages 228 and 248 to answer the questions.

19. How old was Muhammad when he died?

20. When was the Children's Crusade?

GROUP ACTIVITY

Form a group of five or six. Assign each person a role such as a merchant, soldier, king, noble, knight, serf, or child. Have each person write a speech about the reasons he or she wants to go on a Crusade. When the speeches are ready, perform them for the class.

THE RENAISSANCE

Y ou will learn that the word *renaissance* has more than one definition. Beyond those, you might think of it as meaning "a bold, new start." The period in history called the Renaissance meant lots of new learning and new creations. It also meant many new opportunities for those wanting adventure. People faced challenges they had never known before. New kinds of kingdoms developed, under bold new leaders. Now groups competed for control of lands and the way people lived. Thus our recorded history was becoming more detailed and challenging.

Chapters in Unit 5

This detail from the Sistine Chapel illustrates the great thinking that happened during the Renaissance.

New Ideas: The Renaissance

You have read that history is all about change. This could be moving to a different place or shifting focus to a new goal or way of thinking. It could also be the shift from a simple to a more difficult world.

The Middle Ages brought a growth in the Roman Catholic Church as well as in Islam. These religions attracted more and more people. They controlled larger areas and became more powerful. The Renaissance brought a return to learning and creativity. Scientists and artists had more power as did members of the clergy. They began to question their own relationships to religion and the power that came with it.

GOALS FOR LEARNING

- To understand the ideas behind the Renaissance
- To recognize the humanism in Renaissance art
- To describe the advances in knowledge during the Renaissance
- To describe what it means to be a Renaissance man
- To understand how the Reformation came about
- To understand the ideas behind the Counter-Reformation

Reading Strategy: Inferencing

Sometimes you have to make an inference to figure out what the text means. You have to make an inference because the meaning of a text is not directly stated.

What You Know + What You Read = Inference

You can make inferences by thinking "beyond the text." Add what you already know to what you read in the text. This is a helpful strategy for making inferences.

Key Vocabulary Words

Lesson 1

Renaissance The revival of art, literature, and learning in Europe in the 14th through 16th centuries

Humanism A concern with the needs and interests of human beings rather than religious ideas

Criticize To say that someone has done wrong; to find wrong in something

Lesson 2

Patron A wealthy person who supports artists

Sculptor A person who makes statues out of wood, stone, marble, or other material

Architect A person who draws plans for buildings

Masterpiece A piece of art that seems almost perfect

Lesson 3

Astronomer A person who keeps track of the sun, the planets, and the stars

Theory An explanation of how and why something happens, usually based on scientific study

Lesson 5

Reformation A movement that challenged and changed the Catholic religion in Europe

Authority Power

Lutheranism The religious movement founded by Martin Luther

Protestant A reformer who protested against the Catholic Church

Inquisition A special court set up by the Roman Catholic Church to question the beliefs of people to see if they were heretics

Heretic A person who is against the teachings of a church

Lesson 6

Counter-Reformation The Catholic Church's reforms that attempted to fight Protestant beliefs

A Time of New Ideas

- To explain what the word *Renaissance* means
- To explain what the term *humanism* means

Renaissance
The revival of art, literature, and learning in Europe in the 14th through 16th centuries

Humanism
A concern with the needs and interests of human beings rather than religious ideas

History Fact
The Renaissance was a period of great thinking. The Renaissance lasted about 200 years.

During the Middle Ages, the culture and learning of the Greeks and Romans were all but forgotten. For most people it was as if Greece and Rome had never existed. For this reason, the Middle Ages, especially the early part, is sometimes called the Dark Ages.

Were the Middle Ages Really "Dark"?

During the Middle Ages, Christianity united the people of Western Europe. This was not, however, a Dark Age. Great universities were founded. Immense cathedrals were built. Toward the end of the Middle Ages, around A.D. 1300, trade and travel increased. New ideas exploded throughout Europe. The period after the Middle Ages became known as the **Renaissance.** *Renaissance* means "rebirth" or "awakening."

What New Ideas Sprang from the Renaissance?

The Renaissance was a time of new ideas. During the Middle Ages the Catholic Church was all-powerful. Thinking centered on God. Most well-educated people, or scholars, were also people of the church. During the Renaissance, people began to think about themselves as well as about God. People used to worry about whether or not they would go to heaven after they died. Now they thought more about making a good life on Earth. This new belief in the importance of human beings became known as **humanism**. The spirit of humanism sparked new ideas in art, science, literature, and philosophy.

To say that someone
has done wrong;
to find wrong in
something

**Reading Strategy:
Inferencing**

After reading this lesson,
what inferences can
you make about the
Renaissance?

Who Were the Humanists?

Humanists began to question the church and its leaders. A Dutch scholar, Erasmus, eyed the church critically.

"It seems," Erasmus decided, "that the church is more concerned with wealth and power than with helping men find God."

Erasmus wrote books that questioned the church's practices. He believed that simple ways were best. There was too much ritual and ceremony in the church, he said. Erasmus was a humanist. He believed that if people were just shown what was right, they would live that way. Erasmus was among the first Renaissance scholars to **criticize**, or speak out against, the church. However, he certainly was not the last.

On a sheet of paper, write the letter of the answer that correctly completes each sentence.

1. The culture and learning of the Greeks and _____ seemed forgotten during the Middle Ages.

    A Macedonians   **B** Babylonians   **C** Romans   **D** Persians

2. During the Middle Ages, _____ united the people of Western Europe.

    A art   **B** literature   **C** philosophy   **D** Christianity

3. The period after the Middle Ages is known as _____.

    A humanism   **C** the Dark Ages
    B the Renaissance   **D** the Scientific Revolution

4. The Renaissance lasted about _____ years.

    A 100   **B** 200   **C** 1,300   **D** 1,500

5. During the Middle Ages, most scholars were _____.

    A people of the church   **C** knights
    B nobles   **D** kings

6. The Dutch scholar _____ questioned the church's practices.

    A Michelangelo   **B** Gutenberg   **C** Erasmus   **D** Galileo

7. The spirit of _____ sparked new ideas in art, science, literature, and philosophy.

    A humanism   **C** the Middle Ages
    B the Renaissance   **D** the Dark Ages

On a sheet of paper, write the answer to each question. Use complete sentences.

8. Why were the Dark Ages not a "Dark Age"?

9. What does the word *Renaissance* mean? What is the "Renaissance period"?

10. What does the term *humanism* mean?

Renaissance Art

The Renaissance began in Italy. Then it spread northwest across Europe. More and more people began to appreciate beautiful things. The work of Italian craftworkers became fine. People thought of it as art. Europeans showed a new interest in the civilizations of ancient Greece and Rome.

"Perhaps," people said, "that is when civilization was at its best!"

"Look at the art that came out of Greece," they said. "Look at the beautiful statues and the paintings. Look at the fine architecture of the Romans." At first Italian artists tried to copy the work of the ancient Greeks and Romans. Then they began to improve on it.

How Was Art During the Renaissance Different from Art During the Middle Ages?

During the Middle Ages, most paintings were of religious scenes. The people in these pictures were not very lifelike. Renaissance artists studied the human form. They tried to make the people in their pictures look more like real people. For the first time, artists used live models.

Craftworkers could make a good living from their work. It was harder for artists to earn a steady wage. Wealthy Italians served as **patrons** for promising young artists. A patron provided food, housing, and enough money for the artist to live on. Because of their patrons, artists were able to work and study to improve. Some of the world's finest artists lived during the Renaissance.

Sculptor
A person who makes statues out of wood, stone, marble, or other material

Architect
A person who draws plans for buildings

Sculpture
A carving from stone or other hard material

Masterpiece
A piece of art that seems almost perfect

Who Was Michelangelo Buonarroti?

One of the most famous artists of the Italian Renaissance was Michelangelo Buonarroti. During the Renaissance, people were encouraged to be good at many things. Michelangelo, in true Renaissance spirit, was more than just a fine painter. He was also a **sculptor,** a poet, and an **architect.**

Michelangelo earned his greatest fame for his **sculptures,** the carvings he made from stone. He studied the human body. He studied the human form at work and at rest. Michelangelo even studied dead bodies. This helped him understand the lines of bone and muscle. His sculptures seem alive and real. Each muscle is perfect. Each position is totally lifelike.

Michelangelo was born in 1475 in a mountain town in Italy. He began showing artistic talent as a young boy. A wealthy Italian, Lorenzo de' Medici, noticed Michelangelo's brilliance. He became Michelangelo's patron.

At age 24 Michelangelo created his first **masterpiece,** a huge statue called the *Pietà.* Michelangelo sculpted it for St. Peter's Church in Rome. In the *Pietà,* the body of Christ is shown held in his mother's arms. The word *Pietà* came from the Italian word for "pity."

Michelangelo's statue *David* is another of his most famous works. Completed in 1504, it is a perfect example of the Renaissance interest in the human form. "David" is strong and looks alive. The statue is 18 feet high and made of solid marble. Michelangelo's *David* is quite heavy. It took 40 men to move it from the workshop to a central square in Florence, Italy.

Pope Julius II hired Michelangelo to paint the ceiling of the Sistine Chapel in Rome. Michelangelo painted a series of pictures showing events in the Bible. Over 300 figures from the Bible appear on the 60-foot-high chapel ceiling. Michelangelo had to paint the scenes lying on his back. He laid on a platform held by ropes. He worked on that ceiling for four years.

Later in his life, Michelangelo turned to architecture. He worked on the rebuilding of St. Peter's Church. He took no pay. He believed it was a task that would please God.

Michelangelo died when he was 90. He had lived a long life, sculpting, painting, and building. His art brought light and beauty to all of Europe.

Reading Strategy:
Inferencing

How did what you know about Greece and Rome add to what you have just read?

One of Michelangelo's most famous works is the sculpture, Pietà.

On a sheet of paper, write the letter of the answer that correctly completes each sentence.

1. Michelangelo was a fine painter, _____, poet, and architect.

    A engineer   **B** scientist   **C** explorer   **D** sculptor

2. Michelangelo studied _____, which helped to make his art so lifelike.

    A Middle Age art   **C** math books
    B the human body   **D** buildings

3. Lorenzo de' Medici, a wealthy Italian, noted young Michelangelo's artistic brilliance and became his _____.

    A patron   **B** scholar   **C** apprentice   **D** master

4. Michelangelo worked on _____ for four years.

    A *David*   **C** St. Peter's Church
    B the Sistine Chapel   **D** *Pietà*

5. Later in life, Michelangelo accepted no money when he worked to rebuild _____.

    A *David*   **C** St. Peter's Church
    B the Sistine Chapel   **D** *Pietà*

On a sheet of paper, write the answer to each question. Use complete sentences.

6. Where did the Renaissance begin and where did it spread to?

7. What led Renaissance artists to make the people in their art so lifelike?

8. Compare and contrast art in the Middle Ages with that of the Renaissance.

9. What is the role of a patron?

10. What are three famous works of art crafted by Michelangelo?

Advances in Knowledge, Technology, and Science

Objectives

■ To tell how the invention of movable type helped the spread of knowledge

■ To tell about four other inventions that were discovered during the Renaissance

■ To name four important people of the Renaissance

■ To explain why Galileo was in trouble with the church

Reading Strategy:
Inferencing

What can you infer about people's decision to learn how to read at this time?

Remember
Latin, the language of ancient Rome, became the language of the church. Rome was the first place that made Christianity its official religion.

All writing was done by hand during the Middle Ages. Books were copied on parchment made of animal skin. Therefore, books were beautiful, but they were also expensive and few in number. Only wealthy people could buy books of their own. Most books were written in Latin, the language of the church. The only scholars were clergy. The church was the main place where studying went on. The church controlled all learning.

Then things started to change.

How Did the Printing Press Help the Spread of Knowledge?

About 1450, secrets of making paper were brought to Europe from China. They were introduced by the Moors, or Spanish Muslims. Then a new invention eventually made books available to everyone! A German printer named Johannes Gutenberg discovered how to use movable type for printing.

With movable type, letters were molded onto small metal blocks. The letters could be moved around to spell different words. When inked and pressed onto paper, the movable type printed a whole page at one time.

Now books could be made quickly at low cost. Now many people could read the stories of the Greeks and Romans and tales of travel. The ideas of the past and the present were widely available. Books were translated into the languages of the common people, not just that of Latin scholars.

History Fact
The famous *Gutenberg Bible* was not discovered until 1760. It was found in Paris.

With the *Gutenberg Bible* Europeans could read the Bible for themselves. People did not have to rely on the church to tell them what the Bible said. The Bible was translated into English, Italian, French, and German.

It became important to be able to read. More schools opened. Schools that taught Greek and Latin grammar were called "grammar" schools. There were new universities. Studies went beyond religious thought. People studied the world. They also studied about their own place in the world.

What Were Some Other Inventions?

The Renaissance was a time for progress. There were some important changes during the Middle Ages. However, change had come slowly. Now new books—and new ideas—were available for anyone who could read. Universities were growing. With the spirit of the Renaissance, change came rapidly.

People explored new ideas. Gutenberg's printing press was just one of the new inventions. Inventors discovered how to make springs. Then they made watches that were small enough to be carried in a pocket. Before, the only clocks had been huge ones on public buildings. Now people could keep time at home.

New instruments helped sailors find their way on the open seas. New maps improved travel. People experimented with metals. Soon they came up with cast iron to replace expensive bronze.

In medicine, the English doctor William Harvey discovered that the heart pumps blood throughout the body. Around 1600, the microscope was invented. It led to a new look at the world. Suddenly people learned that there were tiny creatures—smaller than the eye could see!

Words from the Past

Newspapers Are Born

When Gutenberg invented movable metal type in the 15th century, printing became easier and cheaper. As a result, newspapers were born. Their purpose was to report news and information to people.

Early newspapers were small. They looked like newsletters. Papers usually consisted of one page. They were published weekly, not daily.

The first known newspaper started in Germany in 1609. It told about events in other countries. The first London paper began in 1622. Then in 1665, The *London News Gazette* started. It was published on a regular basis in newspaper format. The *Boston News-Letter* was the first continuously published American newspaper. It began in 1704. Like papers today, it had news about money and other countries. It also recorded births, deaths, and social events.

Astronomer

A person who keeps track of the sun, the planets, and the stars

Theory

An explanation of how and why something happens, usually based on scientific study

Reading Strategy:
Inferencing

What do you already know about the beginnings of the study of astronomy?

You Decide
Why do you think people were not willing to believe Copernicus?

What Did Scientists Suggest Was at the Center of the Universe?

Some of the greatest scientific discoveries of the Renaissance came in the field of astronomy. Astronomy is the study of the stars, planets, and other heavenly bodies. These new ideas changed people's thinking in many ways. Not only were there new ideas about the way the earth and stars moved. Now there was also a new way of seeing humanity's place in the whole system. These ideas shook up the scientific world as well as the church.

For hundreds of years people had believed that the earth was the center of the universe. They believed that the sun, moon, and stars all moved around the earth. Then, in 1543, the Polish **astronomer** Nicolaus Copernicus wrote a book. He said that the planets, including the earth, revolve around the sun.

Most people would not believe him!

Who Was Galileo Galilei?

The invention of the telescope challenged more old ideas. Now scientists could get a better look at the sky. An Italian scientist, Galileo Galilei, took up where Copernicus had left off. Galileo was born in Pisa in 1564. He made his first important scientific discovery at the age of 20. Galileo watched a great lamp swing from the ceiling of the cathedral in Pisa. Then he came up with the idea of the pendulum. A pendulum is a weight hung so that it swings freely back and forth.

Later, he discovered the "law of falling bodies." Galileo found that gravity pulls all bodies to the earth at the same speed, no matter what their weight. Galileo climbed to the top of the Leaning Tower of Pisa to prove his **theory**. Then he dropped a ten-pound weight and a one-pound weight. He showed that they both hit the ground at the same time.

Some people were angry. They were shocked that Galileo would dare to challenge the ideas of the wise Greek, Aristotle. Galileo's discoveries would bring him a lot of angry words.

The invention of the telescope brought another breakthrough. Galileo was not its inventor, but he was the first to use the telescope to study the heavens. With his telescope, Galileo discovered that the moon did not have its own light. It reflected light. He discovered moons around Jupiter and the mass of stars in the Milky Way. All of Galileo's discoveries led him to support Copernicus's theory. The earth was not the center of the universe. The earth was just another planet revolving around the sun!

No matter how well Galileo proved his theory, the church would not hear of it. Church members were ordered not to read Galileo's books. The church sent Galileo warnings. He was not to teach his theories. In 1632, Galileo was called to a church hearing. There was a long trial. Galileo had to promise that he would give up his belief in Copernicus's theory. The church forced him to say that the earth was the center of the universe. Church officials watched Galileo closely for the rest of his life. He became a prisoner in his own home.

Galileo first used the telescope to search the night sky. His discoveries changed the way people thought about the universe.

Match the description in Column A with the inventor/scientist in Column B. Write the correct letter on a sheet of paper.

Column A

1. invented the microscope

2. wrote a book that said the planets revolve around the Sun

3. the inventor of the printing press

4. a scientist who came up with ideas about gravity and the pendulum

Column B

A Nicolaus Copernicus
B Galileo Galilei
C Johannes Gutenberg
D William Harvey

On a sheet of paper, write the letter of the answer that correctly completes each sentence.

5. The Renaissance was a time for _____.

   A self-reflection   **C** religious worship
   B progress   **D** advancements in farming

6. Many of the greatest scientific studies during the Renaissance came in the field of _____. This is the study of stars, planets, and other heavenly bodies.

   A astronomy   **B** the human body **C** engineering   **D** humanism

7. People were angry that Galileo would challenge the ideas of _____.

   A Copernicus   **B** Michelangelo   **C** William Harvey **D** Aristotle

On a sheet of paper, write the answer to each question. Use complete sentences.

8. How did movable type help the spread of knowledge?

9. What are four other inventions, besides the printing press, that were discovered during the Renaissance?

10. Why was Galileo in trouble with the church?

The Renaissance Man

■ To explain the ways in which Leonardo da Vinci is a Renaissance Man

■ To name three things Leonardo da Vinci is famous for

Leonardo da Vinci's sketchbook contains his ideas for machines. Da Vinci was one of the greatest inventors of all time.

The great artists, writers, and scientists of the Renaissance had many kinds of knowledge, talents, and skills. Michelangelo could paint, sculpt, write poetry, and build. Galileo studied medicine, physics, and astronomy.

Today we think of a Renaissance man as one who was expected to enjoy art, to write poetry, and to play a musical instrument. Renaissance education taught people to read and write Latin and to speak several other languages. People were expected to understand the politics of the day. They were supposed to ride well on horseback and to be good at sports.

A Renaissance man should be able to put up a good fight if necessary. A Renaissance man also had to learn proper manners of courtesy and grace. Great importance was placed on being well educated and well rounded. A perfect example of a Renaissance man was Leonardo da Vinci.

Who Was Leonardo da Vinci?

A list of what Leonardo da Vinci could not do would likely be shorter than a list of what he could do! Italian-born Leonardo was a Renaissance genius in not one field, but many. He was one of the world's greatest artists and scientists. Leonardo was a painter, a sculptor, an architect, and a musician. He was an inventor, an astronomer, and a geologist (he studied the history of the earth). He was one of the first to show an interest in "flying machines."

Leonardo's sketchbooks show drawings of many different machines. His ideas for flying machines were based on the flight of birds. These sketches also show great understanding of the human body and of engineering.

The Mona Lisa *by Leonardo da Vinci.*

Reading Strategy:
Inferencing

After reading this section, what inferences can you make about Leonardo's contributions? What words helped you make your inference?

Leonardo had a sure sense of the way things worked. He understood the way parts joined together to form a whole. This great knowledge helped make him such a good artist.

Leonardo's *Mona Lisa* is a painting of a woman with a mysterious smile. It is one of the world's most famous masterpieces. Today it hangs in the Louvre Museum in Paris, France.

For 17 years Leonardo served the Duke of Milan. He worked as a painter, a sculptor, and an engineer. He was then hired as a painter by the government of Florence. For the last two years of his life, he lived in France at the invitation of King Francis I.

Leonardo, the Renaissance man, used one talent to benefit another. His scientific studies helped him understand people and the world. This understanding made his paintings seem all the more real. He had a desire to know more about everything. It was curiosity like Leonardo's that made the Renaissance a time of new ideas and new inventions.

TECHNOLOGY CONNECTION

Parachutes

Leonardo da Vinci imagined and sketched the parachute in 1514. His design called for a stiff frame shaped like a pyramid. The frame was then covered with a cloth. The cloth was coated to prevent a lot of air from passing through it. In his notes he had said that with his design, a person could safely jump from any height. Da Vinci also had thoughts about flight. Da Vinci's ideas are considered to have come about 400 years "ahead of their time."

A Croatian named Faust Vrancic built a device based on da Vinci's drawing. He jumped from a Venice tower using the parachute in 1617. A French physicist named Louis Sebastien Lenormand is usually credited for inventing the parachute. He made a successful jump from a Paris tower in 1783. Perhaps he gets noticed most often because he coined the word "parachute."

REVIEW

On a sheet of paper, write the answer to each question. Use complete sentences.

1. What is a Renaissance man?

2. Name a perfect example of a Renaissance man.

3. What fields did Leonardo da Vinci experiment in?

On a sheet of paper, write the word from the Word Bank to complete each sentence correctly.

Word Bank

artist

Duke of Milan

France

Mona Lisa

painter

sketchbooks

talent

4. Leonardo was such a great _____ because he understood the way things worked.

5. Leonardo's _____ had drawings for flying machines.

6. The _____ is the painting Leonardo is most famous for.

7. Leonardo served the _____ for 17 years as a painter, sculptor, and engineer.

8. He was also hired as a(n) _____ by the government of Florence.

9. Leonardo lived in _____ the last two years of his life.

10. As a Renaissance man, Leonardo used one _____ to benefit another.

The Reformation

■ To explain what the Reformation was
■ To name two leaders of the Reformation
■ To describe the Inquisition

Reformation
A movement that challenged and changed the Catholic religion in Europe

During the Middle Ages, most of the people in Western Europe were Roman Catholics. The Catholic Church held great power. It owned lands and collected taxes. Popes, bishops, and priests were wealthy men.

During the Renaissance, more people went to school and learned to read. They began to question many things, including the ways of the church.

Was it right for the clergy to be so interested in wealth? Was it right that church officials should have so much power? Some people also questioned the ceremonies and rituals that filled church services. They wondered what had become of the simple ways taught by Jesus.

The movement that questioned the practices of the Catholic Church was called the **Reformation**. Some Europeans set out to reform, or change, the church.

Martin Luther led the Reformation that set out to change the Catholic Church.

Who Was Martin Luther?

A German monk named Martin Luther became a leader among the reformers. Luther was born a German peasant. He grew up as a Roman Catholic. He studied at a university and became a monk. The more Luther studied religion, however, the more he worried. His concern was that the Catholic Church was headed in the wrong direction.

A person did not need fancy rituals or pilgrimages to find God, Luther said. He began to criticize the Catholic Church in public sermons. In 1517, Martin Luther wrote a list of 95 complaints about the church. He nailed it to the door of the Castle Church in Wittenberg, Germany.

Reading Strategy: Inferencing

What can you infer about the way different types of people reacted to Luther?

Luther continued to question church practices. In 1521, he spoke out against the power and **authority** granted the pope. This did not please the pope. Luther was told to recant, or take back, what he had said. Luther refused. He said that unless the Bible itself proved him wrong, he would not recant.

Luther was thrown out of the Catholic Church. Emperor Charles V declared Luther an outlaw. He said that anyone could kill Luther without punishment.

Several German princes supported Luther and his feelings about the church. One prince hid him in a castle. The church could not take him prisoner. Soon Luther had so many supporters that before long he was able to set up a whole new church.

The new church, based on Luther's ideas, simplified religion. Religious practices would be based on what was found in the Bible. In 1529, the Catholic Church declared that no one should practice **Lutheranism.** Lutheran princes decided to speak out, or protest. Because of this, they were called **Protestants.**

Other leaders across Europe also protested against Catholic practice. Other Protestant churches were started. The Reformation was under way.

What Was the Inquisition?

A man named John Calvin developed his own version of Protestantism in Switzerland, called Calvinism. He set up strict rules for Christians to live by. Calvin's teachings were followed in many parts of Europe.

History Fact

The Inquisition held secret trials, and people on trial were not told who their accusers were.

French Calvinists were called Huguenots. However, most French people were Catholic. They began to resent the Huguenots. On St. Bartholomew's Day, in August 1572, the Catholics carried out a plot. They murdered all the Protestants they could find in the city of Paris. The killing then spread throughout France. Thousands died during the next few days.

In Spain, the **Inquisition** was at work. The Inquisition was a special court set up by the Roman Catholic Church. Its purpose was to punish people who spoke out against the teachings of the church, or **heretics.** Besides Spain, the Inquisition was also going on in France, Germany, and Italy. The Inquisition hunted down anyone who was not a practicing Catholic. It forced people to confess their beliefs, often by torturing them. Some of those who would not accept the Catholic faith were burned to death.

On a sheet of paper, write the answer to each question. Use complete sentences.

1. What were Martin Luther's complaints about the church?

2. What happened in Paris on St. Bartholomew's Day in August 1572?

3. What is a heretic?

4. What was the Inquisition?

On a sheet of paper, write the letter of the answer that correctly completes each sentence.

5. As people became more educated during the Renaissance, they began to question many things. In particular, they questioned the ways of the _____.

   A government   B church   C family   D universities

6. The movement that questioned the practices of the Catholic Church is known as _____.

   A Protestants   B Lutheranism   C the Reformation   D Calvinism

7. Luther was thrown out of the Catholic Church and declared a(n) _____.

   A pope   B monk   C scholar   D outlaw

8. After the Catholic Church banned the practice of Lutheranism, Lutherans began to complain. They became known as _____.

   A Protestants   B Huguenots   C Calvinists   D Reformists

9. The people in France who followed John Calvin's teaching were called _____.

   A Protestants   B Huguenots   C Catholics   D Lutherans

10. Some people who denied their beliefs to the Catholic faith were burned to death. This time was known as the _____.

   A Inquisition   B Middle Ages   C Crusades   D early 1400s

The Counter-Reformation

Many people who wanted change had turned away from the Catholic Church. Others hoped to make changes within the church itself. The movement for reform within the Catholic Church was called the **Counter-Reformation.** It is also known as the Catholic Reformation.

What Was the Council of Trent?

In 1545, the pope called a meeting of clergy at Trent in Italy. The Council of Trent looked for ways to keep the Catholic Church from losing followers. The Council clearly spelled out the beliefs of the church and insisted that people obey them. To reawaken faith among the people, church leaders approved of some new religious orders. One of these was the Society of Jesus.

The Council of Trent was formed to help reawaken faith among Catholics.

Inferencing

Consider what you know about what happened with the Counter-Reformation. Then make an inference about why it happened.

Who Was St. Ignatius Loyola?

St. Ignatius Loyola was one of the most powerful leaders of the Counter-Reformation. Once a Spanish soldier, Loyola was crippled when a cannonball hit his leg. While recovering, he read a book about the life of Jesus. He decided to begin a spiritual life. He studied to become a priest at the University of Paris.

In 1534, Loyola gathered six followers and formed the Society of Jesus. Its members were called Jesuits. The society quickly gained more members. Their mission was to win Protestants back to the Catholic Church. The Jesuit order, with ex-soldier Loyola at its head, was run much like an army.

The Jesuits stopped the spread of Protestantism in Europe. However, they carried Catholic ideas to far-off lands. When Loyola died in 1556, the Jesuit order was well established.

Throughout the Reformation, Catholics and Protestants competed for religious control of Europe. The kings and queens of Spain, England, and France became caught up in the struggles of the Reformation. Religion played an important part in shaping Europe's history.

TIMELINE STUDY:

THE RENAISSANCE

When was a council held to reform the Catholic Church?

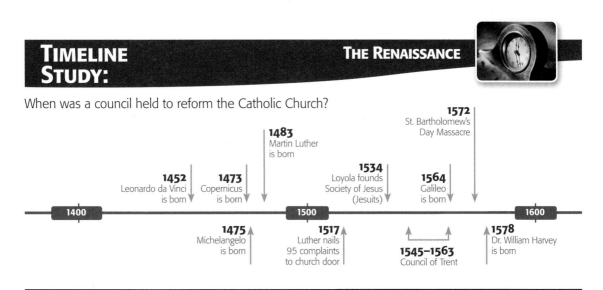

1452 Leonardo da Vinci is born

1473 Copernicus is born

1483 Martin Luther is born

1534 Loyola founds Society of Jesus (Jesuits)

1564 Galileo is born

1572 St. Bartholomew's Day Massacre

1400

1500

1600

1475 Michelangelo is born

1517 Luther nails 95 complaints to church door

1545–1563 Council of Trent

1578 Dr. William Harvey is born

REVIEW

On a sheet of paper, write the answer to each question. Use complete sentences.

1. What was the Counter-Reformation?

2. What was the purpose of the Council of Trent?

3. What was the purpose of the Jesuits?

Word Bank

Catholic ideas

Europe

Italy

Paris

religion

Society of Jesus

St. Ignatius Loyola

On a sheet of paper, write the word from the Word Bank to complete each sentence correctly.

4. The 1545 meeting of clergy at Trent was in _____.

5. Church leaders at the Council of Trent approved a new religious order. The purpose of the _____ was to reawaken faith among the people.

6. One of the most powerful leaders of the Counter-Reformation was _____.

7. Loyola studied to become a priest at the University of _____.

8. The Jesuits stopped the spread of Protestantism in _____.

9. The Jesuits also carried _____ to other lands.

10. _____ played an important part in shaping Europe's history.

SUMMARY

- Renaissance means "rebirth" or "awakening."

- Renaissance Europeans were interested in the art and ideas of the ancient Greeks and Romans.

- The spread of humanism sparked new ideas.

- During the Renaissance, great work was done in art and science. More books became available to more people.

- Human beings were considered important, and the human form in pictures and statues became realistic.

- Michelangelo was a brilliant painter and sculptor of the Renaissance.

- Scientist Galileo's theories caused trouble with the church. He was the first person to use the telescope to study the sky.

- Leonardo da Vinci was known for his many inventions and works of art.

- During the Renaissance, some people began to question the practices of the Catholic Church. Martin Luther led the Reformation.

- People who protested against the Catholic Church were called Protestants.

- Protestants and Roman Catholics competed for the control of Europe.

- The Catholic Church wanted to make changes within the Church itself. This was known as the Counter-Reformation.

Word Bank

astronomer

authority

criticized

heretic

humanism

masterpiece

patron

Renaissance

sculptor

theory

Vocabulary Review

On a sheet of paper, use the words from the Word Bank to complete each sentence correctly.

1. A wealthy person who helps an artist is a(n) _____.

2. *Pietà* was Michelangelo's first _____.

3. Among many other things, Michelangelo was a fine _____.

4. Leonardo da Vinci is a perfect example of a(n) _____ man. It seemed as if there was nothing he could not do.

5. A scientific explanation of why something happens is a(n) _____.

6. Copernicus was a(n) _____. He wrote a book that said the planets—including the earth—revolved around the sun.

7. Martin Luther _____ the Catholic Church.

8. A person who is against certain church teachings is often called a(n) _____.

9. The belief in the importance of human beings is called _____.

10. Luther did not like the power and _____ granted the pope.

Chapter Review Questions

On a sheet of paper, write the answer to each question. Use complete sentences.

11. Where did the Renaissance begin?

12. What is the meaning of the word *Renaissance*?

Test Tip

If you do not know the answer to a question, put a check beside it and go on. Then when you are finished, go back to any checked questions and try to answer them.

13. How was the art of the Renaissance different from the art of the Middle Ages?

14. What changes did the invention of movable type bring about?

15. How did the church react to Galileo's discovery?

16. Who were Martin Luther and John Calvin?

Critical Thinking

On a sheet of paper, write your response to each question. Use complete sentences.

17. How were the Reformation and the Counter-Reformation similar and yet different?

18. During the Renaissance, a well-rounded person was admired. Do you think the same thing is true today? Why or why not?

Using the Timeline

Use the timeline on page 279 to answer the questions.

19. Who was born first, Leonardo da Vinci or Michelangelo?

20. What event shows that some Protestants died for their faith?

GROUP ACTIVITY

Work in a small group to create a biographical dictionary of important people of the Renaissance. If possible, include copies of their works or pictures of their inventions. Be sure to tell why each person was important during the Renaissance and after.

Kings and Queens

The borders of kingdoms were growing clearer. As this happened, the people living in them started feeling a sense of a homeland. People in different lands developed their own customs and languages. In Europe, most of those languages came from Latin.

Monarchs, the kings and queens of these early lands, wanted power. They often gained power by getting more land and goods, and controlling more people. Politics and religion were closely linked to one another. People, and the nations they loved, were certain to change by the power of religion.

GOALS FOR LEARNING

- To describe a country under monarch rule
- To explain the religious goal of the Spanish monarchs
- To describe what King Henry IV did to keep the peace in France
- To explain the struggle between the Catholics and Protestants in England

Reading Strategy: Metacognition

Metacognition means being aware of the way you learn. Use metacognition to become a better reader.

- Write the main idea, details, and any questions you have.

- Make predictions and ask yourself what you already know about the topic.

- Visualize what is happening in the text. If something does not make sense, go back and read it again.

- Summarize what you have read and make inferences about the meaning.

Key Vocabulary Words

Lesson 1

Monarch A ruler, like a king, queen, or emperor

Nationalism Love of one's nation; patriotism

Decline A period of increasing weakness

Lesson 2

Reign The rule of a monarch; to rule as a king, queen, or emperor

Fleet A group of warships under one command

Armada A large fleet of warships

Lesson 3

Massacre The act of killing many people who are often defenseless

Edict A public order by some authority

Lesson 4

Annul To cancel; to make something no longer binding under law

Parliament England's body of lawmakers

Rule by Monarchs

Objectives

■ To explain what a monarch is

■ To name and explain the two powerful forces that shaped 16th-century Europe

Reading Strategy:
Metacognition

Notice the structure of this chapter before you begin reading. Look at the titles, headings, and boldfaced words.

Monarch
A ruler, like a king, queen, or emperor

Nationalism
Love of one's nation; patriotism

Decline
A period of increasing weakness

Spain, France, and England had each become unified into nation-states. Now a separate government ruled each of these three lands. The rulers were **monarchs**—kings and queens who held power over a whole nation.

What Is a Country Under Monarch Rule Like?

The people of each nation were loyal to their rulers. They felt a bond with their country and with each other. Within a country everyone spoke similar languages and followed similar customs. This feeling of pride and loyalty toward one's nation is called **nationalism.** Nationalism and religious beliefs became important. Both were powerful forces that shaped 16th-century European history.

The monarchs of Spain, France, and England followed different religious teachings. Some were Roman Catholics. Some were Protestants. One ruler even started his own church. Because of their separate beliefs, the monarchs led their people into wars. They led them through times of peace, cultural growth, and **declines** (periods of increasing weakness).

The history of each nation affected each of the others. The religions and the personalities of the monarchs changed the lives of the people of Western Europe.

Queen Mary I was one of the many monarchs that ruled England during the 16th century.

REVIEW

Match the definition in Column A with the term in Column B. Write the correct letter on a sheet of paper.

Column A

1. love of one's nation; patriotism

2. a period of decreasing weakness

3. a ruler, like a king, queen, or emperor

Column B

A decline

B monarch

C nationalism

Word Bank

customs

decline

loyal

monarchs

nationalism

religious beliefs

Spain

On a sheet of paper, write the word from the Word Bank to complete each sentence correctly.

4. France, _____, and England are three nation-states that had monarchs in Europe during the 16th-century.

5. People were _____ to their ruler and nation.

6. Within a country, everyone spoke similar languages and followed similar _____.

7. _____ and religious beliefs were both powerful forces that shaped 16th-century European history.

8. The _____ of Western Europe followed different religious teachings.

9. Because of the different _____, the monarchs often led their people into war.

10. Monarchs ruled through times of peace, growth, and _____.

Spanish Monarchs

Reign
The rule of a monarch; to rule as a king, queen, or emperor

Reading Strategy: Metacognition

Remember to ask yourself questions about specific people as you read about them. This will help you make sure you understand what you are reading.

In the late 1400s, King Ferdinand and Queen Isabella ruled Spain. They were Roman Catholics. They wanted no one but Roman Catholics living in their nation.

There were not many Protestants in Spain, but there were Jews and Muslims. Spanish Muslims were called Moors. Ferdinand and Isabella called upon the Inquisition to hunt down anyone who was not Catholic. Many Jews and Moors were tortured and killed. Those who were lucky enough to escape the Inquisition had to flee the country. The Jews left for other European countries and the Middle East. Many of the Moors fled to North Africa.

What Was King Philip's Goal?

King Philip II ruled Spain from 1556 until 1598. He began his rule as the most powerful monarch in all of Europe. At that time, Spain was the strongest European nation. It held many other provinces. Spain controlled rich colonies in the Americas. However, Philip's **reign**, or rule as a monarch, marked the beginning of Spain's decline.

Like Ferdinand and Isabella, Philip II was a Catholic. He also supported the Inquisition and its methods. King Philip saw himself as a man with a job to do.

He wanted to see not only Spain, but all of Europe, under the Catholic Church. King Philip's goal was to crush Protestantism.

You Decide

Do you think that Ferdinand and Isabella were wise rulers? Why or why not?

Reading Strategy: Metacognition

Note the main idea and important details about Philip II. Summarize what you read to make sure you understand it.

Geography Note

Andorra, located between France and Spain, is one of the smallest countries in Europe. It covers only about 181 square miles (468 square km) of land. Beginning in 1278, Andorra was governed by both a French count and a Spanish bishop. In 1505, after the death of Isabella, Spain's King Ferdinand married the daughter of the French count. He brought Andorra under the rule of Spain.

Why Did the Dutch People Rebel Against King Philip and Spain?

Spain ruled the Netherlands. Many Protestants lived there. Philip II would not stand for Protestants living under his rule. He issued a royal command: "People of the Netherlands will accept the Catholic religion!"

Philip did not count on the spirit of the Dutch people. They wanted to worship as they chose. Even the Dutch who were Catholics did not like King Philip. He was a Spaniard, not Dutch. He expected them to send too much tax money to Spain.

The proud people of the Netherlands rebelled. A Dutch prince, William of Orange, led the rebellion in 1568. Things looked grim. However, the Dutch would not give in to Spain. In 1581, the Dutch declared independence. The Netherlands was on its way to freedom from Philip and from Spain.

What Was Preventing Europe from Uniting Under Catholicism?

King Philip was not alone in his dream of a Catholic Europe. Before he became king, Philip had married Queen Mary I of England. Mary was a loyal Catholic, too. She hoped to see all Protestants converted to Catholicism.

That was not to be. Queen Mary only reigned for five years. When she died, the English throne went to her Protestant half-sister, Elizabeth. Although Philip had been her brother-in-law, Elizabeth saw him as England's enemy. She sent aid to the Netherlands in its fight for freedom from Spain. She gave English ships permission to attack Spanish ships on the world's seas. Queen Elizabeth I was definitely getting in the way of Philip's plans to unite Europe under Catholicism.

Fleet

A group of warships under one command

Armada

A large fleet of warships

By defeating the Spanish Armada, England's navy ruled the seas.

LEARN MORE ABOUT IT

The Spanish Armada

King Philip II decided to go to war with England. Philip built up a mighty **fleet,** or a group of warships under one command. It was called the **Armada.** The Armada was the largest fleet of ships that Europe had ever seen. In 1588, 130 Spanish ships set out against England. They were giant ships. There were crosses on their billowing sails. King Philip thought that his Armada could not be beaten.

The Armada reached the English Channel. English ships sailed out to meet it. The English ships were much smaller than the Spanish ships. At first it looked as if they would not stand a chance. However, the English crafts were fast. They could dart among the heavy Spanish galleons (large sailing ships with many decks), firing from all sides. The English had skilled captains like Sir Francis Drake. They kept

King Philip's Armada busy. The Spanish giants could not stop the quick, little English ships.

The fighting lasted for more than a week. Most of the Spanish ships were damaged. The crippled Armada fled to the North Sea. It escaped the English by sailing north around the British Isles. Heavy winds wrecked many ships off the coast of Ireland. What was left of Philip's once-glorious Armada headed back to Spain. Only 67 ships returned home.

Philip's dream of a Catholic Europe ended with the destruction (defeat) of his Armada. He had lost many soldiers. The Armada had cost Spain much money. Instead of conquering Europe, King Philip had sent Spain into a decline.

By defeating the Spanish Armada, England's navy ruled the seas.

On a sheet of paper, write the answer to each question. Use complete sentences.

1. What did the Spanish Inquisition do to the Moors and Jews in Spain?

2. What was the goal of King Philip II of Spain?

3. What happened to the Spanish Armada when it reached the English Channel?

On a sheet of paper, write the letter of the answer that correctly completes each sentence.

4. King Philip would not stand for Protestants living under his rule in _____.

   A Portugal   **B** the Netherlands   **C** the West Indies   **D** England

5. William of Orange led the Dutch rebellion in 1568. In 1581, the Dutch declared _____.

   A independence   **B** a democracy   **C** war   **D** peace

6. King Philip of Spain married Queen Mary I of _____.

   A Portugal   **B** the Netherlands   **C** Italy   **D** England

7. Both King Philip and _____ wanted all Protestants to convert to Catholicism.

   A William of Orange **B** Elizabeth   **C** Queen Mary   **D** Henry VIII

8. Elizabeth, who took the throne from her half-sister Mary, saw _____ as England's enemy.

   A the Netherlands   **C** the Catholic Church
   B King Philip   **D** William of Orange

9. King Philip's dream of a Catholic Europe ended with the destruction of the _____.

   A Protestant Church **B** Catholic Church   **C** Armada   **D** Inquisition

10. Rather than conquering Europe, King Philip sent _____ into a decline.

    A England   **B** the Netherlands   **C** Spain   **D** France

French Monarchs

Objectives

■ To tell why King Henry IV converted to Catholicism

■ To name the good things that Henry IV did for France

Reading Strategy:
Metacognition

Before reading, think about what you can do to help you better understand the text.

Massacre
The act of killing many people who are often defenseless

Edict
A public order by some authority

France had problems of its own. There, too, wars broke out because of religion. Civil wars had torn the country apart for more than 30 years. The Protestant Reformation had started all the trouble. French Protestants, the Huguenots, fought the Catholics. King Philip of Spain and the pope supported the Catholics. England's Queen Elizabeth sent aid to the Huguenots.

In 1572, thousands of Protestants died in the **massacre** on St. Bartholomew's Day.

France's Catholic king was assassinated in 1589. Before he died, he named Henry of Navarre as the next king. Henry of Navarre became King Henry IV. Henry IV was a Huguenot!

What Did King Henry Do for France?

The French Catholics were in an uproar. A Huguenot was king! Henry IV had to fight to keep his throne. He won several battles, but he could not bring peace. The French, especially those in Paris, would not accept a Protestant as king.

To keep the peace, Henry IV declared himself a Catholic. Most French people welcomed this move. Henry IV was then officially crowned king of France. At last he was able to restore peace to the country.

Yet King Henry IV did not turn his back on the Huguenots. In 1598 he issued a public order, the **Edict** of Nantes. This gave religious freedom to the French Protestants. It was better, Henry said, than seeing France torn apart by civil war.

King Henry turned out to be a good king. Once there was religious peace, Henry worked hard to make France rich and strong. He passed laws to help the farmers. He built new roads. He also encouraged trade and manufacturing.

King Henry sent French explorers out on the seas. Under Henry's reign, the first French colony was founded in North America. It was called Quebec. Feelings of nationalism grew. The French called their king "Good King Henry."

Their "good king" was assassinated in 1610. However, the religious freedoms that he had brought to France lasted long after his death.

Thousands of Protestants died in the St. Bartholomew's Day massacre in 1572.

Lesson 14-3

Review

Word Bank

assassinated
Catholic
Edict of Nantes
Huguenot
massacre
Protestant Reformation
Quebec
religious freedoms
rich
trade

On a sheet of paper, write the word from the Word Bank to complete each sentence correctly.

1. The _____ started the civil wars in France.
2. Thousands of Protestants died in the _____ on St. Bartholomew's Day in 1572.
3. French Catholics were upset that King Henry IV was named king. This is because he was a(n) _____.
4. King Henry declared himself a(n) _____ to keep the peace.
5. King Henry issued the _____ that gave religious freedom to the French Protestants.
6. King Henry was a good king who made France _____ and strong.
7. King Henry passed laws to help farmers, built new roads, and encouraged _____ and manufacturing.
8. King Henry founded the first French colony in North America and named it _____.
9. King Henry was _____ in 1610.
10. The _____ that King Henry had brought to France lasted long after his death.

English Monarchs

Objectives

■ To explain why King Henry VIII set up a Church of England

■ To compare life under "The Boy King" with that of "Bloody Mary"

■ To explain why the English people called Queen Elizabeth "Good Queen Bess"

■ To describe life in the Elizabethan Age

Reading Strategy: Metacognition

Make a prediction to tell what you think will happen next. Check your prediction as you read this section and revise if needed.

In England in 1485, a man named Henry Tudor became King Henry VII. His reign ended years of civil war. He was the first of several monarchs from the Tudor family.

Henry VII was not a very colorful character, but he was well-liked. He kept England out of wars. He was good with business matters and built up the country's economy. King Henry VII saw to it that everyone, especially the nobles, paid their taxes.

When Henry VII died in 1509, his son became king of England. King Henry VIII was the second Tudor monarch. He had a more colorful personality than his father. He is well remembered for having six wives.

Why Did King Henry VIII Set Up a Church of England?

The story of Henry VIII and his wives involves religion. To begin with, Henry VIII was a Catholic. The people liked him. His father had been a good king. The new King Henry seemed good humored and kind.

Problems began when Henry no longer wanted to be married to his wife, Catherine of Aragon. Catherine had only been able to have one child. That child was a girl, the princess Mary, who later married King Philip of Spain. Henry wanted a son to follow him on the throne.

Henry showed an interest in Anne Boleyn. She had been one of his wife's maids of honor. Anne, he thought, was beautiful. She would make him a fine wife. She also might give him a son.

Annul

To cancel; to make something no longer binding under law

Parliament

England's body of lawmakers

Reading Strategy: Metacognition

Remember to look at the timelines and illustrations. Also take note of the descriptive words. This will help you visualize what you are reading.

King Henry asked the pope to **annul**, or consent to end, his marriage to Catherine. The pope refused, so Henry VIII took matters into his own hands. In secret he married Anne Boleyn in 1533. His marriage to Catherine was annulled by the man who would become the Archbishop of Canterbury. Henry then broke with the Roman Catholic Church. In 1534, England's body of lawmakers, the **Parliament**, passed a law. The law made Henry the head of the Church of England.

The new Church of England was still Catholic in its practices and beliefs. However, it was not subject to any control by Rome. Henry's break with the church increased his own power and wealth. He seized all the lands, all the gold, and all the silver that had belonged to the Roman Catholic Church in England.

Things did not go so well for King Henry VIII and his new wife, Anne Boleyn. Like Catherine, Anne gave him a daughter, the princess Elizabeth. However, Henry still wanted a son. He wanted a new wife, too. He accused Anne of being unfaithful. He had her imprisoned in the Tower of London. She was sentenced to death and beheaded in 1536.

Henry married a third wife, Jane Seymour. At last Henry fathered a son, Prince Edward. Henry married again after Jane Seymour died. In fact, he married three more times. One wife, he divorced. Another, he ordered killed. The sixth and last wife outlived Henry.

Who Was "The Boy King"?

Prince Edward was Henry's only son. When Henry died, Edward took the throne of England. He became the monarch Edward VI at the age of nine.

Under Edward's rule, the number of Protestants increased in England. Protestantism became the state religion.

Because Edward was so young, the affairs of his country were handled by his uncle, Duke Edward Seymour.

Edward was called "The Boy King." He died after reigning for only six years. Now two women were next in line for the throne of England. They were Henry VIII's two daughters, Princess Mary and Princess Elizabeth.

Why Was Queen Mary Known as "Bloody Mary"?

Henry's older daughter, Mary, reigned after Edward's death. Queen Mary I was a strong Roman Catholic. She was determined to make England Roman Catholic again. First she struck down all the religious laws passed under Edward VI. She made new laws enforcing Catholicism. Mary married Philip II of Spain. Together they planned to reduce the strength of Protestantism in Europe.

History calls Queen Mary "Bloody Mary." She persecuted Protestants. She had more than 300 Protestants burned to death.

The English Parliament did not like it when Mary married Spain's King Philip. They were afraid of Spanish power. They refused Queen Mary's request to make Catholicism the state religion. Queen Mary I died after reigning for five years. Her spirit was broken because she never saw Protestantism crushed.

TIMELINE STUDY: REIGNS OF THE EUROPEAN MONARCHS: 1450–1650

During Elizabeth I's reign, England was united under what church?

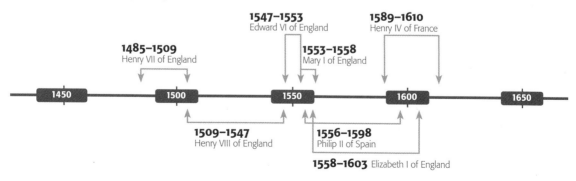

1485–1509
Henry VII of England

1547–1553
Edward VI of England

1553–1558
Mary I of England

1589–1610
Henry IV of France

1450 — 1500 — 1550 — 1600 — 1650

1509–1547
Henry VIII of England

1556–1598
Philip II of Spain

1558–1603 Elizabeth I of England

How Did England Finally Unite?

The next Tudor on the throne of England was Mary's half-sister, Elizabeth. Elizabeth declared that the Church of England was Protestant. The country became firmly united under the one church.

Elizabeth reigned for 45 years, until her death in 1603. Her reign became one of the most glorious periods in English history.

Nationalism grew during Elizabeth's reign. Trouble with Spain only served to strengthen that spirit. England's defeat of the Spanish Armada caused England to cheer.

Queen Elizabeth I did have her faults. She was said to be hot-tempered. She was also called vain. However, the English people loved Elizabeth. Most important, Queen Elizabeth, despite any other faults, loved her England!

Queen Elizabeth I was known as "Good Queen Bess."

Queen Elizabeth never married. Her reign ended the Tudor line. But the English remember her as "Good Queen Bess." She had brought a bright age to England.

What Was Life Like Under Elizabeth?

The reign of Queen Elizabeth became known as the Elizabethan Age. Great writers like William Shakespeare, Edmund Spenser, and Francis Bacon lived in England then. London's Globe Theater was built in 1599. Many of Shakespeare's plays were first performed there.

Elizabeth helped make her people wealthier and England's cities safer. Except for fighting the Spanish Armada, she kept the country out of expensive wars. This left more money to spend on other things. Elizabeth made new laws. The laws gave work to poor people and shelter for those who could not work.

During the Elizabethan Age, ship captains, like Sir Walter Raleigh, brought new products back to England. They brought tobacco and potatoes from America. Daring sailors, like Sir Francis Drake, captured treasures from Spanish ships. In Elizabeth's name, English sailors went out to explore the world.

GREAT NAMES IN HISTORY

William Shakespeare

William Shakespeare (1564–1616) wrote at least 37 plays. *Romeo and Juliet* is about two teenagers from warring families who fall in love. In *Macbeth,* the main character is too ambitious. *Hamlet* is the story of a prince who seeks revenge for his father's death. Although his plays are 400 years old, many are still performed today. Perhaps you have seen one done as a movie.

Many of Shakespeare's plays were first produced in London's Globe Theatre. It has been rebuilt and once again his plays are being performed there. Works by Shakespeare are often seen in major London and New York theaters, too. There are also many Shakespeare festivals. Stratford-upon-Avon, his birthplace, has hosted such an event since 1769.

TIMELINE STUDY:

ENGLAND: 1450–1650

When the Spanish Armada was defeated, who were the monarchs of Spain and England?

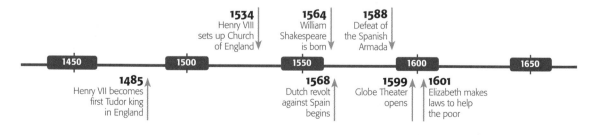

1534 Henry VIII sets up Church of England

1564 William Shakespeare is born

1588 Defeat of the Spanish Armada

1450 — 1500 — 1550 — 1600 — 1650

1485 Henry VII becomes first Tudor king in England

1568 Dutch revolt against Spain begins

1599 Globe Theater opens

1601 Elizabeth makes laws to help the poor

On a sheet of paper, write the letter of the answer that correctly completes each sentence.

1. King Henry VII was the first of several monarchs from the _____ family.

   A English   **B** Seymour   **C** Tudor   **D** Catholic

2. King Henry's son Edward became king at the age of _____.

   A 6   **B** 9   **C** 33   **D** 45

3. Under Edward's rule, _____ was the state religion.

   A Catholicism   **B** Hinduism   **C** Islam   **D** Protestantism

4. Queen Mary I made laws enforcing _____.

   A Catholicism   **B** the monarchy   **C** trade   **D** Protestantism

5. Queen Elizabeth I made the Church of England _____.

   A Catholic   **B** free   **C** Jewish   **D** Protestant

6. During Elizabeth's reign, _____ grew.

   A taxes   **B** civil wars   **C** nationalism   **D** the Armada

7. _____ brought a bright age to England, thus is known as "Good Queen Bess."

   A Catherine   **B** Elizabeth   **C** Anne   **D** Jane

On a sheet of paper, write the answer to each question. Use complete sentences.

8. Why did King Henry VIII set up a Church of England?

9. Why is Queen Mary known as "Bloody Mary"?

10. What was life in the Elizabethan Age like?

- During the 16th century, people throughout Europe developed a new sense of nationalism.

- King Philip II of Spain wanted to make all Europeans Catholic.

- Philip II sent his Armada out to conquer England. However, quicker, smaller English ships sent the Armada home in defeat.

- King Philip's reign sent Spain into a decline.

- The French King Henry IV converted to Catholicism to keep peace in France. Henry IV passed laws giving religious freedom to the Protestants in France.

- The Tudors ruled England from 1485 until 1603.

- King Henry VIII of England broke from the Roman Catholic Church and set up the Church of England.

- After Edward, "The Boy King" died, his sister Mary became queen. She tried to return England to Roman Catholicism by having Protestants put to death.

- The last Tudor monarch was Queen Elizabeth I. Elizabeth made the Church of England Protestant, and she encouraged English nationalism.

- The reign of Elizabeth, which became known as the Elizabethan Age, was one of exploration and relative peace.

- During the Elizabethan Age in England there were many writers who would become famous.

Word Bank

annul

decline

fleet

massacre

monarch

nationalism

Parliament

reign

Vocabulary Review

On a sheet of paper, use the words from the Word Bank to correctly match each definition below.

1. The feeling of pride and loyalty to one's nation

2. A king or queen who holds power over a nation or empire

3. A group of warships under one command

4. The English body of lawmakers

5. A period in which a nation loses strength

6. The act of killing many people who are often defenseless

7. To cancel something as if it had never been

8. The period of time that a monarch rules

Chapter Review Questions

On a sheet of paper, write the answer to each question. Use complete sentences.

9. What are two powerful forces that shaped 16th-century European history?

10. How did the defeat of the Spanish Armada affect England?

11. In what ways was Henry IV a good king of France?

12. Why did Henry VIII of England break with the Roman Catholic Church?

13. What did Henry VII, Henry VIII, Edward VI, Mary I, and Elizabeth I have in common?

14. What was Queen Mary's dream for England?

Test Tip

When studying for a test, learn the most important points. Practice writing this material or explaining it to someone.

15. Why was Queen Elizabeth I called "Good Queen Bess"?

16. In what age did Shakespeare live and write his plays?

Critical Thinking

On a sheet of paper, write your response to each question. Use complete sentences.

17. Which Tudor monarch is the most interesting? Give a reason for your answer.

18. Why did some monarchs want everyone in the nation to belong to one religion?

Using the Timelines

Use the timelines on pages 297 and 299 to answer the questions.

19. For how many years did Henry VIII rule England?

20. Did Elizabeth I make laws to help the poor early or late in her reign?

GROUP ACTIVITY

With your group, practice a scene from one of Shakespeare's plays. Perform it for the rest of the class.

THE AGE OF EXPLORATION AND CONQUEST

People love to go exploring. How excited they may feel at discovering something new, often making it their own. Hundreds of years ago, explorers set out to broaden their horizons—and to become rich and powerful. Discovery often meant conquest, a new group of people found a place and made it their own. Too often this meant that one civilization fell victim to a stronger one. Some of those early civilizations disappeared, except for artifacts found today by archaeologists. Others fought back and continued to live on. Many had a deep effect on the world as it is today.

Chapters in Unit 6

The age of exploration brought together cultures and civilizations that had never crossed paths before.

To the East; To the West

For many centuries the civilizations of the East had no contact with the kingdoms of Europe. As a result, China and Japan were not affected by Great Britain, France, or Spain. This all changed once the traders and missionaries started visiting. The world would start to feel smaller as civilizations became more aware of one another.

Across the ocean from both Europe and Asia lay the Americas. The early people there are thought to have been relatives of those who first settled parts of Asia. These people spread out across the wide open continents they discovered and formed various cultures.

GOALS FOR LEARNING

- To explain how China was advanced even though it was isolated for centuries
- To describe the isolated, feudal society in Japan
- To explain the changes in religion the people of India went through
- To name and describe the early American Indian civilizations

Reading Strategy: Summarizing

When you summarize, you ask questions about what you are reading. That way you can review what you have just read. As you read the text in this chapter, ask yourself these questions:

- What details are most important to the people or this time in history?
- What is the main thing being said about the people?
- What events are pointed out about this time in history?

Key Vocabulary Words

Lesson 1

Forge To work into shape by heating and hammering

Acupuncture Treating pain or illness by putting needles into certain parts of the body

Compass A tool for finding direction by using a magnet

Lesson 2

Samurai A class of warriors in the Japanese feudal system

Privilege A special right given to a person or group

Shogun A great general governing Japan

Enforce To make sure that people follow the laws and rules

Missionary A person sent by a church to other countries to spread a religion

Lesson 4

Mesoamerica The area of North America (including Mexico and Central America) where civilizations developed before Europeans entered the continent

Dweller A person who lives in a place

Advanced Ahead of most others in knowledge, skill, or progress

Terraced Going upward like steps

Barter To trade goods or services without using money

Mosaic A design made by putting together small pieces of colored stone, glass, or other material

China

Objectives

- To name three Chinese inventions
- To explain the Silk Road
- To name the lands conquered by Genghis Khan
- To explain the role Marco Polo played in teaching the Europeans about Chinese discoveries
- To tell what dynasty followed the Mongol rule

Forge
To work into shape by heating and hammering

Acupuncture
Treating pain or illness by putting needles into certain parts of the body

Compass
A tool for finding direction by using a magnet

European nations battled each other. Empires rose and fell. However, Chinese culture continued over the centuries with little change.

What Were Some Things the Chinese Invented?

The Chinese invented many things, but China was isolated. The rest of the world would not learn about Chinese discoveries for hundreds of years. The Chinese kept their secrets.

Papermaking first began during the Han dynasty. The Chinese made paper from wood ash and cloth pulp. The Chinese also knew how to melt iron and how to shape, or **forge,** it. They knew how to mine salt. They learned to use **acupuncture** to cure pain and disease. Later, the Chinese used woodblocks with carved characters to print books. Chinese sailors developed **compasses,** which they used to find their way when on the sea. Gunpowder also was invented in China. It was used first for fireworks. Not until A.D. 1161 were the first explosives used in actual battle.

The Chinese were among the first to use fireworks.

Geography Note

Macao is a province in southeastern China. It is made up of a city on a peninsula in the South China Sea and three nearby islands. The first European known to visit Macao was Vasco da Gama in 1497. The Portuguese established it as a trading port in 1557. The Portuguese paid the Chinese for the use of Macao until 1887 when it became a free port.

History Fact

People still like fine silk cloth. However, today it is made in many places in the world.

TECHNOLOGY CONNECTION

A Gift from the Chinese

A British agricultural advisor named Jethro Tull printed a book of farming methods in 1731. Among many other things, he insisted that planting crops in straight furrows (lines) was the best method. Tull is also thought to be the first European to develop the "seed drill."

However, the Chinese used a seed drill as early as the second century B.C. It was made up of plows that cut furrows in the ground. Seeds were then released from tubes connected to the plows. Then, in a third step, rollers on the plows covered the seeds with dirt. It is believed that visitors to China, probably traders, brought back ideas about farming over many hundreds of years. Eventually, the Europeans presented those ideas as their own.

What Was the Silk Road?

A route known as the *Silk Road* was China's main link to the Western world. A few traders traveled this road. They made their way across deserts and over mountains. They brought Chinese goods to the West. Many Europeans were fascinated with Chinese art and style. They especially liked the fine silk cloth. It was made from threads spun by silkworms.

The Silk Road was not a one-way road. Chinese products came out of China. New ideas filtered into China along this road. Buddhism came to China from India in the second century A.D. In the next centuries it spread across China.

What Lands Did Genghis Khan Conquer?

To the north of China are the vast plains of central Asia. In the second century, the people who lived there were called Mongols. They were nomads, loosely organized into groups. They wandered over their lands with their horses, sheep, camels, oxen, and goats. The Mongols were expert horsemen. They were also skilled at using the bow and arrow. In their camps they lived in felt tents called *yurts*.

Reading Strategy:
Summarizing

What is the main idea of
this section?

In A.D. 1206, a great chief took power over all the
Mongols. His name was Genghis Khan. *Khan* was a
title given to rulers. Genghis Khan believed that he was
destined to rule a great empire. He built up a huge army
of Mongol soldiers. They conquered many lands including
parts of China, Russia, Persia, and India.

Genghis Khan had little education. Yet he was clever and
ruthless. With his soldiers on horseback, he swept across
the countryside. The thunder of hooves of Mongol horses
was a terrifying sound. The Mongols were among the
most fierce conquerors in history. If any city in their path
tried to fight, the Mongols showed no mercy. Every single
person in the city would be killed.

What Role Did Marco Polo Have in Teaching Europeans About the Chinese Culture?

Reading Strategy:
Summarizing

Who is being introduced
in this section?

Marco Polo was a trader and a traveler. He lived in Venice,
Italy. Marco Polo traveled to China with his father and his
uncle. In about 1275 they went to see Kublai Khan. Khan's
palace was in the city of Beijing, then called Cambaluc by
Marco Polo.

GREAT NAMES IN HISTORY

Kublai Khan

Perhaps the greatest of the Khans was Kublai
Khan. He was a grandson of Genghis Khan.
Kublai Khan completed the conquest of China.
Chinese farmers were no match for the Mongol
armies. The Mongols ruled China from A.D.
1260 until A.D. 1368.

Kublai Khan ran his empire well. He was a
Buddhist, but he allowed religious freedom. He
saw to it that roads were good and travel was
pleasant. There were stones to mark the way.

Trees were planted to give shade to travelers.
Kublai Khan developed a postal service. He
wanted to make it easy for people throughout
his empire to communicate. Horsemen carried
messages along China's Great Wall. A post
house stood every 25 miles along the wall. At
each post house messengers could change
horses, and travelers could rest. The Grand
Canal was built to transport goods from north to
south. Chinese boats called junks carried goods
along the miles of waterway.

History Fact
Kublai Khan's kingdom was huge. It extended as far as Russia.

Kublai Khan welcomed the traders. He allowed Marco Polo to travel about his empire. The young Italian stayed in China for 17 years. Marco Polo saw sights that no other European had ever seen.

Then Marco Polo returned to Italy. He got caught up in a war between Venice and another Italian city, Genoa. He was taken as a prisoner of war and thrown into jail in Genoa. There he told amazing tales to a fellow prisoner. The tales eventually became a part of his book, *Description of the World.* The book contained many stories of the great Chinese civilization and of the empire of Kublai Khan.

Many people did not believe Marco Polo's tales. Later, however, the stories proved to be true. Marco Polo had written a good description of his adventures in China.

Marco Polo was impressed with all he saw in China. The Chinese were using gunpowder and compasses, and coal for heat. Marco Polo wrote that coal was "a sort of black stone, which they dig out of the mountainside…." He was interested in their use of paper, especially for money. Europeans were still using heavy, metal coins. He had found China a rich land where travel was quite easy.

Marco Polo's stories gave Europeans their first glimpse of life inside China.

What Dynasty Followed the Mongol Rule?

You Decide
Blue and white Ming porcelain is still much admired. Why do you think antiques, or old things, are often popular with people today?

In the 1300s, the Chinese revolted against Mongol rule. Mongol rule ended in China. The Mongols were driven away. The Ming dynasty reigned.

Ming emperors lived in Beijing in a great palace known as the *Forbidden City.* The Mings ruled there for nearly 300 years. Chinese art and literature thrived during this time. Europeans found Ming art beautiful. They wanted to trade their European goods for the Ming art. China said no. The Chinese would only accept payments of gold and silver.

REVIEW

On a sheet of paper, write the answer to each question. Use complete sentences.

1. What are three things the Chinese invented?

2. What was the route known as the Silk Road?

3. What lands did Genghis Khan conquer?

4. What role did Marco Polo have in teaching the Europeans about Chinese discoveries?

On a sheet of paper, write the letter of the answer that correctly completes each sentence.

5. The Mongols were _____ who roamed the vast plains of central Asia.

   A traders   **B** armies   **C** nomads   **D** farmers

6. The Mongols were among the fiercest _____ in history.

   A conquerors   **B** horsemen   **C** travelers   **D** rulers

7. _____ was a clever, ruthless ruler who built up a huge Mongol army.

   A Marco Polo   **B** Kublai Khan **C** Babar   **D** Genghis Khan

8. _____ was one of the greatest rulers. He allowed religious freedom, ensured roads were good for travelers, and developed a postal service.

   A Marco Polo   **B** Kublai Khan **C** Babar   **D** Genghis Khan

9. Marco Polo was an Italian _____ who traveled throughout China for 17 years.

   A trader   **B** farmer   **C** ruler   **D** inventor

10. The _____ dynasty followed the Mongol rule in China.

   A Khan   **B** Genoa   **C** Chinese   **D** Ming

Japan

Objectives

■ To tell what the Japanese got from their Chinese neighbors

■ To describe the role of samurai and shoguns in Japan

■ To explain why the ruling shogun forbade the Japanese to leave their country

Samurai
A class of warriors in the Japanese feudal system

Privilege
A special right given to a person or group

Reading Strategy:
Summarizing

What part of Japanese history is this section about?

Japan is a group of islands off the coast of China. Little is known about the early history of Japan. The reason is that the ancient Japanese had no system of writing. Writing first came to Japan from China during the fifth century A.D. Customs, crafts, arts, and ideas of government and taxes also came to Japan from China. The Japanese adapted the Chinese calendar system and the ideas of Confucius. About A.D. 552, Buddhism came to Japan from China and Korea.

The Japanese visited China. The Chinese came to Japan. The Japanese began to model their way of life after Chinese ways. In the seventh century, one Japanese emperor was especially drawn to Chinese ways. He ordered changes in Japanese life to make it more like Chinese life.

What Was Japanese Society Like?

Europeans of the Middle Ages lived under a system of feudalism. At the same time, so did the Japanese. Japanese feudal society was divided into classes.

Nobles were at the top. A class of warriors fought for the nobles. Japanese feudal warriors were called **samurai.** Samurai were given many special rights, or **privileges.** The nobles gave them wealth and land. The samurai were respected as an upper class. In return, samurai warriors pledged loyalty and protection to their nobles.

The samurai were highly trained soldiers. They were expected to die, if necessary, for their noble. Samurai fought with huge, two-handed swords. Before attacking, a samurai would first shout his own name. Then he would shout of the bravery of his ancestors. This was meant to scare his enemy.

The nobles and samurai made up the upper classes of Japanese feudal society. However, most of the people in Japan were peasants. They raised the food for the nobles and warriors.

Japanese society also included craftworkers and a few traders. Traders were looked down upon. Buying and selling goods was not considered honorable.

Samurai warriors protected people. They fought with large, two-handed swords.

Shogun
A great general governing Japan

Enforce
To make sure that people follow the laws and rules

Missionary
A person sent by a church to other countries to spread a religion

 History Fact
The shoguns were so powerful that they actually took over leadership from the emperors.

Over time, feudal clans, or families, united into larger groups. Eventually Japan became a nation-state under one emperor. The emperor was called the *mikado*. Japanese people honored their mikado. However, the mikado had no real power. The country was actually ruled by a warlord, a military leader.

One of those warlords was a man called Yoritomo. In A.D. 1192, he began to use the title of **shogun.** For almost 700 years, one powerful shogun after another ruled Japan. Highly trained samurai **enforced** the shogun's rule (they made sure that people followed the laws). Shogun rule lasted until 1867.

Kublai Khan, the Mongol emperor of China, tried twice to conquer Japan. He launched attacks in 1274 and in 1281. Both times, his fleet was defeated because of fierce storms. The Japanese called these raging storms *Kamikaze,* which means "Divine Wind."

Why Was Japan so Isolated from the Rest of the World?

A hermit is someone who lives alone, away from others. Japan under the shoguns could be called a hermit nation. Japan showed little interest in the rest of the world. For years it remained isolated, like China.

The Italian traveler Marco Polo first told Europeans about Japan. He called the country Cipango, land of gold and riches. Europeans liked the sound of "gold and riches"! Traders began to travel to Japan.

At first the Japanese allowed the trade. They even welcomed Christian **missionaries.** A missionary is a person sent by a church to another country to spread a religion. Soon, however, the shogun began to worry.

He thought that Christianity and European ways might upset the Japanese culture. Therefore, the ruling shogun of the Tokugawa family closed the doors to Japan. Only the Dutch were allowed to continue a little trade. Just one Dutch ship a year could come to the port of Nagasaki.

The Japanese were strict about their rules. Stories tell of foreign sailors shipwrecked on Japanese shores being put to death. Their crime was that they had dared to set foot on Japanese soil.

Reading Strategy: Summarizing

What are some important details that relate to Japan as a "hermit nation"?

The shogun also did not allow the Japanese to travel outside of their country. Beginning in about 1600, Japan was totally separated from the rest of the world. For about the next 250 years, Japan remained alone.

REVIEW

On a sheet of paper, write the answer to each question. Use complete sentences.

1. How was the way of life in Japan influenced by its Chinese neighbors?

2. What was the role of the samurai in Japanese society?

3. Why did the ruling shogun family not allow the Japanese to trade with outsiders?

On a sheet of paper, write the letter of the answer that correctly completes each sentence.

4. Japan was a(n) _____ society.

   A feudal　　　**B** friendly　　　**C** democratic　　　**D** artistic

5. Most Japanese were _____ who raised food for the nobles and warriors.

   A mikados　　　**B** shoguns　　　**C** samurai　　　**D** peasants

6. The Japanese emperor, the _____, was honored by the people but had little power.

   A samurai　　　**B** mikado　　　**C** shogun　　　**D** Kamikaze

7. The great general that governed Japan is known as a _____.

   A samurai　　　**B** mikado　　　**C** shogun　　　**D** Kamikaze

8. Japan, like China, was quite _____ the rest of the world.

   A disliked by　　　　　　　**C** friendly with
   B isolated from　　　　　　**D** open to

9. The ruling shogun of the Tokugawa family allowed only the _____ to trade with them.

   A Dutch　　　**B** Italians　　　**C** Chinese　　　**D** Indians

10. The Japanese were not allowed to leave their country for _____ years.

    A 100　　　**B** 250　　　**C** 700　　　**D** 1,600

India

Objectives

■ To explain why the people of India converted to Buddhism under the emperor Asoka
■ To tell what the Moguls brought to India

Reading Strategy: Summarizing

What does this lesson have to say about Hinduism and Buddhism in India?

For a long time India was divided into different kingdoms. Wealthy princes ruled each one. The people followed the Hindu religion. But in about 268 B.C., Asoka became emperor. He converted to Buddhism. Most of India's people turned away from the Hindu religion with its strict caste laws. Many turned to the teachings of Buddha.

Later, however, the Hindu religion became popular in India again. Hindu believers flocked to the Ganges River to wash away their sins. The Hindus believed that all rivers came from the gods. They thought that the Ganges was especially holy.

What Was India Like Under Mogul Rule?

In the eighth century A.D., Muslim warriors began a series of invasions into India.

The first Muslims came from Arabia. Three hundred years later, the invaders came from Persia and Afghanistan. The city of Delhi was captured several times. In 1206, Muslims set up a government in Delhi. In 1398, the conqueror Tamerlane and his army from central Asia raided India and captured Delhi once again.

In 1526, a Muslim prince of Afghanistan named Babar invaded India. He was a direct descendant of Genghis Khan. Babar conquered most of northern India. He established the Mogul Empire and made himself emperor.

The greatest Mogul emperor was Babar's grandson, Akbar. He extended Mogul rule to most of India. He was a wise ruler. He was a Muslim, but he let others worship as they pleased. He tried to bring people of all religions together to live in harmony. Most of the empire remained Hindu.

The Taj Mahal was built by Shah Jahan as a tomb for his wife.

History Fact
It took 20,000 workers 20 years, from 1630 to 1650, to complete the building of the Taj Mahal.

Reading Strategy:
Summarizing

What leaders of India are mentioned in this lesson?

The Mogul Empire lasted for about 200 years. These were good years. The strong central government provided a time of peace. The arts thrived. A special blend of Middle Eastern and Indian culture developed. The Moguls left fine buildings. One of these is the famous Taj Mahal. It was built in Agra by Shah Jahan as a tomb for his wife, Mumtaz Mahal. Shah Jahan was the grandson of Akbar.

Shah Jahan had a son called Aurangzeb. In 1658, Aurangzeb took the throne. Aurangzeb was a harsh ruler. He threw his father in prison. He made Hindus pay a special tax. He destroyed many Hindu temples. Aurangzeb tried to force people to convert to Islam. In central India the Hindus revolted. The empire was weakened. Aurangzeb died in 1707. Shortly after, the Mogul Empire began to break up.

Word Bank

Akbar

Arabia

Aurangzeb

Babar

Buddhism

culture

Muslim

princes

rivers

Taj Mahal

On a sheet of paper, write the word from the Word Bank to complete each sentence correctly.

1. India was divided and ruled by wealthy _____ for a long time.

2. When Asoka became emperor he converted to _____, and many others did the same.

3. The Hindus believed that all _____ came from gods.

4. During the eight century A.D., _____ warriors began a series of invasions into India.

5. Invaders came from _____, Persia, and Afghanistan.

6. _____ conquered most of northern India, establishing the Mogul Empire and making himself emperor.

7. _____ extended Mogul rule to most of India.

8. _____ was a harsh ruler. He forced Hindus to pay a special tax and tried to convert people to Islam.

9. During the Mogul Empire, a strong central government provided peace and the arts thrived. Also, a special blend of Middle Eastern and Indian _____ developed.

10. One of the fine buildings the Moguls left is the famous _____.

The Americas

Mesoamerica
The area of North
America (including
Mexico and
Central America)
where civilizations
developed before
Europeans entered the
continent

Dweller
A person who lives in
a place

Until the end of the 15th century, most Europeans did
not know about the Americas. Only the Vikings knew
that land existed across the western sea. One day the
Europeans would call these lands the New World. To the
American Indians, however, the Americas were home. This
area, at this time in history, is known as **Mesoamerica.**
Mesoamerica refers to the area of North America (including
Mexico and Central America) where civilizations developed
before Europeans entered the continent.

Who Were the Mound Builders and the Cliff Dwellers?

Groups of American Indians lived in different parts of the
Americas. From about 100 B.C. to A.D. 500, the Hopewell
Indians lived in the Ohio River Valley. They built huge
burial mounds. As many as 1,000 people were sometimes
buried in a single mound. Other American Indians lived
along the Mississippi River. They too built giant mounds
of earth around A.D. 1000. They built their temples on top
of the mounds. These Indians were called Mississippians.
They lived mainly by farming.

To the west, in what is now New Mexico, Arizona, and
Colorado, lived the cliff **dwellers.** As their name suggests,
cliff dwellers were people who lived on a cliff. These
Indians were called Anasazi. Some descendants of the
Anasazi are called *Pueblo* Indians, from the Spanish word
for "town." Around A.D. 1000, the Anasazi began building
villages on the sides of cliffs. All building was done
with sandstone blocks and mud. Some homes were on
protected ledges. Others were in hollow spaces in the cliff
walls. Most homes were two or three stories high. As many
as 1,500 people lived in one of these villages.

No one knows why the Anasazi moved away by about A.D. 1300. They left behind their empty villages, which can still be seen today. Perhaps the climate had become too dry to allow farming.

These early American Indians did not have a system of writing. What we know about them comes from the findings of archaeologists.

The Anasazi built dwellings in cliffs.

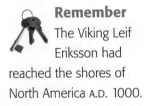

Remember

The Viking Leif Eriksson had reached the shores of North America A.D. 1000.

Who Were the Inuit?

The Inuit, or Eskimos, lived in the far north of North America. The Inuit ate the meat of caribou, seals, whales, and birds. They also ate fish from icy northern waters. They had no greens to eat. They got their vitamins by eating every part of an animal. They often ate the meat raw. The word *eskimo* is an American Indian word. It means "eater of raw meat." The Eskimos call themselves *Inuit,* which means "people."

The Inuit lived in one of the coldest places in the world. They made tools and weapons to fit their cold land. They traveled in sleds made of driftwood and leather. The sleds were pulled by teams of dogs. In the summer the Inuit lived in tents made of animal skins. In winter they lived in houses made of blocks of snow. These houses were called *igloos.*

Reading Strategy:
Summarizing

What are the important details about the different groups of people who settled in North America?

The Inuit loved feasts and celebrations. Their medicine men danced and sang to the spirits of the earth and the air.

The first Europeans to meet the Inuit were the Vikings. The Inuit arrived in Greenland about A.D. 1100. They found Vikings already living there.

Early Civilizations of North America

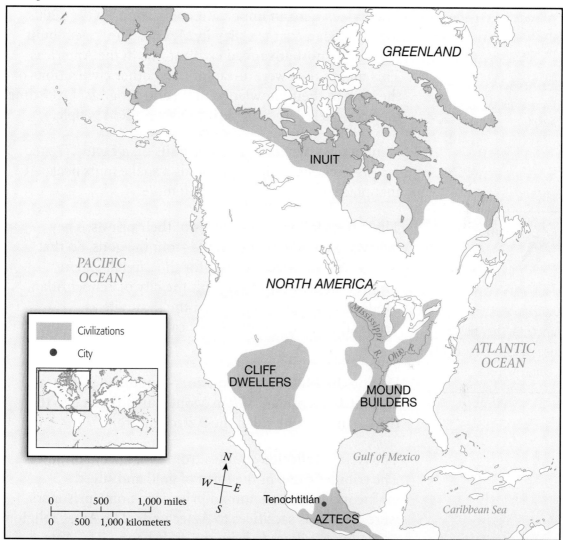

MAP STUDY

1. What were four early civilizations of North America?
2. The mound builders were located near which two rivers?

Remember

The Olmecs and the Maya were some of the earliest civilizations in the Americas. They built their cities in Mexico and Central America.

Who Were the Aztecs?

The Aztecs were an important civilization. In the 1200s they settled in a large valley in Mexico. The Aztecs built one of the most **advanced** civilizations in the Americas. This means they were ahead of most other civilizations of the time in their knowledge, skill, and progress. Over time they conquered and ruled five to six million people.

"Find a place where a great eagle sits on a cactus," Aztec priests declared. "The eagle holds a snake in its beak. At that place, you shall build your temple."

The Aztecs followed the words of their priests. They believed that these words came from the gods. So that is how they decided on a site for the capital. Where they found the eagle, they built the city of Tenochtitlán. Modern-day Mexico City is on the same site as Tenochtitlán, the ancient Aztec capital.

The Aztecs were feared by other American Indians. During the 1400s, Aztec warriors conquered all the lands around Tenochtitlán. When Montezuma II came to the throne in 1502, he ruled the Aztec empire.

The Aztecs collected tributes from those they conquered. The tributes came in the form of gold and silver, craftwork, food, and human prisoners. Some prisoners were offered as sacrifices to Aztec gods. The Aztec religion called for sacrifices to keep the gods happy. The Aztecs developed advanced methods of farming. In mountainous areas, they **terraced**, or stepped, their land to stop the soil from eroding. In dry areas, they used irrigation canals. The Aztecs' greatest achievement, though, was the system of farming called *chinampa*. In this system, the Aztecs farmed in swamps and lakes. They dug drainage ditches and created islands of mud where they grew crops.

Reading Strategy: Summarizing

What is the main idea of this section on the Aztecs?

The Aztecs had a well-ordered society. They invented a form of picture-writing. They also developed a system of numbers to help them keep track of what they owned. They had a calendar stone that recorded time. They built temples and buildings in a pyramid style.

The Aztecs had no need for money since they **bartered**, or traded, for goods. Chocolate was a favorite drink. So cocoa beans were often traded. Our word *chocolate*, in fact, comes from the Aztec language.

The Aztecs made some beautiful craftwork. Archaeologists have found **mosaic** masks made of turquoise and jade. The Aztecs also used colorful feathers to make headdresses and cloaks.

The Aztecs liked games and contests of athletic strength and skill. One of their favorite games was called *tlachiti*. It was a combination of handball and basketball. The players had to put a bouncy rubber ball through rings at either end of a court.

The Aztec empire ended in 1521. Cortés and his army arrived in Tenochtitlán in 1519. They were amazed at what they found. Tenochtitlán was a beautiful city, with floating gardens, drawbridges, and markets. It was larger than any Spanish city of that time.

The Aztecs terraced their land for farming.

The Spaniards were welcomed in friendship. The Aztecs may have believed that Cortés was a long lost Aztec god. The god sailed away across the sea and was expected to return someday. Yet Cortés captured the emperor, Montezuma, and made him a prisoner. In 1520, Aztecs drove the Spaniards away. Montezuma died during the fighting. The next year Cortés returned and destroyed Tenochtitlán.

Who Were the Incas?

The earliest history of the Incas is only legend. What we know for sure is that the Incas lived in the mountains of what is now Peru in South America. Around A.D. 1200 they began to build their empire. In time, the Incas conquered much of western South America. They took over the rest of Peru and parts of what are now Colombia, Bolivia, Ecuador, and Chile.

One man ruled the entire Inca Empire. He was called the *Inca*. His people worshiped him as a direct descendant of the sun. The sun was the Inca people's most powerful god. The Inca's word was law. He had many officials to see that his laws were obeyed.

The Inca ruled over a giant empire from his capital at Cuzco. More than six million people lived under his rule. Communicating with all these subjects was a problem. Therefore, the Incas built a fine network of roads. These roads improved communication. They connected all corners of the empire.

The Incas also built bridges of twisted vines to stretch across steep rain forest valleys. They had no horses or wheeled vehicles. All traveling was done on foot. Llamas carried their goods.

Swift runners raced along the Inca roads to deliver messages. The Incas did not have a system of writing.

Messages were passed by word of mouth. Runners also carried *quipus*. These were different colored ropes with knots to stand for numbers. They used the quipus to keep track of things.

The Incas built rest stops along their roads. At each stop a tired runner could tell his message to a fresh runner. Then that messenger would hurry to the next stop. This relay system kept communication moving across the empire.

The Incas were fine builders. They used huge stone blocks. They fit the blocks together carefully. They needed no mortar or cement of any kind. Some of the stones fit together so tightly that the blade of a knife could not slide between them! Inca buildings still stand at Cuzco today, even after earthquakes have destroyed modern structures.

The Incas had plenty of gold and plenty of silver. Their temples were decorated with both of the valuable metals. Inca artists made beautiful objects of solid gold. These were often inlaid with precious jewels.

It is no wonder that the Spanish explorers were drawn to the Incas. In 1532, tales of great wealth brought Francisco Pizarro to South America. His visit was the beginning of the end of the Inca civilization.

Timeline Study: Asia and the Americas: 1100–1600

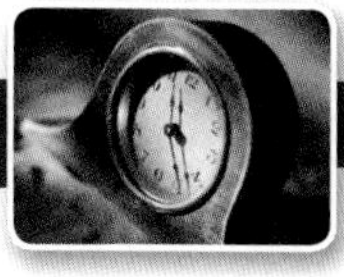

When the Aztecs were first known to be in Tenochtitlán, what group ruled China?

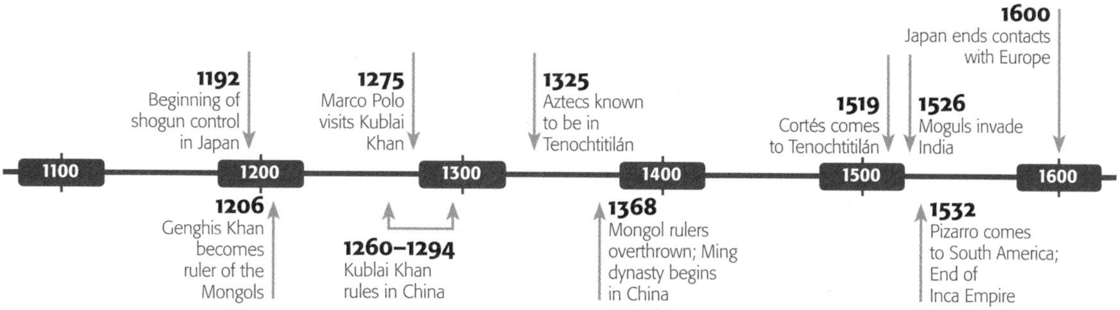
1100
1200
1300
1400
1500
1600
1192 Beginning of shogun control in Japan
1206 Genghis Khan becomes ruler of the Mongols
1275 Marco Polo visits Kublai Khan
1260–1294 Kublai Khan rules in China
1325 Aztecs known to be in Tenochtitlán
1368 Mongol rulers overthrown; Ming dynasty begins in China
1519 Cortés comes to Tenochtitlán
1526 Moguls invade India
1532 Pizarro comes to South America; End of Inca Empire
1600 Japan ends contacts with Europe

On a sheet of paper, write the letter of the answer that correctly completes each sentence.

1. The _____ lived in the Ohio River Valley and built huge burial mounds.

   A Mississippians   **C** Pueblo Indians
   B Hopewell Indians   **D** Inuits

2. The _____ were cliff dwellers. They used sandstone blocks and mud to build their villages on the sides of cliffs.

   A Aztecs   **C** Hopewell Indians
   B Anasazi   **D** Mississippians

3. Early American Indians did not have a system of _____.

   A writing   **B** farming   **C** worship   **D** building

4. The Inuits had no greens to eat, but got their vitamins from eating _____.

   A caribou   **C** birds
   B fish   **D** every part of an animal

5. The Aztecs conquered and ruled five to six million people. It was one of the most _____ civilizations in the Americas.

   A advanced   **B** vicious   **C** simple   **D** dull

6. The _____ invented a form of picture-writing and a calendar stone that recorded time. They also had a number system to help them keep track of what they owned.

   A Inuits   **B** Incas   **C** Aztecs   **D** Spaniards

7. _____ was the Inca people's most powerful god.

   A The sun   **B** The Inca   **C** Montezuma   **D** The cocoa bean

On a sheet of paper, write the answer to each question. Use complete sentences.

8. How did the climate the Inuits lived in affect their daily lives?

9. What methods of farming did the Aztecs develop?

10. What was the system of communication that the Incas developed?

- China was isolated for centuries. Chinese culture changed very little during that time.

- The Chinese were ahead of the Europeans in papermaking and printing. They understood the process of working with iron. The early Chinese also developed the compass and gunpowder.

- The Mongols from the north invaded China. Mongol leader Genghis Khan built a strong army. Khan's army took control of parts of China, as well as Russia, Persia, and India.

- Italian explorer Marco Polo visited Kublai Khan, a Mongol ruler.

- Japan was a feudal society in the Middle Ages. Shoguns and their warriors, or samurais, ruled the country.

- About 1600, the ruling shogun forbade the Japanese to leave their country. Japan was isolated for the next 250 years.

- The people of India turned from Hinduism to Buddhism, then back to Hinduism. The Moguls brought Islam to India in the eighth century A.D.

- Most Europeans did not know about the Americas until the late 1400s. However, Native Americans built civilizations in the Americas long before that time.

- The Hopewell Indians, the Anasazis, and the Inuit lived in North America.

- The Aztecs built a great empire in Mexico.

- The Incas lived in Peru, in South America.

Word Bank

acupuncture

barter

forge

missionaries

mosaic

privileges

samurai

shogun

terraced

Vocabulary Review

On a sheet of paper, use the words from the Word Bank to complete each sentence correctly.

1. _____ were upper-class, feudal warriors who fought for the nobles.

2. A(n) _____ was a great general governing Japan.

3. The Japanese were suspicious of Christian _____, so the ruling shogun closed Japan's doors.

4. The Aztecs _____ their land to stop the soil from eroding.

5. The Aztecs would _____ for goods, exchanging them without the use of money.

6. Small pieces of stone or glass can be used to create a(n) _____.

7. The Chinese invented _____, which uses needles to treat pain and illness.

8. The Chinese knew how to _____ iron and mine salt.

9. Samurai were given many _____, including wealth and land.

Chapter Review Questions

On a sheet of paper, write the answer to each question. Use complete sentences.

10. Where did the Ming emperors of China live?

11. How did Marco Polo feel about what he had seen in China?

12. What were the classes in Japan during the Middle Ages?

When you are reading a multiple-choice question, look for words such as *mainly, most likely, generally, major,* and *best.* Decide which answer choice best fits the meaning of these words.

13. What religion did the Moguls bring to India?

14. How did the Mogul emperor Akbar treat Indians who were not Muslims?

15. Why did some American Indians build mounds?

16. Why were the Spaniards interested in the Incas?

Critical Thinking

On a sheet of paper, write your response to each question. Use complete sentences.

17. Why was the Silk Road important?

18. Why did the early civilizations of the Americas develop in such different ways?

Using the Timeline

Use the timeline on page 327 to answer the questions.

19. How long did Kublai Khan rule in China?

20. What happened in India in A.D. 1526?

GROUP ACTIVITY

Work with a partner to make a poster that compares the civilizations in the Americas before the European explorers arrived. Include categories such as the following: Location, Climate, Building Styles, Religion, and Food. Try to include one picture for each civilization.

Explorers, Traders, and Settlers

The explorers from Europe may have been curious about the world or may have wanted adventure. In most cases, they desired riches for themselves and their countries. On their explorations, they often came upon civilizations in the new lands. However, the explorers did not think about the rights of the people already living on the land. Instead, they forced their own culture on them, often making slaves of them.

Most settlers who journeyed to North America were not hoping to find great fortunes. They were seeking a better life and freedom to make their own choices about religion. As they moved onto lands for farming and trapping, they forced American Indians to surrender to them.

GOALS FOR LEARNING

- To explain the discoveries of explorers
- To tell about the Spanish conquistadors and the lands they claimed
- To explain what the English and French did upon coming to North America
- To explain the importance of trade with Europe and the Americas

Reading Strategy: Questioning

Ask yourself questions as you read. Questioning the text will help you to be a more active reader. You will remember more of what you read if you do this. As you read, ask yourself:

- Why am I reading this text?
- What connections can I make between this text and my own life?
- What decisions can I make about the facts and details in this text?

Key Vocabulary Words

Lesson 2
Conquistador A Spanish conqueror

Lesson 3
Piracy The robbing of ships on the ocean

Pilgrim A person who came to North America for religious freedom and settled in Plymouth, Massachusetts

Puritan A member of a 16th- or 17th-century English group of Protestants who wanted to make the Church of England simpler and stricter

Trapper A person who traps wild animals for their furs

Lesson 4
Stock Shares in a business or company

Shareholder A person who owns one or more parts (shares) of a business

Investment Money given to businesses in order to get even more money back

Interest Money paid for the use of other people's money

Insurance A guarantee that a person or company will be paid money to cover losses

Exploring New Lands

Objectives

■ To tell how Columbus came to land in America

■ To name and tell about two Portuguese explorers and the things they discovered

Reading Strategy: Questioning

What do you already know about early explorations to new lands?

For centuries, the rest of the world did not know about the Americas or the people living there. Then the Vikings landed in North America. They met American Indians, but the Vikings did not stay long in North America. Much later, European explorers found the continent by accident. What they were really looking for was a quicker route to India and the Far East. The place they found instead seemed like a land of wealth and plenty. It seemed well worth exploring and conquering.

What Was Christopher Columbus Looking for and What Did He Find?

Christopher Columbus set sail from Spain in August 1492. He was not out to prove that the world was round, as stories often tell. He was also not out to conquer new lands. Columbus was looking for a water route to Asia. He believed that by sailing west he might find a shorter route to the treasures of Asia. He had convinced Queen Isabella of Spain to support his voyage. Queen Isabella and King Ferdinand gave Columbus three ships for the voyage. They were the *Niña*, the *Pinta*, and the *Santa Maria*.

Columbus sailed westward. Instead of reaching Asia, Columbus landed on an island in the Bahamas. There it was—a new world where no land should have been! Columbus claimed the land in the name of Spain. He named the land San Salvador.

Columbus thought he had reached an island off the coast of India. That is why he called the people living there "Indians." It was not too many years before people realized Columbus was wrong about the land's location. Those islands that Columbus explored are called the "West Indies."

Early Voyages of Exploration

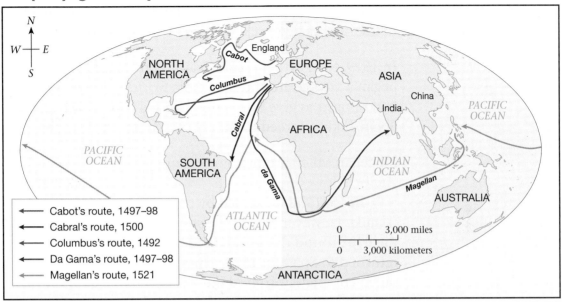

MAP STUDY

1. Which ocean did Columbus cross?
2. How would you describe da Gama's route to India?

Reading Strategy:
Questioning

As you read about the early explorers, notice the details in the text. What questions can you ask yourself about these details?

Remember
Marco Polo had introduced Europeans to the treasures of Asia.

Many places in the Americas have been named after Columbus. The word *America*, however, comes from the name of another explorer, Amerigo Vespucci. He was a European explorer who reached the mainland of South America in 1500. A mapmaker honored his accomplishment by naming the Americas after him.

What Did Portuguese Explorers Discover?

Other explorers searched for that water route to Asia. The Spaniards and the Portuguese led the way in voyages of discovery.

In 1497, Vasco da Gama sailed around Africa's Cape of Good Hope. Vasco da Gama was a Portuguese noble and sailor. He became the first explorer to reach India by a sea route.

Another Portuguese explorer, Pedro Cabral, set out for India in 1500. He sailed wide of Africa and found Brazil. Thanks to Cabral, Brazil was claimed in the name of Portugal.

In 1519, the Portuguese navigator Ferdinand Magellan began a voyage around the whole world. His own king had refused to give him money for his trip. However, the Spanish king agreed to supply five ships and 241 men.

Magellan sailed around South America and across the Pacific. However, Magellan himself did not make it all the way. In 1521, he was killed by people in the Philippine Islands. However, one of the ships, the *Victoria*, completed the trip around the world. With only 18 survivors, it returned to Spain in 1522. This was the first ship to have sailed completely around the world. The *Victoria's* voyage was the first proof that Earth is round.

The voyage of Magellan's ship, the Victoria, *was the first proof that Earth is round.*

Match the description in Column A with the explorer in Column B.
Write the correct letter on a sheet of paper.

Column A

1. discovered Brazil and claimed it in the name of Portugal

2. first explorer to reach India by a sea route

3. discovered America when trying to find a water route to Asia

4. attempted to sail around the whole world

5. the word *America* is named for this explorer

Column B

A Amerigo Vespucci
B Christopher Columbus
C Ferdinand Magellan
D Pedro Cabral
E Vasco da Gama

On a sheet of paper, write the letter of the answer that correctly completes each sentence.

6. Columbus named the land he discovered _____.

   A Bahamas   **B** West Indies   **C** San Salvador   **D** Brazil

7. Columbus called the people living on the island he explored _____.

   A Indians   **C** American Indians
   B Americans   **D** Aztecs

8. The Spaniards and the _____ led the way in voyages of discovery.

   A Dutch   **B** Portuguese   **C** French   **D** English

9. A _____ king supplied five ships and 241 men on Magellan's voyage.

   A Spanish   **B** Portuguese   **C** French   **D** Dutch

10. While Magellan did not make the trip around the world, his ship _____ did.

    A *Niña*   **B** *Santa Maria*   **C** *Pinta*   **D** *Victoria*

Conquering South America

Europeans quickly realized what a prize they had found in the new lands. They thought it did not matter that people already lived there. Europeans did not recognize that the natives had civilizations and cultures of their own. Europeans wanted the new lands for themselves.

What Things Did Spanish Conquistadors Bring to South America?

When the Spanish **conquistadors** (conquerors) arrived in Mexico and South America, they found great civilizations. The conquistadors brought guns and horses to help them claim gold. The American Indians had neither one.

Hernando Cortés met the Aztec ruler, Montezuma. Cortés went on to conquer the Aztec Empire.

You Decide

Many people think the American Indians would have been better off if the Europeans had never set foot in the Americas. What do you think?

Hernando Cortés attacked the Aztec capital of Tenochtitlán in 1521. The Spaniards soon conquered all of Mexico. They called it New Spain.

In South America, Francisco Pizarro attacked the Inca Empire in 1532. Again, the Indians were no match for the new enemy they did not understand. The Spaniards tried to make the Indians accept the Christian religion. Many Indians who refused were burned to death.

The Spaniards treated the Indians cruelly in other ways, too. They used the Indians as slaves, working them harder than animals. Many Europeans thought these people were only savages.

The Europeans caused the Indians to suffer in yet another way. The Europeans brought their diseases with them to the Americas. Thousands of American Indians died from the new diseases.

LEARN MORE ABOUT IT

The Slave Trade

In Africa, too, some Europeans were treating people like work animals. The Europeans discovered that there was money to be made in the slave trade. The Spanish and Portuguese brought ships full of Africans to the Americas, where the Africans were sold into slavery.

For a time the Spanish and Portuguese controlled the slave markets. Soon England and France joined the slave trade, too.

An English naval commander, Sir John Hawkins, was the first English slave trader. In the 1560s, Hawkins made three voyages. On each one, he stopped in Africa to find the strongest, healthiest men. Then Hawkins carried these Africans to Spanish colonies in the Americas. There he sold them into slavery. Slave-trading led the way in setting up trade between England and the Americas.

REVIEW

Match the description in Column A with the name in Column B. Write the correct letter on a sheet of paper.

Column A
1. conquered all of Mexico
2. the first English slave trader
3. attacked the Inca Empire

Column B
A Francisco Pizarro
B Hernando Cortés
C Sir John Hawkins

Word Bank
Christian
diseases
England
Portuguese
slaves
Spanish
Tenochtitlán

On a sheet of paper, write the word from the Word Bank to complete each sentence correctly.

4. Cortés attacked the Aztec capital of _____.

5. Spaniards tried to convert the Indians to the _____ religion.

6. The Spaniards used the Indians as _____.

7. The Europeans brought their _____ with them to the Americas. This caused thousands of American Indians to die.

8. The Spanish and _____ brought ships of Africans to the Americas.

9. Hawkins brought Africans to _____ colonies in the Americas.

10. Trading slaves set up trade between _____ and the Americas.

LESSON 16-3

Settling in North America

Objectives

- To explain what a pirate is
- To name the groups of Europeans who settled the east coast of North America
- To tell how a person made money by trapping

Reading Strategy: Questioning

What do you already know about the settling of North America?

Piracy
The robbing of ships on the ocean

 You Decide
Do you think Drake was an explorer or a pirate?

When the English and French set sail for the Americas, they were a little late. South American land had already been claimed. Therefore, they often turned to **piracy** to claim their share of South American treasures. In other words, they would get the treasures by robbing ships on the ocean.

Sir Francis Drake was English. He was the first English person to sail around the world. The English called him an explorer. The Spanish called him a pirate! Drake made daring attacks on Spanish ships and towns in the West Indies. He brought his treasures home to England. The English loved Drake, but the Spaniards feared his piracy. They called him "The Dragon."

By A.D. 1600, Spain had created an empire in present-day New Mexico, Florida, Central America, the Caribbean islands, and South America. The English, French, and Dutch explored and settled in North America.

How Did the Settlers and American Indians Divide Up the North American Land?

The first Europeans landed on the east coast of North America. There they found American Indians living in villages. Each nation had its own customs and culture. Most of the Indians farmed, hunted, and fished. They grew corn and other vegetables. Although the Indians were friendly at first, they did not fit in with the newcomers. The Europeans brought new ways, new religions, and new diseases. The Indians became wary, or overly cautious, of the settlers.

Pilgrim

A person who came to North America for religious freedom and settled in Plymouth, Massachusetts

Puritan

A member of a 16th- or 17th-century English group of Protestants who wanted to make the Church of England simpler and stricter

In 1607, a group of English colonists settled in Jamestown, Virginia. Another group of English, the **Pilgrims,** arrived on the sailing ship *Mayflower* in 1620. The Pilgrims landed at Plymouth, Massachusetts. They were seeking religious freedom. The **Puritans** were another religious group from England. The Puritans wanted to make the Church of England simpler and stricter. They built several settlements on Massachusetts Bay in the 1630s.

In 1626, the Dutch started a village at the mouth of the Hudson River, in present-day New York state. This village is New York City today. More Europeans came seeking religious freedom, a better life, and adventure. Most of the colonists became farmers. In the south, tobacco became a money-making crop. Slave traders brought Africans to help on the tobacco plantations.

Pilgrims celebrated their first year in Plymouth, Massachusetts, by holding a harvest festival with American Indians.

Ask yourself: "Did I understand what I just read?" If not, read the lesson again.

The settlers on North America's east coast formed 13 colonies. The colonies were under the control of the English government. Trade with Europe helped the colonies grow. Port towns like Boston sprang up.

The American Indians and the Europeans did not continue to live peacefully. Slowly, the Indians were driven westward. Over time, they lost their lands to the newcomers.

The 13 Original Colonies

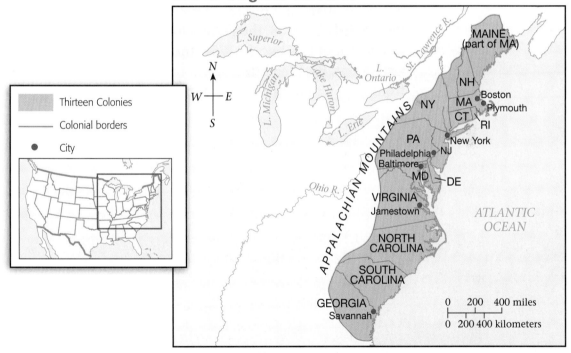

MAP STUDY

1. The colonies bordered on which mountain range?

2. What were the names of the 13 colonies?

Trapper

A person who traps wild animals for their furs

What Did Trappers Do?

Not all of the people who came to North America were interested in settling and farming. Some newcomers were **trappers.** These people made their living by hunting animals and selling the furs. Many French trapped along the Mississippi River. They explored the area, claiming lands in the name of France. Other French trappers went north to Canada. Hunting was good there, and fishing, too. The French created outposts from Canada to south of the mouth of the Mississippi River.

What Happened to Canadian Land?

The English also held land in Canada. This land had been claimed by John Cabot in 1497. Sometimes fights over Canadian land broke out between the French and the English. In 1608, the French founded the Canadian settlement of Quebec. In 1759, the English captured that settlement. By 1763, the English had taken all of Canada from the French during the French and Indian War.

On a sheet of paper, write the letter of the answer that correctly completes each sentence.

1. Sir Francis Drake was known to the English as a(n) _____.

   A conquistador   **B** pirate   **C** explorer   **D** conqueror

2. A person who robs ships in the ocean is known as a(n) _____.

   A voyager   **B** conquistador   **C** explorer   **D** pirate

3. The English, French, and _____ explored and settled in North America.

   A Dutch   **B** Spanish   **C** Portuguese   **D** Indians

4. The Pilgrims landed in Plymouth, Massachusetts, on the sailing ship _____.

   A *Mayflower*   **B** *Pinta*   **C** *Victoria*   **D** *The Dragon*

5. The _____ were a religious group from England. They built several settlements on Massachusetts Bay during the 1630s.

   A Pilgrims   **B** Dutch   **C** Puritans   **D** colonists

6. _____ was a port town.

   A Quebec   **B** Boston   **C** Philadelphia   **D** Savannah

7. _____ made money by hunting animals and selling their furs.

   A Hunters   **B** Traders   **C** Trappers   **D** Farmers

8. _____ was an explorer who claimed land in Canada for the English.

   A Christopher Columbus   **C** Sir Francis Drake
   B Ferdinand Magellan   **D** John Cabot

9. The French founded the Canadian settlement of _____.

   A Jamestown   **B** Quebec   **C** Boston   **D** Baltimore

10. The English had taken all of Canada from the French by _____.

   A 1497   **B** 1608   **C** 1759   **D** 1763

Trading with the Colonies

- To name the three European countries that were leaders in trade
- To describe the effect successful trading with America had on the people in Europe

Stock

Shares in a business or company

Shareholder

A person who owns one or more parts (shares) of a business

Investment

Money given to businesses in order to get even more money back

Interest

Money paid for the use of other people's money

Insurance

A guarantee that a person or company will be paid money to cover losses

Trade between Europe and the Americas became big business. Merchants set up trading companies. The trading companies offered shares of their **stock** for sale. The people who owned the stocks were called **shareholders.** Sea voyages were expensive. Thus, the money the shareholders put in, their **investments,** helped pay for the trips. Profits from successful trips were divided among the shareholders. In 1611, the Amsterdam Stock Exchange was built. This was the first building meant just for the buying and selling of stocks.

What European Countries Were Leaders in Trade?

Three European countries became leaders in trade: the Netherlands, England, and France. These were the trading powers of the 1600s. Banks were set up to help pay for trading trips. They lent money to the merchants and charged a fee called **interest.** London and Amsterdam became important banking cities.

Shipping could be a risky business. There were storms and shipwrecks and lost cargoes. Although merchants could make a lot of money, they could also lose everything. The merchants paid companies a fee for **insurance** to protect their businesses. Then if their ships were lost at sea or attacked by pirates, the insurance companies covered the losses.

Three trading companies became powerful forces in the growing trade between Europe and the East Indies. These were the English East India Company, the Dutch East India Company, and the French East India Company. They brought home ships loaded with spices and rice, diamonds and ivory.

Think beyond the text.
Consider your own
thoughts and experiences
as you read.

Trading became a big business and powerful force during the 1600s.

What Did Successful Trade Create?

Successful trade ventures created a new, rising middle class in Europe. European merchants became wealthy. They often lived in the style of nobility. They built grand houses in the cities or settled on country estates. With their new-found wealth, some merchants became interested only in money, fashion, and fine living. Other merchants used their own good fortune to help others. They paid to set up hospitals, orphanages, and schools.

TIMELINE STUDY: EUROPEAN EXPLORERS IN THE AMERICAS

Were the Aztecs or the Incas conquered by Europeans first?

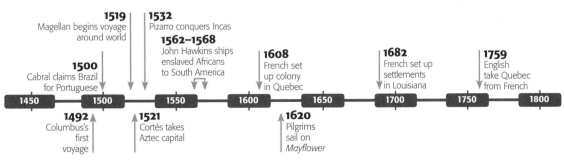

1519
Magellan begins voyage around world

1532
Pizarro conquers Incas

1562–1568
John Hawkins ships enslaved Africans to South America

1608
French set up colony in Quebec

1682
French set up settlements in Louisiana

1759
English take Quebec from French

1500
Cabral claims Brazil for Portuguese

| 1450 | 1500 | 1550 | 1600 | 1650 | 1700 | 1750 | 1800 |

1492
Columbus's first voyage

1521
Cortés takes Aztec capital

1620
Pilgrims sail on *Mayflower*

REVIEW

On a sheet of paper, write the answer to each question. Use complete sentences.

1. What were the three European countries that became leaders in trade?

2. Why might merchants want insurance on their business?

3. What effect did successful trade ventures in America have on the people in Europe?

Word Bank

Amsterdam

Dutch

interest

nobility

rice

risky

stock

On a sheet of paper, write the word from the Word Bank to complete each sentence correctly.

4. Trading companies sold shares of _____.

5. When banks give money to merchants, the fee they charge is called _____.

6. London and _____ were important banking cities.

7. Shipping could be a(n) _____ business.

8. Three trading companies helped trade grow between Europe and the East Indies. These include: the English East India Company, the _____ East India Company, and the French East India Company.

9. Common items to trade include: spices and _____, diamonds and ivory.

10. The new middle class in Europe often lived in the style of _____.

SUMMARY

- Columbus was looking for a sea route to Asia when he landed in the Americas.

- The Spanish and Portuguese led the way in early explorations. Spanish conquistadors like Cortés and Pizarro claimed lands and gold for Spain.

- Europeans forced their own culture on American Indians and took their land.

- Africans were brought to the Americas to be sold into slavery.

- Sir Francis Drake was the first English person to sail around the world.

- The Spanish and Portuguese set up colonies in South America. The Spanish also settled in present-day New Mexico and Florida. The English, French, and Dutch also settled in North America.

- The Pilgrims and Puritans traveled to America from England. Many other groups from various European countries came seeking religious freedom.

- The settlers on North America's east coast formed 13 colonies.

- French trappers explored the Mississippi River and lands in Canada. England and France fought over the lands in Canada.

- The Netherlands, England, and France set up big trading companies. Successful trade created a new, wealthy middle class in Europe.

Word Bank

conquistador

insurance

interest

investment

piracy

Puritans

shareholder

slavery

stock

trappers

Vocabulary Review

On a sheet of paper, use the words from the Word Bank to complete each sentence correctly.

1. Hernando Cortés, a Spaniard who conquered the Aztecs, was a(n) _____.

2. The Spanish and Portuguese were the first to sell Africans into _____.

3. English and French explorers often turned to _____ to claim South American treasures.

4. The _____ wanted to make the Church of England simpler.

5. A person who buys shares of a company will own _____ in the company.

6. A person who makes a(n) _____ is giving money in the hopes of earning more.

7. A(n) _____ holds one or more parts of a business.

8. Merchants had to pay _____ when borrowing money from banks.

9. French _____ hunted animals for their fur.

10. When a business loses money, a(n) _____ company may pay for the losses.

Chapter Review Questions

On a sheet of paper, write the answer to each question. Use complete sentences.

11. What city in Mexico did Hernando Cortés attack?

12. Where does the name *America* come from?

13. Why did the Europeans begin the slave trade?

Test Tip

After you have completed a test, reread each question and answer. Ask yourself: Have I answered the question that was asked? Have I answered it completely?

14. Where did the first settlers in Virginia and Massachusetts come from?

15. Why did the first English colonists come to the eastern coast of North America?

16. What European countries were trading powers in the 1600s?

Critical Thinking

On a sheet of paper, write your response to each question. Use complete sentences.

17. This book uses the term "American Indian" to describe the first people in the Americas. Another term you might hear is "Native American." Why do you think different names are used to describe the same group of people?

18. Do you think trade with the Americas was important to Europe? Give at least one reason.

Using the Timeline

Use the timeline on page 347 to answer the questions.

19. Who conquered the Incas?

20. Did the French settle in Quebec or Louisiana first?

GROUP ACTIVITY

Discuss this question with a partner: What if the European explorers had traded with the American Indians but not conquered them? Write a description of what life might be like in the Americas today. Share your ideas with the rest of the class.

VUURWERK INDE VYVER.

THE BIRTH OF DEMOCRACY

As people became more aware of the world and their place in it, they began to ask questions. Government by a single powerful ruler could last for a time. Then, as a growing number of people began to ask questions, monarch rule started to weaken. It could not answer the questions. It could not give in to demands by the common people. The people listened to one another and heard familiar words. They found strength in their fellow citizens. Democracy would be government of a very different kind.

Chapters in Unit 7

Fireworks explode over the crowning of William and Mary as king and queen of England. William and Mary signed a Bill of Rights that took away many of their royal rights and powers. The change came to be known as the Glorious Revolution.

The Struggle for Democracy

When you hear the word *democracy* you may think about people having a voice in their own government. This is not an idea that is new to the present time. Citizens of the 1600s and 1700s wanted their rights, too. It was a time called the *Enlightenment* or the *Age of Reason.*

Great thinkers at the time believed that every person was born with the ability to reason. They wrote that people should ask questions of their government. They spread ideas about democracy and equal rights for everyone. The ideas they raised sparked revolutions in Europe and in America.

GOALS FOR LEARNING

- To explain the beginnings of democracy
- To describe what happened in England when King Charles I tried to limit democracy
- To explain how the Glorious Revolution gained more power for the Parliament
- To explain why American colonists revolted against British rule

Reading Strategy: Predicting

Preview the text. Think about what you already know about a subject. Look for new information. These things will help you predict what will happen next.

Check your predictions as you read. As you learn more information, you may find you need to change your predictions.

Key Vocabulary Words

Lesson 1
Enlightenment A time in European history when thinkers and writers tried to solve the problems of society by using reason; also known as the Age of Reason

Equality The same rights for everyone

Lesson 2
Divine right The idea that a monarch's right to rule comes directly from God

Petition A written request, often with many signatures, to a person or group in authority

Petition of Right An English document that brought about more democracy

Consent To agree to something

Royalist A supporter of the king or queen during the English Civil War

Roundhead A Puritan who fought for Parliament in the English Civil War

Commonwealth A nation in which the people hold the ruling power

Lesson 3
Glorious Revolution The period in England that involved the overthrow of James II and the crowning of William and Mary

Lesson 4
Representation Sending one or more people to speak for the rights of others before a body of the government

American Revolution The American struggle against Great Britain for independence

Patriot A person who is loyal to his or her own country and shows a great love for that country

Liberty Freedom

Declaration of Independence A document the American colonists signed in which they declared their freedom from Great Britain

The Beginnings of Democracy

Objectives

- To list three main ideas from the Age of Reason
- To explain the revolutionary change King Edward I made to Parliament
- To name the two parts Parliament is divided into

Reading Strategy:
Predicting

Preview the lesson title. Predict what you think you will learn in this lesson.

Enlightenment
A time in European history when thinkers and writers tried to solve the problems of society by using reason; also known as the Age of Reason

Equality
The same rights for everyone

"People have certain natural rights! They have the right to life, liberty, and property!"

"Man is born free! A monarch's right to rule is given to him not by God but by the people!"

"If a monarch rules badly, throw him out!"

Whoever heard of such wild ideas! These were shocking things to say in 17th-century Europe. Yet in the 1600s and 1700s, such ideas were being written and spoken in Europe. It was a time called the *Enlightenment* or the *Age of Reason.*

Philosophers at that time believed that every person is born with the ability to reason. Everyone had the power to decide what was true or false, or good or bad. They also said that people should use their abilities to question things. Why were things the way they were? How might they be better? Why should one person have so much power over others?

Questions like these were asked by the Englishman John Locke and the Frenchmen Voltaire and Jean Jacques Rousseau. These men were thinkers. They believed in freedom of thought, of action, and of speech. Their writings spread ideas of democracy and **equality** throughout the world. Their questions sparked flames of revolution in Europe and in America.

Why Was the Great Council Formed?

In 1215, King John of England was forced to sign the Magna Carta. This document limited certain powers of monarchs, and it granted certain rights. It served to ensure the rights of nobles. It did little for the common people.

Yet the ideas in the Magna Carta marked the beginning of democracy in England.

Now a king or queen could not simply go ahead and order new taxes. He or she first had to bring the matter before a council of nobles. That council was called the Great Council.

What Changes Did King Edward Make to Parliament?

Remember
Parliament is England's body of lawmakers.

The Great Council became known as Parliament. The word *parliament* comes from a French word, *parler*. It means "to speak." Members of Parliament could speak out, advise monarchs, and affect their decisions.

In 1272, King Edward I became king of England. In 1295, when Edward needed more money to fight a war, he called Parliament into session. Edward, however, made some changes. He invited not only nobles to Parliament, but also merchants, knights, and rich landowners. Now more people had a voice in the king's decisions.

After 1295, Parliament was divided into two parts. One group, called the House of Lords, was made up of nobles. Another group was called the House of Commons. Members of the middle class, such as merchants and rich farmers, served in the House of Commons. For those first few hundred years, the House of Lords held the most power. However, the day would come when the House of Commons became the real lawmaking body.

The changes King Edward I made to the Parliament gave more people a voice in his decisions.

17-1   REVIEW

On a sheet of paper, write the answer to each question.
Use complete sentences.

1. Why do we call this time in history the Age
   of Reason?

2. What did John Locke, Voltaire, and Jean Jacques
   Rousseau believe in?

3. How did ideas of democracy and equality spread
   to America?

4. What was the purpose of the Magna Carta?

5. What effect did the Magna Carta have in England?

6. What did a king or queen have to do before ordering
   new taxes?

7. What change did King Edward I make to Parliament
   in 1295?

8. What did members of the Parliament do?

9. What are the two houses of Parliament?

10. At first, which house of Parliament had the
    most power?

The King Tries to Limit Democracy

Objectives

- To tell why a civil war began in England in 1642
- To name and explain the two sides in the civil war
- To describe who Cromwell was and how he ended the reign of King Charles I
- To explain the republic Cromwell set up and what eventually became of the Parliament

Reading Strategy:
Predicting

Predict what you think this lesson will be about.

Divine right
The idea that a monarch's right to rule comes directly from God

You Decide
Should any ruler ever be allowed to claim that he or she rules by "divine right"? Why or why not?

The power of Parliament grew. Some kings did not like that! King Charles I ruled England from 1625 until 1649. He did not want Parliament limiting his power.

In 1603, the line of Stuart kings had begun with the reign of James I. King Charles I was the son of James. He believed in the **divine right** of kings. In other words, he believed that God gave him the right to rule. He also thought he should rule with absolute power.

King Charles decided to ask people to pay higher taxes. When people did not pay the high taxes he demanded, he had them thrown in jail.

Parliament did not like that. "What about the Magna Carta?" Parliament asked. "Rulers must have our approval on new taxes!"

TECHNOLOGY CONNECTION

Halley's Astronomy

Edmond Halley was a British scientist and astronomer who made many of the first advances in the study of space. He drew the first map of the universe in 1686.

In 1705, Halley published a description of the orbits of 24 comets that were seen between 1337 and 1698. Three of these comets had followed the same orbit in 1531, 1607, and 1682. Halley predicted (guessed) that this comet would reappear in 1758. This comet is now known as Halley's Comet.

Halley studied eclipses of the sun by various planets. In 1716, an eclipse by the planet Venus helped him learn more about the solar system. After watching this eclipse, Halley was able to better determine the distance of Earth from the sun.

Petition

A written request, often with many signatures, to a person or group in authority

Petition of Right

An English document that brought about more democracy

Consent

To agree to something

Royalist

A supporter of the king or queen during the English Civil War

Roundhead

A Puritan who fought for Parliament in the English Civil War

Remember

Parliament was created to limit a monarch's power.

Why Did King Charles I Do Away with Parliament?

In 1628, Parliament presented King Charles with a **petition,** or a written request. This petition is known as the **Petition of Right.** The petition said that a king could not demand new taxes without Parliament's **consent** or agreement. It also said the king could not throw people in jail without a jury trial.

King Charles agreed to the petition, but he did not keep his word. He kept raising taxes. When Parliament disagreed with King Charles about money, religion, and relations with other countries, Charles I decided to break up the whole group. King Charles ruled without a Parliament from 1629 until 1640.

Then trouble developed with Scotland. Charles I had been forcing the Scottish people to follow the English religion. Scotland rebelled. In response, Charles called Parliament back into session in 1640. He wanted money to go to war with Scotland.

Again Parliament tried to put reins on the king's power. Charles I reacted by arresting five of the leading members of Parliament. His troops marched right into a session of Parliament and made the arrest! That was too much. The people rebelled.

What Brought an End to King Charles' Reign?

In 1642, a civil war began in England. It lasted until 1649. The nobles who supported the king were called *Royalists.* The greatest supporters of Parliament were the Puritans. They were called *Roundheads* because they cut their hair short. They disagreed with King Charles about the church and other matters.

A man named Oliver Cromwell became a leading figure in the civil war. Cromwell was a member of Parliament. He led the Puritan army against the king.

Commonwealth
A nation in which the people hold the ruling power; a republic or democracy

Reading Strategy:
Predicting

Think about your prediction. What details can you now add to make your prediction more specific?

Cromwell's military victories meant the end of King Charles' reign. In 1649, Charles I was captured and tried by Parliament. He was found to be a "public enemy of the nation." Charles I was beheaded.

What Did Oliver Cromwell Do to the Parliament?

Parliament set up a republic. The republic, known as the **Commonwealth** of England, lasted from 1649 until 1660. Under the Commonwealth, England had no monarch. The country was governed by a committee of Parliament and its leader, Oliver Cromwell.

Cromwell, however, fought with Parliament. To solve the arguments, he put an end to Parliament in 1653. For the rest of the Commonwealth period, Cromwell ruled England alone.

Cromwell had believed in freedom. He had refused the title of king when Parliament once offered it to him. He had been against the total power of kings. Yet, now he had sole power in England. Cromwell's official title was Lord Protector of the Commonwealth. During his rule, he brought Ireland and Scotland under English control. His actions in Ireland were especially cruel.

Oliver Cromwell died in 1658. His son Richard tried to carry on his father's policies. Richard, however, was not as strong as his father. The people of England were also ready to return to the royal Stuart line.

Oliver Cromwell governed the Commonwealth of England. In 1653, he put an end to Parliament.

REVIEW

Word Bank

absolute

divine

ended

Roundheads

Royalists

On a sheet of paper, write the word from the Word Bank to complete each sentence correctly.

1. King Charles believed in the _____ right of kings.
2. King Charles wanted to rule with _____ power.
3. The _____ supported the king during the civil war.
4. The _____ disagreed with the king during the civil war.
5. The reign of King Charles _____ in 1649.

On a sheet of paper, write the letter of the answer that correctly completes each sentence.

6. King Charles forced the people in _____ to follow the English religion.

   A England   **C** Scotland
   B Ireland   **D** Parliament

7. The civil war in England lasted until _____.

   A 1642   **C** 1653
   B 1649   **D** 1658

8. Under the Commonwealth, _____ led the Parliament.

   A Oliver Cromwell   **C** King Charles
   B Richard Cromwell   **D** the Roundheads

9. Oliver Cromwell's official title was _____.

   A Lord Protector of the Commonwealth
   B Roundhead
   C King Oliver
   D General Cromwell

10. Oliver Cromwell put an end to _____ in 1653.

    A military victories   **C** Parliament
    B higher taxes   **D** jury trials

The Glorious Revolution

Glorious Revolution
The period in England that involved the overthrow of James II and the crowning of William and Mary

In 1660, Charles II became king. He restored Parliament, and things were quiet for a while. Unfortunately, new problems came up when James II came to the throne.

King James II became a Catholic. He asked for too much power. In response, Parliament sent word to James II's daughter Mary and her husband William of Orange. Parliament asked them to come from the Netherlands and take over James II's throne.

Did this anger King James? Yes. Did it cause another war? No. James II left the throne quietly. It was a bloodless takeover. Parliament persuaded William and Mary to sign over many of their royal rights and powers. The change came to be called the *Glorious Revolution.*

What Did the Bill of Rights Do for the English Government?

In 1689, William and Mary signed a Bill of Rights. This bill stated that the ruling monarch could act only after consulting Parliament. With that, England took another big step toward democracy. Now Parliament was truly a strong force in government.

One day the Americans would write their own Bill of Rights. The English Bill of Rights would serve as their model.

William and Mary understood the importance of democracy and involved the Parliament in their decisions.

Over time, Parliament itself became more democratic. By the late 1600s, the House of Lords held less power. The House of Commons held more. Members of the House of Lords still inherited their positions. House of Commons members, however, were elected.

REVIEW

Word Bank

Bill of Rights
bloodless
daughter
democracy
English
Glorious Revolution
House of Commons
House of Lords
Parliament
power

On a sheet of paper, write the word from the Word Bank to complete each sentence correctly.

1. King James asked for a lot of _____.

2. William of Orange and Mary took over James II's throne; Mary was James II's _____.

3. King James was upset at having to give up his throne. Nonetheless, it was a(n) _____ takeover.

4. Parliament persuaded William and Mary to sign over many of their royal rights. It came to be known as the _____.

5. William and Mary signed the _____ in 1689.

6. The Bill of Rights stated that the ruling monarch could act only after consulting _____.

7. The Bill of Rights helped England move toward _____.

8. Americans would model their Bill of Rights after the _____.

9. By the late 1600s, the _____ held less power.

10. _____ members were elected to Parliament.

Revolution in America

- To list complaints that colonists in America had against King George III and Britain
- To name five freedoms and rights that Americans won

Reading Strategy:
Predicting

Think about King George's problems. Predict what you may read about next.

Representation
Sending one or more people to speak for the rights of others before a body of the government

American Revolution
The American struggle against Great Britain for independence

Patriot
A person who is loyal to his or her own country

Liberty
Freedom

George III became king of England in 1760. When he came to the throne, England had colonies in North America. George asked for the loyalty of his subjects in America. They seemed happy to give that loyalty.

Why Did the Colonists Revolt Against English Rule?

George III had wars to pay for. Great Britain had fought a major war, the Seven Years' War. In North America this war was sometimes called the French and Indian War. In 1763, the French and Indian War ended in America. The Americans and British had defeated the French and some American Indian nations. Now someone had to pay the bills for war costs. King George decided to demand high taxes from his subjects in the colonies.

"High taxes, but no rights!" the American colonists complained. They had seen that people had won new rights in England. They read the words of Locke, Rousseau, and Voltaire. The Americans wanted rights and freedom, too.

"No taxation without **representation!**" was their cry. If they paid taxes to King George, they wanted a say in the government.

Some colonists wanted more than representation. They wanted freedom!

Many colonists were willing to fight for that freedom. That fight for freedom from British rule was known as the **American Revolution. Patriots** like Thomas Jefferson spoke out for **liberty,** or freedom. Jefferson used his pen to fight for independence. He wrote that Parliament had no right to control the colonies. He also said that unfair acts by the king meant the colonists owed him no loyalty.

The colonies asked Jefferson to write a declaration of independence.

On July 4, 1776, the **Declaration of Independence** was approved. King George sent troops to the colonies. The colonists had to fight the British for their independence. General George Washington led the fight. Washington would later become the first president of the new United States of America.

Thomas Jefferson wrote the Declaration of Independence. Americans signed it on July 4th, 1776.

TIMELINE STUDY:

FIGHTING FOR RIGHTS IN BRITAIN AND NORTH AMERICA

Who ruled England after the Commonwealth?

1649
Parliament sets up Commonwealth

1628
Petition of Right

1660
Stuarts rule again (Charles II)

1689
Glorious Revolution (William and Mary take throne); English Bill of Rights

1776
American colonists declare independence

1600 — 1650 — 1700 — 1750 — 1800

1642
Civil war begins in England

1760
George III takes throne

Words from the Past

The Declaration of Independence

In the Declaration that Thomas Jefferson wrote, he tried to speak for all colonists.

The Declaration was the colonists' announcement that the colonies were becoming a separate nation—the United States of America.

The following passages are from Thomas Jefferson's Declaration of Independence.

We hold these truths to be self-evident, that all men are created equal, that they are endowed by their Creator with certain unalienable Rights, that among these are Life, Liberty and the pursuit of Happiness.

That to secure these rights, Governments are instituted among Men, deriving their just powers from the consent of the governed.

That whenever any form of Government becomes destructive of these ends, it is the Right of the People to alter or to abolish it, and to institute new Government . . .

We, therefore, the Representatives of the United States of America . . . do . . . declare, That these United Colonies are, and of Right ought to be Free and Independent States . . . .

REVIEW

On a sheet of paper, write the letter of the answer that correctly completes each sentence.

1. George III became king of England in _____.

   A 1689 **B** 1760 **C** 1763 **D** 1776

2. The Seven Years' War is also known as the _____.

   A Glorious Revolution **C** Civil War
   B French and Indian War **D** Crusades

3. _____ wrote the Declaration of Independence.

   A George Washington **C** Jean Jacques Rousseau
   B Oliver Cromwell **D** Thomas Jefferson

4. The Declaration of Independence was approved on _____, 1776.

   A June 4 **B** August 6 **C** July 4 **D** December 25

Word Bank

freedom

patriot

representation

On a sheet of paper, write the word from the Word Bank to complete each sentence correctly.

5. Thomas Jefferson was a _____.

6. Colonists cried, "No taxation without _____.

7. Some colonists wanted more than representation, they wanted _____.

On a sheet of paper, write the answer to each question. Use complete sentences.

8. Why did King George demand high taxes from the colonies?

9. What complaints did American colonists have against King George III and Britain?

10. What were five rights that Americans won?

- Ideas of freedom, equality, and fairness came out of the Age of Reason.

- In 1295, the Parliament of England was made up of nobles, merchants, knights, and landowners.

- The English Parliament helped limit the powers of the monarch. Parliament has a House of Lords and a House of Commons. Some rulers did not like asking Parliament to allow them to raise taxes.

- During England's civil war, Oliver Cromwell led Parliament in overthrowing the king.

- After the war, Cromwell headed the Commonwealth from 1653 to 1658. He put an end to Parliament. He brought Ireland and Scotland under English control.

- The Stuart monarchy returned as Charles II took the throne in 1660. Charles restored Parliament. His reign was followed by James II.

- The Glorious Revolution was a bloodless takeover of the throne by William and Mary. The Glorious Revolution brought more power for Parliament and a Bill of Rights for the English people.

- King George III became king in 1760. He demanded high taxes of the American colonies to help pay off England's war debts.

- The English colonies in America resented paying taxes with no rights in return. They had thoughts of fighting for independence.

- In 1776, the American colonists declared their independence. They fought a war and won their freedom.

Word Bank

Commonwealth

consent

Declaration of
Independence

divine right

Enlightenment

liberty

patriot

representation

Vocabulary Review

On a sheet of paper, use the words from the Word Bank to correctly match each definition below.

1. A time when people questioned their way of life, and wanted freedom, equality, and fairness

2. A document American colonists signed; it declared their freedom from Great Britain

3. The idea that a monarch's right to govern comes from God

4. To agree to something

5. When one or more persons are chosen to speak for the rights of others

6. Freedom

7. A nation where people have the power to rule

8. A person, like Thomas Jefferson, who is loyal to his or her country

Chapter Review Questions

On a sheet of paper, write the answer to each question. Use complete sentences.

9. How did Voltaire, Rousseau, and Locke influence Britain and America?

10. Who were the Roundheads?

11. What was the problem between Parliament and King Charles I of England?

12. Who was Oliver Cromwell?

13. What was the Glorious Revolution in England?

Test Tip

It is easier to learn new vocabulary words if you make them part of your speaking and writing in other discussions and subject areas.

14. Why did King George III try to get more money out of American colonists?

15. Why did the American colonists want to revolt against British rule?

16. Who wrote the Declaration of Independence?

Critical Thinking

On a sheet of paper, write your response to each question. Use complete sentences.

17. How were the new ideas of the Age of Reason different from the old idea of divine right?

18. Why were the American colonists affected by the British fight for freedom and rights?

Using the Timeline

Use the timeline on page 366 to answer the questions.

19. Which came first, the Petition of Right or the English Bill of Rights?

20. When the American colonists declared their independence, how long had George III been king of England?

GROUP ACTIVITY

Work with a partner. Read the passages from the Declaration of Independence on page 367. Discuss with your partner what each paragraph means. Look up words in a dictionary if you need to. Then rewrite the paragraphs in your own words.

Revolution in France

Most of the people of France had no voice in their government. They were at the bottom of a country ruled by the upper class. As a group, they could be strong, because their voices were loud and many.

The French Revolution was a colorful, heated time in world history. The common people spoke out against persecution. For many, this led to death for their cause.

The reign of Napoleon began a time in which France thrived. While the people did not gain the freedoms being enjoyed in America, change was being made.

GOALS FOR LEARNING

- To explain why the French began to want freedom and equality
- To explain how the storming of the Bastille led to bloody rebellion in France
- To describe Napoleon Bonaparte's role in French government and war

Reading Strategy: Text Structure

Understanding how text is organized helps you decide which information is most important. Before you begin reading this chapter, do these things:

- Look at how it is organized.

- Look at the title, headings, boldfaced words, and photographs.

- Ask yourself: Is the text a problem and solution, description, or sequence? Is it compare and contrast or cause and effect?

- Summarize the text by thinking about its structure.

Key Vocabulary Words

Lesson 2

Estates-General The French governmental body made up of representatives from the three estates

Oath A serious promise

Bastille A prison in Paris

Symbol An object that stands for an idea

Riot A violent disturbance created by a crowd of people

Arsenal A place where guns and ammunition are stored

French Revolution The war that the common people of France fought against the king, nobles, and one another to achieve freedom

Betray To give help to the enemy

Motto A word or phrase that expresses goals, ideas, or ideals

Fraternity Brotherhood

Execute To kill someone for a crime

Reign of Terror The one-year period in French history when radical leaders put many people to death

Guillotine An instrument used for cutting off a person's head

Lesson 3

Dictator A ruler who has total power

Napoleonic Code The constitution Napoleon set up that contained a single set of laws for all of France and its territories

Colonial Having settlements in far-off lands

The Age of Reason in France

France, in the early 1700s, had a government that was still locked into the Middle Ages. French kings believed they ruled by divine right. No matter how unfair the rule, French people had to accept it. King Louis XIV is said to have declared, "I am the State."

Nobles led lives of luxury. They lived in fine palaces paid for by taxes collected from the lower and middle classes. While the nobles lived splendidly, the peasants often went without enough to eat.

How Did American Independence Affect the French?

By the 1780s, however, the French were listening to new ideas. They read the works of Rousseau and Voltaire. "Look at Britain," the writers said. "The people there are free. Look at the Americans, at their successful fight for freedom. We, too, deserve some rights!" Political conditions did not yet show it, but the Age of Reason had come to France.

The French had helped the Americans in their war for independence from British rule. French nobles were happy to see the British defeated by anyone. French peasants liked the idea of a fight against tyranny—the cruel and unjust use of power. The French noble, Lafayette, went to America and joined the colonists' battle. George Washington gave Lafayette command of a division, and the two fought side by side.

When the Americans won the war, the French began thinking about freedom for themselves.

On a sheet of paper, write the letter of the answer that correctly completes each sentence.

1. The French government in the early 1700s was still locked into _____.

  A war   **B** democracy   **C** the Revolution   **D** the Middle Ages

2. The French kings ruled by _____ and the French people had to accept it.

  A the constitution   **C** the Parliament
  B divine right   **D** the Third Estate

3. Nobles lived comfortable lives in palaces. The palaces were paid for by _____ collected from the lower and middle classes.

  A food   **B** crafts   **C** taxes   **D** goods

4. In contrast, the _____ often went without enough to eat.

  A Parliament   **B** craftworkers   **C** peasants   **D** merchants

5. The French looked at the freedom the _____ and Americans had, and wanted rights too.

  A Persians   **B** Germans   **C** Italians   **D** British

6. The _____ is when common sense began to take over people's thinking.

  A Age of Reason   **C** New Thinking
  B Revolution   **D** Tennis Court Oath

7. _____, a French noble, went to America and fought alongside the colonists.

  A King Louis XIV   **C** Rousseau
  B Lafayette   **D** George Washington

On a sheet of paper, write the answer to each question. Use complete sentences.

8. What did King Louis XIV mean when he declared, "I am the State"?

9. What are two French writers in the 1700s who had new ideas?

10. How did the Age of Reason and the American Revolution lead to revolution in France?

The King Tries to Limit Democracy

Objectives

- To identify the Three Estates
- To explain what the Bastille was and what it stood for
- To describe how the rest of Europe reacted to the French Revolution
- To describe the time known as the Reign of Terror

Estates-General

The French governmental body made up of representatives from the three estates

Reading Strategy:
Text Structure

Notice that the section headings are written as questions. After you read each section, try to answer the question asked in each heading.

By 1788, trouble was brewing in France. The peasants and the middle class were unhappy. The government was in trouble, too. It was out of money. Fancy living and too many wars had resulted in an empty treasury.

Why Was a Meeting of the Estates-General Called?

In 1789, King Louis XVI called a meeting of the **Estates-General.** This was a government body that was something like Britain's Parliament. The Estates-General had not met for 175 years. Now there was to be a meeting at Versailles. This was the name of the fine palace just outside of Paris where King Louis lived with his queen, Marie Antoinette. King Louis wanted the Estates-General to grant him more money in new taxes.

Three groups of people made up the Estates-General. Each group was called an *estate*. The First Estate included wealthy clergy. They arrived at King Louis's meeting dressed in fine clothing and riding in beautiful carriages.

Members of the Second Estate were the nobles. Many were wealthy and came from large country manors. Some of the nobles, however, had lost most of their wealth. They had only their titles left.

The First and Second Estates represented only a tiny part of the French population. The Third Estate represented most of the people of France. It represented a middle class of merchants and city workers and all the peasants.

Each of the three estates had one vote in meetings. This was hardly fair, since the Third Estate represented 98 percent of the population. The First and Second Estates could band together. They could then outvote the Third

Estate every time they wanted to. Members of the Third Estate were ready for change.

At the 1789 meeting in Versailles, the Third Estate asked for more votes. King Louis XVI refused.

What Was the Tennis Court Oath?

The Third Estate rebelled. The members called their own meeting. They declared themselves the National Assembly of France. The king refused to give them a government meeting hall. So the Third Estate held its own meeting at a nearby tennis court.

At the meeting, members of the Third Estate took the Tennis Court **Oath.** They swore that they would give France a constitution. The people of Paris celebrated. They supported the National Assembly. They wanted a constitution.

In the meantime, the king was organizing his troops. When he gathered an army near an assembly meeting, people began to worry. Was the king planning to stop the National Assembly by force? The people grew angry. Force, they said, would be met by force! France was now approaching the boiling point.

Why Did the French Storm the Bastille?

To the people of Paris, the **Bastille** was a terrible **symbol.** It stood for the tyranny of their king and for the injustices they faced. The Bastille was a gloomy fortress built in 1370. It was used as a prison. All that was needed to throw a French person into prison was the say-so of the king.

The Bastille was a dark, mysterious place. People were locked away there for disagreeing with the king or for failing to pay taxes. There were stories of men rotting away in the Bastille's dark dungeons and of terrible tortures. (A dungeon is a dark underground room used as a prison.)

Riot

A violent disturbance created by a crowd of people

Arsenal

A place where guns and ammunition are stored

 History Fact French people celebrate Bastille Day much as Americans celebrate the Fourth of July.

Actually, under earlier kings the prison had done away with dungeons and tortures. However, the horror stories remained. Most French people hated and feared the Bastille.

On July 14, 1789, a **riot** broke out in Paris. The people had become alarmed by the king's gathering of his troops. The people decided it was time to make a stand for freedom. They would attack the symbol of the king's unjust powers—the hated Bastille.

Early in the day, rioters broke into an **arsenal,** a place where guns and ammunition were stored. They took muskets and cannons. Then they attacked. "Down with the Bastille!" the excited rebels shouted. There was no stopping the large group of people, the mob. They murdered the governor of the prison. They carried his head on a stick through the streets.

The rebels then freed the prisoners. They opened the cells to find only seven prisoners inside! However, the Bastille had fallen, and the Revolution had begun.

On this same day, the king returned to his palace at Versailles after a day of hunting. Communication was slow in the 18th century. Therefore, he knew nothing of the riots and murders. It had been poor hunting that day. No deer had been killed. To describe his day, King Louis wrote only one word in his diary on July 14, 1789. He wrote *Rien*, a French word meaning "nothing."

The day that King Louis wrote *nothing* was a day that France would always remember!

An angry French mob stormed the Bastille, the royal prison, on July 14th, 1789. This marked the start of the French Revolution.

French Revolution

The war that the common people of France fought against the king, nobles, and one another to achieve freedom

Betray

To give help to the enemy; to be unfaithful to

Motto

A word or phrase that expresses goals, ideas, or ideals

Fraternity

Brotherhood

Reading Strategy:
Text Structure

As you read the lesson, use a graphic organizer to organize the order of events in the French Revolution.

What Came Out of all the Protests?

Revolutionaries in France were excited by the storming of the Bastille. They began their own protests for freedom. Peasants rose up against feudal lords. Many nobles fled the country because they did not feel safe. In October, a group of women set out from Paris. They wanted the king to give the people more grain. To keep order, the king marched with them from Versailles to Paris.

During the next three years, 1789–1791, the National Assembly wrote the new constitution it had promised. New laws were made that did away with the feudal system. The nobles lost most of their rights and privileges. The king lost much of his power. The old system of taxes was also ended.

On August 26, 1789, the National Assembly adopted the Declaration of the Rights of Man. It was based on the English Bill of Rights and the American Declaration of Independence.

How Was the National Convention Formed?

Rulers throughout Europe saw what was happening in France. They were frightened. They worried that ideas of revolution could spread to their lands. The rulers of Austria and Prussia sent armies into France to try to crush the Revolution.

The leaders of the **French Revolution** were outraged. They thought that their own king had called for the outside armies. They accused Louis XVI of being unfaithful to, or **betraying,** France. They forced him off the throne. Then they held elections for a new lawmaking body called the *National Convention*.

In 1792, the National Convention declared France a republic. The **motto** of the new republic was "Liberty, Equality, and **Fraternity!**" In other words, they demanded freedom, the same rights for everyone, and brotherhood.

Execute

To kill someone for a crime

Reign of Terror

The one-year period in French history when radical leaders put many people to death

Guillotine

An instrument used for cutting off a person's head

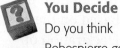

You Decide

Do you think Robespierre got what he deserved? Why or why not?

What Was Happening During the Reign of Terror?

Leaders of the new republic became fearful of their enemies. Their main goal was to seek out those enemies and to do away with them. The Revolution became bloodier.

Revolutionaries found King Louis XVI guilty of betraying his country. In 1793, Louis XVI and Marie Antoinette were **executed,** or killed for their crime. Throughout 1793 and 1794, the new leaders of France arrested and executed many people. Anyone suspected of being against the Republic was attacked. It was a time known as the *Reign of Terror.* "Off with their heads!" became the cry of that stage of the French Revolution.

A Frenchman had invented the **guillotine,** a machine for quickly cutting off heads! Hundreds of suspected enemies of the revolution were beheaded. Carts rolled through the streets of Paris, carrying victims to the guillotine.

A man named Robespierre was one of the most violent leaders of the Revolution. Robespierre believed the Republic would never be safe as long as one enemy lived. Later, the people turned on Robespierre himself. They blamed him for the bloodshed. After sentencing so many others to death, Robespierre lost his own head to the French guillotine.

The country was in turmoil—a state of great confusion. The leaders of the Revolution could not control the people or organize the government. The fighting and bloodshed went on and on.

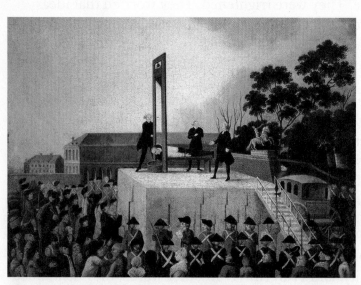

Those considered to be enemies of the new French Republic were executed by guillotine.

On a sheet of paper, write the answer to each question. Use complete sentences.

1. What groups made up each of the Three Estates that met in Versailles in 1789?

2. Why was the National Assembly formed and what was their purpose? (Be sure to mention the oath they took.)

3. What is the Bastille and what does it stand for?

4. What happened on July 14, 1789?

5. What effect did the storming of the Bastille have on the rest of France?

6. What did the Declaration of the Rights of Man promise?

7. How did the rest of Europe react to the French Revolution?

8. Why was Louis XVI forced off the throne? What was formed to take over his position?

9. What did the National Convention declare in 1792? What affect did it have on the Revolution?

10. What was the time known as the Reign of Terror like?

Napoleon Bonaparte

Dictator

A ruler who has total power

Napoleonic Code

The constitution Napoleon set up that contained a single set of laws for all of France and its territories; it remains the basis of French law today

The Revolution had created a strong, new army. That army drove Austrian and Prussian forces out of France. One of the officers in the French army was a young man named Napoleon Bonaparte.

Meanwhile, the National Convention of France had been growing steadily weaker. In October 1795 it came under attack by an army of 30,000 national guardsmen. The guardsmen wanted to get rid of the National Convention and bring back the monarchy. The Convention called on General Napoleon Bonaparte to put down the uprising. Napoleon, a general at age 26, proved his military worth. On October 5, 1795, he brought in a battery of cannons. The uprising ended soon after.

The Directory soon replaced the National Convention in the leadership of France. The Directory eventually became corrupt, meaning it did not rule very honestly.

How Did Napoleon Come to Power?

As Napoleon won battles and gained power, the Directory began to worry. Was Napoleon trying to become the sole ruler of France?

That is exactly what Napoleon did. He pushed out the Directory. Then in 1799, he made himself **dictator** of France. As a dictator, he had total power. One of the first things Napoleon did as ruler was to set up the **Napoleonic Code.** This was a new constitution that contained a single set of laws for all of France and its territories. The Napoleonic Code remains the basis of French law to this day.

Reading Strategy:
Text Structure

Study the map. How does it help you to understand the changes in Napoleon's empire?

France soon discovered that Napoleon was a good politician as well as a good soldier. Napoleon put himself directly in charge of the army. He brought a quick end to the fighting within France. He set up a police force responsible only to him. He invited back the nobles who had fled France during the Revolution. "You will be safe," Napoleon told them, "if you are loyal to me."

Napoleon's Empire, 1812

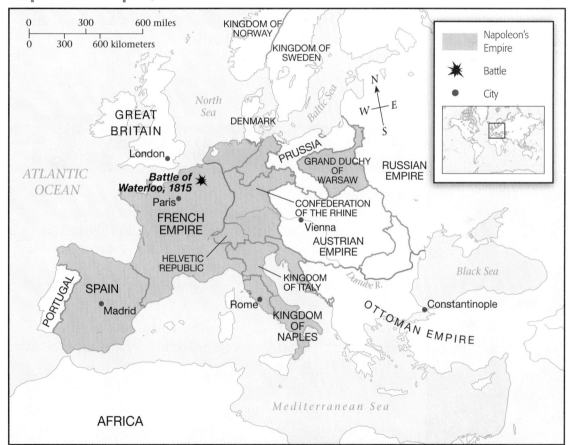

MAP STUDY

1. What are the names of three cities in lands ruled by Napoleon?

2. In which empire is Vienna?

What Did Napoleon Do for France?

Napoleon put an end to the French Republic that the Revolution had won. In 1804, Napoleon had himself crowned emperor. He then crowned his wife, Josephine, empress. He let his ambition and desire for power spread war across Europe. Yet he also made some good changes in the French government.

Napoleon changed unfair tax laws. He required all people, rich and poor, to pay taxes under the same laws. The rich received no favors. Napoleon also strengthened and reorganized the French schools.

History Fact
For 15 years, the history of Europe was the history of Napoleon's conquests.

LEARN MORE ABOUT IT

Napoleon's Mistake

In 1812, Napoleon declared war on Russia. He attacked with an army of nearly 600,000 men. The battle at Borodino resulted in many deaths but no clear winner. However, the Russian armies were clever. They fled eastward, leading Napoleon's army on a chase deep into the heart of Russia. As the Russians retreated, they destroyed everything of value in Napoleon's path.

When Napoleon and his army reached Moscow, they found a deserted city. Most of the people had fled. Those who stayed behind set fire to the city. The French soon found themselves occupying a city of ruins.

Then winter came. It was an icy Russian winter. Napoleon's army had almost run out of food; they were starving and freezing. There was only one thing to do. Napoleon gave the orders to head for home. The Russians attacked again and again as Napoleon's weakened forces struggled toward France. The French suffered terrible losses during the retreat from Russia. Over 500,000 men were killed or died of illness or starvation. Others deserted or were captured. Many simply froze to death. The attack on Russia was Napoleon's big mistake.

Dictator and later emperor of France, Napoleon Bonaparte was very powerful.

Geography Note

Avignon is a city in southeastern France where the Rhone and Durance Rivers meet. It was a Phoenician trading port before it became a thriving city of the Roman Empire. In the 14th century it was home of the pope as the seat of the Roman Catholic Church. During much of this time, the Babylonian Empire controlled Rome. The city remained a territory of the pope for centuries. Its location encouraged a good deal of trading activity, as did its rare bridge over the Rhone River. Avignon was controlled by the Roman church until 1791. At that time, Revolutionary leaders took possession of the city for France.

Napoleon made most things, including education and the press, subject to strict government control. In fact, the French government *was* Napoleon!

Napoleon had a strong, wealthy France behind him now. He had the loyalty of the people. He now set out to conquer a European empire. He led France into war with Great Britain and most of the rest of Europe. Napoleon was a clever general. He won battle after battle. By 1812, Napoleon controlled most of Europe. However, he had been unable to invade and conquer Great Britain.

What Brought Napoleon's Rule to an End?

Other countries took heart when they heard of France's defeat in Russia. Napoleon could be beaten! These countries joined together. Prussia, Sweden, and Austria joined with Great Britain and Russia to march as allies against Napoleon.

The French saw that their emperor was beaten. The French Senate turned against Napoleon. It called for a new king to rule France. On April 11, 1814, Napoleon gave up his throne. Louis XVIII was crowned King of France. Napoleon was exiled and sent to live on the island of Elba off the coast of Italy.

Napoleon was not a man who gave up easily. In less than a year, he had escaped from Elba and returned to France. There he found supporters and actually ruled France again for 100 days. However, Napoleon's dream of ruling Europe was about to come to an end.

What Happened as a Result of the Battle of Waterloo?

The allies against Napoleon joined forces as soon as they heard of his return. With about 75,000 troops, Napoleon marched into Belgium to meet the allied forces. The Duke of Wellington had about 67,000 troops from Britain, Belgium, Hanover, and the Netherlands.

The Battle of Waterloo brought the end to Napoleon's reign.

The fighting began on June 18, 1815, and is known as the Battle of Waterloo. The battle between the French and the allies was just about even for a few hours. Then Prussian troops arrived to back up the allies. That tipped the scale. After one last, fierce attack by France's famous *Old Guard*, the French had to retreat.

Again, Napoleon was sent away as a prisoner. The British sent him to far-off Saint Helena. This was a tiny island off the west coast of Africa. It was there on May 5, 1821, that Napoleon died.

Colonial

Having settlements in far-off lands

What Was France Like After Napoleon?

A royal line of kings ruled France once more. Then, again, there was a revolution. For the next 55 years, France saw change after change—three revolutions in all. There was a Second Republic, a Second Empire, and then, in 1870, a Third Republic.

Under the Third Republic, France built a **colonial** empire. French colonies around the world strengthened French trade and industry. France's Third Republic lasted until World War II when Germany took over France.

After World War II, a Fourth Republic was set up—and then a Fifth. Social revolution continued. Women struggled to take their place in society, to hold property, and to take jobs. Minority groups looked for work, for fair pay, and for good housing. The French still worked toward "Liberty, Equality, and Fraternity."

Reading Strategy:
Text Structure

Study the timeline. How does it help you to understand the sequence of events in this chapter?

TIMELINE STUDY: **FRENCH REVOLUTIONS: 1750–1900**

Which came first, the Second Empire or the Second Republic?

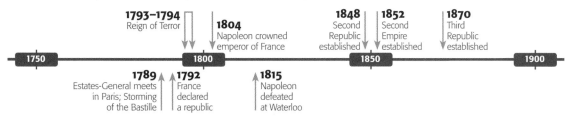

1793–1794 Reign of Terror

1804 Napoleon crowned emperor of France

1848 Second Republic established

1852 Second Empire established

1870 Third Republic established

1750 — 1800 — 1850 — 1900

1789 Estates-General meets in Paris; Storming of the Bastille

1792 France declared a republic

1815 Napoleon defeated at Waterloo

REVIEW

On a sheet of paper, write the answer to each question. Use complete sentences.

1. Why and how was the National Convention replaced?

2. What is the Napoleonic Code?

3. What are two good changes Napoleon made?

4. What was Napoleon's big mistake?

5. What was the Battle of Waterloo?

On a sheet of paper, write the letter of the answer that correctly completes each sentence.

6. In 1799, Napoleon made himself _____ of France.

   A head of the Directory   **C** dictator
   B a soldier   **D** emperor

7. In 1804, Napoleon made himself _____ of France.

   A head of the Directory   **C** dictator
   B a soldier   **D** emperor

8. By 1812, Napoleon controlled most of _____.

   A France   **B** Europe   **C** Russia   **D** Great Britain

9. _____ was crowned King of France after Napoleon gave up his throne.

   A Louis XVIII   **C** Louis XVI
   B Robespierre   **D** Duke of Wellington

10. France went through _____ revolutions in the 55 years after Napoleon.

    A two   **B** three   **C** four   **D** five

- The government of France had changed little since the Middle Ages.

- The Age of Reason and the American Revolution gave the French people ideas about fighting for their own freedom.

- French kings, like Louis XVI, believed that they ruled by divine right.

- The First and Second Estates of the Estates-General represented a tiny piece of the French population. They were mostly wealthy clergy and nobles.

- The Third Estate of the French Estates-General represented all the common people.

- The French Revolution began on July 14, 1789, with the storming of the Bastille.

- King Louis XVI was found guilty of betraying his country. Louis XVI and Marie Antoinette were executed.

- The Reign of Terror from 1793 to 1794 led to increased fear and bloodshed.

- Napoleon Bonaparte stepped in to restore order in France. He conquered much of Europe and brought about many changes in the French government.

- France went through several revolutions in the late 1700s and the 1800s.

- The Third Republic built an empire of colonies. It helped strengthen France's trade and industry.

Word Bank

arsenal

betrayed

dictator

executed

fraternity

guillotine

motto

oath

riot

symbol

Vocabulary Review

On a sheet of paper, use the words from the Word Bank to complete each sentence correctly.

1. The Bastille was a(n) _____ of the injustices the people of France faced.

2. Napoleon took total power and became a(n) _____.

3. A(n) _____ is a serious promise, often given in the name of God.

4. The new French republic encouraged _____.

5. A(n) _____ broke out in July 1789, and the French attacked the Bastille.

6. Weapons are sometimes stored in a(n) _____.

7. When Revolution leaders thought Louis XVI _____ France, they forced him off the throne.

8. After King Louis XVI was found guilty of betraying his country, he was _____.

9. The _____ of the French Revolution was, "Liberty, Equality, and Fraternity!"

10. Robespierre, a violent leader of the Revolution, lost his head to the French _____.

Chapter Review Questions

On a sheet of paper, write the answer to each question. Use complete sentences.

11. What ideas did Rousseau and Voltaire give the French people?

12. What effect did the Age of Reason and the American Revolution have on the French people?

Test Tip

Look for direction details that tell you the correct form of the answer. For example, some directions may ask for a paragraph, and others may require only a sentence or phrase.

13. Why did members of the Third Estate think the Estates-General was unfair?

14. Why did so many people hate the Bastille?

15. What was one of the first things Napoleon did after he made himself dictator of France?

16. What did France do under the Third Republic, established in 1870?

Critical Thinking

On a sheet of paper, write your response to each question. Use complete sentences.

17. Why were European countries afraid the revolution would spread to them?

18. Overall, was Napoleon a success or a failure? Give reasons for your answer.

Using the Timeline

Use the timeline on page 387 to answer the questions.

19. What happened almost immediately after France became a republic?

20. When Napoleon was defeated at Waterloo, how long had he been emperor of France?

GROUP ACTIVITY

Form a group of three or four. Choose an event in the chapter. Write a skit about it. Practice performing the skit. Then present it to the rest of the class.

THE AGE OF IMPERIALISM

Changes in the world over hundreds of years were often connected to power over the earth's resources. In many cases, this meant conquering new lands and controlling new groups of people. As countries learned how to better manufacture different products, they needed more material. Similar knowledge helped them build better methods of transportation to travel to far-off places. Still other learning helped them take control of other lands, using new and stronger weapons. As people's abilities grew, so did their sense of imperialism. At the same time, changes in the makeup of the world seem to happen more rapidly all the time.

Chapters in Unit 8

In 1900, the Chinese rebelled against all foreigners in China. This revolt is known as the Boxer Rebellion. It was one of the many uprisings brought on by imperialism during this time in history.

The Industrial Revolution

The word *revolution* is an interesting one. In the last chapter, it was a fiery battle to upset the unpopular government of France. You have likely learned about the *revolution* of the earth, or the way it moves around the sun. Now, consider the definition you learned in Chapter 1, that *revolution* is another word for "change."

The Industrial Revolution was a huge, rapid change from making goods by hand to making them by machine. It was about more products and a greater need for materials to make those products. It was about more jobs for more people. In some cases, it meant that more people earned money to gain more freedom or, in some cases more power.

GOALS FOR LEARNING

- To tell why the Industrial Revolution began in Great Britain
- To explain inventions of the 1700s
- To explain how the Industrial Revolution changed life
- To explain how the Industrial Revolution made countries more dependent on each other

Reading Strategy: Visualizing

Visualizing is another way to help you understand what you are reading. When you visualize a text, you imagine how it looks. These things will help you visualize a text:

- Use the photographs, illustrations, and descriptive words to "set the stage" for the text.

- Think about experiences you may have faced that are similar to those described in the text.

- Notice the order in which things are happening; try to visualize what will happen next.

Key Vocabulary Words

Lesson 1
Profit The amount of money left over after paying for the cost of doing business

Industrial Revolution The important changes that took place in the way work was done during the 18th and 19th century

Natural resource Materials that are provided by nature

Energy Power that makes machines work

Locomotive A self-propelled vehicle that runs on rails

Investor A person who expects to make a profit by lending money to a business

Raw material Matter in its natural condition

Textile Cloth made by weaving

Import To bring into one country from another

Lesson 2
Internal combustion engine An engine that burns gasoline to produce power

Lesson 3
Labor union A group of workers who join together

Lesson 4
Developed country A nation that has many industries and that imports and exports products

Developing country A nation that is slowly growing its industry and economy

Export To send a product out of one country and into another to sell

Industries Develop

Profit
The amount of money
left over after paying
for the cost of doing
business

**Industrial
Revolution**
The important
changes that took
place in the way work
was done during the
18th and 19th century

Natural resource
Materials that are
provided by nature,
such as forests,
minerals, and water

Energy
Power that makes
machines work

The most dramatic changes in industry began in Great
Britain in about 1750. It is true that people had been
inventing things during earlier years. However, most of
their work centered around scientific theories and ideas.
Now science and invention took a more practical, or
useful, turn. They developed machines especially designed
to increase the production of goods and to help people
make a **profit.**

Why Did the Industrial Revolution Begin in Great Britain?

The **Industrial Revolution** began in Great Britain for
a number of reasons. For one thing, Britain had a large
supply of workers. Women, as well as men, were ready to
leave their homes and join the industrial workforce.

Great Britain also had the **natural resources** needed for
industry. Natural resources are materials that are provided
by nature, such as coal and iron. Indeed, Britain had a
good supply of coal and iron. Coal could produce the
energy to keep the new steam engines running. Coal
was also needed to produce iron. Iron could be used to
improve machines and tools. It could also be used to build
railroad tracks, bridges, and ships.

Britain had the **transportation** that industry needed.
Products had to be marketed and moved. Steam
locomotives and steam-only ocean-going ships were
developed in Britain in the 1700s and 1800s.

Transportation
The act of carrying from one place to another

Locomotive
A self-propelled vehicle that runs on rails

Investor
A person who expects to make a profit by lending money to a business

Market
A place to sell goods

Raw material
Matter in its natural condition, not changed by some human process

Factory
A building where goods are made by machinery

Textile
Cloth made by weaving

Import
To bring into one country from another

Britain had **investors.** These were people with money to back the new businesses.

Britain had colonies to serve as ready **markets** for the goods. British colonies also supplied **raw materials,** like cotton, to the **factories** in London and other cities. It was in the factories where the goods were made by machinery.

Finally, the British government was eager to support growing industry. For all these reasons, Great Britain saw a burst of industrial development. In the late 1700s and 1800s, Britain became known as the "Workshop of the World."

Why Was the Textile Industry in Need of New Development?

Britain's **textile** industry produced cloth. This industry is a good example of what the early Industrial Revolution was all about.

In the earliest days, British merchants **imported** cloth from other lands. Because of the cost of shipping finished goods, cloth was expensive.

Later, in the 1600s, Britain began importing raw cotton. The British spun their own threads and then wove their own cloth.

Farm families did the work. They set up spinning wheels and looms in their cottages. Both spinning wheels and looms were operated by hand. The families who worked this way were called *cottage weavers.*

History Fact

In 1707, Scotland joined England and Wales to become Great Britain, or Britain.

Reading Strategy:
Visualizing

Create a graphic organizer for making simple sketches to illustrate the changes in the textile industry.

Merchants would buy the finished cloth from the cottage weavers. The amounts of cloth produced were never very large. In order to meet their own needs, the weavers had to farm land, too. They could only make cloth in their spare time. There was never enough finished cloth for all the people who wanted to buy it. Therefore, British business leaders looked for ways to improve and increase the production of textiles.

During the 1600s, weavers set up spinning wheels and looms in their cottages. They sold the cloth they wove to merchants.

REVIEW

Word Bank

British

coal

cottage weavers

cotton

imported

small

steam

On a sheet of paper, write the word from the Word Bank to complete each sentence correctly.

1. Britain had a good supply of natural resources such as _____ and iron.

2. In the 1700s and 1800s, Britain developed locomotives and ships that were powered by _____.

3. British colonies supplied raw materials, like _____, to the factories in London and other cities.

4. At first, cloth was _____ from other lands to Britain, making it quite expensive.

5. In the 1600s, the _____ began to import raw cotton to weave their own cloth.

6. _____ operated the spinning wheels and looms by hand.

7. Weavers produced a(n) _____ amount of cloth, which they made in their spare time.

On a sheet of paper, write the answer to each question. Use complete sentences.

8. What dramatic changes in industry happened in Great Britain around 1750?

9. What are four reasons the Industrial Revolution began in Great Britain?

10. Why did British business leaders want to improve the production of textiles?

New Inventions

Objectives

■ To name five machines that improved the making of textiles

■ To name two machines that were powered by steam

■ To describe two uses for oil

Reading Strategy: Visualizing

Draw pictures to help visualize any of the new inventions. How do they help you remember?

In the 1700s some new machines were invented that changed the textile industry. Spinners and weavers left their cottages and went to work in new factories.

What Inventions Helped Move Textile-Making Out of Cottages?

The first important invention in the textile-making revolution was the *flying shuttle.* In 1733, a man named John Kay invented a shuttle, a device on a loom. The shuttle made it possible to weave wider pieces of cloth. Now one worker could do the work of two.

Soon more cotton yarn was needed than could be produced. Business leaders offered prizes to the inventor of a machine to spin yarn. In 1764, James Hargreaves came up with just such a machine. He named it after his wife. The *spinning jenny* used the same ideas as the spinning wheel. But it could spin as many as 80 threads at one time.

The biggest change came in 1769. In that year, Richard Arkwright invented a machine called the *water frame.* Now even more cotton thread could be spun at once. The water frame ran by water power. It was so big that it could not fit into a cottage. It was also an expensive piece of machinery. The water frame required a special building of its own.

New machines forced the textile business out of the English cottages. Mills and factories were built. Workers were no longer their own bosses. They became factory hands. They worked in large mills that often employed up to 600 people.

In 1779, Samuel Crompton put the spinning jenny and the water frame into one machine. He called it the *mule*. The mule could spin much finer threads very rapidly.

Now the weavers had to keep step with the spinners. With so much thread being produced, the textile industry needed a better loom. In about 1785, Edmund Cartwright invented a steam-powered loom.

Workers sometimes feared the new machines. Would the machines completely replace the workers? Would they lose their jobs? At one point, antimachine riots broke out. Mobs smashed machines, shouting, "Men, not machines!" Sometimes progress was a frightening thing. The Industrial Revolution, however, could not be stopped.

Within 50 years, the textile industry had entirely changed. What had been a cottage industry had turned into a big business. As a result, a way of life had changed, too, for thousands of textile workers.

The spinning jenny made spinning yarn faster and easier.

History Fact
The power unit called the *watt* was named in honor of James Watt. He made steam power practical.

How Did the Steam Engine Change the Transportation Industry?

The new machines needed power. Water power was not strong enough to run heavy machines. During the 1600s, inventors had begun experimenting with "fire engines," or steam engines. In 1698, Thomas Savery built the first commercial steam engine. Around 1712, Thomas Newcomen improved on Savery's engine. It was, however, far from perfect. It used too much coal.

In 1769, a Scottish engineer named James Watt invented an improved steam engine. For several years only the textile industry made use of Watt's engine. By 1850, however, it was being used throughout Britain. Then it spread throughout the rest of Europe.

The invention of the steam engine completely changed transportation. In 1804, a British engineer, Richard Trevithick, built the first steam locomotive. Steam locomotives came into general use in Britain in the late 1830s. By 1850, Great Britain had 6,600 miles of railroad track. The United States, France, and Germany built their own rail systems during the next 10 years.

Early steam locomotives were simple but powerful.

An American, Robert Fulton, built the first successful steamboat in 1807. Within a few years, steamboats were being used on British rivers. By the mid-1800s, steam-powered ships were carrying raw materials and finished goods across the ocean.

What Were Some Advances in Electricity and Petroleum?

In 1831, an Englishman named Michael Faraday invented a machine called the *dynamo*. It generated an electric current by using magnets. Faraday's discovery led to the building of more powerful electric generators and electric motors. In time the use of electricity as a source of power would become widespread.

In the 1850s, Americans discovered that petroleum, or unrefined oil, could be used for many things. It could be used to make kerosene, and kerosene could be used for heat and light. Oil could make machinery run more smoothly. Fortunately, there was a good supply of crude oil available in the United States.

Oil was to become one of the most valuable resources in the world. This would come about with the invention of the **internal combustion engine** and the diesel engine. Petroleum could be turned into gasoline and diesel fuel to run those engines. Oil would give some nations new wealth and power.

On a sheet of paper, write the letter of the answer that correctly completes each sentence.

1. The _____, invented in 1764, could spin as many as 80 threads at one time.

    A water frame   **C** steam-powered loom
    B spinning jenny   **D** mule

2. Edmund Cartwright's invention, the _____, helped the weavers keep up with the spinners.

    A steam-powered loom   **C** steam engine
    B spinning jenny   **D** dynamo

3. James Watt's new and improved _____ completely changed transportation.

    A steam locomotive   **C** flying shuttle
    B steam-powered loom   **D** steam engine

4. Because of the _____, many countries laid hundreds of miles of railroad track.

    A diesel engine   **C** spinning jenny
    B dynamo   **D** steam locomotive

5. The American Robert Fulton built the first successful _____.

    A water frame   **C** river steamboat
    B steam-powered loom   **D** diesel engine

6. Michael Faraday invented the _____, which generated an electric current by using magnets.

    A dynamo   **C** internal combustion engine
    B flying shuttle   **D** mule

On a sheet of paper, write the answer to each question. Use complete sentences.

7. What was the first important invention in the textile-making revolution and what did it do?

8. What machine did Richard Arkwright invent in 1769 and what did it do?

9. Why did workers sometimes fear new machines?

10. What are two things oil can be used for?

The Industrial Revolution Changes Life

Objectives

- To explain how the Industrial Revolution encouraged imperialism
- To describe how the Industrial Revolution affected people's lives
- To describe the purpose of a labor union

Reading Strategy: Visualizing

What words in this lesson help you to visualize what you are reading about?

 Remember
Imperialism is the practice of conquering other lands, forming colonies in other lands, or controlling the government and wealth of weaker lands.

As with any revolution, industrialization brought changes to Great Britain. While some of the changes were good, other times they were not.

How Did the Industrial Revolution Encourage Imperialism?

The Industrial Revolution meant new inventions and new products. It also meant new needs. As the ability to produce goods increased, so did the need for more raw materials. Britain needed even more coal to fire the steam engines. It needed more cotton to spin into thread. It also needed more iron to make railroad tracks and machinery.

Imperialism seemed to be a solution to the problems of getting raw materials. Britain took over land in Africa and Asia and formed colonies. The colonies were sources of raw materials. In addition, the colonies became markets for finished products from Britain.

Did the Industrial Revolution Improve Life?

Did the Industrial Revolution improve the lives of the British people? Or did it make life harder? A look at life in Great Britain in the late 1700s and early 1800s gives a mixed picture.

In many ways life was better. Average incomes tripled between 1700 and 1815. Between 1815 and 1836, incomes increased 30 times over! People had better food to eat. They had more meat, sugar, tea, and coffee. Coal not only fueled the industrial machines, it also heated homes and cooked food.

For the merchants, bankers, shipowners, and factory owners, the Industrial Revolution meant wealth. The middle class now had a greater voice in the British government.

New inventions in communication let people learn what was going on in their world. In 1837, Samuel F. B. Morse invented the telegraph. He also invented a code to send telegrams—the Morse code. By 1866, a telegraph cable reached across the Atlantic.

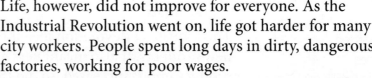
Life, however, did not improve for everyone. As the Industrial Revolution went on, life got harder for many city workers. People spent long days in dirty, dangerous factories, working for poor wages.

At first factory work had paid well. But soon the owners found they could hire women and children for lower wages than men. Soon most of the factory workers were women and children. Many children were very young. Factory wages dropped.

Young children often worked at machines under dangerous conditions.

LEARN MORE ABOUT IT

Child Labor

Many of the children working in factories came from orphanages or poor families. They were treated much like slaves. They often had to work from five in the morning until eight at night. Some factory owners treated the children quite well. Others beat the young workers for such crimes as falling asleep at their work or working too slowly.

In the 1800s there were new laws called Factory Acts. These laws took the very youngest children out of the factories. The laws also put limits on the number of hours children and women could work.

Despite the new laws, work could be dangerous. There were no safety measures or protection against industrial accidents. It is sad to imagine what happened to many little children working on dangerous machines with no safety devices.

Reading Strategy:
Visualizing

Draw a simple sketch of city life showing how it has been shaped by industry. How do these drawings help you remember?

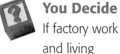

You Decide

If factory work and living conditions in the cities were so awful, why do you think so many people moved to the cities?

How Did the Living Conditions in the Cities Change?

Britain's cities were becoming dark with ash from the new coal-burning factories. As the skies blackened, the factories drew people to the cities. As a result, British cities went through a population explosion. In 1801, about 78 percent of people in Britain lived on farms. By 1901, about 75 percent lived in cities.

Where were all these people going to make their homes? Housing had to be built quickly and cheaply. The results were poorly built slum buildings. Inside were small apartments where whole families often shared one room. Sewage and garbage could not be disposed of properly. These conditions led to the outbreak and spread of disease.

1700–1850   *The Industrial Revolution*   *Chapter 19*   **407**

Earning a living became difficult as more people moved into cities.

History Fact

An American visited a British textile mill in 1810. Within a few years he built the first textile factory in the United States. It was located in Waltham, Massachusetts.

It would not be long before people began to protest against this kind of life. They protested against factories that employed young children and paid terrible wages. They protested against having to work with dangerous machines that had no safety devices.

The Industrial Revolution taught workers that they had to band together. They formed **labor unions** to demand better, fairer conditions. Of course factory owners were not in favor of the workers' unions. Until 1825, unions were against the law in Great Britain.

Word Bank

children

coal

disease

incomes

middle

population explosion

telegraph

On a sheet of paper, write the word from the Word Bank to complete each sentence correctly.

1. Average _____ increased as a result of the Industrial Revolution.

2. _____ was used to heat homes and cook food.

3. The Industrial Revolution allowed the _____ class to have a greater voice in the British government.

4. The invention of the _____ allowed people to communicate across the ocean.

5. Factory wages dropped when factories began to employ women and _____.

6. The cities experienced a(n) _____ because of the Industrial Revolution.

7. Without a proper way to dispose of sewage and garbage, _____ spread more rapidly.

On a sheet of paper, write the answer to each question. Use complete sentences.

8. How did the Industrial Revolution encourage imperialism?

9. What were the Factory Acts?

10. What was the purpose of a labor union?

The Industrial Revolution Spreads

Objectives

■ To explain the role of industrial countries
■ To tell how the less-developed countries profited from the revolution

Developed country

A nation that has many industries and that imports and exports products

Developing country

A nation that is slowly developing its industry and economy

Export

To send a product out of one country and into another to sell

Industrialization began in Great Britain. But during the 1800s, it spread to France, Germany, the United States, Russia, and finally Japan.

How Did the Relations Between Nations Change?

Over time industrialization forced nations of the world to depend on each other. Countries had to work out trade agreements. The more industrialized countries, known as **developed countries,** built the factories and produced the goods. They often depended on other nations for raw materials. Less developed countries, known as **developing countries,** needed finished products. Many of these countries profited from their natural resources.

The United States, Germany, Japan, and Great Britain are considered developed countries. They depend on Saudi Arabia, Mexico, Indonesia, Nigeria, and other developing countries for crude oil. They get uranium from nations in Africa. Chile and Peru **export** copper, meaning they ship copper to another country to sell.

The results of the Industrial Revolution can be seen in British coal mines, in Japanese electronics factories, in cities, and on farms. The Industrial Revolution has changed the way people live and where they live. It has changed the way they depend on each other.

Reading Strategy:
Visualizing

How could this lesson be written differently to create a stronger picture in your mind?

At one time, some people thought that the Industrial Revolution would come to an end. They thought that all the great changes and developments had already happened. In the late 1800s, it was actually suggested that the United States Patent Office be closed. Surely, some people thought, everything possible had already been invented. We know now that the revolution is far from over. New developments continue every day. In fact, in recent years, large international companies have made their finished products in developing countries. There, labor is cheap. Developed countries may produce many services and fewer finished products.

TIMELINE STUDY:
THE INDUSTRIAL REVOLUTION

When was the machine invented that was a combination of the spinning jenny and the water frame?

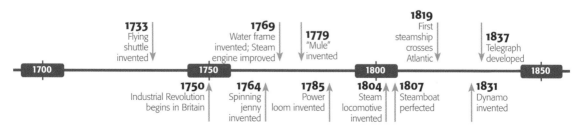

1733 Flying shuttle invented

1769 Water frame invented; Steam engine improved

1779 "Mule" invented

1819 First steamship crosses Atlantic

1837 Telegraph developed

1700 — 1750 — 1800 — 1850

1750 Industrial Revolution begins in Britain

1764 Spinning jenny invented

1785 Power loom invented

1804 Steam locomotive invented

1807 Steamboat perfected

1831 Dynamo invented

REVIEW

Word Bank

crude oil

finished products

industrialization

live

raw materials

services

trade agreements

On a sheet of paper, write the word from the Word Bank to complete each sentence correctly.

1. _____ forced nations to depend on each other.

2. Countries had to work out _____.

3. Industrialized countries depended on other nations for _____.

4. Less developed countries needed _____.

5. The United States and Great Britain relied on countries like Saudi Arabia and Nigeria for _____.

6. The Industrial Revolution changed the way and where people _____.

7. These days, developed countries may produce many _____ and fewer finished products.

On a sheet of paper, write the answer to each question. Use complete sentences.

8. What nations were affected by industrialization?

9. What are three countries that developed nations rely on for natural resources?

10. Why, in the 1800s, was it suggested that the U.S. Patent Office be closed?

CHAPTER 19

SUMMARY

- During the Industrial Revolution, people went from making goods by hand to making goods by machine.

- Great Britain led the Industrial Revolution with rapid changes beginning around 1750.

- Great Britain had a good supply of resources such as coal and iron.

- Machines forced Britain's textile industry from country cottages to city factories.

- The invention of steam power changed manufacturing and transportation.

- To gain additional raw materials, Europe established new colonies.

- During the Industrial Revolution, people tried new things. Their discoveries led to important developments in electricity and the use of oil products in industry.

- Industrialization caused a rapid growth in city populations. Life for many people improved. A strong wealthy middle class grew. Life for many became harder.

- Working conditions in the factories were often unsafe and unhealthy. This eventually led people to form labor unions.

- By the late 1800s, France, Germany, the United States, Russia, and Japan became industrialized.

- Nations became dependent on each other for needed goods and services. Many wrote trade agreements for products such as oil, uranium, and copper.

Word Bank

energy

factory

import

Industrial Revolution

investors

labor union

natural resources

raw materials

textile

transportation

Vocabulary Review

On a sheet of paper, use the words from the Word Bank to complete each sentence correctly.

1. A place where goods are made is a(n) _____.

2. A(n) _____ is an organization of workers.

3. Water, cotton, and wool are _____ that may be needed to make cloth.

4. Coal has the ability to supply the _____ needed to keep steam engines running.

5. The steam locomotive is an example of a development in _____ that helped advance industry.

6. Great Britain was a leader in the cloth, or _____ industry.

7. Many countries _____, or bring in, cloth from other countries.

8. Coal and iron are examples of _____.

9. _____ are people with money to back business.

10. During the _____, people stopped making goods by hand and instead made them with machines.

Chapter Review Questions

On a sheet of paper, write the answer to each question. Use complete sentences.

11. What natural resources did Britain have that were important for industry?

12. How did new inventions in the textile industry change the lives of workers?

Test Tip

Learn from your mistakes. Review corrected homework and tests to understand your errors.

13. What are five inventions that changed industry in the late 1600s and in the 1700s?

14. How did industrialized nations get the raw materials that they so needed?

15. How did industrialization change relationships between nations?

Critical Thinking

On a sheet of paper, write your response to each question. Use complete sentences.

16. Why did factory owners like to hire women and children?

17. The Industrial Revolution made countries more dependent on each other. Do you think this was good or bad? Give at least one reason.

Using the Timeline

Use the timeline on page 411 to answer the questions.

18. When did the Industrial Revolution begin in Britain?

19. When was the steam locomotive invented?

20. How many years after the steamboat was perfected did the first steamship cross the Atlantic?

GROUP ACTIVITY

With a partner, debate this question: Should labor unions be allowed in Great Britain? One should take the part of a factory owner in 1810. The other should take the part of a factory worker. Before the debate, prepare some notes to help you remember the points you will make.

Independence in Latin America

Spain and Portugal ruled most of the colonies of Latin America. Their leaders were wealthy Europeans who took advantage of people who were native to the land. They became dictators who made slaves of the native people and Africans they had enslaved.

The desire for independence was felt not only by Europeans or the American colonies. People of the colonies of South America and Central America also wanted to gain their freedom. With the help of some rebel leaders, many of these countries found liberty during this time.

GOALS FOR LEARNING

- To explain the Latin American colonies' relationship with the countries that conquered them
- To describe the Latin American colonies' fight for independence
- To understand the influences on Latin America culture

Reading Strategy: Inferencing

Sometimes the meaning of a text is not directly stated. You have to "read between the lines" to understand what is really being said.

What You Know + What You Read = Inference

As you read, look for clues that help you understand what is happening. Predicting what will happen next and explaining cause and effect are helpful strategies for making inferences.

Key Vocabulary Words

Lesson 1
Mother country A nation that controls a colony

Descendant A person who comes from a specific group of people; a family member

Discrimination Treating a person or people unfairly because of his or her race or religion

Lesson 2
Liberator One who frees a group of people

Viceroy The governor of a country or province who rules as the representative of the king

Political Having to do with governing

Lesson 3
Mural A large picture painted on a wall

Dominate To control; to be most important, most powerful, strongest

Influence The power to affect other people or things

Colonization

Objectives

- To explain how Central and South America came to be called "Latin America"
- To describe the control Spain and Portugal had over the Latin American colonies
- To tell why the Creoles and mestizos were ready to fight for independence

Reading Strategy:
Inferencing

What do you already know about colonization?

Mother country
A nation that controls a colony

For 300 years, Spaniards built colonies in the Americas. From about 1500 until 1800, they controlled areas of Mexico, Central America, and South America. Some Portuguese settled in the eastern part of South America. The French also founded a few settlements. Most of the lands in this area are called *Latin America.* That is because the Spanish, Portuguese, and French languages came from Latin.

Wherever Spaniards settled, they took power. Many Spanish settlers came from wealthy families. They felt they should not do certain kinds of work. Therefore, they made the natives work for them. The Spaniards also brought Africans to the Americas to work as enslaved persons on farms and in mines.

Many wealthy Spaniards lived on *haciendas.* These were large cattle ranches with rich farmlands. Much of the work on the haciendas was done by native field hands or by enslaved Africans.

Why Was Latin America Late to Industrialize?

Spain and Portugal controlled all trade in their colonies. The colonies were not allowed to trade among themselves or with other nations. They were kept dependent on the **mother country.** In addition, any effort to develop industry in the colonies was crushed. Latin America had to sell all its raw materials to Spain and Portugal. It had to buy all its finished products from them, too.

This kind of control kept industry from developing in Latin America. Eventually the people of Latin America rose up against their foreign rulers. The 1800s saw waves of revolution sweep through Latin America.

What Was the Social Structure in the Latin American Colonies?

Most people who had been born in Spain felt superior to the other Latin Americans. This means that they felt they were better than, or above, the other Latin Americans. The Spaniards did not adopt any native customs. Instead, they tried to make the new land as much like Spain as possible.

The Creoles were people of Spanish blood who were born and raised in Latin America. Many Creoles resented the self-important attitude of Spanish-born people. The Creoles would play a large part in the soon-to-come struggles for independence.

Many wealthy Spaniards lived on large cattle ranches with rich farmlands, called haciendas.

You Decide

Is there discrimination against any groups of people in the United States today? If so, what kind of discrimination do they face?

Reading Strategy: Inferencing

How does what you already know about colonization add to what you have just read?

Most of the Spaniards and Portuguese who settled in Latin America did not bring their families. Many were soldiers and fortune-seekers. They did not plan to stay any longer than it took to get rich. Some Spaniards fathered the children of native women. These children and their **descendants** became part of a large class of people of mixed race, called *mestizos*.

Many of the mestizos were angered by their lack of social standing. They hated the unfair treatment, or **discrimination,** they felt from their Spanish rulers. The mestizos were ready for freedom from European rule.

The native people and the enslaved Africans were certainly ready for a change of government. Year after year, they worked hard yet remained poor. They had nothing for themselves under European rule—no land, no wealth, no power, little hope.

The poor people of Latin America were now ready to fight for freedom. They saw Britain's colonies in North America win their freedom. They saw the people of France rise up against tyranny. Now they needed leaders to call them together and organize revolts.

Match the description in Column A with the term in Column B.
Write the correct letter on a sheet of paper.

Column A

1. large ranch or country home that wealthy Spaniards lived in

2. people of Spanish blood who were born and raised in Latin America

3. a mixed race; typically refers to one that is born from a Spanish father and a native mother

Column B

A Creole

B hacienda

C mestizos

On a sheet of paper, write the answer to each question. Use complete sentences.

4. How did Central and South America come to be called "Latin America"?

5. What kept industry from developing in Latin America?

6. What does it mean to discriminate against someone?

7. Why were the Creoles and mestizos ready to fight for independence?

On a sheet of paper, write the letter of the answer that correctly completes each sentence.

8. The Spaniards that settled in Latin America believed they were above certain kinds of work. They made the native people work for them and brought _____ to work as slaves.

   A Asians   B Europeans   C Africans   D Americans

9. The people born in Spain felt _____ to the other Latin Americans.

   A enslaved   B superior   C inferior   D equal

10. The British colonies in _____ and the French inspired the poor people of Latin America.

   A Europe   B Britain   C Germany   D North America

Colonies Fight for Independence

The time for revolution in Latin America was ripe. The poor people were ready to back revolutionaries that would lead them to independence.

What Did Toussaint L'Ouverture Do?

Haiti covers the western third of the island of Hispaniola in the Caribbean Sea. Haiti was the first Latin American colony to fight for freedom. Haiti was a French colony. When news of revolution in France reached Haiti, the people of the colony got excited. They began to think about freedom, too.

In 1791, the enslaved people rebelled against their French masters. A black revolutionary named Toussaint L'Ouverture became a leader in Haiti's fight for freedom. L'Ouverture was an enslaved person himself until he was 50. He led the slave revolt until 1793, when France freed all enslaved people. In 1801, Napoleon sent a French army to Haiti. He planned to reestablish slavery in the country. War broke out again. The French threw L'Ouverture into prison, where he died in 1803. However, by 1804, the French army was defeated, and French rule in Haiti ended. Haiti declared its independence.

Wars of revolution continued. Other Latin American countries demanded freedom.

Toussaint L'Ouverture led slaves in a rebellion.

Liberator
One who frees a group of people

What Did Hidalgo and Morelos Do?

Miguel Hidalgo and José Morelos led Mexico's revolt against Spain. Both men were Catholic priests. They organized the native people in a revolution.

On September 16, 1810, in the town of Dolores, Miguel Hidalgo rang church bells. He shouted the *grito de Dolores*, or "cry of Dolores": "Long live independence! Down with bad government!"

Both Hidalgo and Morelos lost their lives fighting for Mexico's independence. By 1821, the fight was won. Now Mexico celebrates September 16th as its independence day. Furthermore, the town of Dolores is now called Dolores Hidalgo.

What Did Simón Bolívar Do?

Perhaps the best-known Latin American **liberator** was Simón Bolívar. Today he is called "The Liberator" and the "George Washington of South America."

History Fact
Bolívar died alone and poor. It was not until his death that he became honored as South America's liberator.

Bolívar spent much of his life fighting for the independence of South American nations. He was a Creole, born in Venezuela. His parents were wealthy Spaniards. To keep his wealth and social position, Bolívar might have sided with Spain. Instead, he spent all his money backing revolutions because he believed in freedom from European rule. Starting in 1810, Simón Bolívar helped to organize an army. He then led the army in a series of victories against the Spanish. He liberated, or freed, one country after another. At one time he ruled the newly formed Republic of Gran Colombia. This was made up of Colombia, Venezuela, Ecuador, and Peru. Then, one by one, each country withdrew from the union. By 1828, Bolívar ruled only Colombia. His own people did not appreciate him. After a failed attempt on his life, he resigned as president in 1830.

Viceroy

The governor of a country or province who rules as the representative of the king

Political

Having to do with governing

What Did Bernardo O'Higgins Do?

Chile owes its liberation to the son of an Irishman. Bernardo O'Higgins's father had been a **viceroy,** or governor, of Peru. Bernardo O'Higgins led a revolution that began in 1810. After winning Chile's independence from Spain in 1818, O'Higgins acted as the country's dictator. He planned to bring about reform in Chile. He taxed wealthy landowners to pay for new schools and roads. He also tried to break up their big estates. A revolt by the landowners in 1823, however, sent O'Higgins into exile.

GREAT NAMES IN HISTORY

José de San Martín

Bernardo O'Higgins was helped in his struggle against Spain by another great leader, José de San Martín. San Martín was born in Argentina, but was educated in Spain. While in Spain, he fought with the Spanish army against Napoleon. When he returned to Argentina, the fight for independence had already begun in South America.

In 1812, San Martín took command of a rebel army. For the next several years he fought to free Argentina from Spain's rule. In 1816, Argentina declared its independence. Then San Martín decided to help the rest of South America become free. He planned a daring surprise attack against the Spanish army in Chile. In 1817, he joined forces with Bernardo O'Higgins. Together, they led their army across the Andes Mountains. It was a difficult and dangerous march. Blizzards struck without warning. The men had to plow through deep snowdrifts. Slowly they made their way across the icy mountain passes. Many men died along the way. Finally, the brave leaders and their army came down from the mountains in Chile. There they attacked the Spanish army. The Spaniards were completely taken by surprise, and they were easily defeated.

San Martín then went on to help win independence for Peru in 1821. When he finally returned to Argentina, a fierce struggle for **political** power was going on. San Martín felt bad about this and would have nothing to do with it. He went back to Europe and lived in France for the rest of his life.

What Did Dom Pedro Do?

Dom Pedro led Brazil to independence without bloodshed. He was a Portuguese prince. He inherited the Brazilian kingdom when it was still under Portuguese rule. The Brazilian people wanted independence. They also wanted Dom Pedro to go home to Portugal.

"I remain!" he stated. Then on September 7, 1822, he declared Brazil an independent country. He took the throne of the newly independent nation as Pedro I.

What Were the Governments of the New Nations Like?

The Latin American countries' struggles for independence did not necessarily mean freedom for the people. Most of the countries did not become democracies. Life did not change much for many native peoples and mestizos in those lands.

Dictators ruled most of the new nations. These dictators were powerful men with strong armies behind them. Any changes in government usually came only by military takeovers.

Match the description in Column A with the revolutionary(ies) in Column B. Write the correct letter on a sheet of paper.

Column A

1. a black revolutionary who led the slave revolt in Haiti

2. a Creole who helped organize an army in present-day Colombia, Venezuela, Ecuador, and Peru; led them to victories against the Spanish; known as "The Liberator"

3. the Catholic priests who led Mexico's revolt against Spain

4. the Portuguese prince who led Brazil to independence without bloodshed

5. the son of a viceroy of Peru; led the revolution that won Chile's independence from Spain

6. the leader who commanded a rebel army and helped Argentina win freedom from Spain's rule

Column B

A Bernardo O'Higgins

B Dom Pedro

C José de San Martín

D Miguel Hidalgo and José Morelos

E Simón Bolívar

F Toussaint L'Ouverture

On a sheet of paper, write the letter of the answer that correctly completes each sentence.

7. A person who frees a group of people is known as a _____.

A viceroy   **B** liberator   **C** descendant   **D** mestizos

8. A _____ is a governor of a country or province who rules as the monarch's representative.

A descendant   **B** dictator   **C** senator   **D** viceroy

9. Despite the Latin American countries' struggles for independence, not all people were _____.

A Creole   **B** liberators   **C** free   **D** in the army

10. _____ ruled most of the new nations.

A Liberators   **B** Dictators   **C** Descendants   **D** Viceroys

Latin American Culture

- To explain how the language, religion, and architecture of Latin America reflect European influence
- To describe Latin American music and its influences

Mural
A large picture painted on a wall

Latin American culture is really more than one culture. It is a mixture of several different peoples: native people, Spanish, Portuguese, African, and French.

What Are the Influences of Latin American Culture?

Some native peoples who live in rural areas still live much like their ancestors. They wear woven shawls and take their goods to market along mountain roads on burros (small donkeys) and llamas. They play music on handmade wooden instruments and weave baskets of cane and reed. Native women still spin and weave colorful cloth. There is often a note of sadness to the native people's art. A **mural** in Mexico City shows natives suffering at the hands of Spanish conquistadors.

Although Spain colonized Latin America, native cultures are still strong. These natives of Peru are an example of people who have kept their own traditions.

Reading Strategy:
Inferencing

After reading this lesson, what can you infer about the lasting effects of the early Latin American culture? What words helped you make your inference?

The Spanish and Portuguese brought their languages and religion to Latin America. Most of the people of Latin America speak Spanish. Portuguese is the main language of Brazil. The different native groups speak their own native languages. Roman Catholicism is the main religion.

Spanish architecture is common in Latin America. Many homes, churches, and public buildings have a Spanish flavor. However, much Latin American music reflects the music of Africa. The Africans brought their songs and dances with them when they came to Latin America as enslaved people.

Different races and cultures **dominate** different areas of Latin America. In some countries, most of the people are natives. The art, music, dress, and customs in Guatemala, Bolivia, and Peru are strongly **influenced**, or affected, by the cultures of the native peoples. In some countries, like Haiti, the people are mostly descendants of Africans.

Latin America gets its name from the colonization and influence of Latin peoples—the Spanish, the Portuguese, and the French. However, the natives and Africans have played a large part in making Latin America what it is today.

TIMELINE STUDY: FROM COLONIES TO INDEPENDENCE IN LATIN AMERICA: 1500–1900

During what time period did many Latin American countries win their independence?

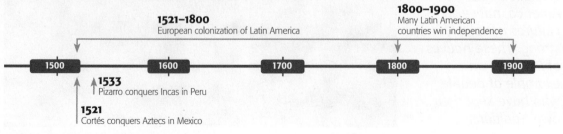

1521–1800
European colonization of Latin America

1800–1900
Many Latin American countries win independence

| 1500 | 1600 | 1700 | 1800 | 1900 |

1533
Pizarro conquers Incas in Peru

1521
Cortés conquers Aztecs in Mexico

Latin American Nations Become Independent

Year of Independence

Country	Year
Antigua and Barbuda	1981
Argentina	1816
Bahamas	1973
Barbados	1966
Belize	1981
Bolivia	1825
Brazil	1822
Chile	1810
Colombia	1819
Costa Rica	1821
Cuba	1902
Dominica	1978
Dominican Republic	1844
Ecuador	1822
El Salvador	1841
Grenada	1974
Guatemala	1821
Guyana	1966
Haiti	1804
Honduras	1821
Jamaica	1962
Mexico	1821
Nicaragua	1838
Panama	1903
Paraguay	1811
Peru	1824
St. Kitts-Nevis	1983
St. Lucia	1979
St. Vincent	1979
Suriname	1975
Trinidad and Tobago	1962
Uruguay	1828
Venezuela	1821

MAP STUDY

1. In what year did Brazil become independent?

2. Which Latin American country shares a border with the United States?

REVIEW

Word Bank

African

ancestors

art

burros

colorful

influence

mural

music

Portuguese

Spanish

On a sheet of paper, write the word from the Word Bank to complete each sentence correctly.

1. Latin American culture mixes several different peoples: native people, Spanish, Portuguese, _____, and French.

2. Some people native to Latin America still live like their _____.

3. _____ are used to carry goods to market.

4. The cloth the native women weave is quite _____.

5. Native _____ often has a hint of sadness to it.

6. A(n) _____ is a large picture painted on a wall.

7. Most Latin Americans speak Spanish, but _____ is the main language of Brazil.

8. The architecture in Latin America has a(n) _____ flavor.

9. Latin American _____ reflects the customs that the Africans brought to Latin America.

10. When something has the power to affect other people or things, it has _____.

- Most areas of Latin America were settled by the Spanish. The Portuguese settled some areas, particularly on the eastern side of South America.

- The European settlers made workers of the native people and enslaved Africans.

- Spain and Portugal, as colonial powers, did not allow industry to develop in Latin America. Their colonies could supply raw materials only to them.

- Between 1500 and 1900, Europeans, Creoles, mestizos, natives, and enslaved Africans lived in Latin America.

- As social classes developed in Latin America, many people became the victims of discrimination.

- During the 1800s, revolutions gained independence for many Latin American countries.

- Haiti was a French colony. With the help of Toussaint L'Ouverture, Haitians fought and gained their freedom in 1804.

- There were other Rebels, too, such as: Hidalgo, Morelos, Bolívar, O'Higgins, San Martín, and Dom Pedro. They helped lead countries of South America to independence.

- Newly formed countries in Latin America were often ruled by dictators.

- Latin American culture is a blend of Spanish, Portuguese, French, native, and African cultures.

Word Bank

descendant

discrimination

dominate

influence

liberator

mother country

mural

political

viceroy

Vocabulary Review

On a sheet of paper, use the words from the Word Bank to correctly match each definition below.

1. A nation that controls a country

2. Having to do with governing

3. Unfair treatment of a person, often based on race or religion

4. The power to affect the way that people or nations act

5. A person from a particular ancestor

6. A leader who frees a group of people

7. A large painting on a wall

8. A representative of the monarch that rules a country or province

9. To be most important, most powerful, or strongest

Chapter Review Questions

On a sheet of paper, write the answer to each question. Use complete sentences.

10. Why was Latin America late to industrialize?

11. How did the people born in Spain feel about Latin Americans and their culture?

12. Who were the Creoles and the mestizos?

13. What factors led the poor people of Latin America to fight for freedom?

14. Why does Mexico celebrate September 16th as independence day?

Test Tip

To study for a chapter test, use the headings within the chapter to write an outline. Review this outline to help you recall and organize the information.

15. What kind of leaders governed Latin American nations after independence?

16. Where does Latin American culture come from?

Critical Thinking

On a sheet of paper, write your response to each question. Use complete sentences.

17. How did the American and French revolutions affect Latin America?

18. Why do you think O'Higgins wanted to break up the big estates in Chile?

Using the Timeline

Use the timeline on page 428 to answer the questions.

19. How long did European colonization of Latin America last?

20. What happened in 1533?

GROUP ACTIVITY

Work with a group to make a large wall chart of Latin American revolutionaries. Include their personal background, nicknames, famous words, countries they liberated, and other information.

The United States Gains Power

The new United States attracted more people who came in search of a new life. The Industrial Revolution brought growth in manufacturing, trade, and transportation. People were no longer on the move.

During the 1800s, the size of the United States grew. The growth was a result of a number of land purchases from other nations. The United States tried to protect the western hemisphere from further European involvement. In doing so, it also gained territories. However, the growth of America came with new problems.

GOALS FOR LEARNING

- To explain the growth of the United States in the early 1800s
- To list the problems the United States faced in establishing its northern and southern borders
- To identify the causes and main events of the American Civil War
- To explain the expansion of the United States

Reading Strategy: Metacognition

Metacognition means being aware of the way you learn. It will help you become a better reader.

- Preview the text, noting the main idea, details, and any questions you have.

- If you do not understand something, go back and read it again.

- Summarize what you have read. Make inferences about the meaning.

Key Vocabulary Words

Lesson 1
Monroe Doctrine The document stating that Europe should not try to get more territory in North or South America

Territory The land ruled by a nation or state

Lesson 2
Interfere To mix in another's affairs without being asked

Lesson 4
Expansion Growth; to increase in size

Sympathy Feeling sorry for another's suffering

Victor The winner of a battle, war, struggle, or contest

Rebellion A fight by people against a government; a struggle for change

Economic Having to do with money

International Having to do with many nations

Imperialism and Growth

Objectives

- To explain European imperialism and the Monroe Doctrine
- To tell how the United States gained the Louisiana Territory

Reading Strategy:
Metacognition

Notice the structure of this chapter. Look at the titles, headings, and boldfaced words.

Monroe Doctrine
The document stating that Europe should not try to get more territory in North or South America

Territory
The land ruled by a nation or state

Smaller nations are often threatened by larger and stronger nations. The new, independent countries in Latin America struggled to survive. The United States wanted these countries to remain independent.

What Is the Monroe Doctrine?

In 1823, James Monroe, president of the United States, spoke before Congress. He said that the United States would not allow Europe to set up new colonies in North or South America. The United States would also not allow any existing colonies to take over more land. The President's statement against European imperialism was later called the **Monroe Doctrine.**

How Did the United States Gain the Louisiana Territory?

The United States grew rapidly during the early 1800s. Settlers moved west, taking lands from the American Indians.

In 1803, Thomas Jefferson was president of the United States. He arranged for the United States to buy the Louisiana **Territory,** a large piece of land, from France. The United States paid about $15 million for 828,000 square miles of land. The Louisiana Purchase almost doubled the size of the United States.

American pioneers streamed into the new land. They settled first in what would become the states of Louisiana, Arkansas, and Missouri.

The Louisiana Purchase

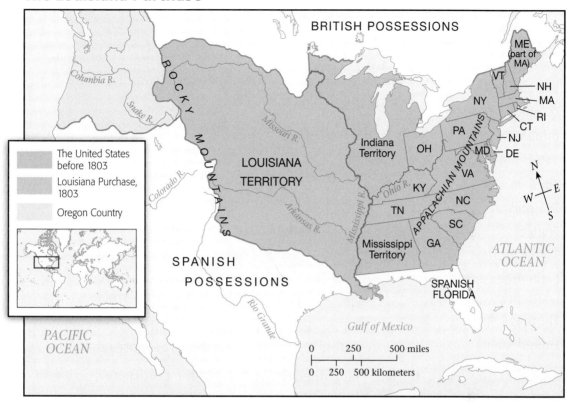

BRITISH POSSESSIONS

ME (part of MA)

VT

NH

MA

RI

CT

NJ

DE

Columbia R.

Snake R.

ROCKY MOUNTAINS

Missouri R.

NY

PA

OH

Indiana Territory

MD

VA

APPALACHIAN MOUNTAINS

Ohio R.

KY

NC

TN

SC

LOUISIANA TERRITORY

Colorado R.

Arkansas R.

Mississippi R.

Mississippi Territory

GA

ATLANTIC OCEAN

SPANISH POSSESSIONS

SPANISH FLORIDA

Rio Grande

Gulf of Mexico

PACIFIC OCEAN

The United States before 1803

Louisiana Purchase, 1803

Oregon Country

N
W E
S

0   250   500 miles
0 250 500 kilometers

MAP STUDY

1. Which river formed the eastern border of the Louisiana Territory?

2. Which mountain range bordered the Louisiana Territory on the west?

REVIEW

Word Bank

colonies

doubled

1803

1823

$15 million

France

James Monroe

Latin American
    countries

Thomas Jefferson

United States

On a sheet of paper, write the word from the Word Bank to complete each sentence correctly.

1. The United States wanted the newly independent _____ to remain independent.

2. The Monroe Doctrine was U.S. President _____'s statement against European imperialism.

3. The Monroe Doctrine was put into action in _____.

4. The _____ took a stand against European imperialism in the Monroe Doctrine. It said Europe could not set up new colonies in North or South America.

5. The Monroe Doctrine also forbid (did not allow) any existing _____ from taking over more land.

6. The United States bought the Louisiana Territory from _____.

7. President _____ arranged for the United States to buy the Louisiana Territory.

8. The Louisiana Territory was purchased in _____.

9. The United States paid _____ for the Louisiana Purchase.

10. The Louisiana Purchase practically _____ the size of the United States.

Border Problems

Objectives

- To explain the reasons for the War of 1812
- To describe the Battle of the Alamo
- To explain the importance of the Treaty of Guadalupe Hidalgo

Reading Strategy:
Metacognition

Make a prediction to tell what you think will happen next. Check your prediction as you continue reading and revise if needed.

Interfere

To mix in another's affairs without being asked

 History Fact
General Santa Anna made himself dictator of Mexico in 1834. Americans in Texas did not want to live under his rule.

The United States needed to set up clear northern and southern borders. Britain still controlled Canada to the north. War broke out between Britain and the United States in 1812. However, the United States-Canadian border was not the cause. Other problems had led to the war. Britain had been **interfering** with United States trade. In other words, Britain was mixing in U.S. trade without being asked. A peace treaty was signed in December 1814. The border remained the same.

In the southern United States, however, border disagreements *were* the cause of war. What is now the state of Texas once belonged to the Republic of Mexico. Many settlers from the United States moved into Texas.

The Mexicans worried about the large numbers of settlers from the North. They said that no more settlers could come in from the United States. In response, the settlers rebelled. In November 1835, they declared themselves free from Mexico. Then the battles began.

What Was the Result of the Battle of the Alamo?

The Battle of the Alamo was one of the most famous battles in the Texas war of independence. The Alamo was an old Spanish mission in San Antonio that the Texans were using as their fort.

The Alamo was a fort in San Antonio, Texas, where a famous battle was fought in 1836.

It was February of 1836. Around 5,000 Mexican soldiers stormed the fort. Inside the Alamo were fewer than 200 Texans, among them Davy Crockett and James Bowie. They managed to hold the fort for 13 days. In the end, nearly all the Texans defending the Alamo were killed. However, their brave fight gave spirit to the struggle and helped the Texan forces to win the war.

"Remember the Alamo!" became the battle cry of the Texan forces. By April 1836, the Mexican army was defeated. The Mexican general Santa Anna signed a peace treaty. Texas became an independent nation.

Gold was discovered in California in 1848. More than 100,000 people moved west in search of their fortune. So many people settled in California that it was allowed to become a state the following year. Across the Pacific Ocean in 1851, gold was found in Australia. During the Australian Gold Rush of the 1850s, about 350,000 people traveled to that continent in search of gold. By the end of the 1850s, Australia was producing more than one-third of all gold in the world.

How Was the Boundary Between Mexico and Texas Decided?

In 1845, Texas became the 28th state to join the United States. Many in the Mexican government had not approved of the treaty Santa Anna had signed in 1836. As a result, the declaration of statehood led to war in 1846 between the United States and Mexico.

Mexico lost the war in 1848. The United States and Mexico signed the Treaty of Guadalupe Hidalgo. In the treaty, Mexico accepted the Rio Grande as the boundary between Mexico and Texas. Also, in return for $15 million, the United States gained vast new territory that had belonged to Mexico. This included what are now the states of Utah, California, Nevada, and most of Arizona, New Mexico, Wyoming, and Colorado.

On a sheet of paper, write the letter of the answer that correctly completes each sentence.

1. The War of 1812 began because Britain was interfering with U.S. _____.

   A government **B** trade   **C** borders   **D** wars

2. The state that is now Texas once belonged to _____.

   A Mexico   **B** Britain   **C** France   **D** Santa Anna

3. The disagreements about _____ in the southern United States caused the war.

   A government **B** trade   **C** borders   **D** wars

4. The Alamo was a fort in San Antonio, _____.

   A Louisiana   **B** Mexico   **C** Texas   **D** Oregon

5. The Battle of the Alamo gave Texans _____.

   A another victory   **C** independence from Mexico
   B the determination to win **D** the land up to the Rio Grande

6. Mexican general _____ signed a peace treaty that made Texas independent.

   A Santa Anna **B** Davy Crockett **C** James Bowie **D** James Monroe

7. In 1846, _____ declared itself a state.

   A Oregon   **B** Louisiana   **C** Mexico   **D** Texas

8. The Treaty of Guadalupe Hidalgo was signed in 1848 when Mexico _____.

   A defeated the Texans   **C** lost the war
   B won the Battle of the Alamo **D** declared independence

9. The Treaty of Guadalupe Hidalgo said the _____ was the border between Mexico and Texas.

   A Rio Grande **B** Alamo   **C** Gulf of Mexico **D** Mississippi River

10. The Treaty of Guadalupe Hidalgo also gave _____ new territory.

   A Texas   **B** Mexico   **C** Louisiana   **D** the United States

The American Civil War

Reading Strategy: Metacognition

Note the main idea and the important details of this section. Summarize what you have read to make sure you understand it.

History Fact
The word Union (with a capital U) means the Union of all the states. In the Civil War, Union also meant those on the side of the North, such as Union soldiers.

Like European history, American history is scarred with war. Between 1861 and 1865, Americans fought a bloody civil war between the northern and southern states.

What Caused the Civil War?

Slavery was an important issue between the North and South. However, it was not the immediate cause of the war. After Abraham Lincoln was elected president, the southern states broke away from the United States. They formed a separate nation called the Confederate States of America. Lincoln could not allow the South to break up the Union. He felt he had no choice but to go to war to save the Union.

The North had many more people than the South. The North also had more manufacturing and industry. It was able to produce more guns and cannons. The South was still mainly agricultural. Its main crops were cotton and tobacco. The southern plantations depended on enslaved workers.

Northerners expected the war to be over soon. They were also sure they would be the winners. However, they were in for a surprise. The first major land battle of the war, at Bull Run on July 21, 1861, was easily won by the South! Furthermore, the Confederate army went on to win one battle after another. The army was led by brilliant generals such as Robert E. Lee and Stonewall Jackson.

What Was the Turning Point of the War?

The turning point of the war came at Gettysburg, Pennsylvania. Lee and his forces retreated from the battlefield.

The Union won the battle at Gettysburg, making it the turning point of the war.

Reading Strategy:
Metacognition

Remember to ask yourself questions as you read. This will help you make sure that you understand what you are reading.

In 1863, Lincoln's *Emancipation Proclamation* took effect, outlawing slavery in areas rebelling against the Union. By the end of the war, about 200,000 African Americans had fought for the North.

By 1864, Ulysses S. Grant had won many Union victories in the West. In that year, Lincoln appointed, or made, Grant commander of all Union forces. By 1865, much of the South lay in ruins. The southern armies had also become much weaker. The North had cut off all of the South's supply routes. Lee's army was trapped in Virginia by Grant's army. Lee decided it was hopeless to keep on fighting. He surrendered to Grant on April 9, 1865, at Appomattox Court House in Virginia.

The bloodiest war in American history was over. More than 600,000 people were killed. Many cities and farms were destroyed. However, the North had won the war and the Union was saved. All of the states were now united.

REVIEW

Word Bank

agricultural

Confederate States
of America

*Emancipation
Proclamation*

General Grant

General Lee

Gettysburg

industry

slavery

South

Union

On a sheet of paper, write the word from the Word Bank to complete each sentence correctly.

1. _____ was an important issue between the North and the South. It was not, however, the immediate cause of the Civil War.

2. When Abraham Lincoln was elected president, the southern states broke away from the United States. They formed the _____.

3. The main reason for the Civil War was to save the _____.

4. The North had more people and more manufacturing and _____.

5. The South was mainly _____ and depended on slave labor.

6. The _____ won the first battle of the war—Bull Run.

7. _____ was the turning point of the war.

8. Lincoln's _____ outlawed slavery in the south.

9. _____ was the commander of all Union forces.

10. After the North had cut off all of the South's supply routes, _____ surrendered.

U.S. Expansion

Reading Strategy: Metacognition

Before you read this section, think about what you can do that will help you better understand the text.

Expansion

Growth; to increase in size

After the Civil War was over, the United States set its sights on **expansion,** or growth. With the battles of the country settled, the United States could finally grow its industry, territory, and control.

How Did Industry in the United States Change During the 1800s?

Many changes occurred in the United States during the early 1800s. The introduction of the steam locomotive led to great improvements in overland transportation. Samuel F. B. Morse's telegraph, first demonstrated in 1837, led to greatly improved communication. In 1834, Cyrus McCormick invented a mechanical reaper. This machine cut down and gathered crops, allowing farmers to harvest grain more quickly than before. Beginning in the early 1800s, some businesses began building factories. Inside the factories were machines that allowed workers to produce goods more rapidly.

After the Civil War, changes occurred more quickly. More and more factories were built. Machines began to replace hand labor as the main means of manufacturing. At this time, a new nationwide network of railroads was being built. In 1869, the transcontinental railroad was completed. This linked up the eastern and western parts of the country. It also helped speed up the settlement of the West.

The railroad system helped businesses distribute their goods more quickly. In addition, there were more goods available. Inventors developed new products. Businesses were able to make the products in large quantities. The United States now had its own industrial revolution.

Many big businesses developed during this period. Some involved the production of coal, petroleum, steel, and industrial machinery. New England, New York, and Pennsylvania became important industrial centers in the North. The United States was on its way to becoming an industrial giant.

How Did the United States Gain Alaska and Hawaii?

"A foolish purchase!" "Who wants a hunk of frozen land?" Many Americans said that about the territory known as Alaska. In 1867, Secretary of State William Seward had persuaded the United States to buy Alaska from Russia. Its price was just over $7 million. In 1897, gold was discovered in Alaska. It was only then that Americans began to realize the value of the purchase.

The United States' interest in Hawaii began in 1820. That year a group of Protestant missionaries from New England arrived there. In 1835, the first sugar plantation began operating. It was owned by an American company. Commercial development of pineapple began in the mid-1800s. Also, around this time, hundreds of U.S. whaling ships began to visit Hawaii regularly. In 1887, the United States signed a treaty with Hawaii. It gave the United States the right to use Pearl Harbor as a naval base. The United States' interests were now well-established on the islands.

In 1893, the Hawaiians staged a revolution against Liliuokalani, queen of Hawaii. Americans, who by that time owned most of Hawaii's industry, encouraged and led the revolt. Queen Liliuokalani left her throne. In 1900, Hawaii became a territory of the United States.

The United States used the Monroe Doctrine to keep European interests out of the Americas. Meanwhile the United States gained more territory for itself.

Remember
The United States also made a huge land purchase in 1803, the Louisiana Purchase.

Reading Strategy: Metacognition

Remember to look at the illustrations and to note the descriptive words. This will help you visualize what you are reading.

After Queen Liliuokalani left her throne, Hawaii became a territory of the United States.

Sympathy
Feeling sorry for another's suffering

Victor
The winner of a battle, war, struggle, or contest

You Decide
Today some experts believe the explosion of the *Maine* was probably an accident. Were Americans right to declare war? Why or why not?

What Was the Outcome of the Spanish-American War?

A war broke out between the United States and Spain in 1898. As a result of this war, the United States gained still more territory.

The United States wanted Spain out of the Caribbean. Many Americans felt sorry, or **sympathy,** for the Cubans who lived under harsh Spanish rule. Some Americans also saw a chance for the United States to gain more power.

Relations between the United States and Spain were tense. Then, in February 1898, the U.S. battleship *Maine* exploded in the harbor at Havana, Cuba. Many Americans blamed Spain. By April the Spanish-American War had begun.

By August of that same year, the war was over. The United States was the winner, or **victor.** In December, Spain and the United States sent representatives to Paris to sign a treaty. The Treaty of Paris gave the United States possession of Puerto Rico, the Philippines, and the Pacific Island of Guam. Spain gave Cuba its freedom.

Why Was the Panama Canal so Important?

By the early 1900s, the United States was the strongest country on the American continents. It held control over lands gained in the Spanish-American War. During that war, the U.S. Navy sent a battleship from San Francisco to Cuba. It had to sail all the way around the tip of South America. This is a distance of 13,000 miles. If there had been a canal across Central America, the trip would have been about 5,000 miles.

U.S. President Theodore Roosevelt wanted to build such a canal across Panama. However, Colombia ruled Panama. Furthermore, Colombia would not grant the United States the land it needed for the canal. To get around this problem, the United States encouraged Panama to declare its independence from Colombia.

The Panama Canal was completed in 1914. Ships can now sail from the Atlantic to the Pacific Ocean without going around South America.

Panama's **rebellion,** or fight against the government, in November 1903 was a success. The United States gained the right to build the canal. Panama sold the United States a canal zone that was 10 miles wide. The Panama Canal and the Canal Zone belonged to the United States. However, in 1977, the United States and Panama signed a treaty. In keeping with the treaty, Panama regained control of the Canal Zone in 1979. Then in 1999, Panama gained control of the canal itself.

Rebellion
A fight by people against a government

Economic
Having to do with money

International
Having to do with many nations

With the canal built, the United States grew as an **economic,** military, and industrial power. It became important in **international** affairs. The United States was becoming a major force in the modern world.

TIMELINE STUDY: THE U.S. GAINS POWER AND TERRITORY

From the information on the timeline, do you think the United States felt the Monroe Doctrine applied to itself? Why or why not?

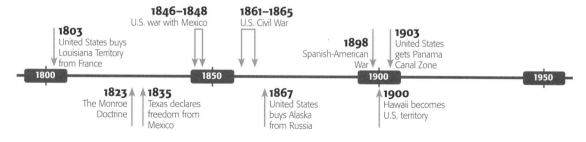

1803
United States buys Louisiana Territory from France

1823
The Monroe Doctrine

1835
Texas declares freedom from Mexico

1846–1848
U.S. war with Mexico

1861–1865
U.S. Civil War

1867
United States buys Alaska from Russia

1898
Spanish-American War

1900
Hawaii becomes U.S. territory

1903
United States gets Panama Canal Zone

1800   1850   1900   1950

On a sheet of paper, write the answer to each question. Use complete sentences.

1. What impact did the transcontinental railroad have on the United States?

2. What made Americans change their minds about the "foolish" purchase of Alaska?

3. How did the United States keep European interests out of the Americas?

4. How did the United States gain Hawaii?

5. Why did the United States want Spain out of the Caribbean?

6. Who won the Spanish-American war?

7. Who signed the Treaty of Paris and what did it promise?

8. How did the United States gain the right to build the Panama Canal?

9. Who has control of the Panama Canal?

10. Why was the Panama Canal so important to the United States?

- The Monroe Doctrine said that the United States would not allow Europeans to set up new colonies in the Americas.

- The United States expanded with the Louisiana Purchase.

- Great Britain and the United States went to war in 1812 over trade disagreements.

- In 1835, Texas went to war with Mexico. By 1845, Texas was a U.S. state.

- The United States fought with Mexico from 1846 to 1848. The United States purchased Mexican lands that later became the states of Utah, California, Nevada, and most of Arizona, New Mexico, Wyoming, and Colorado.

- The Treaty of Guadalupe Hidalgo established the southern border of the United States.

- The United States was torn apart by a bloody civil war from 1861 to 1865. The North won the war and the Union was preserved. More than 600,000 people died in that war.

- The completion of the transcontinental railroad aided business. It also helped speed up the settlement of the West.

- During the 1800s, farming methods improved, as did communication with the telegraph.

- Alaska (in 1867) and Hawaii (in 1900) became territories of the United States.

- In the Spanish-American War, the United States gained Puerto Rico, the Philippines, and Guam.

- The United States built the Panama Canal. It connected the Atlantic and Pacific Oceans.

Word Bank

economic

international

Monroe Doctrine

rebellion

sympathy

territory

victor

Vocabulary Review

On a sheet of paper, use the words from the Word Bank to complete each sentence correctly.

1. The _____ is the statement that the United States made against European imperialism.

2. Many thought that the purchase of the Alaska _____ was foolish.

3. The Cubans lived under harsh Spanish rule in 1898. Americans felt _____ for the Cubans.

4. The Union army was the _____ of the Civil War.

5. Americans encouraged _____ in Hawaii in hopes of gaining Hawaii as a territory.

6. The United States is an important power in _____ affairs.

7. The Panama Canal gave the United States _____, military, and industrial power.

Chapter Review Questions

On a sheet of paper, write the answer to each question. Use complete sentences.

8. What did the Monroe Doctrine forbid (not allow) Europe to do?

9. How did the United States gain the Louisiana Territory?

10. What did the Treaty of Guadalupe say?

11. How did the United States gain Utah, Nevada, and California?

12. Who won the Battle of Bull Run?

Test Tip

Take time to organize your thoughts before answering a question that requires a written answer.

13. How did the United States gain Alaska and Hawaii?

14. How did the United States gain Puerto Rico, the Philippines, and Guam?

15. In what ways was the transcontinental railroad good for the United States?

16. What events led to the building of the Panama Canal?

Critical Thinking

On a sheet of paper, write your response to each question. Use complete sentences.

17. What do you think would have happened to the United States if the South had won the Civil War?

18. Why might some countries have objected to the way the United States obtained the Panama Canal Zone?

Using the Timeline

Use the timeline on page 449 to answer the questions.

19. How many years passed between the time Texas declared freedom from Mexico and the U.S. war with Mexico?

20. How long did the Civil War last?

GROUP ACTIVITY

With a partner, debate the purchase of Alaska. One should be for the purchase, and the other should be against it. Before the debate, prepare a few notes to help you remember the points you hope to make. Make sure you review that information to support the argument on the opposing side. This will help prepare you to respond to the other person's arguments.

Imperialism and the Far East

You have learned about how China and Japan spent many years isolated from other countries. Some contact developed as trade with Europe began. However, governments such as the Manchus in China put tight limits on trade. This kept most of the Far East in isolation.

The poverty of the Chinese peasants led to revolution. The Chinese were also at war with Japan over control of Korea. As a result, the Chinese government would struggle for many years. On the other hand, Japan was growing powerful. It was now open to trade with many countries. It gained a wealth of new materials from Korea to aid in its growing industries.

GOALS FOR LEARNING

- To describe China under Manchurian rule
- To explain the unrest in China under Manchurian rule
- To explain how Japan became less isolated

Reading Strategy: Summarizing

When readers summarize, they look for key ideas and phrases. Then they rewrite them in their own words, using as few words as possible. A summary of key points will help you remember the important ideas you have read. As you read the text, ask yourself these questions:

- What are some important ideas or phrases in the text?
- How can I write these ideas or phrases in a few words?
- Will this remind me of the main idea in the section or the lesson?

Key Vocabulary Words

Lesson 1

Policy A rule; a method of action or conduct

Addicted Having a strong habit that is hard to give up

Smuggle To move something into or out of a country secretly because it is against the law

Lesson 2

Interference Mixing in another's affairs without being asked

Open-Door Policy The American approach to China around 1900 that allowed open trade relations between China and other nations

China Under Manchurian Rule

Objectives

■ To describe the Manchus' attitude toward other Chinese people and the world
■ To explain the Opium War and the Treaty of Nanjing

Reading Strategy:
Summarizing

What is the main idea of this first paragraph?

Manchuria is a region in the northeastern part of China. At one time, it did not belong to China. In 1644, the Manchus—the people of Manchuria—invaded northern China. They overthrew the Ming dynasty that was then in power. Then they conquered the rest of China. The Manchus set up their own dynasty called the Qing dynasty. The Manchus would remain in power for more than 250 years. However, the Qing dynasty would be the last of the Chinese dynasties.

What Was the Manchus' Attitude Toward Others?

The Manchus were a proud people—too proud, perhaps. They thought they were better than the other Chinese people. They passed a law saying that a Manchu could not marry a Chinese. They forced Chinese men to wear a Manchu hairstyle. This was a long braid down the back of the head. The British later called the long braid a *queue*. The word *queue* comes from a Latin word meaning "tail."

Empress Cixi, of the Qing dynasty, was a Manchu ruler who wanted to stop any change in China.

The Manchus not only looked down on other Chinese, they looked down on the rest of the world. Until the mid-1800s, foreign trade was allowed through only one Chinese city—Guangzhou, or Canton. When European nations and the United States asked for more trade with China, the Manchu rulers always refused.

China Under the Qing Dynasty

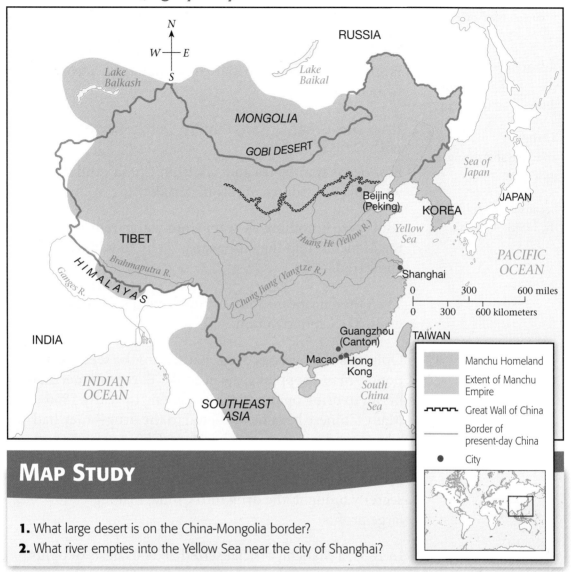

MAP STUDY

1. What large desert is on the China-Mongolia border?
2. What river empties into the Yellow Sea near the city of Shanghai?

During the first 150 years of Manchu rule, China enjoyed prosperity.

Agriculture increased, and the handicraft industry did, too. The population expanded rapidly. However, by the late 1700s, the times had changed. The population had increased more quickly than the food supply. Life became harder for most people.

Policy

A rule; a method of action or conduct

Addicted

Having a strong habit that is hard to give up

Smuggle

To move something into or out of a country secretly because it is against the law

China also suffered because of the Manchus' isolationist **policies.** Once China had been a leader in science and medicine. By the 1800s, however, the Chinese had fallen behind the Europeans in all areas of science and invention. From this point on, the Manchus would rule a troubled China.

How Did Great Britain Finally Get to Trade with China?

Europeans wanted tea and silk from China. And they wanted a new source of raw materials.

"But there is nothing we want from you in return," the Manchus told the Europeans. "Why should we allow trade?"

Then the Europeans found something the Chinese did want. They found opium.

Opium is a dangerous drug made from the seeds of a poppy. Many poppies grew in India. European merchants began to bring opium to China during the early 1800s. Many Chinese became **addicted** to the drug—they had a hard time giving it up. Therefore, China passed a law making the opium trade illegal. However, the demand for opium was still there. Now the Europeans **smuggled,** or secretly brought, the drug into China, making large profits.

In 1839, a Manchu official seized 20,000 chests of opium from British merchants in Guangzhou. He had the opium burned. The British were angry. They said valuable property had been destroyed. Great Britain went to war with China, demanding better trading rights. China had little chance against Britain's armies. In 1842, the Chinese surrendered. They signed the Treaty of Nanjing.

You Decide

Do you think the major powers today would be more likely to go to war to protect the drug trade or to destroy it? Why?

This was the first of what the Chinese called the Unequal Treaties. China not only had to pay for the lost opium, but also for the cost of the war. China had to open five ports to British trade. China also had to give the island of Hong Kong to Great Britain. The new treaties totally protected British merchants from Chinese law. No British citizen could be tried for any crime in a Chinese court—even if the crime were committed in China. The Chinese felt helpless.

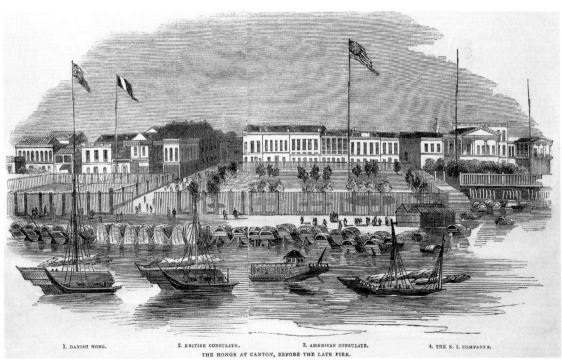

1. DANISH HONG. 2. BRITISH CONSULATE. 3. AMERICAN CONSULATE. 4. THE E. I. COMPANY S.

THE HONGS AT CANTON, BEFORE THE LATE FIRE.

Danish, British, and American ships used harbors to trade with China, such as this one in Canton.

REVIEW

Word Bank

agriculture

Chinese

food supply

opium

Qing

silk

trade

On a sheet of paper, write the word from the Word Bank to complete each sentence correctly.

1. The Manchu dynasty was known as the _____ dynasty.

2. The Manchus were proud people. They thought they were better than other _____ people and the rest of the world.

3. The Manchu rulers refused to _____ with the European nations and the United States.

4. _____, the handicraft industry, and the population increased in the first 150 years of Manchu rule.

5. Unfortunately, the population increased more quickly than the _____.

6. The Europeans wanted tea, _____, and a new source of raw materials from China.

7. The Europeans found that many Chinese wanted _____.

On a sheet of paper, write the answer to each question. Use complete sentences.

8. In what ways did China suffer from the Manchus' isolationist policies?

9. What did the Treaty of Nanjing force China to do?

10. In what ways did Great Britain benefit from the Unequal Treaties?

LESSON 22-2

Chinese Rebellion

Objectives

- To explain the outcome of the Taiping Rebellion
- To describe the Open-Door Policy
- To tell how Sun Yatsen put an end to the Manchu rule in China

Reading Strategy: Summarizing

Write the main idea, details, and any questions you may have.

Remember
During the late 1700s, French peasants rose up against their lords.

The Manchus had trouble with foreigners as well as with people in China.

What Was the Result of the Taiping Rebellion?

Chinese farmers were not happy under Manchu rule. They said that the rulers were greedy and unfair. Most Chinese farmers were poor. Finally the peasants rebelled.

Peasants in China rose up against the Manchu rulers in 1850. By the end of the Taiping Rebellion in 1864, the Manchus were still in power.

1600–1950   *Imperialism and the Far East   Chapter 22*   **461**

They called their rebellion *Taiping*, meaning "Great Peace." The Taiping Rebellion lasted from 1850 to 1864. Millions of lives were lost. When it was over, the Manchus still ruled China.

The peasants might have won their fight. They might have overthrown the Manchu government. Yet foreign **interference** worked against them. Western governments wanted to keep the Manchus in power. Western powers worried that they might lose their trade rights if the Manchus were overthrown. Great Britain, the United States, and other Western nations supported the Manchus. Western governments sent military help, and the peasants were defeated.

Why Did China Fight with Japan?

Next, the Manchus faced war with Japan. China had staked claims on Korea for hundreds of years. When a rebellion broke out in Korea in 1894, the Chinese sent troops in to crush it. Japan had interests in Korea, too. Japan also sent in its troops. The rebellion was put down. Then, neither Japan nor China would withdraw its troops. Instead, the two countries began fighting each other.

By April 1895, the Japanese had defeated the Chinese. China had to give up much of its claim on Korea. China also had to give the island of Taiwan to the Japanese. By 1910, Japan would take complete control of Korea.

The Chinese-Japanese war left China weak. From then on, Manchu rulers got little respect. The Manchus feared that European nations might step in and divide China into colonies. The United States suggested an **Open-Door Policy**. This meant that all countries would have equal rights to trade in China. The Manchus agreed to this policy. The Chinese had once kept everyone out. Now, they opened their ports to the world.

The Boxer Rebellion

In 1898, the Manchu empress Cixi ruled the Qing dynasty. She was very old-fashioned. She wanted to stop any change in China. Perhaps she remembered China's glorious past. If she had her way, she would keep China the way it was.

Then something happened in 1900, during the empress's reign. A group of Chinese rebelled against all foreigners in China. The revolt was called the Boxer Rebellion. And the empress Cixi secretly supported the rebels.

The Boxers were members of a secret society. Westerners called them Boxers because they practiced Chinese exercises that resembled shadow-boxing. The Boxers attempted to kill all foreigners in China. They were put down by an international army that included soldiers from the United States.

China was forced to make payments to the foreign countries to make up for the rebellion. However, the United States used much of the money it received to educate Chinese students. Because of this, the United States won China's favor.

How Did China Move Into the Modern World?

The Qing dynasty would be the last dynasty to rule China. Rebellions had weakened the government. The war with Japan had cost China both land and power. Many foreign countries had interests in China now. In addition, the weak Manchus were unable to protect China against the foreigners. China needed a new government if it were to survive.

In 1911, a Chinese doctor named Sun Yatsen was in Denver, Colorado. He had been traveling throughout Japan, Europe, and the United States. He was trying to raise money to help overthrow the Manchu government. When he heard about sparks of revolution in China, he returned there. He led the revolution and overthrew the Manchu empire. On January 1, 1912, he became the first president of China's new republic. The last Manchu emperor, Puyi, gave up the throne on February 12, 1912. He was only six years old at the time.

History Fact
In China, Sun Yatsen is called "the father of the Revolution."

Yatsen's term as president was short, less than two months. Then a strong military officer, Yuan Shikai, took over. Yatsen and his followers remained. They organized the Nationalist Party. For years the Chinese people suffered under harsh rulers who fought each other for power.

By 1922, the republic had failed and civil war was widespread. With the support of the Soviet Union and of Chinese Communists, Yatsen and his Nationalist Party trained an army. They set out to bring China together under a Nationalist government.

Reading Strategy:
Summarizing

What are the most important details that helped you understand this lesson?

Sun Yatsen died in 1925, but his work was finished by Chiang Kai-shek. By 1928, Chiang was able to set up a Nationalist government in China.

More days of war and revolution were ahead. However, China had left its great dynasties behind and moved into the modern world.

TIMELINE STUDY:

CHINA: 1600–1950

How long did the Qing dynasty last?

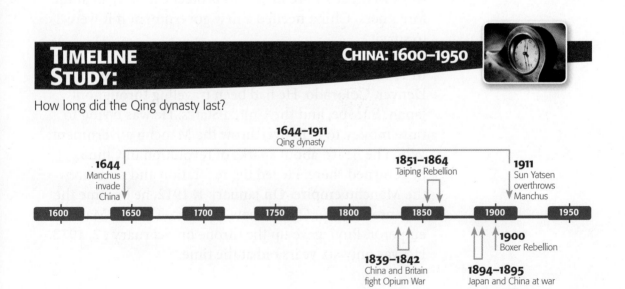

1644–1911
Qing dynasty

1644
Manchus invade China

1851–1864
Taiping Rebellion

1911
Sun Yatsen overthrows Manchus

1600 1650 1700 1750 1800 1850 1900 1950

1900
Boxer Rebellion

1839–1842
China and Britain fight Opium War

1894–1895
Japan and China at war

On a sheet of paper, write the answer to each question. Use complete sentences.

1. Why did the Chinese peasants rebel against the Manchus from 1850 to 1864?

2. What factors led to the Manchu victory over the peasants?

3. China was forced to make payments to make up for the Boxer Rebellion. What did the United States do with the money?

4. How did Sun Yatsen put an end to the Manchu rule in China?

On a sheet of paper, write the letter of the answer that correctly completes each sentence.

5. China and Japan fought for control of _____.

   A Korea **B** Taiwan **C** Japan **D** Hong Kong

6. The _____ gave all countries equal rights to trade with China.

   A Taiping Rebellion **C** Open-Door Policy
   B Boxer Rebellion **D** Treaty of Nanjing

7. The _____ was when a group of Chinese rebelled against all foreigners in China.

   A interference **C** Taiping Rebellion
   B civil war **D** Boxer Rebellion

8. _____ overthrew Sun Yatsen after less than two months as president.

   A Puyi **B** Cixi **C** Chiang Kai-shek **D** Yuan Shikai

9. Yatsen and his followers organized the _____.

   A republic **C** Boxer Rebellion
   B Nationalist Party **D** Taiping Rebellion

10. By _____, China had a Nationalist government.

    A 1912 **B** 1922 **C** 1925 **D** 1928

Japan Opens Its Doors

Objectives

■ To tell how Commodore Matthew C. Perry opened the doors of trade to Japan

■ To list the ways Japan modernized after a powerful emperor took over in 1867

■ To explain how Japan's industrialization led to Japanese imperialism

Reading Strategy: Summarizing

What American is introduced in this lesson?

After 1600, Japan had become an isolated nation. The whole country was under the rule of the Tokugawa family. Foreign trade and travel were not allowed. Japan did not allow foreign products to enter its ports. Japan did not send any products to other lands either. Japan would not accept visitors from other countries. In fact, if a foreign seaman were shipwrecked on Japan's shores, he was in for trouble. He could be arrested or even killed.

How Did Commodore Perry Get Japan to Open Its Ports to Trade?

In 1853, an American naval officer, Commodore Matthew C. Perry, changed all that. Commodore Perry sailed four U.S. warships into Tokyo Bay. He brought a letter from the U.S. president. The letter asked the Japanese to change their policies. It asked for better treatment of any shipwrecked American sailors. It asked that American whaling ships be allowed to buy supplies at Japanese ports. It asked that Japan agree to trade with the United States.

The Japanese were impressed by Perry and his U.S. ships. They had never seen such large vessels or such mighty guns. Perry was a stern man. He met the Japanese with dignity. He refused to speak to anyone except the highest officials. Perry left his requests for the Japanese to consider.

The next year, Commodore Perry returned to Japan. This time, he brought even more ships. The ruling shogun spoke with Perry. Then the Japanese ruler signed a treaty with the United States. Japanese ports would be open to U.S. ships. It was the beginning of a new Japan.

Commodore Matthew C. Perry arrives in Tokyo in 1853 and is greeted by Japanese officials.

How Did Mutsuhito Modernize Japan?

In 1858, Townsend Harris, a U.S. diplomat, signed a more extensive treaty with Japan. That same year, Japan signed trade treaties with Great Britain, France, the Netherlands, and Russia. Japan was no longer an isolated nation.

Then came years of change. Japan was torn between its old ways and the new. Some Japanese wanted to drive the foreigners out of Japan again. They said the treaties Japan had signed were Unequal Treaties. Others wanted to accept the Western world and learn what they could. They realized that their feudal system of government was outdated. The rule of the shoguns with their samurai warriors had to end.

You Decide
Why do you think some Japanese considered the treaties to be "unequal"?

In 1867, a young emperor named Mutsuhito came to power. He and his followers began to modernize Japan. Their motto was, "Knowledge shall be sought throughout the world." The emperor adopted *Meiji* as his title, which means "enlightened rule." He was to rule Japan until 1912. These years are known as the Meiji period. The Japanese traveled to other nations. They wanted to learn what they could about industry, education, transportation, and banking. They built thousands of schools and they invited foreigners to teach in Japan.

In 1889, Japan's first constitution was written. The Japanese still considered their emperor to be godlike. The emperor still held the power, but he accepted advice from elected representatives.

By the 1890s, Japan was keeping step with the modern world. Japan had done away with the samurai and now had a modern army and navy. Japan had steel mills, shipyards, and electrical power plants. In just over 25 years, Japan had made amazing progress. It had gone from an isolated, feudal nation to one of the world's industrial powers.

What are some of the ways in which Japan changed during this time in history?

What Brought About Japanese Imperialism?

As industry grew, Japan needed more raw materials. Like many strong nations, Japan decided to set up overseas colonies to supply those raw materials. However, gaining such colonies meant war.

From 1894 to 1895, Japan was at war with China. China and Japan had a strong difference of opinion over the control of Korea. Japan, with its new, modern military, easily defeated China, and took the island of Taiwan.

In 1904, Russia tried to stake claims in Korea. Japan declared war. The Russo-Japanese War was costly to both sides, but the war was over in 1905. Again the Japanese were the victors. Japan took over some lands in China that had been controlled by Russia. And in 1910, Japan took complete control of Korea. Japan's victory over Russia surprised the world. For the first time, an Asian nation had proved to be stronger than a European nation. And this was to be only the first chapter in the story of Japanese imperialism.

TIMELINE STUDY: JAPAN: 1600–1950

From 1600 to 1854, Japan remained a relatively quiet country. Why are there few events on the timeline?

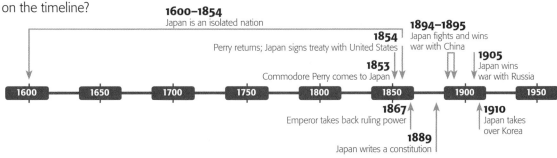

1600–1854
Japan is an isolated nation

1854
Perry returns; Japan signs treaty with United States

1853
Commodore Perry comes to Japan

1894–1895
Japan fights and wins war with China

1905
Japan wins war with Russia

| 1600 | 1650 | 1700 | 1750 | 1800 | 1850 | 1900 | 1950 |

1867
Emperor takes back ruling power

1889
Japan writes a constitution

1910
Japan takes over Korea

REVIEW

On a sheet of paper, write the answer to each question. Use complete sentences.

1. How did Commodore Matthew C. Perry open the doors of trade to Japan?

2. Why did Japan need more raw materials and how did it solve that problem?

3. Why did Japan declare war on Russia?

Word Bank

constitution

Korea

Meiji

Mutsuhito

isolated

Taiwan

treaties

On a sheet of paper, write the word from the Word Bank to complete each sentence correctly.

4. Japan remained _____ after 1600, forbidding trade and foreign visitors.

5. Some Japanese thought the _____ they signed with other nations were good. Others thought they were unequal.

6. The emperor _____ worked to modernize Japan.

7. The emperor adopted _____ as his title, meaning "enlightened rule."

8. Japan's first _____ was written in 1889.

9. Japan won the island of _____ from China in 1895.

10. Japan took complete control of _____ by 1910.

- The Manchus conquered China in 1644 and established the Qing dynasty.

- The Manchus tried to limit foreign trade in China.

- By the late 1700s, the population of China had grown too large for its food supply.

- Europeans started smuggling opium into China.

- Great Britain went to war against China for better trading rights.

- As a result of a treaty signed in 1842, China opened five ports to British trade. China had to give the island of Hong Kong to the British.

- Chinese peasants rebelled in the Taiping Rebellion of 1851. The rebellion was put down by the Manchus and the Westerners.

- Disagreements over claims to Korea led to a war between Japan and China. Eventually Japan gained control of all of Korea.

- The United States persuaded China to have an Open-Door Policy toward foreign trade.

- In 1900, the Boxers tried to drive foreigners out of China. They were crushed by foreign armies.

- In 1911, Chinese Nationalists overthrew the Manchus and ended dynasty rule in China.

- In 1853, Commodore Perry negotiated trade treaties with Japan.

- In 1867, a young emperor began to modernize Japan. It became a powerful industrial nation in just over 25 years.

- To gain raw materials, Japan began to practice imperialism. This led to costly wars with China and Russia.

Word Bank

addicted

interference

Open-Door Policy

policy

smuggle

Vocabulary Review

On a sheet of paper, use the words from the Word Bank to complete each sentence correctly.

1. Foreign _____ during the Taiping Rebellion in China may have changed the outcome of the uprising.

2. A person who is _____ to something must work hard to break the habit.

3. If you _____ goods into a country, they are not legal in that country.

4. The _____ gave all countries equal rights to trade with China.

5. A nation's foreign _____ determines the way the nation acts toward other nations.

Chapter Review Questions

On a sheet of paper, write the answer to each question. Use complete sentences.

6. What was the Manchu dynasty called?

7. How did the Manchus feel about other Chinese?

8. Why did the Chinese pass a law making opium trade illegal?

9. What was the Treaty of Nanjing known as?

10. Who won the Taiping Rebellion: the peasants or the Manchus? Why?

11. Why did the Manchus agree to the Open-Door Policy?

12. Who helped put an end to Manchu rule in China?

13. Who was the American naval officer who got Japan to sign a trade treaty?

14. How did Emperor Mutsuhito help to change Japan?

15. Why was Japan's victory over Russia so surprising to the world?

Critical Thinking

On a sheet of paper, write your response to each question. Use complete sentences.

16. Why did the dynasties come to an end in China?

17. Why did Japan become an imperialist nation?

Using the Timelines

Use the timelines on pages 464 and 469 to answer the questions.

18. What is the topic of each timeline?

19. How many years did the Taiping Rebellion last?

20. What happened in China one year after Japan took over Korea?

GROUP ACTIVITY

With a partner, create a large timeline that shows events in both China and Japan. Display the timeline on a wall of your classroom.

Imperialism and India

The situation in India during this time was far different from that of China and Japan. India had established strong trading ties with Europe for many years. Many Europeans had come to feel comfortable in India in various areas of trade. They had become quite powerful.

Like the native people of the Americas, the people of India wanted freedom from European control. They did not want to see their own culture taken over by another, especially the British. One man named Gandhi helped the people gain power using some very different methods.

GOALS FOR LEARNING

- To describe India after the fall of the Mogul Empire
- To explain the path of British rule in India
- To identify Mahatma Gandhi, and tell what was different about his way of revolution

Reading Strategy: Questioning

You will understand and remember more information if you ask yourself questions as you read. As you read, ask yourself:

- What is my reason for reading this text?

- What connections can I make between this text and my own life, or something I have read before?

Key Vocabulary Words

Lesson 1

Agent A person who has the authority to act for some other person or company

Impose To force one's ideas or wishes on another

Indirectly In a roundabout way

Cartridge A small metal or cardboard tube that holds gunpowder and a bullet

Lesson 2

Superiority A feeling of being better than others

Lesson 3

Nonviolent resistance The act of opposing or working against without using force or causing injury

Civil disobedience The refusal to obey rules, orders, or laws

Fast To go without food

The British East India Company

Objectives

■ To tell how the British East India Company came to rule India
■ To explain how the Sepoy Rebellion began and how it led to direct British rule

Reading Strategy: Questioning

What do you think you will learn about by reading this lesson?

Aurangzeb, the last powerful Mogul emperor, died in 1707. The Moguls had ruled India for almost 200 years. Aurangzeb, a Muslim, had been a harsh ruler. He had angered the Hindus by destroying many of their temples. He had tried to force non-Muslims to convert to Islam.

After the death of Aurangzeb, the Mogul Empire began to break up. Once again, India was divided into small kingdoms. The rajas of the different kingdoms quarreled with one another. The Mogul rulers no longer had any real power.

As the Moguls weakened, stronger countries saw their chance. Europeans would take advantage of the unsteady government in India.

What European Trading Companies Fought for Control of the Indian Trade?

Trading between Europe and India had been going on for a long time. In 1498, the Portuguese explorer Vasco da Gama reached India by sailing around Africa. From that time on, European merchants made regular voyages to India. Dutch, Portuguese, French, and British traders fought each other for control of Indian trade.

In 1600, a private business called the British East India Company was formed. Its purpose was to trade with India. It set up trading posts along India's coastline at Bombay, Calcutta, and Madras. At around this time, the Dutch East India Company was formed. It began operating out of Java, in Indonesia.

The Europeans gained little in India as long as the Mogul Empire was strong. But by the mid-1700s, there was no

Agent

A person who has the authority to act for some other person or company

Impose

To force one's ideas or wishes on another

Indirectly

In a roundabout way

longer a strong central government in India. The British East India Company became involved in what went on in that country. It took sides in Indian civil wars. And it supported rulers who gave it favorable trade rights.

After the French began the French East India Company, the British went to war with the French. In 1757, Robert Clive led the British to victory against the French. Both Clive's army and the French army used Indian soldiers to fight their war. The Indian soldiers were called *sepoys*. The British drove the French out of India. After that, the British East India Company became a powerful force in India.

How Did the British East India Company Come to Rule India?

Soon, **agents** of the East India company became stronger than the local rajas. An agent is a person who has the authority to act for some other person or company. By 1850, the British agents controlled more than half of the land in India. The British put their own men into all the important positions. The British led sepoy armies. They became wealthy landholders.

The British **imposed,** or forced, their own ways on Indian society. They built Christian churches and spoke out

against the Hindu caste system. Many of the Indians did not like the English ways. They did not like the East India Company either. For almost 100 years, Britain **indirectly** ruled India through the British East India Company. India was not officially a British colony, but the British held all the power.

As ruler of Britain, Queen Victoria was eventually named empress of India.

Cartridge

A small metal or cardboard tube that holds gunpowder and a bullet

Reading Strategy: Questioning

As you read, notice the details in the text. What questions can you ask yourself about these details?

LEARN MORE ABOUT IT

The Sepoy Rebellion

To protect their own power, the East India agents from Britain built up armies of sepoys. Most of the British army officers did not try to understand Indian customs and culture. They insisted that the Indians accept British ways.

The sepoys grumbled about this. Then, in 1857, the British started using a new kind of bullet in India. To open the **cartridge,** a soldier had to bite off its end. A cartridge is the small metal or cardboard tube that holds gunpowder and a bullet. The new cartridges were greased with the fat from cows and pigs. The Muslim religion does not allow its followers to eat pork. Hindus are not allowed to eat the meat of a cow. Therefore, the sepoys refused to bite the bullets. When British officers ordered them to bite open the cartridges, the sepoys rebelled.

The British put down the Sepoy Rebellion in 1858. Many lives were lost in the battle. Britain saw that the East India Company could no longer be trusted with control of India.

Sepoys rebelled after they were ordered to bite bullets that were greased with animal fat.

On a sheet of paper, write the letter of the answer that correctly completes each sentence.

1. Europeans saw a chance to profit as the _____ power weakened.

   A sepoy   **B** Mogul   **C** trading   **D** Hindu

2. In 1600, the British East India Company was formed to _____.

   A get more soldiers for Britain   **C** trade with India
   B get more land from India   **D** convert Indians to Catholicism

3. By the mid-1700s, India no longer had a strong central _____.

   A religion   **B** government   **C** army   **D** trade route

4. At this time, the _____ became very involved with what went on in India.

   A sepoys   **C** French East India Company
   B Dutch East India Company   **D** British East India Company

5. Defeating _____ made the British East India Company powerful in India.

   A the French East India Company   **C** the Indians
   B the Dutch East India Company   **D** Clive's army

6. For almost _____ years, Britain indirectly ruled India.

   A 50   **B** 100   **C** 150   **D** 200

7. An Indian soldier is called a _____.

   A Bombay   **B** raja   **C** sepoy   **D** Java

8. The _____ imposed their ways and customs on Indian society.

   A British   **B** French   **C** Dutch   **D** sepoys

9. It went against the sepoys' _____ to bite the bullets greased with animal fat.

   A laws   **B** customs   **C** ways   **D** religion

10. Britain realized that the East India Company could not handle _____ India.

    A trade with   **B** control of   **C** treaties with   **D** war with

British Rule

Objectives

■ To list five good things Britain did for India

■ To explain why many Indians were unhappy with British rule

■ To tell of the turning point in British-Indian relations

Reading Strategy: Questioning

What do the details of this section tell you about a likely outcome?

Superiority
A feeling of being better than others

Remember
In China the Manchus looked down on the rest of the people. In 1912, the Manchus were overthrown.

In 1858, the British Parliament took over the rule of India. India became a colony of Great Britain. It was now called "British India," or the "British Raj."

A viceroy ran the colony. He was appointed by the British monarch. In 1877, the British held a splendid ceremony in India. On this occasion, Queen Victoria was named empress of India.

The British profited from their Indian colony. They called India the "Jewel of the British Empire." In turn, the British government tried to treat Indians more fairly than the British East India Company had.

The British tried to solve the problems of poverty that had always troubled India. They helped farmers dig irrigation canals. They set up hospitals in cities and in some villages. They built railroads and factories, roads and schools. The British tried to do away with the harsh caste system that kept many people so poor.

Why Were Some Indians Unhappy with British Rule?

Many Indians were still unhappy. Some were poorer than ever. India's raw materials were all going to British industry. Manufactured goods were brought in from Britain, killing off India's own industries. Machine-made cloth poured in from Britain. This resulted in Indian spinners and weavers being put out of work. Furthermore, all of India's top jobs went to the British.

It was clear to the Indians that the British looked down on them. The British did not allow Indians in their restaurants or hotels. It seemed that British imperialism encouraged British feelings of **superiority.**

As Europeans moved into India, they brought Western ideas with them. They built railroad stations, such as this one in Agra, Utter Pradesh, India.

Where Did Indians Get Ideas of Independence?

The British chose some Indian students to send off to school in Great Britain. They planned to give the students "English" ideas and training. The plan backfired. Once the students from India learned about English democracy, they wanted independence for their own people.

In 1885, a group called the Indian National Congress was founded. It was made up of educated Indians. They said they were meeting to improve relations with Britain. In truth, they were discussing revolution. In the early 1900s, there were some violent uprisings. The British always crushed them. To improve the situation, the British allowed a few Indians to be included in the government. A few years later, the British increased the number of Indians in the government. But the protests continued.

On April 13, 1919, British troops fired on an unarmed crowd in Amritsar. Nearly 400 Indians were killed, and at least 1,200 were wounded. The Amritsar Massacre marked a turning point in British-Indian relations. From then on, Indians knew what they could expect from the British. They were determined to keep fighting for independence. No real progress toward independence came until leadership went to a man called Gandhi.

Reading Strategy:
Questioning

Think beyond the text. Consider your own thoughts and experiences as you read.

On a sheet of paper, write the letter of the answer that correctly completes each sentence.

1. The British Parliament took control of India in 1858, making India a(n) _____ of Britain.

   A island   **B** republic   **C** colony   **D** supporter

2. The British monarch appointed a(n) _____ to run the colony.

   A raja   **B** empress   **C** viceroy   **D** queen

3. The British government tried to treat Indians more fairly than the _____ had.

   A French East India Company   **C** Dutch East India Company
   B British East India Company   **D** raja

4. The British _____ their hotels and restaurants.

   A did not allow Indians into   **C** forced Indians to build
   B allowed Indians into   **D** spent Indian money on

5. British _____ seemed to encourage British feeling of superiority.

   A religion   **B** democracy   **C** trade   **D** imperialism

6. When Indian students learned about _____, they wanted independence for their own people.

   A imperialism   **C** British railroads
   B English democracy   **D** British industry

On a sheet of paper, write the answer to each question. Use complete sentences.

7. What are five good things the British did in India?

8. Why were many Indians unhappy with British rule?

9. What was the Indian National Congress really meeting about?

10. What was the turning point in British-Indian relations?

Mahatma Gandhi

Objectives

- To define and provide an example of nonviolent resistance
- To define and provide an example of civil disobedience
- To explain what happened after India won independence

Reading Strategy: Questioning

What do you already know about Gandhi?

Nonviolent resistance
The act of opposing or working against without using force or causing injury

Civil disobedience
The refusal to obey rules, orders, or laws

 You Decide
Do you think nonviolent resistance is a good way to make change today?

Mohandas K. Gandhi was born in 1869. He was a Hindu. His family belonged to the merchant caste. Gandhi studied law in London. He worked as a lawyer in South Africa for 21 years. At that time, South Africa was ruled by Great Britain. Gandhi worked for the rights of Indians who were being discriminated against. In 1914, Gandhi returned to India. There he began to work for independence from Britain. By 1920, he had become the leader of the Indian National Congress.

How Did Gandhi Suggest Indians Gain Their Independence?

Gandhi had new ideas. He said that the way to freedom was not through violence or bloodshed. Instead, Gandhi taught **nonviolent resistance** and **civil disobedience.**

Calmly and peacefully, Gandhi led Indians to refuse to obey the British government. "Conquer by love," he taught. His followers called him *Mahatma* Gandhi. *Mahatma* means "Great Soul."

"We cannot win against British guns," Gandhi said. "The British only know how to fight against guns. We will show them a new kind of resistance." Gandhi said that civil disobedience was a weapon stronger than guns. He told Indians to refuse to work in British mines, shops, and factories.

Gandhi led a revolution for independence. It was, for the most part, a revolution of the poor. Although he was a Hindu, he did not believe in the caste system. He lived among the poorest Indians, the untouchables, for many years. He lived simply, often wearing only a linen loincloth (a small cloth worn about the hips).

India and Pakistan, 1950

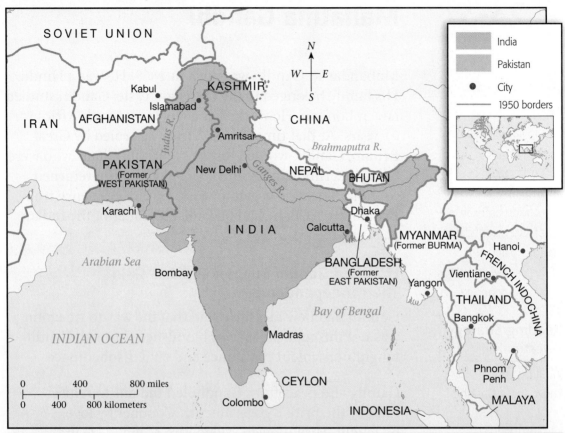

MAP STUDY

1. What are two cities in Pakistan?
2. What city in India is located near the Ganges River?

Reading Strategy: Questioning

What problems in your own life can help you understand Gandhi and the struggles of the Indian people?

In one act of resistance, Gandhi led thousands of Indian women to the train tracks. There they lay down, stopping the British trains. When the British put an unfair tax on salt, Gandhi peacefully led a march 240 miles to the sea to get salt from the ocean.

Gandhi was often arrested for his activities. He spent a total of seven years in jail. But in time, the British began to listen to Gandhi and his followers.

Fast
To go without food

Mahatma Gandhi became an important leader in India's fight for independence.

What Did Gandhi Do to Keep the Peace in India?

The British knew that the Indian people no longer wanted them in their country. They knew it was just a matter of time before they would be forced to leave. So they offered independence to India. The Muslims however, demanded a separate nation. Their protests led to bloody rioting between Muslims and Hindus. As a result, India was divided into two nations. Pakistan would be a Muslim nation, and India would be Hindu.

Mahatma Gandhi saw his country gain independence in 1947. Unfortunately, more fighting between Hindus and Muslims came with independence. There was terrible loss of life. Entire villages were wiped out. Gandhi insisted that the fighting stop. He went on a **fast,** refusing to eat until the bloodshed ended. He almost starved to death. At last, Hindu and Muslim leaders promised to stop the fighting. They did not want their leader to die. Gandhi's fast had come to an end.

Shortly after Gandhi's fast ended, he was shot down by a Hindu gunman. Both Hindus and Muslims mourned their great leader.

TIMELINE STUDY:

INDIA: 1600–1950

After Gandhi began nonviolent resistance against the British, how many years passed before Indian independence?

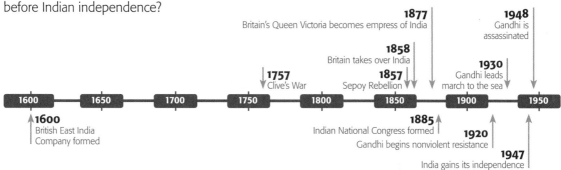

1877
Britain's Queen Victoria becomes empress of India

1948
Gandhi is assassinated

1858
Britain takes over India

1757
Clive's War

1857
Sepoy Rebellion

1930
Gandhi leads march to the sea

| 1600 | 1650 | 1700 | 1750 | 1800 | 1850 | 1900 | 1950 |

1600
British East India Company formed

1885
Indian National Congress formed

1920
Gandhi begins nonviolent resistance

1947
India gains its independence

REVIEW

Match the definition in Column A with the term in Column B.
Write the correct letter on each line.

Column A

1. to go without food

2. the act of opposing without using force; working against without causing injury

3. to refuse to do as told, especially when the rule, order, or law is bad

Column B

A civil disobedience

B fast

C nonviolent resistance

Word Bank

conquer by love

Gandhi

Great Soul

Hindu

On a sheet of paper, write the word from the Word Bank to complete each sentence correctly.

4. _____ worked for the rights of Indians who were being discriminated against.

5. Gandhi taught Indians to _____.

6. *Mahatma* means "_____."

7. Gandhi was a _____, but did not believe in the caste system.

On a sheet of paper, write the answer to each question. Use complete sentences.

8. What is an example of civil disobedience?

9. What is an example of nonviolent resistance?

10. What happened after the British offered India independence?

CHAPTER 23 SUMMARY

- Mogul rule in India weakened in the 1700s.

- The British East India Company gradually built a strong trading presence in India. It became involved in what took place in the country.

- When the French East India Company was formed, the British went to war against them. They were aided by Indians.

- The British East India Company began to rule India. They imposed British ways on Indian society.

- Indian soldiers, called sepoys, rebelled against the British East India Company in 1857.

- The British brought some improvements to India. However, the British felt superior to Indians and did not allow them to control their own country.

- A group of educated Indians formed the Indian National Congress to talk about gaining independence from Great Britain.

- In 1919, 400 Indians were killed and 1,200 wounded in the Amritsar Massacre. After that, the Indians were determined to end British rule.

- Mahatma Gandhi led India to independence by encouraging nonviolent civil disobedience.

- In 1947, India won independence and was divided into India and Pakistan.

- Unfortunately, independence brought more fighting between Hindus and Muslims.

Word Bank

agent

cartridge

civil disobedience

fast

impose

indirectly

nonviolent
  resistance

superiority

Vocabulary Review

On a sheet of paper, use the words from the Word Bank to correctly match each definition below.

1. To go without eating for a considerable time

2. Refusal to obey bad rules, orders, or laws

3. Working against something without using force

4. To force one's will on another person or group

5. A feeling of being better than somebody else

6. A small tube that holds gunpowder and a bullet

7. To go about something in a roundabout way

8. A person who has the authority to act for someone or something else

Chapter Review Questions

On a sheet of paper, write the answer to each question. Use complete sentences.

9. What was the purpose of the British East India Company?

10. What gave the Europeans the chance to take advantage of India?

11. Why did the British Parliament take over rule of India?

12. Why was the Indian National Congress formed?

13. What two new ideas did Gandhi teach?

14. Why did Gandhi lead a march to the sea?

15. Why was India divided into two nations?

Test Tip

Studying together in small groups and asking questions of one another is one way to review for tests.

Critical Thinking

On a sheet of paper, write your response to each question. Use complete sentences.

16. Why do you think the British called India the "Jewel of the British Empire"?

17. Why do you think so many Indian people followed Gandhi?

Using the Timeline

Use the timeline on page 485 to answer the questions.

18. Did the Sepoy Rebellion take place before or after Britain took over India?

19. How many years after the British East India Company was formed did Britain officially take over India?

20. When was the Indian National Congress formed?

GROUP ACTIVITY

Form groups of four students. Discuss a problem in your community or nation. List some ways to solve the problem. Would nonviolent resistance help to solve it? Why or why not?

Imperialism and Africa

Many civilizations grew up south of the African Sahara beginning around 1000 B.C. Arabs were the first to trade with these civilizations. Later, traders from Europe began to visit these parts of Africa too. They made people aware of these civilizations. Trade increased and trading posts were established on the coast. Soon, the Africans, like the native people of the Americas, became affected by Europeans.

European explorers began to establish colonies. An increasing number of African people faced foreign control in their own land. Others became enslaved and many were taken away in ships, as if they were a raw material. It would be many years before much change would end outside control.

GOALS FOR LEARNING

- To name and describe the early kingdoms of Africa
- To describe Africa after the first century A.D.
- To describe the African slave trade
- To explain why Europeans wanted colonies in Africa

Reading Strategy: Predicting

Previewing a text helps prepare readers to look for new information—to predict what will come next. A prediction is your best guess about what might happen next.

- As you read the text, notice details that could help you make predictions.

- While you read, check your predictions. You may have to change your predictions as you learn more information.

Key Vocabulary Words

Lesson 1
Caravan A group of people traveling together, often through a desert

Lesson 4
Dominance The act of ruling, controlling, or being most powerful

Prejudice Dislike of people just because they are of a different race or religion, or are from another country

Racism The idea that one race is better than another

Conference A meeting of people to discuss something

Inferior Not as good as someone or something else

Early Kingdoms of Africa

Objectives

- To describe the Kush civilization
- To tell what the caravans brought and to explain their impact on Ghana
- To tell how Mali became a wealthy kingdom
- To describe the end of the kingdom of Songhai

Reading Strategy: Predicting

Preview the lesson title. Predict what you think you will learn in this lesson and the lessons to follow.

One of the world's earliest civilizations was that of the ancient Egyptians in northern Africa. The Egyptian pharaohs built great pyramids and temples. In time, other nations founded colonies in northern Africa. The Phoenicians built the city of Carthage. Then the Romans came and built their own cities. Still later came the Arab conquerors. Their armies swept across northern Africa, bringing Islam with them.

All this happened in northern Africa. However, there were civilizations in the rest of the continent, south of the Sahara.

How Long Did the Kush Civilization Last?

Along the Nile River, just south of Egypt, is a country called Sudan. During the time of ancient Egypt, this land was called Nubia. A civilization arose there about 2000 B.C. The people of Nubia, or Kush, as it was also called, were black. In about 1500 B.C., Egypt conquered Kush. For the next 500 years, Kush was ruled by the Egyptians. The Kushites were greatly influenced by them. Kush became an important center of art, learning, and trade. But by about 1000 B.C., the Egyptians had lost much of their power. The Kushites were able to drive out the Egyptians.

At about this time, Kushites began mining iron. They used the iron to make tools and weapons. The Kushites kept growing stronger. In about 750 B.C., they conquered Egypt and ruled there until about 670 B.C.

Caravan

A group of people traveling together, often through a desert

This ancient statue of a lion holding a shield dates back to the Kush civilization.

The civilization of Kush lasted until about A.D. 350. Kush was then conquered by the neighboring kingdom of Aksum. By then, both Kush and Aksum had come under the influence of the Roman Empire and Christianity. Kush was to remain Christian until the 1300s when Arabs appeared in the region. The Kushites then converted to the Muslim religion.

How Were Goods Traded Across the Sahara?

In western Africa, on the southern side of the Sahara, is a vast area of grasslands. Great kingdoms of black Africans grew up there.

By about A.D. 1000, Arab traders from northern Africa began to cross the Sahara in **caravans**. The trade caravans brought goods that the people of western Africa needed. They brought tools and clothing. They also brought the thing that the people needed most—salt. The climate south of the Sahara is hot and dry. People needed salt to stay healthy. They needed salt to preserve their food. Salt was so important that the people were willing to trade gold for it. Luckily there was plenty of gold available in western Africa.

TIMELINE STUDY: THE KUSHITES: 2000 B.C.–A.D. 500

How long did the Kush civilization last?

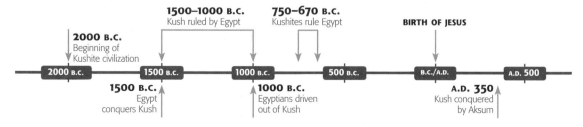

1500–1000 B.C.
Kush ruled by Egypt

750–670 B.C.
Kushites rule Egypt

BIRTH OF JESUS

2000 B.C.
Beginning of Kushite civilization

2000 B.C. | **1500 B.C.** | **1000 B.C.** | **500 B.C.** | **B.C./A.D.** | **A.D. 500**

1500 B.C.
Egypt conquers Kush

1000 B.C.
Egyptians driven out of Kush

A.D. 350
Kush conquered by Aksum

Ancient Kingdoms of Africa, 1500

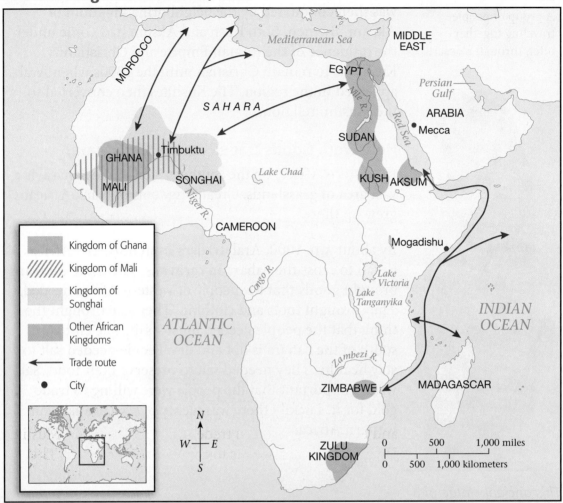

MAP STUDY

1. What large island is located off the coast of eastern Africa?

2. What are four rivers in Africa?

What Impact Did Arab Trading Caravans Have on the Kingdom of Ghana?

During the A.D. 400s, a kingdom called Ghana grew up in western Africa. The kingdom began to prosper about A.D. 1000. This is when the Arabs from northern Africa became interested in trade with Ghana. They had learned that Ghana was rich in gold. However, trade turned out to be a mixed blessing for Ghana. The Arab trading caravans brought not only goods but also religion to Ghana. In time, Ghana's rulers became Muslims. In contrast, most of the people living in Ghana did not convert. They still practiced their own ancient worship of many gods.

Muslim rulers tried to force the people to practice Islam. This weakened the kingdom. The Mandingo people of a kingdom called Mali took over Ghana near the end of the 13th century. By 1300, the kingdom of Ghana was gone.

How Did Mali Become a Wealthy Kingdom?

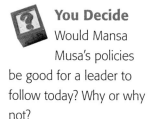

You Decide
Would Mansa Musa's policies be good for a leader to follow today? Why or why not?

From 1312 to 1337, the Mali kingdom was ruled by a man named Mansa Musa. *Mansa* means "king." Mansa Musa was a good king. He built Mali's wealth by encouraging and then taxing caravan trade. Mansa Musa was a Muslim. He invited Arab scholars to come to Mali to teach. The city of Timbuktu became a center of Muslim learning.

Mansa Musa became famous when he made his pilgrimage to the holy city of Mecca, in Arabia. He decided to show the rest of the world just how wealthy his kingdom was. He took a splendid caravan with him on his pilgrimage to Mecca. Across the grasslands and deserts he went, along with thousands of his people. Mansa Musa also took thousands of enslaved people with him. Many of the slaves carried a solid gold staff, which was used for support when walking. He also took at least 80 camels, each loaded with bags of gold dust. Everywhere he went, the Mali ruler gave out gold and other gifts. Stories quickly spread about the fabulous wealth of the kingdom of Mali.

Reading Strategy:
Predicting

Think about your
prediction. What details
can you now add to
make your prediction
more specific?

What Was the Kingdom of Songhai Like?

When Mansa Musa died, Mali weakened. A kingdom
called Songhai took control of Mali during the 1400s.
One of the Songhai rulers was a king named Askia
Mohammed. Askia ruled from 1493 to 1528. This was a
time of growth in Songhai power. The city of Timbuktu
reached its height as an important center of trade and
learning. Songhai remained strong until the late 1500s.
At that time, the Moroccan king, Mohamed al-Mansur,
The Victorious, attacked. The Moroccans had guns.
The Songhai warriors fought with spears. Songhai
was defeated.

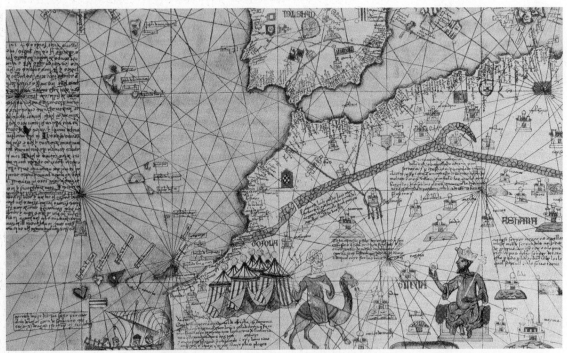

*This Spanish map, created in 1375, includes a drawing of Mansa Musa. It gives clues
about Musa's power, his wealth, and the extent of his rule.*

Match the definition in Column A with the term in Column B.
Write the correct letter on a sheet of paper.

Column A

1. the civilization that arose around 2000 B.C. along the Nile River

2. a kingdom that began to prosper in A.D. 1000

3. the kingdom that took over Ghana near the end of the 13th century

4. the kingdom that took control of Mali during the 1400s

5. the ruler of the Mali kingdom from 1312 to 1337; was Muslim

6. the ruler of Songhai from 1493 to 1528

Column B

A Askia Mohammed

B Ghana

C Kush

D Mali

E Mansa Musa

F Songhai

On a sheet of paper, write the answer to each question. Use complete sentences.

7. What was the Kush civilization like during Egyptian rule (1500–1000 B.C.)?

8. What goods and ideas did the people of western Africa and the Arabs trade?

9. How did the ruler of Mali's kingdom from 1312 to 1337 build Mali's wealth?

10. What was the importance of the city of Timbuktu in the kingdom of Songhai?

LESSON 24-2

Africa After the First Century A.D.

Objectives

- To name two southern African kingdoms
- To explain why Europe had little contact with southern Africa before the 1400s

Reading Strategy:
Predicting

Think about what you predicted earlier. Does your prediction still work or do you need to revise your prediction?

History Fact
Swahili is a Bantu language that uses many Arabic words.

Early in the first century A.D., a great migration began in Africa. Black peoples of what is now Nigeria and Cameroon moved southward into the forests of central Africa. The population had been growing, and the people needed more land. Migration continued over the next 1,000 years. The people spoke Bantu languages. They settled in many parts of central, eastern, and southern Africa.

By about A.D. 1100, trading cities dotted the eastern African coast. A city called Mogadishu was one of the largest. The people living in coastal towns had frequent contact with Arab traders. They became Muslims, and they followed many Arabic customs. They spoke Swahili. The language is still used in much of central and southern Africa.

What Kingdoms Arose in South Africa?

A number of kingdoms arose in southern Africa. One of these was the kingdom of Zimbabwe. Another was the kingdom of the Zulus. The Zulus moved into southern Africa in the 1600s. They were powerful warriors. During the 1800s, they had a strong military under a fierce ruler named Shaka.

Shaka led his armies to conquer other kingdoms. Meanwhile, southern Africa was being settled by the Dutch and the British. The Zulus fought against European rule. In 1879, the British conquered the Zulu kingdom.

What Riches Did Europeans Find in Africa?

Africa was not an easy continent to explore. The Sahara kept many European traders from traveling south by land.

---

498   *Unit 8   The Age of Imperialism*

During the Renaissance, however, interest in travel grew. Seamen sailed better ships. In the 1400s, the Europeans began to arrive in Africa by sea routes.

The Portuguese were the first to sail the waters along Africa's coast. Prince Henry the Navigator sent ships along the west coast. He was searching for a trade route to India. Portuguese sailors soon learned of the gold in western Africa. They called a section of the African coastline the *Gold Coast*.

Reading Strategy:
Predicting

Think about the arrival of Europeans in Africa. What do you predict they will do?

In 1497, the Portuguese sea captain Vasco da Gama discovered the sea route around Africa. Soon, Portugal set up trading posts along Africa's coasts. In 1571, Angola, in southwestern Africa, became a Portuguese colony.

Then the Portuguese found something in Africa that was a better money-maker than gold. They found that they could get rich by buying and selling human beings.

This map from 1547 is of the Gold Coast in Africa. It is drawn upside-down as if viewed from Europe.

Word Bank

British

Gold Coast

human beings

Mogadishu

Portuguese

Sahara

south

Vasco da Gama

Zimbabwe

Zulus

On a sheet of paper, write the word from the Word Bank to complete each sentence correctly.

1. Africans began to migrate _____ in the first century A.D.

2. _____ was a large trading city on the eastern African coast around A.D. 1100.

3. The kingdom of _____ and the kingdom of the Zulus arose in southern Africa.

4. The _____ was a kingdom in Africa made up of powerful warriors.

5. The Zulus fought hard, but in 1879 the _____ conquered the Zulu kingdom.

6. Europe had little contact with Africa. This is because the _____ made it hard to travel south by land.

7. The _____ were the first to explore Africa's coast.

8. The western section of the African coast is known as the _____.

9. _____ discovered the sea route around Africa, which was then used for trading.

10. The Portuguese found that buying and selling _____ made better money than gold.

The African Slave Trade

Objectives

- To explain the differences in the ways Africans and Europeans treated slaves
- To list the European nations that took part in the slave trade

Reading Strategy: Predicting

Think about the slave trade by Europeans. What do you predict will happen to end this serious problem?

There had been enslaved people in Africa for a long time. When Africans conquered other Africans, they often made slaves of their captives. However, African slavery was quite different from the kind of slavery the Europeans practiced. The Africans treated enslaved people like human beings. Children of African slaves were free. But the Europeans treated their slaves like goods to be traded and sold, not like people.

How Did the African Slave Trade Come About?

The Portuguese were the first European slave traders. By the mid 1400s, the Portuguese were capturing Africans and packing them onto crowded ships. Many Africans died on the terrible voyages. Those who survived had to work as slaves in mines and on plantations in the West Indies. Soon the Spanish were also shipping slaves to the Americas.

PUBLIC SALE OF NEGROES.—Under the authority of a decree of the Circuit Court of Albemarle county, pronouced in the case of Michie's administrator and others, on the 30th day of October, 1855, I will offer for sale, at public auction, on MONDAY, the 5th day of May next, being Albemarle Court day, if a suitable day, if not, on the next suitable day thereafter, at the Court House of Albemarle county, *Five Negroes*, of whom the late David Tichis died possessed, consisting of a Negro Woman, twenty years of age and child two years old, a woman fifty-five years old, a negro man twenty-five years old, who has been working at the slating business, and a negro man twenty-two years old, a blacksmith.—The above lot of negroes is equal to any that has ever been offered in this market.

TERMS OF SALE—Five months credit, negotiable notes with approved endorsers, with the interest added.

ap24—ctds   GEO. DARR, Commissioner.

This 18th century slave trade ad demonstrates the horrors of slavery. Africans were sold like they were objects, rather than human beings.

By the mid-1600s, the French, English, and Dutch had joined in the profitable slave trade. Some Africans helped supply the Europeans with slaves. Sometimes, tribes fought each other to capture people to supply the slave traders. The fighting between tribes weakened Africa.

The slave markets wanted only the healthiest, strongest young Africans. Over time, at least 10 million men and women were taken out of Africa to be sold into slavery. The loss of some of its finest people also weakened Africa. Africa was in no position to defend itself against European imperialism.

Fortunately, people finally recognized that slavery was wrong. By the 1800s, many countries made slave trading illegal. In 1834, Britain outlawed, or did not allow, slavery in its colonies. Other European countries soon did the same. The United States abolished, or did away with, slavery in 1865. By 1888, slavery was illegal throughout the Americas.

Words from the Past

Songs of Slavery and Freedom

When enslaved Africans arrived in the Americas, they brought rich cultures with them. In the Americas, their cultures were forbidden. However, enslaved Africans created a rich culture of their own, based on their memories of Africa and their life on the plantations of America.

From the 1600s through the mid-1800s, enslaved Africans created songs called *spirituals*. Spirituals are religious songs that use African music and rhythms. The words of spirituals tell of enslavement and struggle.

This music served many purposes. As their ancestors had done in Africa, enslaved Africans sang while they worked.

During the mid-1800s, some spirituals helped enslaved people escape to freedom in the North on the Underground Railroad. For example, the song "Swing Low, Sweet Chariot," is about the Underground Railroad.

The spirituals were important to the development of today's gospel music, the blues, and jazz.

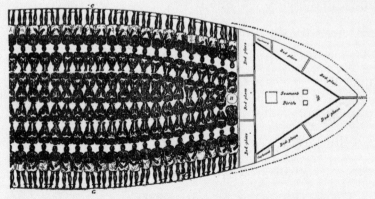

This is a diagram showing the inside of a slave ship.

REVIEW

On a sheet of paper, write the letter of the answer that correctly completes each sentence.

1. The _____ were the first European slave traders.

   A Portuguese **B** Spanish **C** Dutch **D** English

2. In the mid 1400s, slaves worked in mines and on plantations in _____.

   A the Americas **B** France **C** the West Indies **D** Portugal

3. Sometimes, African tribes fought each other to capture people to _____, weakening Africa.

   A kill them **C** get information from them
   B force them into the army **D** supply the slave traders

4. Africans lost at least _____ men and women to slavery.

   A 10,000 **B** 1 million **C** 10 million **D** 100 million

5. Having lost many people, Africa was in no position to defend itself against European _____.

   A religion **B** trade **C** imperialism **D** armies

6. Britain outlawed slavery in its colonies in 1834, and in 1865 _____ did the same.

   A Portugal **B** the United States **C** Spain **D** France

7. Religious songs that use African music and rhythms, called _____, tell of enslavement and struggle.

   A spirituals **B** musicals **C** rap **D** odes

On a sheet of paper, write the answer to each question. Use complete sentences.

8. What are the differences in the way Africans and Europeans treated slaves?

9. Which European countries were involved in slave trade in Africa?

10. What types of music of today are influenced by spirituals?

European Imperialism

Objectives

- To explain how and why racism led Europeans into Africa
- To detail how Europeans set up colonies in Africa
- To tell of ways that Europeans made Africans feel inferior

Dominance

The act of ruling, controlling, or being most powerful

Prejudice

Dislike of people just because they are of a different race or religion, or are from another country

Racism

The idea that one race is better than another

Conference

A meeting of people to discuss something

American and European slave trade in Africa finally came to an end. However, Africa had not seen the end of European **dominance** and **prejudice**. In the 1800s there had been an industrial revolution in Europe. Now Europeans needed raw materials and new markets for finished products. European nations wanted new colonies. These nations saw that the continent of Africa had lots of land.

The Industrial Revolution led to imperialism. However, there was another reason that led the Europeans into Africa. That was **racism**. Some Europeans simply thought they were better than the dark-skinned peoples of the world. Some thought it was their duty to bring their own culture to the black Africans. Therefore, the Europeans took over Africa.

How Were Colonies Set up in Africa?

In 1884, European nations held a **conference**, or a meeting, in Berlin, Germany. The United States and the Ottoman Empire sent representatives, too. No one invited African representatives. The conference set up rules for forming colonies in Africa. By 1914, Europeans had taken over almost all the land in Africa.

The Europeans formed some of their colonies easily. They made agreements with local tribal chiefs. They gave the chiefs presents and promised chances for trade. Some of the tribal leaders simply gave away their kingdoms.

European missionaries helped set up colonies. They had come to convert the Africans to Christianity. Often they were unwelcome. Yet again, the Europeans felt it was their duty to show Africans the idea of a better way.

Soon there were only two independent countries left in all of Africa. Ethiopia, in the northeast, was the larger one. Liberia, on the west coast, was the other. Founded in 1822 by freed American slaves, Liberia had declared its independence in 1847.

TECHNOLOGY CONNECTION

The Suez Canal

The Suez Canal was built by a French company from 1859 to 1869. It was constructed under the direction of canal expert Ferdinand de Lesseps. This waterway linked the Gulf of Suez and the Red Sea with Port Said on the southeastern Mediterranean Sea. The total original cost of building the canal was about $100 million. It is 105 miles (169 km) long and 197 feet (300 meters) at its narrowest point. The Mediterranean and the Gulf of Suez are at about the same water level. Because of this, the canal was built without locks. (Locks are part of some canals. They are used to raise and lower boats as they move to different water levels.)

The Suez Canal revolutionized trade by providing a faster route from Europe to the Far East. The British government was responsible for protecting the Canal soon after it was completed. In 1956, Egypt took over that role. In recent years it has been widened so larger ships can pass through.

Inferior

Not as good as someone or something else

Remember

Religion came along with invaders at many points in history. Sometimes the new religion was welcomed. Often it was resisted.

How Did the Europeans Affect the Africans and Their Culture?

It is easy to see the wrongs and injustices of European imperialism in Africa. African culture was damaged. The Europeans did not understand tribal differences and tribal customs. Most did not even try to understand.

The Europeans forced the Africans to learn new ways. They tried to make the Africans feel **inferior**, or not as good as Europeans. They forced the Africans to accept European government, religion, and languages. They drew up colonial boundaries without giving any thought to splitting up tribes.

Some of the things the Europeans did in Africa helped the natives. However, most of those helped the Europeans. Railway systems, roads, and schools were built, and the continent of Africa was opened up to the rest of the world.

In the years ahead, new ideas would come to Africa. These would be ideas of freedom, of self-government—and, in some cases, of revolution.

TIMELINE STUDY:

CHANGES IN AFRICA: A.D. 400–1900

What happened 31 years after Britain outlawed slavery?

450–1224
Kingdom of Ghana

1493–1541
Kingdom of Songhai

1642
French join slave trade

1621
Dutch join slave trade

1661
English join slave trade

1865
United States outlaws slavery

1834
Britain outlaws slavery

1888
Slavery illegal throughout Americas

| 400 | 1200 | 1300 | 1400 | 1500 | 1600 | 1700 | 1800 | 1900 |

1300–1500
Kingdom of Mali

1500
Portuguese begin slave trade

1600–1883
Kingdom of Zulu in southern Africa

1884

Conference in Berlin begins; Europeans scramble for colonies in Africa

REVIEW

Match the definition in Column A with the term in Column B.
Write the correct letter on a sheet of paper.

Column A

1. the idea that one race is better than another

2. not as good as someone or something else

3. disliking people because they are a different race or religion, or are from another country

4. the act of ruling, controlling, being most powerful

5. a meeting of people to discuss something

Column B

A conference

B dominance

C inferior

D prejudice

E racism

On a sheet of paper, write the answer to each question. Use complete sentences.

6. What factors (besides racism) led the Europeans into Africa?

7. How and why did racism lead Europeans into Africa?

8. How did Europeans go about setting up colonies in Africa?

9. What are the only two independent countries in Africa?

10. How did Europeans make Africans feel inferior?

- The Kush civilization of ancient Egypt was one of the earliest in Africa.

- The Kushites were greatly influenced by 500 years of Egyptian rule, beginning in 1500 B.C.

- The Kush civilization lasted until about A.D. 350. At that time, it was taken over by the neighboring kingdom of Aksum.

- Ghana, Mali, and Songhai were rich kingdoms in western Africa.

- The population grew in what is now Nigeria and Cameroon. Thus more people moved into the forests of central Africa.

- European ships began arriving in Africa in the 1400s.

- The Portuguese found that they could make money by taking and selling Africans as slaves.

- The British, French, and Dutch soon joined the slave trade.

- The Industrial Revolution and racial prejudices played a part in European colonization of Africa.

- In 1884, a conference in Berlin laid down ground rules for colonizing Africa.

- By 1914, almost the entire continent of Africa had fallen under European imperialism.

CHAPTER 24
REVIEW

Word Bank

caravans

conference

dominance

inferior

prejudiced

racism

Vocabulary Review

On a sheet of paper, use the words from the Word Bank to complete each sentence correctly.

1. When people show _____ toward others, they rule over them or use their power on them.

2. In colonial Africa, Europeans tried to make Africans feel _____, or not as good as Europeans.

3. About A.D. 1000, trade _____ crossed the desert to bring goods to Africa.

4. _____ is the mistaken idea that one race is better than another.

5. A(n) _____ is a meeting to discuss something.

6. Even though the slave trade had ended, Europeans were still _____ against Africans.

Chapter Review Questions

On a sheet of paper, write the answer to each question. Use complete sentences.

7. Where was the Kush civilization?

8. Why did Europeans have little contact with Africa south of the Sahara before 1400?

9. What goods and ideas did the people of western Africa and the Arabs trade?

10. Which people took over Ghana near the end of the 13th century?

11. How did the kingdom of Mali become rich?

12. During Songhai rule, what happened to Timbuktu?

13. What European nations took part in the slave trade in Africa during the 1600s?

14. What two factors led to European imperialism in Africa?

15. The Europeans colonized all but what two countries in Africa?

Critical Thinking

On a sheet of paper, write your response to each question. Use complete sentences.

16. How can salt be as valuable as gold?

17. How did the colonial powers show that they thought Africans were inferior?

Using the Timelines

Use the timelines on pages 493 and 507 to answer the questions.

18. How long did the Kushite civilization last?

19. Were the Kushites in power a longer time before or after the birth of Jesus?

20. How many years after the Dutch did the English join the slave trade?

GROUP ACTIVITY

Form groups of four students. Make a booklet of the early kingdoms of Africa. Describe the way of life and the accomplishments, or triumphs, of each kingdom.

NATIONALISM AND THE SPREAD OF WAR AND REVOLUTION

N ationalism is a feeling of strong loyalty to one's country. It may lead people to honor the flag or sing the anthem of that country. It may give them reason to risk their lives. The French had a sense of nationalism that made them fight for their rights within their country. The same was true of the American colonists.

Throughout history, a sense of nationalism gave even the poorest of people a real purpose. If they believed in their country, no government could abuse them in that country. They would revolt, if necessary, to make change. Sometimes the imperialism of one nation threatened the nationalism of another. This conflict often led to war.

Imperialism often leads to war. Japan thought the United States stood in the way of its control of the Pacific Ocean. So, Japan bombed the Pearl Harbor naval base in Hawaii, on December 7, 1941. The attack brought the United States into World War II.

Chapters in Unit 9

The Unifications of Italy and Germany

In the 19th century, the people of Italy and of Germany became much more unified. They had a homeland. Many were proud that their parents and grandparents were born in the same place they lived. All around them were people with whom they shared a common language, customs, and culture. Their sense of nationalism made them realize that they must defend their home, if necessary.

GOALS FOR LEARNING

- To tell how the spirit of nationalism led to the unification of Italy
- To tell how the spirit of nationalism led to the unification of Germany

Reading Strategy: Text Structure

Readers can look at the organization of the text to help them identify the most important information.

- Preview the chapter before you begin reading. Look at the chapter title and the names of the lessons and sections. Also review the boldfaced words and the maps and photographs.

- You will notice that the section titles are in the form of questions. The answer to each question is provided in the paragraph(s) in that section. In this way, the text is structured in a question and answer format.

Key Vocabulary Words

Lesson 1

Anthem The official song of a country

Unification Bringing together into one whole

Boundary The dividing line between one country and another

Unify To connect; to bring together as one

Society A group of people joined together for a common purpose

Prime minister The chief official of the government in some countries

Diplomat A person in government whose job is dealing with other countries

Lesson 2

Confederation A group of independent states joined together for a purpose

Legislature A group of people who make the laws of a nation or state

Reich The German word for "empire"

Kaiser The emperor of Germany

Chancellor The head of government, or prime minister, in some European countries

Militarism A national policy of maintaining a powerful army and constant readiness for war

Nationalism in Italy

Nationalism is a feeling of strong loyalty to one's country and culture. Such a feeling often develops among people who speak the same language and follow similar customs. Nationalism leads people to honor their flag and to sing a national song, or **anthem**. It leads people to risk their lives to support their nation.

The spirit of nationalism helped the French fight off countries that were against their revolution. It gave the colonies in the Americas the strength to break away from the European imperialists.

In the 19th century, the spirit of nationalism led to the **unification** of Italy and of Germany. In each place, people were feeling the bonds of language, customs, and culture. They decided it was time to unite as a single nation.

What Role Did Napoleon Have in Italian Nationalism?

During the early Roman times, Italy had been a united country. It was the center of the Roman Empire. But late in the fifth century A.D., the Roman Empire fell. Italy was divided into many small kingdoms. For more than 1,000 years, different nations and monarchs fought for control of the Italian territories. French troops, Spanish troops, and German troops marched through Italy. Then in 1796, Napoleon Bonaparte invaded the Italian peninsula and took power.

Napoleon granted Venetia to Austria. Venetia was the kingdom that included the city of Venice. Napoleon put the rest of the small kingdoms under his own rule. In 1804, he crowned himself ruler of the new kingdom. The crown he wore had these words on it: "God gave it [the Italian peninsula] to me; woe to him who dares touch it."

Boundary
The dividing line between one country and another

Unify
To connect; to bring together as one

Society
A group of people joined together for a common purpose

 Remember
In India in the late 1800s, British leaders did not know their policy of sending Indians to school in Britain would encourage ideas of Indian independence.

Reading Strategy:
Text Structure

As you read this lesson, use three separate graphic organizers (such as webs) to gather details about Mazzini, Cavour, and Garibaldi.

Napoleon's actions gave rise to the spirit of nationalism. This spirit would one day carry Italy to independence. Napoleon did away with old **boundary** lines, the lines that divided one country from another. Then he joined the little kingdoms together. By doing this, he gave Italians a chance to look at themselves as members of one group. The idea that all of them were Italians began to grow.

Why Did Italians Form Secret Societies?

As feelings of nationalism grew, Italians began to think about unity. They dreamed about one independent Italy. However, by 1815, Italy was once again divided into many kingdoms and states. Most of these were ruled either by Austria or by the pope. The Italians who wanted to bring together, or **unify,** Italy had some barriers to overcome.

Austria tried to crush any ideas of unity. Austria wanted Italy to remain weak and divided. The pope also tried to crush any ideas of unity. He feared nationalism as a threat to his own power.

The people, however, wanted to be free. They wanted to join together as one nation. So secret revolutionary **societies**, groups of people joined together for a common purpose, sprang up. During the mid-1800s, three men became leaders of the movement toward a unified Italy. Italians called these men "The Soul," "The Brain," and "The Sword."

What Did "The Soul" Do?

"The Soul" of Italy was a man named Giuseppe Mazzini. In 1830, he joined a group that was working to unify Italy. That same year, he was exiled because of his political activities. He would remain in exile for 18 years. In 1831, Mazzini organized a secret society known as "Young Italy." The society's goal was to free the Italian peninsula from Austrian rule. Young Italy wanted to join the country together under one government.

Italy Before Unification

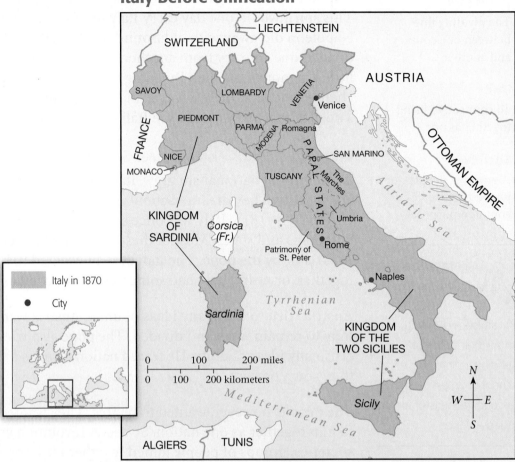

Map legend:
- Italy in 1870
- ● City

MAP STUDY

1. Italy is bordered by which three seas?

2. Which main islands are part of Italy?

In 1848, revolutions broke out in many European countries. Mazzini returned to Italy to stir up a revolution there. The ruler of the kingdom of Sardinia favored the revolutionaries. He tried to help their cause by declaring war on Austria. However, Austrian and French armies helped put down the Italian revolt.

Italy Today

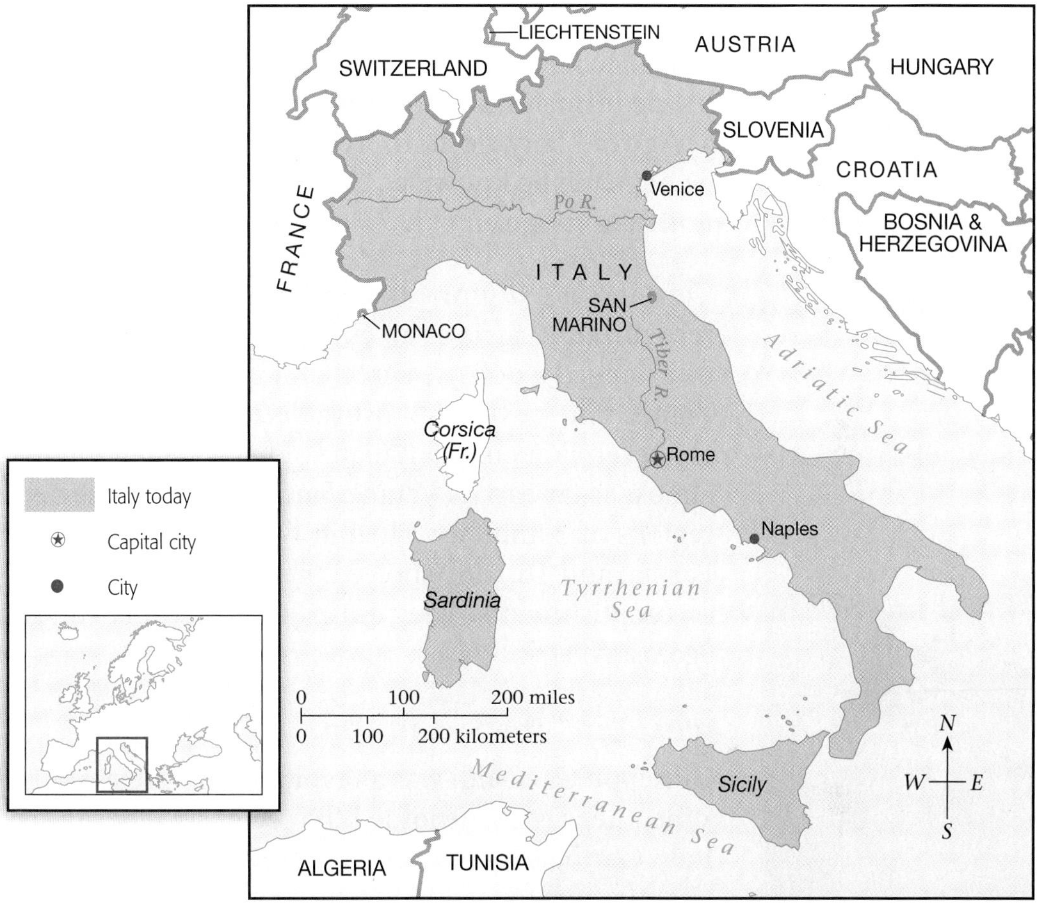
LIECHTENSTEIN
AUSTRIA
SWITZERLAND
HUNGARY
SLOVENIA
CROATIA
FRANCE
Venice
Po R.
BOSNIA & HERZEGOVINA
ITALY
SAN MARINO
MONACO
Tiber R.
Adriatic Sea
Corsica (Fr.)
Rome
Naples
Sardinia
Tyrrhenian Sea
0 100 200 miles
0 100 200 kilometers
N
W E
S
Mediterranean Sea
Sicily
ALGERIA
TUNISIA
Italy today
Capital city
City

Map Study

1. What river runs through the capital of Italy?
2. What island off the coast of Italy is still under French control?

Not only did the revolution fail, but Sardinia was also defeated. Mazzini had to go into exile once again.

The Austrians forced the Sardinian king from his throne. His son, Victor Emmanuel II, became king of Sardinia in 1849.

Prime minister
The chief official of the government in some countries

Diplomat
A person in government whose job is dealing with other countries

What Did "The Brain" Do?

The new king of Sardinia was also in favor of Italian unity. He named Camillo Benso, Conte di Cavour, as his **prime minister,** the chief official of the government. This act moved Italy closer to freedom. Camillo di Cavour would soon be known as "The Brain," the leader of the unification movement.

Cavour was a **diplomat,** a master of foreign affairs. He recognized Austria as an enemy of unification. In 1858, he arranged a defense agreement between Sardinia and France. The next year Austria declared war on Sardinia. However, French and Italian soldiers pushed the Austrians almost as far east as Venice. Sardinia gained the nearby regions of Lombardy. Then in 1860, Romagna, Modena, Parma, and Tuscany showed their respect for Sardinia's accomplishments. They united with Sardinia and turned against Austria.

What Did "The Sword" Do?

Giuseppe Garibaldi was a revolutionary most of his life. When he was 26, he joined the secret society, Young Italy. Garibaldi was a soldier in the battle for freedom. His attempts to lead Italy to independence won him the nickname of "The Sword."

Giuseppe Garibaldi fought for Italian independence.

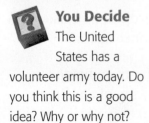

You Decide
The United States has a volunteer army today. Do you think this is a good idea? Why or why not?

Failed rebellions forced Garibaldi to flee Italy or face death. He returned in 1848 to fight under Mazzini. When this revolution failed, he went into exile again.

In 1859, Garibaldi was back in Italy. He joined the fight for freedom led by King Victor Emmanuel of Sardinia. Garibaldi led an army of 1,000 volunteers to Sicily. His men were called "Red Shirts" because they wore red shirts as uniforms.

When Garibaldi and his army reached Sicily, many Sicilians joined them. Sicily was soon free.

Then Garibaldi, "The Sword," led his army north on the Italian mainland. He headed for Naples. Cavour, "The Brain," sent an army south. By the end of 1860, the two armies had freed most of Italy. In 1861, Victor Emmanuel II became ruler of an almost completely united Italy.

How Did Rome Become a Part of Italy?

Only Rome and the northern kingdom of Venetia were still not free. The pope ruled Rome, and Austria ruled Venetia. In 1866, the Italians helped Prussia defeat Austria in war. In return for its support, Italy was given Venetia.

Then came Rome. Garibaldi tried to take Rome twice, but failed. He was defeated by French troops who came to aid the pope. In 1870, Italy got another chance at Rome. France was fighting a war against Prussia. France took its troops out of Rome to help fight the Prussians. It was Italy's time to move! The pope's own small army could not fight off the Italian troops. Rome finally became part of the united nation of Italy. In 1870, Rome became the capital of Italy.

TECHNOLOGY CONNECTION

Marconi, the Telegraph, and the Radio

An Italian engineer named Guglielmo Marconi invented the wireless telegraph in 1895. In 1901, he transmitted, or sent, a signal on radio waves across the Atlantic Ocean. The signal went from England to Newfoundland. Marconi went on to build communication products for ships at sea. A few years later, Canadian Reginald Fessenden and American Ernst Alexanderson made related advances. They learned how to send speech and music on the same radio waves. Another American named Lee de Forest created a device to make these radio messages louder. By 1906, the beginnings of radio were established.

Large-scale worldwide radio broadcasting began about 1922. The number of radio stations in the United States grew from eight to nearly 600. Broadcasting services developed in Britain, Russia, and France about the same time.

REVIEW

On a sheet of paper, write the answer to each question. Use complete sentences.

1. What is nationalism and why does it develop?

2. What role did Napoleon have in Italian nationalism?

3. How did Rome become a part of Italy?

Match the description in Column A with the revolutionary in Column B. Write the correct letter on a sheet of paper.

Column A

4. organized a secret society whose goal was to free the Italian peninsula from Austrian rule; known as "The Soul"

5. prime minister of Sardinia who is considered the leader of the unification movement; known as "The Brain"

6. led the "Red Shirts" and freed Sicily; known as "The Sword"

Column B

A Camillo di Cavour

B Giuseppe Garibaldi

C Giuseppe Mazzini

On a sheet of paper, write the letter of the answer that correctly completes each sentence.

7. "_____" was the secret society formed to free the Italian peninsula from Austrian rule.

   A Red Shirts   **B** Young Italy   **C** The Sword   **D** The Soul

8. In 1861, _____ was the ruler of an almost completely unified Italy.

   A the pope   **C** Victor Emmanuel II
   B Giuseppe Garibaldi   **D** Camillo di Cavour

9. Italy was given _____ in return for helping Prussia defeat Austria in war.

   A Venetia   **B** Rome   **C** Sicily   **D** Tuscany

10. Rome became the capital of Italy in _____.

    A 1848   **B** 1859   **C** 1866   **D** 1870

Nationalism in Germany

Objectives

■ To explain Napoleon's role in German nationalism

■ To tell how Bismarck united Germany under a Prussian kaiser

■ To describe two main features of the new German nation

Confederation

A group of independent states joined together for a purpose

Legislature

A group of people who make the laws of a nation or state

History Fact
The 39 states agreed to be members of the German Confederation, but each one remained an independent state.

Just as he did in Italy, Napoleon lit the first flames of nationalism in Germany. Napoleon took over large parts of Germany in 1806. These lands were made up of many small kingdoms. Napoleon decided to join them together to rule them more easily. He called the group of kingdoms the **Confederation** of the Rhine. A confederation is a group of independent states joined together for a purpose. People living within the Confederation began to have a sense of loyalty toward one another.

When Napoleon was defeated in 1815, a new German Confederation was formed. The Confederation joined 39 states together, including Austria and Prussia. Since Austria was large, it considered itself the leader. However, Prussia had a well-organized government and real strength—military strength.

Many Germans thought about unifying the states under a central government. Only Austria was against German unity. Austrians thought they could remain more powerful with the German states divided. It was not until 1862 that Germany moved toward becoming one nation.

Who Was Otto von Bismarck?

The king of Prussia, Wilhelm I, was having problems with his law-making group, the **legislature**. King Wilhelm wanted to add to his already mighty army. However, the legislature would not give him the money that he needed. King Wilhelm turned to a Prussian landowner and soldier to help him. His name was Otto von Bismarck. In 1862, Wilhelm appointed Bismarck prime minister.

Otto von Bismarck had a strong sense of loyalty to Prussia. He was not interested in democracy or individual rights. He believed that duty to one's country was most important.

Reading Strategy:
Text Structure

Study the map of the unification of Germany. How does this map help you to understand what this lesson is about?

The Unification of Germany, 1871

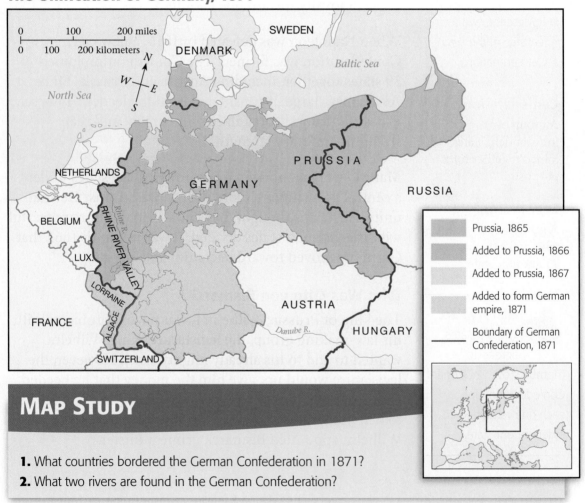

SWEDEN
DENMARK
Baltic Sea
North Sea
PRUSSIA
NETHERLANDS
GERMANY
RUSSIA
BELGIUM
Rhine R.
RHINE RIVER VALLEY
LUX.
LORRAINE
ALSACE
AUSTRIA
FRANCE
Danube R.
HUNGARY
SWITZERLAND

0   100   200 miles
0   100   200 kilometers

Prussia, 1865
Added to Prussia, 1866
Added to Prussia, 1867
Added to form German empire, 1871
Boundary of German Confederation, 1871

MAP STUDY

1. What countries bordered the German Confederation in 1871?

2. What two rivers are found in the German Confederation?

Words from the Past

Otto von Bismarck expanded and unified Germany.

? You Decide
Bismarck was called the "Iron Chancellor." Why do you think he was given this name?

Bismarck's Policy of "Blood and Iron"

Bismarck thought the goals of the individual and the state were the same. He promised the Prussian king a firm hand over the legislature and the people. The new prime minister thought that could be done with a strong army. "The importance of a state," Bismarck said, "is measured by the number of soldiers it can put into the field of battle . . . ."

Bismarck followed a policy of "blood and iron." In other words, it was a policy of war. "The great questions of our day," he said, "cannot be settled by speeches and majority votes, but by blood and iron."

Bismarck encouraged King Wilhelm to unite the German states under one rule—Prussian rule. "My highest ambition is to make the Germans a nation," Bismarck said.

How was this to be done? Bismarck's answer was war!

Reich
The German word for "empire"

Kaiser
The emperor of Germany

Chancellor
The head of government, or prime minister, in some European countries

Reading Strategy:
Text Structure

Create an organizer (such as a simple chart) to record what Otto von Bismarck did during his reign. Be sure to put it in the correct order.

History Fact
The title *kaiser* came from the Latin word *Caesar*.

How Was the Second Reich Formed?

In 1864, Bismarck began a war with Denmark. After just seven months of fighting, Prussia seized two provinces from Denmark. In 1866, Prussia and Italy defeated Austria in the Seven Weeks' War. This brought the German Confederation to an end.

Then Prussia formed the North German Confederation in 1867, without Austria. Most of the German states joined. The Confederation's seat of power was Prussia, and at its head was Wilhelm I.

Bismarck would not be satisfied until all the German states were united under Wilhelm's rule. He decided on the best way to join the states. He would rally them together against one common enemy. For that purpose, in 1870, Bismarck started a war with France. Prussia's mighty armies won easily. They took the provinces of Alsace and Lorraine as their prize.

At the end of the war, all German states joined with Prussia. They formed a united German empire. On January 18, 1871, the new German empire was officially declared. It was also called the *Second **Reich*** (*reich* is the German word for "empire"). King Wilhelm I of Prussia was crowned its emperor, or ***kaiser***.

What Were the Two Main Features of the New German Nation?

There were two main features of the new Germany. First, Germany was not a democratic nation. Germans accepted rule by a single person. Bismarck became the head of government, the **chancellor**, of Germany. He was responsible only to Kaiser Wilhelm I. Neither the kaiser nor the chancellor had to answer to any legislature or to any elected representatives. These two men alone had complete power in Germany.

Militarism
A national policy of maintaining a powerful army and constant readiness for war

Second, Germany had a strong tradition of **militarism**. Militarism was Germany's policy where they kept a powerful army and were always ready for war. Bismarck's "blood and iron" policy became the German way. German nationalism meant pride in a mighty military force.

Germans gave their soldiers respect and honor. It was a German's privilege to belong to a great army. It was an honor to fight for the glory of the empire.

Much of Germany was geared toward a strong military. Large businesses supported the army. Major industrialists, like Friedrich Krupp of the Krupp Iron and Steel Works, devoted factories to making war machines. Krupp built guns and cannons. The whole nation stood behind the military effort. Germany was ready for war!

TIMELINE STUDY: UNIFICATION OF ITALY AND GERMANY

Which people had a revolution, the Italians or the Germans?

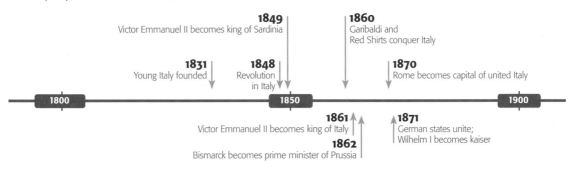

1849
Victor Emmanuel II becomes king of Sardinia

1860
Garibaldi and Red Shirts conquer Italy

1831
Young Italy founded

1848
Revolution in Italy

1870
Rome becomes capital of united Italy

1800

1850

1900

1861
Victor Emmanuel II becomes king of Italy

1871
German states unite; Wilhelm I becomes kaiser

1862
Bismarck becomes prime minister of Prussia

REVIEW

On a sheet of paper, write the answer to each question.
Use complete sentences.

1. What role did Napoleon have in German nationalism?

2. Why did Bismarck start a war with France?

3. What are two features of the new German nation?

On a sheet of paper, write the word from the Word Bank to complete each sentence correctly.

Word Bank

Austria

chancellor

King Wilhelm I

military

Otto von Bismarck

Second Reich

war

4. _____ was the only state against German unity.

5. In 1862, Wilhelm I, king of Prussia, appointed _____ prime minister.

6. Otto von Bismarck believed in a policy of _____, and that duty to one's country was most important.

7. The new German empire formed in 1871 was known as the _____.

8. _____ was crowned kaiser of the new German empire.

9. In the new German nation, the kaiser and the _____ had complete power.

10. Germans placed great pride in their _____.

- The spirit of nationalism led the people of Italy to unite under a central government. During the 19th century, the Italians worked toward independence and unification.

- Giuseppe Mazzini was the leader of a secret society called "Young Italy," which worked to unify Italy.

- Camillo di Cavour was a diplomat and leader of the unification movement in Italy.

- Giuseppe Garibaldi led a revolutionary army that fought for a unified Italy.

- Almost all of Italy was united by 1860. Sardinia's king, Victor Emmanuel II, became its ruler.

- In 1870, Italy was totally united. Rome became its capital city.

- During the 19th century, many Germans wanted to see a unified Germany. Austria opposed the unification of Germany.

- The prime minister of Prussia, Otto von Bismarck, started a war to unify Germany.

- Bismarck won his wars, and in 1871 Germany was united. Prussia's Wilhelm I became the kaiser of the German empire.

- Germans accepted rule by a single person, known as the chancellor.

- Germany developed a tradition of militarism and loyalty to strong leaders.

Word Bank

anthem

confederation

diplomat

kaiser

legislature

militarism

prime minister

reich

societies

unification

Vocabulary Review

On a sheet of paper, use the words from the Word Bank to complete each sentence correctly.

1. The _____ is the most important official in some countries, such as Britain.

2. Germany's strong tradition of _____ made them always ready for war.

3. Italians were interested in _____ to bring together people with a common language, customs, and culture.

4. A national _____ is a national song.

5. A(n) _____ is a person who deals with other countries for his or her own country.

6. _____ is the German word for "empire."

7. Prussia's _____ would not give King Wilhelm money to add to his army.

8. Many revolutionary _____ sprang up in Italy; they shared the same purpose: freedom.

9. Napoleon joined many small kingdoms of Germany together to rule them more easily. He called the group the _____ of the Rhine.

10. The emperor of Germany is the _____.

Chapter Review Questions

On a sheet of paper, write the answer to each question. Use complete sentences.

11. What was the purpose of Young Italy?

Test Tip

Pay special attention to key words in a set of directions—words such as *first, second, most important, least important, all, some, only, more than one, best,* and *none.*

12. What three men helped unify Italy?

13. How did the Italians take control of Rome?

14. How did Bismarck manage to form a united Germany?

15. What was the Second Reich?

16. How did German industry help the nation get ready for war?

Critical Thinking

On a sheet of paper, write your response to each question. Use complete sentences.

17. How did Napoleon help to develop a spirit of nationalism among Italians?

18. What are some positive ways to unite a country?

Using the Timeline

Use the timeline on page 527 to answer the questions.

19. When did Victor Emmanuel II become king of Italy?

20. When did Wilhelm I become kaiser of Germany?

GROUP ACTIVITY

Write a paragraph that compares and contrasts the way Italy and Germany became nations. Exchange your paragraph with a partner. Discuss the ideas in your paragraphs. Revise your paragraphs to make your ideas clearer.

World War I

The major powers in Europe had been gathering military strength for many years. For most countries, a sense of national pride seemed to call for an army. Of course, some built strong armies to help them conquer weaker nations. Others needed armies simply to avoid being conquered.

Finally, war began on July 28, 1914. It involved many countries, most of them in Europe. The battles featured modern weapons that caused great destruction. Years later it would come to be called "World War I."

GOALS FOR LEARNING

- To describe the beginnings of World War I
- To describe the fighting during the war
- To describe the terms of peace at the end of the war

Reading Strategy: Visualizing

When readers create pictures in their head about what they are reading, they are using visualization. This is another strategy that helps readers understand what they are reading. Use the following ways to visualize a text:

- Notice the order in which things are happening and what you think might happen next.

- Look at the photographs, illustrations, and words.

- Think about experiences in your own life that may add to the images.

Key Vocabulary Words

Lesson 1

Alliance A group of nations joined together for some purpose; an agreement to help one another

Central Powers The nations of Germany, Austria-Hungary, Turkey, and later Bulgaria

Allied Powers The nations of Great Britain, France, Russia, Italy, and eventually, the United States and Japan during World War I

Balance of power The condition that exists when all countries or all sections of government have equal strength

Sniper A person who shoots from a hidden spot

Lesson 2

Neutral Joining neither side in a war

Trench A long ditch dug in the ground to protect soldiers in battle

Front A place where the actual fighting is going on during a war

Torpedo To attack or destroy with a large, exploding, underwater missile

U-boat A German submarine

Lesson 3

Armistice An agreement to stop fighting; a truce before a formal peace treaty

Treaty of Versailles The treaty that ended World War I

Disarm To stop having armed forces or to reduce their size

Casualty A soldier who has been killed, wounded, captured, or is missing

Conflict Fighting

The War Begins in Europe

Objectives

- To explain what is meant by a "balance of power"
- To name the two alliances made by 1914
- To tell what event directly triggered World War I

Alliance

A group of nations joined together for some purpose

Central Powers

The nations of Germany, Austria-Hungary, Turkey, and later Bulgaria

Allied Powers

The nations of Great Britain, France, Russia, Italy, and eventually, the United States and Japan during World War I

Balance of power

The condition that exists when all countries have equal strength

Relations between countries were strained in the early 1900s. By 1914, Europe had divided itself into two sides. Nations formed **alliances**. They promised to protect each other and to help each other in case of war.

What Two Alliances Were Formed?

One group of nations was called the **Central Powers**. The nations of the Central Powers included Germany, Austria-Hungary, the Ottoman Empire (Turkey), and, for a short time, Italy. (Bulgaria joined later.) The other group of nations was called the **Allied Powers**, or *Allies*. On that side were Britain, France, Russia, and many smaller nations.

Each alliance tried to keep the other from getting too strong. The two alliances wanted to keep a "**balance of power**" in Europe.

Why Were Countries Getting Ready for War?

As the year 1914 began, there was tension throughout Europe. France and Germany had been bitter enemies for years. France had lost a war against Bismarck's armies in 1871. Ever since then, France wanted to get back the provinces of Alsace and Lorraine.

Russia and Austria-Hungary had an ongoing quarrel. They disagreed about the territorial borders and control of areas, including Bosnia, in the Balkans. The Balkans is a southern peninsula of Europe.

Nations watched each other as each one built up its military forces. Airplanes, bigger warships, and machine guns made armies more capable of destruction or ruin. One country would build new arms. Then another would panic and race to keep up. No one wanted war, but everyone was getting ready for it.

What Event Started World War I?

It took a single incident in June 1914 to explode the already tense situation in Europe. The Austrian archduke Francis Ferdinand was assassinated. This is named as the incident that began the First World War.

Archduke Ferdinand was the next in line to the throne of Austria-Hungary. He and his wife, Sophie, were visiting Sarajevo, a city in the Austrian province of Bosnia. Many Serbs also lived in Bosnia. Some of them believed Bosnia should belong to Serbia.

The assassination of Archduke Francis Ferdinand led to the start of World War I.

Archduke Ferdinand and his wife were traveling by motor car on a road in Sarajevo. They were a fine-looking pair. The archduke wore a white uniform, and his wife wore a matching white gown. Riding in an open car, they were clear targets. As the royal procession drove through the streets, two shots rang out. Archduke Ferdinand and his wife were both killed by a **sniper**. A sniper is a person who shoots from a hidden spot.

The assassin, Gavrilo Princip, was a Serb. He was a member of a Serbian revolutionary group called the "Black Hand."

Austria-Hungary blamed the Serbian government for the assassination. On July 28, 1914, it declared war on Serbia. Now the alliances came into play. Germany stood behind Austria-Hungary. Russia came to the aid of Serbia. France came to Russia's aid. Soon, Britain joined in to help its allies. World War I had begun.

Europe, 1914

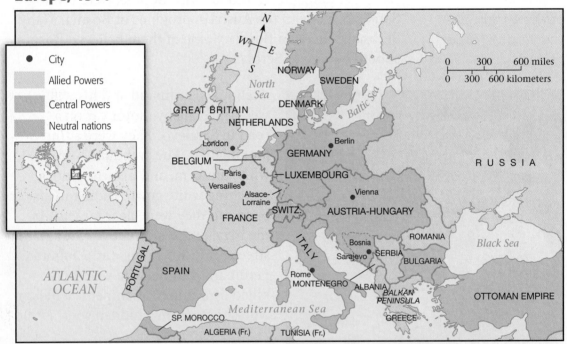

MAP STUDY

1. In 1914, which countries were neutral in Europe?
2. Did more nations belong to the Allied Powers or the Central Powers in 1914?

On a sheet of paper, write the answer to each question. Use complete sentences.

1. What nations were included in the Central Powers?

2. What nations were included in the Allies?

3. The European alliances wanted to keep a "balance of power." What does that mean?

4. What event directly triggered World War I?

On a sheet of paper, write the letter of the answer that correctly completes each sentence.

5. Tensions between countries were growing, and by 1914 _____ had divided itself into two sides.

   A Russia   **B** Germany   **C** Europe   **D** Austria-Hungary

6. France wanted to get back at _____ for losing the provinces of Alsace and Lorraine.

   A Russia   **B** Germany   **C** Europe   **D** Austria-Hungary

7. _____ and Austria-Hungary disagreed about the borders and control of areas, including the Balkans.

   A Russia   **B** Germany   **C** Europe   **D** Italy

8. Countries raced to keep up with the latest _____.

   A fashions   **B** computer technology   **C** weapons   **D** space technology

9. Archduke Ferdinand was the next ruler of _____.

   A Russia   **B** Germany   **C** Europe   **D** Austria-Hungary

10. Austria-Hungary blamed _____ for the killing, and declared war.

   A Serbia   **B** France   **C** Russia   **D** Italy

The Fighting

Neutral
Joining neither side in a war

Trench
A long ditch dug in the ground to protect soldiers in battle

Front
A place where the actual fighting is going on during a war

Reading Strategy:
Visualizing

What clues on this page help you visualize the fight to take France?

World War I is sometimes called "The Great War." It was not really a "worldwide" war. Most of the fighting took place in Europe. Furthermore, not every country in the world was fighting. However, more than 30 countries, including all the major powers, were involved. The Great War's effects were certainly felt worldwide.

At first the Central Powers seemed to be winning. Germany and Austria-Hungary and their allies made gains. Italy had been allied with the Central Powers. However, Italy remained **neutral** in the early part of the war (they did not join either side). Then in 1915, Italy changed its alliance. It joined forces with the Allies.

What Is Trench Warfare?

The Central Powers wanted to take France. They came within 25 miles of Paris. However, the French and British held them off in a major battle, the Battle of the Marne. Then both sides dug in. The soldiers dug long **trenches**. Armies could hide in the trenches and shoot at each other. Some trenches were more than a mile long.

The **fronts** were lined with networks of trenches. A front is a place where the actual fighting is going on during a war. There were three fronts in Europe. The western front ran from Belgium to Switzerland. The eastern front ran from the Baltic Sea to the Black Sea. The Italian, or southern, front ran between Italy and Austria-Hungary.

The battle trenches along the fronts became home for the soldiers. They ate in the trenches and slept in the trenches. Many soldiers died in the trenches.

Torpedo
To attack or
destroy with a
large, exploding,
underwater missile

History Fact
Switzerland was
one of the
few European nations
to remain neutral
throughout the war. It
would also stay neutral
during World War II.

**Reading Strategy:
Visualizing**

How could this section
on the *Lusitania* be
written differently to help
you better visualize it?

Most of the battles of World War I were fought in Europe.
However, there was also some fighting in Africa and in
the Middle East. The powerful British navy kept control of
most of the seas.

Why Did the United States Enter the War?

Despite Britain's great navy, German submarines were
terrorizing the oceans. A submarine is a warship that
travels under water. They attacked enemy merchant
ships without warning. Then in 1915, Germany attacked
a British luxury liner. The *Lusitania* was **torpedoed**
(attacked with a large, exploding, underwater missile)
and sunk. The death list of 1,198 people included 128
Americans. In 1917, German submarines began attacking
ships of neutral nations. Several American merchant ships
were sunk.

*During World War I, soldiers dug trenches six to eight feet
deep to hide and defend themselves.*

U-boat

A German submarine

History Fact
The submarine was the most deadly military vessel of World War I.

In April 1917, U.S. President Woodrow Wilson made an announcement. He said that it was time to "make the world safe for democracy." The United States declared war on Germany and joined the Allies. The United States entered the battlefields just in time. The Allies needed help. The United States sent fresh soldiers and supplies of arms to Europe. The scale in the balance of power was now tipped in favor of the Allies.

Then in November 1917, a revolution took place in Russia. The new government signed a peace treaty with Germany and pulled out of the war.

LEARN MORE ABOUT IT

Wartime Inventions

The war brought many changes in the world. New inventions were perfected in a hurry to meet war needs. The Germans developed submarines to travel under the water, like sharks. The submarines were also called "U-boats" (underwater boats). Like a shark, they moved unseen, seeking their prey.

Allied countries could not find a defense against the submarines for the first three years of the war. Eventually depth charges were used to destroy the submarines. Fast British ships known as subchasers carried the depth charges. These ships also used zigzag courses to avoid German submarines.

The submarines were very successful. Only 203 German submarines were destroyed during the whole war. But the German submarines sank 6,604 Allied ships.

For the first time, airplanes were used for war. At first they were just used for scouting, watching the enemy, and taking pictures.

They were not used for fighting until later in the war.

Planes improved rapidly. In 1914, an airplane could go 60 to 70 miles an hour. By 1917, they were flying at 130 miles an hour or faster. They carried bombs and machine guns. Some pilots became famous as war aces for shooting down five or more enemy airplanes.

Germany used zeppelins in the air. Zeppelins were huge, cigar-shaped crafts, 600 feet long. They were filled with hydrogen gas and used in bombing raids over Britain and France.

British engineers invented the tank, an armored vehicle with caterpillar tracks. The big tanks rumbled their way across the battlefields of Europe. There were other new weapons, like poison gas and flame throwers. Each side tried to outdo the other with more powerful weapons.

On a sheet of paper, write the answer to each question. Use complete sentences.

1. Describe trench warfare.

2. Why did the United States enter the war?

3. What are three wartime inventions used during World War I?

Match the description in Column A with the term in Column B.
Write the correct letter on a sheet of paper.

Column A

4. the front that stretched from Belgium to Switzerland

5. the front that ran from the Baltic Sea to the Black Sea

6. the front that ran between Italy and Austria-Hungary

Column B

A eastern

B southern

C western

On a sheet of paper, write the letter of the answer that correctly completes each sentence.

7. More than 30 countries were involved in the Great War. Most of the fighting took place in _____.

A the ocean
B Germany
C Austria-Hungary
D Europe

8. The _____ kept control of most of the seas, even without submarines.

A Germans
B British
C French
D Russians

9. At first _____ remained neutral, but then in 1915 it joined forces with the Allies.

A France
B the United States
C Italy
D Serbia

10. U.S. soldiers and supplies helped tip the balance of power in favor of the _____.

A Allies
B Central Powers
C Germans
D Italians

The End of the War

Objectives

- To describe how the war ended
- To explain the Treaty of Versailles
- To explain the League of Nations and why the Americans opposed it

Armistice

An agreement to stop fighting; a truce before a formal peace treaty

Treaty of Versailles

The treaty that ended World War I

Disarm

To stop having armed forces or to reduce their size

History Fact
When the German government finally agreed to the Allies' terms, Kaiser Wilhelm II gave up his throne.

With new American soldiers and supplies, the Allies began to push back the Germans. The other Central Powers had given up. Germany stood alone, and German armies were losing ground.

Germany asked for an end to the war. On November 11, 1918, an **armistice** was declared. All fighting was to stop at 11:00 A.M. that day.

What Demands Did the Treaty of Versailles Make?

After the war, leaders of the Allied nations and Germany met in Versailles, France. Their purpose was to write a peace treaty to end the war. The treaty, known as the **Treaty of Versailles**, was signed in 1919 and made many demands on Germany.

Germany lost all of its colonies and had to return Alsace and Lorraine to France. Germany took all blame for the war, so it had to pay for many of the war's costs. Germany also promised to **disarm**. The nation was not supposed to rebuild its navy or air force. It was allowed to maintain only a small army. This was quite a blow to a nation that had taken such pride in a powerful military.

Turkey was another big loser in the war. In 1919, most of the Middle East and North Africa was still ruled by the Ottoman Empire, or Turkey. However, the end of the war brought about the end of the Ottoman Empire. Most of the Arab lands that had been ruled by the Turks now fell under British control.

Europe After World War I

New nations

NORWAY
SWEDEN
FINLAND
RUSSIA
ESTONIA
LATVIA
LITHUANIA
EAST PRUSSIA
(Germany)
North Sea
Baltic Sea
DENMARK
UNITED KINGDOM
NETHERLANDS
GERMANY
POLAND
CZECHOSLOVAKIA
ATLANTIC OCEAN
BELGIUM
LUXEMBOURG
FRANCE
SWITZERLAND
AUSTRIA
HUNGARY
ROMANIA
YUGOSLAVIA
Black Sea
PORTUGAL
SPAIN
ITALY
BULGARIA
GREECE
TURKEY
Mediterranean Sea
ALBANIA
AFRICA

0 200 400 miles
0 200 400 kilometers

Map Study

1. What were the new nations in Europe after World War I?

2. What countries now bordered Germany to the east?

Some Casualties of World War I	
Allies	
Russia	9,150,000
British empire	3,190,235
France	6,160,800
Italy	2,197,000
United States	323,018
Central Powers	
Germany	7,142,558
Austria-Hungary	7,020,000
Turkey	975,000
Bulgaria	266,919

Why Was the League of Nations Formed?

The Great War ended four years after it had begun. Those four years meant the loss of almost eight million soldiers. Millions of others died of disease and starvation, side effects of war. Russia suffered the most **casualties** in World War I. In other words, they had the most soldiers who had been killed, wounded, captured, or missing.

The total cost of the war to all countries involved was more than $337 billion. All of Europe was weakened.

When the war ended, leaders of the world's nations looked at the results. They decided there must be a better way to solve **conflicts**, or fights, between nations. President Wilson proposed setting up a League of Nations. European leaders welcomed the idea. They knew that their people would support such a league. Wilson was confident that the American people would support it as well.

In 1920, the League of Nations was set up. Its headquarters were in Geneva, Switzerland—a neutral, peaceful country. Representatives of member nations could meet there to discuss their problems. It was the first organization designed to keep the peace of the entire world.

The League of Nations was formed to keep the peace of the entire world.

Many nations joined the League. Some, including the United States, did not. Wilson was greatly disappointed. Many people in the United States did not like the idea of the League. In particular, Article Ten of the plan caused major problems. It mentioned threats to any member nation of the League. It said that if any threats were made, the other members would aid the threatened nation.

Americans felt they had seen too much of war. They did not want to have anything to do with Europe's problems. They thought Article Ten seemed to invite trouble.

President Wilson put up a strong fight. He made speeches all around the country. He did everything he could to try to convince Americans to join the League. However, the Senate voted against it in March 1920. Wilson died in 1924, a defeated man. He had warned that another world war was not far off. He had said that only the League of Nations could prevent it. Many Americans did not want to hear him.

The League of Nations had no army to enforce its decisions. The League was based on goodwill and the idea that nations wanted peace. The war years, 1914 to 1918, had left everyone fearful of war. Now the whole world was anxious to avoid war. People everywhere were hopeful that a war would never be fought again.

TIMELINE STUDY: WORLD WAR I AND AFTER

How long did World War I last?

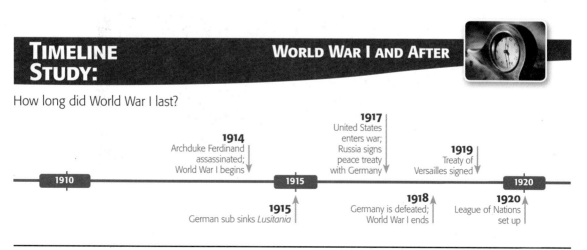

1914
Archduke Ferdinand assassinated; World War I begins

1917
United States enters war; Russia signs peace treaty with Germany

1919
Treaty of Versailles signed

1910

1915

1920

1915
German sub sinks *Lusitania*

1918
Germany is defeated; World War I ends

1920
League of Nations set up

REVIEW

On a sheet of paper, write the answer to each question. Use complete sentences.

1. How did World War I end?

2. What are three demands the Treaty of Versailles made on Germany?

3. Why was the United States against the League of Nations?

Word Bank

four

League of Nations

peace

Russia

Switzerland

Turkey

Wilson

On a sheet of paper, write the word from the Word Bank to complete each sentence correctly.

4. The Great War lasted _____ years.

5. _____ suffered the most casualties in World War I.

6. _____ lost control of most of its Arab lands as part of the peace treaty.

7. President _____ suggested setting up a League of Nations. Unfortunately, he died still fighting to convince Americans of its value.

8. The _____ was designed to keep the peace of the entire world.

9. The League of Nations was headquartered in _____ because it was a neutral, peaceful country.

10. The League of Nations had no army. It was based on goodwill and the idea that nations wanted _____.

SUMMARY

- World War I began in 1914. The assassination of the Austrian archduke Francis Ferdinand started World War I.

- The war was fought between the Central Powers and the Allies. The Central Powers included Germany, Austria-Hungary, and in the early part of the war, Italy. The Allies included Britain, France, and Russia.

- Italy joined the Allies in 1915.

- The United States entered the war on the side of the Allies in 1917.

- Most battles of World War I took place in Europe.

- For the most part, the strong British navy controlled the seas. German U-boats caused a good deal of damage to ships at sea.

- Wartime developments and inventions included submarines, special planes, zeppelins, tanks, and weapons such as poison gas.

- World War I ended in 1918. The Treaty of Versailles, signed in 1919, set up terms for peace.

- The League of Nations was founded after the war in hopes of maintaining world peace.

Word Bank

alliance
armistice
balance of power
casualties
conflict
disarm
fronts
neutral
trench
U-boats

Vocabulary Review

On a sheet of paper, use the words from the Word Bank to complete each sentence correctly.

1. A solider lived, fought, and often died in the long _____ he dug.

2. Three places where fighting went on, called _____, extended across much of Europe.

3. Nations could form a(n) _____ to protect and help each other in time of war.

4. German underwater ships, called _____, attacked enemy ships without warning.

5. Russia suffered the most _____ in World War I.

6. Some nations did not take sides in the war. They were _____.

7. An agreement to stop fighting is called a(n) _____.

8. A(n) _____ means that no one country becomes stronger than another.

9. Russia and Austria-Hungary had an ongoing quarrel, or _____, about territorial borders.

10. Germany promised to _____ after the war.

Chapter Review Questions

On a sheet of paper, write the answer to each question. Use complete sentences.

11. What two alliances were formed in Europe before World War I?

12. What event is usually named as starting World War I?

13. Why was World War I called the Great War?

Test Tip

Be sure you
understand what
a test question is
asking. Read it twice
if necessary.

14. How did the United States help the Allies beginning in 1917?

15. What was the peace treaty signed by the Allied nations and Germany in 1919?

16. What international organization was set up after World War I ended?

Critical Thinking

On a sheet of paper, write your response to each question. Use complete sentences.

17. Do you think the Treaty of Versailles made too many demands on Germany? Why or why not?

18. Do you think the League of Nations was a weak organization? Why or why not?

Using the Timeline

Use the timeline on page 545 to answer the questions.

19. After the Germans sank the *Lusitania*, how long did it take for the United States to enter the war?

20. What happened in 1919?

GROUP ACTIVITY

With a partner, prepare an illustrated talk about a ship, plane, or weapon of World War I. Prepare a drawing, with parts labeled. Have one person explain how the ship, plane, or weapon was used in war. Have the other person explain the drawing. Then switch roles if you wish.

Revolution in Russia: The Birth of the Soviet Union

In earlier chapters, you read about the Byzantine Empire that came out after the fall of Rome. You read how the empire fell to the Ottoman Turks in 1453. However, much of the Byzantine Empire continued on in a new nation in eastern Europe. That nation was Russia. The people of Russia are as varied as the geography of the country. Stories of their history are both exciting and colorful. This is especially true of the revolution that took place in Russia in the early 1900s.

GOALS FOR LEARNING

- To list the main events in Russia's early history
- To understand the reasons for unrest in Russia in the early 1900s
- To explain how Russia became the Union of Soviet Socialist Republics

Reading Strategy: Inferencing

Sometimes the meaning of a text is not directly stated. You have to make an inference to figure out what the text means.

What You Know + What You Read = Inference

To make inferences, you have to think "beyond the text." Predicting what will happen next and explaining cause and effect are helpful strategies for making inferences.

Key Vocabulary Words

Lesson 1

Geography The natural surface features of the earth, or any part of it

Steppe A wide plain

Dialect A form of a language used only in a certain place or among a certain group

Czar The ruler of Russia; a Russian title that means "caesar"

Economy The system of making and trading things

Lesson 2

Socialism An economic and political system where the government owns and controls all industry

Communism A political system where there are no social classes and a common ownership of industries and farms, as well as a sharing of work and of goods produced

Shortage Too small an amount; not enough

Lesson 3

Bolshevik A revolutionary Communist group in Russia; means "member of the majority"

Soviet A Russian council

Collective Run by a group

Oppose To be against something

Censor To examine communications before they are released and to remove any parts that are objected to

Iron Curtain The invisible boundary between Western Europe and Eastern Europe after World War II

The Early History of Russia

Objectives

■ To name the ancient civilization in eastern Europe that became Russia

■ To explain why Ivan IV was so terrible

■ To explain why Peter the Great wanted to open a "window to the West"

■ To describe the reign of Catherine the Great

**Reading Strategy:
Inferencing**

What do you already know about Russia?

Geography
The natural surface features of the earth, or any part of it

Steppe
A wide plain

Dialect
A form of a language used only in a certain place or among a certain group

The **geography** of Russia is varied. The country takes in frozen wastelands, thick forests, and wide plains known as **steppes**. There are also sandy deserts and huge snow-capped mountains. In addition, some of the longest rivers in the world are in Russia.

The people of Russia are just as varied as the geography. Some are tall and blond-haired, others are olive skinned and dark-haired. Some have European backgrounds, while others have Asian backgrounds. Altogether, Russian people speak dozens of different languages and **dialects**. A dialect is a form of language used only in a certain place or among a certain group.

Russia is the largest country on Earth. However, the country was not always so large or strong.

How Did Russia Become a Part of the Mongol Empire?

As far back as A.D. 400, a people known as Slavs lived in forests north of the Byzantine Empire. The Slavs became traders. Along their trade route, a town called Novgorod was established.

The Slavs of Novgorod were threatened by a wandering people of Turkish descent. The Vikings, a tribe of Northmen from Scandinavia, came to help the Slavs defend Novgorod. The Vikings were also called the Rus. In 862, Rurik the Viking became the ruler of Novgorod. The land of the Rus and the Slavs became known as Russia.

Czar
The ruler of Russia

Around 882, the Vikings captured the town of Kiev to the south of Novgorod. Kiev and Novgorod united under the rule of Viking Prince Oleg. Oleg set up the first Russian state and ruled from its capital at Kiev. The state was called Kievan Russia.

In 980, Vladimir I, great-grandson of Rurik, became the ruler of Kievan Russia. Vladimir wanted to unite Kievan Russia under one religion. He admired the Eastern Orthodox church and saw that it was established as the official religion of Kiev.

In 1019, the son of Vladimir I became the able ruler of Kievan Russia. He was known as Yaroslav the Wise because he made Kiev a center of learning.

Around 1237, a huge army of Asian warriors invaded Russia. Their leader was Batu Khan, a grandson of Genghis Khan. They destroyed one town after another, including Kiev. Russia became part of the Mongol Empire.

Why Was Ivan IV So Terrible?

The Mongols ruled for over 200 years. Then they grew weaker because of fighting among their leaders. Finally, in 1480, a group of Russian princes defeated the Mongols. Ivan III and his son, Basil III, led those princes. In 1547, Basil's son became the ruler, the first **czar** of all Russia. The first czar's name was Ivan IV. He became known as *Ivan the Terrible*.

Ivan IV changed Russian government. Earlier rulers, called Grand Dukes, had accepted advice and criticism from other nobles. Not Ivan IV—as czar, he moved the head of the government to Moscow and made himself all-powerful. It is said that one nobleman who dared to disagree with Ivan IV was tossed to the hounds (dogs). The hounds tore him to shreds!

Ivan the Terrible ruled by terror.

Economy
The system of making
and trading things

Ivan ruled by terror. With threats of cruel punishment, he frightened the Russian people into doing what he wanted them to do. Hundreds of people were murdered by Ivan and his special police force. Ivan even killed his oldest son with his own two hands.

Ivan fought many wars. He increased Russia's territory. However, he made the daily lives of his people worse. Under Ivan the Terrible, the peasants were dreadfully poor. There was lots of land, but there were not enough people to keep the **economy** strong. The economy is the system of making and trading things.

Ivan did grant the right to trade in Russia. This brought in money for the upper classes. Yet it did little to improve the lives of the common people. After Ivan, most Russian rulers would seem kindly in comparison.

During the 1600s, Russia added to its territory. It took more of the Ukraine. It also extended its control of Siberia eastward to the Pacific Ocean. Slowly, Russia increased its contact with the rest of the world. Czar Michael Romanov took the throne in 1613. He encouraged trade with the Netherlands and England. He brought foreign engineers and doctors to Russia. Michael's son Alexis followed him. He, too, was open to European customs and cultures.

Why Did Peter the Great Want to Open a "Window to the West"?

Toward the end of the 17th century, a czar named Peter ruled in Russia. Peter had big plans. He wanted to make Russia more powerful. His goal was to make Russia equal to the nations of western Europe. Peter brought more Europeans into Russia. He brought engineers, artists, soldiers, and scientists to teach Russians the ways of western Europe.

Still, Peter did not learn all he wanted to know. To learn more, he went on a journey.

He traveled to the Netherlands to study shipbuilding. He continued his studies in England, where he visited factories, schools, and museums. He also visited France, Germany, and Austria.

When Czar Peter returned, he had many new ideas. He wanted to "westernize" his people. He ordered his subjects to wear European-style clothing instead of long, Asian-styled robes. He demanded that all Russian men cut off their beards to look more European. To set an example, Peter called his nobles together and cut off their beards himself. When people rebelled against Peter's no-beard orders, he demanded a tax from any man wearing a beard.

Peter changed the old Russian calendar to make it match the European calendar. He gave women more freedom. He put the Russian church under complete control of his government.

Peter the Great wanted to make Russia like the nations of western Europe. He wanted Russian men to cut off their beards to look more European.

Peter's desire to westernize Russia led him to seek a "window to the West." Peter wanted to open a Russian port on the ice-free Baltic Sea. Sweden stood in his way, so in 1700 he attacked Sweden. In 1721, a peace treaty gave Russia land along the eastern Baltic coast.

Meanwhile, in 1703, Peter began building the city of St. Petersburg. It would be Peter's European "window." It was built along the Neva River, where the river flows into the Gulf of Finland. In 1712, Peter moved the nation's capital from Moscow to St. Petersburg.

Peter brought new ideas, industrialization, and strength to Russia. That is why he was given the name *Peter the Great*. However, he did little for the common people. Russian peasants were still poor and completely at the mercy of their czar.

What Did Catherine II Do During Her Reign?

In 1762, Empress Catherine II became ruler of Russia. Catherine continued many of Peter's policies. She kept the "window to the West" open. She brought French culture to the nobles of Russia and improved their education. She was called *Catherine the Great*. However, she, too, did little for the peasants. In 1773, Catherine's armies had to put down a peasant revolt. Catherine ruled Russia for 34 years. She joined forces with the rulers of Austria and Prussia. Together they conquered Poland, and they divided up the land. Russia's territory was greatly increased during the reign of Catherine II.

In 1812, Russia's relations with the West took a turn for the worse. That year, France's Napoleon Bonaparte invaded Russia. In Chapter 18 you read how this turned out to be Napoleon's big mistake. After taking Moscow, Napoleon's army began to run out of supplies as the weather turned bitter cold. Napoleon had to order a retreat. Only about one out of six of the men in his army lived to reach France.

Reading Strategy: Inferencing

How does what you already know about Russia add to what you have just read?

History Fact
The great Russian author Tolstoy wrote about Napoleon's invasion of Russia in his famous novel, *War and Peace.*

REVIEW

Word Bank

Byzantine

French

industrialization

Mongol

peasants

Sweden

territory

terror

trade

traveled

On a sheet of paper, write the word from the Word Bank to complete each sentence correctly.

1. During the 1400s, the _____ civilization in eastern Europe became Russia.

2. In 1237, Russia was invaded and became a part of the _____ Empire.

3. Ivan IV was the first czar after the Russians defeated the Mongols. He ruled by _____ and made the daily lives of people worse.

4. Although Ivan allowed _____ in Russia, it only brought in money for the upper classes.

5. Peter's goal was to make Russia equal to the nations of western Europe. Thus, he _____ to learn more about the western culture.

6. Peter fought _____ to win land along the eastern Baltic coast. The Russian port would serve as a "window to the West."

7. Peter brought new ideas, _____, and strength to Russia.

8. Catherine brought _____ culture and education to Russian nobles.

9. Catherine II greatly increased Russia's _____ during her reign.

10. Neither Peter nor Catherine did much for the _____ of Russia.

Unrest in the Early 1900s

Objectives

- To explain how Bloody Sunday started a revolution in 1905
- To describe how Russians felt about their country taking part in World War I
- To identify Karl Marx and define Communism

Reading Strategy: Inferencing

What can you infer about the way the Russian peasants were feeling?

You Decide

Czar Nicholas II did not trust his people. In fact, he feared them. Do you think a ruler who fears the people can rule well? Why or why not?

Russian peasants had lived under a feudal-type of system for hundreds of years. Wealthy nobles owned all the farmlands. In 1861, peasants were freed, but their lives were not much better.

How Did Bloody Sunday Prompt a Revolution in 1905?

As industrialization came to Russia, factories sprang up in the cities. Thousands of peasants left the farms. They moved to the cities to work in the factories. Often, the peasants found the factory owners as unfair and uncaring as the land-owning nobles had been. In 1905, many of the peasants protested to demand changes. On January 22, 1905, workers and their families marched in the streets of St. Petersburg. Workers wanted higher wages and a voice in government. In response, the czar's soldiers killed or wounded hundreds of men, women, and children that day. January 22, 1905, became known as Russia's "Bloody Sunday."

In 1905, protests by Russian workers led to violence in the streets.

Reading Strategy:
Inferencing

What inferences can you make about the Russian people's attitude? What words helped you make this inference?

 History Fact

In 1918, Czar Nicholas and his family were executed by a revolutionary Communist group called the Bolsheviks. The remains of the royal family were discovered in 1991.

Bloody Sunday was the end of any peaceful demand for change. Strikes, riots, and revolutionary battles broke out. In order to put a stop to the revolt, Nicholas II agreed to set up an elected Duma, or parliament. The Duma would have the power to rule on any proposals for new laws. Some people were satisfied with this change. Others felt that the Duma was not enough. The Duma lasted until 1917. The problems in Russia continued.

What Did the Revolutionaries Want?

Many Russians thought that **socialism** would solve Russia's problems. Socialism is an economic and political system where the government owns and controls all industry. Many of the revolutionaries in Russia had read the works of Karl Marx. Marx was a German thinker of the 1800s. Marx pictured a perfect world in which there would be no classes and in which government would be unnecessary. Marx's ideas were known as **Communism**. Communism is a form of socialism. Some of the revolutionaries in Russia wanted to see Marx's ideas become a reality in their country.

Why Were Russians Against Their Country's Involvement in World War I?

Russia entered World War I shortly after it began in 1914. The war brought severe food **shortages** to Russia (there was not enough food). The poor people became even poorer. The common people of Russia were not interested in fighting Germany. However, Czar Nicholas II had plunged Russia into the war.

In March 1917, the people of Russia demanded more food. The starving workers and peasants revolted. Czar Nicholas II was overthrown, and a new government took over. The czar and his family gave up the throne. The government promised democracy in Russia, but it did not end Russia's involvement in World War I. The people were against the war. It was draining supplies, killing men, and taking food.

Words from the Past

Karl Marx and the *Communist Manifesto*

Karl Marx is often called the father of Communism.

In 1848, Karl Marx and his friend Friedrich Engel wrote a pamphlet called the *Communist Manifesto*. "A spectre [spirit or ghost] is haunting Europe—the spectre of Communism," the *Manifesto* began. "Workingmen of all countries, unite," the *Manifesto* ended.

The *Manifesto* said that all history is the history of class struggles. It said that just as the serfs had gained their freedom from the nobles, workers in industry would revolt against the factory owners. The *Manifesto* described the first steps toward Communism. One step was that children would not be allowed to inherit their parents' money when their parents died.

Marx was born in Prussia (Germany) in 1818. His parents were middle class. Although they were Jewish, Marx's father converted to Christianity. Karl Marx was raised as a Christian. Later in life, he was famous for saying, "Religion is the opium [drug] of the people."

Das Kapital was Marx's most famous book. It was published in 1867. Part of the book described the poor conditions of the working class. Marx said that eventually capitalism would die and another better, classless, or Communist, society would take its place.

For most of Marx's adult life, he and his family lived in London, England. He researched his pamphlets and books at the British Museum. After Marx died in 1883, he was buried in Highgate Cemetery, in London. His ideas continue to have influence. They were important to the development of the USSR, a Communist state.

On a sheet of paper, write the answer to each question. Use complete sentences.

1. Why was January 22, 1905, called "Bloody Sunday"?

2. Who was Karl Marx and what was the main idea he promoted?

3. Why were the Russians against involvement in World War I?

On a sheet of paper, write the letter of the answer that correctly completes each sentence.

4. Russian peasants lived under a _____ type of system for hundreds of years.

　A feudal　　　　**B** democratic　　　**C** republic　　　**D** monarch

5. More strikes, _____, and revolutionary battles followed Bloody Sunday.

　A trade　　　　**B** riots　　　　　**C** peace　　　　**D** farming

6. Nicholas II set up a parliament, called a _____, but it only lasted until 1917.

　A Manifesto　　　　　　　　**C** Communist Party
　B soviet　　　　　　　　　　**D** Duma

7. Many Russian revolutionaries read the works of _____.

　A Nicholas II　　**B** Catherine II　　**C** Karl Marx　　**D** Lenin

8. Marx imagined a perfect world with a classless society and no _____.

　A trade　　　　**B** government　　**C** factories　　**D** Communism

9. Russia entered World War I in 1914. As a result, poor people became even poorer and there were severe _____ shortages.

　A worker　　　**B** water　　　　**C** soldier　　　**D** food

10. Even though _____ was overthrown in 1917, Russia stayed involved in World War I.

　A Czar Nicholas II　　　　　　**C** the Duma
　B Karl Marx　　　　　　　　　**D** the working class

Russia Becomes the USSR

In 1917, a man named Vladimir Ilyich Lenin returned to Russia from exile in Switzerland. Lenin had always hated the government of the czar. His brother had been hanged as a revolutionary. And Lenin himself had been exiled.

Lenin read Karl Marx. He became a Communist revolutionary who believed in rebellion and in a classless society. On his return to Russia, Lenin became the leader of a Communist group called the **Bolsheviks**. *Bolshevik* means "member of the majority." Lenin and the Bolsheviks promised to give the people what they wanted: "Peace, land, and bread."

What Was the Bolshevik Revolution?

In November 1917, the Bolsheviks overthrew the government. Karl Marx had pictured a society that would someday have no need for government. However, Lenin felt that a strict Communist Party should be in charge in Russia. The country would need a planned economy. Furthermore, the Communist Party would draw up the plans. The country would be governed by councils called *soviets*. The soviets would be headed by Bolsheviks.

What Was Life Like in the Union of Soviet Socialist Republics?

In 1918, Moscow became the nation's capital once again. That year, Russia was torn apart by a civil war. The Communists had taken power in the large cities of central Russia. However, resistance developed in many other parts of the country. The "Whites," or anti-Communists, had moved quickly to organize armies to fight the "Reds," or Communists. By 1921 most of the fighting was over. The Whites had been defeated.

Lenin led the Bolsheviks to power in Russia.

Reading Strategy:
Inferencing

Reread this section as necessary in order to make inferences about why Russia became the USSR.

In 1922, Russia became the Union of Soviet Socialist Republics (USSR). By then, Lenin had put the Communists firmly in charge. He had organized a strong police force. Every day, the police arrested, jailed, and even killed enemies of Communism. The police force often made their arrests secretly at night. Many members of the clergy were arrested. Communists believed that religion was in the way. Religion misguided people, the Communists said.

The Soviet Union, 1922

MAP STUDY

1. What oceans border the Soviet Union?

2. Name two rivers in the Soviet Union.

Some members of the nobility and of the middle class were labeled enemies of the state. They were arrested, jailed, and executed. The government took their businesses. Lenin and his secret police ruled by fear.

The Bolshevik Revolution was supposed to help the peasants. Now Lenin ordered farmers to turn their crops over to the government. Some farmers rebelled. There was more fighting. Throughout the early 1920s, the Communists struggled to maintain power. For a brief period, the Communists let up on their hold over factories and farms in order to win support.

Collective
Run by a group

Oppose
To be against
something

Then, in 1924, Lenin became ill and died. He is remembered as the "Father of the Revolution." After his death, Joseph Stalin, a well-known Communist Party member, took control.

What Did Joseph Stalin Do?

Joseph Stalin was born in 1879 in the country of Georgia. He was educated in a religious school. His mother wanted him to become a priest. Then Joseph Stalin read the works of Karl Marx. "There is no God!" he announced at age 13. When he grew up, he became a revolutionary and then a leader in the Communist Party.

Stalin's real name was Dzhugashvili. But in 1913, he adopted the name *Stalin*, which means "man of steel" in Russian. Stalin took power after Lenin's death. He ruled the Soviet Union from 1924 until his death in 1953.

Stalin built up Russia's economy and industry. He saw to the building of new factories and heavier machinery. The peasants were forced to work on farms run by a group, called **collective** farms. He insisted that farmers use the new government machines. However, he did not show the farmers how to operate them. Farm production went down. There were food shortages again.

Stalin made himself strong by destroying anyone who was against, or **opposed**, him. Suspected enemies were shot or exiled to Siberia. People learned to be loyal to the Communist Party and to Stalin.

Many people were unhappy living under such a tyrant. Stalin made life especially hard for Soviet Jews. Yet throughout the country, there were food shortages for everyone. In addition, certain goods, like clothing, were hard to come by.

Soviet newspapers and radio programs told nothing of the country's problems. Sources of news said only what Stalin wanted them to say. Also, Stalin would **censor** any news that came in from the rest of the world. This means that he would examine the news before it was released. Then, he would remove any parts he did not like. Stalin did not allow the Soviet people to travel outside the Soviet Union. This was one reason the Soviet Union was said to be surrounded by an **Iron Curtain**. The Iron Curtain refers to the invisible boundary between Western Europe and Eastern Europe after World War II.

Joseph Stalin controlled the Soviet Union through fear and terror.

British prime minister Winston Churchill made the term *Iron Curtain* popular. He used it in a speech in the United States in 1946.

Stalin had statues of himself put up all over Russia. He insisted that the statues be built to make him look taller and more handsome than he really was. Stalin actually rewrote Soviet history. He tried to make it sound as if the Russian people had actually chosen him to be their leader.

Russia has a long history of being ruled by tyrants. Ivan the Terrible, Peter the Great, and many other czars were cruel dictators. However, many people think that Stalin was the most destructive tyrant and dictator of all.

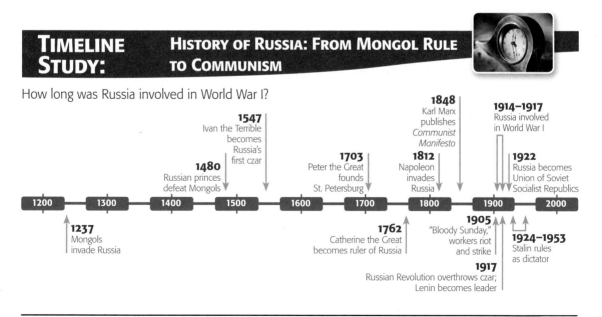

TIMELINE STUDY: HISTORY OF RUSSIA: FROM MONGOL RULE TO COMMUNISM

How long was Russia involved in World War I?

1237 Mongols invade Russia

1480 Russian princes defeat Mongols

1547 Ivan the Terrible becomes Russia's first czar

1703 Peter the Great founds St. Petersburg

1762 Catherine the Great becomes ruler of Russia

1812 Napoleon invades Russia

1848 Karl Marx publishes *Communist Manifesto*

1905 "Bloody Sunday," workers riot and strike

1914–1917 Russia involved in World War I

1917 Russian Revolution overthrows czar; Lenin becomes leader

1922 Russia becomes Union of Soviet Socialist Republics

1924–1953 Stalin rules as dictator

1200 1300 1400 1500 1600 1700 1800 1900 2000

Match the description in Column A with the person in Column B.
Write the correct letter on a sheet of paper.

Column A

1. known as the "Father of the Revolution"; he helped to overthrow the Russian government in 1917
2. British prime minister known for his speech about the Iron Curtain
3. a leader in the Communist Party who ruled the Soviet Union from 1924–1953; he helped build up Russia's economy and industry

Column B

A Lenin
B Stalin
C Winston Churchill

On a sheet of paper, write the letter of the answer that correctly completes each sentence.

4. The _____ were a Communist group whose name means "member of the majority."

   A Soviets   **B** Bolsheviks   **C** Reds   **D** Whites

5. The civil war that began in _____ put the "Whites" against the "Reds."

   A 1917   **B** 1918   **C** 1920   **D** 1921

6. The Whites, who were _____, were defeated in 1921.

   A Bolsheviks   **B** Soviets   **C** anti-Communist   **D** Communist

7. The Communists believed that _____ misguided people.

   A religion   **B** books   **C** governments   **D** factories

On a sheet of paper, write the answer to each question. Use complete sentences.

8. Did the Bolshevik Revolution help the peasants? Explain.

9. Why was it said that the Soviet Union was surrounded by an Iron Curtain?

10. What are two ways that Stalin made himself appear better than he really was?

- Much of the former Byzantine civilization lived on in Russia.

- Russia covers a good deal of land. It is home to many types of people. This includes descendants of the Vikings and Asian leader Genghis Khan.

- Russian czars came to power after 200 years of Mongol rule. Ivan the Terrible, who ruled by terror, was the first czar.

- Peter the Great westernized Russia. He brought teachers from Europe. He helped strengthen the industry of the country.

- Catherine the Great continued Peter's policies. She promoted education and culture.

- Bloody Sunday, in 1905, began a revolt of the Russian workers.

- Czar Nicholas II led Russia into World War I in 1914. The war was unpopular. In 1917, Nicholas II was overthrown.

- In 1917, the Bolsheviks took control of the government. The Bolsheviks, who followed Communist ideas, supported Lenin as head of Russia's government.

- In 1922, Russia became the Union of Soviet Socialist Republics.

- Joseph Stalin followed Lenin as leader of the Communist Party and the nation.

- Many Russians were hungry and unhappy living under the iron hand of Stalin.

Word Bank

Bolsheviks

censor

collective

Communism

dialect

economy

geography

opposed

shortage

soviets

Vocabulary Review

On a sheet of paper, use the words from the Word Bank to complete each sentence correctly.

1. _____ is a political system based on common ownership of industries and farms.

2. You can study _____ to learn about the natural features of the earth.

3. A(n) _____ is a form of language used in a certain place or by a certain group.

4. Stalin decided to _____ news so that Soviets would not know about events around the world.

5. The _____, a revolutionary Communist group, overthrew the Russian government in 1917.

6. Stalin built up Russia's _____, or system of making and trading things.

7. A(n) _____ is when there is not enough of something.

8. The Communist Party drew up a plan where Russia was governed by councils called _____.

9. Under Communism, peasants were forced to work on _____ farms (farms run by a group).

10. Stalin became powerful by destroying anyone who was against, or who _____, him.

Chapter Review Questions

On a sheet of paper, write the answer to each question. Use complete sentences.

11. Where did Russia get its name?

Test Tip

To choose the answer that correctly completes a sentence, read the sentence using each answer choice. Then choose the answer that makes the most sense when the entire sentence is read.

12. Why do you think Czar Ivan IV became known as *Ivan the Terrible?*

13. Why did Czar Peter want to open a "window to the West"?

14. What kind of government did Lenin think the Russians needed?

15. Why did Russian peasants revolt in 1917?

16. Lenin put Communists in charge in the Soviet Union. What was their attitude toward religion?

Critical Thinking

On a sheet of paper, write your response to each question. Use complete sentences.

17. Was life ever easy for Russian peasants? Why or why not?

18. What kind of person was Stalin? Give examples to support your answer.

Using the Timeline

Use the timeline on page 567 to answer the questions.

19. When did Peter the Great found St. Petersburg?

20. What happened in 1922?

GROUP ACTIVITY

Form a group of three or four. Write a skit about a person (or people) involved in the Russian Revolution. Base it on a historical event and make sure it follows some historical facts. You can also include fictional details (e.g., dialogue and actions). Perform your skit for the class.

World War II

After World War I, many nations struggled with great economic depressions. People in various places were jobless and homeless. Nations such as China and Spain had civil wars. Other nations, such as Germany and Japan, had begun building empires.

World War I had been costly in lives and in money. No one was anxious for another war. Yet only 20 years after World War I ended, another war began.

GOALS FOR LEARNING

- To describe dictators who, in the years between the world wars, wanted an empire
- To understand how World War II began
- To describe the fighting during World War II
- To describe how the war ended
- To tell the results of the war

Reading Strategy: Metacognition

When you think about your thinking, you are using metacognition. Use metacognition to be a better reader.

- Preview the text. Ask yourself what you already know about the topic, and make predictions.

- Note the main idea, details, and any questions you have. Try to visualize what is happening in the text.

- Summarize and make inferences about what you read.

Key Vocabulary Words

Lesson 1

Depression A period of low business activity and high unemployment

Fascist People who follow the political system that honors the state over the individual

Anti-Semitism Prejudice against Jews

Scapegoat A person or group blamed for the mistakes and problems of others

Concentration camp A prison camp for people thought to be dangerous to a ruling group

Axis Powers The alliance of Germany, Italy, and Japan during World War II

Allied Powers The nations united against the Axis Powers in World War II; includes Britain, France, and later the United States and the Soviet Union

Lesson 2

Civilian A person who is not in the military

Lesson 3

Genocide An attempt to kill all the people of a certain race or religious group

Holocaust Hitler's killing of many of the Jews in Europe

Pact An agreement

D-Day The Allied invasion of France in 1944

Lesson 4

Kamikaze A Japanese pilot who crashed his plane into an enemy ship, destroying it and killing himself

Nuclear Having to do with atoms or energy from atoms

Atomic bomb A bomb that uses nuclear energy and has much destructive power

Lesson 5

Organization A group of people joined together for a common purpose

The Rise of Dictators

Objectives

- To name three dictators who came to power before World War II
- To identify the Axis and Allied Powers
- To describe the theory that Adolf Hitler used to explain Germany's troubles

Depression

A period of low business activity and high unemployment

Fascist

People who follow the political system that honors the state over the individual

Benito Mussolini took control of Italy in 1922.

The 20 years between World War I and World War II were troubled years. In the early 1930s, nations struggled through **depressions**. Businesses went broke. Millions of workers were out of jobs. Farmers could not sell crops to unemployed people. Banks closed. Poverty spread throughout the world. Historians would call the 1930s the "Great Depression."

There were other troubles, too. In India, people were fighting for freedom from British rule. Civil wars were raging in China and Spain. In addition, Japan, Italy, and Germany began building empires.

The years between World War I and World War II brought new governments to several nations. They were governments ruled by dictators. The Great Depression created a perfect climate for the rise of dictators. Hungry, hopeless people wanted to see changes. They were ready to turn to a strong leader who promised a better future. Most of the dictators, however, were men with evil ideas and purposes. They wanted power and control.

Who Was Benito Mussolini?

A man named Benito Mussolini took control of Italy in 1922. He and his followers were called **fascists**. Fascists are people who honor the state over the individual. Mussolini won favor with his people by building roads and factories. He improved his country's economy and industry, but insisted on absolute rule. Anyone who refused to obey Mussolini was jailed or killed.

Mussolini wanted Italy to become a great empire. He wanted to win colonies, to make war, and to take new lands by force.

Invade

To attack or march into another country

General Hideki Tojo had all the power in Japan by 1941.

In 1935, Mussolini sent troops into Ethiopia, a free African country. The League of Nations protested. However, it could not stop Mussolini's drive into Africa.

Who Was General Hideki Tojo?

In Japan, General Hideki Tojo arose as a dictator. He wanted to build an empire in Asia. Under the leadership of Tojo and other generals, Japanese forces **invaded**, or attacked, the Chinese province of Manchuria in 1931. When the League of Nations protested, Japan left the League. By 1932, Japan had claimed Manchuria. Japan invaded China again in 1937, taking over miles of coastal lands. By 1938, Japan controlled all of China's major ports and industrial centers.

During the 1930s, Japanese military officers began taking over their own government. Anyone who got in their way or protested was either jailed or assassinated. By 1940, Tojo had become minister of war. Finally, in 1941, he became premier. Japan still had an emperor, but the emperor had no real power.

Who Was Adolf Hitler?

The country that was most willing to accept a dictator and to follow him without question was Germany. Germany had suffered greatly after World War I. German pride had been crushed. A country whose nationalistic spirit was based on military greatness had been beaten in war. German armies had been reduced to almost nothing. And the Treaty of Versailles had not allowed the Germans to rebuild their military.

The depression hit hard, and Germany still had war debts to pay. Germans were out of work and hungry. Many were angry and ready to get even.

Scapegoat
A person or group blamed for the mistakes and problems of others

Concentration camp
A prison camp for people thought to be dangerous to a ruling group

Reading Strategy:
Metacognition

Make a prediction as to what you think will happen next. Check your prediction as you read and revise if needed.

Adolf Hitler promised to win Germany's lost lands back.

This situation in Germany led people to accept Adolf Hitler as their leader in 1933. Hitler was the head of the National Socialist, or *Nazi*, party. The Nazis seemed to have an answer to Germany's problems. Hitler appealed to the Germans' wounded pride. He told them that they were a "super race" who should rule the world. He promised to return Germany to a position of power and glory.

Hitler spoke of winning back Germany's lost lands. He promised a new German empire, the Third Reich. In 1935, Hitler began rebuilding Germany's armed forces. This had been forbidden by the Treaty of Versailles. However, nothing was done to stop the Nazis from arming themselves.

As Hitler gave Germany new hope and national pride, he built his own strength. Few people dared speak out against Adolf Hitler!

How Did Hitler Explain Germany's Troubles?

Hitler tried to bind his people together with the feeling of hatred. He aimed that hate at all people who were not white and Germanic. Hitler believed that the German race was stronger, better, and smarter than any other. He gave fiery speeches that stirred German emotions. He told the people that Germans should be "masters of the world."

Hitler directed his fiercest hatred at the Jewish people. He encouraged **anti-Semitism**, a mindless hatred of Jews. He told the German people that the Jews were the cause of all their troubles. Hitler's lies gave the unhappy Germans a **scapegoat**. Now they had a simple way to explain away their troubles: they blamed them all on the Jews.

Hitler united Germany under a banner of hatred and fear. He made people afraid to disobey, or go against, him. Hitler's secret police backed his rule. They arrested anyone who spoke against him. **Concentration camps** were built to imprison Hitler's enemies. Many were killed in these camps.

Axis Powers

The alliance of Germany, Italy, and Japan during World War II

Allied Powers

The nations united against the Axis Powers in World War II; includes Britain, France, and later the United States and the Soviet Union

---

Remember

Long before Hitler, Alexander the Great wanted to conquer the world. Later, so did Napoleon.

Hitler won Germany's loyalty. Then he turned to the rest of Europe. "Today Europe," Hitler declared, "tomorrow the world!"

What Two Alliances Were Formed?

The three dictators—Hitler, Mussolini, and Tojo—each wanted an empire. In 1936, Hitler and Mussolini joined forces. They called their alliance the Rome-Berlin axis. They chose the name "axis" to suggest that all of Europe revolved around Germany and Italy. In 1940, Japan joined the **Axis Powers**. Germany, Italy, and Japan planned to conquer the world and divide it up!

On the other side, countries like Britain, France, and later the Soviet Union and the United States united against the Axis Powers. These nations were known as the **Allied Powers**.

With these two alliances formed, the sides were set for one of the worst wars in history.

Concentration camps imprisoned Hitler's enemies. Buchenwald concentration camp, pictured here, was one of the largest Nazi concentration camps.

REVIEW

Match the description in Column A with the dictator in Column B.
Write the correct letter on a sheet of paper.

Column A

1. the fascist ruler who took control of Italy in 1922 and insisted on absolute rule

2. the man who, as premier of Japan in 1941, had more power than the emperor

3. head of the Nazis; believed Germans were a "super race" and should rule the world

Column B

A Adolf Hitler

B Benito Mussolini

C Hideki Tojo

On a sheet of paper, write the letter of the answer that correctly completes each sentence.

4. Germany's defeat in World War I had crushed German _____.

   A trade   **B** pride   **C** weapons   **D** inventions

5. _____ and Italy named their alliance "axis," suggesting that all of Europe revolved around them.

   A Britain   **B** France   **C** Germany   **D** Russia

6. In 1940, _____ joined the Axis Powers.

   A Japan   **B** Italy   **C** Russia   **D** the United States

7. By rebuilding Germany's armed forces, Hitler was going against the _____.

   A National Socialist party   **C** Treaty of Versailles
   B Axis Powers   **D** United Nations

On a sheet of paper, write the answer to each question. Use complete sentences.

8. How did Hitler appeal to the Germans' wounded pride?

9. What countries were included in the Allied nations?

10. What was Adolf Hitler's theory to explain Germany's troubles?

World War II Begins in Europe

Objectives

- To explain how Germany helped to bring about World War II
- To identify Hitler's style of warfare and explain what happened when Germany invaded France
- To describe the Battle of Britain
- To describe the problems Hitler had after his army invaded the Soviet Union

Reading Strategy: Metacognition

Note the main idea and supporting details of *blitzkrieg*. Summarize what you have read to make sure you understand it.

In 1938, Hitler set forth on his conquest of Europe. His troops marched into Austria and took over the country. Austria was now a part of Germany.

"This is wrong," said Great Britain and France. "Hitler has broken the Treaty of Versailles." However, they did not act to stop him.

Next Hitler turned to Czechoslovakia. Hitler claimed that Germans living there were treated poorly. He asked for a border region in Czechoslovakia. He said that this would be his last request for territory. Great Britain and France had sworn to protect Czechoslovakia. To keep peace, however, they signed a treaty with Hitler. They gave him 11,000 square miles of Czech lands. This area was known as the Sudetenland. Six months later, Hitler took over the rest of Czechoslovakia. The British and French policy of trying to satisfy Hitler by giving in had not worked.

On September 1, 1939, German armies invaded Poland. This time Great Britain and France acted. On September 3, 1939, they declared war on Germany. World War II had begun.

What Was Hitler's *Blitzkrieg?*

The German army took Poland in less than a month. Then Hitler pushed west. Norway and Denmark fell to Germany, too.

Hitler's style of warfare was called a *blitzkrieg*, which means "lightning war." His armies moved fast, using quick attacks with planes, tanks, and troops. First, German planes bombed railroads, highways, and cities. Then, the armored cars moved in, followed by the Nazi foot soldiers.

Words from the Past

Winston Churchill, June 4, 1940

Winston Churchill had become prime minister of Great Britain on May 10, 1940. That was the same day that Germany invaded Belgium, Luxembourg, and the Netherlands. Soon after that, Belgium surrendered to Germany. It looked as if it would only be a matter of days until France fell to the Nazis. People in Britain began to worry about what would happen to their own country.

On June 4, Churchill gave a speech to the British House of Commons. He wanted to raise the spirits of the British people. He said that even though all of Europe might fall, " . . . we shall not flag or fail. We shall go on to the end . . . we shall fight in the seas and oceans . . . we shall fight on the beaches, we shall fight on the landing-grounds, we shall fight in the fields and in the streets, we shall fight in the hills; we shall never surrender . . . ."

Civilian

A person who is not in the military

Remember

France had been Germany's bitter enemy since losing a war to Bismarck in 1871.

You Decide

Britain's spirit remained strong in spite of the constant bombing. Do you think your country would be as strong in this situation? Explain.

The German *blitzkrieg* moved in on the Netherlands, Luxembourg, and Belgium. Next came France.

When the Germans attacked France, they had some help from Italy. France's armies were unable to stop Hitler. With Germans at the gates of Paris and planes overhead, the French surrendered. In June 1940, the French admitted their defeat. It is said that Hitler received the news of France's surrender with great joy. A story went around that he danced a little "victory jig."

Who Won the Battle of Britain?

With the fall of France, only Britain remained in Hitler's way. Hitler decided not to attack the island of Great Britain by sea. Britain's navy was too powerful. Hitler would launch an air attack instead.

The Battle of Britain was the first major air war in history. Beginning in July 1940, thousands of German planes attacked Britain. They bombed cities and airfields. However, the British would not be defeated.

Readers choose books in a London library damaged by bombs.

British **civilians** (those not in the military) worked out air raid plans to protect their neighborhoods. Citizens even strung piano wire from balloons to catch Nazi planes. The skilled young pilots of the British Royal Air Force (RAF) fought hard. With speedy Spitfire planes and with newly developed radar, they fought off the German planes.

Reading Strategy:
Metacognition

Review the prediction you made during the last lesson. Make changes to it as needed.

From September 1940 until May 1941, German planes bombed London almost every night. These attacks became known as the *London Blitz*. By May 1941, it was clear that the German bombing attacks had failed. Germany had lost more than 2,600 planes. It was Germany's first defeat in World War II.

World War II in Europe, 1942–1945

MAP STUDY

1. Which nations were neutral in World War II?

2. What three cities in the USSR were near the area of Axis control?

What Nations Did Hitler Conquer?

Unable to take Britain, Hitler's armies moved eastward. The Germans took Romania and its oil fields. Then Italy invaded Greece. Greece's armies fought bravely against the Italians. However, when Hitler joined the Italians, Greece had to surrender.

Next, the Axis nations invaded Yugoslavia. Most of Europe had now fallen under Hitler. His next goal would be the conquest of the Soviet Union. Germany had been allies with the Soviets, but Hitler decided to invade anyway.

What Happened When Hitler Invaded the Soviet Union?

Like Napoleon Bonaparte, Hitler chose June 22 as the day to attack Russia. Napoleon had attacked on June 22, 1812. Now Hitler attacked on June 22, 1941, with three million German soldiers. He expected Russia to fall in a matter of weeks.

The Russians surprised the world by fighting back with amazing strength and determination. Soldiers and civilians alike stood up against the Germans. However, the Germans advanced toward Moscow. Just as in the fight against Napoleon, Russians burned whatever they could not move. They destroyed food, supplies, machinery, and factories so the Germans could not use them. The Germans approached Moscow, but they were unable to take the city. People from all over Russia poured in to defend it.

History Fact
Hitler made the same mistake in 1941 that Napoleon did in 1812.

Like Napoleon, Hitler did not count on the fierce Russian weather. Hitler's soldiers did not even have winter clothing. Furthermore, the winter of 1941–1942 turned out to be the worst in years. Nazi soldiers froze on the icy Russian plains. It was beginning to look as if Hitler might have made a mistake by invading Russia. Indeed, by 1944 the Soviets had pushed the Germans out of the Soviet Union.

REVIEW

Word Bank

blitzkrieg

Britain

Czechoslovakia

France

Greece

Moscow

Romania

On a sheet of paper, write the word from the Word Bank to complete each sentence correctly.

1. _____ was Hitler's style of warfare, which means "lightning war."

2. To keep peace, Britain and France signed a treaty that gave Hitler parts of _____. Ignoring the treaty, Hitler took over the rest of the nation six months later.

3. With help from Italy, Germany invaded _____ who surrendered, unable to stop Hitler.

4. Germany's loss to _____ was its first defeat in World War II.

5. Germany took _____ and its oil fields.

6. _____ surrendered to the Italians.

7. Germany was unable to take _____ because Russians from all over came to defend it.

On a sheet of paper, write the answer to each question. Use complete sentences.

8. What action by Germany started World War II?

9. What steps did the British take to defend their neighborhoods during the Battle of Britain?

10. What mistake did Hitler make when invading the Soviet Union in 1941?

The Holocaust and Allied Victories

Hitler forced his own ideas on the people he conquered. They were evil ideas of a "super race." People who did not fit Hitler's ideal of the super race were considered inferior. They were used as slave laborers or thrown into concentration camps.

What Was the Holocaust?

Some Europeans fought the Nazi ideas. They formed resistance groups and waged secret, undercover wars. They wrecked telephone and telegraph lines to stop German communication. They blew up bridges and derailed trains. They killed Nazi officers. They helped Allied prisoners escape.

The Nazis answered the resistance by murdering hundreds of innocent men, women, and children. Nazi terror was aimed most directly at Europe's Jews. First, Hitler forced Jews out of their jobs. He took their businesses and their property. Then Jews were made to live in special areas.

In 1941, Hitler's plans reached their evil peak. He announced his "final solution" to what he called the "Jewish problem." That solution was **genocide**—to kill all of Europe's Jews.

Hitler sent millions of people to concentration camps. Worse than any prison, these camps were slave-labor camps. In the camps, millions of men, women, and children were executed. Many people were spared execution only to be worked or starved to death.

Over six million Jews died in Nazi concentration camps. Hitler's efforts to destroy all Jews is called the **Holocaust**.

The Nazis captured millions of Jewish men, women, and children and sent them to concentration camps.

History Fact

Healthy prisoners were sometimes hired out as slaves for private businesses. Often, they were worked and starved to death in factories and other businesses.

The Nazis also murdered millions of others—Russians, Poles, Gypsies, Slavs—all "inferior" enemies of Hitler.

The Nazi death camps are one of history's greatest horrors. "How could the world have let this happen?" question the ghosts of Hitler's victims. Survivors of the Holocaust tell of wishing for death in a world too evil to bear.

Why Did the United States Declare War on Japan?

The United States was a neutral nation from 1939 until 1941. It was not directly involved in the war.

Even so, the United States did send aid to Germany's enemies. The United States sent food, arms, and raw materials to Great Britain and Russia. However, it took a direct blow from Japan to bring the United States into World War II.

Pact
An agreement

You Decide
Why do you think the United States remained neutral until December 1941?

Japan was trying to create its empire in Asia. Japan felt that the United States stood in the way of its control of the Pacific Ocean. On December 7, 1941, Japanese planes bombed the Pearl Harbor naval base in Hawaii. The attack took the United States by surprise. Japan sank or damaged 13 ships and about 170 planes. Nearly 2,500 U.S. soldiers, sailors, and civilians died in the surprise attack.

In Japan, Emperor Hirohito declared war on the United States. In the United States, President Franklin D. Roosevelt asked Congress to declare war on Japan. After a vote in Congress, Roosevelt addressed the nation. "We are now in this war," he declared. "We are in it all the way."

Four days later, Germany and Italy honored their agreement, their **pact**, with Japan. They declared war on the United States.

By the end of 1941, the war really had become a world war. The Axis countries stood on one side. The Allied countries, which now included the United States, stood on the other.

GREAT NAMES IN HISTORY

Anne Frank

Anne Frank's diary has made her a symbol of Nazi cruelty. In July 1942, Nazi troops began rounding up Jews in Amsterdam. With her parents and sister, Anne went into hiding. She had just turned 13. The family and others lived in a secret attic above her father's former business. Anne also began a diary, writing about her hopes and dreams. For two years, non-Jewish friends brought them food. Then in August 1944, the secret police force, the Gestapo, found them. They sent them to concentration camps. Only her father lived past the horrors of the war. Anne died at Bergen-Belsen. After the war, her father found the diary and published it.

Why Was the Battle of Stalingrad so Important?

In 1942, Soviet and German armies were locked in battle. The battlefront stretched about 2,000 miles through the Soviet Union, from the Arctic to the Black Sea. In the north, Leningrad (formerly St. Petersburg) was under siege by the Nazis. The siege began in August 1941 and would last until January 1944. About a million Russians died during the siege, most of them from starvation.

History Fact
The name *Leningrad* was changed back to St. Petersburg in 1991.

In September 1942, the German Sixth Army attacked Stalingrad (now called Volgograd). For five months, Soviet soldiers fought the Germans. The battle raged back and forth from one block to the next. Finally, on January 31, 1943, the German Sixth Army surrendered. Only 90,000 of the original force of 350,000 German soldiers were still alive.

The Battle of Stalingrad marked a major turning point in the war. Now the Soviet army went on the offensive. The Soviets began to take back cities that had been captured by the Germans.

Meanwhile, fighting had been going on in northern Africa. Hitler had taken over most of Europe. Now he could be attacked only from Britain, the Soviet Union, or from North Africa. North Africa became important.

General Erwin Rommel, known as the clever "Desert Fox," led the Germans in Africa. Early in 1943, U.S. General Dwight D. Eisenhower set a trap for the Desert Fox and defeated the Germans. In May 1943, German and Italian forces in Africa surrendered.

The Allies invaded Italy next. It was, according to President Roosevelt, the "beginning of the end" for the Axis countries. The Allies accepted the Italian surrender in 1943. However, German forces continued to fight in Italy. Rome was finally freed on June 4, 1944.

**Reading Strategy:
Metacognition**

Make a prediction to tell what you think will happen next. Check your prediction as you continue reading and revise if needed.

What Was D-Day?

Hitler still felt sure of his strength in Europe. But the Allies were preparing an invasion. By 1944 they were ready to free France.

German forces protected the Normandy coast facing Great Britain. The Allies planned to invade Normandy. The day of the invasion was called "**D-Day.**"

D-Day came at 2 A.M. on June 6, 1944. General Eisenhower was in charge of the attack. The first wave of troops crossed the English Channel. By 6:30 A.M. more than 150,000 Allied soldiers waded ashore on the beaches of Normandy. Within five days the Allies had fought many miles inland.

The Allies began their sweep through France. In August, they freed Paris. By October the Nazis were driven from all of France, as well as from Belgium and Luxembourg.

Allied soldiers landed in Normandy, France, for the longest land and sea attack in history.

On a sheet of paper, write the letter of the answer that correctly completes each sentence.

1. People who did not fit Hitler's ideal of the _____ were considered inferior. They were used as slave laborers or thrown into concentration camps.

   A super race   **B** Jewish   **C** Russian   **D** Gypsies

2. Some Europeans waged secret wars to fight the _____. It only seemed to fuel Hitler's purpose.

   A Russians   **B** Nazi ideas   **C** Italians   **D** Japanese

3. During the Holocaust, over _____ Jews died in Nazi concentration camps.

   A 600   **B** 6,000   **C** 60,000   **D** 6 million

4. German and Italian forces in _____ surrendered in May 1943.

   A Greece   **B** Romania   **C** Africa   **D** Britain

5. The Allies invaded _____ and accepted their surrender in 1943.

   A Japan   **B** France   **C** Belgium   **D** Italy

6. The day that the Allies planned to invade Normandy was called "_____."

   A Battle of Stalingrad   **C** D-Day
   B London Blitz   **D** Holocaust

7. By October 1944, the Nazis were driven from all of _____, Belgium, and Luxembourg.

   A France   **B** Russia   **C** Africa   **D** Germany

On a sheet of paper, write the answer to each question. Use complete sentences.

8. What was Hitler's solution to the "Jewish problem?"

9. How did the United States become involved in the war?

10. Why was the Battle of Stalingrad a major turning point in the war?

The End of the War

Objectives

- To explain the Battle of the Bulge and its outcome
- To explain what became of Mussolini and Hitler
- To tell the purpose of kamikaze pilots
- To describe how the war finally ended in Japan

Reading Strategy: Metacognition

Note the main idea and important details about the ending of World War II. Summarize what you have read to make sure you understand it.

The Germans were soundly defeated in December 1944 in the Battle of the Bulge. According to Winston Churchill, it was the greatest U.S. victory of the war.

At last, early in 1945, the Allies invaded Germany. Germany's capital, Berlin, fell on May 2. On May 7, 1945, Germany surrendered. The war in Europe was over.

What Happened to Hitler and Mussolini?

The leaders of Germany and Italy had created terrible death and destruction. What became of the leaders of these fallen powers?

In Italy, fascist leader Benito Mussolini met an ugly end. Mussolini tried to escape from Italy, to run from the antifascists. When captured, he begged for his life.

Despite his pleas, Mussolini was executed—shot without a trial. His body was hung upside down outside a gas station in Milan, Italy. Italians shouted at the body, kicking it and throwing stones at it. A man who had lived by cruelty and terror met a cruel end.

Germany's Hitler died two days later. On April 30, 1945, reports came that the dictator had killed himself. He had been hiding in a bomb shelter beneath the flaming, shattered city of Berlin. Unable to face defeat, Hitler and his wife, Eva Braun, killed themselves.

Kamikaze

A Japanese pilot who crashed his plane into an enemy ship, destroying it and killing himself

Nuclear

Having to do with atoms or energy from atoms

Atomic bomb

A bomb that uses nuclear energy and has much destructive power

Why Did the Japanese Keep Fighting?

The war had ended in Europe, but not in the Pacific. After Pearl Harbor, the Japanese had taken the Philippines, most of Southeast Asia, and islands in the Pacific.

General Douglas MacArthur led the U.S. forces against the Japanese in the Pacific. Although his campaigns were successful, the Japanese would not give up. Most of Japan's navy and air force had been destroyed by August 1945. However, there was no surrender. The Japanese felt it was their duty and honor to fight to the very end.

The Japanese turned to desperate measures. **Kamikaze** pilots became human bombs. They did this by strapping themselves into planes filled with explosives. Then they flew their planes into U.S. warships.

It seemed time for the terrors of war to end. However, the greatest terror was still to come.

Why Did the United States Drop Two Atomic Bombs on Japan?

Scientists had discovered how to split the atom to create great energy, **nuclear** energy. This nuclear energy could be used as a weapon. By 1940, German scientists were working to develop an **atomic bomb**. An atomic bomb uses nuclear energy to create a powerful weapon.

In 1942, the Manhattan Project began to develop the bomb in the United States. Working on the project in the United States were scientists such as Enrico Fermi and J. Robert Oppenheimer. They, with the help of many others, finally built the powerful weapon.

U.S. President Harry S. Truman made the difficult decision. The atomic bomb would be the quickest way to end the war.

Geography Note

Hiroshima is on the southwest coast of Japan's Honshu Island. The River Ota splits into seven branches as it flows into the Seto Inland Sea. Hiroshima is made up of the six islands created by those branches. The islands are connected by 81 bridges. The Aioi Bridge was a T-shaped bridge connecting three of those islands. It was the target of the atomic bomb dropped in 1945. The bomb missed its target, but it damaged the bridge. After the war, the Japanese repaired the bridge. They replaced it many years later. Damaged pieces from the original bridge are preserved in Hiroshima's Peace Memorial Park.

Japan was warned, but the Japanese refused to surrender. Therefore, on August 6, 1945, an American plane dropped the atomic bomb on Hiroshima, Japan. In seconds, more than 60,000 people were killed, and Hiroshima was gone.

Still, Japan did not surrender, and three days later, a second A-bomb was dropped. This bomb fell on Nagasaki's 250,000 people.

At last, on September 2, 1945, the Japanese surrendered. It was their first military defeat in 2,000 years. General Tojo was arrested and convicted as a war criminal. He was hanged on December 23, 1948.

REVIEW

atomic bombs

Battle of the Bulge

committed suicide

energy

Europe

executed

hanged

kamikaze

Pacific

surrender

On a sheet of paper, write the word from the Word Bank to complete each sentence correctly.

1. The Germans were soundly defeated in the _____.

2. When Berlin fell and Germany surrendered, the war in _____ was over.

3. Mussolini was _____.

4. Hitler and his wife Eva _____.

5. Although the war in Europe was over, the Japanese still had control of the _____.

6. Although most of Japan's navy and air force had been destroyed by August 1945, they did not _____.

7. _____ pilots became human bombs. They strapped themselves into planes filled with explosives and flew the planes into U.S. warships.

8. An atomic bomb uses the _____ from a split atom to create a powerful weapon.

9. After the United States dropped _____ on Hiroshima and Nagasaki, Japan finally surrendered.

10. General Tojo was convicted as a criminal and _____.

The Results of the War

Objectives

■ To list three reasons why World War II was the most expensive war in history

■ To explain the pact known as the *Declaration by United Nations*

Reading Strategy: Metacognition

Remember to ask yourself questions as you read. This will help you better understand what you are reading.

World War II was over at last. It was the most expensive war in history.

What Were the Costs of the War?

The figures of World War II were shocking:

- Over a trillion dollars had been spent for arms and war machinery.

- About 55 million lives were lost. (This includes civilian and military losses.)

- Germany lost almost 3 million soldiers.

- Japan lost more than 2 million soldiers.

- Italy lost about 160,000 soldiers.

- Russia lost about 7,500,000 soldiers.

- Britain lost about 270,000 soldiers.

- The United States lost more than 400,000 soldiers.

- France lost about 200,000 soldiers.

Many millions of civilians had died. Millions of others were homeless. The world was left with questions to answer. How could people have so easily accepted the horrors of the Nazi concentration camps? What about the atomic bomb? What was to become of a world that possessed such a terrible and powerful weapon?

Why Was the United Nations Formed?

The League of Nations had tried to keep the peace after World War I. However, the League had failed. How could future wars be prevented?

U.S. President Franklin D. Roosevelt and other national leaders were thinking about how to keep peace. They had been since the beginning of World War II. Finally, in June 1941, representatives of nine countries met in London to talk about it. There, those officials signed a pledge to work for a free world. This pledge was called the *Inter-Allied Declaration.*

By early 1942, the idea of a "United Nations" gained wide support. In January, representatives from 26 nations met in Washington, D.C. There they signed a pact calling for world peace and freedom for all people. The agreement also called for eventual disarmament and economic cooperation. The pact they signed was called the *Declaration by United Nations.*

At that time, of course, there was still a world war going on. By 1944, however, it was clear that the Allies would win the war. Allied representatives began planning the new **organization**. In February 1945, a date was set for a United Nations meeting in San Francisco. As scheduled, the meeting was held on April 25.

At that first meeting of the United Nations, a constitution was established. Representatives from 50 nations signed the United Nations Charter. The delegates also set up a Security Council with permanent members from five countries. They were the United States, the Soviet Union, Great Britain, France, and China. Each member had veto power over any decision the Security Council made. Just one veto would keep a decision from going into effect.

On October 24, 1945, the United Nations became official. The new organization had a big job ahead of it. Its aim was to protect world peace and human rights throughout the world. In 1949, the cornerstone was laid for the UN headquarters in New York City.

The United Nations building is in New York City.

Whenever a world problem comes up, the United Nations meets to work for a peaceful settlement. Delegates from every member nation attend meetings of the United Nations' General Assembly. They try to solve problems without war. Other branches of the UN work on problems of education, trade, labor, health, and economics.

The weapons of the world have grown to unbelievable destructive power. The purpose of the United Nations has become more and more important. The United Nations has one victory as its major goal—the victory over war.

Reading Strategy:
Metacognition

Remember to look at illustrations such as this timeline. This will help you understand what you have read.

TIMELINE STUDY:

WORLD WAR II

What event happened the same year that France fell to Germany?

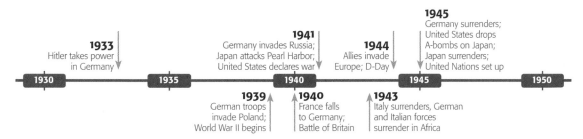

1933 Hitler takes power in Germany

1941 Germany invades Russia; Japan attacks Pearl Harbor; United States declares war

1944 Allies invade Europe; D-Day

1945 Germany surrenders; United States drops A-bombs on Japan; Japan surrenders; United Nations set up

1930 — 1935 — 1940 — 1945 — 1950

1939 German troops invade Poland; World War II begins

1940 France falls to Germany; Battle of Britain

1943 Italy surrenders, German and Italian forces surrender in Africa

On a sheet of paper, write the answer to each question. Use complete sentences.

1. What are three reasons why World War II was the most expensive war in history?

2. Describe the *Inter-Allied Declaration*.

3. What did the *Declaration by United Nations* call for?

On a sheet of paper, write the letter of the answer that correctly completes each sentence.

4. A _____ was established at the first meeting of the United Nations.

   A treaty   **B** war   **C** constitution   **D** trade agreement

5. The United Nations set up a Security Council from five countries. The countries were: the United States, the Soviet Union, Great Britain, France, and _____.

   A China   **B** Japan   **C** Germany   **D** Belgium

6. Each member of the Security Council had _____ power over any decision the council made.

   A little   **B** one-fifth   **C** unequal   **D** veto

7. The _____ became official on October 24, 1945.

   A *Inter-Allied Declaration*   **C** UN headquarters
   B Security Council   **D** United Nations

8. The UN headquarters are in _____.

   A Geneva   **B** New York City **C** Moscow   **D** London

9. The UN has branches that address education, trade, labor, health, and_____.

   A religion   **B** air travel   **C** economics   **D** computer technology

10. The UN becomes important as _____ grow to even more destructive power.

   A weapons   **B** countries   **C** dictators   **D** computers

- Mussolini improved the economy and industry of Italy, then he became its dictator.

- Tojo rose up from the military to become dictator of Japan.

- Hitler, as head of the Nazi party, made bold promises to the people of Germany. The Germans were eager to regain their sense of national pride, so they made him their leader.

- Two alliances fought each other in World War II. The Axis Powers were Germany, Italy, Japan, and many smaller nations. The Allied Powers were Britain, France, Russia, the United States, and many smaller nations. The United States joined the war in 1941, after Japan attacked Pearl Harbor.

- Hitler had ideas of a "super race" that was meant to rule the world. He especially hated the Jews and he tried to destroy them. In the Holocaust, he imprisoned and murdered millions of Jews. He also murdered millions of other people who did not fit into his idea of the super race.

- World War II began in 1939, after Germany invaded Poland. The war was fought in Europe, Asia, and Africa.

- D-Day, in June 1944, began the Allied sweep to regain Europe. Within four months the Allies had freed France, Belgium, and Luxembourg.

- Terrible weapons, including two atomic bombs dropped by the United States on Japan, were used in the war.

- World War II ended after Germany surrendered in May 1945 and Japan surrendered in September 1945.

- About 55 million soldiers and civilians died in World War II.

- World War II cost more than any other war in history.

- The United Nations officially began in 1945. It was another attempt to promote world peace.

CHAPTER 28
REVIEW

Word Bank

anti-Semitism

atomic bomb

concentration camps

depression

fascist

genocide

invaded

organization

pact

scapegoat

Vocabulary Review

On a sheet of paper, use the words from the Word Bank to complete each sentence correctly.

1. Hitler made the Jews into a(n) _____ by blaming them for all the troubles in Germany.

2. Business activity goes down and unemployment goes up during a(n) _____.

3. Germany, Italy, and Japan signed a(n) _____ to support each other in World War II.

4. A follower of the dictator Mussolini was a(n) _____.

5. The killing of people of a certain race or religion is _____.

6. Japan _____ China several times. By 1938 it controlled all of China's major ports and industrial centers.

7. Japan finally surrendered after a second _____ was dropped.

8. Hitler encouraged _____, or prejudice against Jews.

9. The United Nations is a(n) _____ formed to protect world peace and human rights.

10. Hitler sent millions of people to _____, which were built to imprison his enemies.

Chapter Review Questions

On a sheet of paper, write the answer to each question. Use complete sentences.

11. How did the Great Depression help the rise of dictators?

12. What were the three Axis Powers and the dictators who ruled them?

13. How did Hitler use hate as a weapon?

14. How did Germany help cause World War II?

15. Which country lost the most soldiers in the war?

16. What are three world problems that the United Nations works to solve?

Critical Thinking

On a sheet of paper, write your response to each question. Use complete sentences.

17. Do you think the Holocaust could happen again? Why or why not?

18. How did the dropping of the atomic bombs on Japan change the world?

Using the Timeline

Use the timeline on page 597 to answer the questions.

19. When the United States entered the war, how long had it been going on?

20. When was D-Day?

GROUP ACTIVITY

Form a group of four. Make a large wall chart about World War II. Use the information in this chapter and in encyclopedias and other books. Suggested headings are: Battles, Weapons, Leaders, Nations and Their Flags, Famous Speeches, the Holocaust, the Atomic Bomb, Costs of War, the United Nations, and Winners and Losers.

THE WORLD SINCE 1945

You have read that history is all about change. People move, people learn, and people develop ideas. Disagreements among groups often lead to wars. Countries change as their citizens change. That is the history you read about in books. These last chapters cover history that many people in the world recall as news. It is history they remember. It is history they lived through. It might even be history that affected their daily lives. You may have some knowledge to bring to your reading. Use your knowledge and experience when reading these coming chapters.

Chapters in Unit 10

The quality of life on Earth is at risk as overpopulation threatens our environment. It is more important than ever for people to be responsible citizens of our planet.

The Cold War

After six years of fighting, World War II had come to an end. More than ever before, people all over the world hoped to see the end of war. Millions had lost loved ones. Millions of others were homeless or their cities had been destroyed. Many people and countries began to work for peace.

This time in history was not one without fear. New enemies were growing. New challenges were facing those who wanted to return to the happiness before the war. People wanted to live beyond war.

GOALS FOR LEARNING

- To describe the world after World War II
- To identify major crisis periods in relations between the Soviet Union and United States
- To describe the changing relations between the Soviets and Americans

Reading Strategy: Summarizing

When summarizing, a good reader asks questions about what he or she is reading. When reading this chapter, ask yourself these questions:

- Who or what am I reading about?
- Why am I reading about this topic?
- What is the most important idea related to this topic?

Key Vocabulary Words

Lesson 1

Marshall Plan The American plan to rebuild Europe after World War II

Satellite A country that depends on and is controlled by a more powerful country

Berlin Wall The wall that divided the people of East and West Berlin

Isolationism A policy of staying out of the affairs, or business, of other countries

Lesson 2

Superpower A nation that has more power and money than other countries

Cold war The tension and hostility between the United States and the Soviet Union after World War II; was a war of ideas

Capitalist Having business and industry privately owned and operated for profit

Truman Doctrine U.S. President Truman's plan to stop the spread of Communism

Currency The form of money a country uses

Nuclear weapon A powerful weapon, such as an atomic bomb or missile

Crisis A time of danger; a turning point in events

Lesson 3

Disaster Something that causes harm or problems

Détente An easing of tensions between countries

Ratify To formally approve

The World After World War II

Marshall Plan
The American plan to rebuild Europe after World War II

Satellite
A country that depends on and is controlled by a more powerful country

Reading Strategy:
Summarizing

What is the main idea of this first section?

Europe was weakened by World War II. European countries were no longer the powerful nations they had been. It was time for these nations to rebuild. Many nations, including Italy and France, set up democratic governments. Charles de Gaulle served as the first president of postwar France.

What Was the Marshall Plan?

U.S. President Harry S. Truman called for a plan to help put Europe back on its feet. The **Marshall Plan**, named for U.S. Secretary of State George C. Marshall, provided money for European recovery. From 1947 until 1951, the United States gave $13 billion of food, raw materials for industry, and machinery to European nations.

War-torn nations welcomed the aid. However, the Soviet Union and its Communist **satellites** refused to accept the Marshall Plan. This refusal was just one act that would divide the world into two camps.

The Eastern European countries did not turn to democracy. They became Communist satellites of the Soviet Union. They had been freed from the Germans by the Soviet Union at the end of the war. But they remained under Soviet control.

How Was Germany Divided After World War II?

Germany was a mess after World War II. Cities and farms had been bombed. The economy was ruined.

The winning nations divided Germany into four sections. Great Britain, France, the United States, and the Soviet Union each took control of a section. Each country put troops inside its zone to keep order.

Berlin Wall
The wall that divided the people of East and West Berlin

After a few years the United States, France, and Britain tried to bring Germany together as one republic. However, the Soviet Union refused. As a result, the democratic nations combined their regions to form West Germany, or the Federal Republic of Germany. The Soviet-controlled zone became known as East Germany, or the German Democratic Republic.

The city of Berlin is located in the eastern part of Germany. It was divided into East Berlin, a Communist section, and West Berlin, under democratic West German control. In 1961, the Communists built the **Berlin Wall** to separate the city's two sections. They also wanted to keep East Berliners from leaving to live in the West.

The Division of Germany After World War II

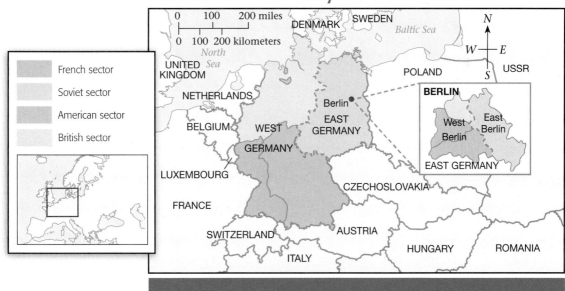

MAP STUDY

1. What were the four sections of Germany after World War II?

2. What were the three parts of West Berlin?

Isolationism
A policy of staying out of the affairs, or business, of other countries

Reading Strategy: Summarizing

What are some important details to help you understand this section?

How Did World War II Alter the United States' Policies?

The United States, unlike Europe, was not shattered by World War II. No battles tore apart U.S. lands. Wide oceans kept the United States separate and safe. The United States also had the power of the atomic bomb. At the end of World War II, the United States was the strongest nation in the world.

Except for its involvement in World War I, the United States had mostly kept to its own business. It followed a policy of **isolationism**. World War II connected the United States with the rest of the world. In 1945, the United States became one of the first countries to join the United Nations. The world was changing. Countries were becoming more dependent on each other. The United States could no longer stand alone, minding its own business.

On a sheet of paper, write the letter of the answer that correctly completes each sentence.

1. The Soviet Union and its Communist satellites refused to accept the _____.

  A peace treaty   **C** Marshall Plan
  B policy of isolationism   **D** détente

2. After World War II, the Eastern European countries were freed from the Germans. However, they remained under _____ control.

  A U.S.   **B** Japanese   **C** Soviet   **D** German

3. _____ economy was ruined after its defeat in World War II.

  A The United States'   **C** The Soviet Union's
  B Japan's   **D** Germany's

4. The democratic nations combined their regions to form _____ Germany.

  A North   **B** South   **C** East   **D** West

5. The Soviet-controlled zone became _____ Germany.

  A North   **B** South   **C** East   **D** West

6. _____ was the strongest nation in the world at the end of World War II.

  A The United States   **C** The Soviet Union
  B Japan   **D** Germany

7. After World War II, the United States could no longer follow _____.

  A Communist rule   **C** the Marshall Plan
  B its policy of isolationism   **D** its democratic government

On a sheet of paper, write the answer to each question. Use complete sentences.

8. What was the Marshall Plan?

9. How was Germany divided after World War II?

10. Why was the Berlin wall built?

The Cold War Begins

Objectives

- To explain why the cold war began
- To explain the alliances formed as a result of the cold war
- To name the bomb that was more powerful than the atomic bomb
- To describe life in the Soviet Union under Nikita Khrushchev
- To explain the Cuban missile crisis

Superpower

A nation that has more power and money than other countries

Cold war

The tension and hostility between the United States and the Soviet Union after World War II

Capitalist

Having business and industry privately owned and operated for profit

During World War II, the United States and the Soviet Union were allies. After World War II, the two countries became the most powerful nations on Earth. In fact, they were known as *superpowers*. This is because they had more money and power than other countries. Each had different ideas about what an ideal society should be like. Soviet peoples lived under Communism, while Americans lived in a free democracy. Disagreements and tensions between the two nations grew. The "**cold war**" had begun.

What Was the Cold War?

The cold war was not an outright conflict. It did not involve actual battles or bombings. The cold war was a war of ideas.

Both the Soviet Union and the United States had their own allies in the cold war. The United States and its allies thought Communism was bad. They pointed out that people in Communist countries usually had little freedom. The Communist nations criticized the United States for being a **capitalist** nation. A capitalist nation is one that has business and industry privately owned and operated for profit. They pointed out that some people in the United States were very rich and some were very poor. They said that because of this, the United States was an unfair society.

Americans worried about a Communist takeover of the whole world. President Truman announced that the United States would give aid to any country fighting Communism. He made a plan for military and economic support. This plan became known as the **Truman Doctrine**. Both Greece and Turkey were given aid under this plan.

Truman Doctrine
U.S. President
Truman's plan to
stop the spread of
Communism

Reading Strategy:
Summarizing

What are some important details about the Soviet idea of Americans? What are some important details about the American idea of Soviets?

You Decide
Do you think the Communist criticism of the United States was fair? Why or why not?

Remember
The world was also divided into alliances before and during the two world wars.

Communism often grew strong in poor countries. Financial aid under the Marshall Plan helped European nations resist Communist ideas.

What Military Alliances Were Formed?

In 1949, sides were clearly drawn in the cold war. The United States led the setting up of the North Atlantic Treaty Organization (NATO). Members of NATO included the United States, Britain, France, Italy, Canada, and several smaller nations. In 1954, West Germany became a member.

NATO began as a defense against Communism. Member nations promised to help each other. They said that an attack against any one of them would be taken as an attack against all.

In 1955, the Soviet Union created its own alliance to balance the NATO alliance. It was called the Warsaw Pact. It included the Soviet Union and its Communist allies in Eastern Europe.

What Economic Alliances Were Formed?

NATO and the Warsaw Pact were military alliances. The cold war also prompted European nations to form economic alliances. The Soviet Union developed ties with its European allies. These ties gave the Soviet Union a market for its manufactured products. The economic allies, in turn, supplied the Soviets with raw materials.

Many Western European countries joined together to promote trade and common interests. The organization that these countries formed was known as the European Union by the late 1990s. The European Union consisted of 15 full member nations: Austria, Belgium, Denmark, Finland, France, Germany, Greece, Ireland, Italy, Luxembourg, the Netherlands, Portugal, Spain, Sweden, and the United Kingdom.

Currency
The form of money a
country uses

*The euro is the form
of currency used in
the European Union.*

You Decide
Do you think the
nuclear arms
race made people feel
safer? Why or why not?

**Reading Strategy:
Summarizing**

What event in history is
this section about?

*The atomic bomb
killed everything in
Nagasaki in a matter
of seconds. With
the discovery of the
hydrogen bomb, the
atomic bomb was
no longer the most
destructive weapon.*

The European Union was best known as a supporter for
a single form of **currency**, or money, called the euro. The
euro has now been introduced in some member countries.
The European Union also worked to lower trade barriers
between the member countries.

Why Was There a Nuclear Arms Race?

The Soviet Union and the United States tried to stay in
step with each other. Each superpower feared that the
other would become more powerful.

One measure of power is the buildup of weapons. When
the United States exploded the atomic bomb in 1945, it
made America fearsome and powerful. Other nations
wanted that power, too. In 1949, the Soviet Union
exploded its first atomic bomb. By 1952, Great Britain
also had the atomic secret. Then the United States pulled
ahead again in the race for destructive power. In 1954, the
United States tested a hydrogen bomb. It was thousands of
times more powerful than the atomic bomb that had fallen
on Hiroshima and Nagasaki. Soon Great Britain, France,
and the Soviet Union had hydrogen bombs, too.

Nuclear weapon

A powerful weapon, such as an atomic bomb or missile

Now the People's Republic of China had the bomb. So did India, Israel, and Pakistan. The world had given itself something to fear. As nations struggled to keep pace in the cold war, the stakes became higher. There are now enough **nuclear weapons** in existence to destroy the world many times over.

What Was Life Like in the Soviet Union After World War II?

After World War II, Joseph Stalin worked to rebuild Soviet industry. He set up labor camps, forcing workers to build, build, and build some more. Between 1945 and 1965, Soviet industry boomed. Yet life was not easy for the Russian worker. Stalin had caused shortages of food and clothing with his stress on heavy industry.

After Stalin's death in 1953, there was a struggle for power. Then a new leader, Nikita Khrushchev, rose to the top of the Communist Party.

Khrushchev accused Stalin of the arrests and deaths of many citizens. Khrushchev promised that now the country would be led by the party rather than by a single dictator.

Under Khrushchev, life became better for the people of the Soviet Union. Khrushchev halted some of the activities of the secret police. The government allowed somewhat greater freedom of speech. The workweek was shortened to 40 hours. In addition, Khrushchev tried to raise the standard of living for ordinary people. His economic plan included a greater production of consumer goods. However, progress was slow.

Crisis
A time of danger; a turning point in events

History Fact
Kennedy promised not to invade Cuba. He also said the United States would remove missiles from Turkey.

Where Did Communism Spread?

The Soviet Union helped spread Communism to other parts of the world. China, Mongolia, North Korea, and some nations in Southeast Asia and Africa, turned to Communism. Cuba, only 90 miles from the United States, became a Communist dictatorship under Fidel Castro.

In 1962, the Soviets tried to build missile bases in Cuba. To stop Soviet ships, U.S. President John F. Kennedy set up a blockade around Cuba. The cold war nearly turned hot at that point. The Cuban missile **crisis** brought the world to the edge of another big war. But Khrushchev agreed to take the missiles out of Cuba, and the situation cooled.

In 1963, Khrushchev's farm program fell apart. Russia had to buy a huge quantity of grain from the West. That year Soviet industrialization slowed down. Then Khrushchev came under heavy criticism for the way he had handled the Cuban situation. In 1964, he was forced to retire. Leonid Brezhnev and Alexei Kosygin replaced him as leaders of the Communist Party. Now life became worse for the people of the Soviet Union. Once again, people had to be careful about what they said.

REVIEW

Word Bank

European Union

hydrogen bomb

NATO

superpowers

Warsaw Pact

On a sheet of paper, write the word from the Word Bank to complete each sentence correctly.

1. The United States and the Soviet Union were both _____.

2. _____ began as a defense against Communism.

3. To balance the NATO alliance, the Soviet Union and its Communist satellites formed the _____.

4. While NATO and the Warsaw Pact were military alliances, the _____ was an economic alliance. It is best known for its support of a single currency, the euro.

5. The United States tested the first _____, which was more powerful than the atomic bomb.

On a sheet of paper, write the answer to each question. Use complete sentences.

6. What was the cold war?

7. Why did the cold war begin?

8. What was the Truman Doctrine?

9. Life in the Soviet Union was better under the rule of Nikita Khrushchev. Name three reasons why.

10. What was the Cuban missile crisis?

Changing Relations Between the Soviets and Americans

Objectives

- To explain the SALT agreement
- To describe how the détente between the Soviet Union and the United States ended

Disaster
Something that causes harm or problems

Détente
An easing of tensions between countries

Reading Strategy:
Summarizing

What important idea is being introduced in this section?

Both the United States and the Soviet Union realized that another world war would bring **disaster**. Between the quarrels and the peaks of tension, they met to try to solve their problems. The two countries even set up a "hot line" to prevent the cold war from turning into a "hot" war. The hot line was a telephone line between the leaders of the United States and the Soviet Union.

Soviet and American officials began to talk about more cooperation between their countries. The new relationship was called **détente**. The nations began to share ideas in science and space exploration. Trade relations improved.

U.S. President Richard M. Nixon and Leonid Brezhnev, general secretary of the Soviet Communist Party, signed the SALT agreement on May 26, 1972.

Ratify
To formally approve

History Fact
To protest the Soviet invasion of Afghanistan, the United States did not send its athletes to the Summer Olympics in Moscow in 1980. The USSR boycotted the Olympics in Los Angeles in 1984.

In 1972, the two powers held Strategic Arms Limitation Talks (SALT). They agreed to set some limits on nuclear arms. A second SALT agreement was later proposed. However, SALT II was never **ratified**, or approved, by the U.S. Senate.

What Ended the Détente?

In 1979, the Communists took over the government of Afghanistan. The Muslim people of Afghanistan rebelled. Soviet troops went in to put down the rebellion. The United States and many other nations were angered by the Soviet invasion of Afghanistan.

During the early 1980s, tensions between the United States and the Soviet Union continued to increase. The United States sent more missiles to Europe. Then, in 1983, a Korean Air Lines passenger jet was shot down over Soviet territory. More than 200 people were killed, many of them Americans. The Soviets said the jet was spying. The United States was angry. Détente was over, and Soviet–U.S. relations grew even colder.

TIMELINE STUDY:
CHANGES IN EUROPE: 1940–1990

In what year was a wall built to separate East and West Berlin?

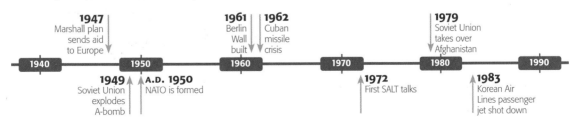

| 1947 Marshall plan sends aid to Europe | 1961 Berlin Wall built | 1962 Cuban missile crisis | 1979 Soviet Union takes over Afghanistan |

1940 — 1950 — 1960 — 1970 — 1980 — 1990

| 1949 Soviet Union explodes A-bomb | A.D. 1950 NATO is formed | 1972 First SALT talks | 1983 Korean Air Lines passenger jet shot down |

On a sheet of paper, write the letter of the answer that correctly completes each sentence.

1. The _____ was an attempt to prevent the cold war from turning into a real war.

   A "hot line"   **B** Warsaw Pact **C** Marshall Plan **D** Truman Doctrine

2. The Soviet and _____ effort to improve relationships between their countries is known as *détente.*

   A German   **B** Muslim   **C** American   **D** Korean

3. Soviets and Americans tried to cooperate by sharing ideas in science and _____.

   A government   **B** capitalism   **C** nuclear arms   **D** space exploration

4. In _____, the Soviet Union and United States held the Strategic Arms Limitation Talks (SALT).

   A 1970   **B** 1972   **C** 1979   **D** 1983

5. In the SALT agreement, the United States and Soviet Union set limits on _____.

   A space exploration **B** nuclear arms **C** Communism **D** trade

6. SALT II was never approved by _____.

   A the United States **B** Korea   **C** Afghanistan **D** the Soviet Union

7. The Communists took over the government of _____ in 1979.

   A the United States **B** Germany   **C** Afghanistan **D** Korea

8. The United States sent more _____ to Europe during the early 1980s.

   A hydrogen bombs **B** soldiers   **C** airplanes   **D** missiles

9. The Soviets shot down a Korean Air Lines passenger jet in _____.

   A 1970   **B** 1972   **C** 1979   **D** 1983

10. The shooting down of the Korean plane ended the _____.

    A SALT agreement **B** détente   **C** Warsaw Pact **D** Cuban missile crisis

- Under the Marshall Plan, the United States gave aid to war-torn Europe.

- The Soviet Union and its Communist satellites refused Marshall Plan aid.

- The Soviet Union gained Communist satellites in Eastern Europe after World War II. The Soviet Union encouraged the spread of Communism throughout the world.

- After World War II, Germany was divided into two parts. West Germany was democratic and East Germany was controlled by Communists.

- The United States and the Soviet Union were allies during World War II. However, after the war a cold war began between the two nations.

- The two superpowers had different ideas about what a country should be. The Communist nations criticized the United States as a capitalist nation.

- The United States began the development of NATO, an alliance of defense against Communism.

- The Soviets formed the Warsaw Pact, an alliance of Communist nations.

- After World War II, a nuclear arms race began. Nations worked to develop powerful new types of weapons.

- The Soviet Union helped spread Communism to many different parts of the world.

- The two superpowers held peace talks to try to limit the buildup of nuclear arms.

CHAPTER 29
REVIEW

Word Bank

capitalist

cold war

crisis

currency

détente

disaster

isolationism

nuclear weapon

ratify

satellite

Vocabulary Review

On a sheet of paper, use the words from the Word Bank to correctly match each definition below.

1. To officially approve

2. Running business and industry for profit

3. The relaxing of tensions between countries

4. The idea of staying out of international affairs

5. A country that is controlled by a more powerful country

6. The form of money a country uses

7. The war of ideas between the United States and the Soviet Union

8. Something that causes harm or problems

9. A dangerous time; a turning point in events

10. A powerful weapon, like a missile

Chapter Review Questions

On a sheet of paper, write the answer to each question. Use complete sentences.

11. What did the Marshall Plan promise?

12. How did the Communists decide to keep people from leaving East Berlin?

13. What nations were the superpowers after World War II?

14. What U.S. plan promised aid to any country fighting Communism?

15. What is NATO?

16. What were the SALT treaties?

Critical Thinking

On a sheet of paper, write your response to each question. Use complete sentences.

17. Why do you think progress was slow when Khrushchev tried to improve the standard of living in the Soviet Union?

18. Suppose you lived in 1962. How do you think you would feel about the Cuban missile crisis?

Using the Timeline

Use the timeline on page 617 to answer the questions.

19. In what year was NATO formed?

20. In what year did the Soviets invade Afghanistan?

GROUP ACTIVITY

Form a group of three or four. Discuss whether you think the Olympics should be canceled or boycotted for political reasons. Write up your conclusion to share with the rest of the class.

Changes in Asia and Africa

The years after World War II brought huge changes to many countries of Africa and Asia. Some countries were forming new governments after winning their independence from large European powers. Some faced major upsets as different political groups struggled to gain control from within. Civil wars brought violence and ruin to many countries. Many people faced starvation and homelessness. Western nations such as the United States worked to fight the spread of Communism.

GOALS FOR LEARNING

- To describe India's problems of civil war, religious differences, and widespread poverty
- To describe China and Korea under Communist rule
- To explain why Korea is split into two parts
- To explain Japan and Southeast Asia after World War II
- To describe the conflict in Vietnam
- To understand Africa's progress after World War II

Reading Strategy: Questioning

Questioning what you are reading helps you understand and remember more information. It also makes you a more active reader. When reading this chapter, ask yourself:

• Why am I reading this text?

• What key points can be drawn from this text?

• How can I connect this text to my life experiences?

Key Vocabulary Words

Lesson 1
Security Safety

Violence Great physical force; actions that hurt others

Lesson 2
Corrupt Dishonest, evil, selfish

Commune A group of people working or living closely together, often sharing property and tasks

Lesson 4
Pollution Waste materials in the air or water

Invest To put money into something with the hope of making more money

Lesson 5
Guerilla One of a group of fighters who are not part of a regular army, and who usually make surprise raids behind enemy lines

Domino theory The belief that if one country became Communist, neighbors would fall to Communism too

Refugee A person who flees his or her country or home

Lesson 6
Starvation The condition of dying from not having enough food to eat

Famine A time when crops do not grow and there is no food

Minority Less than half

Sanction An action taken by one nation against another for breaking international law

Majority More than half

Apartheid The separation of races based mainly on skin color

Curfew A time after which certain people cannot be on the streets

Repeal To cancel; put an end to

Standard of living A way to judge how well a person or family is living

India

Objectives

■ To describe the fighting between the Hindus and Sikhs over Punjab

■ To explain the steps the Indian government has taken to end poverty

Reading Strategy: Questioning

What do you think you will learn about by reading this lesson?

Security
Safety

Violence
Great physical force; actions that hurt others

History Fact
With its population of about 1 billion, India is the world's largest democracy.

In Chapter 23, you read about India winning its independence from Britain in 1947. At that time, Indian leaders agreed to divide India into two separate nations, India and Pakistan. India fell under the control of the Hindus. The Muslims controlled Pakistan. Furthermore, Pakistan was divided into East and West Pakistan.

India held its first general election in 1951. Jawaharlal Nehru was elected as the first prime minister of the Republic of India. Nehru led India until he died in 1964. In 1966, his daughter, Indira Gandhi, was elected prime minister.

Why Did the Hindus and Sikhs Fight?

There were food shortages and labor strikes in India during Mrs. Gandhi's years as leader. For a time she lost her position. But she returned to power in 1980. In 1984, Indira Gandhi was assassinated by members of her own **security,** or safety, force. The assassins were members of the Sikh religion. Sikh rebels were seeking a separate state in Punjab, their region of India. After Gandhi's assassination, her son Rajiv became prime minister. Rajiv resigned (gave up his job) in 1989.

The late 1980s and early 1990s brought **violence,** or fighting, to several parts of India. A decision to bring the state of Punjab under control of the central government led to fighting between Hindus and Sikhs. Muslim and Hindu Indians clashed over possession of a holy temple. In 1991, Rajiv Gandhi made another bid for the office of prime minister. He was assassinated during that election campaign.

Reading Strategy:
Questioning

As you read, notice the details in the text. What questions can you ask yourself about these details?

How Was Bangladesh Formed?

Over the years, India has had border disputes with its neighbors. This led to fighting between India and China in 1959 and in 1962. In 1965, India and Pakistan fought a three-week-long war. Both countries claimed the same land, called Kashmir, in northern India.

In 1971, civil war broke out in Pakistan. The people of East Pakistan complained because the center of government was based in West Pakistan. The war led to East Pakistan becoming a separate nation called Bangladesh. In 1998, India and Pakistan continued their fighting. Both nations tested nuclear weapons to prove they could launch a nuclear attack on each other.

How Is India Working to End Poverty?

India has always had to deal with poverty and food shortages. The country has a huge population. It must struggle to provide enough food for all its people. Even though India is a major producer of farm products, there is never enough food to go around. It is said that almost two-thirds of India's people go to bed hungry every night.

The government has tried to teach farmers new methods to increase production. They have allowed Western businesses to come in and build chemical factories. There was hope that the chemicals would increase crops. In general, India benefited from the chemicals. However, in 1984, an accident at one U.S. chemical plant caused the worst industrial disaster in history. There was an explosion at a factory in Bhopal, India. A cloud of highly toxic (deadly) gas spread into the heavily populated area around the plant. Several thousand people who breathed the poisonous fumes died horrible deaths.

Poverty and food shortages affect many people in India.

You Decide

Millions of poor people live on the streets of India's cities. How do you think rich countries can help homeless people?

India is trying to end its poverty with programs for economic growth. Indian leaders try to build industry. They want to make better use of their country's resources, such as coal and iron ore. And India spends billions of dollars building dams to provide power.

Age-old customs contribute to the food shortages. While India has tried to industrialize, some of its people still hold on to old ideas. In 1950, the government tried to improve life by outlawing the "untouchable" category in the Hindu caste system. Until then, people called *untouchables* had been forced to live in the dirtiest, poorest parts of villages. Their children were not allowed to go into schools. They had to sit on the steps outside and listen. When untouchables walked through village streets, they were supposed to brush away their footsteps with a broom. India has had to move beyond some old ideas to make life better for its people. In 1997, India's first lowest caste president, K. R. Narayan, took office.

REVIEW

Word Bank

Bangladesh

coal

disaster

Kashmir

population

Sikh

Western

On a sheet of paper, write the word from the Word Bank to complete each sentence correctly.

1. The people that assassinated Indira Gandhi were members of the _____ religion.

2. India and Pakistan both claimed the same land, called _____, in northern India.

3. A civil war led to East Pakistan becoming a separate nation called _____.

4. India has food shortages and poverty because of its large _____.

5. India's government has allowed _____ businesses to build factories to help increase production.

6. In 1984, an accident at a U.S. chemical plant caused the worst industrial _____ in history.

7. India is trying to make use of their natural resources, such as _____ and iron ore.

On a sheet of paper, write the answer to each question. Use complete sentences.

8. Why did a civil war break out in Pakistan in 1971?

9. What has India's government done to deal with poverty?

10. Before 1950, what was life like for the "untouchables"?

China

In the years after World War II, a power struggle was going on in China between two political parties. They were the Nationalists and the Communists.

Who Won the Battle for Power in China?

Back in 1928, Chiang Kai-shek and his Nationalist Party had come to power. Some members of the Nationalist Party believed in Communism. The Communists felt that Chiang showed favor to rich landowners and businesspeople. So the Communists broke away from the Nationalists. In 1927, they took over the city of Shanghai.

Mao Zedong set up a Communist government in mainland China.

Chiang expelled (removed) the Communists from the Nationalist Party. A struggle began between Chinese Nationalists and Chinese Communists. Stalin and the Soviet Union supported the Communists. Stalin encouraged them to win the support of China's factory workers.

However, China's strength did not lie in the city workers. It lay in the farm peasants. A man named Mao Zedong, who had been born a peasant, turned to the peasants for support.

Corrupt
Dishonest, evil, selfish

During World War II, the Communists helped defend the peasants of northern China against the Japanese. Mao and the Communists won the peasants' loyalty.

After the war, the Communists and Nationalists continued their struggle for China. There were four years of civil war. The Nationalists had better supplies and a larger army. However, they no longer had the support of the people. Many Nationalist leaders were dishonest, or **corrupt.** They wanted to become rich themselves while the Chinese people went hungry. The Communists divided land and food fairly among the people. In this way, they received the peasants' support.

By 1948, the war had turned in favor of the Communists. Chiang Kai-shek and the Nationalists decided it was time to get out. They left mainland China to live in Taiwan. In 1949, mainland China was taken over by Mao Zedong and the Communists. They called their nation the People's Republic of China.

The Soviet Union was quick to recognize the new government. So were many other nations. Yet the United States refused to recognize the Communist government.

You Decide
Why do you think it took so long for the United States to recognize the People's Republic of China?

The United States recognized the Nationalist government in Taiwan and supported it. Taiwan, calling itself the Republic of China, kept China's seat in the United Nations. In 1971, mainland China replaced Taiwan in the United Nations. In 1972, U.S. president Richard Nixon made an eight-day visit to the People's Republic. In 1979, the United States recognized the People's Republic of China, or mainland China, as the only legal government in China. However, the United States continued many unofficial contacts with Taiwan.

Commune

A group of people working or living closely together, often sharing property and tasks

What Was Life Like Under Communist Rule?

More than one-fifth of the population of the world lives in China! Producing enough food to feed more than 1.25 billion people is no simple matter. The Communists knew they had to solve that problem. They took land away from rich farmers. They set up huge farm **communes.** A commune is a group of people working closely together, often sharing property and tasks. The peasants had to work on these communes. Sometimes as many as 10,000 people worked on a single commune. In addition, the government took over industries, built new factories, and trained workers.

The Communists insisted on the support and loyalty of all the people. Workers had to attend meetings where they read aloud from Mao Zedong's writings. They talked about how Mao's ideas could make them better citizens of a better China.

What Was the Cultural Revolution?

Mao and the Communists worried that people might prefer the Old China to the New China. They held meetings to teach people to think the Communist way. Enemies of Communism were punished. They were brainwashed, or forced to accept the Communist way of thought.

For a while, Mao's harsh policies worked. However, China's economy declined for a time. From 1965 to 1969, Mao called his policies a "Cultural Revolution." The Cultural Revolution was supposed to build loyalty for the Communists. Young students, called "Red Guards," became soldiers for Communism. They helped Mao carry out his policies.

Farm production fell. China closed its doors to visitors from the rest of the world. The Chinese leaders wanted to make sure that no anti-Communist ideas could filter in.

Red Guards helped Mao carry out his Communist policies.

After Mao's death in 1976, trade relations between China and the rest of the world improved. Under Deng Xiaoping and other leaders, China went through a period of modernization. In other words, they worked to make China more up-to-date and modern.

Deng was willing to give the Chinese more economic freedom. However, he was not willing to grant political freedom. In the spring of 1989, hundreds of thousands of students gathered in Tiananmen Square in Beijing to demand more democracy. The demonstration was crushed by the army, as tanks rolled through the square. Since then, China and the West have disagreed over China's treatment of protesters and others in the country. China had a fast-growing economy in the 1990s. China has allowed people to own businesses and trade with the West. In 2000, the U.S. Congress voted to give China permanent normal trade relations. Many people in the United States still worried about the lack of freedom and human rights in China.

Reading Strategy:
Questioning

What details are
important to
understanding what this
lesson is about?

GREAT NAMES IN HISTORY

Aung San Suu Kyi

Since 1988, Aung San Suu Kyi has led the fight for democracy in
Myanmar (Burma). Leadership seems to run in her family. Her father,
Aung San, is called the father of independent Burma.

In 1988, Myanmans protested against military rule. As a result, troops
shot or arrested thousands. Aung San spoke out for human rights.
She helped the National League for Democracy win 80 percent of
the seats in Parliament. The rulers ignored the results and held her
prisoner in her own home for six years. In 1991, she won the Nobel
Peace Prize. However, the generals still limit her freedom to speak
and travel.

How Did Hong Kong Come Under Chinese Rule?

China had to give Hong Kong to Britain in 1842. This was
a part of the treaty that ended the Opium War. Britain got
the mainland peninsula of Kowloon, a mainland region
called the New Territories, and 230 small islands in the
South China Sea. These areas became known as Hong
Kong. Hong Kong lies off the southeastern coast of China.

After the Communist revolution in China, the population
of Hong Kong grew rapidly. This is because people fled
there from China. It became an important manufacturing
and business center.

China and Britain signed an agreement in 1984. In it,
Britain agreed to give up control of Hong Kong in 1997.
The agreement stated that Hong Kong would become a
protected region. It would also remain a free port. Britain
returned Hong Kong to China on July 1, 1997.

REVIEW

Word Bank

commune

democracy

Hong Kong

Nationalists

peasants

population

United States

On a sheet of paper, write the word from the Word Bank to complete each sentence correctly.

1. The political parties that struggled for power after World War II were the _____ and the Communists.

2. The Communists gained strength with loyalty to the _____.

3. In 1949, the _____ did not recognize the Communist government in mainland China.

4. More than one-fifth of the world's _____ lives in China.

5. As many as 10,000 peasants worked at a single _____ to help feed its population.

6. In 1989, hundreds of thousands of students gathered in Tiananmen Square to demand more _____.

7. The area that lies off the southeastern coast of China is called _____.

On a sheet of paper, write the answer to each question. Use complete sentences.

8. What did the Communists do to gain the support and loyalty of their people?

9. Why did Mao Zedong create the "Red Guards"?

10. Why did China have to give Hong Kong to Britain in 1842?

Korea

Reading Strategy: Questioning

What do the details of Korea's past tell you about what happened there?

Korea, with its northern border on China, became a hot spot in the world in 1950. Korea had been controlled by the Japanese from 1910 to 1945. In 1945, the country was divided into two parts. North Korea had the support of Soviet Communists. South Korea had American support.

How Did Korea Become Divided Into Two Parts?

In 1950, North Korea suddenly attacked South Korea. The Communists threatened to take over the whole country.

South Korea turned to the United Nations for help. A UN army made up mostly of U.S. soldiers came to South Korea's aid. The UN troops and South Koreans pushed the Communists back, almost to the Chinese border. The Chinese sent 780,000 soldiers to help North Korea.

The U.S.-South Korean troops fought the Chinese-North Korean troops for three years. In 1953, a truce was finally declared. The division between North and South Korea remained. Today the United States supports efforts to reunify Korea. In 2000, North Korea and South Korea held a conference. Later, some family members who had been separated held reunions in the capitals of South Korea and North Korea.

Why Did North Korea Build Up Its Supply of Nuclear Weapons?

For many years, North Korean authorities insisted that the country needed its own nuclear weapons. Otherwise it would have no way to prevent or discourage other nations from attacking it.

It began building a supply of plutonium, a material used in making nuclear weapons. Then in 2002, North Korea forced UN inspectors looking for weapons out of the country. Leaders from five other nations began meeting with North Korea. They hoped to limit the country's production of nuclear weapons. In 2006, North Korea conducted its first nuclear missile test in eight years.

In February 2007, North Korea signed a deal with the United States and four other nations. It agreed to shut down its main nuclear facility, or factory, within 60 days. The other nations, in return, would send a total of $400 million in economic aid, beginning with fuel oil. This aid would help after severe floods in the late 1990s. The floods had left many North Koreans homeless and hungry. However, world nations became concerned almost immediately. North Korean authorities said the facility was being shut down "temporarily"—or for a short time.

North Korea's test of nuclear weapons drew much protest around the world. Here, protesters from South Korea rally against North Korea's 2006 nuclear missile test.

REVIEW

On a sheet of paper, write the letter of the answer that correctly completes each sentence.

1. Korea was controlled by the _____ from 1910 to 1945.

    A French **B** Japanese **C** Chinese **D** English

2. In 1950, North Korea suddenly attacked _____.

    A South Korea **B** Britain **C** Japan **D** China

3. The United Nations created an army made up of _____ soldiers.

    A Japanese **B** British **C** U.S. **D** Vietnamese

4. The fighting in Korea lasted _____ years.

    A 30 **B** eight **C** four **D** three

5. North Korean authorities insisted that the country needed _____.

    A nuclear weapons **C** stronger schools
    B economic growth **D** more laws

6. Five nations sent aid to North Korea in the late 1990s. It was to help North Korea recover after severe _____.

    A drought **B** floods **C** crime **D** poverty

On a sheet of paper, write the answer to each question. Use complete sentences.

7. How did South Korea defend itself against North Korea?

8. Who helped North Korea in trying to defeat South Korea?

9. Why was North Korea building up a supply of plutonium?

10. In 2007, North Korea signed a deal to shut down their main nuclear facility. Why were some nations concerned about the agreement?

Japan and Southeast Asia

Reading Strategy: Questioning

As you read, notice the details about Japan and Southeast Asia. What new questions can you ask yourself about this section?

 You Decide
Japan is now one of the richest countries in the world. Why do you think Japan became a great industrialized country after its defeat in World War II?

The explosion of the atomic bomb left Japan in shock. Japan surrendered, and World War II was over. Then the Allied forces occupied Japan. U.S. general Douglas MacArthur was the supreme commander. His job was to build a democracy in Japan.

A new democratic constitution, written in 1946, gave power to an elected prime minister. It also gave women the right to vote. Japan would be allowed to keep its emperor, but he would have no power. In 1951, the government was put back into the hands of the Japanese. The Allied occupation had ended.

The new Japanese constitution stated that Japan would not maintain a strong military. As a result, the Japanese turned from a policy of war to one of industrial and economic growth.

What Southeast Asian Countries Gained Independence from Japan?

Japan took over much of Southeast Asia during World War II. Before the war all of the area, except Thailand, was colonized by European nations. After the war, anticolonial feelings were strong. The nations of Southeast Asia wanted to be free.

Some countries gained independence easily. Others had to struggle. When nations such as the Philippines, Burma (now Myanmar), Indonesia, Malaysia, and Singapore became independent, they all faced problems. In many of them, there were bitter civil wars.

What Is Japan's Role in the World Economic Community?

Today Japan has become a world leader in industry. Japan is one of the world's largest steel producers. It is the second largest manufacturer, or maker, of automobiles and **electronics** equipment. It is also a leading shipbuilder. This is quite an achievement since Japan has few natural resources of its own. The country's industrial success depends on trade, the import of raw materials, and the export of finished products.

Japan is a small, crowded country. There is little room to grow food. Again, Japan depends on imports, bringing in at least 30 percent of its food. Japan has also had to deal with problems caused by overcrowding, such as lack of housing. Another problem Japan faces is **pollution,** which is when waste materials get into the air and water. Despite these problems, Japan has made amazing progress.

Japan's economic success brought negative remarks from other nations. The Japanese were able to **invest** heavily in industry because of their very low defense budget.

Japan, a small, crowded country, faces pollution and lack of housing.

During the 1980s, some countries began to complain that the competition from Japanese exports was hurting their own industry. They also said that Japan was discouraging the import of foreign products. In 1981, Japan agreed to limit its exports of automobiles to Canada, the United States, and West Germany. It also began to remove some restrictions, or limits, on imports. In 1990, Japan and the United States signed a trade agreement. This made it easier for foreign companies to do business in Japan. By the late 1990s, Japan, like other world powers over the years, had trade and economic difficulties.

Word Bank

atomic bomb

automobiles

democracy

free

imports

industry

invest

On a sheet of paper, write the word from the Word Bank to complete each sentence correctly.

1. The explosion of the _____ left Japan in shock.

2. Douglas MacArthur's job after the war was to build a(n) _____ in Japan.

3. Japan is now a world leader in _____.

4. Japan is the second largest maker of _____ and electronics equipment in the world.

5. Japan is a small, crowded country with few natural resources. Thus, it relies heavily on _____.

6. The Japanese have been able to _____ a lot in industry. This is because they spend very little on national defense.

7. After World War II, the other Southeast Asian countries wanted to be _____ from Japan.

On a sheet of paper, write the answer to each question. Use complete sentences.

8. What new laws did the Japanese constitution include?

9. What are some problems that Japan faces?

10. Why did Japan agree (in 1981) to limit its exports to Canada, the United States, and West Germany?

Vietnam

Objectives

- To describe how Vietnam was divided
- To explain U.S. involvement in Vietnam and why so many Americans were against it
- To explain why there were so many refugees after the capital of South Vietnam fell

Reading Strategy: Questioning

What do you already know about Vietnam?

In the 1800s, France took over an area of Southeast Asia called Indochina. Indochina was made up of the countries of Vietnam, Laos, and Cambodia. During World War II, Japan took Southeast Asia from the French. Then France regained Southeast Asia after the war.

How Was Vietnam Divided?

Southeast Asia was not anxious to return to French rule. Nationalists and Communists had gained some support there. In 1946, the fighting began. The Vietnamese Communists wanted to force the French out of Vietnam. The French set up a government in the South. The Communists, under their leader, Ho Chi Minh, set up a government in the North. The Communists defeated the French in 1954.

Then a conference was held in Geneva, Switzerland, to decide what would happen next. Vietnamese Communists and representatives from France, Cambodia, Laos, China, Britain, the United States, and the Soviet Union all came to that conference. They made their decision. Vietnam was divided into two zones. Ho Chi Minh and the Communists would continue to rule the North. South Vietnam was supposed to hold an election to choose its own form of government.

But a free election never took place. Ngo Dinh Diem took leadership and refused to hold elections. Meanwhile, North Vietnam grew stronger with the support of Communist China and the Soviet Union. The political situation in South Vietnam remained unsettled.

Guerilla
One of a group of fighters who are not part of a regular army, and who usually make surprise raids behind enemy lines

Domino theory
The belief that if one country became Communist, neighbors would fall to Communism too

The Vietcong, Communist **guerilla** fighters, began an attempt to take over South Vietnam in 1957. Guerillas are a group of fighters who are not part of a regular army. In 1963, South Vietnam's leader, Diem, was assassinated. The country's problems increased. The government changed hands nine times in three years.

Why Did the United States Get Involved?

The Soviet Union and China continued to give aid to North Vietnam. In the 1960s, the U.S. government sent aid to South Vietnam because it believed in the **domino theory.** If dominoes are stood in a line together, the fall of one domino will knock down the others. The domino theory was the idea that if one country became Communist, neighbors would fall to the Communists, too.

At first, the United States sent money and supplies. Then in 1965, U.S. President Lyndon B. Johnson sent more than 3,500 U.S. marines to Da Nang, South Vietnam. They were the first United States combat troops to join the fight. Thousands more would follow. By 1969, there were more than 543,000 U.S. troops in Vietnam.

Why Were So Many Americans Against U.S. Involvement in Vietnam?

Many Americans did not want the United States to get into the war in Southeast Asia. When American soldiers began dying in Vietnamese jungles, the protests grew stronger. Hundreds of thousands of people marched against the war, in cities all across America. "Bring home our troops!" they shouted.

However, the war went on. More and more Americans were killed or wounded. The Vietcong remained strong. There did not seem to be any end in sight.

You Decide

Antiwar protesters felt that the war in Vietnam was a matter that should be fought and decided by the Vietnamese themselves. Do you think they were right to protest against the war? Why or why not?

By the end of the decade, the United States was a nation in turmoil, or unrest. The growing antiwar movement had helped to touch off a general youth protest movement. The middle-class youth of America were questioning and protesting against all the values of their parents.

Also during the 1960s, there had been a series of assassinations that had shocked the nation. President John F. Kennedy, in 1963, and his brother Robert F. Kennedy, in 1968, had been shot to death. So had African American leaders Malcolm X, in 1965, and Martin Luther King, Jr., in 1968. This was the last straw for many African Americans. They were becoming angry and frustrated at not being able to share in the success of white America. Now feeling that they had nothing to lose, they took their cause to the streets. Rioting occurred in many U.S. cities.

In 1973, the United States decided to take its troops out of Vietnam. About 58,000 Americans had been killed, and about 365,000 had been wounded. And the war had not been won.

How Did People Escape Communist Rule?

In 1975, Saigon, the capital of South Vietnam, fell to the Vietcong. The name of the city was changed to Ho Chi Minh City. Vietnam was united as a Communist country in 1976. Then the "dominoes" fell. Communists took power in Laos and Cambodia.

History Fact

As the Communists closed in on Saigon, the remaining Americans were forced to flee the city.

The Communist rulers of Cambodia, called the *Khmer Rouge,* murdered millions of Cambodians. The situation in Cambodia became very unstable. In 1978, Vietnam invaded Cambodia. For the next 10 years, Vietnam had control of the country. In 1989, Vietnam withdrew from Cambodia, giving in to pressure from the Soviet Union. The Khmer Rouge lost its power. National elections were held in 1998.

Refugee

A person who flees his or her country or home

Many people in Vietnam, Laos, and Cambodia did not want to live under Communist rule. They fled their homelands. These people, called **refugees,** escaped by boat. They became known as "boat people"—people who no longer had a home. A large number came to the United States. Some died making their escapes. All suffered hardships along their way. Today many boat people have made successful lives in the United States.

Vietnamese refugees wanted freedom from Communism.

What Is Vietnam Like Today?

The Communist government of Vietnam continued through aid from the party's Central Committee. When the Soviet Union ended, much of that aid stopped. The government had to accept the development of private business to help the failing economy. The Vietnamese tried to encourage foreign investment in the country. The United States insisted on an updated account of American soldiers imprisoned or missing in Vietnam.

The Vietnamese gave in. In 1995, American firms began operating in Vietnam. Many Western nations opened factories and businesses in Vietnam, beginning in the late 1990s. The United States signed a long-term trade agreement with Vietnam. The Communist government wants to remain in control even though it allows private business in its country. In June 2005, Phan Van Khai was the first Vietnamese leader to visit the American White House.

On a sheet of paper, write the letter of the answer that correctly completes each sentence.

1. In 1946, the Vietnamese wanted to force the _____ out of Vietnam.

   A United States   **B** French   **C** Japanese   **D** Chinese

2. After the conference in Geneva, Vietnam was divided into _____ zones.

   A six   **B** four   **C** three   **D** two

3. North Vietnam grew stronger with support from Communist China and _____

   A Japan   **B** the United States   **C** the Soviet Union   **D** Africa

4. In the 1960s, the U.S. government sent aid to South Vietnam. This is because it believed in _____.

   A building leadership   **C** helping the poor
   B the domino theory   **D** expanding borders

5. By 1969, there were more than _____ U.S. troops in Vietnam.

   A 543,000   **B** 780,000   **C** 220,000   **D** 43,000

6. The United States decided to take its troops out of Vietnam in _____.

   A 1969   **B** 1972   **C** 1973   **D** 1978

7. To help the failing economy, Vietnam's Communist government had to accept the development of _____.

   A communes   **C** natural resources
   B a stronger military   **D** private business

On a sheet of paper, write the answer to each question. Use complete sentences.

8. Why did a free election never take place in South Vietnam?

9. How did Americans protest the war in Vietnam?

10. Why did the United States think South Vietnam would fall to Communism?

Africa

- To describe the development of former colonies in Africa after World War II
- To explain the effects of apartheid inside South Africa
- To name three problems Africa faces today

Reading Strategy:
Questioning

Think about the purpose of this text. Ask yourself what you hope to learn by reading this lesson.

During the 19th century, Africa had been divided into European-ruled colonies. In 1945, at the end of World War II, most of Africa remained under European rule. Only the countries of South Africa, Ethiopia, Liberia, and Egypt were not. Many Africans had joined the armies of their European colonizers during the war. When they returned to Africa, they wanted independence.

How Did the African Colonies Gain Freedom?

The years after 1945 saw European colonies in Africa gain freedom, one by one. Some won their independence peacefully. For other nations, such as Algeria, freedom came only through struggle and revolt.

Several colonies ruled by the British gained independence during the 1950s. Sudan, the largest nation in Africa, won freedom from Britain in 1956. Some of the free nations changed their names. When the Gold Coast won its freedom in 1957, it became Ghana.

Kenya was an African nation that had to struggle for independence from Britain. A rebellion by a group known as the *Mau Mau* lasted from 1952 until 1956. Jomo Kenyatta was their leader. He was thrown in jail in 1953. Britain granted independence to Kenya in 1963. Kenyatta became the leader of the new, free nation. In the 1990s, Kenya suffered unemployment and conflict within the country. In 1998, the U.S. embassy in Nairobi was bombed.

Starvation

The condition of dying from not having enough food to eat

Famine

A time when crops do not grow and there is no food

Drought

A long period of time without much rain

Minority

A smaller number, less than half

Sanction

An action taken by one nation against another for breaking international law

---

 History Fact

In April 2000, Ethiopia's president Robert Mugabe introduced a new way to divide land. Violence against white farmers resulted. White people hold 70 percent of the land in Ethiopia, although they make up only 1 percent of the population.

What Problems Did Freedom Bring?

Freedom did not always mean an end to problems and unrest. The new nations had troubles of their own. In 1967, the eastern part of Nigeria separated and became a country called Biafra. This led to civil war. With the war came **starvation** (dying because of a shortage of food), disease, and death. Biafra was defeated by the Nigerian government in 1970. As a separate country, Biafra no longer existed.

Problems plagued Uganda when General Idi Amin took over the independent government in 1971. Amin arrested and executed anyone he thought was against him. Finally, the people revolted. In 1979, they forced Amin from power. Civil wars and military conflict have also taken place in Angola, Ethiopia, Rwanda, Sudan, and other countries. In Ethiopia, this conflict contributed to a **famine** that killed about one million people in the 1980s. Famine is a time when crops do not grow and there is no food. Again, in 2000, Ethiopia was threatened with famine after a three-year **drought**. A drought is a long period of time without rain.

How Was Zimbabwe Formed?

Independence did not bring an end to racial prejudice in some new African nations. Sometimes those nations had more problems with the new governments than with the European rulers. When Rhodesia gained independence from Britain in 1965, black Africans had no voice in government. Even though they were smaller in number, a white **minority** ruled for 15 years.

Britain wanted black Rhodesians to have rights. However, the new white rulers said no. Britain asked the United Nations to place **sanctions** on Rhodesia. A sanction is an action taken by one nation against another for breaking international law. Because of this request for a sanction, black revolutionaries began a guerilla war.

Majority
A greater number, more than half

Apartheid
The separation of races based mainly on skin color

Curfew
A time after which certain people cannot be on the streets

In 1980, Rhodesia's first black **majority** government finally came to power through a general election. (It was a majority government because there was a greater number of blacks in Rhodesia.) The new government officially changed the nation's name. Rhodesia became Zimbabwe, an ancient African name for that part of the continent.

What Effects Did Apartheid Have on South Africa?

Of all the independent countries in Africa, South Africa was ruled by a white minority for the longest period of time. It was ruled by *Afrikaners* for many years. They were descendants of Dutch colonists who began settling in South Africa as early as 1652. The Afrikaners believe that the country belongs to them. They helped win South Africa's independence from Britain in 1910.

The Afrikaners wanted to keep white people in control. So in 1948, they set up a policy of **apartheid,** or separation of races. They passed laws to separate people according to race. By law, people of certain races can live, own property, or run businesses only in certain zones.

Curfews determined the time black people had to be off the streets of South Africa. Separate trains, beaches, schools, and other facilities were provided for blacks and whites. Laws did nothing to stop whites from getting the best facilities and blacks the worst.

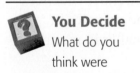

You Decide
What do you think were the worst aspects of apartheid?

Many people in South Africa and around the world were strongly against apartheid. However, many South Africans who protested were arrested, and apartheid continued.

During the 1980s, the United States and other countries placed sanctions on South Africa. The white South African government now came under growing pressure to do something about ending apartheid.

In 1990, South African president F.W. de Klerk decided to "unban" the African National Congress (ANC).

Signs such as this were common in South Africa during apartheid.

Repeal

To cancel; put an end to

This meant that the ANC, a black anti-apartheid political party, would now be legal. De Klerk also released the jailed leader of the ANC, Nelson Mandela. Both leaders began working together on a difficult task. They had to find a way to end apartheid that would be acceptable to both blacks and whites.

In 1990 and 1991, the South African government **repealed,** or ended, its apartheid laws. No longer was separation of hotels, restaurants, and public places required by law. No longer could laws determine where a person could live. Nelson Mandela, as well as other anti-apartheid leaders, looked forward to the day when the black majority would be heard in government. A constitution giving nonwhites full voting rights was completed in 1994. After the repeal of the apartheid laws, countries around the world lifted most of their sanctions against South Africa.

African Nations Become Independent

Year of Independence

Algeria	1962
Angola	1975
Benin	1960
Botswana	1966
Burkina Faso	1960
Burundi	1962
Cameroon	1960
Central African Republic	1960
Chad	1960
Comoros	1975
Congo	1960
Côte D'Ivoire	1960
Djibouti	1977
Egypt	1922
Equatorial Guinea	1968
Eritrea	1993
Ethiopia	1941
Gabon	1960
Ghana	1957
Guinea	1958
Guinea-Bissau	1974
Kenya	1963
Lesotho	1966
Liberia	1847
Libya	1951
Madagascar	1960
Malawi	1964
Mali	1960
Mauritania	1960
Morocco	1956
Mozambique	1975
Namibia	1990
Niger	1960
Nigeria	1960
Rep. of Congo	1960
Rwanda	1962
São Tomé & Principe	1975
Senegal	1960
Sierra Leone	1961
Somalia	1960
South Africa	1910
Sudan	1956
Swaziland	1968
Tanzania	1961
The Gambia	1965
Togo	1960
Tunisia	1956
Uganda	1962
Zambia	1964
Zimbabwe	1980

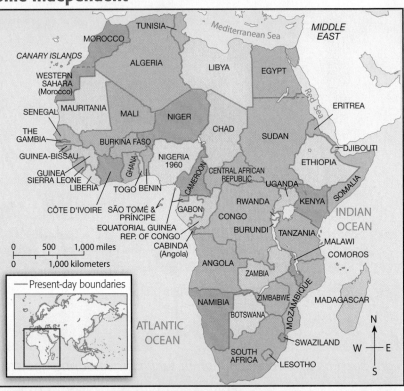

MAP STUDY

1. What are two countries that became independent in 1960?

2. What are two countries that became independent in 1962?

Change does not often come easily. There were many South Africans who resisted the end of apartheid. However, change did come. A new constitution protected the rights of all South Africans. In 1994, Nelson Mandela became the president of South Africa. He served until 1999, when he chose not to run for reelection.

South Africans celebrate the end of apartheid together.

Reading Strategy:
Questioning

Think again about the purpose of the text. Ask yourself, "Am I learning what I expected to learn when I began reading?"

There have been other political changes in South Africa, but they often came slowly. A conflict dating back to 1915 came to an end. In that year, South Africa took its neighbor, Namibia, away from Germany. For the next 75 years, South Africa ruled Namibia. The United Nations declared South Africa's rule of Namibia to be illegal. Black nationalists fought to rule their own country. In 1990, Namibia became independent.

Why Were So Many People Killed in Sudan?

Sudan is a large African country south of Egypt. Most of its people are native black Sudanese. For years the country has been controlled by the Arabic National Islamic Front. In 2003, native rebel groups began attacking government targets in Darfur, a western area of Sudan. They were protesting treatment by the government. The Janjaweed is a military group sponsored by the government. This group began attacking rebels as well as innocent civilians. More than 200,000 Sudanese were killed and more than two million were left homeless. Thousands of women and girls were sexually assaulted. Many have been taken as slaves by Janjaweed fighters.

Many Sudanese fled to neighboring Chad, and that country was drawn into the fighting. Raids by Janjaweed into Chad have left many thousands of people from Chad homeless too.

Government representatives promised to give native Sudanese a greater representation in the government. United Nations and African Union groups have made unsuccessful attempts to bring peace to Sudan. Even into 2007, more than 14,000 aid workers from UN organizations fear for their lives as the fighting around them continues.

What Is Africa Like Today?

At one time, Africa was mistakenly called the "Dark Continent." To outsiders, it was an unexplored land of mystery. Later, it became a land to be owned, and it was divided up among strong European countries. Then World War II ended the days of European-ruled colonies in Africa. The new nations of Africa, however, continue to face serious problems such as poverty, disease, and food shortages. Many areas lack schools, hospitals, and medical equipment.

Severe droughts have added to Africa's food shortages. During the 1980s, many Africans starved to death in the worst drought in the continent's history. The death toll was especially high in Ethiopia.

In recent years, drought and civil war left over one million Africans starving in the tiny nation of Somalia. Since 1960, various Somali warlords had battled for control of parts of the country. Their armies blocked attempts to get food to starving people. In December 1992, the United States and the UN approved a plan to aid the Somalis. U.S. troops led an international force to Somalia. Soon after, UN forces left because of the fighting.

Standard of living

A way to judge how well a person or family is living

After continued violence and food shortages in Somalia, a peace agreement was signed in January 2004. In August of that same year, Somalia got its first legislature in 13 years. Despite the new parliament, the unrest continues.

Africa is the second largest continent on Earth. It has been slow to develop. Today, however, free African nations are growing stronger. More Africans are attending school. They are developing the skills needed to improve their **standard of living.** African nations are learning to work together. The Organization of African Unity (OAU) is an association of African nations that tries to find peaceful solutions to quarrels between African countries. They hope that unity will lead to economic and political progress. As the nations grow stronger, Africa takes a place of greater importance in the world.

TIMELINE STUDY:

ASIA AND AFRICA: 1945–2010

When did the United States first pull out of Vietnam?

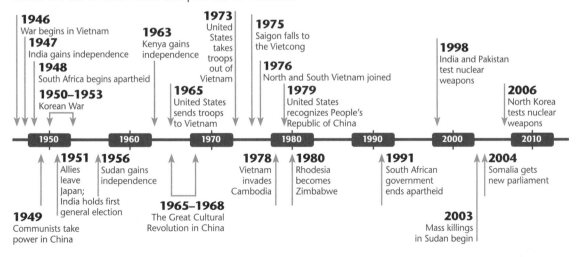

1946
War begins in Vietnam

1947
India gains independence

1948
South Africa begins apartheid

1950–1953
Korean War

1963
Kenya gains independence

1973
United States takes troops out of Vietnam

1965
United States sends troops to Vietnam

1975
Saigon falls to the Vietcong

1976
North and South Vietnam joined

1979
United States recognizes People's Republic of China

1998
India and Pakistan test nuclear weapons

2006
North Korea tests nuclear weapons

1949
Communists take power in China

1951
Allies leave Japan; India holds first general election

1956
Sudan gains independence

1965–1968
The Great Cultural Revolution in China

1978
Vietnam invades Cambodia

1980
Rhodesia becomes Zimbabwe

1991
South African government ends apartheid

2003
Mass killings in Sudan begin

2004
Somalia gets new parliament

REVIEW

Africa

apartheid

Britain

Darfur

Europe

famine

Nelson Mandela

On a sheet of paper, write the word from the Word Bank to complete each sentence correctly.

1. At the end of World War II, most of Africa remained controlled by _____.

2. In 1963, Kenya was granted independence by _____ after a long battle.

3. A time when crops do not grow and there is no food is called _____.

4. In 1948, the Afrikaners set up a policy of _____ to keep white people in control of South Africa.

5. In 1994, _____ became the president of South Africa.

6. Native rebel groups began attacking government targets in _____, a western area of Sudan.

7. _____ is the second largest continent on Earth.

On a sheet of paper, write the answer to each question. Use complete sentences.

8. Why did Africans want their independence after World War II?

9. What problems did nations have after gaining their independence?

10. How did the repeal of apartheid laws affect South Africa?

- India and its neighbors, Pakistan and Bangladesh, face many problems. These include: border disputes, religious conflicts, and food shortages.

- India is continually working to improve farming techniques. There is never enough food for the country's large population.

- Indian leaders are trying to build industry. They are doing this while learning to make better use of the country's natural resources.

- The Communists and the Nationalists fought a four-year civil war in China.

- In 1949, the Communists gained power in mainland China. They called their nation the People's Republic of China. The Nationalists left the mainland for Taiwan. They called their nation the Republic of China.

- Communist China has not granted its people political freedom, but it has allowed more private ownership and trade with the West.

- The United States fought wars in Korea and Vietnam on the anti-Communist side. Many Americans protested against U.S. involvement in the Vietnam War.

- Many European colonies in Africa gained independence after 1945.

- In South Africa, apartheid officially began in 1948 and ended in 1991. In 1990, Nelson Mandela, head of the African National Congress, was released from jail. He eventually became president of the country.

- African nations struggle to solve problems such as poverty, disease, and food shortages. Many are growing stronger, despite their history of colonial rule.

Word Bank

corrupt
curfew
electronic
guerilla
majority
minority
sanction
security
starvation
violence

Vocabulary Review

On a sheet of paper, use the words from the Word Bank to correctly match each definition below.

1. Powered by electricity

2. Great physical force; actions that hurt others

3. An action taken by one nation against another for breaking international law

4. A greater number, more than half

5. Safety

6. Dishonest, evil, selfish

7. A time after which certain people cannot be on the streets

8. A smaller number, less than half

9. The act of dying from not having enough food to eat

10. One of a group of fighters who are not part of a regular army, and who usually make surprise raids behind enemy lines

Chapter Review Questions

On a sheet of paper, write the answers to each question. Use complete sentences.

11. What was outlawed in India in 1950?

12. How did Mao and the Communists win the support of the Chinese peasants?

13. How did the United Nations help South Korea?

14. Why did Japan and the United States sign a trade agreement in 1990?

Test Tip

Restate test directions in your own words. Tell yourself what you are expected to do.

15. What major change happened in Africa after World War II?

Critical Thinking

On a sheet of paper, write your response to each question. Use complete sentences.

16. Do you think the limits on the Japanese military helped the Japanese economy after World War II? Give two examples to support your answer.

17. Do you think you would have liked being a young person in the 1960s? Be sure to include Vietnam and other important events in your answer.

Using the Timeline

Use the timeline on page 653 to answer the questions.

18. When did India gain its independence?

19. After World War II ended, how long did the Allies stay in Japan?

20. When did apartheid end in South Africa?

GROUP ACTIVITY

Work with a partner. Find a recent news story about one of the countries in this chapter. Write three questions that can be answered by the news story. Then read the story to your class, or tell about it in your own words. After you finish the story, ask your classmates the questions.

The Middle East

Religious differences have brought people to war against one another for many centuries. This is particularly true in the Middle East. Jews and Muslims have fought for the right to lands along the eastern Mediterranean. These disagreements continue. In countries such as Lebanon, Muslims and Christians fight for control. In other countries, Muslim groups with different beliefs fight one another. With the power of religion comes the power of money. The countries of the Middle East cover lands rich in valuable oil resources. Foreign nations are dependent on that oil, and thus become involved in the political struggles.

GOALS FOR LEARNING

- To explain why there is fighting over Palestine
- To list the conflicts that continue in the Middle East today
- To discuss the importance of oil to the Middle East and the world
- To describe life in the Middle East

Reading Strategy: Predicting

In order to predict what will come next, it is helpful to preview a text. Previewing helps readers think about what they already know about a subject. When making predictions, consider the following:

- Consider what you already know about the topic. Make your best guess as to what might happen next.

- Be sure to include details that support your prediction.

- As you read, you may learn new information that changes your prediction. Check your predictions from time to time.

Key Vocabulary Words

Lesson 1

Homeland The land that belongs to people

Zionism The movement to set up a Jewish nation in Palestine

Arms Weapons used to attack or defend

Cease-fire An end in military operations, especially to try and discuss peace

Hostile Unfriendly, showing hate or dislike

Traitor One who betrays a cause, a friend, or a nation

Lesson 2

Terrorist A fighter who hopes to achieve certain goals by using force or violence

Terrorism The use of force or random violence to frighten people or groups

Negotiate To talk together, make bargains, and agree on something

Stalemate To put in a position in which no action can be taken

Shah An Iranian ruler

Ayatollah A Muslim religious leader

Embassy The home and offices of a person sent to represent his or her government in another country

Hostages People held prisoner by an enemy until certain demands are met

Weapons of mass destruction A means of attack or defense that uses powerful weapons; an atomic bomb is an example

The Fight for Palestine

Objectives

- To describe the conflict between the Jews and Arabs over Palestine
- To explain how Israel was formed and how it became more powerful
- To explain why many Palestinians ended up in refugee camps

Reading Strategy: Predicting

Preview the lesson title. Predict what you think you will learn in this lesson.

People in the Middle East were often ruled by other lands. For hundreds of years, the Middle East was part of the Ottoman Empire. After World War I, most of the Middle East fell under British control. Egypt, however, gained its independence from Britain in 1922. Meanwhile, France took control of Syria and Lebanon.

World War II weakened the European countries. This left the door open for Arab nationalists to gain independence for their countries. However, with this independence came conflict.

The Middle East Today

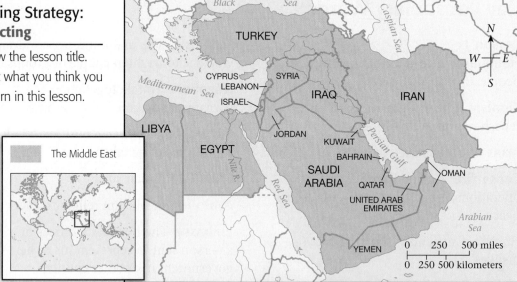

MAP STUDY

1. Which country borders the Red Sea and the Persian Gulf?
2. Turkey borders which two seas?

Homeland

The land that belongs to people

Zionism

The movement to set up a Jewish nation in Palestine

 History Fact

This scattering of the Jews is called the *diaspora*.

What Was the Zionist Movement?

In ancient days, the Jews considered Palestine their **homeland.** They called it a land promised to them by God. They built a temple in Jerusalem, the holy city.

Almost 2,000 years ago, the Romans drove the Jews out of Palestine. Some Jews settled in an area of Palestine called Galilee. However, most of the Jews fled from Palestine. They scattered around the world.

Many Jews never gave up their dream of the promised homeland. In the late 1800s, Jews in eastern Europe were persecuted. Some Jews started a movement called **Zionism.** Their goal was to make Palestine an independent Jewish nation. Jews from Europe began to settle in Palestine, which at that time was ruled by the Ottoman Turks.

By 1914, about 85,000 Jews were living there. After World War I, Britain promised to create a Jewish homeland in Palestine. Meanwhile, the Arab population of Palestine had been increasing, too. There was a problem. The Arabs living there did not like that Jews were moving into Palestine.

After World War II, Zionism became more popular. Jews who had felt Hitler's persecution were ready for a homeland of their own. Many came to Palestine.

How Was the State of Israel Formed?

In 1947, the United Nations voted to end British rule over Palestine. The UN knew there was a conflict between Arabs and Jews in Palestine. Arabs said the land had been theirs for 2,000 years. Jews said it had been theirs before the Arabs. Therefore, the United Nations divided Palestine into two parts. One part was for Jews and the other for Arabs. The Jews agreed to the UN plan. However, the Arabs were angry. They wanted all of Palestine to be an Arab state.

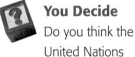 **You Decide**

Do you think the United Nations was wise to divide Palestine into two parts?

On May 14, 1948, David Ben-Gurion, the Zionist leader in Palestine, read a declaration of independence. He declared that the Jewish part of Palestine was the new state of Israel.

Israel was recognized immediately by the United States and then by the Soviet Union. The Arab nations declared war on Israel. On May 15, 1948, Israel was invaded by armies from the Arab nations of Syria, Egypt, Lebanon, Iraq, and Jordan.

GREAT NAMES IN HISTORY

Golda Meir

Golda Meir was born in Ukraine. Her family moved to Milwaukee in 1906. She later taught school there and worked with the Labor Zionist Party.

In 1921, Meir and her husband moved to Palestine. There she worked for the Zionist movement. After Israel became a nation, Meir was elected to the Knesset, the Israeli parliament. She was labor minister and then foreign minister. Later, she helped organize the Labor Party. As prime minister (1969–1974), Meir tried to bring peace to the Middle East.

Why Was the Palestine Liberation Organization Formed?

The Israelis were greatly outnumbered and had a shortage of weapons. However, Israel won the war against many odds. An agreement between Israel and Arab states was signed in 1949. The state of Israel was firmly established. The lands left to the Arabs became part of Jordan.

About 700,000 Arabs fled Israel, becoming refugees. The homeless Palestinian Arabs lived in crowded refugee camps outside of Israel. Many still live there. They believed that their homes were stolen. Some of them formed a group of fighters called the Palestine Liberation Organization (PLO). Their goal is to win back their land.

After the war in 1948, about 700,000 Jews living in Arab nations were forced to leave. Jews left Iraq, Yemen, Libya, and other countries. Most went to live in Israel.

Israel had won the 1948 war. However, the problems of the Middle East were far from settled.

How Did Israel Broaden Its Control?

Soon the superpowers became involved in the Israeli-Arab conflict. In 1955, the Soviets offered to sell weapons, or **arms,** to Egypt. This was followed by a conflict over the Suez Canal.

In 1956, Egypt took over the canal from Britain and France. Britain, France, and Israel then attacked Egypt. The United Nations arranged an end in military operations—a **cease-fire.** The Suez Canal was held by Egypt. The Arabs, however, became even more unfriendly and **hostile** toward Israel.

Families in the disputed area of Palestine live in sometimes hostile surroundings.

Traitor

One who betrays a cause, a friend, or a nation

Reading Strategy: Predicting

Think about what you predicted earlier. Does your prediction still work or do you need to revise your prediction?

 You Decide

What do you think would have happened to Israel if it had lost any of its wars?

In June 1967, another war began. Israel fought the Arab nations of Egypt, Jordan, and Syria. In the first few minutes of the war, Israeli planes attacked the Arab airfields. Almost all of the Arab airplanes were destroyed on the ground. Then the Israeli army pushed through the Sinai Peninsula all the way to the Suez Canal. The war was over in six days! Israel occupied all of the Sinai Peninsula, the Gaza Strip, and the West Bank. The West Bank was the section of Palestine that had become part of Jordan. Israel also took control of East Jerusalem.

Arab nations grew angrier. In 1973, Egypt, Syria, Jordan, and Iraq launched a surprise attack on Israel. It was called the *Yom Kippur War* because the Arabs attacked on the Jewish holy day called *Yom Kippur.* This time, the Arabs almost won. Israel managed to defend itself. However, it paid a high price in the number of lives lost.

LEARN MORE ABOUT IT

Anwar Sadat

In 1977, Egypt's President Anwar el-Sadat visited Israel. His visit surprised the world. It was the first move toward peace with Israel that any Arab leader had ever made. Then, U.S. President Jimmy Carter invited Sadat and Israel's prime minister, Menachem Begin, to the United States. There the three leaders held discussions on how to end the Israeli-Arab conflict. These meetings led to the signing of the Camp David Accords in 1979. Israel promised to return all of the Sinai Peninsula to Egypt in exchange for peace. Israel also promised to allow the Palestinians in Gaza and on the West Bank to govern themselves.

Much of the world praised Sadat. In 1978, Sadat and Begin shared the Nobel Peace Prize. However, many Arab nationalists were angry. They said that Sadat was a **traitor** to the Arab cause, meaning he betrayed it. In 1981, Sadat was assassinated by extremists.

Israel and Its Neighbors, After the Six-Day War

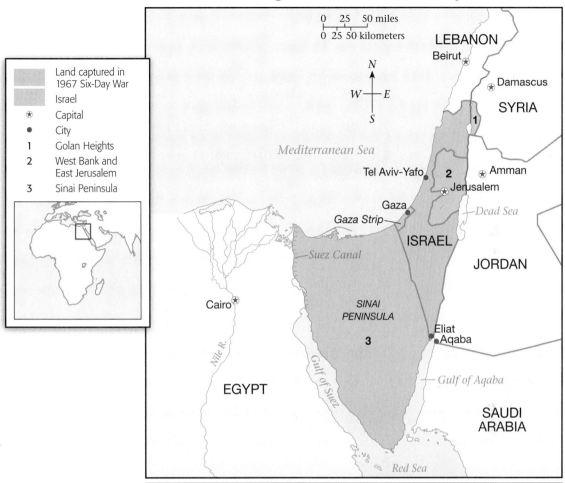

0   25   50 miles
0   25   50 kilometers

Legend:

- Land captured in 1967 Six-Day War
- Israel
- ⊛ Capital
- • City
- 1 Golan Heights
- 2 West Bank and East Jerusalem
- 3 Sinai Peninsula

LEBANON
Beirut ⊛

⊛ Damascus
SYRIA

Mediterranean Sea

Tel Aviv-Yafo •

1

2   ⊛ Amman
⊛ Jerusalem

Gaza •
Gaza Strip ⟵

Dead Sea

ISRAEL

Suez Canal

JORDAN

Cairo ⊛

*SINAI
PENINSULA*

3

Eliat
• Aqaba

Nile R.

Gulf of Suez

Gulf of Aqaba

EGYPT

SAUDI
ARABIA

Red Sea

MAP STUDY

1. What areas were captured by Israel in the 1967 Six-Day War?

2. What connects the Mediterranean Sea to the Red Sea?

REVIEW

Word Bank

British

Egypt

homeland

Israel

refugees

Palestine

On a sheet of paper, write the word from the Word Bank to complete each sentence correctly.

1. Long ago, the Jews considered Palestine their _____.

2. The United Nations voted to end _____ rule over Palestine.

3. The United Nations divided _____ into two parts.

4. Palestinian _____ formed the Palestine Liberation Organization to win back their land.

5. After the United Nations arranged a cease-fire, _____ held control over the Suez Canal.

6. _____ gained the Sinai Peninsula, the Gaza Strip, and the West Bank after the Six-Day War.

On a sheet of paper, write the answer to each question. Use complete sentences.

7. What was the goal of the Zionist movement?

8. Why was Palestine divided by the United Nations?

9. Why did so many Palestinians end up in refugee camps after the war in 1948?

10. Why did Egypt, Syria, Jordan, and Iraq attack Israel on *Yom Kippur* in 1973? Who won?

The Middle East Remains in Conflict

The fighting in the Middle East was not over. The Palestine Liberation Organization (PLO) still wanted a home for the Palestinians.

Why Was There Fighting in Lebanon?

In 1970, the PLO was forced out of Jordan. In 1975, it became involved in a civil war in Lebanon. From bases in Lebanon, the PLO carried out **terrorist** attacks into Israel. Terrorists use force or violence to achieve certain goals. Palestinian terrorists were also active in other parts of the world.

In 1982, Israel invaded Lebanon in order to destroy PLO bases. The PLO was forced to leave Lebanon. However, once the Israeli army withdrew from Lebanon, the PLO came back.

In December 1987, violent protests by Palestinians broke out in the West Bank and Gaza. The uprising, known as the *intifada,* continued until the 1990s. The Palestinians wanted an independent state. They were especially angry that Israel allowed Jewish settlers to take away some of their land. However, the Israelis have given control of some of the Gaza Strip and the West Bank back to the Palestinians.

Lebanon's civil war began in 1975 and lasted until 1990. Muslims battled Christians for power. Different Muslim groups also battled each other. In 1983, the United States became involved with the war. U.S. troops were taken out of Lebanon only after many U.S. Marines were killed by Muslim terrorists. Syria also sent troops into Lebanon, who used force to end the civil war in 1990.

The civil war all but destroyed Lebanon, leaving its cities in shambles. Beirut, the capital of Lebanon, had been known as the "Paris" of the Middle East. Much of it was left in ruins.

The PLO agreed to stop acts of **terrorism,** or the use of force or violence to frighten people. It also began talking and working toward agreement, or **negotiating,** with Israel. Israelis had a difficult choice to make as they negotiated with the Palestinians and Arabs. They could give up the occupied lands and hope that it would bring about a lasting peace.

In January 2001, hopes for peace seemed to be **stalemated** again (they were in a position in which no action could be taken). Despite U.S. President Bill Clinton's involvement, sticking points, such as Jerusalem's future, remained unresolved.

Israeli Prime Minister Yitzhak Rabin, left, and PLO chairman Yasser Arafat shake hands after signing a peace agreement. U.S. President Bill Clinton looks on.

Shah

An Iranian ruler

Ayatollah

A Muslim religious leader

Embassy

The home and offices of a person sent to represent his or her government in another country

Hostages

People held prisoner by an enemy until certain demands are met

The country of Iran has seen its share of conflict, too. Iranians were unhappy with their leader, the **Shah.** The Shah had a vicious secret police who made sure he kept power.

In 1979, a 76-year-old Muslim leader, the **Ayatollah** Khomeini, returned to Iran from exile in France. Khomeini led a successful revolution against the Shah. He then set up a Muslim republic following strict Islamic rules. Khomeini's followers wanted the Shah to stand trial for crimes they said he had committed. However, the Shah had fled to the United States. Then in November 1979, Iranians captured the U.S. **embassy** in Tehran, Iran's capital. An embassy is the home and offices of a person sent to represent their government in another country. They took American prisoners, called **hostages,** and they demanded the Shah's return.

Much of the world was angered by the Iranian action. However, Iran would not give up the hostages. The Shah died in Egypt in July 1980. Finally, in January 1981, the American hostages were freed.

Meanwhile, in 1980, Iran was attacked by its neighbor, Iraq. There had been bitter fights over territory. Iraq hoped to win a quick victory over Iran. Saddam Hussein, leader of Iraq, thought that Iran had been weakened by the Islamic revolution. However, neither nation could beat the other. The war dragged on for many years.

There were huge land battles. Then both sides began firing missiles at each other's cities. In addition, each country began to attack oil tankers in the Persian Gulf. In 1987, the United States sent its navy to the Gulf to protect the flow of oil.

Finally, in 1988, the United Nations was able to arrange a cease-fire between Iran and Iraq. Both countries had suffered such huge losses that they were willing to begin talking about ending the war.

Why Did Iraq Invade Kuwait?

In August 1990, Iraq invaded the small neighboring nation of Kuwait. Iraqi leader Saddam Hussein wanted to make Kuwait and its rich oil fields a part of his country. Kuwait fell only hours after the Iraqi attack.

The United Nations protested Iraq's capture of Kuwait. Then Iraq threatened the border of Saudi Arabia. The United States and other nations sent their own military forces to the Persian Gulf. They were ready to defend Saudi Arabia against a possible Iraqi invasion. They were also ready to liberate Kuwait.

Saddam Hussein wanted to make oil-rich Kuwait a part of Iraq.

On November 29, 1990, the United Nations sent Hussein a warning. It would use "all necessary means" if Iraq did not withdraw (pull out) from Kuwait. They gave Hussein until January 15, 1991 to do so. Hussein did not respond to the warning. So, on the evening of January 16, bombs and missiles began to fall on Iraq. A ground war began on February 23. By February 28, Kuwait was free, and a cease-fire had begun.

The Gulf War ended when Kuwait was freed. The war did not, however, destroy Saddam Hussein's control of Iraq or his threats of attack.

Weapons of mass destruction

A means of attack or defense that uses powerful weapons

Reading Strategy: Predicting

Based on what you have just read, what do you predict you will read about in the upcoming paragraphs?

Hussein refused to cooperate with UN inspections to make sure he was not building **weapons of mass destruction.** An example of a weapon of mass destruction is an atomic bomb.

What Progress Did Peace Talks Bring to the Middle Eastern Nations?

In the 1990s, the United States and Russia sponsored peace conferences between Israel and the Arab nations of the Middle East. Israeli, Palestinian, and Arab leaders agreed to meet to try to cool heated conflicts. They wanted to make the Middle East more stable. Progress is slow. Israel has given the Palestinians control over some of the occupied lands. Israel and Jordan have also signed a peace treaty. In early 2000, the United States helped move Syria and Israel toward peace. However, by early 2001, the peace talks had broken down because Israel refused to give up the Golan Heights.

How Did Middle Eastern Terrorism Spread to the Larger World?

Many Middle Eastern countries have become home to terrorist groups. These people commit acts of violence against citizens of various countries. They often use bombs to kill people. Terrorists may disagree with the politics or religion of a particular nation or group. In some cases, they may not like the presence of foreign governments in their countries. Often this foreign presence is due to oil resources. Since 1998, there have been about 2,000 terrorist attacks worldwide.

As mentioned in Chapter 30, the U.S. Embassy in Nairobi, Kenya was bombed in 1998. Nearly 300 people were killed, and more than 5,000 were injured. Most victims were native Kenyans. The al Qaeda group, guided by Osama bin Laden, was blamed for these attacks.

On September 11, 2001, two planes crashed into the World Trade Center in New York City. Shortly afterward, another plane flew into the Pentagon. A fourth plane, redirected from another Washington target, crashed into a field in Pennsylvania. A total of 3,025 people were killed. Again, al Qaeda and Osama bin Laden were held responsible.

In March 2004, al Qaeda-related terrorists planted bombs in Madrid, Spain train stations. Three separate bombs there killed almost 200 people and wounded another 1,400.

Middle Eastern terrorism has spread to the larger world. On September 11, 2001, two planes crashed into the World Trade Center buildings in New York City.

On a sheet of paper, write the letter of the answer that correctly completes each sentence.

1. In 1975, the _____ became involved in a civil war in Lebanon.

   A PLO   **B** British   **C** United States   **D** Iranians

2. _____ use force or violence to achieve their goals.

   A Americans   **B** Iranians   **C** Israelites   **D** Terrorists

3. _____ sent troops into Lebanon to end the civil war in 1990.

   A The United States   **B** Kuwait   **C** Syria   **D** Palestine

4. Iran had a leader called the _____. He had secret police to make sure he kept his power.

   A president   **B** Shah   **C** prime minister   **D** dictator

5. In 1976, _____ returned to Iran from exile in France.

   A Ayatollah Khomeini   **C** Bill Clinton
   B David Ben-Guiron   **D** the Shah

6. In 1980, Iran was attacked by _____.

   A Lebanon   **B** Iraq   **C** Israel   **D** Russia

7. In 1987, the United States sent its military to the Gulf to protect the _____.

   A water   **B** people   **C** oil   **D** leader

8. The Gulf War ended when _____ was free.

   A Palestine   **B** Lebanon   **C** Chad   **D** Kuwait

9. In 2001, Israel broke down peace talks because it refused to give up _____.

   A Kuwait   **B** Iraq   **C** the Golan Heights **D** the oil fields

10. In 2001, two planes crashed into the World Trade Center in _____.

   A Washington, D.C.   **B** New York City   **C** Palestine   **D** Los Angeles

---

Oil

Objectives

■ To explain how Middle Eastern nations manage their oil power

■ To explain what happened when Libya tried to expand its borders

■ To describe how Middle Eastern nations can impact oil prices

Reading Strategy: Predicting

Preview the lesson title. Predict what you think you will learn in this lesson.

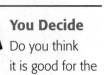

You Decide

Do you think it is good for the United States to be so dependent on Middle East oil?

As you may remember from Lesson 1, Arab nationalists gained independence for their countries after World War II. Most important, Arabs took control of their own oil fields. Oil deposits had been discovered in Iraq in 1927 and in Saudi Arabia in 1938. More huge oil fields were later found along the Persian Gulf. European and U.S. oil companies had moved in to control the oil fields. The Middle Eastern nations saw little of their own oil wealth. However, after World War II, many Arab nations gained tremendous riches and power because of their oil.

How Do Middle Eastern Nations Control Their Oil?

Much of the Middle East has oil. All nations need oil, and world supplies are limited. The Middle East's oil fields give Arab countries power.

An organization called OPEC (Organization of Petroleum Exporting Countries) manages that power. OPEC members include the oil-producing nations of the Middle East, Asia, and Africa, as well as the South American country of Venezuela.

OPEC sets the price of oil. OPEC can force up oil prices or deny oil from certain countries. This gives OPEC tremendous power. During the Israeli-Arab wars of 1967 and 1973, the Arabs used their oil as a weapon. They cut off the flow of oil to the West. In 1973, this resulted in a severe oil shortage in the United States. Drivers were forced to wait in long lines at the gas pumps. They also had to pay a much higher price for each gallon they bought. Through the 1990s and into the 21st century, OPEC used its power to control other countries.

Oil pipelines run through Saudi Arabian oil fields. Saudi Arabia has the richest known oil reserves of any country in the world.

Some people in the Middle East are very, very wealthy because of oil. However, much of the oil wealth remains in the hands of a few. Most profits from oil sales go toward building a strong Arab military.

What Happened When Libya Tried to Expand Its Borders?

Most Middle East oil comes from Saudi Arabia. Another important oil producer is Libya. In 1969, Muammar al-Qaddafi came to power after he and his followers overthrew the king of Libya. Al-Qaddafi has shown great interest in expanding his country's borders. He tried to seize territory from Chad, the country that borders Libya on the south.

In April 1986, a disco in West Berlin that was popular with American service people was bombed. Two people were killed and 200 were injured. The United States learned that Libya was responsible for this act. In response, U.S. warplanes struck targets in Libya.

Al-Qaddafi spent much of Libya's oil profits on new weapons and a stronger army. He also supported terrorist actions against Americans and Israelis. However, in 2001, a top official in Libya said his country was prepared to restore its ties with the United States. By 2003, Libya announced that it would give up its nuclear weapons program. The United States returned to having full political relations with the country by 2006.

Why Do Oil Prices Continue to Change?

Oil prices rose sharply at the end of the Persian Gulf War. Hussein's Iraqi troops set fire to the oil fields of Kuwait as they left that country. This decreased the supply of oil exported from Kuwait. Other OPEC nations increased supplies and repairs to lines in Kuwait. This made prices come back down.

Reading Strategy: Predicting

Think about the prediction you made in the last lesson. What details can you now add to make your prediction more specific?

During the 2000s, oil prices rose to an all-time high. The price per barrel of crude oil was $25 in September 2003. By August 2005, it had risen to $60 per barrel. It reached the highest price ever in July 2006, at $78.40 per barrel. Experts believe the prices may have risen due to fears about nuclear arms advances in North Korea and Iran. As those fears eased up a bit, the price of oil decreased slightly. However, oil prices continue to change and are still an issue today.

REVIEW

Word Bank

Kuwait

Libya

military

oil fields

OPEC

Saudi Arabia

weapon

On a sheet of paper, write the words from the Word Bank to complete each sentence correctly.

1. The Middle East's _____ give Arab countries power.

2. An organization called _____ manages the oil for several parts of the world.

3. During the Israeli-Arab wars, the Arabs used their oil as a(n) _____.

4. Most profits from oil go toward building a strong Arab _____.

5. Most of the oil in the Middle East comes from _____.

6. Muammar al-Qaddafi came to power after overthrowing the king of _____.

7. Hussein's Iraqi troops set fire to the oil fields of _____ before leaving the country.

On a sheet of paper, write the answer to each question. Use complete sentences.

8. Why did U.S. warplanes strike targets in Libya?

9. Why does OPEC have such tremendous power?

10. What do experts think caused oil to go up in price?

Life in the Middle East

The Middle East is, without a doubt, a land of war and conflict. It faces serious problems that will have to be dealt with. Still, the Middle East has fine, modern cities, well-educated people, farmlands, and productive industries.

What Is Life in the Middle East Like?

Israel is one of the most industrialized and advanced nations of the Middle East. About 85 percent of Israel's people live and work in modern cities. Israel's farms are a source of pride. Most of Israel's land is poor. Some of the land is too rocky or steep for farming. Other areas get little rainfall. Only through hard work and agricultural know-how could those lands be productive. Still, Israel produces most of its own food.

Huge irrigation systems pump in water through underground pipelines. Scientists experiment with turning saltwater from the Mediterranean and Red seas into fresh water to soak their fields.

The Israelis have not won the perfect land. However, they have worked hard to build their nation.

Long before the first century A.D., the first civilizations were forming along the Tigris and Euphrates rivers and along the Nile River. Those early peoples concerned themselves with producing food and irrigating dry lands. They battled invaders who would take their lands. They argued over how they would worship their gods. In some ways, those people had much in common with today's Middle Eastern people.

Land in Israel along the Sea of Galilee is fertile. This is because of irrigation systems and the hard work of the Israeli people.

TIMELINE STUDY:

THE MIDDLE EAST: 1945–2010

During which year did militant Iranians capture the U.S. embassy in Tehran?

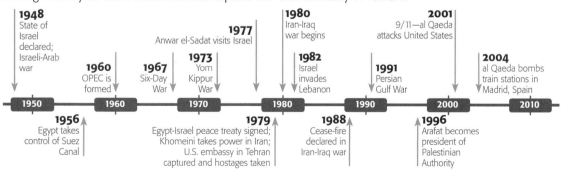

1948 State of Israel declared; Israeli-Arab war

1956 Egypt takes control of Suez Canal

1960 OPEC is formed

1967 Six-Day War

1973 Yom Kippur War

1977 Anwar el-Sadat visits Israel

1979 Egypt-Israel peace treaty signed; Khomeini takes power in Iran; U.S. embassy in Tehran captured and hostages taken

1980 Iran-Iraq war begins

1982 Israel invades Lebanon

1988 Cease-fire declared in Iran-Iraq war

1991 Persian Gulf War

1996 Arafat becomes president of Palestinian Authority

2001 9/11—al Qaeda attacks United States

2004 al Qaeda bombs train stations in Madrid, Spain

1950 | 1960 | 1970 | 1980 | 1990 | 2000 | 2010

REVIEW

Word Bank

cities

irrigation

Israel

land

Nile

saltwater

war

On a sheet of paper, write the word from the Word Bank to complete each sentence correctly.

1. The Middle East is a land of _____ and conflict.

2. _____ is one of the most advanced nations in the Middle East.

3. About 85 percent of Israel's people work and live in modern _____.

4. Large _____ systems pump water through underground pipelines.

5. Scientists are experimenting with turning _____ into fresh water to soak their fields.

6. Early civilizations formed along the Tigris and Euphrates rivers and the _____ River.

7. Early civilizations battled invaders who would try and take their _____.

On a sheet of paper, write the answer to each question. Use complete sentences.

8. Despite the problems, what good things are happening in the Middle East?

9. How are Israel's farms productive even with poor land?

10. What do early civilizations have in common with today's Middle Eastern people?

CHAPTER 31

SUMMARY

- Most Middle Eastern countries gained independence from Britain and France after World War II.

- Zionists wanted to set up a Jewish state in Palestine. The United Nations divided Palestine between Arabs and Jews.

- In 1948, the Jews set up the state of Israel. The remaining lands of Palestine became part of the Arab state of Jordan. Since 1948, Arabs and Israelis have fought wars for control of these lands. Conflict or the threat of conflict continues.

- Many Palestinians who had fled from Israel were forced to live in crowded refugee camps. They formed the PLO and demanded their lands back.

- Lebanon had a civil war between Muslims and Christians that lasted from 1975 to 1990.

- Iran captured the U.S. embassy in its capital in 1979. It happened after its former Shah came to the United States in exile. Americans from the embassy were taken hostage.

- Territory disputes caused a war between Iran and Iraq that lasted for nearly eight years.

- In 1990, Iraq invaded its neighbor, Kuwait. In the Persian Gulf War, the United States and other nations used military force to free Kuwait.

- Terrorism by Middle Eastern groups has spread to many other locations around the globe. Some of these places include: Spain, England, and the United States.

- Many nations of the Middle East have wealth and power because the world depends on their oil.

Word Bank

arms

embassy

homeland

hostages

hostile

negotiate

stalemate

terrorism

traitor

Zionism

Vocabulary Review

On a sheet of paper, use the words from the Word Bank to complete each sentence correctly.

1. When countries _____, they begin to talk and work toward agreement.

2. The situation in Palestine has turned more _____, or unfriendly, over the years.

3. Middle Eastern _____ has spread to the larger world.

4. The Jews consider Palestine to be their _____.

5. _____ is the movement to set up a Jewish nation in Palestine.

6. Arab nationalists called Sadat a(n) _____ because they thought he had betrayed the Arab cause.

7. The U.S. _____ in Tehran, Iran was captured in 1979.

8. In 1979, Iranians took American _____ and demanded the Shah's return.

9. The Soviets offered to sell _____, or weapons, to Egypt in 1955.

10. Talks over the future of Palestine are at a(n) _____. They are in a position where no action can be taken.

Chapter Review Questions

On a sheet of paper, write the answers to each question. Use complete sentences.

11. Why did the Jews consider Palestine their homeland?

12. Why did the Arabs think Palestine belonged to them?

13. Why did many Palestinians end up in refugee camps in the late 1940s?

14. Why did the United States and other nations fight against Iraq in the Gulf War?

Critical Thinking

On a sheet of paper, write your response to each question. Use complete sentences.

15. Do you think the United States should try to help bring peace to the Middle East? Why or why not?

16. The United States and other countries are dependent on Middle Eastern oil. How do you think they could become less dependent?

17. Do you think it was right for the United Nations to divide Palestine into two parts?

Using the Timeline

Use the timeline on page 679 to answer the questions.

18. When did the oil-rich nations of the Middle East form their own organization?

19. Which came first, the Six-Day War or the Yom Kippur War?

20. When did Egypt take control of the Suez Canal?

GROUP ACTIVITY

Form a group of four or five. Assign group members to be either a news anchor or a field reporter. Choose an event that happened in the Middle East after 1945. Use that event as the basis for a 5-minute newscast. (Look at the timeline on page 679 for some major events in the Middle East.) The event should focus on at least two different religious groups in the city (e.g., Jews, Christians, Muslims). Report the news "live" to the class.

The End of the Soviet Union

The Soviet Union began to change rapidly during the late 1980s and early 1990s. The Soviet people started having greater freedoms and focusing less on the strength of their army. The cold war, which had caused such fear among Americans, was coming to an end.

A man named Mikhail Gorbachev came to power in the Soviet Union in 1985. Like no Soviet leader before, he wanted to work together with other nations. He introduced bold new policies for the Soviet Union. Many nations would come to feel the effects of these historic changes.

GOALS FOR LEARNING

- To describe how Mikhail Gorbachev improved the Soviet Union's relations with Western nations
- To explain how the Soviet Union disbanded and became an alliance of independent republics
- To describe the freedom gained by Eastern European satellites and the unrest that often followed

Reading Strategy: Text Structure

The way a text is organized can help readers determine which information is most important. Before you begin reading, page through this chapter to see how it is organized. When doing so, pay special attention to the title, headings, boldfaced words, maps, and photographs. When reading, ask yourself:

- How is this text organized?

- Is it a problem and solution, description, or sequence?

- Is it compare and contrast or cause and effect?

Think about the structure of the text and then summarize what you have just read.

Key Vocabulary Words

Lesson 1
Glasnost The Soviet policy of open discussion of political and social issues

Perestroika The Soviet policy of economic and government reform

Coup A bold, sudden move to bring about change in a government

Lesson 2
Disband To break up

Lesson 3
Reunification The act of joining together again

Changes in the Soviet Union

Objectives

■ To list three changes in the Soviet Union for which Mikhail Gorbachev was responsible

■ To describe the attempted coup and the effect it had on Communism in the Soviet Union

**Reading Strategy:
Text Structure**

Preview this lesson. Notice the headings, features, and boldfaced words.

Some of the biggest changes in recent history happened within the Soviet Union and its Eastern European satellites. Soviet policy turned from militarism and hostility to a freer and more open society. After years of cold war, the Soviet Union and the United States, the world's two superpowers, began to make peace.

Changes in the Soviet Union began in 1985 when a man named Mikhail Gorbachev came to power. Gorbachev introduced new policies within the Soviet Union and improved Soviet relations with other nations.

How Did Mikhail Gorbachev Improve Relations?

Friendly relations with Western countries were important to Gorbachev's plans for the Soviet Union. Good relations, he hoped, would lead to trade agreements and economic improvements. They might also lead to a more secure and peaceful world. In 1987, Gorbachev and U.S. President Ronald Reagan signed the INF Treaty (Intermediate-Range Nuclear Force Treaty). For the first time, both sides agreed to get rid of an entire class of nuclear weapons. In 1991, the Strategic Arms Reduction Treaty (START) was signed in Moscow. Gorbachev and U.S. President George Bush agreed to the treaty. It would reduce nuclear weapons on both sides by 30 percent.

Gorbachev took other steps to show that his country had changed its attitude toward the West. In 1989, he brought Soviet troops home from Afghanistan. He agreed to stop supplying military aid to the Communist Sandinista government in Nicaragua (see Chapter 33). He pressured Cuba's Communist leader, Fidel Castro, to bring home the Cuban troops from Angola in Africa. They had been involved in a civil war there. Gorbachev also persuaded Vietnam to withdraw its forces from Cambodia.

What Was Gorbachev's *Glasnost* Policy?

Glasnost

The Soviet policy of open discussion of political and social issues

Perestroika

The Soviet policy of economic and government reform

 You Decide

How would you feel if you were a Soviet citizen and were able to vote for the first time?

Although Mikhail Gorbachev was a Communist, he encouraged his nation to be more open to information and ideas from the democratic West. He put into action a policy of **glasnost** or "openness." Suddenly, Soviet citizens had more freedom of speech and basic human rights than ever before.

A new branch of the government was set up. Its members were directly elected by the people. Soviet citizens could choose people they wanted to represent them in the government. The newly elected people did not even have to be members of the Communist Party. For the first time, the Communist leaders had to listen to the opinions and complaints of the Soviet people.

The policy of *glasnost* led many of the republics within the Soviet Union to demand the right to manage their own affairs. The Baltic states of Estonia, Latvia, and Lithuania even went so far as to seek independence from Moscow.

One unfortunate result of *glasnost* was an increase in hostilities between different national groups within the Soviet Union. In many places, long-standing disagreements boiled over into outbreaks of violence. For example, violence broke out between Armenians and Azerbaijanis as to who owned a particular territory in the Caucasus Mountains. Many people were killed as a result.

Gorbachev knew that by the late 1980s, the Soviet economy was in serious trouble. He also knew that he would have to make major changes in order to see any improvement. Therefore, he proposed a policy of **perestroika,** or "restructuring." Factories and businesses around the country would no longer be controlled by Moscow. Each would be responsible for running its own operations. In addition, individual Soviet citizens would be allowed to engage in small-scale private business.

Coup

A bold, sudden move
to bring about change
in a government

Reading Strategy:
Text Structure

Notice that the section
headings are written
as questions. After you
read each section, try
to answer the question
asked in the heading.

Gorbachev also welcomed U.S. corporations to set up joint operations in the Soviet Union. A number of U.S. companies signed agreements with the Soviets. In Moscow, the largest fast-food restaurant of a major U.S. chain of restaurants opened for business.

Many people in both the Soviet Union and the United States were declaring that the cold war was finally over. Yet in spite of all the changes taking place, Soviet citizens had questions. Would Gorbachev's plans be successful? What would happen if Gorbachev were to fall from power?

Why Did Communist Leaders Attempt a Coup?

Hard-line Soviet Communists criticized Gorbachev's new policies. During 1990, the Soviet Union was faced with a widespread economic crisis. Food shops in many cities were empty. Conflicts continued in some of the republics. Some Soviets believed that Gorbachev was changing things too quickly.

Mikhail Gorbachev
introduced policies of
openness and restructuring
to the Soviet Union.

In August 1991, a group of hard-line Communist leaders made a move to take over power in the Soviet Union. They announced that Gorbachev had been "taken ill" and had left Moscow for a "rest." However, the **coup** failed. Since Gorbachev had begun reform in 1985, Soviet citizens had been introduced to new freedoms. Despite hard times, they were not ready to give up their rights.

Following the failure of the coup, change came even more rapidly. Citizens toppled statues of Communist heroes that had long stood in city squares. The city of Leningrad took back the name it held before the coming of Communism. It became St. Petersburg again. The country became known as the Union of Sovereign States. The attempted coup only sped up the death of Communism inside the Soviet Union.

LESSON 32-1

REVIEW

Word Bank

Afghanistan

cold war

coup

glasnost

Mikhail Gorbachev

Ronald Reagan

St. Petersburg

On a sheet of paper, write the word from the Word Bank to complete each sentence correctly.

1. The Soviet Union and the United States began to make peace in the 1980s. This peace was after years of _____.

2. Changes were made in 1985 when _____ came to power in the Soviet Union.

3. Gorbachev met with _____ in 1987 to begin limiting nuclear weapons.

4. In 1989, Soviet troops were taken out of _____ and brought home.

5. Gorbachev put into action a policy of _____ or "openness."

6. In 1991, a(n) _____ tried to take over the Soviet government and failed.

7. As Communism was dying, the city of Leningrad changed its name back to _____.

On a sheet of paper, write the answer to each question. Use complete sentences.

8. What was one bad result of *glasnost*?

9. What is the meaning of *perestroika*?

10. What changes occurred after the takeover of the Soviet government failed?

The End of the Soviet Union and the Cold War

In December 1991, the Soviet Union **disbanded,** or broke up. It was replaced by 15 independent nations. Gorbachev had returned to power, but was unable to hold the union together. Three of the 15 republics that made up the Soviet Union—Latvia, Estonia, and Lithuania—had declared their independence earlier that year. On December 21, leaders of 11 of the 12 remaining republics signed agreements creating the Commonwealth of Independent States (CIS). This was a loose alliance of fully independent states. The Communist Party was no longer in charge. Mikhail Gorbachev stepped down. Boris Yeltsin, president of the republic of Russia, became a leader and spokesman for the new Commonwealth. Yeltsin had long been calling for an end to Communist rule.

Boris Yeltsin led Russia to democracy and freedom after the Soviet Union collapsed.

How Did the Cold War End?

On February 1, 1992, Boris Yeltsin met with U.S. President George H.W. Bush. The leaders declared an end to "cold war hostility." The United States and other nations of the free world pledged to send aid to help rebuild the economy of the new nations.

The Soviet Union died, and 15 new nations were born with many problems. The people still faced economic woes. Food and medicine continued to be in short supply. In some of the new nations, lives continued to be lost as different groups battled for control.

Russia, or the Russian Federation, is the largest and most powerful of the new nations. It took the seat at the UN that had been held by the Soviet Union.

What Did Vladimir Putin Do While In Office?

Yeltsin appointed Vladimir Putin prime minister in 1999. Putin was the fifth prime minister to be appointed in 18 months. The following year, Yeltsin resigned because of poor health. That same year, in 2000, Putin was elected president. He won more than half of all votes, as one of 11 candidates for president.

Vladimir Putin began his presidency by getting two weapons reduction agreements passed by the legislature. In talks with the United States and other Western nations, he said he wanted to reduce nuclear arms. He also wanted to take part in the fight against terrorism. Putin brought many important social reforms to Russia. He worked to build up Russia's vast energy supplies. He promoted changes to make the central Russian government stronger. Putin was reelected in 2004 for a four-year term.

REVIEW

Word Bank

Boris Yeltsin

energy

George H.W. Bush

independent

president

Russia

Vladimir Putin

On a sheet of paper, write the word from the Word Bank to complete each sentence correctly.

1. In 1991, the Soviet Union broke up into 15 _____ nations.

2. After Gorbachev stepped down from power, _____ became the leader of the new commonwealth.

3. Boris Yeltsin met with U.S. President _____ in 1991 to end the cold war.

4. The Soviet Union disbanded in 1991. The largest and most powerful of the new nations was _____.

5. Boris Yeltsin made _____ prime minister in 1999.

6. In 2000, Vladimir Putin was elected _____.

7. Putin has worked hard to build Russia's _____ supply.

On a sheet of paper, write the answer to each question. Use complete sentences.

8. When the Soviet Union ended, what problems did the 15 new nations have?

9. Why did Boris Yeltsin step down from office?

10. List two examples of what Vladimir Putin has done while in office.

Changes in Eastern Europe

The Soviet Union was not the only country going through changes during the late 1980s and early 1990s. As a result of Gorbachev's *glasnost* policy, the Soviets loosened their control over their satellite countries in Eastern Europe.

How Did Soviet Satellites Gain Their Freedom?

Back in 1956, Hungary had tried to cut its ties with the Soviets. It wanted to set up its own government, free of Soviet influence. However, Soviet troops marched into Hungary, crushing the movement for independence.

Then in 1968, there was trouble in Czechoslovakia. The Soviet government felt that the Czechoslovakian Communist Party was losing control of the country. The Russians were afraid that too much freedom of speech would turn the people away from Communism. So in August 1968, Soviet tanks rumbled through Czechoslovakia. Soon, new people were running the Czech government—people chosen by Moscow.

During the 1970s, many workers rioted in Poland. They were demanding higher pay and better working conditions. They wanted a labor union, something unheard of under Communist rule. In 1980, the Polish government allowed the workers to form the union. The new workers' union was called Solidarity. Its leader was a man named Lech Walesa.

In 1982, the government began to fear that many of Solidarity's demands went against Communist ideals. That year, the Communists arrested Solidarity's leaders and declared the union illegal. Many people inside Poland and in the West insisted that the Soviet Union had forced the Polish government to outlaw Solidarity.

Reunification
The act of joining together again

History Fact
In 1993, the country of Czechoslovakia split into two separate nations: The Czech Republic and Slovakia.

Throughout the 1980s, economic conditions in Poland continued to worsen. By 1989, Polish leaders were ready to try a different approach. Encouraged by the radical changes taking place inside the Soviet Union, they made Solidarity legal again. Solidarity then formed a political party. When the first free elections in Poland were held, the union's leaders were voted into office to run the government. Lech Walesa became president. However, in 1995, after Poland experienced economic troubles, Walesa lost the presidency. A former Communist was elected president.

In 1990, free elections in East Germany led to a non-Communist government. East Germany and West Germany then began the process of **reunification.** Later that year, they were joined together again.

In Hungary and in Czechoslovakia, the Communist leaders decided to set up multi-party political systems through free elections. The Communist leaders of Bulgaria gave in to the wishes of their people and resigned. In Romania, a bloody revolt in 1989 ended in the arrest and execution of the Communist dictator, Nicolae Ceausescu, and his wife, Elena.

Eastern European countries wanted to establish closer ties with the West. It now seemed to people all over the world that the Iron Curtain had finally lifted.

In Germany, people celebrated the fall of the Berlin Wall.

The Fall of the Berlin Wall and the Reunification of Germany

For 28 years, a 26-mile-long wall had divided East Berlin from West Berlin. Ever since it had been built, East Berliners had been risking their lives to cross the wall to freedom. The Berlin Wall symbolized the split between a free, democratic West and an oppressed, nondemocratic East.

Then, in late 1989, democratic movements swept the Soviet Union and much of Eastern Europe. In September 1989, thousands of East Germans crossed the newly opened border from Hungary to Austria. From there they made their way to West Germany. The East German government recognized that it could no longer keep its citizens prisoners behind a wall.

After the East Germans agreed to open the gates to the Wall, people took matters into their own hands. They began to tear down the Wall.

In 1990, East Germany held its first free elections since World War II. The Communists were voted out of office. The new leaders of East Germany worked out a plan with West Germany to join into a single, reunified country. Helmut Kohl was elected the first chancellor of the reunified Germany. Once combined, the two Germanys had over 80 million people, more than any other nation in Europe. It would have a powerful economy and a strong military. A united Germany would be a mighty force in the European community.

Reading Strategy:
Text Structure

Study the map in this lesson. What is it showing you about this lesson?

Independent Republics

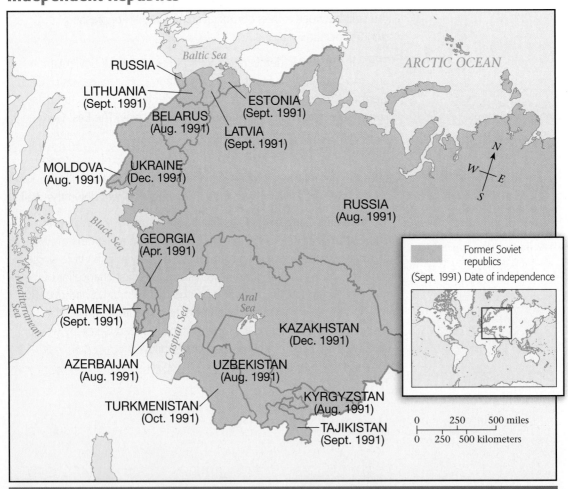

RUSSIA

LITHUANIA
(Sept. 1991)

ESTONIA
(Sept. 1991)

BELARUS
(Aug. 1991)

LATVIA
(Sept. 1991)

MOLDOVA
(Aug. 1991)

UKRAINE
(Dec. 1991)

Baltic Sea

ARCTIC OCEAN

RUSSIA
(Aug. 1991)

Black Sea

GEORGIA
(Apr. 1991)

Mediterranean Sea

Aral Sea

ARMENIA
(Sept. 1991)

Caspian Sea

KAZAKHSTAN
(Dec. 1991)

AZERBAIJAN
(Aug. 1991)

UZBEKISTAN
(Aug. 1991)

TURKMENISTAN
(Oct. 1991)

KYRGYZSTAN
(Aug. 1991)

TAJIKISTAN
(Sept. 1991)

Former Soviet republics
(Sept. 1991) Date of independence

0 250 500 miles
0 250 500 kilometers

MAP STUDY

1. Name four former Soviet republics.

2. Which two former Soviet republics were the last to gain independence?

Why Did Yugoslavia Break Up?

New freedoms did not necessarily mean peace in Eastern Europe. As Communism released its hold on Yugoslavia, separate republics began declaring their independence. Yugoslavia was made up of six republics: Serbia, Croatia, Slovenia, Bosnia-Herzegovina, Macedonia, and Montenegro. Though it covered an area the size of Wyoming, it was home to 30 nationalities. The largest groups of people were Serbs and Croats. In Yugoslavia, 41 percent were Eastern Orthodox Christians, 32 percent were Roman Catholics, and 12 percent were Muslims.

Fierce fighting in Bosnia ended when the Dayton Accords was signed in 1995. Ten years later, a Bosnian man stands in front of a damaged building in Sarajevo.

In June 1991, the republics of Croatia and Slovenia formally declared themselves independent. Civil war began in Croatia as Croats and ethnic Serbs fought for control. By the end of 1991, at least 6,000 people had been killed and 15,000 wounded in the Serbian-Croatian conflict.

The republic of Bosnia-Herzegovina declared itself independent in February 1992. Independence was supported by the Bosnian Muslims. They made up about 44 percent of the republic's population. The Eastern Orthodox Serbs (about 34 percent of the population) opposed the declaration. Violence broke out between Serbs and Bosnians. Thousands of Bosnians were killed. Fierce fighting continued until 1995 when a peace plan called the Dayton Accords was signed. The plan was sponsored by the United States. NATO troops, including American troops, were sent to Bosnia to keep the peace.

Geography Note

In the 9th century, Bohemia was an independent country in central Europe. Prague was its largest city. It later became part of the Holy Roman Empire. Under Emperor Charles IV (1347–1378), Prague grew into one of the most successful cities in Europe. After World War I, Bohemia, Moravia, and Slovakia became independent as Czechoslovakia. The country was taken over by Communists in 1948. Czechoslovakia broke up in 1993. Bohemia and Moravia joined to form the Czech Republic.

Trouble in the area that was once Yugoslavia has continued. Soon after Bosnia left Yugoslavia, another republic, Macedonia, declared its independence. Yugoslavia still appears on many maps, but now it only consists of two republics—Serbia and Montenegro. Ethnic Albanians living inside Serbia began to push for freedom.

In Serbia, the Serbs terrorized and killed many ethnic Albanians in Kosovo. Kosovo had been a self-ruling province in Serbia. Serbia's president, Slobodan Milosevic, started ruling Kosovo and forcing many ethnic Albanians to leave. In response, NATO bombed Serbia in 1999. More ethnic Albanians, or Kosovars, fled to nearby countries. After the bombing, NATO peacekeeping troops, including U.S. troops, went to Kosovo to protect the people. Many ethnic Albanians who had been forced from their homes returned to Kosovo.

A UN court charged Serbia's president, Slobodan Milosevic, with war crimes. In the year 2000, Serbs rejected him when he ran for president. When Milosevic would not accept election results, the Serbs protested. Milosevic finally accepted defeat in October 2000.

Why Was There War in Chechnya?

Chechnya is a region in southwestern Russia. After the fall of the Soviet Union, it remained part of Russia. However, in 1992 Chechnya declared its independence. Russian troops invaded the area to bring peace. Fighting continued until 1996, when troops left the area. Fighting began again in 1999. Heavy fighting took place on and off for years.

The Russian army was criticized for bombing civilian areas of Chechnya. Likewise, Chechen suicide bombers killed many innocent people throughout Russia. In 2002, Chechens held more than 800 hostages in a Moscow theater. Of the 800 hostages, 129 were killed. The number of civilian deaths in the two wars is not certain. Most sources estimate that anywhere from 100,000 to 200,000 people were killed in the two wars. In 2003, Russia approved a new constitution for Chechnya, giving it more power within the Federation.

TIMELINE STUDY: THE FALL OF COMMUNISM IN THE SOVIET UNION AND EASTERN EUROPE

Did the Soviet Union disband before or after reform swept Eastern Europe?

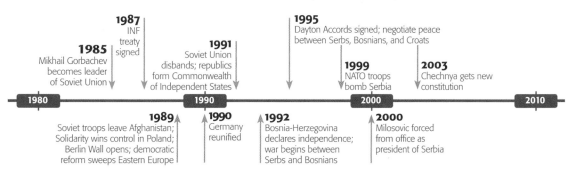

1985 Mikhail Gorbachev becomes leader of Soviet Union

1987 INF treaty signed

1991 Soviet Union disbands; republics form Commonwealth of Independent States

1995 Dayton Accords signed; negotiate peace between Serbs, Bosnians, and Croats

1999 NATO troops bomb Serbia

2003 Chechnya gets new constitution

1980   1990   2000   2010

1989 Soviet troops leave Afghanistan; Solidarity wins control in Poland; Berlin Wall opens; democratic reform sweeps Eastern Europe

1990 Germany reunified

1992 Bosnia-Herzegovina declares independence; war begins between Serbs and Bosnians

2000 Milosovic forced from office as president of Serbia

On a sheet of paper, write the letter of the answer that correctly completes each sentence.

1. In 1956, _____ tried to cut its ties with the Soviet Union.

   A Yugoslavia   **B** Moscow   **C** Hungary   **D** Romania

2. The Russians were afraid that Czechoslovakians had too much freedom of _____.

   A speech   **B** government   **C** Communism   **D** Moscow

3. In 1980, the Polish government allowed workers to form a(n) _____ to better working conditions.

   A government **B** coup   **C** army   **D** union

4. When the first free elections were held in Poland, _____ became president.

   A Nicolae Ceausescu   **C** Helmut Kohl
   B Lech Walesa   **D** Boris Yeltsin

5. In 1990, free elections in East Germany led to a non-_____ government.

   A radical   **B** Communist   **C** union   **D** political

6. Fierce fighting in _____ continued until a peace plan called the Dayton Accords was signed.

   A Serbia   **B** Albania   **C** Croatia   **D** Bosnia

7. NATO bombed _____ in 1999 because Slobodan Milosevic was forcing Albanians out of Kosovo.

   A Serbia   **B** Bosnia   **C** East Germany   **D** West Germany

On a sheet of paper, write the answer to each question. Use complete sentences.

8. Why did workers riot in Poland in the 1970s?

9. What is the meaning of the word *reunification*?

10. Why did civil war begin in Croatia?

SUMMARY

- After he came to power in 1985, Mikhail Gorbachev introduced new policies. He gave Soviet citizens more freedoms and improved Soviet relations with Western nations.

- New treaties between the Soviet Union and the United States promised to reduce nuclear arms.

- Soviet citizens faced economic problems as well as shortages of food and medicine.

- During the late 1980s, democratic reform swept Eastern Europe, spurred by changes in the Soviet Union. The wave of freedom reached its height when the Berlin Wall fell in late 1989.

- In 1991, the Soviet Union disbanded. Eventually nations formed a loose alliance called the Commonwealth of Independent States. Boris Yeltsin became leader of independent Russia and the Commonwealth of Independent States.

- Upon the resignation of Yeltsin in 1999, Vladimir Putin became president of the Russian Federation. He was elected in 2000 and again in 2004.

- Putin made bold strides to begin social programs to help the people of his country. He worked to develop strong communication with Western nations.

- As the Soviet Union disbanded in 1991, Chechnya declared its independence from the Russian Federation. Two separate wars followed, during which at least 150,000 people have been killed to date.

- During the break up of the former Yugoslavia, the Serbian-Croatian conflict began. At least 6,000 people were killed and 15,000 were wounded.

- Parts of Eastern Europe have been unstable as nations and ethnic groups struggle to move forward.

Word Bank

coup

disband

glasnost

perestroika

reunification

Vocabulary Review

On a sheet of paper, use the words from the Word Bank to correctly match each definition below.

1. _____ is a word that means "to break up."

2. When the Berlin Wall fell, East and West Germany began the process of _____.

3. Gorbachev's policy of _____ led many republics in the Soviet Union to seek independence.

4. Hard-line Communist leaders attempted a _____ in 1991 to take over power in the Soviet Union.

5. Gorbachev's policy of _____ allowed other countries to open businesses in the Soviet Union.

Chapter Review Questions

On a sheet of paper, write the answers to each question. Use complete sentences.

6. How did Gorbachev change the Soviet economy?

7. What alliance did most of the former Soviet republics form?

8. What happened to Germany after the fall of the Berlin Wall?

9. How did the Soviet Union and the United States reduce nuclear arms?

10. Why did the hard-line Soviet Communists criticize Gorbachev's new policies?

11. In 1991, which three countries declared their independence from the Soviet Union?

12. The Russian Federation took the seat in the UN that was held by the Soviet Union. Why?

13. What did the Soviet government do to limit Czechoslovakia's freedom of speech?

14. Why did Poland's government declare unions illegal?

Critical Thinking

On a sheet of paper, write your response to each question. Use complete sentences.

15. In your opinion, why has there been so much civil war in the area of former Yugoslavia?

16. In your opinion, why did the Soviet Union end?

17. Should the United States send troops to try to resolve conflicts in Eastern Europe? Explain.

Using the Timeline

Use the timeline on page 699 to answer the questions.

18. When did Solidarity win control in Poland?

19. What happened during the same year Bosnia-Herzogovina declared independence?

20. When did Mikhail Gorbachev become leader of the Soviet Union?

GROUP ACTIVITY

Form a group of four or five. Create a television newscast about the end of the Soviet Union and the fall of Communism in Eastern Europe. One classmate is the anchor. The three other classmates report from three different areas of Eastern Europe. Be sure to make notes to use during the newscast.

Latin America After World War II

After World War II, Communism began to grow throughout Asia and Europe. The United States grew more concerned about keeping the countries of Latin America free of Communist control. In 1948, the Organization of American States (OAS) was founded. The OAS members pledged to defend one another and to work out any problems among them peacefully. Since that time, the United States has sent billions of dollars to Latin American countries for education, industry, and health care programs.

GOALS FOR LEARNING

- To describe the United States' role in Latin American affairs
- To describe the unrest in Central America
- To explain the trouble in Mexico and Haiti
- To describe Latin America today

Reading Strategy: Visualizing

It is often useful to create a movie in your mind as you read. This reading strategy is known as visualizing. It helps you better understand what you are reading. The following tips can help you visualize a text:

- Look at the maps, timelines, photographs, and illustrations.

- Think about your own experiences that may add to the images.

- Observe the order in which things are happening. Use your past knowledge and experiences to consider what you think might happen next.

Key Vocabulary Words

Lesson 1
Good Neighbor Policy The policy in which the United States said it would not interfere with Latin American affairs

Lesson 2
Stronghold A place dominated by a certain group which they have made safe and secure

Politics The work of government

Ban To get rid of; to make something not legal

Moderate To make or become less extreme or violent

Humane Kind; showing care for others

Lesson 3
Tariff A tax that countries put on goods they import or export

Immigration The act of coming into a country or region to live there

Refuge Shelter or protection from danger

Lesson 4
Global warming The heating up of Earth from the burning of wood, coal, oil, and gasoline

Environment The land, sea, and air of our world

The United States in Latin American Affairs

Objectives

- To explain why the Organization of American States was formed
- To describe the effect of Fidel Castro's takeover of Cuba on U.S.-Cuban relations

Reading Strategy: Visualizing

What clues on this page help you visualize the changes that took place in Cuba?

Good Neighbor Policy

The policy in which the United States said it would not interfere with Latin American affairs

Before World War II, representatives from the nations of the Americas met in a Pan-American conference. They pledged themselves to a **Good Neighbor Policy**. They promised that no nation would interfere with the affairs of another nation. Then came World War II. During the war all Latin American nations supported the Allies. Brazil and Mexico even provided troops.

When World War II ended, the United States took a renewed interest in Latin America. The U.S. government hoped to keep Communism out of the Western Hemisphere and to encourage good relations between the nations of the Americas. In 1948, the Organization of American States (OAS) was founded. Among its members were the United States and all the independent countries of Latin America. OAS countries pledged to join together in defending the Americas and in peacefully settling any quarrels.

Since the 1950s, the United States has sent billions of dollars to help Latin American countries solve their social and economic problems. Technical experts from the United States have helped improve Latin American agriculture, industry, education, and health care.

In more recent years, U.S. aid was sometimes unwelcome. Some Latin Americans said the United States was not really interested in helping them but was sending aid to protect its own interests. They said the United States should stay out of the affairs of other nations.

Why Are Relations Between the United States and Cuba Strained?

The first half of the 20th century was a time of change and instability in Latin America. Revolutions overthrew a number of dictators. However, the end of dictatorship did not always bring about stability. New governments did not always grant rights to its people.

A 1959 revolution led to major changes on the island nation of Cuba. A former lawyer named Fidel Castro and his army of guerrilla fighters overthrew the military dictatorship of Fulgencio Batista. Castro set up a Communist dictatorship. Under Communism, Cuba became closely allied with the Soviet Union. Castro pledged to help Communist rebels gain control in other Latin American countries. The United States refused to recognize the Castro government in Cuba. Friendly relations ended between the United States and the small country only 90 miles from its shores.

Thirty years later, the situation was not much better. The collapse of the Soviet Union and the end of Communism upset Cuba's economy. It left the country even more unstable. As a result, thousands of Cubans left Cuba for the United States. In recent years, this has strained Cuba's relationship with its U.S. neighbor.

Fidel Castro has been in power as the dictator of Cuba since 1959.

Word Bank

Communism

Cuba

dictatorship

Good Neighbor
Policy

Organization of
American States

Pan-American

United States

On a sheet of paper, write the word from the Word Bank to complete each sentence correctly.

1. The Good Neighbor Policy came out of the _____ conference held before World War II.

2. The _____ promised that no nation would interfere with the affairs of another nation.

3. The U.S. government took renewed interest in Latin America after World War II. They hoped to prevent _____ from entering the Western Hemisphere and to encourage good relations.

4. The _____ pledged to defend the Americas and peacefully settle any quarrels.

5. When Castro came to power after the 1959 revolution, he set up a Communist _____.

6. The United States refused to recognize the Castro government in _____.

7. After Castro came to power, friendly relations between the _____ and Cuba ended.

On a sheet of paper, write the answer to each question. Use complete sentences.

8. The United States has sent billions of dollars to help solve problems in Latin America. What are three social and economic problems U.S. support has helped improve?

9. Why was U.S. aid unwelcome in recent years?

10. Under Fidel Castro, Cuba allied itself with what superpower?

Unrest in Central America

Objectives

■ To explain why the United States aided Nicaraguan rebels in their fight against the Sandinistas

■ To describe why the United States helped the government of El Salvador stay in power

■ To discuss the reasons the United States invaded Panama in 1989

Reading Strategy: Visualizing

Create a graphic organizer with boxes and arrows to help you understand the sequence of events in Nicaragua.

Stronghold
A place dominated by a certain group which they have made safe and secure

Politics
The work of government

The social and economic situation of Latin American countries is unstable at times. The United States has provided aid to some countries, but that aid is not always welcome. However, the United States is physically close to Central America. It is not surprising, then, that the United States continues to get tangled in Latin American affairs.

Why Did a Civil War Break Out in Nicaragua?

After the Castro revolution, Communist activity increased in Latin America. In 1979, Cuban Communists supported a revolution in Nicaragua. A Communist group called the Sandinista National Liberation Front overthrew Nicaragua's dictator, Anastasio Somoza. The Sandinistas took control of the government. Although Somoza had done little to improve life for his people, he had supported U.S. policies throughout Central America. The United States criticized Somoza's use of violence. The United States also feared that a new Sandinista government would provide a Communist **stronghold** in Central America. A stronghold is a place dominated by a certain group that has been made safe and secure. The United States accused the Nicaraguan Sandinistas of helping Communist rebels in neighboring El Salvador. They also accused the Sandinistas of relying on Soviet aid and support.

A group called the Contras (*contra* means "against" in Spanish) rebelled against the Sandinistas. U.S. President Ronald Reagan announced that the United States would provide military and economic aid to the Contras. Many Latin Americans criticized the United States for interfering in the **politics** of another nation. In other words, they did not think the United States should mix in the workings of another nation's government.

Ban
To get rid of; to make something not legal

Remember
Ronald Reagan feared that the domino theory, one nation after another falling to Communism, could apply to Latin America.

Some U.S. citizens also questioned their country's involvement. In 1984, the U.S. House of Representatives voted to **ban** aid to the Contras—they made giving aid to the Contras illegal. However, it was later discovered that in spite of the ban, illegal aid continued for several years.

A civil war went on in Nicaragua until 1989. Then President Daniel Ortega signed a treaty with Contra rebels. The Contras agreed to lay down their arms and refuse outside aid. Ortega promised that Nicaragua would hold democratic elections in 1990. That year, in a surprise victory, Violeta Barrios de Chamorro defeated Ortega and became the new president of Nicaragua.

LEARN MORE ABOUT IT

The Iran-Contra Affair

The United States Congress banned military aid to the Nicaraguan Contras in 1984. However, in 1986, the American people learned of a secret arms deal that gave money to Nicaragua. The affair had two parts.

Part One: It was discovered that U.S. officials secretly sold missiles and missile parts to the Middle Eastern nation of Iran. This was at a time when the United States was publicly speaking out against Iran, calling it a terrorist nation. As a result of the weapons sales, Iranians persuaded terrorists in Lebanon to release some U.S. hostages. U.S. policy, however, strictly forbade (did not allow) trading arms for political hostages.

Part Two: The U.S. Congress had specifically refused military aid to the Contras. However, profits from the Iranian arms sales were illegally used to aid the Contras in Nicaragua.

Reading Strategy:
Visualizing

What words about El Salvador help you visualize what you are reading?

Why Was There Fighting in El Salvador?

Nicaragua was not the only Central American country engaged in a civil war during the 1980s. Unrest had rocked El Salvador for many years. In 1979, the military took control of the government. Anti-government rebels were backed by Cuba and by the Communists in Nicaragua. The United States sent aid to El Salvador's military government. President Reagan said the United States had to defend itself against Communism. Again, some U.S. citizens protested the aid. They said that the military government was not worthy of support because it promoted violence that had killed thousands of Salvadoran civilians.

Soldiers fought a civil war in El Salvador for over 12 years.

Moderate
To make or become less extreme or violent

Humane
Kind; showing care for others

In 1984, El Salvadoran voters elected Jose Napoleon Duarte to the presidency. He promised a more **moderate** and **humane** government. A moderate government is one that is less extreme or violent; a humane government is one that is more kind and shows care for people. However, rebel guerrilla attacks continued. The civil war finally ended in 1992.

A peace treaty between the government and rebel forces promised military and political reform. The war in El Salvador had lasted about 13 years and took the lives of nearly 75,000 people.

Why Did the United States Invade Panama?

As civil war raged in El Salvador, a storm was brewing in the Central American nation of Panama. In 1987, General Manuel Noriega was commander of the Panamanian defense forces. Although Panama's president was Eric Arturo Delvalle, all the real power lay in the hands of General Noriega.

Noriega was corrupt. He was an accused drug smuggler (he secretly brought illegal drugs into and out of the country). He was known to tamper with election votes so his candidates would win. In other words, he would interfere with votes so his candidates would be elected. When a national election was held in May 1989, the man who ran against him, Guillermo Endara, won the most votes. Noriega ignored the election results. He claimed victory.

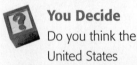

You Decide
Do you think the United States had the right to send troops to Panama to drive Noriega from power? Why or why not?

The U.S. government wanted to see General Noriega removed from power. On December 23, 1989, U.S. President George H.W. Bush sent 24,000 U.S. troops to Panama to drive Noriega from power. At a U.S. military base, Guillermo Endara was sworn in as president.

General Noriega spent 10 days in hiding before he surrendered to American military forces. He was brought back to the United States to stand trial on drug charges. In 1992, a U.S. District Court in Miami, Florida, convicted Noriega of drug trafficking.

Throughout the 1980s, protest against military governments grew in several Latin American countries. In many cases, these protests brought free elections. By the early 1990s, civilian leaders elected by the people had replaced military governments in such places as Guatemala, Argentina, Brazil, Chile, and Paraguay.

LEARN MORE ABOUT IT

War in the Falklands

In April 1982, Argentina launched an attack on a British colony in South America. The Falklands, a group of islands off the Argentinian coast, had been a British colony since 1833. Most of the people living there are British. When Argentina tried to seize control of the Falklands, Margaret Thatcher, Britain's prime minister, sent forces to protect the colony. It was a short but bloody war. On June 14, Argentina surrendered. The Falklands remained under British control.

Today the Falkland Islands are a territory of the United Kingdom. The islands are also claimed by Argentina.

On a sheet of paper, write the letter of the answer that correctly completes each sentence.

1. The _____ controlled the Nicaraguan government after the 1979 revolution.

   A military   **B** Sandinistas   **C** Contras   **D** civilians

2. The United States provided _____ military and economic aid because they rebelled against the Sandinistas.

   A Communists   **B** Panamanians   **C** Contras   **D** civilians

3. Nicaragua's civil war ended in _____ when the president signed a treaty with Contra rebels.

   A 1979   **B** 1984   **C** 1989   **D** 1990

4. The U.S. government sent money to support El Salvador's _____ government.

   A military   **B** Communist   **C** rebel   **D** Contra

5. El Salvador's civil war ended after a peace treaty promised _____ and political reform.

   A economic   **B** military   **C** social   **D** Communism

6. _____ was finally sworn in as president after U.S. troops invaded Panama.

   A General Manuel Noriega   **C** George H.W. Bush
   B Eric Arturo Delvalle   **D** Guillermo Endara

On a sheet of paper, write the answer to each question. Use complete sentences.

7. Why did U.S. President Reagan believe it was important to support anti-Communist forces in Latin America?

8. Why were some U.S. citizens upset at the aid sent to El Salvador?

9. Why did U.S. troops invade Panama in 1989?

10. Name three Latin American nations where civilian governments replaced military governments by the early 1990s.

LESSON 33-3

Trouble in Mexico and Haiti

Objectives

■ To explain Mexico's political and economic situation

■ To explain why so many Haitians are fleeing their country

Mexico and Haiti have similar political and economic situations—they are unstable. Both have large gaps between the rich and the poor. Both have people who flee their country to try and make a home in the United States. This has strained the relationships between these two countries and the United States.

What Changes Were Happening in Mexico?

Political corruption and a growing population put Mexico into an economic crisis during the 1980s. During the 1970s, the discovery of vast oil fields in southern Mexico had promised new riches. The government increased spending on public works and on industry. It expected to pay for new development with income from oil. In the early 1980s, however, the price of oil fell, and so did Mexico's hopes for success. The country was left in serious debt.

This cathedral in Mexico City was built on top of the ruins of an Aztec temple.

Reading Strategy:
Visualizing

How could this section on Mexico be written differently to create a stronger picture in your mind?

History Fact
On July 2, 2000, Vincent Fox Quesada became the president of Mexico. The election may have been the fairest in Mexican history.

Mexico's economic crisis caused rising unemployment. The population kept growing rapidly, adding to the number of unemployed. A growing population, high foreign debt, and falling oil income meant economic troubles for Mexico.

Many Mexicans turned their anger and disappointment toward the government. Political unrest increased. During the oil boom, Mexico's peasants and the poor who lived in the city saw hope for their future. Now that hope was gone. They became more aware than ever of the great gap that existed between the few rich people and the many poor ones. As Mexico's economy weakened, the number of Mexicans illegally entering the United States grew. They crossed the border in search of work and a better standard of living.

In 1992, the United States, Canada, and Mexico announced plans for the North American Free Trade Agreement (NAFTA). The agreement offered a chance for economic growth for all three nations. Among the terms of the agreement were proposals to eventually end **tariffs** on all farm products and many other goods. A tariff is a tax that a country puts on goods they import or export. The treaty also aimed to ease **immigration** laws for business executives and professionals (when a person immigrates, he or she comes into a country to live there). Finally, the treaty allowed trucks free access to border routes between the three countries. The agreement was approved by the governments of the three nations. It promised a boost to Mexico's economy. After some difficult years, the Mexican economy grew from 1997 to 2000.

In the mid-1990s, rebels in the state of Chiapas demanded more land for the people. The Mexican government is in control of the state today. However, some fighting between armed civilians over land claims still happens.

Reading Strategy:
Visualizing

Draw a picture to help
you visualize what
you are reading in this
section on Haiti. How
does this image help you
remember?

Why Was There Unrest in Haiti?

Civil unrest has plagued the Caribbean island nation
of Haiti in recent years. Revolutions and government
takeovers have been spurred by poverty, drought,
hurricanes, and famine. Between early 1986 and mid-
1990, Haiti had five different governments. In the 1990s,
the United States led a force from many nations to restore
Haiti's elected leader to office.

Violence against civilians has led many Haitians to flee
their country. In 1991 and 1992, over 65,000 Haitian
refugees were stopped by the U.S. Coast Guard. They were
trying to enter the United States illegally. Most of them
were returned to Haiti, although many in the United States
felt they should be allowed to seek **refuge** (shelter) in the
United States.

Violence against civilians forced many Haitians to flee their country in 1991 and 1992.

On a sheet of paper, write the letter of the answer that correctly completes each sentence.

1. _____ was discovered in Mexico during the 1970s, and promised new riches.

   A Gold   **B** Oil   **C** An ancient ruin   **D** NAFTA

2. In the early 1980s, the price of oil fell, leaving Mexico in serious _____.

   A drought   **B** success   **C** debt   **D** riches

3. As Mexico's economy weakened, more Mexicans entered the United States _____.

   A illegally   **B** to avoid work   **C** in search of water   **D** looking for oil

4. Mexicans came to the United States in search of _____ and a better standard of living.

   A oil   **B** work   **C** food   **D** water

5. The North American Free Trade Agreement (NAFTA) offered economic growth for the United States, _____, and Mexico.

   A Cuba   **B** El Salvador   **C** Haiti   **D** Canada

6. Poverty, drought, hurricanes, and _____ have prompted civil unrest in Haiti.

   A famine   **B** the military   **C** unemployment   **D** violence

7. Haiti had _____ different governments between early 1986 and mid-1990.

   A three   **B** five   **C** seven   **D** nine

On a sheet of paper, write the answer to each question. Use complete sentences.

8. What are three factors that have contributed to the economic troubles in Mexico?

9. What were the terms of the North American Free Trade Agreement?

10. Why are so many Haitians fleeing their country?

Latin America Today

Objectives

- To explain what happened to the Latin American economy by the late 1970s
- To explain the positive changes that have taken place in Latin America since 2000

Throughout its history, Latin America has faced many problems. However, in recent years the region has become more democratic and financially stable.

What Is Latin America Like Today?

Latin America's economy grew during the 1960s and early 1970s. By the late 1970s, however, economic growth declined. Latin American industry depended upon certain imports. It needed refined goods and machinery. This became a problem when prices on these imports rose sharply. At the same time, the prices on Latin America's raw agricultural and mineral exports dropped.

Latin America Today

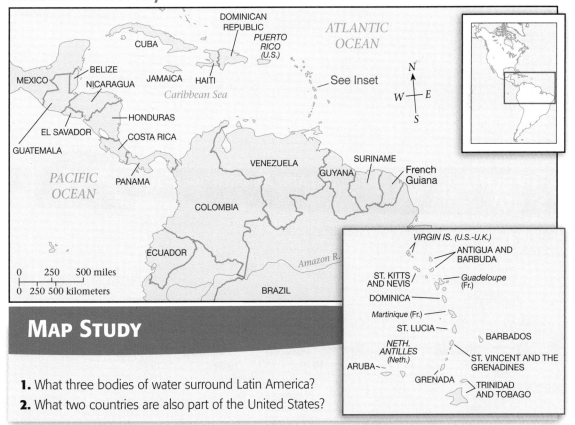

MAP STUDY

1. What three bodies of water surround Latin America?
2. What two countries are also part of the United States?

During this period, the Latin American nations were spending more and making less. Many had to borrow huge sums of money. Some of these nations have had trouble raising the money they need to repay their loans. By 2000, many positive changes had taken place in Latin America. In most countries, the economy had been improving. Democracy was growing. Women were gaining rights. Education had become a priority.

Brazil has the largest economy in South America. In fact, Brazil has the ninth largest economy in the world. Although the Brazilian government had to devalue its money in 1999, the economy still grew.

Reading Strategy:
Visualizing

Study the timeline in this lesson. How does it help you visualize the events in this chapter?

TIMELINE STUDY:

LATIN AMERICA: 1945–2010

In what year did Cuba become a Communist country?

1990 Nicaragua holds democratic elections

1992 War ends in El Salvador

1988 Democratic elections end military rule in Chile

2000 Fox wins presidency in Mexico

1948 OAS is founded

1982 Falklands War

1959 Castro sets up Communist government in Cuba

1979 Sandinistas take power in Nicaragua

1989 U.S. troops go to Panama

1994 North American Free Trade Agreement takes effect

1983 U.S. troops go to Grenada; Democratic rule returns to Argentina

1950   1960   1970   1980   1990   2000   2010

Global warming
The heating up of Earth from the burning of wood, coal, oil, and gasoline

Environment
The land, sea, and air of our world

Destruction of the rain forests not only threatens the world's climate. It also threatens the one-of-a-kind animals, such as this Cassowary, that live there.

LEARN MORE ABOUT IT

Brazil Pledges to Protect Its Rain Forest

The rain forests of South and Central America are an important resource to the whole world. The forests are not only beautiful. They have a direct effect on the world's climate. Yet in many regions, vast areas of the rain forests have been burned or cut down to make way for cattle ranches and farms. In 1987 and 1988, pictures taken from space showed the huge damage being done to Brazilian forest lands.

The world will pay a price for the destruction, or ruin, of its rain forests. Trees remove carbon dioxide (CO_2) from the air. Many scientists believe that a buildup of CO_2 will result in **global warming.** Global warming is the term used to describe the heating up of Earth from the burning of wood, coal, oil, and gasoline.

Global warming is sometimes called the "greenhouse effect." In addition, Brazilian fires set to burn the rain forests add CO_2 to the atmosphere. This increases the greenhouse effect.

In 1988, Brazil's president promised an end to the mass burning of the Amazon forests. In 1989, Brazil began a program aimed at protecting its rain forests. Brazil demonstrated its concern for the **environment** by hosting representatives from 178 countries at an Earth Day Summit in June 1992. Today, Brazil has adopted an environmental plan. It has also adopted the Environmental Crimes Law with strong penalties.

REVIEW

Word Bank

Amazon

Brazil

carbon dioxide
   (CO_2)

climate

democracy

economies

global warming

loans

machinery

mineral

On a sheet of paper, write the word from the Word Bank to complete each sentence correctly.

1. Latin American industry was dependent on refined goods and _____.

2. The price of Latin America's raw agricultural and _____ exports dropped as the price for imports rose.

3. Some Latin American nations were having trouble repaying their _____.

4. By 2000, many Latin American _____ were improving.

5. Also, _____ was growing, women were gaining rights, and education was becoming a priority.

6. _____ has the ninth largest economy in the world.

7. Rain forests have a direct effect on the world's _____.

8. By cutting down trees in the rain forests, _____ is being removed from the air.

9. _____ is also known as the "greenhouse effect."

10. Since 1988, Brazil has worked to protect the _____ forests.

SUMMARY

- After World War II, the United States tried to keep Communism out of Latin America.

- In a 1959 revolution, Fidel Castro set up a Communist dictatorship in Cuba.

- A Communist group called the Sandinistas took over the government of Nicaragua in 1979. The United States provided aid to a group called the Contras, a rebel group opposed to the Sandinistas. A civil war went on until 1989.

- A civil war in El Salvador went on for over 12 years. It took the lives of nearly 13,000 people.

- The United States invaded Panama to remove General Manuel Noriega from power.

- Many Latin Americans and U.S. citizens criticized the U.S. government for interfering in the affairs of other nations. They also did not think the United States should aid harsh governments.

- Mexico faced an economic and political crisis in the 1980s and 1990s.

- In 1992, the United States, Canada, and Mexico announced plans for the North American Free Trade Agreement.

- The island nation of Haiti has faced great hardship in recent years. Poverty, drought, hunger, and damage from hurricanes have caused many revolutions.

- The countries of Latin America have struggled with many different problems. However, in recent years some have become more democratic and financially stable.

Word Bank

ban
environment
global warming
humane
immigration
moderate
politics
refuge
stronghold
tariff

Vocabulary Review

On a sheet of paper, use the words from the Word Bank to complete each sentence correctly.

1. The U.S. feared a Communist _____ in Central America.

2. A(n) _____ government cares about poor people.

3. Some people believe that the United States should not interfere in the _____ of other nations.

4. A(n) _____ government is not extreme in its policies or actions.

5. Burning wood, coal, oil, and gasoline heats up Earth, causing _____.

6. _____ laws are rules about people coming into a country or region to live there.

7. The rain forests are an important part of our _____.

8. A(n) _____ is a tax a country puts on goods they import or export.

9. When you _____ aid to someone or something, you make providing aid illegal.

10. A(n) _____ is a safe place away from danger.

Chapter Review Questions

On a sheet of paper, write the answer to each question. Use complete sentences.

11. What happened to Cuba-U.S. relations after Castro took power in Cuba?

12. Why did the United States fight on the side of the rebels in Nicaragua?

13. Why did the United States fight on the side of the government in El Salvador?

14. What happened after General Manuel Noriega claimed victory in Panama's 1989 election?

15. What countries does NAFTA include and what does the agreement offer?

16. What four factors have contributed to the unrest (the revolutions and government takeovers) in Haiti?

Critical Thinking

On a sheet of paper, write your response to each question. Use complete sentences.

17. Why do events in Mexico affect the United States?

18. How could the destruction of the rain forests in Brazil affect your life?

Using the Timeline

Use the timeline on page 720 to answer the questions.

19. Which came first, the Falklands War or the U.S. invasion of Panama?

20. When was the Organization of American States founded?

GROUP ACTIVITY

With a group of three or four students, discuss U.S. relations with Cuba. Do you think the United States should have friendly relations with Cuba even if it is a Communist country? List the reasons your group says yes or no.

The World Today

People call the present time the "Nuclear Age," the "Computer Age," or the "Age of Technology." Today's world is full of brand new inventions and discoveries. People today are seeing advances in technology at a faster rate than ever before. At the same time, the world's challenges are rapidly increasing. Overpopulation, food shortages, and disease present important needs for change. Damage to the environment threatens the well-being of generations to come. Preventing ongoing global terrorism is a main concern of many world governments.

GOALS FOR LEARNING

- To describe the uses of nuclear power
- To explain the advances made in space exploration
- To describe the many ways we can get information in today's world
- To explain the global issues we face today
- To describe the current state of our environment and population
- To tell about the threat of global terrorism
- To consider what the future holds

Reading Strategy: Inferencing

You have to infer the meaning of a text when it is not directly stated. When making inferences, start with what you already know. Then try to think "beyond the text" by considering what you have just read.

What You Know + What You Read = Inference

When inferencing, consider what you are reading and then predict what will happen next. Also, explain cause and effect to help you make quality inferences.

Key Vocabulary Words

Lesson 1
Nonrenewable Cannot be replaced once it is used up

Lesson 2
Satellite An object put into orbit around the earth

Astronaut A person trained to make space flights

Cosmonaut Russian word meaning "astronaut"

Lesson 4
Multinational corporation A company that hires people and has business interests around the world

Technology Science put to use in practical work

Lesson 5
Overpopulation The state of having too many people; can ruin the environment or the quality of life

Extinction The act of bringing to an end; dying out

Epidemic The rapid spread of a disease

Lesson 6
Agency A group that provides a service

Humanity The human race

The Nuclear Age

Reading Strategy:
Inferencing

What do you already know about the use of nuclear energy?

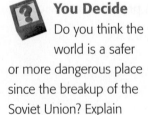

You Decide
Do you think the world is a safer or more dangerous place since the breakup of the Soviet Union? Explain why or why not.

The last half of the 20th century is sometimes called the "Nuclear Age." Actually, the idea of nuclear power began about 1905, with Albert Einstein. Einstein suggested that energy was contained in every atom. The first use of that energy came in 1945 when the United States exploded two atomic bombs over Japan. Those explosions ended World War II and began an age of development for atomic energy.

The explosion of the first atomic bomb started the powerful nations of the world on a race. It was a deadly race to build bigger weapons. Countries tried to outdo each other in the number and size of the bombs they built.

Now many nations have a weapon so destructive that the results of another world war are impossible to imagine. So, nations try to avoid that war. They meet and talk about peace. They discuss ways to limit the buildup of nuclear arms. The United States and the Soviet Union held talks and signed treaties.

In 1991, the Soviet Union broke up. Its separate republics became 15 new nations. The nuclear weapons of the old Soviet Union are no longer under control of a single government. The cold war is over, and old enemies have friendlier relations. However, there is concern whether these new nations will handle their nuclear arms responsibly. Nuclear weapons in the hands of unstable governments or of terrorists threaten the safety of the whole world. It is a reality that today's people must live with.

Nonrenewable
Cannot be replaced once it is used up

What Are Some Peaceful Uses of Nuclear Energy?

Although it was first used in a bomb, nuclear power has peacetime uses, too. The most important use is as a source of energy.

All nations use oil, coal, and natural gas for energy. These are all **nonrenewable** energy sources. Once they are used up, they are gone. As the population grows, the demand for energy also grows. People worry that we will run out of those traditional sources of energy.

The energy created in the nucleus of an atom can be used to run factories, heat homes, and light cities. Today this energy is produced in nuclear power plants around the world. Nuclear power is expensive. However, it can provide unlimited energy for thousands of years. The question is: Is it safe?

What Are the Risks to Using Nuclear Power?

History Fact
In a meltdown, the cooling system fails and the core of the nuclear reactor actually melts.

Nuclear power plants have strict safety regulations, or rules. Accidents, however, can happen. In 1979, there was an accident at the Three-Mile Island nuclear power plant in Pennsylvania. Failing equipment and human mistakes caused a near meltdown. While there were no tragic results, the public was frightened. People became aware that a disaster could happen. Stricter safety rules were set up. Yet, some people still wondered about the future of nuclear power. They worried that the risk was too great.

In 1986, a nuclear disaster occurred in the Soviet Union. There was a meltdown and explosion at the Chernobyl nuclear power plant. Nuclear explosions cause radiation. Radiation is when the rays and tiny pieces from a nuclear explosion are spread out. These rays and tiny pieces are very harmful and dangerous to anything living.

The explosion at the Chernobyl nuclear power plant killed 23 people. It also forced many people to evacuate, or leave, nearby towns. The radiation from the explosion badly polluted the soil for 1,000 square miles. It sent a cloud of radiation across the Ukraine and other parts of the Soviet Union, and across several other European nations. Thousands of Soviet citizens—men, women, and children—were exposed to the radiation. Many of these people may die of cancer or other diseases. Traces of radiation were also found in animals, milk, and plant life far from the site of the accident. No one is sure just what the long-range effects of such radiation might be.

Many people protest the building of nuclear power plants. They say that no amount of energy is worth the risk of nuclear disaster. Others maintain that nuclear power is a safe answer to the world's energy crisis. They point out that many people have died in coal mine accidents over the years. Compared to this, only a few have died in accidents related to nuclear power plants.

Those in favor of nuclear power also point out that it is clean. It causes much less pollution than coal or oil. However, those against nuclear power have one very solid argument for their point of view. No safe method has yet been discovered for disposing of nuclear waste.

Reading Strategy:
Inferencing

After reading this section, what can you infer about the future use of nuclear energy? What words helped you make your inference?

Word Bank

Einstein

energy

Japan

meltdown

nuclear

nucleus

Soviet Union

On a sheet of paper, write the word from the Word Bank to complete each sentence correctly.

1. The last half of the 20th century is sometimes called the "_____ Age."

2. In 1905, nuclear power began with the idea from _____.

3. In 1945, the United States exploded two atomic bombs over _____.

4. The most important peacetime use of nuclear power is as a renewable source of _____.

5. The _____ of an atom creates enough energy to heat homes and light cities.

6. In 1979, there was almost a(n) _____ at the Three-Mile Island nuclear power plant.

7. In 1986, a nuclear disaster happened in the _____.

On a sheet of paper, write the letter of the answer that correctly completes each sentence.

8. Nuclear explosions cause _____.

    A heat   B radiation   C energy   D light

9. Nuclear power causes much less _____ than coal or oil.

    A pollution   B energy   C heat   D light

10. There is not a safe method yet to dispose of nuclear _____.

    A energy   B power   C weapons   D waste

The Space Age

History Fact
Sputnik I weighed 184 pounds and was only 23 inches wide. It looked like a shooting star as it moved across the sky.

Sometimes the present era is called the "Space Age." The Space Age began in 1957. That is when the Soviet Union launched the first **satellite** made by humans into orbit around the earth. The satellite was called *Sputnik I*. Soon after, the United States launched its first satellite, *Explorer I.* The space race had begun.

Why Was There a Race Into Space?

An **astronaut** is a person who is trained to make space flights. In 1961, the Russians put the first human being into space. He was **cosmonaut** Yuri Gagarin (*cosmonaut* is the Russian word for "astronaut"). Then, in 1969, U.S. astronaut Neil Armstrong became the first person to walk on the moon. This event was watched on TV by 600 million people around the world.

The first woman went into space in 1963. She was the Soviet cosmonaut Valentina V. Tereshkova. In 1983, the United States sent its first woman astronaut, Sally Ride, into space aboard the shuttle *Challenger.*

The exploration of space is exciting. But it is also difficult, expensive, and dangerous. In January 1986, the space shuttle *Challenger* exploded shortly after takeoff. All the people on board were killed. There have been other accidents in which people have died. However, many people feel that the rewards from space exploration are worth the risks.

The space shuttle program provides a way for astronauts to learn more about our universe.

What Are the Benefits and Risks of Space Exploration?

Space has been an area in which the United States and the Soviet Union race to be the best. Space, however, can also be an arena for peace. In July 1975, three American astronauts and two Russian cosmonauts met in space. As planned, their two spaceships hooked up. U.S. space shuttles regularly delivered supplies and people to the Russian space station *Mir.* American and Russian astronauts lived and worked together in space. They conducted scientific experiments together and both nations shared the results.

In early 2001, an American and two Russians were living on the International Space Station (ISS). The ISS is an orbiting science laboratory. It will be completed in space.

The *Columbia* was the first space shuttle to be launched into orbit, in April 1981. During the next 22 years it flew a total of 28 missions. It was completely rebuilt three times, most recently in 1999. On February 1, 2003, the *Columbia* was returning from a 16-day scientific mission. It broke apart as it reentered the earth's atmosphere. The *Columbia's* seven crew members were killed. Researchers believe that a piece of insulation broke off the shuttle's outside fuel tank. (Insulation is material used to cover and protect something.) The falling insulation seriously damaged one of the shuttle's wings.

The Space Age has only begun. Many people expect that before too long, we will have colonies on the moon. People from Earth may someday live on Mars and on other planets. Spaceships that do not include humans to operate them have already landed on Mars and Venus and sent back pictures. Other ships have flown close to Jupiter, Saturn, Uranus, and Neptune. Perhaps someday, we may even go to other solar systems!

Reading Strategy:
Inferencing

Consider what you just read. What can you infer about the future progress of space exploration?

TECHNOLOGY CONNECTION

The Hubble Space Telescope
In the late 1970s, the National Aeronautics and Space Agency (NASA) teamed up with the European Space Agency. Together they built the Hubble Space Telescope. In 1990, the space shuttle *Discovery* sent the telescope into space, about 350 miles above the earth. This was the first telescope in space that could take photographs. Since that time, the telescope has sent back better photos of the universe than any taken from the ground. Among the many images captured by the Hubble were those of two distant galaxies. A galaxy is a large group of stars and planets. In 1997 these galaxies, named *Antennae*, collided. At first, this crash created blue light from gases and hot star clusters. Scientists counted over 1,000 clusters of new stars. The brightest cluster was believed to have contained a million new stars.

REVIEW

Word Bank

astronaut

Challenger

Neil Armstrong

Soviet Union

Space Age

Sputnik I

Yuri Gagarin

On a sheet of paper, write the word from the Word Bank to complete each sentence correctly.

1. The _____ began in 1957.

2. The _____ launched the first satellite made by humans into orbit around the earth.

3. The first satellite to orbit around the earth was called _____.

4. A(n) _____ is a person who is trained to make space flights.

5. In 1961, the Russians launched the first human into space. The cosmonaut's name was _____.

6. _____ was the first person to walk on the moon.

7. In 1986, the space shuttle _____ exploded shortly after takeoff.

On a sheet of paper, write the letter of the answer that correctly completes each sentence.

8. In 1975, Americans and Russians started working together in a Russian space station named _____.

   A *Columbia*   **B** *Mir*   **C** *Challenger*   **D** *Explorer*

9. In _____, the *Columbia* was the first space shuttle to be launched into orbit.

   A 1957   **B** 1975   **C** 1981   **D** 2004

10. More than _____ people watched on television as the first man walked on the moon.

    A 12 million   **C** 200 million
    B 60 million   **D** 600 million

The Computer Age

Reading Strategy: Inferencing

What do you already know about computers?

History Fact
Supersonic airplanes fly faster than sound can travel. (At sea level, sound travels 740 miles per hour.)

You Decide
The present era is often called the "Information Age." Do you think the name fits? Why or why not?

Computers are electronic machines. They solve problems, answer questions, and store information. Computers are used around the world to help people do their work, find information, communicate with others, and play games.

Computers have improved steadily since World War II. At first they were very large, very expensive, and difficult to run. Now they are much smaller and are used by millions of people. A computer that once filled an entire room now fits into the palm of a hand!

At first people worried that computers would replace humans in many jobs. In some cases, this has happened. However, computers have created many more new jobs. Computers give people the time and freedom to get more work done. They also provide entertainment for millions of people.

In What Ways Is the World "Shrinking"?

Developments in transportation and communication have made the world seem smaller. People in one part of the world now know what is happening across the ocean. In fact, a trip across an ocean that used to take months, now takes only hours!

Television also has the ability to transport people across the ocean—all while they sit on their couch! Without a doubt, TV has greatly changed 21st-century life. Many Americans protested involvement in the Vietnam War because television cameras brought the action to them. They saw for themselves the suffering of American soldiers and Vietnamese villagers.

Television news brought the Israeli-Arab conflict into millions of homes. People of the world witnessed the injustices of apartheid in South Africa. They also saw hunger in Ethiopia and Somalia with their own eyes.

We also get information from the hundreds of communication satellites that circle the earth. They beam radio, television, telephone, and computer signals around the world. Satellites in space can take weather pictures to make forecasts anywhere in the world.

Reading Strategy:
Inferencing

How does what you already know about computers add to what you have just read?

With computers and the Internet, workers can trade or share information almost instantly.

Words from the Past

The Internet

Communication around the world is advancing almost daily. Satellites and under-ocean cables provide connections for global telephone and Internet service.

The Internet links people all over the world in a way like never before. We can write to one another, send photos and videos, and even communicate "live" using webcam. Consumers can buy countless products from companies all over the world. We can book a hotel room in Tokyo, arrange car rental in Cairo, or sign up for scuba lessons in New Zealand. The number of people using the Internet has tripled since 1997. More than one billion people worldwide now use the Internet regularly.

Personal computers and cell phones bring people together, even when they are on the move. Using handheld devices, people can type instant messages (IMs), share music, and talk. They can snap and then send photos. They can surf the Internet while riding on a bus, or send e-mails from a coffee shop in a foreign country. They can watch movies or do research while sitting under a tree in a park.

Thousands of people have created their own spaces on the Internet. They can link to friends through these sites, and share ideas instantly with other people all over the world. Workers can trade or share files with one another using other Internet sites.

REVIEW

Word Bank

bigger

billion

cell phones

computers

humans

Internet

satellites

smaller

Vietnam War

World War II

On a sheet of paper, write the word from the Word Bank to complete each sentence correctly.

1. _____ solve problems, answer questions, and store information.

2. Computers have improved steadily since _____.

3. People were afraid computers would replace _____ in many jobs.

4. Development in transportation and communication make the world seem _____.

5. Many Americans did not like the _____ because television cameras showed the action to them.

6. Communication _____ beam radio, television, and computer signals all over the world.

7. The _____ links people all over the world.

8. More than one _____ people worldwide regularly use the Internet.

9. Personal computers and _____ bring people together, even when they are on the move.

10. Computers used to be much _____ than they are today.

Global Issues

Objectives

Objectives

- To describe a global economy
- To explain the relationship between developed nations and developing nations

As the world seems to grow smaller, nations have a greater influence on each other. Trade has long affected cultures and civilizations, and ideas have always been shared while trading. Now it is common for nations to trade their goods and ideas worldwide. They depend on each other for an exchange of raw materials and manufactured goods.

What Is a "Global Economy"?

The Pacific Rim is a term used to describe lands bordering the Pacific Ocean. During the 1980s, the Pacific Rim became the world's fastest-growing trading area. Electronic equipment, cars, and other products leave Japan, Taiwan, and Korea for foreign markets.

The popularity of foreign products weakened the economy of the United States. Since the 1970s, the United States has imported more goods from other nations than it has exported. Since that time, hundreds of U.S. factories have closed or laid off workers. This is because these foreign products are being purchased in large quantities by U.S. consumers.

At first the United States tried to solve its economic problems by setting up trade restrictions. Congress set limits on the number of imports that could enter the country. Foreign companies found ways to get around the restrictions. Japanese automakers built factories in the United States. By 1989, many "American-made" cars were manufactured in U.S. plants owned by Japanese companies.

Multinational corporation

A company that hires people and has business interests around the world

Remember

Trade developed among early civilizations. Many things you own are imports.

This was not a new strategy. The United States had been setting up factories all over the world for years. During the 1980s, many U.S. companies built factories in foreign lands to take advantage of cheap labor. Today many are **multinational corporations**—companies that hire people and have business interests around the world. Japanese companies own some entertainment and food business in the United States. U.S. auto companies have interests in auto companies in other countries.

The health of one nation's economy depends greatly on that of other nations. All countries need places to export the goods they make. All countries need to import some. Countries made trade alliances and free-trade agreements to tear down barriers and encourage fair trade. In 1988, the United States and Canada signed a free-trade pact. It ended restrictions and tariffs on almost all products. In 1994, the United States, Canada, and Mexico began free trade between all three nations.

European nations have joined together in the European Union (EU). The goal of the EU is to ensure completely free trade and free movement of money and people between member nations. The World Trade Organization (WTO) has 150 member nations. In 2000, some people in the United States protested against the WTO. In Seattle, protesters included workers who were afraid their jobs would go to other countries. Environmentalists who wanted stronger protection for the environment were there, too.

What Is the Difference Between a Developed Nation and a Developing Nation?

The Industrial Revolution split the nations of the world into two camps: developed nations and developing nations. Developed nations have many industries. They import and export products. Most people who live in developed nations have a fairly high standard of living.

Most people there can read and write. They benefit from
the advances of modern science and its practical uses, or
technology. The United States, Russia, Canada, France,
Great Britain, Japan, the Scandinavian countries, and
Germany are just some of the developed nations.

Developing nations are the countries that are less
developed. Many people in developing nations are
poor. Many people farm the land, but their methods of
agriculture are often outdated. There are fewer industries
in developing nations. Their standard of living is lower,
and many people cannot read or write.

History Fact
Developing
countries include
about 120 countries and
more than half of the
world's people.

In developing countries, many people live in traditional
ways. It is important to preserve aspects of traditional life
while making economic gains. Haiti, Afghanistan, and
Mexico are examples of developing countries. Many South
American and African nations are developing countries.
Some of these nations, like Nigeria and Venezuela, have
rich oil deposits.

Developed nations have many industries and a fairly high standard of living. New York
City is an excellent example of a city in a developed nation.

Developing countries are more dependent on other nations. Their economies can be easily upset by weather, a year of bad farm crops, or a war. Sometimes the more developed nations help the developing nations by lending money or sending supplies. The United States has sent thousands of Peace Corps volunteers to developing countries all over the world. There the volunteers teach modern farming methods, health care, and engineering.

Developing nations often use outdated methods of agriculture and live in traditional ways. Afghanistan is an example of a developing country.

Reading Strategy:
Inferencing

After reading this section, what inference can you make about the problems of hunger in developing nations?

GREAT NAMES IN HISTORY

Mother Teresa of Calcutta

Agnes Gonxha Bojaxhiu was born in Macedonia in 1910. At age 18, she joined the Sisters of Loreto, an order of nuns with missions in India. She became Sister Teresa. She started teaching in a convent school in Calcutta, India. Sister Teresa saw great suffering beyond the convent walls. After many years she left the school to work in the poorest neighborhoods of Calcutta. By this time she was known as Mother Teresa.

Mother Teresa started helping people who were sick and had little food. She had no money, yet she founded an open-air school for the children of the poor neighborhoods. She began to attract volunteers to help her. Organizations started giving money for the school. In 1959, she founded the Missionaries of Charity to help needy people in other parts of the world. Mother Teresa won many awards for her kindness, including the Nobel Peace Prize in 1979.

On a sheet of paper, write the letter of the answer that correctly completes each sentence.

1. It is now common for nations to trade their goods and ideas _____.

   A worldwide   **B** yearly   **C** monthly   **D** by telegraph

2. During the 1980s, the _____ became the world's fastest-growing trading area.

   A United States   **B** Soviet Union   **C** Pacific Rim   **D** Canadian border

3. The popularity of _____ weakened the economy in the United States.

   A farming   **B** the Internet   **C** gold   **D** foreign products

4. The United States set up _____ to try and solve economic problems.

   A allowances   **B** restrictions   **C** agreements   **D** companies

5. In 1988, the United States and Canada signed a _____.

   A peace treaty   **B** free-trade pact   **C** trade restriction   **D** technology pact

6. There is free trade and movement of resources between nations in the _____.

   A free-trade pact   **B** WTO   **C** Peace Corps   **D** European Union

7. The _____ has 150 member nations.

   A World Trade Organization   **C** Pacific Rim
   B European Union   **D** United States

8. The _____ split nations into developed nations and developing nations.

   A Agricultural Revolution   **C** European Union
   B World Trade Organization   **D** Industrial Revolution

9. Many people in developing countries are _____.

   A wealthy   **B** scientists   **C** poor   **D** exporters

10. U.S. _____ volunteers teach modern farming methods in developing countries.

   A Army   **B** Navy   **C** Peace Corps   **D** Air Force

Environment, Overpopulation, and Disease

Objectives

- To describe the effects of overpopulation
- To explain some alternative sources of energy
- To describe the diseases that threaten our world today

Reading Strategy:
Inferencing

What do you already know about concerns regarding the environment, overpopulation, and disease?

Overpopulation

The state of having too many people; can ruin the environment or the quality of life

Humankind has made big progress since the first civilizations in Sumer. However, with progress comes problems. The technological advances we have made, along with our growing population, can negatively affect Earth.

What Is the Growing Population Doing to Our Environment?

As the number of people increases around the world, so does the damage to the environment. More people are driving cars. More factories are using more energy to make products. More space is needed to house and grow food for the population. Indeed, our planet has reached a state of **overpopulation.** Overpopulation, the state of having too many people, can ruin the environment or quality of life.

Vehicles, factories, and some plants produce gases from burning fuels such as oil or coal. These gases pollute the air. They may contribute to breathing illnesses in people. They produce acid rain, which damages plants and harms animals that eat those plants. Dangerous global warming happens when gases surrounding the earth trap the heat from sunlight. Factories, careless farming practices, and misplaced trash is affecting water quality in many countries of the world.

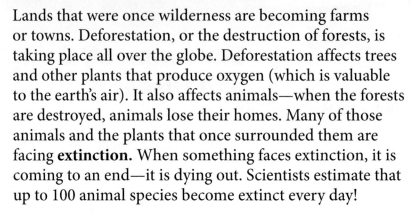

Extinction
The act of bringing to an end; dying out

Lands that were once wilderness are becoming farms or towns. Deforestation, or the destruction of forests, is taking place all over the globe. Deforestation affects trees and other plants that produce oxygen (which is valuable to the earth's air). It also affects animals—when the forests are destroyed, animals lose their homes. Many of those animals and the plants that once surrounded them are facing **extinction.** When something faces extinction, it is coming to an end—it is dying out. Scientists estimate that up to 100 animal species become extinct every day!

What Are Some Alternative Sources of Energy?

The world's energy needs are increasing. However, the supplies of fossil fuels such as oil, coal, and natural gas are decreasing. Scientists in many countries are working to find ways to use energy from renewable sources. Renewable sources are sources that can be replaced.

Wind, sunlight, water, and heat from the ground are renewable sources, because supplies are endless. Many countries now have wind farms in open areas, often near oceans, which get strong winds. One such collection of windmills near Ireland produces electricity for 16,000 homes. Since the 1980s, many homes and office buildings have used solar panels to collect energy from the sun. New technology is making the use of solar energy better and less expensive. An increasing number of cities are capturing underground heat for use in buildings. Areas near oceans and rivers are exploring new ways of using waves or falling water to produce electricity.

Governments are working to encourage the use of alternative energy such as wind energy.

Manufacturers have developed cars that run on electricity or ethanol. Ethanol is a fuel that is made from something that can be grown, such as sugar. People of many nations are working to create laws to improve air and water quality. Laws are being passed to preserve animal homes and to protect animals that are facing extinction.

Deadly Storms

Horrible natural disasters have occurred in recent years on opposite sides of the globe.

A tsunami up to 30 feet high hit the Indian Ocean in late 2004. A tsunami is a giant wall of water usually caused by an earthquake under the sea. It killed nearly 200,000 people, mostly in Indonesia, India, and on the island of Sri Lanka. A second tsunami hit Java, Indonesia's main island, in 2006, killing 530 people. This wave was six feet high, small compared to the one in 2004.

Hurricane Katrina hit the Florida coast on August 25, 2005. Then it moved into the Gulf of Mexico and gained strength. It hit the coast of Louisiana and Mississippi on August 29. The force of the storm broke the levees around New Orleans, Louisiana. The levees were made to hold back water. Almost all of that city became badly flooded. More than 1,800 people were killed and more than a million were left homeless by this storm.

What Diseases Are Threatening Our World?

Millions of poor people die from illnesses related to dirty living conditions. Others simply do not have enough of the right foods to remain healthy. In wealthier countries, many people overeat, use tobacco, and get too little exercise. These habits often lead to heart disease and diabetes, two major causes of early deaths in these countries.

Various new diseases prompted concern in the 1990s and 2000s. Insects and other flying creatures spread many of them. A disease called SARS (Severe Acute Respiratory Syndrome) is spread by close person-to-person contact. More than 8,000 people in 26 countries have become infected with SARS. Lyme disease, spread by deer ticks, infected 25,000 people in the United States alone during 2002. The West Nile virus is most often spread to people and animals through mosquitoes.

The bird flu, spread through infected poultry, has infected about 300 people worldwide. Scientists are working to learn more about how to control all of these diseases.

Malaria is not a new disease, by any means, but it is also transmitted by mosquitoes. About a million people in Africa die each year from malaria. During the 1950s, the disease was eliminated (gone) from the United States. In recent years it has returned, with over 1,000 cases reported in America in 2002.

AIDS (acquired immune deficiency syndrome) continues to infect people all over the world. Doctors discovered that AIDS was caused by a virus—the human immunodeficiency virus (HIV). Since 1981, AIDS has shown up in some 140 countries around the world. It exploded into the most widespread **epidemic**—the rapid spread of a disease—in central Africa. High numbers were also found in the small Caribbean nation of Haiti. By the end of the 1990s, there were very few countries in which this killer disease had not struck. In 2006, nearly 40 million people worldwide were living with HIV. New medications are helping more people with HIV avoid developing AIDS. Despite these new advances, the number of AIDS cases is growing worldwide. Doctors continue to search for ways to stop the AIDS epidemic and to save those who already have the virus.

Reading Strategy:
Inferencing

How does what you already know about these issues add to what you have just read?

Word Bank

AIDS

deforestation

fossil fuels

global warming

malaria

overpopulation

renewable

On a sheet of paper, write the word from the Word Bank to complete each sentence correctly.

1. _____ happens when gases surrounding the earth trap heat from the sunlight.

2. _____ can ruin the environment or quality of life for people.

3. _____ affects animals' homes as well as trees and plants that produce oxygen.

4. The supplies of _____, such as oil, coal, and natural gas, are decreasing.

5. _____ sources are energy sources that can be replaced. Wind, sunlight, water, and heat from the ground are examples.

6. About a million people die in Africa each year because of _____.

7. Since 1981, _____ has shown up in 140 countries around the world.

On a sheet of paper, write the answer to each question. Use complete sentences.

8. What are two forms of alternative energy sources?

9. What are governments doing to help the environment?

10. What are two common diseases in wealthier countries that are major causes of death?

The Threat of Global Terrorism

Objectives

- To explain how terrorism has affected the entire world
- To describe what can be done to prevent future terrorist attacks

As you may remember from Chapter 31, Middle Eastern terrorism has spread to the larger world. With the threat of terrorism so real, nations are coming together to prevent future attacks.

How Has the Threat of Terrorism Changed the World?

Terrorism has existed for many years. It has not been limited to the Middle East. Terrorists throughout the world use violence to frighten people and leaders. They use fear in hope of having their demands met.

After the September 11 terrorist attacks on the United States, all planes were grounded for two days. When they started flying again, airport security screening for all passengers was much stricter. Security was also increased near public places where large groups of people gather, such as sports arenas.

Lawmakers in the United States began developing the new Department of Homeland Security. This department would organize all security and emergency agencies as one branch of government. By doing so, the department wanted to better prepare for and prevent future terrorist attacks.

How Did Wars Start in Iraq and Afghanistan?

The Taliban in Afghanistan was known to allow training camps for al Qaeda members. (The Taliban is the group that controls the government in Afghanistan.) The United States government had asked that the Taliban turn over Osama bin Laden. He had admitted leading the 9/11 terror attacks on America. The Taliban refused to turn bin Laden in.

Agency
A group that provides a service

Humanity
The human race

So, the United States attacked Taliban sites in Afghanistan in October 2001. They destroyed al Qaeda camps. The Taliban and al Qaeda members fled the country, as did bin Laden. American and NATO troops stayed in Afghanistan to help rebuild the country under a new government.

A report published by the American CIA (Central Intelligence **Agency**) in 2002 warned that Iraq was hiding weapons of mass destruction. Iraq refused to cooperate with United Nations inspectors looking for weapons. President George W. Bush insisted that Saddam Hussein's government was aiding terrorist groups. Hussein had to be removed and the people of Iraq had to be freed of his tyranny. On March 19, 2003, troops from the United States, Britain, and many smaller nations invaded Baghdad, the capital of Iraq. Operation Iraqi Freedom had begun. Saddam Hussein went into hiding. Within 43 days the troops had taken over the country.

Saddam Hussein's sons were killed in a raid in July 2003. Hussein was captured in December of the same year. An Iraqi court found him guilty of crimes against the human race, or **humanity.** He was executed in December 2006. The American and British troops found no weapons of mass destruction.

Reading Strategy: Inferencing

After reading this section, what inference can you make about the best way to control terrorism? What words helped you make your inference?

The Americans wanted to help establish a democratic government in Iraq. Aided by other governments, the Iraqis began forming a representative government. They wrote a constitution and held their first free elections in 2005. Unfortunately, since that time, fighting between groups for control of the country has increased. As of early 2007, more than 10,000 Iraqis had been killed. More than 3,000 American soldiers were killed and about 20,000 had been injured. Many Americans did not support increasing troop activity in the country.

Have There Been Other Terrorist Attacks?

According to the U.S. State Department, there were 9,474 terrorist attacks worldwide between 1982 and 2003. In the five-year period between 1998 and 2003, there were 1,865. Regular acts of terror continue in both Iraq and Afghanistan.

In many countries of the world, increased security seems to be reducing the number of terrorist attacks. However, they continue to happen. For instance, bombs planted on a subway and buses in London killed 52 people in 2005.

What Can Be Done to Prevent Further Attacks?

Further attacks can be prevented by increasing our awareness of dangers. This is especially important with travel and in situations involving large groups of people.

Passengers on a flight from Paris to New York in December 2001 noticed another passenger acting suspiciously. They were able to control him before he could light bombs in his shoes.

In August 2006, British officials discovered a plot to blow up nine or ten planes. The planes were traveling from London to the United States. The 24 men arrested planned to blow up the planes mid-air. They would use liquid bombs that they had in their carry-on bags. As a result, all liquids in carry-on bags were banned for future flights.

Reading Strategy:
Inferencing

Based on what you have read, what can you infer about the threat of global terrorism in the years to come?

The U.S. State Department has identified dozens of terrorist groups training members in different countries. One important task for the Department of Homeland Security is to monitor the activities of such groups. Agents and offices in foreign countries help them do this. A law called the Patriot Act helps too. It gives the U.S. government more power to check on backgrounds of people in the country. Firmer rules on entering the United States will also help prevent terrorist acts.

On a sheet of paper, write the letter of the answer that correctly completes each sentence.

1. _____ became much stricter at airports and public places after September 11.

    A Troops   **B** Governments   **C** Lawmakers   **D** Security

2. U.S. lawmakers began developing the Department of _____ after the attacks.

    A Defense   **B** Transportation   **C** Homeland Security **D** Terrorism

3. The _____ in Afghanistan allowed training camps for al Qaeda members.

    A Iraqis   **B** Americans   **C** Taliban   **D** CIA

4. The American CIA warned that Iraq was hiding _____ in 2002.

    A guns   **C** energy sources
    B military troops   **D** weapons of mass destruction

5. In 2003, _____ was found guilty of crimes against the human race.

    A Tony Blair   **B** Saddam Hussein   **C** Osama bin Laden   **D** George W. Bush

6. In 2005, Iraq wrote a _____ and held free elections.

    A constitution **B** trade-pact   **C** news release   **D** speech

7. According to the U.S. State Department, _____ terrorist attacks were made between 1982 and 2003.

    A 7,000   **B** 9,474   **C** 16,300   **D** 42,714

8. Bombs planted on a subway and in buses in _____ killed 52 people in 2005.

    A Kuwait   **B** New York City   **C** Washington, D.C.   **D** London

9. The _____ gives the U.S. government power to check people's backgrounds.

    A Patriot Act   **B** Terrorism Act   **C** Security Act   **D** Humanity Bill

10. The United States has identified _____ of terrorist groups in different countries.

    A dozens   **B** hundreds   **C** thousands   **D** millions

Looking to the Future

Picture the days of ancient Greece and a Greek athlete running an Olympic race. It is 776 B.C. The young man pulls ahead of the other racers on a dusty road. He gasps the warm air. His lungs ache with the effort. As he crosses the finish line, he closes his eyes and raises his arms over his head in victory.

When he opens his eyes again, he expects to find himself surrounded by cheering Greeks. He can almost feel the crown of olive leaves about to be placed on his head.

Instead the racer finds himself in a crowded, modern stadium. It is A.D. 2004, Athens, Greece, the 28th Summer Olympics. People are cheering, but they are not all Greeks. There are people from around the whole world. Furthermore, no olive leaves await the racer. Instead he is awarded a shiny, gold medal. Somehow our racer has been jolted forward in time more than 2,000 years.

What will he find? What undreamed-of wonders will our racer discover?

What Does the Future Hold?

The racer will find a whole new world of medicine. Doctors can actually replace worn-out or diseased body parts. Sometimes those replacements come from people who have died. Other times the parts are manufactured. The young Greek time-traveler can hardly believe it. These modern doctors can even replace a person's heart!

People treat each other in a different way now. The Greek racer is surprised to find women athletes around him. Women, he will discover, have a whole new role in society. In many places they are treated as equals with men.

They work side by side with men in all kinds of jobs. Women have become leaders in science, medicine, and business.

Spaceships to the moon, automobiles that speed people to their destinations, airplanes, television, telephones . . . the list of new wonders is endless.

Has anything remained the same? Most people still live in family groups, although many of those groups are smaller. People still have the same basic needs for food and shelter. People still have trouble getting along. There are still those who want to be conquerors and who seek power at all costs. There are still those who must struggle to hold on to their cultures and their homes. People from different backgrounds still do not know and understand each other well enough. People still fear what they do not understand.

Human beings are still curious, too. They still need to learn, explore, and discover. There will always be some questions to answer: What lies beyond the sun? Are there worlds and peoples other than our own? Can the people of this world ever live together completely at peace?

Reading Strategy:
Inferencing

What can you infer about the most important concerns as we look to the future? What details helped you make your inference?

TIMELINE STUDY:

THE WORLD: 1945–2010

Who was the first woman in space? When did she make her flight?

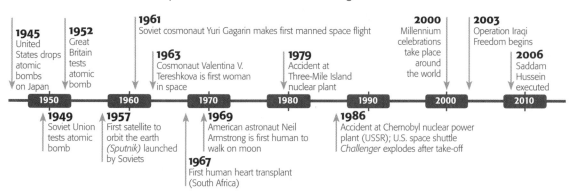

1945 United States drops atomic bombs on Japan

1952 Great Britain tests atomic bomb

1961 Soviet cosmonaut Yuri Gagarin makes first manned space flight

1963 Cosmonaut Valentina V. Tereshkova is first woman in space

1979 Accident at Three-Mile Island nuclear plant

2000 Millennium celebrations take place around the world

2003 Operation Iraqi Freedom begins

2006 Saddam Hussein executed

1949 Soviet Union tests atomic bomb

1957 First satellite to orbit the earth (*Sputnik*) launched by Soviets

1969 American astronaut Neil Armstrong is first human to walk on moon

1986 Accident at Chernobyl nuclear power plant (USSR); U.S. space shuttle *Challenger* explodes after take-off

1967 First human heart transplant (South Africa)

1950   1960   1970   1980   1990   2000   2010

REVIEW

backgrounds

curious

doctors

fear

Greece

groups

olive leaves

questions

science

women

On a sheet of paper, write the word from the Word Bank to complete each sentence correctly.

1. In 2004, the Summer Olympics were held in _____.

2. At the first Olympics, winners received _____ instead of shiny, gold medals.

3. _____ can now replace worn-out or diseased body parts.

4. In many places in society, _____ are now treated as equals with men.

5. Many people today still live in family _____.

6. People from different _____ still do not know and understand each other well enough.

7. Even today, people _____ what they do not understand.

8. Still today, humans are as _____ as they were before.

9. Women have become leaders in _____, medicine, and business.

10. Throughout time, there will always be _____ to be answered.

- Nuclear power is used for weapons and as a source of energy in peacetime. People worry about the dangers of an accident in a nuclear power plant. There are also concerns about how to safely get rid of nuclear waste.

- Countries can explore space by working together. Space exploration is both costly and, at times, dangerous. Many people feel that the knowledge gained is well worth the sacrifices.

- Television and other forms of international communication help bring people of the world closer together.

- Computers and the Internet are improving the ways of communication like never before. Handheld devices and the chance to "talk" to people anywhere at any time shrink the distance across the globe.

- Nations have become economically dependent on each other. Many are forming free-trade alliances that remove barriers to international trade.

- Developed nations have advanced technology, a higher standard of living, and strong trade programs. Developing nations are less developed, poorer, and more dependent on other countries.

- It is important to improve living conditions for everyone on Earth.

- The world has much to learn about controlling deadly diseases. Oftentimes, these diseases affect people without doctors or medicines.

- The increase in terrorist attacks in recent years has prompted nations to increase their security.

- Many breakthroughs in energy, space, and communication have taken place in the present age. However, people still have to deal with problems of ignorance, prejudice, persecution, and war.

Word Bank

agency

astronaut

cosmonaut

epidemic

extinction

humanity

nonrenewable

overpopulation

satellite

technology

Vocabulary Review

On a sheet of paper, use the words from the Word Bank to complete each sentence correctly.

1. A(n) _____ travels into space for the United States.

2. A(n) _____ from the Soviet Union was the first person into space.

3. A(n) _____ resource cannot be replaced once people use it all.

4. Computers, the Internet, and cell phones are examples of _____.

5. The United States has put a(n) _____ into space, which orbits around Earth.

6. A group that provides a service is called a(n) _____.

7. Deforestation is causing the _____ of plants and animals.

8. The rapid spread of AIDS is an example of a(n) _____.

9. _____ means "the human race."

10. The state of having too many people is called _____.

Chapter Review Questions

On a sheet of paper, write the answer to each question. Use complete sentences.

11. What are two uses of nuclear power?

12. When did the Space Age begin?

13. Why does the world seem to be shrinking?

14. Why is the last half of the 20th century sometimes called the "Nuclear Age"?

Critical Thinking

On a sheet of paper, write your response to each question. Use complete sentences.

15. What are some dangers of a global economy?

16. What is the major difference between a developed nation and a developing nation?

17. Do you think that nuclear energy is worth the possible risks?

Using the Timeline

Use the timeline on page 755 to answer the questions.

18. When was the first human heart transplant?

19. When did Neil Armstrong walk on the moon?

20. What satellite orbited the earth in 1957?

GROUP ACTIVITY

Suppose you are an Olympic racer from 776 B.C. Your partner is an Olympic athlete at the 2008 Olympics. Write a conversation the two of you would have about changes in the world. Practice the conversation and share it with some of your classmates.

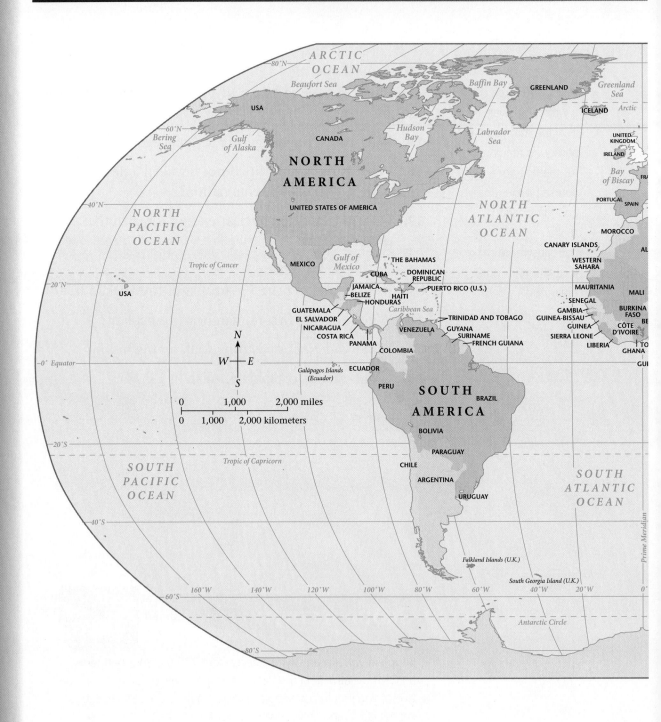

ARCTIC OCEAN

Beaufort Sea

Baffin Bay

GREENLAND

Greenland Sea

80°N

ICELAND

Arctic

USA

Hudson Bay

Labrador Sea

UNITED KINGDOM

CANADA

60°N

Bering Sea

Gulf of Alaska

IRELAND

Bay of Biscay

FRA

NORTH AMERICA

NORTH ATLANTIC OCEAN

40°N

NORTH PACIFIC OCEAN

UNITED STATES OF AMERICA

PORTUGAL

SPAIN

MOROCCO

CANARY ISLANDS

Tropic of Cancer

MEXICO

Gulf of Mexico

THE BAHAMAS

WESTERN SAHARA

CUBA

DOMINICAN REPUBLIC

20°N

USA

JAMAICA

HAITI

PUERTO RICO (U.S.)

MAURITANIA

MALI

BELIZE

SENEGAL

GUATEMALA

HONDURAS

GAMBIA

BURKINA FASO

EL SALVADOR

TRINIDAD AND TOBAGO

GUINEA-BISSAU

BE

NICARAGUA

VENEZUELA

GUYANA

GUINEA

CÔTE D'IVOIRE

COSTA RICA

SURINAME

SIERRA LEONE

TO

PANAMA

FRENCH GUIANA

LIBERIA

GHANA

COLOMBIA

GUI

Caribbean Sea

N

Galápagos Islands (Ecuador)

ECUADOR

0° Equator

W—E

S

PERU

SOUTH AMERICA

BRAZIL

0   1,000   2,000 miles

0   1,000   2,000 kilometers

BOLIVIA

20°S

PARAGUAY

Tropic of Capricorn

CHILE

SOUTH ATLANTIC OCEAN

SOUTH PACIFIC OCEAN

ARGENTINA

URUGUAY

40°S

Falkland Islands (U.K.)

South Georgia Island (U.K.)

Prime Meridian

160°W   140°W   120°W   100°W   80°W   60°W   40°W   20°W   0°

Antarctic Circle

80°S

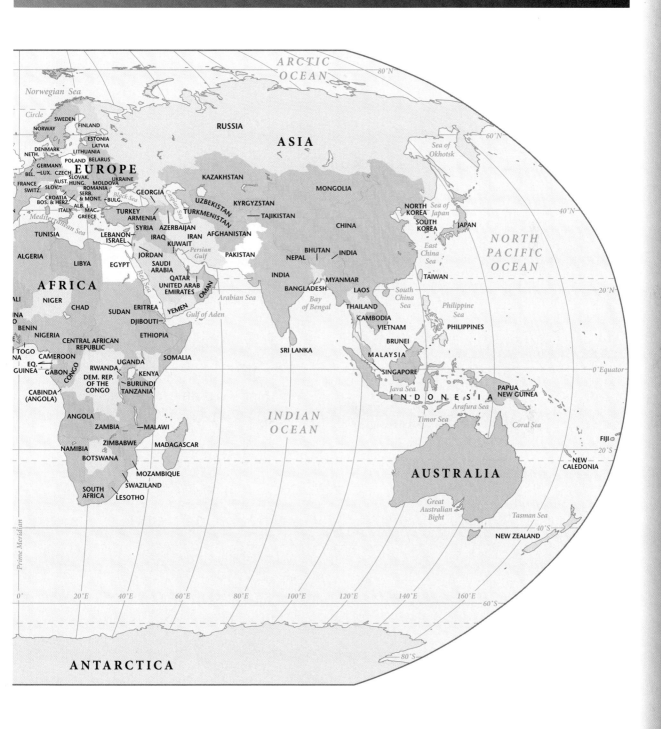

ARCTIC OCEAN

Norwegian Sea

Circle

SWEDEN
NORWAY
FINLAND

DENMARK
NETH.
GERMANY
BEL. LUX. CZECH
AUST. HUNG.
FRANCE
SWITZ. SLOV.
CROATIA
BOS. & HERZ.
ITALY
GREECE

EUROPE

ESTONIA
LATVIA
LITHUANIA
POLAND BELARUS

UKRAINE
MOLDOVA
ROMANIA
SERB.
& MONT. BULG.
ALB. MAC.

RUSSIA

ASIA

60°N

KAZAKHSTAN

GEORGIA
ARMENIA
TURKEY
SYRIA AZERBAIJAN
IRAQ
LEBANON
ISRAEL
JORDAN
KUWAIT

UZBEKISTAN
TURKMENISTAN
TAJIKISTAN

KYRGYZSTAN

MONGOLIA

Black Sea
Caspian Sea

Sea of Okhotsk

NORTH KOREA
SOUTH KOREA
JAPAN

Sea of Japan

40°N

CHINA

Mediterranean Sea

TUNISIA
ALGERIA
LIBYA
EGYPT

AFRICA

MALI
NIGER
CHAD
NA
BENIN
NIGERIA
TOGO
EQ.
GUINEA
GABON
CABINDA
(ANGOLA)

AFGHANISTAN

IRAN
Persian Gulf
PAKISTAN

SAUDI
ARABIA
QATAR
UNITED ARAB
EMIRATES
OMAN
YEMEN

Red Sea

ERITREA
SUDAN
DJIBOUTI
CENTRAL AFRICAN
REPUBLIC
ETHIOPIA
SOMALIA

CAMEROON
CONGO
RWANDA
DEM. REP.
OF THE
CONGO
BURUNDI
TANZANIA
UGANDA
KENYA

Arabian Sea

Gulf of Aden

NEPAL
INDIA

BHUTAN
INDIA
BANGLADESH

MYANMAR
LAOS
THAILAND
CAMBODIA
VIETNAM

Bay of Bengal

SRI LANKA

South China Sea

TAIWAN

NORTH
PACIFIC
OCEAN

East China Sea

Philippine Sea

PHILIPPINES

BRUNEI
MALAYSIA
SINGAPORE

20°N

0° Equator

ANGOLA
ZAMBIA
MALAWI
ZIMBABWE
NAMIBIA
BOTSWANA
MADAGASCAR

MOZAMBIQUE
SWAZILAND
SOUTH
AFRICA
LESOTHO

INDIAN
OCEAN

INDONESIA

Java Sea
Arafura Sea
Timor Sea

PAPUA
NEW GUINEA

Coral Sea

FIJI

NEW
CALEDONIA

20°S

AUSTRALIA

Great Australian Bight

Tasman Sea

40°S

NEW ZEALAND

Prime Meridian

0°   20°E   40°E   60°E   80°E   100°E   120°E   140°E   160°E

60°S

80°S

ANTARCTICA

80°N

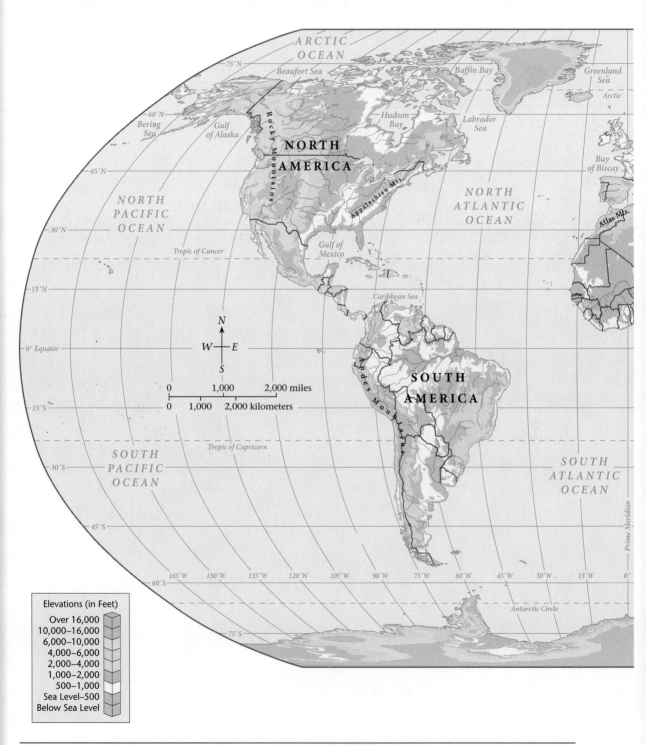

ARCTIC
OCEAN

75°N

Beaufort Sea

Baffin Bay

Greenland
Sea

Arctic

60°N

Bering
Sea

Gulf
of Alaska

Hudson
Bay

Labrador
Sea

Bay
of Biscay

NORTH
AMERICA

45°N

NORTH
PACIFIC
OCEAN

NORTH
ATLANTIC
OCEAN

Atlas Mts.

Appalachian Mts.

30°N

Tropic of Cancer

Gulf of
Mexico

15°N

Caribbean Sea

N

0° Equator

W   E

S

SOUTH
AMERICA

0   1,000   2,000 miles

15°S

0   1,000   2,000 kilometers

Tropic of Capricorn

SOUTH
PACIFIC
OCEAN

30°S

SOUTH
ATLANTIC
OCEAN

Prime Meridian

45°S

165°W   150°W   135°W   120°W   105°W   90°W   75°W   60°W   45°W   30°W   15°W   0°

60°S

Antarctic Circle

75°S

Elevations (in Feet)

Over 16,000
10,000–16,000
6,000–10,000
4,000–6,000
2,000–4,000
1,000–2,000
500–1,000
Sea Level–500
Below Sea Level

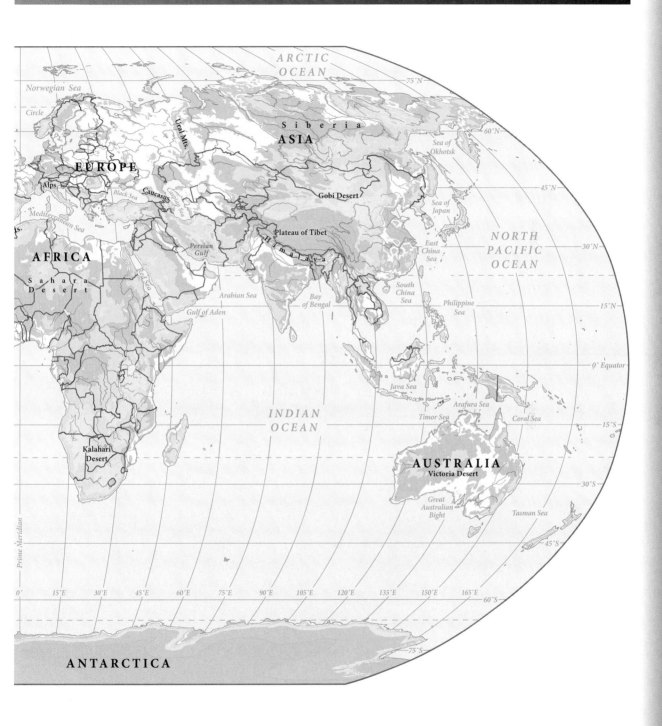

ARCTIC
OCEAN

75°N

Norwegian Sea

60°N

Circle

S i b e r i a
ASIA

Ural Mts.

Sea of
Okhotsk

EUROPE

45°N

Alps

Black Sea

Caucasus

Gobi Desert

Sea of
Japan

Mediterranean Sea

Caspian Sea

30°N

East
China
Sea

**NORTH
PACIFIC
OCEAN**

Persian
Gulf

Plateau of Tibet

H i m a l a y a

AFRICA

S a h a r a
D e s e r t

Arabian Sea

Bay
of Bengal

South
China
Sea

15°N

Gulf of Aden

Red Sea

Philippine
Sea

0° Equator

Java Sea

Arafura Sea

15°S

Timor Sea

Coral Sea

**INDIAN
OCEAN**

Kalahari
Desert

AUSTRALIA
Victoria Desert

30°S

Great
Australian
Bight

Tasman Sea

Prime Meridian

45°S

0°   15°E   30°E   45°E   60°E   75°E   90°E   105°E   120°E   135°E   150°E   165°E

60°S

75°S

ANTARCTICA

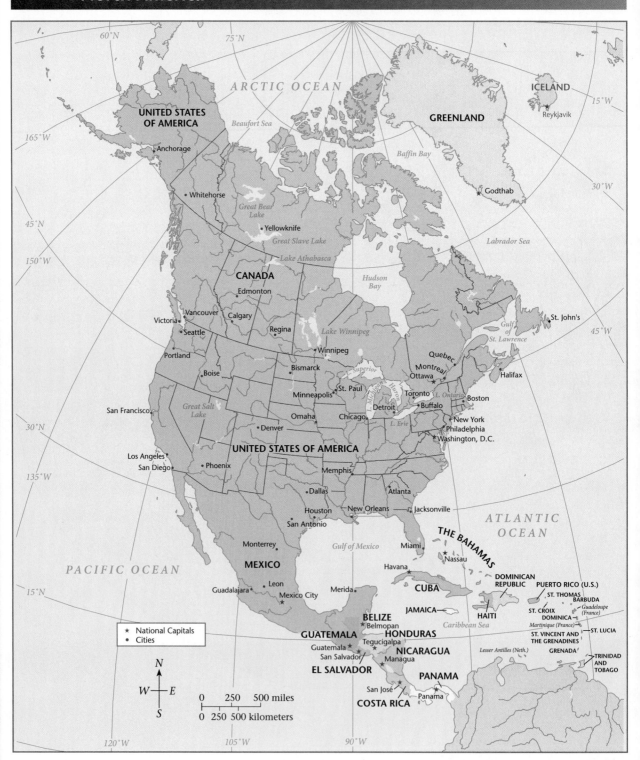

North America

ARCTIC OCEAN

60°N 75°N 15°W

UNITED STATES OF AMERICA

ICELAND

• Reykjavik

165°W

• Anchorage

Beaufort Sea

GREENLAND

Baffin Bay

30°W

• Whitehorse

Great Bear Lake

• Godthab

45°N

• Yellowknife

Great Slave Lake

Labrador Sea

150°W

Lake Athabasca

Hudson Bay

CANADA

• Edmonton

Gulf of St. Lawrence

• St. John's

• Vancouver • Calgary

• Victoria

• Seattle • Regina

Lake Winnipeg

45°W

• Portland

• Winnipeg

• Quebec

• Montreal

• Halifax

• Boise

• Bismarck

• Ottawa

Superior

• Minneapolis • St. Paul

Huron Toronto L. Ontario • Boston

• San Francisco

Great Salt Lake

• Omaha • Chicago • Detroit • Buffalo

L. Erie • New York

30°N

• Denver

UNITED STATES OF AMERICA

• Philadelphia

• Washington, D.C.

• Los Angeles

• San Diego

• Phoenix

135°W

• Memphis

• Dallas

• Atlanta

• Houston • New Orleans • Jacksonville

• San Antonio

ATLANTIC OCEAN

• Monterrey

Gulf of Mexico

• Miami

THE BAHAMAS

★ Nassau

PACIFIC OCEAN

MEXICO

• Leon

• Havana

DOMINICAN REPUBLIC

PUERTO RICO (U.S.)

15°N

• Guadalajara

• Mexico City ★

• Merida

CUBA

ST. THOMAS

BARBUDA

JAMAICA

HAITI

ST. CROIX Guadeloupe (France)

DOMINICA

BELIZE

Belmopan ★

Martinique (France)

ST. LUCIA

GUATEMALA

HONDURAS

ST. VINCENT AND THE GRENADINES

Guatemala ★ Tegucigalpa ★

NICARAGUA

Caribbean Sea

Lesser Antilles (Neth.)

GRENADA

San Salvador ★

Managua ★

EL SALVADOR

PANAMA

TRINIDAD AND TOBAGO

San José ★

• Panama ★

COSTA RICA

★ National Capitals
• Cities

N
W—E
S

0   250   500 miles

0 250 500 kilometers

120°W 105°W 90°W

Caribbean Sea

Managua

San José

Panama

Barranquilla

Caracas

TRINIDAD AND TOBAGO

Valencia

VENEZUELA

Cúcuta

Medellín

Georgetown

Paramaribo

GUYANA

Cayenne

Bogotá

SURINAME

FRENCH GUIANA

COLOMBIA

Mitú

Quito

Manaus

Belém

ECUADOR

Guayaquil

Galápagos
Islands
(Ecuador)

Talara

PERU

Fortaleza

Recife

Trujillo

Pôrto Velho

BRAZIL

Huánuco

Lima

Ica

Cuzco

Salvador

BOLIVIA

La Paz

Brásilia

Goiânia

Santa Cruz

Sucre

Iquique

Rio de Janeiro

Antofagasta

PARAGUAY

São Paulo

CHILE

Asunción

Córdoba

Rosario

URUGUAY

Santiago

Buenos Aires

Montevideo

Concepción

ARGENTINA

Valdivia

ATLANTIC OCEAN

Puerto Montt

PACIFIC OCEAN

10°N

0°
Equator

10°S

20°S

30°S

40°S

50°S

Comodoro Rivadavia

★ National Capitals
• Cities

0   250   500 miles

0 250 500 kilometers

N
W   E
S

Falkland Islands
(U.K.)

South Georgia Island
(U.K.)

90°W   80°W   70°W   60°W   50°W   40°W

15°W 0° 15°E 45°E

Reykjavik ★ ICELAND

60°N

Norwegian Sea

Faroe Islands (Denmark)

FINLAND

SWEDEN

NORWAY

Helsinki ★

RUSSIA

NORTH ATLANTIC OCEAN

Oslo ★

Stockholm ★

Gulf of Bothnia

Tallinn ★
ESTONIA

Moscow ★

Baltic Sea

LATVIA
Riga ★

North Sea

Belfast ★

Dublin ★

IRELAND

UNITED KINGDOM

DENMARK

Copenhagen ★

LITHUANIA
Vilnius ★

Minsk ★

RUSSIA

BELARUS

NETHERLANDS

London ★

Amsterdam ★

Berlin ★

Warsaw ★

POLAND

Kiev ★

UKRAINE

English Channel

Brussels ★

BELGIUM

GERMANY

Prague ★

CZECH REP.

SLOVAKIA

45°N

Paris ★

LUXEMBOURG

LIECHTENSTEIN

Vienna ★ ★ Bratislava

MOLDOVA

Chisinau ★

FRANCE

Bern ★

SWITZERLAND

AUSTRIA

★ Budapest

HUNGARY

ROMANIA

Bay of Biscay

SLOVENIA

Ljubljana

Zagreb ★

Belgrade ★

Bucharest ★

ITALY

MONACO ★

CROATIA

BOSNIA AND HERZEGOVINA

Sarajevo ★

SERBIA AND MONTENEGRO

BULGARIA

Black Sea

PORTUGAL

ANDORRA

Corsica

Adriatic Sea

Sofia ★

Skopje ★

Madrid ★

Rome ★

Tirana ★

MACEDONIA

Lisbon ★

SPAIN

Sardinia

Tyrrhenian Sea

ALBANIA

Aegean Sea

Ankara ★

Balearic Islands

GREECE

TURKEY

Gibraltar (U.K.) ★

Algiers ★

Sicily

Athens ★

Ionian Sea

Rabat ★

Tunis ★

N

W E

S

★ Valletta

MALTA

Crete

AFRICA

Mediterranean Sea

Alexandria ★

Tripoli ★

★ National Capitals

0 200 400 miles

0 200 400 kilometers

Red Sea

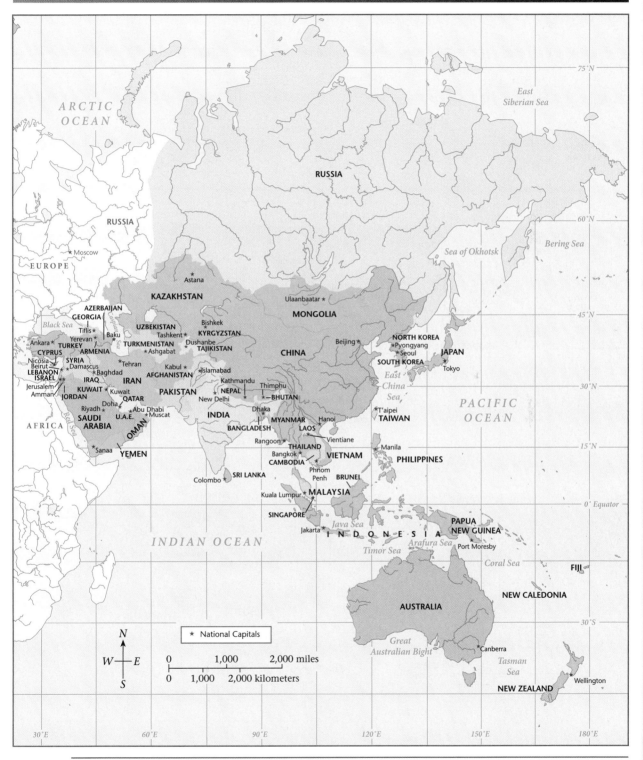

ARCTIC OCEAN

East Siberian Sea

RUSSIA

75°N

EUROPE

Moscow

RUSSIA

60°N

Bering Sea

Sea of Okhotsk

Astana

KAZAKHSTAN

Ulaanbaatar

MONGOLIA

45°N

AZERBAIJAN
GEORGIA
Black Sea
Tiflis
Yerevan
Baku
Ankara
TURKEY
ARMENIA
CYPRUS
Nicosia
Beirut
SYRIA
Damascus
LEBANON
ISRAEL
Baghdad
Jerusalem
Amman
JORDAN
IRAQ
KUWAIT
Kuwait
QATAR
Riyadh
Doha
Abu Dhabi
SAUDI
ARABIA
U.A.E.
Muscat
OMAN

UZBEKISTAN
Tashkent
Bishkek
KYRGYZSTAN
TURKMENISTAN
Dushanbe
Ashgabat
TAJIKISTAN

Tehran
IRAN
Kabul
AFGHANISTAN
Islamabad

PAKISTAN

Beijing

CHINA

NORTH KOREA
Pyongyang
Seoul
SOUTH KOREA

JAPAN
Tokyo

30°N

East China Sea

T'aipei
TAIWAN

PACIFIC OCEAN

Kathmandu
NEPAL
New Delhi
Thimphu
BHUTAN
Dhaka

INDIA

Hanoi
MYANMAR
LAOS
BANGLADESH
Rangoon
Vientiane

AFRICA

Red Sea

Sanaa
YEMEN

Colombo
SRI LANKA

THAILAND
Bangkok
CAMBODIA
VIETNAM
Phnom
Penh
BRUNEI

Manila
PHILIPPINES

15°N

Kuala Lumpur
MALAYSIA

SINGAPORE

Jakarta
INDONESIA

Java Sea

0° Equator

INDIAN OCEAN

Timor Sea
Arafura Sea
Port Moresby

PAPUA
NEW GUINEA

Coral Sea

FIJI

NEW CALEDONIA

N
W—E
S

★ National Capitals

0   1,000   2,000 miles
0 1,000 2,000 kilometers

AUSTRALIA

Great
Australian Bight
Canberra

30°S

Tasman
Sea

Wellington

NEW ZEALAND

30°E   60°E   90°E   120°E   150°E   180°E

Africa

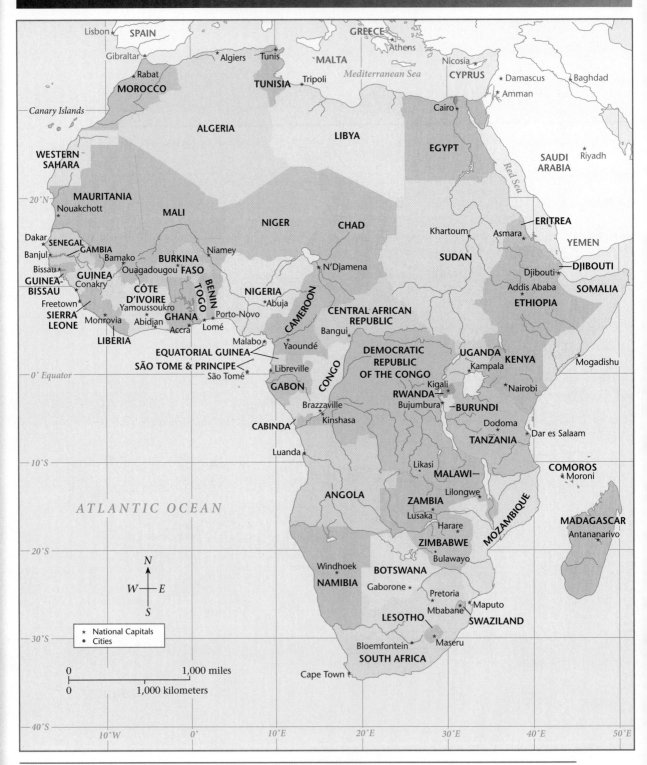

National Capitals ★
Cities •

0 — 1,000 miles
0 — 1,000 kilometers

World Climate Zones

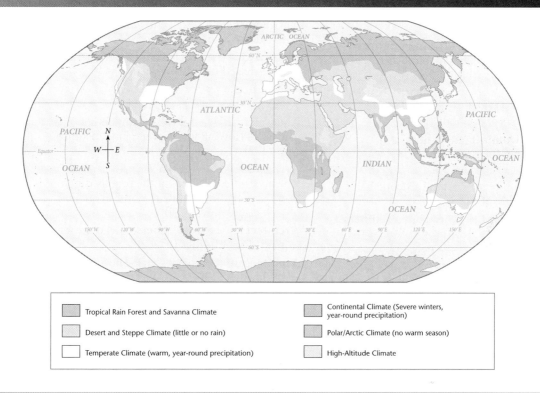

- Tropical Rain Forest and Savanna Climate
- Desert and Steppe Climate (little or no rain)
- Temperate Climate (warm, year-round precipitation)
- Continental Climate (Severe winters, year-round precipitation)
- Polar/Arctic Climate (no warm season)
- High-Altitude Climate

World Time Zones

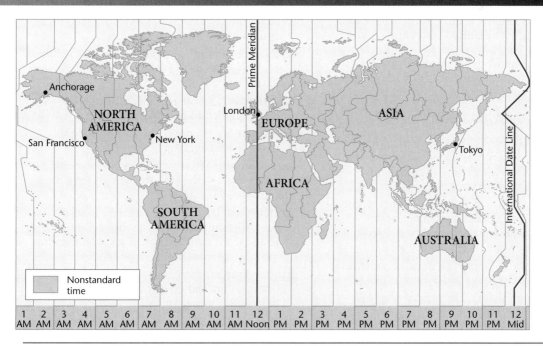

Nonstandard time

| 1 AM | 2 AM | 3 AM | 4 AM | 5 AM | 6 AM | 7 AM | 8 AM | 9 AM | 10 AM | 11 AM | 12 Noon | 1 PM | 2 PM | 3 PM | 4 PM | 5 PM | 6 PM | 7 PM | 8 PM | 9 PM | 10 PM | 11 PM | 12 Mid |

Glossary

A

Acropolis (ə krop´ ə lis) The hill on which the people in a Greek city built their main temple (p. 126)

Acupuncture (ak´ yu̇ pungk chər) Treating pain or illness by putting needles into certain parts of the body (p. 308)

A.D. (Anno Domini) (an´ ō dom´ ə nī) Dating from the time Jesus Christ was born (p. 12)

Addicted (ad´ ikt əd) Having a strong habit that is hard to give up (p. 458)

Advanced (ad vanst´) Ahead of most others in knowledge, skill, or progress (p. 324)

Agency (ā´ jən sē) A group that provides a service (p. 751)

Agent (ā´ jənt) A person who has the authority to act for some other person or company (p. 477)

Agriculture (ag´ rə kul chər) The use of land for growing crops and raising animals; farming (p. 5)

Alliance (e lī´ əns) A group of nations joined together for some purpose; an agreement to help one another (p. 534)

Allied Powers (al´ īd pou´ ərs) The nations of Great Britain, France, Russia, Italy, and eventually, the United States and Japan during World War I (p. 534); The nations united against the Axis powers in World War II; includes Britain, France, and later the United States and the Soviet Union (p. 577)

Ambition (am bish´ ən) The drive to become powerful, successful, or famous (p. 145)

American Revolution (ə mar´ ə kən rev ə lü´ shən) The American struggle against Great Britain for independence (p. 365)

Ancestor (an´ ses tər) A person from whom one is descended; for example, your grandfathers, grandmothers, and so on back, are your ancestors (p. 106)

Annul (ə nul´) To cancel; to make something no longer binding under law (p. 296)

Anthem (an´ thəm) The official song of a country (p. 516)

Anti-Semitism (an ti - sem´ ə tiz əm) Prejudice against Jews (p. 576)

Apartheid (ə pärt´ hīt) The separation of races based mainly on skin color (p. 648)

Apprentice (ə pren´ tis) A person who learns a trade under a master (p. 244)

Aqueduct (ak´ wə dukt) A channel that carries flowing water over a long distance (p. 172)

Archaeologist (är kē ol´ ə jist) A scientist who studies cultures of the past by digging up and examining the remains of ancient towns and cities (p. 9)

Architect (är´ kə tekt) A person who draws plans for buildings (p. 262)

Architecture (är´ kə tek chər) The art of building (p. 136)

Armada (är mä´ də) A large fleet of warships (p. 290)

Armistice (är´ mə stis) An agreement to stop fighting; a truce before a formal peace treaty (p. 542)

Arms (ärmz) Weapons used to attack or defend (p. 663)

Arsenal (är´ sə nəl) A place where guns and ammunition are stored (p. 378)

Artifact (är´ tə fakt) A handmade object, such as a tool or weapon (p. 9)

Artisan (är´ tə zən) A person who works with his or her hands to create something (p. 217)

Assassinate (ə sas´ n āt) To kill a leader or other important person (p. 145)

Astronaut (as´ trə nȯt) A person trained to make space flights (p. 732)

Astronomer (ə stron´ ə mər) A person who keeps track of the sun, the planets, and the stars (p. 268)

Athlete (ath´ lēt) A person trained to take part in competitive sports; the ancient Greek word *athlete* means "one who tries to win a prize in a contest" (p. 137)

Atomic bomb (ə tom´ ik bom) A bomb that uses nuclear energy and has much destructive power (p. 592)

Authority (ə thôr′ ə tē) Power; the right to tell someone what to do (p. 275)

Axis Powers (ak′ is pou′ ərs) The alliance of Germany, Italy, and Japan during World War II (p. 577)

Ayatollah (ä yä tō′ lə) A Muslim religious leader (p. 669)

B

Balance of power (bal′ əns ov pou′ ər) The condition that exists when all countries or all sections of government have equal strength (p. 534)

Ban (ban) To get rid of; to make something not legal (p. 710)

Barbarians (bär bâr′ ē ənz) Uncivilized, primitive people; people living outside Greece or Rome in the days of the Roman Empire (p. 193)

Barrier (bar′ ē ər) Something that blocks the way; a wall (p. 109)

Barter (bär′ tər) To trade goods or services without using money (p. 325)

Bastille (ba stēl′) A prison in Paris (p. 377)

B.C. (Before Christ) (bi fôr′ krīst) Dating from before the time Jesus Christ was born (p. 12)

Berlin Wall (bər lin′ wòl) The wall that divided the people of East and West Berlin (p. 607)

Betray (bi trā′) To give help to the enemy; to be unfaithful to (p. 379)

Bible (bī′ bəl) The ancient Israelite and Christian book that is thought to be holy (p. 78)

Bishop (bish′ əp) A high-ranking church official in charge of other priests and a number of churches; from the Latin word that means "overseer" (p. 181)

Bolshevik (bōl′ shə vik) A revolutionary Communist group in Russia; means "member of the majority" (p. 562)

Border (bôr′ dər) The dividing line between two countries (p. 8)

Boundary (boun′ dər ē) The dividing line between one country and another (p. 517)

Buddha (bü′ də) A name meaning the "Enlightened One"; the name given to Siddhartha Gautama, the founder of Buddhism (p. 102)

Buddhism (bü′ də izm) A religion based on the teachings of Buddha (p. 102)

C

Campaign (kam pān′) A series of battles all aimed at one military end (p. 145)

Canal (kə nal′) A man-made waterway (p. 41)

Capital (kap′ ə təl) A city or town where the government of a nation or state is located (p. 80)

Capitalist (kap′ ə təl ist) Having business and industry privately owned and operated for profit (p. 610)

Caravan (kar′ ə van) A group of people traveling together, often through a desert (p. 493)

Cartridge (kär′ trij) A small metal or cardboard tube that holds gunpowder and a bullet (p. 478)

Caste (kast) A social class in India (p. 100)

Casualty (kazh′ ü əl tē) A soldier who has been killed, wounded, captured, or is missing (p. 544)

Cease-fire (sēs′ - fīr) An end in military operations, especially to try and discuss peace (p. 663)

Censor (sen′ sər) To examine communications before they are released and to remove any parts that are objected to (p. 566)

Central Powers (sen′ trəl pou′ ərs) The nations of Germany, Austria-Hungary, Turkey, and later Bulgaria (p. 534)

Chancellor (chan′ sə lər) The head of government, or prime minister, in some European countries (p. 526)

Chariot (char′ ē ət) An open two-wheeled cart, pulled by horses (p. 47)

a	hat	e	let	ī	ice	ò	order	ù	put	sh	she	ə {	a	in about
ā	age	ē	equal	o	hot	oi	oil	ü	rule	th	thin		e	in taken
ä	far	èr	term	ō	open	ou	out	ch	child	ᵺ	then		i	in pencil
â	care	i	it	ȯ	saw	u	cup	ng	long	zh	measure		o	in lemon
													u	in circus

Charter (chär´ tər) A constitution; a set of statements that explains a group's purpose (p. 248)

Christianity (kris chē an´ ə tē) The religion based on the teachings of Jesus Christ and the Bible (p. 79)

Citizen (sit´ ə zən) A person who has certain rights and duties because he or she lives in a particular city or town (p. 126)

City-state (sit´ ē - stāt) An independent city and the surrounding land it controls (p. 43)

Civil disobedience (siv´ əl dis´ ə bē´ dē əns) The refusal to obey rules, orders, or laws (p. 483)

Civilian (sə vil´ yən) A person who is not in the military (p. 581)

Civilization (siv ə lə zā´ shən) A group of people who have cities and government; a large group of people with a high level of development as a group (p. 9)

Civil war (siv´ əl wôr) Fighting between people who live in the same country (p. 166)

Class (klas) A group of people according to social rank (p. 100)

Clergy (klėr´ jē) The people who lead a religion (p. 213)

Code (kōd) A group of laws (p. 84)

Cold war (kōld wôr) The tension and hostility between the United States and the Soviet Union after World War II; was a war of ideas (p. 610)

Collapse (kə laps´) To fall apart (p. 109)

Collective (kə lek´ tiv) Run by a group; for example, a collective farm (p. 565)

Colonial (kə lō´ nē əl) Having settlements in far-off lands (p. 387)

Colony (kol´ ə nē) A group of people who settle in a far-off land but are still under the rule of the land they came from (p. 74)

Commandment (kə mand´ mənt) A law or order, most often a religious law, as in the Ten Commandments in the Bible (p. 78)

Commonwealth (kom´ ən welth) A nation in which the people hold the ruling power; a republic or democracy (p. 361)

Commune (kə myün´) A group of people working or living closely together, often sharing property and tasks (p. 630)

Communism (kom´ yə niz əm) A political system where there are no social classes and a common ownership of industries and farms, as well as a sharing of work and of goods produced (p. 559)

Compass (kum´ pəs) A tool for finding direction by using a magnet (p. 308)

Concentration camp (kon sən trā´ shən kamp) A prison camp for people thought to be dangerous to a ruling group (p. 576)

Confederation (kən fed ə rā´ shən) A group of independent states joined together for a purpose (p. 523)

Conference (kon´ fər əns) A meeting of people to discuss something (p. 505)

Conflict (kon´ flikt) Fighting; not being able to agree on something (p. 544)

Conquer (kong´ kər) To get control by using force, as in a war (p. 80)

Conqueror (kong´ kər ər) A person who gains control by winning a war (p. 99)

Conquistador (kon kē´ stə dôr) A Spanish conqueror (p. 338)

Consent (kən sent´) To agree to something (p. 360)

Constitution (kon stə tü´ shən) The basic laws and rules of a government (p. 130)

Contract (kon´ trakt) A written agreement between two or more people (p. 47)

Convert (kən vėrt´) Change from one religion to another (p. 180)

Corrupt (kə rupt´) Dishonest, evil, selfish (p. 629)

Cosmonaut (koz´ mə nôt) Russian word meaning "astronaut" (p. 732)

Counter-Reformation (koun´ tər - ref ər mā´ shən) The Catholic Church's reforms that attempted to fight Protestant beliefs; also known as the Catholic Reformation (p. 278)

Coup (kü) A bold, sudden move to bring about change in a government (p. 688)

Craft (kraft) A trade or art that takes special skill with the hands (p. 26)

Create (krē āt´) To make something (p. 48)

Crisis (krī′ sis) A time of danger; a turning point in events (p. 614)

Criticize (krit′ ə sīz) To say that someone has done wrong; to find wrong in something (p. 259)

Crusade (krü sād′) Any of the military journeys taken by Christians to win the Holy Land from the Muslims (p. 232)

Culture (kul′ chər) The way of life—religion, ideas, arts, tools—of a certain people in a certain time (p. 5)

Cuneiform (kyü nē′ ə fôrm) A wedge-shaped form of writing used in ancient Sumer (p. 46)

Curfew (kėr′ fyü) A time after which certain people cannot be on the streets (p. 648)

Currency (kėr′ ən sē) The form of money a country uses (p. 612)

Czar (zär) The ruler of Russia; a Russian title that means "caesar" (p. 553)

D

D-Day (dē′ - dā) The Allied invasion of France in 1944 (p. 589)

Declaration of Independence (dek lə rā′ shən ov in di pen′ dəns) A document the American colonists signed in which they declared their freedom from Great Britain (p. 366)

Decline (di klīn′) A period of increasing weakness (p. 286)

Democracy (di mok′ rə sē) A government that gives the people the ruling power (p. 126)

Democratic (dem ə krat′ ik) Having to do with a government in which all people have equal rights (p. 133)

Depression (di presh′ ən) A period of low business activity and high unemployment (p. 574)

Descendant (di sen′ dənt) A person who comes from a specific group of people; a family member (p. 420)

Desert (dez′ ərt) Dry, sandy land with little or no plant life (p. 58)

Détente (dā tänt′) An easing of tensions between countries (p. 616)

Developed country (di vel′ əpəd kun′ trē) A nation that has many industries and that imports and exports products (p. 410)

Developing country (di vel′ ə ping kun′ trē) A nation that is slowly growing its industry and economy (p. 410)

Development (di vel′ əp mənt) Growth of something (p. 5)

Dialect (dī′ ə lekt) A form of a language used only in a certain place or among a certain group (p. 552)

Dictator (dik′ tā tər) A ruler who has total power (p. 382)

Dike (dīk) A wall built along a river or sea to hold back the water from low land (p. 41)

Diplomat (dip′ lə mat) A person in government whose job is dealing with other countries (p. 520)

Disarm (dis ärm′) To stop having armed forces or to reduce their size (p. 542)

Disaster (də zas′ tər) Something that causes harm or problems (p. 616)

Disband (dis band′) To break up (p. 690)

Discrimination (dis krim ə nā′ shən) Treating a person or people unfairly because of his or her race or religion (p. 420)

Divine right (də vīn′ rīt) The idea that a monarch's right to rule comes directly from God (p. 359)

Document (dôk′ yə mənt) An important paper (p. 248)

Dominance (dom′ ə nəns) The act of ruling, controlling, or being most powerful (p. 505)

Dominate (dom′ ə nāt) To control; to be most important, most powerful, strongest (p. 428)

Domino theory (dom′ ə nō thir′ ē) The belief that if one country became Communist, neighbors would fall to Communism too (p. 641)

a	hat	e	let	ī	ice	ô	order	ù	put	sh	she	ə {	a	in about
ā	age	ē	equal	o	hot	oi	oil	ü	rule	th	thin		e	in taken
ä	far	ėr	term	ō	open	ou	out	ch	child	ᴛʜ	then		i	in pencil
â	care	i	it	ȯ	saw	u	cup	ng	long	zh	measure		o	in lemon
													u	in circus

Drought (drout) A long period of time without much rain (p. 647)

Dweller (dwel´ ər) A person who lives in a place (p. 321)

Dynasty (dī´ nə stē) A family that rules a country for a long period of time (p. 107)

E

Economic (ek ə nom´ ik) Having to do with money (p. 449)

Economy (i kon´ ə mē) The system of making and trading things (p. 554)

Edict (ē´ dikt) A public order by some authority (p. 292)

Elect (i lekt´) To choose someone for an office by voting (p. 161)

Electronic (i lek tron´ ik) Powered by electricity (p. 638)

Embassy (em´ bə sē) The home and offices of a person sent to represent his or her government in another country (p. 669)

Emperor (em´ pər ər) A person who rules a group of different countries, lands, or peoples (p. 104)

Empire (em´ pīr) A group of lands all ruled by the same government or ruler (p. 84)

Energy (en´ ər jē) Power that comes from wood, coal, electricity, oil, the sun, water, and wind; makes machines work; and produces heat (p. 396)

Enforce (en fôrs´) To make sure that people follow the laws and rules (p. 315)

Enlightened (en līt´ nd) Knowing the truth (p. 102)

Enlightenment (en līt´ n mənt) A time in European history when thinkers and writers tried to solve the problems of society by using reason; also known as the Age of Reason (p. 356)

Enslaved (en slāvd´) When a person is forced to become a slave (p. 177)

Environment (en vī´ rən mənt) The land, sea, and air of our world (p. 721)

Epidemic (ep ə dem´ ik) The rapid spread of a disease (p. 748)

Equality (i kwol´ ə tē) The same rights for everyone (p. 356)

Estate (e stāt´) A large piece of land with a large home on it (pp. 210–211)

Estates-General (e stāts´ - jen´ ər el) The French governmental body made up of representatives from the three estates (p. 376)

Execute (ek´ sə kyüt) To kill someone for a crime (p. 380)

Exiled (eg´ zīld) Forced to live away from home in a foreign land (p. 200)

Expand (ek spand´) To grow; to stretch (p. 126)

Expansion (ek span´ shən) Growth; to increase in size (p. 446)

Exploration (ek splə rā´ shən) The act of looking around some unknown place (p. 238)

Export (ek spôrt´) To send a product out of one country and into another to sell; a product that is sent from one country to another (p. 410)

Extinction (ek stingkt´ shən) The act of bringing to an end; dying out (p. 746)

F

Factory (fak´ tər ē) A building where goods are made by machinery (p. 397)

Faith (fāth) To believe in God; a religion (p. 228)

Famine (fam´ ən) A time when crops do not grow and there is no food (p. 647)

Fascist (fash´ist) People who follow the political system that honors the state over the individual (p. 574)

Fast (fast) To go without food (p. 485)

Fertile (fėr´ tl) Able to produce large crops, as in rich soil (p. 28)

Fertile Crescent (fėr´ tl kres´ nt) The area of land in the Middle East shaped like a quarter moon (crescent) (p. 28)

Feudalism (fyü´ dl iz əm) A political and military system based on the holding of land (p. 210)

Fleet (flēt) A group of warships under one command (p. 290)

Foreign (fôr´ ən) From another country; having to do with another country (p. 104)

Forge (fôrj) To work into shape by heating and hammering (p. 308)

Fortress (fôr´ tris) A building with strong walls for defense against an enemy (p. 211)

Forum (fôr´ əm) A public square in an ancient Roman city; lawmakers met there (p. 167)

Founded (foun´ ded) To have begun a country or city; to have built a city (p. 148)

Fraternity (frə tėr´ nə tē) Brotherhood (p. 379)

Freemen (frē´ men) People who are free, not slaves, and who have the rights of citizens (pp. 210–211)

French Revolution (french rev ə lü´ shən) The war that the common people of France fought against the king, nobles, and one another to achieve freedom (p. 379)

Front (frunt) A place where the actual fighting is going on during a war (p. 538)

Frontier (frun tir´) Land just beyond the border of a country (p. 192)

G

General (jen´ ər əl) A high-ranking military officer (p. 149)

Genocide (jen´ ə sīd) An attempt to kill all the people of a certain race or religious group (p. 585)

Geography (jē og´ rə fē) The natural surface features of the earth, or any part of it (p. 552)

Glacier (glā´ shər) A large, slow-moving mass of ice and snow (p. 20)

Glasnost (glas´ nost) The Soviet policy of open discussion of political and social issues (p. 687)

Global warming (glō´ bəl wôrm´ ing) The heating up of Earth from the burning of wood, coal, oil, and gasoline (p. 721)

Glorious Revolution (glôr´ ē əs rev ə lü´ shən) The period in England that involved the overthrow of James II and the crowning of William and Mary (p. 363)

Goddess (god´ is) A female god (p. 43)

Good Neighbor Policy (güd nā´ bər pol´ ə sē) The policy in which the United States said it would not interfere with Latin American affairs (p. 706)

Goods (güdz) The things for sale or trade (p. 41)

Gospel (gos´ pəl) One of four books of the New Testament part of the Bible; a word that means "good news" (p. 177)

Govern (guv´ ərn) To rule (p. 125)

Governor (guv´ ər nər) A person chosen to run a province or territory (p. 165)

Guerilla (gə ril´ ə) One of a group of fighters who are not part of a regular army, and who usually make surprise raids behind enemy lines (p. 641)

Guild (gild) An organization formed to protect the interests of workers in one craft or trade (p. 244)

Guillotine (gil´ ə tēn) An instrument used for cutting off a person's head; it has two posts crossed by a heavy blade (p. 380)

H

Heretic (her´ ə tik) A person who is against the teachings of a church (p. 276)

Hieroglyphics (hī ər ə glif´ iks) A system of writing using pictures or symbols to represent objects, ideas, or sounds (p. 66)

Hinduism (hin´ dü iz əm) The main religion of India; Hindus worship many gods (p. 99)

Historian (hi stôr´ ē ən) Someone who writes about the past; an expert in history (p. 8)

History (his´ tər ē) The record of past events and the story of what happened to people in the past (p. 4)

Holocaust (hol´ ə kȯst) Hitler's killing of many of the Jews in Europe (p. 585)

a	hat	e	let	ī	ice	ȯ	order	ů	put	sh	she	ə	a	in about
ā	age	ē	equal	o	hot	oi	oil	ü	rule	th	thin		e	in taken
ä	far	ėr	term	ō	open	ou	out	ch	child	ŦH	then		i	in pencil
â	care	i	it	ȯ	saw	u	cup	ng	long	zh	measure		o	in lemon
													u	in circus

Holy Land (hō´ lē land) Palestine; the area where Jesus of Nazareth lived (p. 227)

Homage (hom´ ij) A pledge of loyalty; a promise to serve that was made to kings and lords during the Middle Ages (p. 210)

Homeland (hōm´ land) The land that belongs to people (p. 661)

Hostages (hos´ tij ez) People held prisoner by an enemy until certain demands are met (p. 669)

Hostile (hos´ tl) Unfriendly, showing hate or dislike (p. 663)

Hostility (ho stil´ ə tē) Feelings of hate or acts of war (p. 126)

Humane (hyü mān´) Kind; showing care for others (p. 712)

Humanism (hyü´ mə niz əm) A concern with the needs and interests of human beings rather than religious ideas (p. 258)

Humanity (hyü man´ ə tē) The human race (p. 751)

Human rights (hyü´ mən rīts) The right to life, liberty, and pursuit of (the attempt to get) happiness (p. 248)

I

Ice Age (īs āj) A period of time when much of Earth and Earth's water was frozen (p. 20)

Idol (ī´ dl) An image of a god that is used as an object of worship (p. 224)

Immigration (im ə grā´ shən) The act of coming into a country or region to live there (p. 716)

Imperialism (im pir´ ē ə liz əm) The practice of conquering other lands, forming colonies in other lands, or controlling the government and wealth of weaker lands (p. 5)

Import (im pôrt´) To bring into one country from another (p. 397)

Impose (im pōz´) To force one's ideas or wishes on another (p. 477)

Independence (in di pen´ dəns) Being free; being able to govern one's self (p. 235)

Independent (in di pen´ dənt) Self-governing, separate, free (p. 43)

Indirectly (in də rekt´ lē) In a roundabout way (p. 477)

Industrial Revolution (in dus´ trē əl rev ə lü´ shən) The important changes that took place in the way work was done during the 18th and 19th century (p. 396)

Industry (in´ də strē) Business and manufacturing (p. 5)

Inferior (in fir´ ē ər) Not as good as someone or something else (p. 507)

Influence (in´ flü əns) The power to affect other people or things (p. 428)

Inquisition (in kwə zish´ ən) A special court set up by the Roman Catholic Church to question the beliefs of people to see if they were heretics (p. 276)

Insurance (in shùr´ əns) A guarantee that a person or company will be paid money to cover losses (p. 346)

Interest (in´ tər ist) Money paid for the use of other people's money (p. 346)

Interfere (in tər fir´) To mix in another's affairs without being asked (p. 439)

Interference (in tər fir´ əns) Mixing in another's affairs without being asked (p. 462)

Internal combustion engine (in tėr´ nl kəm bus´ chən en´ jən) An engine that burns gasoline to produce power (p. 403)

International (in tər nash´ ə nəl) Having to do with many nations (p. 449)

Invade (in vād´) To attack or march into another country (p. 575)

Invest (in vest´) To put money into something with the hope of making more money (p. 638)

Investment (in vest´ ment) Money given to businesses in order to get even more money back (p. 346)

Investor (in ves´ tər) A person who expects to make a profit by lending money to a business (p. 397)

Iron Curtain (ī´ərn kėrt´ n) The invisible boundary between Western Europe and Eastern Europe after World War II (p. 566)

Irrigate (ir´ ə gāt) To bring water to dry land by means of canals (p. 41)

Isolate (ī´ sə lāt) To set apart from others; alone (p. 109)

Isolationism (ī sə lā´ shə niz əm) A policy of staying out of the affairs, or business, of other countries (p. 608)

J

Judaism (jü´ dē iz əm) The religion developed by the ancient Israelites that Jews practice today (p. 79)

Jury (jür´ ē) A group of people who listen to the facts and decide if a person on trial is guilty or not guilty (p. 130)

K

Kaiser (kī´ zər) The emperor of Germany (p. 526)

Kamikaze (kä mi kä´ zē) A Japanese pilot who crashed his plane into an enemy ship, destroying it and killing himself (p. 592)

Knight (nīt) A high-ranking soldier of the Middle Ages who received his title from a noble (p. 213)

Koran (kô rän´) The holy book of the Muslims that contains the teachings of Islam; also spelled *Qur'an* (p. 227)

L

Laborer (lā´ bər ər) A person who does hard work with his or her hands (p. 129)

Labor union (lā´ bər yü´ nyən) A group of workers who join together to protect their wages, working conditions, and job benefits (p. 408)

Legal (lē´ gəl) Lawful; based on the law of the government (p. 180)

Legislature (lej´ ə slā chər) A group of people who make the laws of a nation or state (p. 523)

Liberator (lib´ ə rā´ tôr) One who frees a group of people (p. 423)

Liberty (lib´ ər tē) Freedom (p. 365)

Locomotive (lō kə mō´ tiv) A self-propelled vehicle that runs on rails (pp. 396–397)

Lord (lôrd) A king or noble who gave land to someone else (pp. 210–211)

Lutheranism (lü´ thər ə niz əm) The religious movement founded by Martin Luther (p. 275)

M

Majority (mə jôr´ ə tē) A greater number, more than half (p. 648)

Manor (man´ ər) The lands belonging to a medieval lord, including farmland, a village, and the home of the owner (pp. 210–211)

Market (mär´ kit) A place to sell goods (p. 397)

Marshall Plan (mär´ shəl plan) The American plan to rebuild Europe after World War II (p. 606)

Massacre (mas´ ə kər) The act of killing many people who are often defenseless (p. 292)

Masterpiece (mas´ tər pēs) A piece of art that seems almost perfect (p. 262)

Medieval (med ē´ vəl) Belonging to the Middle Ages (p. 211)

Merchant (mėr´ chənt) A person who buys and sells goods for a profit; a trader (p. 41)

Mesoamerica (mes ō ə mer´ ə kə) The area of North America (including Mexico and Central America) where civilizations developed before Europeans entered the continent (p. 321)

Middle Ages (mid´ l āj´ əz) The period of European history extending from the Fall of Rome in A.D. 476 to about A.D. 1450 (p. 192)

Migrate (mī´ grāt) To move away from one country or region to settle in another (p. 243)

Militarism (mil´ ə tə riz əm) A national policy of maintaining a powerful army and constant readiness for war (p. 527)

Military (mil´ ə ter ē) Having to do with soldiers or the armed forces (p. 89)

Minority (mə nôr´ ə tē) A smaller number, less than half (p. 647)

a	hat	e	let	ī	ice	ô	order	ù	put	sh	she		a	in about
ā	age	ē	equal	o	hot	oi	oil	ü	rule	th	thin	ə	e	in taken
ä	far	ėr	term	ō	open	ou	out	ch	child	ŦH	then		i	in pencil
â	care	i	it	ò	saw	u	cup	ng	long	zh	measure		o	in lemon
													u	in circus

Missionary (mish´ ə ner ē) A person sent by a church to other countries to spread a religion (p. 315)

Moderate (mod´ ər it) To make or become less extreme or violent (p. 712)

Monarch (mon´ ərk) A ruler, like a king, queen, or emperor (p. 286)

Monk (mungk) A man who has taken religious vows and usually lives in a monastery (p. 213)

Monroe Doctrine (mən rō´ dok´ trən) The doctrine stating that Europe should not try to get more territory in North or South America; taken from U.S. President James Monroe's speech to Congress (p. 436)

Mosaic (mō zā´ ik) A design made by putting together small pieces of colored stone, glass, or other material (p. 325)

Mother country (muŦH´ ər kun´ trē) A nation that controls a colony (p. 418)

Motto (mot´ ō) A word or phrase that expresses goals, ideas, or ideals (p. 379)

Multinational corporation (mul ti nash´ ə nəl kôr pə rā´ shən) A company that hires people and has business interests around the world (p. 741)

Mummy (mum´ ē) A dead body kept from rotting by being treated with chemicals and wrapped in cloth (p. 63)

Mural (myür´ əl) A large picture painted on a wall (p. 427)

Muslim (muz´ ləm) A follower of the religion that Muhammad founded in Arabia in the seventh century (p. 225)

Myth (mith) A story, often about gods or goddesses, that is handed down through the years and sometimes used to explain natural events (p. 128)

N

Napoleonic Code (nə pō´ lē ən ik kōd) The constitution Napoleon set up that contained a single set of laws for all of France and its territories; it remains the basis of French law today (p. 382)

Nationalism (nash´ ə nə liz əm) Love of one's nation; patriotism (p. 286)

Natural resource (nach´ ər əl ri sôrs´) Materials that are provided by nature, such as forests, minerals, and water (p. 396)

Navigate (nav´ ə gāt) To plan the course of a ship; to sail or steer (p. 74)

Negotiate (ni gō´ shē āt) To talk together, make bargains, and agree on something (p. 668)

Neutral (nü´ trəl) Joining neither side in a war (p. 538)

Noble (nō´ bəl) A person of high social rank (p. 51)

Nomad (nō´ mad) A person who moves from place to place (p. 78)

Nonrenewable (non ri nü´ ə bl) Cannot be replaced once it is used up (p. 729)

Nonviolent resistance (non vī´ ə lənt ri zis´ təns) The act of opposing or working against without using force or causing injury (p. 483)

Nuclear (nü´ klē ər) Having to do with atoms or energy from atoms (p. 592)

Nuclear weapon (nü´ klē ər wep´ ən) A powerful weapon, such as an atomic bomb or missile (p. 613)

Nun (nun) A woman who has taken religious vows and enters a convent (p. 213)

O

Oath (ōth) A serious promise, often pledged in the name of God (p. 377)

Open-Door Policy (ō´ pən - dôr pol´ ə sē) The American approach to China around 1900 that allowed open trade relations between China and other nations (p. 462)

Oppose (ə pōz´) To be against something (p. 565)

Organization (ôr gə nə zā´ shən) A group of people joined together for a common purpose (p. 596)

Organize (ôr´ gə nīz) To set up (p. 210)

Overpopulation (ō vər pop yə lā´ shən) The state of having too many people; can ruin the environment or the quality of life (p. 745)

Pact (pakt) An agreement (p. 587)

Papyrus (pə pī´ rəs) A writing paper the Egyptians made from water plants of the same name (p. 66)

Parliament (pär´ lə mənt) England's body of lawmakers (p. 296)

Patriot (pā´ trē ət) A person who is loyal to his or her own country and shows a great love for that country (p. 365)

Patron (pā´ trən) A wealthy person who supports artists (p. 261)

Pax Romana (paks rō mä´ nə) The Roman peace that began during the reign of Augustus Caesar (p. 169)

Peasant (pez´ nt) A poor farmer or farm worker (p. 217)

Peninsula (pə nin´ sə lə) A long piece of land almost completely surrounded by water; from the Latin word meaning "almost an island" (p. 160)

Perestroika (per ə stoi´ kə) The Soviet policy of economic and government reform (p. 687)

Persecute (pėr´ sə kyüt) To treat in a cruel way; to hurt or injure (p. 178)

Petition (pə tish´ ən) A written request, often with many signatures, to a person or group in authority (p. 360)

Petition of Right (pə tish´ ən ov rīt) An English document that brought about more democracy (p. 360)

Pharaoh (fâr´ ō) A ruler of ancient Egypt (p. 60)

Pictograph (pik´ tə graf) A drawing that represents an actual thing; for example, a picture of an eye represents an eye (p. 48)

Pilgrim (pil´ grəm) A person who came to North America for religious freedom and settled in Plymouth, Massachusetts (p. 342)

Pilgrimage (pil´ grə mij) A visit to a holy place (p. 231)

Piracy (pī´ rə sē) The robbing of ships on the ocean (p. 341)

Plague (plāg) A deadly disease that spreads quickly (p. 134)

Policy (pol´ ə sē) A rule; a method of action or conduct (p. 458)

Political (pə lit´ ə kəl) Having to do with governing (p. 424)

Politics (pol´ ə tiks) The work of government (p. 709)

Pollution (pə lü´ shən) Waste materials in the air or water (p. 638)

Pope (pōp) The head of the Roman Catholic Church (p. 181)

Population (pop yə lā´ shən) People living in a place, or the total number of those people (p. 243)

Prejudice (prej´ ə dis) Dislike of people just because they are of a different race or religion, or are from another country (p. 505)

Priest (prēst) A religious leader (p. 43)

Primary source (prī´ mer ē sôrs) A first-hand account of a historical event (p. 8)

Prime minister (prīm min´ ə stər) The chief official of the government in some countries (p. 520)

Primitive (prim´ ə tiv) Of long ago; very simple (p. 192)

Privilege (priv´ ə lij) A special right given to a person or group (p. 313)

Profit (prof´ it) The amount of money left over after paying for the cost of doing business (p. 396)

Prophet (prof´ it) A religious leader who claims to speak for God; one who tells what will happen in the future (p. 225)

Protestant (prot´ ə stənt) A reformer who protested against the Catholic Church (p. 275)

Province (prov´ əns) A part of a country, with its own local government; much like a state in the United States (p. 165)

a	hat	e	let	ī	ice	ȯ	order	u̇	put	sh	she		a	in about
ā	age	ē	equal	o	hot	oi	oil	ü	rule	th	thin	ə	e	in taken
ä	far	ėr	term	ō	open	ou	out	ch	child	ᴛʜ	then		i	in pencil
â	care	i	it	ȯ	saw	u	cup	ng	long	zh	measure		o	in lemon
													u	in circus

Puritan (pyür´ ə tən) A member of a 16th- or 17th-century English group of Protestants who wanted to make the Church of England simpler and stricter (p. 342)

Pyramid (pir´ ə mid) A huge stone structure with a square base and four triangular sides that meet in a point at the top; Egyptian rulers were buried in the pyramids (p. 62)

R

Racism (rā´ siz əm) The idea that one race is better than another (p. 505)

Raid (rād) To attack suddenly; a surprise attack (p. 109)

Ratify (rat´ ə fī) To formally approve (p. 617)

Raw material (rȯ mə tir´ ē əl) Matter in its natural condition, not changed by some human process (p. 397)

Rebellion (ri bel´ yən) A fight by people against a government (p. 449)

Reformation (ref ər mā´ shən) A movement that challenged and changed the Catholic religion in Europe (p. 274)

Refuge (ref´ yüj) Shelter or protection from danger (p. 717)

Refugee (ref yə jē´) A person who flees his or her country or home (p. 643)

Reich (rīk) The German word for "empire" (p. 526)

Reign (rān) The rule of a monarch; to rule as a king, queen, or emperor (p. 288)

Reign of Terror (rān ov ter´ ər) The one-year period in French history when radical leaders put many people to death (p. 380)

Reincarnation (rē in kär nā´ shən) A belief that living souls are reborn in a new body (p. 100)

Religious (ri lij´ əs) Having to do with a belief in a higher being (p. 80)

Renaissance (ren´ ə säns) The revival of art, literature, and learning in Europe in the 14th through 16th centuries (p. 258)

Repeal (ri pēl´) To cancel; put an end to (p. 649)

Representation (rep ri zen tā´ shən) Sending one or more people to speak for the rights of others before a body of the government (p. 365)

Representative (rep ri zen´ tə tiv) A person who is chosen to act or speak for others (p. 161)

Republic (ri pub´ lik) A government in which the citizens have the right to elect (or choose) their representatives to make laws (p. 160)

Reunification (rē yü nə fi kā´ shən) The act of joining together again (p. 694)

Revolt (ri vōlt´) To rise up against a government; to refuse to obey the people in charge (p. 130)

Revolution (rev ə lü´ shən) A complete change, especially in a way of life or a government (p. 4)

Riot (rī´ ət) A violent disturbance created by a crowd of people (p. 378)

Roundhead (round´ hed) A Puritan who fought for Parliament in the English Civil War (p. 360)

Royalist (roi´ ə list) A supporter of the king or queen during the English Civil War (p. 360)

S

Saga (sä´ gə) A long story of brave deeds (p. 201)

Samurai (sam´ ú rī) A class of warriors in the Japanese feudal system (p. 313)

Sanction (sangk´ shən) An action taken by one nation against another for breaking international law (p. 647)

Satellite (sat´ l īt) A country that depends on and is controlled by a more powerful country (p. 606); an object put into orbit around the earth (p. 732)

Scapegoat (skāp´ gōt) A person or group blamed for the mistakes and problems of others (p. 576)

Scribe (skrīb) A person whose job it was to write out copies of contracts and other important papers; people worked as scribes before the invention of printing (p. 46)

Sculptor (skulp´ tər) A person who makes statues out of wood, stone, marble, or other material (p. 262)

Sculpture (skulp´ chər) A carving from stone or other hard material (p. 262)

Security (si kyúr´ ə tē) Safety (p. 624)

Senate (sen´ it) A governing or lawmaking body (p. 161)

Senator (sen´ ə tər) A person who is a member of the senate (p. 165)

Serf (sėrf) A poor farm worker who was bound to the land and whose life was controlled by the lord of the manor (pp. 210–211)

Settlement (set´ l mənt) A small group of homes in a newly established place or region (p. 24)

Shah (shä) An Iranian ruler (p. 669)

Shareholder (sher´ hōl dər) A person who owns one or more parts (shares) of a business (p. 346)

Shogun (shō´ gun) A great general governing Japan (p. 315)

Shortage (shôr´ tij) Too small of an amount; not enough (p. 559)

Shrine (shrīn) A place of worship believed to be sacred or holy (p. 114)

Siege (sēj) The surrounding of a city by soldiers who are trying to capture it so that food, water, and other supplies cannot get in or out (p. 89)

Slavery (slā´ vər ē) The owning of human beings with the belief that they are property (p. 4)

Smuggle (smug´ əl) To move something into or out of a country secretly because it is against the law (p. 458)

Sniper (snī´ pər) A person who shoots from a hidden spot (p. 535)

Socialism (sō´ shə liz əm) An economic and political system where the government owns and controls all industry (p. 559)

Society (sə sī´ ə tē) A group of people joined together for a common purpose (p. 517)

Soul (sōl) A person's spirit (p. 100)

Soviet (sō´ vē et) A Russian council (p. 562)

Specialize (spesh´ ə līz) To work in, and know a lot about, one job or field (p. 26)

Stalemate (stāl´ māt) To put in a position in which no action can be taken (p. 668)

Standard of living (stan´ dərd ov liv´ ing) A way to judge how well a person or a family is living (p. 653)

Starvation (stär vā´ shən) The condition of dying from not having enough food to eat (p. 647)

Steppe (step) A wide plain (p. 552)

Stock (stok) Shares in a business or company (p. 346)

Stone Age (stōn āj) The earliest known period of human culture where people used tools and weapons made from stone (p. 21)

Stronghold (strông´ hōld) A place dominated by a certain group which they have made safe and secure (p. 709)

Superiority (sə pir ē ôr´ ə tē) A feeling of being better than others (p. 480)

Superpower (sü´ pər pou ər) A nation that has more power and money than other countries (p. 610)

Surplus (sėr´ pləs) More than what is needed (p. 240)

Swamp (swomp) An area of low, wet land (p. 41)

Symbol (sim´ bəl) An object that stands for an idea; for example, the dove is a symbol of peace (p. 377)

Sympathy (sim´ pə thē) Feeling sorry for another's suffering (p. 448)

T

Tablet (tab´ lit) A small, flat piece of clay used for writing (p. 46)

Tariff (tar´ if) A tax that countries put on goods they import or export (p. 716)

Tax (taks) Money paid to support a government (p. 60)

Technology (tek nol´ ə jē) Science put to use in practical work (p. 742)

Temple (tem´ pəl) A building used to honor and praise a god or gods (p. 43)

a	hat	e	let	ī	ice	ô	order	ù	put	sh	she
ā	age	ē	equal	o	hot	oi	oil	ü	rule	th	thin
ä	far	ėr	term	ō	open	ou	out	ch	child	ᴛʜ	then
â	care	i	it	ȯ	saw	u	cup	ng	long	zh	measure

ə { a in about / e in taken / i in pencil / o in lemon / u in circus

Terraced (ter´ ist) Going upward like steps (p. 324)

Territory (ter´ ə tôr ē) The land ruled by a nation or state (p. 436)

Terrorism (ter´ ər ism) The use of force or random violence to frighten people or groups (p. 668)

Terrorist (ter´ ər ist) A fighter who hopes to achieve certain goals by using force or violence (p. 667)

Textile (tek´ stīl) Cloth made by weaving (p. 397)

Theory (thir´ ē) An explanation of how and why something happens, usually based on scientific study (p. 268)

Tomb (tüm) A grave, usually one that is enclosed in stone or cement (p. 62)

Torpedo (tôr pē´ dō) To attack or destroy with a large, exploding, underwater missile (p. 539)

Tradition (trə dish´ ən) A custom, idea, or belief handed down from one person to the next (p. 202)

Traitor (trā´ tər) One who betrays a cause, a friend, or a nation (p. 664)

Translate (tran slāt´) To change the words of one language to another (p. 67)

Transport (tran spôrt´) To move from one place to another (p. 62)

Transportation (tran spər tā´ shən) The act of carrying from one place to another (pp. 396–397)

Trapper (trap´ ər) A person who traps wild animals for their furs (p. 344)

Treaty (trē´ tē) An agreement, usually having to do with peace or trade (p. 87)

Treaty of Versailles (trē´ tē ov ver sī) The treaty that ended World War I (p. 542)

Trench (trench) A long ditch dug in the ground to protect soldiers in battle (p. 538)

Tribute (trib´ yüt) A payment or gift demanded by rulers of ancient kingdoms (p. 90)

Truce (trüs) A time when enemies agree to stop fighting (p. 234)

Truman Doctrine (trü´ mən dok´ trən) U.S. President Truman's plan to stop the spread of Communism (p. 611)

Tyrant (tī´ rənt) A ruler who has complete power (p. 125)

U

U-boat (yü´ - bōt) A German submarine (p. 540)

Uncivilized (un siv´ ə līzd) Without training in arts, science, or government (p. 192)

Unification (yü nə fə kā´ shən) Bringing together into one whole (p. 516)

Unify (yü´ nə fī) To connect; to bring together as one (p. 517)

Unite (yü nīt´) To bring together as one (p. 60)

Upstream (up´ strēm) In the direction against the flow of the river; at the upper part of a river (p. 59)

V

Vassal (vas´ əl) A noble who received land from a king in return for loyalty and service (p. 210)

Viceroy (vīs´ roi) The governor of a country or province who rules as the representative of the king (p. 424)

Victor (vik´ tər) The winner of a battle, war, struggle, or contest (p. 448)

Violence (vī´ ə ləns) Great physical force; actions that hurt others (p. 624)

Vision (vizh´ ən) Something seen in the mind or in a dream (p. 225)

Vote (vōt) To choose leaders and pass laws (p. 126)

W

Weapons of mass destruction (wep´ ənz ov mas di struk´ shən) A means of attack or defense that uses powerful weapons; an atomic bomb is an example (p. 671)

Worship (wėr´ ship) To honor and praise a god (p. 78)

Z

Zionism (zī´ ə niz əm) The movement to set up a Jewish nation in Palestine (p. 661)

Index

Christianity, 79, 177–181, 185, 493
  defined, 79
Churchill, Winston, 567, 580
Church of England, 295–296, 298, 301
CIA. *See* Central Intelligence Agency
Circus Maximus, 173
CIS. *See* Commonwealth of Independent States
Cities, development of, 26, 33, 43–44
Citizen, defined, 126
City-state, 43–44, 51, 53, 122, 125–126, 128–130, 139
  defined, 43
Civil disobedience, defined, 483
Civilian, defined, 581
Civilization, defined, 9
Civil war, defined, 166
Cixi, 463
Class, defined, 100
Cleopatra, 169, 185
Clergy, 213, 256
  defined, 213
Clinton, Bill, 668
Code, defined, 84
Code of Hammurabi, 84, 93, 152
Cold war, 610–614, 619, 691
  defined, 610
Collapse, defined, 109
Collective, defined, 565
Colonial, defined, 387
Colony, defined, 74
Colonies/Colonization, 397, 413, 418–420, 431, 509
Columbus, Christopher, 334–335, 349
Commandment, defined, 78
Commonwealth, defined, 361
Commonwealth of Independent States (CIS), 690–691, 701
Commune, defined, 630
Communism, 559–561, 567, 569
  after World War II spread of, 606–607, 611, 614, 619
  Cuba and, 707
  defined, 559
  domino theory and, 641, 710
  Latin America and, 704, 706–707, 709, 723
  North Korea and, 634

North Vietnam and, 640–641, 655
  Red Guard, 630
  U.S. and, 704, 706–707, 723
Communist Manifesto, 560
Communist Party, 562–565, 569, 614, 687
Compass, defined, 308
The Computer Age, 736–737, 757
Concentration camp, 576–577
  defined, 576
Confederation, defined, 523
Conference, defined, 505
Conflict, defined, 544
Confucius, 110
Conquer, defined, 80
Conquerors, defined, 99
Conquistador, defined, 338
Consent, defined, 360
Constantine, 179–180, 185
Constitution, defined, 130
Contract, defined, 47
Contras, 709–710, 723
Convert, defined, 180
Copernicus, Nicholas, 268
Corrupt, defined, 629
Cortés, Hernando, 325–326, 339, 349
Cosmonaut, defined, 732
Council of Trent, 278
Counter-Reformation, 278–279, 281
  defined, 278
Coup, defined, 688
Crafts, 26, 33
  defined, 26
Create, defined, 48
Creoles, 419
Crisis, defined, 614
Criticize, defined, 259
Croatia, 697
Cromwell, Oliver, 360–361, 369
Crusades, 231–235, 237–238, 248, 251
  defined, 232
Cuba, 707, 723
Cuban missile crisis, 614
Cultural Revolution, 630
Culture, 5–6, 65–66, 106–107, 152, 155, 306, 427–428, 431
  defined, 5
Cuneiform, 46, 48
  defined, 46
Curfew, defined, 648

Currency, defined, 612
Cyrus the Great, 132
Czar, defined, 553
Czechoslovakia, 579, 693–694, 698

D

Darius III, 147, 149
Das Kapital, 560
David and Goliath, 80
Dayton Accords, 697
D-Day, 589–599
  defined, 589
Declaration by United Nations, 596
Declaration of Independence, 366–367, 369, 379
  defined, 366
Declaration of the Rights of Man, 379
Decline, defined, 286
Democracy, 126, 136, 139, 354, 356–357, 376–380, 624, 720
  defined, 126
Democratic, defined, 133
Department of Homeland Security, 750
Depression, defined, 574
Descendant, defined, 420
Description of the World, 311
Desert, defined, 58
Détente, defined, 616
Developed country, 410, 741, 757
  defined, 410
Developing country, 410, 741, 757
  defined, 410
Development, defined, 5
Dialect, defined, 552
Diaspora, 661
Dictators, 382, 425, 431, 574–577
  defined, 382
Dike, defined, 41
Diocletian, 179
Diplomat, defined, 520
The Directory, France, 382
Disarm, defined, 542
Disaster, defined, 616
Disband, defined, 690
Discrimination, defined, 420
Diseases, 747–748
Divine right, 359, 374
  defined, 359
Document, defined, 248
Dominance, defined, 505

Hinduism, 99, 102–104, 117, 318–319, 485, 487, 624
    defined, 99
Hiroshima, 593, 612
Historian, 8, 15
    defined, 8
History, defined, 4
Hitler, Adolf, 575–577, 579, 581–583, 588, 591, 599
    blitzkrieg, 579, 581
Hittite empire, 86–87, 91, 93
HIV. *See* human immunodeficiency virus
Ho Chi Minh, 640
Holocaust, 585–587, 599
    defined, 585
Holy Land, 227, 232, 235, 251
    defined, 227
Homage, defined, 210
Homeland, defined, 661
Hong Kong, 459, 632
Hopewell Indians, 321, 329
Hostages, defined, 669
Hostile, defined, 663
Hostility, defined, 126
House of Commons, 357, 369
House of Lords, 357, 369
How to Use This Book: A Study Guide
    As You Read the Lesson, xxi
    Before Beginning Each Chapter, xix
    Before Beginning Each Lesson, xxi
    Before Beginning Each Unit, xix
    How to Study, xviii
    Note These Features, xx
    Preparing for Tests, xxiv
    Reading Checklist, xxv
    Reading Strategy, xx
    Taking Notes, xxii
    Using a Three-Column Chart, xxiii
    Using the Bold Worlds, xxi
    Using the Reviews, xxiv
    Using the Summaries, xxiv
    Word Study Tips, xxii
Huang He Valley, 96, 106, 117
Hubble Space Telescope, 734
Huguenots, 276, 292
Humane, defined, 712
Human immunodeficiency virus (HIV), 748

Humanism, 258, 261, 281
    defined, 258
Humanists, 259, 261
Humanity, defined, 751
Human rights, defined, 248
Hungary, 694
Huns, 194
Hunters, 20–21, 33
Hussein, Saddam, 670–671, 751

I

Ice Age, 20, 33
    defined, 20
Idol, defined, 224
Immigration, defined, 716
Imperialism, 5, 15, 405, 436, 454, 469, 471, 474, 490, 505–507, 509
    defined, 5
Import, defined, 397
Impose, defined, 477
Incas, 326–327, 329
Independence, defined, 235
Independent, defined, 43
India, 102, 117, 624, 743. *See also* Ancient India
    Amritsar Massacre, 481, 487
    Bangladesh and, 625, 655
    British East India Company, 346, 476–477, 487
    British rule, 480–481, 487
    Buddhism, 318
    caste system, 100, 104, 626
    democracy, 624
    European trading companies, 476
    farming methods, 625–626, 655
    French East India Company, 346, 477, 487
    Hinduism, 103, 104, 117, 318, 319
    Hindus *vs.* Muslims, 485, 487
    Hindus *vs.* Sikhs, 624
    imperialism and, 474
    independence, 481, 483–485, 487, 517
    Indian National Congress, 481, 487
    industry, 625–626, 655
    Islam in, 318–319, 329
    Mogul rule, 318–319, 329, 476, 487
    natural resources, 626, 655

Pakistan and, 484–485, 487, 624, 655
    population, 624, 625–626, 655
    poverty, 625–626, 655
    Sepoy Rebellion, 478
    Taj Mahal, 319
    untouchables, 626
Indirectly, defined, 477
Indus River Valley, 96, 98, 99, 117
Industrial Revolution, 394, 396, 411
    in Africa, 505, 509
    beginnings, 396–398
    British colonies and, 396–397, 413
    child labor, 406–407
    cities, 407–408
    defined, 396
    developed, developing countries and, 410–411
    electricity, 403
    Factory Acts, 407
    Great Britain, 396–397, 413
    growth, 410–411, 413
    housing, 407
    imperialism and, 405
    inventions, 400–403, 406, 413
    labor and, 405–407, 413
    labor unions, 408
    Latin America and, 419
    living conditions, 407
    middle class, 406, 413
    nations and, 410–411, 413
    petroleum, crude oil, 403
    population, 407, 413
    quality of life and, 405–408, 410, 413
    steam power and, 402–403, 413
    telegraph, 406, 446, 451
    textile industry and, 397–398, 400–401
    trade agreements, 410, 413
    U.S. and, 411, 434, 446–447
    U.S. Patent Office and, 411
    wages and, 405–406
    working conditions, 405–407, 413
Industry, 5, 15, 397–398, 400–401, 413, 625–626, 638, 655
    defined, 5
Inferior, defined, 507
Influence, defined, 428

INF Treaty. *See* Intermediate Range Nuclear Force Treaty
Inquisition, 275–276
    defined, 276
Insurance, defined, 346
Inter-Allied Declaration, 596
Interest, defined, 346
Interfere, defined, 439
Interference, defined, 462
Intermediate Range Nuclear Force Treaty (INF Treaty), 686
Internal combustion engine, defined, 403
International, defined, 449
International Space Station (ISS), 733
Internet, 738
Intifada, 667
Inuit, 322, 329
Invade, defined, 575
Inventions, 46–47, 53, 66, 75–76, 91, 265–266, 281, 308, 329, 400–403, 406, 413, 540
Invest, defined, 638
Investment, defined, 346
Investor, defined, 397
Iran, 669–670, 676, 681
Iran-Contra Affair, 710
Iran-Iraq war, 669–670, 681
Iraq, 670–671, 751
Iron Curtain, 566–567
    defined, 566
Irrigate, defined, 41
Islam, 224–228, 251, 318–319, 329, 493. *See also* Muslims
Isolate, defined, 109
Isolationism, defined, 608
Israel, 661–662, 667, 678, 681. *See also* Ancient Israelites
Israelites. *See* Ancient Israelites
ISS. *See* International Space Station
Italy, 518, 520–521, 527, 529
    fascism and, 574–575, 591, 599
    nationalism in, 516–521, 529
    Rome, 521, 529
    secret societies, 517
    World War I and, 538, 547
    Young Italy secret society, 517
Ivan the Terrible, 553–554, 567, 569

J

James II, 363
Japan, 466–469
    after World War II, 637
    China and, 313, 469
    Chinese-Japanese war, 462–463, 471
    craftworkers, traders, 314
    economy, 638
    exports, 638
    feudal society, 313–314, 329, 467
    foreign trade, 466
    imperialism, 469, 471
    industry, 638
    investment in, 638
    isolation of, 315–316, 329, 454, 466
    kamikaze, 315
    Korea and, 462, 471
    mikado, 315
    modernization, 467–468
    nation-state formation, 315
    pollution, 638
    raw materials, 469, 471
    Russia and, 469, 471
    Southeast Asia and, 637
    trade, 315–316, 638
    treaties with, 467
    world economy and, 638
    World War II and, 575, 586–587, 592–593, 599, 637
Jefferson, Thomas, 365–366
Jericho, 28–29
Jerusalem, 81, 93, 227, 231–233, 251
Jesuits, 279
Jesus Christ, 177–179, 185
Jews, diaspora, 661
Johnson, Lyndon, 641
Judaism, 79, 81, 93
    defined, 79
Julius Caesar, 165–167, 185
Jury, defined, 130

K

Kaiser, defined, 526
Kamikaze, 315, 592
    defined, 592
Kay, John, 400
Kennedy, John F., 614
Kenya, 646
Kenyatta, Jomo, 646

Khomeini, Ayatollah, 669
Khrushchev, Nikita, 613–614
Kingdoms, development of, 26, 33
Klerk, F. W. de, 648–649
Knights, 213–214
    defined, 213
Kohl, 65
The Koran, 227, 229
    defined, 227
Korea, 655. *See also* North Korea; South Korea
    Chinese-Japanese war, 462–463, 471
Kublai Khan, 310–311, 315, 329
Kush civilization, 492–493, 509
Kuwait, Persian Gulf War, 676, 670–671, 679, 681

L

Laborer, defined, 129
Labor union, defined, 408
Laden, Osama bin, 671, 750
Lafayette, 374
Land bridge, 112, 117
Latin, 174, 197, 265
Latin America, 429, 719. *See also specific countries*
    architecture, 428
    colonies, 422–425
    Communism and, 704, 706–707, 709, 723
    Creoles, 419
    culture, 427–428, 431
    democracy in, 720
    dictators, 425, 431
    discrimination, 420, 431
    independence, 416, 422–425, 428, 429
    Industrial Revolution and, 419
    languages, 428
    mestizos, 420
    native people, 420, 431
    1945–present, 719–720, 723
    protest against military governments, 713
    social structure, 420
    U.S. and, 704, 706–707, 723
Laws, 26, 174, 185, 192, 384
League of Nations, 544–545, 547, 595
Leakey, Louis and Mary, 9

Acknowledgments

Photo Credits

Cover (Bkgd) (T) © Royalty-Free/Corbis; Cover (Bkgd) (T) © Getty Images; Cover (Bkgd) (B) © Getty Images; Cover (C) © Val Duncan/Kenebec Images/Alamy; Cover (B) © Royalty-Free/Corbis; Cover (R) © Getty Images; page xviii © Blend Images/SuperStock; page xxxii © SuperStock, Inc./SuperStock; page 5 © Tamir Niv/Shutterstock; page 6 © Bettman/CORBIS; page 9 © Nancy Carter/North Wind Picture Archives; page 20 © Charles Knight/National Geographic Image Collection; page 25 © Robert Adrian Hillman/Shutterstock; page 29 The Granger Collection, New York; page 36 © Peter M. Wilson/CORBIS; page 44 The Granger Collection, New York; page 46 The Art Archive/Musee du Louvre Paris/Dagli Orti; page 50 © Tom Lovell/National Geographic Image Collection; page 63 The Art Archive/Dagli Orti; page 65 © Vova Pomortzeff/Shutterstock; page 67 © Vladimir Korostyshevskiy/Shutterstock; page 76 © Scala/Art Resource, NY; page 79 © Topham/The Image Works; page 83 © Francoise de Mulder/CORBIS; page 87 The Art Archive/Museum of Anatolian Civilisations Ankara/Dagli Orti; page 90 The Art Archive/British Museum/Dagli Orti (A); page 103 The Art Archive/Musee Guimet Paris/Dagli Orti (A); page 108 © Thomas Barrat/Shutterstock; page 115 © Ales Liska/Shutterstock; page 120 © Peter M. Wilson/Alamy; page 126 © Palis Michael/Shutterstock; page 129 © Emily Goodwin/Shutterstock; page 133 Bust of Pericles (495–429 B.C.) copy of a Greek original, Roman, 2nd century A.D. (marble) (see also 99060)/British Museum, London, UK, Index/The Bridgeman Art Library International; page 145 © Dhoxax/Shutterstock; page 147 © Mimmo Jodice/CORBIS; page 152 © Mansell/Time&Life Pictures/Getty Images; page 163 © Araldo de Luca/CORBIS; page 166 Bust of Julius Caesar (100–44 B.C.) (marble), Roman, (1st century B.C.)/Galleria degli Uffizi, Florence, Italy, Alinari/The Bridgeman Art Library International; page 174 © Will Iredale/Shutterstock; page 178 © Erich Lessing/Art Resource, NY; page 179 The Art Archive/Museo Capitolino Rome/Dagli Orti (A); page 188 The Granger Collection, New York; page 194 © Erich Lessing/Art Resource, NY; page 198 © Giraudon/Art Resource, NY; page 201 © Hulton Archive/Getty Images; page 202 © Ted Spiegel/CORBIS; page 214 The Art Archive/Museo di Roma Palazzo Braschi/Dagli Orti (A); page 216 © North Wind/North Wind Picture Archives; page 224 © Keren Su/CORBIS; page 229 © Archivo Iconografico, S.A./CORBIS; page 234 © Ann Ronan Picture Library/HIP/Art Resource, NY; page 238 The Granger Collection, New York; page 241 © Gianni Dagli Orti/CORBIS; page 246 © Snark/Art Resource, NY; page 249 © Bettman/CORBIS; page 254 © Scala/Art Resource, NY; page 263 © Bartlomiej K. Kwieciszewski/Shutterstock; page 269 © Bettman/CORBIS; page 271 Facsimile of Codex Atlanticus f.386v Water Wheel with Cups (original copy in Biblioteca Ambrosiana, Milan, 1503/4-07), Vinci, Leonardo da (1452–1519)/Private Collection,/The Bridgeman Art Library; page 272 © Scala/Art Resource, NY; page 274 Portrait of Martin Luther (1483–1546) (oil on panel), Cranach, Lucas, the Elder (1472–1553) / Germanisches Nationalmuseum, Nuremberg, Germany/The Bridgeman Art Library; page 278 The Art Archive/Farnese Palace Caprarola/Dagli Orti (A); page 286 Queen Mary I of England (1516–58) 1550s (oil on panel), Mor, Anthonis (Antonio Moro) (c.1519–1576/77) (studio of)/© Isabella Stewart Gardner Museum, Boston, MA, USA,/The Bridgeman Art Library; page 290 The Art Archive/Eileen Tweedy; page 293 St. Bartholomew's Day Massacre, 24th August 1572 (oil on panel), Dubois, Francois (1529–1584)/Musee Cantonal des Beaux-Arts de Lausanne, Switzerland, Photo © Held Collection/The Bridgeman Art Library; page 298 © Scala/Art Resource, NY; page 304 © Mary Evans Picture Library/The Image Works; page 308 Celebration with Fireworks and Kites (painted textile), Chinese School, (19th century)/Private Collection, Archives Charmet/The Bridgeman Art Library; page 314 © Hulton Archive/Getty Images; page 319 © Taolmor/Shutterstock; page 322 © Nancy Carter/North Wind Picture Archives; page 325 Wikipedia.org; page 336 Ferdinand Magellan (c.1480–1521) from the 'Sala del Mappamondo' (Hall of the World Maps) (fresco), Varese, Antonio Giovanni de (16th century)/Villa Farnese, Caprarola, Lazio, Italy,/The Bridgeman Art Library; page 338 © Michel Zabe/Art Resource, NY; page 342 © Burstein Collection/CORBIS; page 347 Wijdships offshore running in a stiff breeze on a cloudy day (oil on panel), Vlieger, Simon Jacobsz. (c.1600–53)/Private Collection, Johnny Van Haeften Ltd., London/The Bridgeman Art Library; page 352 The Granger Collection, New York; page 357 Edward I (1239–1307) King of England (engraving), English School, (19th century)/Private Collection, Ken Welsh/The Bridgeman Art Library; page 361 © Nancy Carter/North Wind Picture Archives; page 363 Presentation of the Bill of Rights to William III (1650–1702) of Orange and Mary II (1662–94) (engraving) (b/w photo), English School/British Museum, London, UK,/The Bridgeman Art Library; page 366 © Victorian Traditions/Shutterstock; page 378 ullstein bild/The Granger Collection, New York; page 380 The Art Archive/Musee Carnavalet Paris/Dagli Orti (A); page 384 © Reunion des Musees Nationaux/Art Resource, NY; page 386 Battle of Waterloo, 18th June 1815, 1898 (colour litho), Sullivan, William Holmes (fl.1870–d.1908)/Private Collection,/The Bridgeman Art Library; page 392 The Art Archive/Bibliotheque Municipale Dijon/Dagli Orti; page 398 Interior of a Weaver's Cottage with a Mother and Child, 1663 (oil on panel), Decker, Cornelius (d.1678)/Private Collection, Johnny Van Haeften Ltd., London/The Bridgeman Art Library; page 401 The Granger Collection, New York; page 402 The Granger Collection, New York; page 406 © Bettmann/CORBIS; page 408 © John Thomson/Hulton Archive/Getty Images; page 419 © CORBIS; page 422 © British Library/HIP/Art Resource, NY; page 427 © Galen Rowell/CORBIS; page 440 © Brandon Seidel/Shutterstock; page 444 The Granger Collection, New York; page 447 The Granger Collection, New York; page 449 © Kevin Schafer/CORBIS; page 456 © Bettmann/CORBIS; page 459 The Granger Collection, New York; page 461 The Granger Collection, New York; page 467 © Bettmann/CORBIS; page 477 © David Cumming; Eye Ubiquitous/CORBIS; page 478 The Granger Collection, New York; page 481 © Jeremy Horner/CORBIS; page 485 © Hulton-Deutsch Collection/CORBIS; page 493 © Jonathan Blair/CORBIS; page 496 The Granger Collection, New York; page 499 The Granger Collection, New York; page 501 © Kenneth V. Pilon/Shutterstock; page 503 © Henry Guttmann/Hulton Archive/Getty Images; page 512 The Art Archive/National Archives Washington DC; page 520 The Art Archive/Museo Civico Modigliana Italy/Dagli Orti (A); page 525 © Bettmann/CORBIS; page 535 © Bettmann/CORBIS;

page 539 © Hulton Archive/Getty Images; page 544 © Hulton-Deutsch Collection/CORBIS; page 553 © Bettmann/CORBIS; page 555 The Granger Collection, New York; page 558 © Archivo Iconografico, S.A./CORBIS; page 560 Library of Congress; page 563 © Erich Lessing/Art Resource, NY; page 566 The Granger Collection, New York; page 574 © Topham/The Image Works; page 575 The Granger Collection, New York; page 576 The Art Archive/Imperial War Museum/Eileen Tweedy; page 577 © A/P Images; page 581 © Hulton Archive/Getty Images; page 586 © Keystone/Hulton Archive/Getty Images; page 589 © Hulton Archive/Getty Images; page 597 © Natalia Bratslavsky/Shutterstock; page 602 © The Image Bank/Getty Images; page 612a © Mario Lopes/Shutterstock; page 612b © CORBIS; page 616 © Wally McNamee/CORBIS; page 626 © Jeremy Horner/CORBIS; page 628 © BoonLeng Woo/Shutterstock; page 631 © Bettmann/CORBIS; page 635 © Jeon Heon-Kyun/epa/Corbis; page 638 © Bettmann/CORBIS; page 643 © Peter Turnley/CORBIS; page 649 © UN Photo/A Tannenbaum; page 651 © David Turnley/CORBIS; page 663 © Peter Turnley/CORBIS; page 668 © Reuters/CORBIS; page 670 © Bob Strong/epa/Corbis; page 672 © Spencer Platt/Getty Images; page 675 © John Moore/The Image Works; page 679 © Hanan Isachar/CORBIS; page 688 © Don Emmert/AFP/Getty Images; page 690 © Peter Turnley/CORBIS; page 694 © Lionel Cironneau/AP Images; page 697 © Danilo Krstanovic/Reuters/Corbis; page 707 © Alejandro Ernesto/epa/Corbis; page 711 © John Hoagland/Getty Images; page 715 © Colman Lerner Gerardo/Shutterstock; page 717 © Jacques Langevin/CORBIS SYGMA; page 721 © Luc Sesselle/Shutterstock; page 733 NASA; page 737 © LWA-Dann Tardif/zefa/Corbis; page 742 © Mityukhin Oleg Petrovich/Shutterstock; page 743 © Kevin Frayer/AP Images; page 746 © ExaMedia Photography/Shutterstock

Staff Credits

Mel Benzinger, Nancy Condon, Barb Drewlo, Marti Erding, Daren Hastings, Brian Holl, Mariann Johanneck, Julie Johnston, Patrick Keithahn, Mary Kaye Kuzma, Marie Mattson, Daniel Milowski, Carol Nelson, Carrie O'Connor, Jeff Sculthorp, Julie Theisen, LeAnn Velde, Mike Vineski, Peggy Vlahos, Amber Wegwerth, Charmaine Whitman, Sue Will